rational passions

rational passions

Women and Scholarship in Britain, 1702-1870

[A Reader]

Felicia Gordon and Gina Luria Walker

broadview press

Library and Archives Canada Cataloguing in Publication

Rational passions : women and scholarship in Britain, 1702-1870 : a reader / [edited by] Felicia Gordon and Gina Luria Walker.

Includes bibliographical references and index.
ISBN 978-1-55111-643-3

1. English literature—Women authors. 2. English literature—18th century. 3. English literature—19th century. 4. Women—Great Britain—Intellectual life—18th century. 5. Women—Great Britain—Intellectual life—19th century. 6. Academic writing—Sex differences—Great Britain—History—18th century. 7. Academic writing—Sex differences—Great Britain—History—19th century. 8. Women and literature—Great Britain—History—18th century. 9. Women and literature—Great Britain—History—19th century. 10. Women—Great Britain—Literary collections. I. Gordon, Felicia II. Walker, Gina Luria

AC5.R27 2008   820.8'0928709033   C2008-900360-8

Broadview Press is an independent, international publishing house, incorporated in 1985. Broadview believes in shared ownership, both with its employees and with the general public; since the year 2000 Broadview shares have traded publicly on the Toronto Venture Exchange under the symbol BDP.

We welcome comments and suggestions regarding any aspect of our publications—please feel free to contact us at the addresses below or at broadview@broadviewpress.com.

North America
PO Box 1243, Peterborough, Ontario, Canada K9J 7H5
2215 Kenmore Ave., Buffalo, New York, USA 14207
Tel: (705) 743-8990; Fax: (705) 743-8353
email: customerservice@broadviewpress.com

UK, Ireland, and continental Europe
NBN International, Estover Road, Plymouth, UK PL6 7PY
Tel: 44 (0) 1752 202300; Fax: 44 (0) 1752 202330
email: enquiries@nbninternational.com

Australia and New Zealand
UNIREPS, University of New South Wales
Sydney, NSW, Australia 2052
Tel: 61 2 9664 0999; Fax: 61 2 9664 5420
email: info.press@unsw.edu.au

www.broadviewpress.com

Typesetting by Aldo Fierro.

This book is printed on paper containing 100% post-consumer fibre.

PRINTED IN CANADA

Contents

Acknowledgements

We wish to thank the following for their contributions to and encouragement for our project:

Clarissa Campbell Orr for her historical acuity, scholarly advice, and friendship; Patricia Fara who revised our book's title to "Rational Passions" and to whose work on women in science we are indebted: Christine Corton; Jenny Fellows; Robert Inglesfield; Lockwood Morris; Barbara Taylor; Sarah Knott; and the many contributors to the Feminism and Enlightenment Seminars at the University of London.

Mical Moser, former Broadview Press History Editor, for her support in the initial planning of the project.

Natalie Fingerhut and Tara Lowes for their attentiveness and help.

Stefanie Bendik, Samantha Paul, and Clara Drew for their assistance in producing the manuscript.

Karen E. Taylor for her efficient and good-humoured work as copyeditor and her enthusiasm for our work.

The British Library; Cambridge University Library; The Elmer Holmes Bobst Library, New York University; the Raymond Fogelman Library, New School University; Bodleian Library, University of Oxford; the Carl H. Pforzheimer Collection of Shelley and His Circle at NYPL, Astor, Tilden, and Lenox Foundations; Dr. David L. Wykes, Director, and the Trustees of Dr. Williams's Library; and New School University for a Faculty Development Grant in support of the project.

Ian Gordon and Chauncey Walker for their support, good humour, editorial assistance, and patience during the research and writing of this book.

Introduction

This critical anthology of primarily non-fiction[1] prose works by British women, 1702 to 1870, aims to introduce readers to a range of lesser-known texts and to examine their authors' ambitions and achievements and the social and political contexts in which they wrote. The texts collected here illustrate the complex cultural inheritance of British women intellectuals: a feminised rationalism, a largely Protestant language of equality before God, a civic humanist language of republicanism, and a discourse of enlightened self-interest in an increasingly commercial society.[2] Our chronological reach, 1702–1870, begins with the reign of Queen Anne and ends in the middle of Victoria's reign, when women were first admitted to British universities. Though a great deal changed for women in the course of the century and a half covered, their economic position in law did not significantly alter until the Married Women's Property Acts (1870 and 1882), constituting the biggest revolution in property ownership since the Dissolution of the Monasteries (1539). Yet in spite of their lack of civil and political rights prior to the economic and political reforms in the latter half of the nineteenth century, as the texts included here demonstrate, elite women were involved in print culture, and their often considerable earnings through publication contributed to their independence, activity, and engagement with many facets of public life.

This collection is part of contemporary re-evaluations of the effects of gender on women's education, textual production, and the cultural reception of their work. We have chosen selections that "add women in" to traditional narratives of the history of ideas, grouping them according to received academic categories. *Rational Passions* also contributes to ongoing efforts to chart the separate evolution of women's intellectual history that addresses the absence of women from more conventional accounts. Thus, we draw attention to what Judith Zinsser describes as the actual ways in which women have functioned "not only [as] facilitators of men's intellectual endeavors, but also as agents and contributors in their own right."[3] Our hope is that, individually and as an ensemble, the selections in this reader will further consideration of the extent to which women contributed to the early feminist dialectics that Siep Stuurman argues form "one of the critical discourses that went into the *making* of the Enlightenment."[4] In addition, in brief biographies of each woman, we have highlighted evidence that addresses significant historical questions. How can we accurately understand "female education" in the context of women's accounts of their necessary autodidactism?[5] How do we assess women's textual production in spite of the persistence of what Michèle Le Doeuff describes as women's "conditional access to knowledge"?[6] In other words, what parts did these women play in the making of modernity?

With these questions in mind, our principles of selection have centred on works of intrinsic interest that have not already been much anthologised or that are not readily accessible to students.[7] We aim to offer readers compelling examples of the writers represented, as an introduction to further exploration. The texts are supported by biographical profiles and short commentaries. Although we have instituted thematic divisions: History and Politics, Education, Philosophy and Religion, Art and Literary Criticism, and Science and Mathematics, these categories can be anachronistic and deceptive. Many of our writers wrote in other genres or "disciplines": philosophers were successful playwrights, historians also published educational tracts, polemicists were better known as poets. We have taken a slice of what is a rich vein of non-fiction prose writing, conscious that it is only part of a much wider story.[8] We wish to show some of the range and richness of women's writing, while avoiding what E.J. Clery terms the "unreflecting triumphalism at women's achievements."[9] The inter-relationship between writers is another important aspect of the texts presented, constituting an ongoing debate, sometimes in a spirit of amity and sometimes the reverse. Women writers examined and often contested each other's views, testifying to a vigorous polemical culture. Finally, in spite of the generally limited opportunities for women's formal education in Britain (see "Education" below), the texts collected here reveal a significant group of women intellectuals in the eighteenth and nineteenth centuries, who sought and enjoyed exceptional training and whose achievements, by any criteria, were outstanding.[10]

Our title, *Rational Passions*, a deliberate oxymoron, serves to indicate the way in which women, who lived in a culture that could simultaneously admire and deplore women's intellectual development, pursued their scholarly interests with passionate commitment. It is this rather than any unanimity of opinion on politics, religion, or women's rights that unites them. We think that the term "scholarship" in our title is justified, although the texts range from erudite to more popular works disseminating scientific or educational theories.[11] All the authors in this volume were "scholars" in the strict sense of pursuing learning in their chosen areas.[12] Whereas Elizabeth Elstob, Elizabeth Carter, Mary Somerville, Catharine Macaulay, Mary Hays, Elizabeth Hamilton, and Ada Byron probably conform to the modern academic meaning of "scholar," having done original research or advancing knowledge, all our writers fulfil scholarly characteristics in their desire to study and in their pursuit of learning. They were not always representative of high culture, namely classical learning, but almost half had all or some of the elements of that culture. Some of the texts included here are more journalistic or educative in the popular culture sense, but their authors all participated in significant forms of intellectual exploration and scholarly activity.

All the women represented in *Rational Passions* aspired to the project of Enlightenment. Whatever their religious or political persuasions, they shared the progressive impulse to demonstrate that women could contribute to knowledge, and were compelled to do so, often in the face of dismissal, rejection, and condescension. Thus, this collection also points to further inquiry: How did women make use of the knowledge that they were able to attain? To what extent did their work contribute to the evolving academic disciplines and professions? What were the reactions to their texts by educated men, the general public, and each other? Progress in women's ability to turn their learning to professional advantage was distinctly uneven. The disparity between men and women's educational standing, in the course of the nineteenth century, actually broadened, as the professions increasingly drew on those with formal qualifications acquired both at the old and the newer universities, all of which excluded women.[13] Nevertheless, some women intellectuals made their way both against these practical difficulties and contemporary currents of ideological belief thick with "conflicting messages about [women's] roles, predispositions, and abilities."[14]

PRECURSORS

An impressive legacy of seventeenth-century women's scholarly writing underpins the aspirations and achievements of writers featured in this volume. The work of Mary Astell (1666–1731) inspired her contemporary, Elizabeth Elstob (1683–1756) with a standard of intellectual distinction.[15] Astell, who wrote both on theological questions and in defence of women's education, derived her conviction in women's right to develop their intellectual powers both from her Anglican faith and her adherence to Cartesian rationalism, a philosophy that described the human mind as ungendered.[16] Though deeply conservative on religious and political questions, Astell argued that women should control their own lives, an aspiration impossible, she thought, within marriage. Her *Serious Proposal to the Ladies for the Advancement of the True and Greatest Interest* (Part I, 1694 and Part II, 1697) advocated higher education for women in a celibate women's college, partly as an antidote to the frivolous pursuits that trained young women in husband hunting. Astell's *A Serious Proposal* forms the backcloth to many of the eighteenth and nineteenth century debates on women's capacity and potential and to proposals for educational training.

MARKETS AND MOTIVES

Women writers did not operate in a social or economic vacuum. Though partly impelled to write by their intellectual interests, they were also constrained or assisted by their own material conditions and the structure of the literary marketplace. The latter was largely determined by the growth of the reading public.[17] Improved literacy resulted in a much wider market for writing of almost every description, from the most serious to the most scurrilous. This increased market, especially for popular or fashionable novels, as well as shifts in the economics of production from subscription based works to a highly commercialised book trade, shaped what authors wrote and the audiences they wrote for.[18]

Literary production in the course of the eighteenth century shifted gradually from the patronage system, in which writers depended on aristocratic patrons to finance their writing, to publication by subscription, and, finally, to the dominance of commercial booksellers who operated in the marketplace for profit. When Elisabeth Elstob and Elisabeth Carter produced their scholarly works (1715 and 1758, respectively), publication was guaranteed by subscribers, who pledged to buy a copy or copies of the forthcoming volumes. Such editions could, as in Carter's case, bring substantial financial rewards, but subscription publication depended on a network of patronage, though representing a wider social base than pure aristocratic patronage. The Bluestockings formed one such network, as did those writers in Dr. Johnson's circle, like Chapone, More, Burney, and Catharine Talbot.[19] The fact that the first bluestocking generation published relatively little indicates the extent to which female success could imply an unladylike appetite for fame and fortune.[20]

A combination of factors served to commercialise the book trade. After 1774, cheap reprints of books out of copyright were allowed for the first time. Booksellers moved from publication by subscription to publication by direct sale of copyright. Profit based economics dominated the booksellers and publishers, and writers necessarily adapted themselves to the marketplace. Many of the women writers included in this volume wrote from financial necessity. Those whom Cheryl Turner has termed "dependent literary professionals," women who earned their living through writing, became increasingly respectable from the late eighteenth century onwards. Among these writers can be ranked Aikin, Barbauld, Edgeworth, Hays, Marcet, Martineau, Piozzi, Shelley, Strickland, Wakefield, and Wollstonecraft. Harriet Martineau (1802–1876) was a good example of someone turning to authorship as an honourable profession for the educated middle-class woman. Others like Macaulay, Marcet, and Somerville became successful professional writers, though they were not dependent on their earnings through publication.

Apart from the economic imperative, women's justification for writing varied, but it may be loosely grouped under the rubric "moral improvement." The tradition of didactic and educational texts for well-born young women that proliferated in the eighteenth century merged almost seamlessly in the nineteenth century into moral homilies for the working class or books designed to introduce children and adults to the newer scientific disciplines. In most cases, the assumptions of subordination of status and of gender were built into such educational and didactic narratives.[21] The imagined audience of docile young ladies in earlier texts greatly expanded in the nineteenth century with the growth of a wider literate public, as Harriet Martineau's immensely successful narratives on political economy attest. The popularisations of Priscilla Wakefield or Jane Marcet rank as part of a continuum with the serious works of scientific synthesis by Mary Somerville. All, however, aimed at expanding knowledge in a wider audience.[22]

Women themselves might resist their classification as "women writers," considering it belittling or provocative. When in 1804 Anna Barbauld, the poet, educationist, and polemicist, was asked by Maria Edgeworth to edit a journal devoted to women's writing, she refused. Women, she pointed out, do not all think alike on any given subject. Politics, class, religion, and even age divide them, a point that Simone de Beauvoir would make in almost exactly the same terms one hundred and fifty years later.[23] Barbauld argued that any grouping of female writers risked alienating other women of different outlook:

> There is no bond of union among literary women, any more than among literary men; different sentiments and different connec-tions separate them more than the joint interest of their sex would unite them. Mrs. Hannah More would not write along with you or me, and we should probably hesitate at joining Miss Hays, or if she were living, Mrs. Godwin.[24]

Barbauld thought the proposed title, *The Lady's Paper,* would invite male condescension and an assumption that the journal was devoted to frivolous top-ics. She had shown her credentials as a poet, critic, and eloquent supporter of radical causes, and did not relish being pigeonholed as a lady's writer. Though mindful of Barbauld's strictures, in this anthology we nevertheless celebrate the very diversity of which she complained. Some of the writers included here were political and social conservatives, some were radicals or republicans, some were Anglicans and some Rational Dissenters, and a few were non-believers. Their feminism or their lack of it did not necessarily follow a left-right divide.

To what extent do Barbauld's reservations remain valid? Does the gathering of disparate texts under the rubric of "women's scholarship" rank as mere anti-quarianism? Does it patronise women? As one of our earliest authors, Elizabeth Elstob, amply demonstrated, antiquarianism, if it is really empirical research, is not "mere." The effect of reading, analysing, and reproducing the texts in this volume has been to demonstrate an impressive range of scholarly labour and intellectual confidence. Often, this scholarly activity flourished in the face of material or social difficulties; equally, many of our writers were supported by their families and wider society. In other words, these texts, grouped together, help to throw light on such issues as the degree to which women intellectuals' writings constituted a political project, the cultural shifts in gender prescrip-tions, the influence these had on individual women, the importance of religious affiliation for gifted women's educational prospects, the impact of domestic or separate spheres' ideology, and the material factors affecting women who par-ticipated in the cultural revolution of the long eighteenth century.[25]

5

EDUCATION

Female education, its theory and practice, was an obvious site for competing notions about gender in general and women's mental capacities in particular. Conduct books for women by men continued a long tradition, begun by Juan Vives in the sixteenth century, which warned that, without proper restraint, a woman and her thoughts were likely to go wandering out from home to heaven knew what dangers.[26] This conduct book tradition did not go unchallenged. Mary Wollstonecraft's particular animus against the Scottish Enlightenment writers James Fordyce and John Gregory, which she displayed in *A Vindication of the Rights of Woman*, lay in her perception that their texts educated girls to consider a weak physical and intellectual self as culturally acceptable and, therefore, desirable. Yet, as Wollstonecraft and other writers featured in this volume attest, there were many exceptions to female intellectual and physical frailty. Conduct books may have drawn the ideological parameters for female education and manners, but that they were written at all—and the wilder flights of fantasy and anxiety evinced in some writers, most notably Rousseau, about women's potential to undermine men's powers—reflects the fact that "conduct" was far more varied and many girls' education was more diverse than the moralists allowed.[27] Conduct books responded to cultural anxieties about shifting gender relations rather than necessarily describing social realities.

What was education for? Young gentlemen were supposed to learn the classics, understood as necessary for gentility, but, according to Catharine Macaulay, their usual public school education did not mould them as citizens but rather as dilettantes.[28] Nevertheless, a classical education did qualify a young man for the Church or for a political career. For well-born young women, for whom marriage was the presumed destiny, learning was often considered an impediment to matrimony. Mothers, aunts, and grandmothers worried that too much erudition might transform a girl into a "learned lady" and render her less likely to succeed in the marriage market.[29] Nevertheless, others, like Catharine Trotter's or Ada Byron's mother, were determined to see that their daughters' education prospered. Even the conservatively-minded were aware that ignorant young women were ill-equipped to become the mother-educators of their children, an equally popular pedagogical model. Authors as ideologically opposed as Hannah More and Mary Wollstonecraft condemned frivolous female education. Of the writers included in this volume, at least eleven (Chapone, Piozzi, Macaulay, Wollstonecraft, Hays, Edgeworth, Marcet, Martineau, More, Wakefield, and Hamilton) wrote specifically on women's education, and, in a general sense, many of the texts included here have an educational, popularising function.

What education was actually available to aspiring women from the early eighteenth to the mid-nineteenth centuries? Most girls were taught letters and numbers at home, and those of the middle and upper classes sometimes attended boarding schools of uneven academic quality. There were also informal alternatives. Marjorie Reeves has described how, in a provincial group of families in the southwest of England through the eighteenth century, "the real education of intellectual young women was fostered by the men in their social environment."[30] The breadth of elite women's education depended largely on parental views as well as on their incomes.[31] In spite of advice manuals, some parents, confronted with highly intelligent daughters, eager to learn, shared the delight of watching them flourish.[32] Some, like Jane Marcet's or Agnes Strickland's parents, were committed to an equal education for boys and girls. Others, like Mary Wollstonecraft's, discriminated against their daughters' education in favour of their sons'. However, the possibility of learning was part of most of our authors' inheritance. Ada Byron's hothouse education stemmed from her aristocratic mother's own intellectual training. Jane Marcet benefited from her Swiss father's belief that children of both sexes should be well-educated. Harriet Martineau, from a Unitarian background, attended a co-educational school; Catharine Macaulay devoured her father's excellent library; and Carter, Trotter, Elstob, and Montagu, encouraged and taught by fathers, brothers or mothers, acquired the classical learning that was supposedly the monopoly of their male peers. The idea that young women did not learn Greek or Latin may well have been true of the majority of girls, as of the majority of the male population, but, of our twenty-three authors, seven had both Latin and Greek, eight had Latin, and eight absorbed a wide-ranging liberal education. A thorough grounding in modern languages, literature, history, philosophy, and sometimes mathematics was also a distinguishing feature of this perhaps accidental curriculum. Some of our writers attended school for some period (Wollstonecraft, More, Hamilton, Lamb, Martineau, Shelley, and Edgeworth), though not always happily.[33] Most were taught at home, and all pursued their studies independently into adult life. The intellectual hunger of women like Hays, Wollstonecraft, Lamb, Piozzi, or Barbauld mirrors that of Elstob, Carter, Montagu, or Trotter, in earlier generations.

The high proportion of women writers in this collection who are from a Rational Dissent background (at least nine out of twenty-two) is far in excess to the proportion of Dissenters in the general population and reveals another facet of British educational development. The general term "Dissenter" referred to Protestants who rejected the Thirty-Nine Articles, which included the requirement by clergy to accept the British king as head of the Anglican Church. Increasingly after the mid-eighteenth century, Dissenters functioned as a vocal minority in opposition to British establishment culture. By the 1770s, Rational Dissent was a strongly liberal, intellectual brand of Dissent. Rational Dissenters held a materialist view of human knowledge (derived from the empiricism of Newton, Locke, Collins, and Hartley) and argued for nurture rather than nature as determining human character. The most progressive advocated unfettered inquiry and toleration of differing points of view; education as a liberating force; and, most radically, the idea of "an equal representation of the people in the great council of the nation, annual elections, and the universal right of suffrage."[34] Spiritual nonconformity often led to reformist politics, scepticism, and theological heterodoxy. Most radical male Dissenters, however, did not include women's claim to natural rights in their radical agenda.[35] In response to their exclusion (like Catholics and Jews) from English universities, Dissenters established a network of Dissenting academies, which were frequently open not only to radical ideas but also to learning about the newer scientific disciplines.[36] Some of these academies evolved into academic laboratories in which tutors produced new textbooks, incorporated the literature of living languages and modern history into traditional academic curricula, and encouraged free inquiry into topical controversies, in deliberate contrast to Cambridge and Oxford.[37] Though women in the Dissenting community benefited informally from continuity with the academic cultures to which tutors at the newer institutions were connected, even among the most enlightened male Dissenters disparities endured "between the urbane liberalism professed by Unitarians, and the conservative, patriarchal tenor which overshadowed their personal relationships and codes of etiquette."[38]

WOMEN IN THE PUBLIC SPHERE

Recent historiography has seen a great deal of interest in the role of British women in politics, as campaigners, as supporters of philanthropic projects, or as consumers of cultural spectacles.[39] This debate, more widely, concerns the presence or absence of women in Jürgen Habermas's conception of the newly expanded public sphere.[40] Did every public appearance by women—from shopping, to theatre attendance, to political canvassing, to entering the public realm as a signed author—constitute a political act? To the extent that such actions challenged gender prescriptions, women in public, in the broadest sense, were acting politically. However, on the level of *Realpolitik*, it is important to recognize that they had no direct power nor control over the laws that most affected their lives, for example, laws on property ownership, divorce, or child custody.

Anna Clark has distinguished between the different senses of "public" and "political" in Britain prior to and after the French Revolution of 1789.[41] Parliament, controlled by aristocratic families, represented the reality of political power. Radical intellectuals, emerging from the prosperous manufacturing classes, and Rational Dissenters sought to reform what was an often corrupt system of patronage through the formation of extra parliamentary associations, thereby creating an alternative public sphere. Clark details women's quasi-political involvement under four headings—aristocrats, intellectuals, political radicals, and feminists—none representing the direct exercise of political power. Their participation was conditioned by class or status as much as by gender. Aristocratic women wielded influence through their dynastic connections. Some women intellectuals participated in salon culture, philanthropy, and writing. Women radicals wrote or spoke on political topics but not necessarily for women's rights, and a few feminists argued for women's rights as part of a wider platform of the "Rights of Man," generically understood.

THE PUBLIC FACE OF FEMALE GENIUS

How were women scholars viewed by their contemporaries? Richard Samuel's painting "The Nine Living Muses of Great Britain," first exhibited in 1779, consecrated his subjects—women writers, painters, and musicians—as legitimately enjoying the fame that their talents had brought them and as exemplars of female excellence.[42] Yet, for women, a scholar's situation, between public exposure and private decorum, was a complex one. That the Bluestockings achieved iconic status encapsulates the gender contradictions running through much eighteenth- and nineteenth-century culture—on the one hand, celebrating "ladies'" scholarly and artistic achievements as demonstrating social refinement and progress, on the other hand, reconfiguring women intellectuals as exceptions to the general rule of legitimate gender inequality.[43] In a similar vein, *The British Lady's Magazine* in its 1815 prospectus announced its conviction that "the female is partaking to an unprecedented extent, in that taste for intellectual acquirement, so perceptible in every department of civilised life." However, the female was expected to partake of this richer intellectual diet "in the calm recesses of private life."[44] Women participating in the public realm, part of which was print culture, always risked the imputation that they were "public" or scandalous women. It is not surprising that a life of domestic retirement could be preferred to the competition of the marketplace.[45]

Nevertheless, by publishing and being read, women did participate in the public sphere. Though only some of our writers in this volume engage directly with politics or history (Macaulay, Barbauld, Hays, Wollstonecraft, Aikin, Hamilton, and Martineau), all engage with shifts in political consciousness in a broad sense and shifts, if not revolutions, in gender politics. Even in the mid-eighteenth century, public sensitivity to "women of letters" and their possibly disruptive gender roles can be gauged in reactions to the socially and intellectually secure Mrs. Montagu, "Queen of the Blues." As William Wraxall, diplomat, traveller, historian, and amiable gossip, recalled in his memoirs of the period, excerpted in *The British Lady's Magazine*:

> Mrs. Montagu, in 1776, verged towards her sixtieth year; but her person, which was thin, spare, and in good preservation, gave her an appearance of less antiquity.... She possessed great natural cheerfulness, and a flow of animal spirits; loved to talk, and talked well on almost every subject ... but her manner was more dictatorial and sententious, than conciliating or diffident. There was nothing feminine about her.... Destitute of taste in disposing the ornaments of her dress, she nevertheless studied or affected those aids more than would seem to have become a woman professing a philosophic mind, intent on higher pursuits than the toilet. Even when approaching to fourscore, this female weakness still accompanied her; nor could she relinquish her

9

diamond necklaces and bows ... the perpetual ornament of her emaciated person.... Notwithstanding the defects and weaknesses that I have enumerated, she possessed a masculine understanding, enlightened, cultivated and expanded by the acquaintance of men as well as of books.[46]

The message conveyed to the female readers of *The British Lady's Magazine* was clear. For a woman to retain good health, intelligence, cheerfulness, and a love of fine dressing were not enough to counter the comment that "there was nothing feminine about her," even though, in a contradictory vein, Wraxall presents Montagu's ostentatious recourse to ornament as evidence of female weakness. On the plus—or was it the minus—side she possessed a "masculine understanding." Intellectual women could not escape their objectification as feminine or non-feminine, handsome or ugly. In a similar vein, Wraxall undermines his praise for Mrs. Chapone, author of one of the best known educational texts for young women of the period, by describing her as one who, "under one of the most repulsive exteriors that any woman ever possessed, concealed very superior attainments and extensive knowledge." Mary Hays came in for particularly *ad feminam* attacks. One reviewer described Hays as the "baldest disciple of Mrs. Wollstonecraft." Hays's hair—or lack of it—continued to be a sore subject in public and private.[47] In light of a social climate in which such judgments were commonplace, the intellectual confidence, or combativeness, of writers such as Elstob, Trotter, Carter, Macaulay, Hays, or Wollstonecraft seems even more remarkable.

On a broader canvas, women intellectuals can be understood as products of Enlightenment optimism and as part of a cultural revolution "carried out by and for the professional middle class," as well as players in the growing "feminisation" of British culture.[48] If this interpretation runs the danger of denying agency to the cultural revolution's participants, it does help to place many of our writers in a wider social and political context. On the political front, the climate of repression from the 1790s onwards in Britain clearly affected what women wrote, for whom they wrote, and how they justified their writing.[49] After the French Revolution and in the face of the Napoleonic threat, overt political activity for women became unfashionable, if not subversive, or at least it required a different rationale. The term "Bluestocking" changed from its earlier connotations of approval to those of ridicule. Women intellectuals, it is argued, ceased writing history or philosophy and wrote novels instead.[50] According to this reading, by the 1790s, the woman of letters ceased to exist as a cultural category. Women's writing focused on domesticity as a means of tackling wider political issues.[51]

Yet the extraordinary attempts by Mary Wollstonecraft in multiple genres to "interrupt the fraternal conversation of political thought"[52] transformed her, Wendy Gunther-Canada argues, from "rebel reader" to radical writer and revolutionary thinker. The effects of Wollstonecraft's "complex critique of the impact of power relations on the feminine psyche" (Barbara Taylor's words) were seismic.[53] After her premature death, a heterogeneous cluster of women refused to allow either Wollstonecraft's infamy or their own to deter them from insisting that Enlightenment advances be applied to female education, marriage, domestic violence, civic participation, vocational training, the new science of the mind, and the arts. Kathryn Gleadle comments, "feminism was alive and kicking in early nineteenth-century Britain. Indeed, to many it was a palpable threat."[54] This had significant implications for women's cognitive aspirations and achievements in the new century and beyond, both to support and subvert them.[55]

As many of the texts in this volume demonstrate, the thesis that post-Enlightenment women's writing narrowed to a domestic agenda and that the novel was the principal vehicle for its expression is only part of the story. When we turn to the newer scientific disciplines, the picture is very different, although it carries forward previous narrative, didactic traditions. Literature comprised more than fiction, drama, and poetry. It encompassed history, political economy, and science. The distinction we make today between scientific and literary activity did not obtain. If we focus on style, genre, and the textual strategies employed to attract a wide audience, it is clear that Enlightenment ideas of popularising knowledge, making it available to more than an elite, flourished even in the British counter-revolutionary climate.[56] So in the 1790s, while there was a backlash in Britain against radical ideas, a backlash orchestrated by Burke's attack on the English Radicals and the French Revolution, at the same time, the growth of empire and industrial expansion created a new market for revolutionary ideas about the material world.[57]

Mental adventurousness, however, could go hand in hand with gender conservatism. This is reflected in the way we have come to understand the industrial and scientific revolutions as being effected by heroic male individuals rather than by groups. The idea of the lonely genius "voyaging through strange seas of thought alone"[58] has remained for us as the paradigm of the male scientist/mathematician. It may have been true of Newton, Wordsworth's subject, but it is deceptive as a cultural construct. Many masculine intellectual adventurers voyaged with a full complement of domestic comforts provided by mothers, wives, sisters, and daughters, who were often collaborators in their researches. The enthusiasm of the eighteenth and early nineteenth centuries for scientific study operated as an amateur pursuit of leisured but well-educated gentlemen, with their collections of natural objects, experiments, and discoveries, typically carried out in a domestic context.[59]

The fascination with the natural world and the new explanations emanating from experimenters and theoreticians were not confined to a scientific coterie. In what was termed "polite society," everyone was potentially a natural philosopher or scientist.[60] Texts on all branches of scientific activity enlarged the imaginations of a generation of young people, as Faraday attested in his tribute to Mrs. Marcet's *Conversations on Chemistry*, which gave him the confidence to pursue chemical experiments. "Mrs Marcet was a good friend to me as she must have been to many in the human race."[61] Joseph Priestley encouraged entrepreneurship in the emerging field of electricity. He vividly

11

described the excitement of scientific experimentation, which he compared to new geographical discoveries:

> In electricity, in particular, there is the greatest room to make new discoveries. It is a field but just opened, and requires no great stock of particular preparatory knowledge; so that any person who is tolerably well versed in experimental philosophy may presently be upon a level with the most experienced electricians. Nay, this history shows that several raw adventurers have made themselves as considerable as some who have been, in other respects, the greatest philosophers ... The pleasure arising from the most trifling discoveries of one's own far exceeds what we receive from understanding the much more important discoveries of others; and a mere reader has no chance of finding new truths, in comparison of him who now and then amuses himself with philosophical experiments.[62]

Scientific studies were not restricted to universities or to the holders of academic degrees. "Even women" could participate in scientific learning, though they could not join the rapidly proliferating scientific academies. Similarly, although mathematics in the eighteenth century was a required subject at Oxford and Cambridge, mathematical scholarship could flourish elsewhere, as we see in the careers of William Frend, Charles Babbage, and Ada Byron. Some talented women profited from the lesser compartmentalisation of learning, and, even when Victorian male scholars founded scientific and medical societies that excluded women, there was an assumption that scientific knowledge should be part of general knowledge. Institutions such as the *Society for the Diffusion of Useful Knowledge* (founded by Lord Brougham in 1826) point to a widespread hunger for greater educational opportunities by and for the general public. Writers like Marcet, Somerville, Wakefield, and Martineau responded to a popular demand for authoritative but accessible texts that would explain the world of the new sciences. Women not only wrote successful scientific educational texts but also argued for women to read them and saw female education as encompassing chemistry, physics, astronomy, and, above all, botany. However, as Jenny Uglow observes, if enlightened fathers, such as members of the Lunar Society, encouraged their daughters to study botany, chemistry, and mechanics, this was not with a view to equipping them, like their brothers, for the professions but as part of a general education for their future role as intelligent wives and educating mothers.[63]

DOMESTICITY

Women writers typically wrote at home, and their domestic context affected them more centrally than it did men because an external professional life was denied to women. The literary market place was one of the few areas where middle-class women, if successful, could earn a good living. In Hilda L. Smith's words, "While ... women's training for future domestic duties, religious piety, and their appropriate place within the nuclear family may seem unremarkable, when contrasted with the educational and social goals for men, they remind us of how men's life courses were equated with human aspirations in ways women's were not."[64] A common strategy was for women with intellectual interests to adopt what Sylvia Harcstark Myers has termed "'rational domesticity' [which] gave the individual intellectual freedom within a supportive family network."[65] Conversely, the domestic ideal could stifle creativity and ambition in women. Material security, whether founded by inheritance, marriage, or wider family support, was the key to scholarly production since, unlike men, women could not gain their living in the Church or professions. Of the writers included in this volume, ten were single and twelve married at some point in their adult lives. Among single women, at the most economically vulnerable end of the scale, we have Elizabeth Elstob, (1683–1756) rendered destitute after the death of her clergyman brother. Elstob's eclipse from the world of scholarship into dire poverty and her subsequent rescue by noble patrons formed a cautionary tale for the next generation of women scholars. Whether married or single, the writers featured in this volume, unless they were very wealthy like Ada Byron, took their domestic responsibilities seriously. Elizabeth Carter, who never married and who was memorably praised by Dr. Johnson for her ability to make puddings as well as to translate Greek, was perhaps the pre-eminent contemporary example of a woman balancing domestic life and scholarship in order to lead an independent life on her own terms.[66] Sixty years on, little seemed to have changed. Mary Somerville, though an eminent scientist, mathematician and avowed feminist, appeared acceptable to her contemporaries not only thanks to the kindness and generosity of her nature but also for her graceful feminine persona. Harriet Martineau, herself no slave to convention, endorsed the feminine domestic ideal when speaking of Mrs. Somerville:

> It was delightful to see her always well dressed and thoroughly womanly in her conversation and manners, while unconscious of any peculiarity in her pursuits. It was delightful to go to tea at her house at Chelsea, and find every thing in order and beauty;—the walls hung with her fine drawings; her music in the corner and her tea table spread with good things.[67]

The popularity of didactic literature aimed at preparing young women for marriage as women's natural destiny testifies to the pervasiveness of the domestic ideal. On the one hand, Wollstonecraft, in *A Vindication*, protested against the educational theories for women of Rousseau, Fordyce, and Gregory; Catharine Macaulay argued for educational equality for girls and boys; Mary Hays, in *An Appeal of the Men of Great Britain in Behalf of Women* (1798, published anonymously), urged that women could be trained for various occupations; and

13

Mary Robinson, in her *Letter to the Women of England on the Injustice of Mental Subordination* (1799), echoed Mary Astell's call for a women's academy for higher education. On the other hand, many writers like Chapone and More endorsed the prevailing ethos of limited educational opportunities for women, geared to their assumed domestic role.[68]

If marriage was a woman's assumed destiny, a suitable marriage was a key factor in making or breaking a woman's social and intellectual reputation. Marriage to a younger man or to a man not of one's class (Macaulay, Piozzi) could be almost as damning as a relationship out of wedlock (Wollstonecraft). Contradictions and hypocrisies abounded, but all our writers were conscious of maintaining or losing their reputations as respected intellectuals if they overstepped social decorum.

Whereas the ethos governing marriage assumed a total commitment to husband and children, in reality many women writers depended on encouragement and intellectual stimulation from other like-minded women. The Bluestocking Circle was perhaps the pre-eminent example of a positive network for women. For those women who remained single and for whom scholarship ranked well above marriage as a life choice, the prospect of women friends marrying meant the end of a close relationship, as Elizabeth Carter explained ironically to her friend Catharine Talbot:

> The splenetic fit of which you enquire the cause, was occasioned by some apprehensions, that a person for whom I have a great love was going to be married; and as I have read in a book [a conduct book?] that people when they marry are dead and buried to all former attachments; I could not think of resigning a friendship which constitutes some of the brightest intervals of my life, without a very severe uneasiness.[69]

The lack of reasonably paid employment for women of all classes became a growing concern, as we see in Wakefield's *Reflections on the Present Condition of the Female Sex* (1798). In the mid-eighteenth century, sewing still employed much of the leisure time of middle-class and upper-middle-class women. Elizabeth Carter's rueful comment is symptomatic: "I have not read any thing time immemorial, as I have been greatly engaged in the important affair of working a pair of ruffles and handkerchief, to which I have attached myself more than would do me good."[70] The time devoted to such tasks was time taken away from improving the mind. Paid labour for women of whatever class was always justified by economic need. To write for money, as Chapone or Wakefield did, required the plea of necessity. More positively, the cult of domesticity, especially in the nineteenth century, can be understood as enabling to women, allowing them to fulfil quasi-public roles in their maternal educative function. For Elizabeth Hamilton and Lucy Aikin, for example, domesticity was a site from which an oppositional discourse could be articulated.

HISTORICAL WRITING

History was the principal non-fiction genre and assumed to be a distinctively male preserve. Indeed, the absence of female historical actors and women historians was accepted as "natural" and normative. Catharine Macaulay, when she researched and composed her *History of England from the Accession of James I to that of the Brunswick Line*, was fully conscious that she was entering into competition not only with David Hume's *History of England*, written between 1753 and 1761, but also with a long tradition of male historical writing. She was recognised as a phenomenon, lauded for her scholarship and intellect, but eventually vilified by men and women alike for ill-advised self-promotion and for marrying a much younger man. Macaulay, however, was not the only woman historian, though she was unique in writing a frankly political history. We have included Elstob, as a linguistic historian; Mary Hays for her original research in her entry for Macaulay in *Female Biography*; Lucy Aikin for her "memoirs" of the courts of Elizabeth I, James I, and Charles I; Agnes Strickland for her *Lives of the Queens of England*; and Mary Shelley who wrote lives of eminent literary and scientific European men. Macaulay, Strickland, Hays, and Aikin all extended the bounds of historical scholarship by basing their work on often previously untouched archival sources. Apart from Macaulay's republican history and Elstob, who sought to validate the Anglo-Saxon past as a part of a national heritage, Aikin, Hays, Shelley, and Hamilton focused on biographical or social history. For these writers, history functioned to some extent as a didactic exercise in the sense that the behaviour of historical figures was to be emulated or shunned.

Increasingly, in the course of the nineteenth century, publishers were eager to exploit the public appetite for life-writing. Readers accepted female authors of this genre more readily than they might accept women as philosophers or theologians. Hays experimented with writing women's history in her "memoirs" of Wollstonecraft and in the 288 entries in *Female Biography*. Mary Shelley attempted to "add women in" to Lardner's *Cabinet Cyclopaedia* in *Lives of the Most Eminent Literary and Scientific Men of Italy, Spain, and Portugal* and in separate volumes of French *Lives*. Nevertheless, when Hays's six-volume *Female Biography* was published, the author and publisher were criticized for including scandalous women, even by readers who could have been expected to be natural allies.[71] Many women historians did not write as feminists.[72] Macaulay's *History* is largely a defence of republican not feminist principles. She saved her feminist views for her *Letters on Education*.

RELIGION AND PHILOSOPHY

For the majority of women intellectuals, it was their belief in the equality of souls before God that fuelled their desire to attain their potential, which they believed had a Divine source. This was true whether they were Catholic,

Anglican, Dissenter (Baptist, Quaker, Unitarian, or Presbyterian), or influenced by Methodism, although the Protestant emphasis on "the right to private judgement" did encourage these convictions. Writers as diverse as Carter, Trotter, Chapone, Wollstonecraft, Marcet, and Somerville justified their scholarly work as fulfilling the capacities given them by God. Female self-fulfilment, as Barbara Taylor writes, was understood as an aspiration to human usefulness based on a belief in God's goodness.[73] Religion was not an addition to women's lives; it was for many the bedrock of their intellectual inspiration.

Sectarian differences loomed large. Religious conformity (in British terms) with the Church of England could, but did not necessarily, imply conservative political and social views. Though the Bluestocking Circle was firmly Anglican (Church of England) and socially conservative, Catharine Macaulay, also Anglican, had strong links with Dissenters and held republican and feminist views. Women nurtured in the Rational Dissenting tradition (Wollstonecraft, Hays, Barbauld, Martineau, and Wakefield) were often committed to social activism in philanthropy, anti-slavery agitation, religious toleration, and feminism. Somerville, whose religious views were considered heterodox by some critics, saw no contradictions among faith in a benevolent deity, scientific knowledge, and campaigning for women's emancipation. Marcet justified popularising the new scientific disciplines because, she argued, scientific knowledge developed pupils' understanding of God.

What of those without faith? Atheism or agnosticism based on a philosophically materialist view of the world remained a shocking concept, as seen in the response to Darwin's theories of evolution or in debates generated from geological discoveries about the antiquity of the world, which some argued pre-dated Biblical time. When Harriet Martineau publicly declared her repudiation of religious belief, even admirers like Charlotte Brontë broke off their friendship. The fact that Wollstonecraft, quite wrongly, was suspected of atheism because she had twice attempted suicide helped to compromise her posthumous reputation.

The major philosophic influence underpinning intellectual enquiry from the late seventeenth century onwards was John Locke (1632–1704), who rejected Cartesian notions of innate ideas and argued that all knowledge was derived from experience; sensations were turned into ideas by reason and reflection. Though, of our authors, Catharine Trotter, who wrote so ably in his defence, was the only writer to engage explicitly with Locke, his influence was pervasive and lay behind the conviction of many women intellectuals that they were not born with innate qualities that debarred them from seeking knowledge. They proceeded on the assumption that there is a material basis to consciousness, that external stimuli produce clusters of sensation in the human brain associating with one another to form ideas, and that each human being is born without innate knowledge and spends a lifetime acquiring it through experience. It follows that each individual, female as well as male, has an equivalent possibility of development or improvement. The implications for gender relations of these views were rejected, however, by so committed a Lockean as Rousseau. In *Émile* (1762), Rousseau reinstated

16

innate gender differences, asserting that the female foil to the natural man is the natural woman, whom Rousseau, with perhaps unintended irony, named "Sophie," the Greek word for "knowledge." He insisted that her inborn passivity could be trained to make her a perfect wife, always under the authority of man. For Rousseau, Sophie's knowledge must be restricted to the purely utilitarian aspects of household management. Many of the debates between women writers about female potential centre on this divide between Locke and Rousseau.

FEMINISM OR PROTO-FEMINISM

Reading these authors today, we may tend to focus on their feminism or lack of it, but we need to be wary of reading the past too closely in terms of the present. Like atheism or democratic representation in politics, feminist concerns, in the sense of full autonomy for women, were deeply radical and dangerous-seeming ideas. Nevertheless, even someone as socially conventional as Elizabeth Carter "was much inclined to believe that women had not their proper station in society, and that their mental powers were not related sufficiently high."[74] Some writers like Chapone and More, promulgated a conservative gender ethos while pursuing an alternative discourse within a religious framework, finding there a locus of social responsibility to temper the philosophic materialism and individualism of Enlightenment rationalism.[75] Only the most courageous, publicly espoused the rights of women, though, as noted above, the idea of female emancipation usually derived from a religious belief in the equality of souls. Macaulay, Wollstonecraft, and Hays, in particular, were exceptional, not only in their ideas but also in their willingness to express them. Lucy Aikin's cautionary voice when speaking of Hays's *Female Biography* is characteristic of an age when women knew the price to be paid for "unwomanly" views. "Alas, alas! Though Miss Hayes has wisely addressed herself to the ladies alone, I am afraid the gentlemen will get a peep at her book and repeat with tenfold energy that women have no business with anything but nursing children and mending stockings."[76] Aikin, however, was committed to women's educational advancement. Her reservations about Hays were about means not ends.

LINKS BETWEEN WRITERS

Though exceptional, learned women writers were neither alone in their endeavours nor isolated from one another. Informal social circles were central to facilitating women's exchanges of ideas with their male colleagues and with one another. Friendships between women, as well as critiques, criticisms, and reviews, formed a loose network, allowing them to draw on and respond to one another's work.

The best known eighteenth-century grouping of women intellectuals, a set that drew on concepts of friendship and sociability, was without doubt the

Bluestockings. A circle of women committed to the life of the mind and linked to, but not dependent on male mentors such as Dr. Johnson and Samuel Richardson, the Bluestockings are often divided into two generations. The first included Elizabeth Montagu, Elizabeth Carter, Catharine Talbot, and Hester Chapone. Among the second (though it often overlapped with the first) can be grouped Hester Thrale, Hannah More, Fanny Burney, Maria Edgeworth, and Anna Barbauld.[77] Their links with other social circles and individuals, from aristocratic patrons to eclectic publishers like Joseph Johnson, demonstrate that the Bluestocking Circle formed only one part of the intellectual lives of these women. However, for many, the Bluestockings were crucially supportive, as reflected in Hannah More's praise for the group's conversation as "The noblest commerce of mankind/Whose precious merchandise is MIND!"[78] Finally, women linked to the religious Rational Dissenting communities, for example, Macaulay, Wollstonecraft, Hays, Barbauld, and Aikin, found there a network of like-minded male and female intellectuals often in the context of political radicalism.

While they may have held a wide array of opinions,[79] women of disparate political persuasions occasionally presented strikingly similar views. Elizabeth Hamilton, Mary Wollstonecraft, Hays, and More shared many of the same ideas on female education. Mary Berry commented, that she found it "amazing, or rather ... not amazing, but impossible ... [that Hannah More and Mary Wollstonecraft] agree on all the great points of female education."[80] Wollstonecraft, Hamilton, and the socially conservative Chapone also found themselves in agreement regarding their support for companionate marriage over romantic attachment. Kate Davies argues that, despite their obvious differences, for erudite women like Macaulay and the American, Mercy Otis Warren, "it was often useful ... to think of themselves as connected rather than opposed."[81] In addition, women read each other's texts, conscious that, as outsiders in the masculine republic of letters, gender prejudices limited women to less established genres. Women writers responded to these constraints by blending traditional forms to produce hybrids: Wollstonecraft advanced her political critique in fiction and book reviews; Hannah More espoused Evangelical tenets in wildly successful novels, though she disparaged the form as "a complicated drug"; and Anna Jameson practiced art history as feminist commentary.

Not all relationships between intellectual women were complimentary and by no means were all friendly. For these women, as for any people competing to make places for themselves in the republic of letters, rivalries and disagreements persisted as they reviewed and commented on one another's work. Martineau wrote harshly of Wollstonecraft: "Women who would improve the condition ... of the sex must, I am certain, be not only affectionate and devoted, but rational and dispassionate. But Mary Wollstonecraft was, with all her powers, a poor victim of passion...." Fanny Burney vented her frustration with Hester Chapone in her play *The Woman-Hater*, in which a young daughter throws down the improving books she has been reading and cries, "Decamp, Mrs. Chapone." The relationship between Mary Hays and Elizabeth Hamilton was particularly fraught, involving attacks and defences as each struggled to gain her footing in

18

the new and complex, concomitantly public and private sphere of publishing and reviewing.[82] Particularly after the French Revolution, women necessarily took sides in the print war between radicals and conservatives; whatever possibilities may have existed for them to come together around issues of gender were lost in the exigencies of larger political demands.

CONCLUSION

The texts reproduced in this volume, dating from the early eighteenth to the late nineteenth centuries, were not merely the products of individual minds—they reflect a responsive, and at times confrontational, matrix of cultural influences. These writings constitute clear evidence of intellectual women's published achievements as well as of the uneven fortunes of women's gradual emancipation in British life. They also help to puncture our perhaps unexamined assumptions that higher intellectual attainment is necessarily the product of formal higher education. At the beginning of our period (1702), most men and all women were excluded from British universities. Nonetheless, as we have seen, some parents educated their daughters to the highest standards of the day, and some daughters, even with minimal or no encouragement, found ways of becoming learned.

Though post-Enlightenment culture in Britain rejected the radical legacy of the French Revolution, the social and political issues raised by radical thinkers, including those of gender relations, did not disappear. The "woman question" (if woman is a question, what is the answer?), which might seem like a logical non-problem, became one of the major social, political, and moral issues in nineteenth century British life. The combination of rapid industrial change, accompanied by political reaction, and increasing social tensions was felt not only in the public sphere but also in private relations between men and women. Freud asked, "What do women want?" The Victorians tended to ask, "What are they for?" If, as traditionally understood, they existed for matrimony and motherhood, what was to be done about the vast army of "redundant" or "surplus" middle-class women who remained unmarried?

Class blindness as well as gender blindness affected this debate. Middle-class women were deemed too fragile for "work" and were believed likely to be corrupted by exposure to public life. Marriage, as well as their destiny, was supposedly their economic safeguard. The fact that a woman's property became her husband's after marriage, and that this inheritance often became *his* economic safeguard, makes comprehensible the resistance to the Married Women's Property Acts, long campaigned for and finally passed in 1870 and 1882. In the period in which our authors were writing, married women could not own property, they had no legal share in the house in which they lived and no control over the money they might earn or inherit. Meanwhile, working class women, labouring in mines, in factories, as servants, as prostitutes, or as gang labourers in the fields, were the virtually invisible side of the imagined fragile female persona.

If the women writing in the late eighteenth and early nineteenth centuries tended to avoid political confrontation by structuring their works within a domestic ethos—and the powerful exceptions of Wollstonecraft, Macaulay, Hays, Martineau, and Barbauld go far to undermining such a generalisation— the question arises as to the degree to which a largely conservative gender and political ethos allowed such writers to flourish. Did women writers of non-fiction write only on topics considered suitable for women? Though a female audience was clearly in the publishing sights of most of the writers included in this volume, theirs was by no means only or even principally a female audience. We have argued that the emphasis on educational texts formed part of a wider democratisation of education responding to the demands of an emerging industrial society. Popularisations of all kinds answered to a growing public demand. The concept of the mother educator, though grounded in separate spheres theories, did require that this maternal icon acquire the tools to teach her children, helping to subvert the stultifying effects of domesticity.

With the increasing professionalisation of life in industrial Britain, women's exclusion from higher education, seen as a road to professional qualifications and thus to higher status employment, became a contested issue. The gradual demise of the amateur in science and technology, the growth of professional organisations, for example in medicine, all served to curtail women's possibilities. This goes some way to explaining why women's writing for publication in the nineteenth century became so important, whether women wrote anonymously in periodical reviews, under their own names, or under a pseudonym (the Brontës, as Currer and Ellis Bell; Mary Ann Evans, as George Eliot).[83] Writing for publication, as Harriet Martineau conclusively proved, was, for gifted women, a way out of the twin prisons of poverty and boredom.

For Victorian reformers, it became evident that women's access to formal education at all levels was the key to professional qualifications and, by extension, proof that they possessed the intellectual capacity and moral worth to vote. These proofs had never been required of men, for whom a franchise based on property had been the major hurdle. Thus, for women in particular, education became the lynchpin of change. The writers on education represented in this volume, such as Wakefield, Hays, Chapone, Macaulay, Marcet, and More, presciently combine the intellectual development of young women with increasing their capacity for civic responsibility.

In 1845, Elizabeth Barrett Browning contrasted the Elizabethan age unfavourably with her own:

> England has had many learned women, not merely readers, but writers of the learned languages in Elizabeth's time and afterwards—women of deeper acquirements than are common now in the greater diffusion of letters.... I look everywhere for grandmothers and see none.[84]

This volume is a tribute to the grandmothers, or perhaps foremothers, whom Barrett Browning had never known or forgotten. In recent years, these writers have been rediscovered, studied, and, in many cases, republished by feminist scholars. We present the works included in this volume, and our descriptions of the contexts in which these women wrote, to be imagined as a frieze, tapestry, or film in which the figures converse with each other, sometimes amicably and sometimes not. This intellectual conversation, this overarching narrative conveys a passion for the life of the mind coupled with a pragmatic desire to gain either fame or fortune by the published word—to the extent that the world would allow.

ENDNOTES

1   Where authors such as Jane Marcet, Patricia Wakefield, or Harriet Martineau adopt a fictional format in dialogues, letters, or didactic tales, these belong less to the novel or romance and more to the Socratic method in which the pupil learns by questioning and empirical demonstration.

2   Tjitke Akkerman and Siep Stuurman, eds., introduction to *Perspectives on Feminist Political Thought in European History from the Middle Ages to the Present* (London and New York: Routledge, 1998), 15.

3   Judith P. Zinsser, "The Many Representations of the Marquise du Châtelet," in *Men, Women, and the Birthing of Modern Science*, ed. Judith P. Zinsser (DeKalb: Northern Illinois University Press, 2005), 62.

4   Siep Stuurman, "The Deconstruction of Gender: Seventeenth-Century Feminism and Modern Equality," in *Women, Gender and Enlightenment*, ed. Barbara Taylor and Sarah Knott (Houndmills: Palgrave Macmillan, 2005), 371.

5   Barbara J. Whitehead argues that "the principle to be questioned is whether formal training in the humanities was required in order for a woman to be 'educated.'" "Introduction," in *Women's Education in Early Modern Europe: A History 1500–1800* (New York: Garland, 1999), xi.

6   George Eliot addressed these issues in her portrayal of Dorothea Brooke's aspirations in *Middlemarch:* "[Dorothea] would not have asked Mr. Casaubon at once to teach her the [classical] languages, dreading of all things to be tiresome instead of helpful; but it was not entirely out of devotion to her future husband that she wished to know Latin and Greek. Those provinces of masculine knowledge seemed to her a standing-ground from which all truth could be seen more truly. As it was, she constantly doubted her own conclusions, because she felt her own ignorance." For a more contemporary view, see Michèle Le Doeuff, *The Sex of Knowing*, trans. Kathryn Hamer and Lorraine Code (New York: Routledge, 2003), 24.

7   A number of excellent scholarly reprints are now available: *Bluestocking Feminism: Writings of the 1738–1785*, ed. Garry Kelly, 6 vols. (Oxford: Clarendon Press, 1993); Judith Hawley, ed., *Literature and Science 1660–1834*, 8 vols.

(London: Pickering and Chatto, 2003–04); James A. Secord, *Collected works of Mary Somerville*, 9 vols. (Bristol: Toemmes Continuum, 2004); Mary Shelley, *Literary Lives and Other Writings*, ed. Nora Crook, 4 vols. (London: Pickering and Chatto, 2002).

8   For example, we have not included, largely for considerations of space, the important category of travel writing, where the richness of material seems to demand fuller treatment in a separate study, though we have included Piozzi's *Observations and Reflections*.

9   E.J. Clery, "Bluestocking 'Feminism' and the Fame Game," *British Journal for Eighteenth-Century Studies* 28, no. 2 (Autumn 2005): 277–78.

10   For an analysis on the ways in which women's intellectual contributions have been minimised or misrepresented, see Berenice A. Carroll, "The Politics of 'Originality': Women and the Class System of Intellect," *The Journal of Women's History*, 2 (Fall 1990): 136–62.

11   The claim to scholarly status for women has a long history. As Brita Rang writes, the "overriding aim of the authors [of Renaissance catalogues of learned women] was to demonstrate that women were capable of engaging in scholarly work. The biographies are usually embedded in detailed argumentation in favour of the scientific pursuits of women, while the individual *exempla* 'proved' that women could actually do scientific work." See Brita Rang, "A 'learned wave': Women of Letters and Science from the Renaissance to the Enlightenment," in *Perspectives on Feminist Thought in European History: From the Middle Ages to the Present*, ed. Tjitske Akkerman and Siep Stuurman, 50–67 (London: Routledge, 1998), 53.

12   The *OED*, though defining "scholar" as one who studies in the "schools or universities," not the case with our women writers, also characterises a scholar as "a learned or erudite person, especially one who is learned in the classical languages and their literatures," a definition fitting most of the women featured in this volume.

13   Rosemary O'Day comments, "Women were unable to enter the learned professions because they were excluded from the institutions that conferred the qualifications that gave access to those professions." "Women and Education in Nineteenth-Century England," in *Women, Scholarship and Criticism: Gender and Knowledge c. 1790–1900*," ed. Joan Bellamy, Anne Laurence, and Gill Perry, 91–109 (Manchester: Manchester University Press, 2000), 92.

14   Joan Bellamy, Anne Laurence, and Gill Perry, "Introduction: Gender and Women's History," in *Women, Scholarship and Criticism: Gender and Knowledge c. 1790-1900*, ed. Joan Bellamy, Anne Laurence, and Gill Perry, 1–15 (Manchester: Manchester University Press), 11.

15   See Hilda L. Smith, *Reason's Disciples: Seventeenth-Century English Feminists* (Urbana: University of Illinois Press, 1982) for the contributions of twelve seventeenth-century feminists including Mary Cavendish, Duchess of Newcastle; Bathsua Makin; Mary Astell; Elizabeth Elstob; and Anne Finch, Countess of Winchelsea. Astell has received increased critical attention since

the publication of *Women and the Enlightenment*, by Margaret Hunt, Margaret Jacob, Phyllis Mack, and Ruth Perry (New York: Haworth Press, 1984) and Ruth Perry's biography, *The Celebrated Mary Astell* (Chicago: University of Chicago Press, 1986), which contextualises Astell with her female contemporaries such as Aphra Behn, Mary de la Rivière Manley, Elizabeth Elstob, and Lady Mary Wortley Montagu. More recently, various publications have contributed to the growing scholarship on this seminal feminist writer: Hilda L. Smith, *Women Writers and the Early Modern British Political Tradition* (Cambridge: Cambridge University Press, 1998); E. Derek Taylor and Melvyn New, eds. *Mary Astell and John Norris: Letters Concerning the Love of God* (Aldershot: Ashgate, 2005); Ruth Perry, "Mary Astell and the Enlightenment," in *Women, Gender and Enlightenment*, ed. Sarah Knott and Barbara Taylor, 357–70 (Basingstoke: Palgrave/Macmillan, 2005); and Patricia Springborg, *Mary Astell: Theorist of Freedom from Domination* (Cambridge: Cambridge University Press, 2006).

23

16 For the influence of the French Cartesians, i.e., Jacques Du Bosc, author of *The Excellent Woman* (1692), and Poulain de la Barre, who wrote *De l'égalité des sexes* (1673), see Hilda L. Smith, *Reason's Disciples: Seventeenth-Century English Feminists* (Urbana: University of Illinois Press, 1982), 6; Ruth Perry, *The Celebrated Mary Astell*, 16; and Siep Stuurman, "The Deconstruction of Gender: Seventeenth-Century Feminism and Modern Equality," in *Women Gender and Enlightenment*, 371–88. See also, Anna Maria van Schurman, *Whether a Christian Woman Should be Educated*, ed. and trans. Joyce L. Irwin (Chicago: University of Chicago Press, 1998).

17 In the course of the seventeenth-century, female literacy gradually improved, and, by the mid-eighteenth century, a nation-wide survey of marriage registers showed that 60 per cent of males could sign their names as could 35 per cent of females, rising to 45 per cent in 1800: Rosemary O'Day, *Education and Society 1500–1800* (New York: Longman, 1982), 190–191.

18 For the literary marketplace, see James Raven, "Introduction: The Historical Novel Comes of Age" in *The English Novel 1770-1829: A Bibliographical Survey of Prose Fiction Published in the British Isles*, vol. 6, *1770–1799*, ed. James Raven and Antonia Foster (Oxford: Oxford University Press, 2000), 15–121; William St. Clair, *The Reading Nation in the Romantic Period* (Cambridge: Cambridge University Press, 2004); and Cheryl Turner, *Living by the Pen: Women Writers in the Eighteenth Century* (London and New York: Routledge, 1994).

19 Norma Clarke, *Dr. Johnson's Women* (London: Hambledon and London, 2000); Betty A. Schellenberg, *The Professionalization of Women Writers in Eighteenth-Century Britain* (Cambridge: Cambridge University Press, 2005).

20 See E.J. Clery, *The Feminization Debate in Eighteenth-Century England; Literature Commerce and Luxury* (Basingstoke: Palgrave, 2004), 13–139. For an assessment of women as facilitators of salon culture in France, see Dena Goodman, *The Republic of Letters: A Cultural History of the French Revolution* (London: Cornell University Press, 1994) and Judith Zinsser, *La Dame d'Esprit: A Biography of the Marquise du Châtelet* (New York: Viking, 2006).

24

21 See Norma Clarke, "Bluestocking Fictions: Devotional Writings, Didactic Literature and the Imperative of Female Improvement," in *Women, Gender and Enlightenment*, ed. Sarah Knott and Barbara Taylor, 460–73 (Basingstoke, Hampshire: Palgrave, 2005); Deidre David, *Intellectual Women and Victorian Patriarchy* (London: Macmillan, 1987), 33; and Greg Meyers, "Science for Women and Children: The Dialogue of Popular Science in the Nineteenth-Century," in *Nature Transfigured: Science and Literature 1700–1900*, ed. John Christie and Sally Shuttleworth, 171–200 (Manchester: Manchester University Press, 1989).

22 James A. Secord has argued that Somerville's posthumously published and immensely popular *Personal Recollections* (1891), read as an exemplary story of struggle, intellectual growth, and moral commitment, tended to overshadow her purely scientific texts. "Introduction," *Collected Works of Mary Somerville* (Bristol: Theommes Continuum, 2004), xxxvii.

23 "They [women] have no past, no history, no religion of their own; and they have no such solidarity of work and interest as that of the proletariat.... They live dispersed among the males, attached through residence, housework, economic condition, and social standing to certain men—fathers or husbands—more firmly than they are to other women." Simone de Beauvoir, *The Second Sex*, trans. H.M. Parshley (Harmondsworth: Penguin Books 1949, 1983), 19.

24 Ann Laetitia Le Breton, *Memoir of Mrs. Barbauld* (London: George Bell and Sons, 1874), 87.

25 See Hannah Barker and Elaine Chalus, eds., "Introduction," in *Gender in Eighteenth-Century England: Roles, Representations and Responsibilities* (London: Longman, 1997).

26 "Womans thought is swyfte, and for the most parte unstable, walking and wandrynge out from home, and soon wyl slyde, by the reason of hit owne slypernes, I wot nat how far." Juan Luis Vives, *The Instruction of a Christen Woman (1524)*, ed. Virginia Walcott Beauchamp, Elizabeth H. Hageman, and Margaret Mikesell (Urbana: University of Illinois Press, 2002), 16.

27 Rousseau's animadversions against women's castrating potential, if not curbed by a sense of acquired shame and modesty and his insistence on separate moralities for men and women, drew trenchant criticisms from Wollstonecraft and Macaulay and from feminists ever since. See J.J. Rousseau, *Émile* (1760), Book V.

28 Catharine Macaulay Graham, *Letters on Education with Observations on Religious and Metaphysical Subjects* (London: C. Dilly, 1790), Letter XXI.

29 Catharine Harrison, later Cappe, was distressed at the inferior education available to young women, but she received more formal training at a girls' seminary in York. Harrison pressed for and finally won the privilege to have private tutors teach her arithmetic and French at school. When she was forced to leave the seminary and return home, she suffered when her female relations advised her that needlework was her only appropriate task. For Cappe's career as a Unitarian reformer and philanthropist, see Helen Plant, *Unitarianism, Philanthropy and Feminism in York, 1782–1821: The Career of Catharine Cappe*, Borthwick Paper

No. 103 (Borthwick: Borthwick Institute of Historical Research. 2003). See also Ruth Watts's discussion of Cappe, "Women, Philanthropy and Class Relations," in *Gender, Power and the Unitarians in England 1760-1860* (London: Longman, 1998), 70–76.

30 Marjorie Reeves, "Eighteenth-century young women: How were they educated?" in *Pursuing the Muses: Female Education and Nonconformist Culture, 1700–1900* (London: Leicester University Press, 1997), 18–29; Michèle Cohen, "'To think, to compare, to combine, to methodise': Girls' Education in Enlightenment Britain," *Women, Gender and Enlightenment*, ed. Sarah Knott and Barbara Taylor, 224–42 (Basingstoke: Palgrave, 2005), 238.

31 See Jane Rendall, "Women and the Enlightenment in Britain c. 1690–1800" and Deborah Simonton, "Women and Education" in *Women's History: Britain, 1700–1850*, ed. Hannah Barker and Elaine Chalus, 9–32, 33–56 (London: Routledge, 2005).

32 Educational advice manuals proliferated throughout the eighteenth and nineteenth centuries led by Locke and Rousseau's educational theories. Among the best known one can mention Vicesimus Knox, *Liberal Education* (1781), John Gregory, *A Father's Legacy to His Daughters* (1774), and James Fordyce, *The Character and Conduct of the Female Sex* (1776).

33 For the development of girls' boarding schools and a discussion of female literacy, see Rosemary O'Day, *Education and Society 1500-1800* (New York: Longman, 1982), 179–95; and for women's education more generally, see Janet Todd, "Introduction," *Female Education in the Age of Enlightenment*, Vol. I (London: William Pickering, 1996); Michèle Cohen, "To think, to compare, to combine, to methodise"; Hilda L. Smith, *All Men and Both Sexes, Politics and the False Universal in England 1640–1832* (University Park, PA: Pennsylvania State University Press, 2002), 167–171.

34 John Jebb, "Report of the Sub-Committee of Westminster...," 27 May 1780, reprinted in S. Maccoby, ed., *The English Radical Tradition 1763–1914* (New York: New York University Press, 1957), 35–36.

35 Arianne Chernock, "Extending the 'Right of Election': Men's Arguments for Women's Political Representation in Late-Eighteenth-Century Britain" (paper presented at the 8th Gender and Enlightenment Colloquium, *Gender and Enlightened Utopias*, University of York, UK, June 7, 2003).

36 J.W. Ashley Smith, "Tutors Constructing their own Curricula," in *The Birth of Modern Education: The Contribution of the Dissenting Academies 1660–1800* (London: Independent Press Ltd., 1954), 129–87; Ruth Watts, "Ideals into Practice: Unitarians in Education," in *Gender, Power and the Unitarians in England 1760–1860* (London: Longman, 1998), 56–63. For a trenchant history of the varieties of pedagogy at the academies, see David L. Wykes, "The contribution of the Dissenting Academy to the Emergence of Rational Dissent," in *Enlightenment and Religion: Rational Dissent in Eighteenth-Century Britain*, ed. Knud Haakonssen, 99–139 (Cambridge: Cambridge University Press, 1996).

37 J.W. Ashley Smith, *The Birth of Modern Education*, 154 ff.

25

38　Kathryn Gleadle, *The Early Feminists: Radical Unitarians and the Emergence of the Women's Rights Movement, 1831–51* (New York: St. Martin's Press, 1995), 8; see also Ruth Watts, "Part One: 1760–1815," in *Gender, Power and the Unitarians in England 1760-1860* (London: Longman, 1998), 34. Kathryn Gleadle remarks that "the relationship between Unitarianism and early feminism is far more complex than has traditionally been assumed.... there existed no natural corollary between Unitarian liberalism and a commitment to feminist principles" (31).

39　See Hannah Barker and Elaine Chalus, eds., *Gender in Eighteenth-Century England: Roles, Representations and Responsibilities* (London: Longman, 1997); Amanda Vickery, *The Gentleman's Daughter, Women's Lives in Georgian England* (New Haven and London: Yale University Press, 1998); and Joan B. Landes, *Women in the Public Sphere in the Age of the French Revolution* (Ithaca, NY: Cornell University Press, 1988).

40　Jürgen Habermas, *The Structural Transformation of the Public Sphere*, trans. T. Burger (1962; repr., Cambridge, MA: MIT Press, 1989).

41　Anna Clark, "Women in Eighteenth-Century British Politics," in *Women, Gender and Enlightenment*, ed. Sarah Knott and Barbara Taylor, 570–586 (Basingstoke, Hampshire: Palgrave, 2005).

42　The "Nine Muses" not drawn from life were Elizabeth Montagu, Elizabeth Griffith, Elizabeth Carter, Charlotte Lennox, Elizabeth Linley, Angelica Kauffman, Catharine Macaulay, Anna Barbauld, and Hannah More. For a detailed analysis of the painting and its implications, see Elizabeth Eger, "Representing Culture: *The Nine Living Muses of Great Britain* (1789)," in *Women Writing and the Public Sphere, 1700–1830*, ed. Elizabeth Eger, Charlotte Grant, Clíona ó Gallchoir, and Penny Warburton 104–32 (Cambridge: Cambridge University Press, 2001).

43　E.J. Clery, "Bluestocking 'Feminism' and the Fame Game," 275.

44　*The British Lady's Magazine* 1 (January to June 1815): 3–4.

45　See Caroline Gonda, "Misses, Murderesses and Magdalens, Women in the Public Eye," in *Women, Writing and the Public Sphere*, 53–74; and Felicia Gordon, "*Filles publiques* or public women: The Actress as Citizen: Marie Madeleine Jodin (1741–90) and Mary Darby Robinson (1758–1800)" in *Women, Gender and Enlightenment*, ed. Sarah Knott and Barbara Taylor, 610–29 (Basingstoke: Palgrave, 2005).

46　William Wraxall, *Historical Memoirs of my own Time, Part the First from 1772–1780; Part the Second, from 1781–1784*, 2 vols. (London: T. Cadwell and W. Davies, 1815) (Excerpts in *British Lady's Magazine*, 1815).

47　For example, a conservative reviewer of Hays's *Letters and Essays, Moral and Miscellaneous* (1793) described Hays as "the baldest disciple" of Wollstonecraft, and Elizabeth Hamilton satirized Hays's appearance in *Memoirs of Modern Philosophers*.

48　Gary Kelly, *Women, Writing and Revolution 1790–1827* (Oxford: Clarendon Press, 1993), 3, and E.J. Clery, *The Feminization Debate in Eighteenth-Century England: Literature, Commerce and Luxury* (Basingstoke: Palgrave, 2004). For the impact

26

of Enlightenment thought on women, see Hilda L. Smith, *All Men and Both Sexes* and, for a wide-ranging reassessment of the Enlightenment for women, see Sarah Knott and Barbara Taylor, eds., *Women, Gender and Enlightenment.*

49 It was not, of course, only women who felt the effects of counter-revolutionary repression. Joseph Priestley, the scientist and radical Unitarian, immigrated to Pennsylvania in 1794, after a mob in Birmingham had burnt down his house, library, and laboratory. Of the unusually high number of English émigrés that year (about 10,000), many had played an active role in the English radical movement. See Jenny Graham, *Revolutionary in Exile: The Emigration of Joseph Priestley to America 1794–1804* (Philadelphia: The American Philosophical Society, 1995).

50 Sylvia Harcstark Myers, *The Bluestocking Circle: Women, Friendship, and the Life of the Mind in Eighteenth-Century England* (Oxford: Clarendon Press, 1990); Norma Clarke, *Dr. Johnson's Women* (London: Hambledon and London, 2000); Norma Clarke, *The Rise and Fall of the Woman of Letters* (London: Pimlico, 2004).

51 Gary Kelly, *Women, Writing and Revolution*, 183.

52 Wendy Gunther-Canada, *Rebel Writer: Mary Wollstonecraft and Enlightenment Politics* (DeKalb: Northern Illinois University Press, 2001).

53 Barbara Taylor, *Mary Wollstonecraft and the Feminist Imagination* (Cambridge: Cambridge University Press, 2003), 56.

54 Kathryn Gleadle, *Radical Writing on Women, 1800–1850: An Anthology* (Houndsmills, Basingstoke: Palgrave Macmillan, 2002), 1.

55 Lucy Newlyn, *Reading, Writing, and Romanticism: The Anxiety of Reception* (Oxford: Oxford University Press, 2000), 38.

56 Ludimilla Jordanova, *Nature Displayed: Gender, Science and Medicine 1760–1820* (London and New York: Longman, 1999), 103.

57 See Jennifer S. Uglow, *Lunar Men: The Friends who made the Future* (London: Faber, 2002); Patricia Fara, *Pandora's Breeches: Women, Science and Power in the Enlightenment* (London: Pimlico, 2004); Deidre David, *Intellectual Women and Victorian Patriarchy* (London: Macmillan, 1987); Greg Meyers, "Science for Women and Children: The Dialogue of Popular Science in the Nineteenth-Century," in *Nature Transfigured: Science and Literature 1700–1900*, ed. John Christie and Sally Shuttleworth, 171–200 (Manchester: Manchester University Press, 1989).

58 William Wordsworth, *The Prelude* (1850), bk. 3, line 63.

59 See Patricia Fara, *Pandora's Breeches*, who documents the collaborative and domestic nature of much early scientific research and Judith Zinsser, *Men, Women and the Birthing of Modern Science* (DeKalb, IL: Northern Illinois University Press, 2005).

60 The term "scientist" as opposed to "natural philosopher" was coined only in 1833 by William Whewell.

61 Quoted in Bette Polkinghorn, *Jane Marcet: An Uncommon Woman* (Aldermaston: Forestwood Publications, 1993), 29–30.

62   "Preface," *The History and Present State of Electricity* (1767).

63   Jenny Uglow, "But What About the Women? The Lunar Society's Attitude to Women and Science, and to the Education of Girls," in *The Genius of Erasmus Darwin* (Aldershott: Ashgate, 2005), 165.

64   Hilda L. Smith, *All Men and Both Sexes*, p. 171.

65   Sylvia Harcstark Myers, *The Bluestocking Circle: Women, Friendship, and the Life of the Mind in Eighteenth-Century England* (Oxford: Clarendon Press, 1990), 16.

66   Norma Clarke, in *Dr Johnson's Women*, provides a telling reading of Johnson's comment, "Knowing Greek, and being known to know Greek as comprehensively as she did, was in many ways the bedrock of Elizabeth Carter's independent life. No man could condescend to her.... [Dr Johnson's] comment ... was actually about what men wanted, not what women could or could not do" (26–27).

67   Harriet Martineau, *Autobiography*, vol. 1 (1877; repr., London: Virago Press, 1983), 357.

68   Jean-Jacques Rousseau, *Émile* (1762); James Fordyce, *The Character and Conduct of the Female Sex* (1776); John Gregory, *A Father's Legacy to his Daughters* (1774).

69   Judith Hawley, *Bluestocking Feminism* (London: Pickering and Chatto, 1999), 2: 382.

70   Hawley, *Bluestocking Feminism*, 2: 381.

71   "There is a singular work lately published, of which I should much like to hear your opinion, Mary Hayes's [sic] 'Female Biography'. She is a great disciple of Mrs. Godwin, you know, and a zealous stickler for the equal rights and equal talents of our sex with the other; but, alas, though I would not so much as whisper this to the pretended lords of creation—

     Her arguments directly tend
     Against the cause she would defend.

At the same time as she attempts to make us despise 'the frivolous rivalry of beauty and fashion', she holds forth such tremendous examples of the excesses of more energetic characters, that one is much inclined to imitate those quiet, good folks who bless God they are no geniuses." Lucy Aikin to Mrs. Taylor, 27 January 1803, in *Memoirs, Miscellanies and Letters of the Late Lucy Aikin*, ed. Philip Hemery Le Breton (London: Longman, Green, Longman, Roberts and Green, 1864), 124.

72   See Devoney Looser, *British Women Writers and the Writing of History, 1670–1820* (Baltimore: John Hopkins University Press, 2000).

73   Barbara Taylor, "Feminism and Enlightened Religious Discourses," in *Women, Gender and Enlightenment*, 410.

74   Montagu Pennington. *Memoirs of the Life of Mrs. Elizabeth Carter* (London: F.C. and J. Rivington, 1807), 447–48.

75   See Clarissa Campbell Orr, "Aristocratic Feminism, the Learned Governess, and the Republic of Letters," in *Women, Gender and Enlightenment*, 306–25.

28

76 71 Letter to Mrs. Taylor, January 27 1803, *Memoirs, Miscellanies and Letters of the late Lucy Aikin*, ed. Philip Hemery Le Breton (London: Longman, Green, Longman, Roberts and Green, 1864), 124.

77 Norma Clarke, *Dr. Johnson's Women* (London: Hambledon and London, 2000) traces the circle of women around Dr. Johnson, who delighted in the company of clever women though, as in his vexed relationship with Catharine Macaulay, he could prove himself a vitriolic critic of women intellectuals.

78 See Elizabeth Eger, "'The noblest commerce of mankind': Conversation and Community in the Bluestocking Circle," *Women, Gender, and Enlightenment*, 290.

79 See Barbauld's comment to Edgeworth above.

80 Quoted in Ann Stott, *Hannah More: The First Victorian* (Oxford: Oxford University Press, 2003), 224–25.

81 Kate Davies, *Catharine Macaulay and Mercy Otis Warren: The Revolutionary Atlantic and the Politics of Gender* (Oxford: Oxford University Press, 2005).

82 For a general discussion of "The Woman Critic," including Barbauld, Wollstonecraft, Hays, and Martineau, see Mary Waters, *British Women Writers and the Profession of Literary Criticism, 1789–1832* (Houndsmill: Palgrave Macmillan, 2004). For the interactions between Hays and Hamilton, see Gina Luria Walker, "Whirlwind and Torrent," in *Mary Hays (1759–1843): The Growth of a Woman's Mind* (Aldershot: Ashgate, 2006), 159–86.

83 See Alexis Easley, *First Person Anonymous: Women Writers and the Victorian Print Media, 1830–1870* (Aldershot: Ashgate, 2006).

84 Elizabeth Barrett Browning, Letter to Mr. Chorley, 7 January 1845.

Chronology

1702	Catharine Trotter, *A Vindication of an Essay Concerning Human Understanding*
1715	Elizabeth Elstob, *The Rudiments of Grammar for the English-Saxon Tongue, First given in English with an Apology for the study of Northern Antiquities*
1750	Elizabeth Carter, "On Religion," *The Rambler*, XLIV
1750–51	Hester Mulso Chapone, "A Matrimonial Creed"
1755	Elizabeth Carter, *Letter to Catherine Talbot*
1758	Elizabeth Carter, *All the Works of Epictetus*
1769	Catharine Macaulay, *The History of England From the Accession of James I to the Elevation of the House of Hanover* (Published in 1763 under the title *The History of England, from the accession of James I to that of the Brunswick Line*)
1769	Elizabeth Montagu, *Essay on the Writings and Genius of Shakespear, Compared with the Greek and French Dramatic Poets. With some remarks Upon the Misrepresentation of Mons. De Voltaire*
1773	Hester Mulso Chapone, *Letters on the Improvement of the Mind. Addressed to a Young Lady*
1789	Hester Lynch Piozzi, *Observations and Reflections Made in the Course of a Journey through France, Italy, and Germany*
1789	Mary Wollstonecraft, review of Hester Lynch Piozzi's *Observations and Reflections Made in the Course of a Journey through France, Italy, and Germany*
1790	Anna Lætitia Barbauld, *An Address to the Opposers of the Repeal of the Corporation and Test Acts;* Catharine Macaulay, *Letters on Education with Observations on Religious and Metaphysical Subjects;* Catharine Macaulay, *Observations on the Reflections of the Right Hon. Edmund Burke on the Revolution in France, In a Letter to the Right Hon. The Earl of Stanhope;* Mary Wollstonecraft, review of Catharine Macaulay's *Letters on Education*
1792	Anna Lætitia Barbauld, "Remarks on Mr. Gilbert Wakefield's *Enquiry into the Expediency and Propriety of Public or Social Worship*"
1793	Mary Hays, "Letter IV," *Letters and Essays, Moral, and Miscellaneous*
1794	Hester Lynch Piozzi, *British Synonymy; Or An Attempt at Regulating the Choice of Words in Familiar Conversation*
1795	Maria Edgeworth, *Letters for Literary Ladies*
1796	Priscilla Wakefield, *An Introduction to Botany, in a series of familiar letters*
1798	Priscilla Wakefield, *Reflections on the Present Condition of the Female Sex*
1799	Hannah More, *Strictures on the Modern System of Female Education. With a view of the principles and conduct prevalent among women of rank and fortune*

PART 1

History and Politics

Elizabeth Elstob (1683–1756)

"The incomparably learned and ingenious Mrs. Elstob," as the antiquarian George Ballard termed her, was revered throughout the eighteenth and nineteenth centuries as a remarkable scholar.[1] Born in Newcastle-upon-Tyne, September 29, 1683 of a prosperous merchant family, she was encouraged by her mother to study Latin. After her mother's death when Elizabeth was eight, she lived in Canterbury with her uncle, the Reverend Charles Elstob, who while disapproving of women learning languages—"one tongue is enough for a woman"—nevertheless did allow his niece to study French.[2] The fact that she addressed a 1713 pamphlet (*Some Testimonies of Learned Men in Favour of the Intended Edition of the Saxon Homilies*) to her uncle suggests that his early opposition to women's learning may have weakened with time.

Elizabeth's scholarly prospects improved when she was taken under the wing of her brother William, who, "being impressed with more liberal sentiments concerning the education of women, very joyfully assisted and encouraged her studies for the whole time he lived."[3] Ten years older than his sister, William had studied classics, theology, and Anglo-Saxon at Oxford and was elected a fellow of University College in 1696. Elizabeth may have joined her brother at Oxford and, through him, met the antiquarians' circle, scholars devoted to Anglo-Saxon studies, the most eminent of whom was the Reverend Dr. George Hickes. In 1702, William moved to London as rector of St Swithin's and St Mary Bothaw, taking his sister with him. This was the happiest and most productive period of Elizabeth Elstob's life, when she formed links with Mary Astell.[4] She continued her studies, gaining a sound knowledge of French, Latin, Greek, Hebrew, German, Anglo-Saxon, and "the Teutonic languages."

With William Elstob's early death in 1715 and that of George Hickes in the same year, Elizabeth lost her only financial security and the two great encouragers of her scholarly work. Her brother, though recognised as an authority in Anglo-Saxon studies and holding a living as a rector, had never been successful in gaining preferment from wealthy patrons. His sister said of him rather sadly, "... He was a most dutiful son, affectionate to his relations, a most sincere friend, very charitable to the poor, a kind master to his servants, and generous to all, which was his greatest fault."[5] Probably as a result of this generosity and the Elstobs' attempts to publish necessarily expensive editions of scholarly texts, which led them into debt, Elizabeth Elstob was left almost penniless. University fellowships or church livings, two recourses of otherwise impecunious scholars, were not open to women. She eventually moved to Evesham in Worcestershire, where she set up a school for poor children, a precarious employment that gave her no time for study, though she prized the opportunity to spread some learning even in this sphere: "I should think it as glorious an employment to instruct these poor children as to teach the children of the greatest monarch."[6] Worse than the burden of poverty, her books and papers, consigned to the care of a friend, were lost. Eventually, she made the acquaintance of influential people in the town, among them George Ballard, an antiquarian, who, when preparing his *Memoirs of Several Ladies of Great Britain* (1752), found Elstob a fount of information, especially on Mary Astell. He and Mrs. Chapone raised an annuity of 20 guineas by subscription for Elstob. Queen Caroline also contributed £100 for a five-year period. Though the Queen's death in 1737 put an end to this source of income, Elizabeth Elstob was again recommended by friends in 1739 to the Duchess of Portland, who appointed her governess to her children. Once more able to pursue her studies and live in comfort, Elizabeth Elstob remained in the duchess's household until her death on May 30, 1756. She was buried at St Margaret's, Westminster.

Elizabeth Elstob became the first woman authority on Anglo-Saxon language and literature. Contemporaries, and, more recently, twentieth-century scholars, attest to her pre-eminence in Anglo-Saxon studies.[7] A rare and somewhat disapproving perspective on her devotion to scholarship over worldly advantage emerges from the recollections of Mr. Rowe Mores, an antiquarian, who visited her in her old age: "She was a Northern lady of an antient family and a genteel fortune; but she pursued too much the drug called learning, and in that pursuit failed of being careful of any one thing necessary."[8] Her intoxication with learning, if that is what it was, produced some remarkable scholarship. In 1708, after publishing an English translation of Mlle de Scudéry's *Discours de la gloire* (1671), she embarked, with the encouragement of Dr. George Hickes, the doyen of Anglo-Saxon scholars at Oxford, on a transcript of Latin/Saxon versions of the Creed. In 1709, her scholarship focused on Ælfric, a tenth-century grammarian and writer of sermons; she published an edition of his *Life of Pope Gregory the Great*, entitled *An English-Saxon Homily on the Birthday of St Gregory*, with copious notes and an English translation of the Old English text. Her next major project was a complete edition of Ælfric's *Catholic Homilies*, which she only partially published and abandoned due to lack of funds on her brother's death in 1715. As Mechthild Gretsch comments, "had Elizabeth Elstob been able to complete this massive project, her edition of the *Catholic Homilies* would have antedated the first critical and annotated edition of that important text by almost three centuries."[9]

THE RUDIMENTS OF GRAMMAR FOR THE ENGLISH-SAXON TONGUE (1715)

Elizabeth Elstob's last publication, *Rudiments of Grammar for the English-Saxon Tongue*, was the first Saxon language grammar in English. It was based on authoritative Anglo-Saxon grammar in Latin (1703) written by her mentor, George Hickes, and on a shorter version (1711) by Edward Thwaites. The preface defends Anglo-Saxon studies against its detractors, making two major arguments. The first is a justification for writing an Anglo-Saxon grammar in English. The second constitutes an attack on detractors of Anglo-Saxon studies, especially Dean Swift. In relation to the first point, Elstob explains that she chose to write in English, rather than the more usual scholars' Latin, in order to reach those readers, chiefly cultivated women, who would not have had access to a classical education. She conveys her delight in intellectual effort and justifies her aim of passing it on to other women: "Considering the pleasure I myself had reaped from knowledge I have gained from this original of our Mother Tongue, and that others of my own sex, might be capable of the same satisfaction: I resolved to give them the rudiments of the language in an English dress."

Most of the preface deals with her second argument, namely the defence of Anglo-Saxon studies. Her indignation had been aroused when Jonathan Swift, published a pamphlet in 1712 in which he proposed the creation of an academy for "Correcting, Improving and Ascertaining the English Tongue." It was not Swift's proposal for improving spoken and written English, or for establishing a standard idiom, that Elstob objected to, but the fact that he had dismissed Anglo-Saxon studies as irrelevant to a correct knowledge of English. Such studies, as he pithily but, unfortunately, phrased it, were pursued by "men of low genius," among whom he would have classed George Hickes and William Elstob. Elizabeth Elstob's riposte is copious, witty, and trenchant and exposes Swift's ignorance of a subject, which he had dismissed, she demonstrates, without understanding it.

Swift's *Proposal* repeated traditional criticisms of Teutonic-based languages, including Anglo-Saxon, as being full of monosyllables (thought simplistic) and given to harsh consonants. To refute the charge that the use of monosyllables was peculiar to Anglo-Saxon or was a vice of style, Elstob quoted at least seventy-nine examples of verse by eminent poets from Homer to the major English poets, including Dryden, Pope, and Swift himself. She joked at Swift's expense, quoting from his translation of Horace's *Seventh Epistle*, Book I, 137–38:

> Then since you now have done your worst,
> Pray leave me where you found me first.

In these two lines, Swift employs sixteen monosyllables and not a single polysyllable—this from the great despiser of monosyllables.

Elizabeth Elstob's undoubted scholarship, comprehensive literary culture, linguistic skills (her examples range from Greek,[10] Latin, Old French, and Old English to Modern English), and her rhetorical boldness and wit show her in complete command of her subject. Reading this preface we hear the voice of a confident, pugnacious intelligence, secure in her learning but admiring of the scholars and poets who had forged an English tradition.

The Rudiments of Grammar for the English-Saxon Tongue, First given in English with an Apology for the Study of Northern Antiquities (1715)

Elizabeth Elstob

The Preface

To the Reverend Dr. Hickes.

Soon after the publication of the Homily on St. Gregory, I was engaged by the importunity of my friends, to make a visit to Canterbury, as well to enjoy the conversation of my friends and relations there, as for that benefit which I hoped to receive from change of air, and freer breathing, which is the usual expectation of those who are used to a sedentary life and confinement in the great city, and which renders such an excursion now and then excusable. In this recess, among the many compliments and kind expressions, which their favourable acceptance of my first attempt in Saxon had obtain'd for me from the ladies, I was more particularly gratified, with the new friendship and conversation, of a young lady, whose ingenuity and love of learning, is well known and esteem'd, not only in that place, but by your self: and which so far indear'd itself to me, by her promise that she wou'd learn the Saxon Tongue and do me the honour to be my scholar, as to make me think of composing an English Grammar of that language for her use. That ladies fortune hath so disposed of her since that time, and hath place her at so great distance, as that we have had no opportunity, of treating farther on this matter, either by discourse or correspondence. However though a work of a larger extent, and which hath amply experienced your encouragement, did for some time make me lay aside this design, yet I did not wholly reject it. For having re-assumed this task, and accomplish'd it in such manner as I was able, I now send it to you, for your correction, and that stamp of authority, it must needs receive from a person of such perfect and exact judgement in these matters, in order to make it current, and worthy of reception from the publick. Indeed I might well have spared my self the labour of such an attempt, after the elaborate work of your rich and learned *Thesaurus*, and the ingenious compendium of it by Mr. Thwaites; but considering the pleasure I my self had reaped from knowledge I have gained from this original of our Mother Tongue, and that others of my own sex, might be capable of the same satisfaction: I resolved to give them the rudiments of that language in an English dress. However not 'till I had communicated to you my design for your advice, and had received your repeated exhortation, and encouragement to the undertaking.

The method I have used, is neither entirely new, out of a fondness and affectation of novelty: nor exactly the same with what has been in use, in teaching the learned languages. I have retained the old division of the parts of speech, nor have I rejected the other common terms of grammar; I have only endeavour'd to explain them in such a manner, as to hope they may be competently understood, by those whose education, hath not allowed them an acquaintance with the grammars of other languages. There is one addition to what your self and Mr. Thwaites have done on this subject, for which you will, I imagine, readily pardon me: I have given most, if not all the grammatical terms in true old Saxon, from Ælfrick's Translation of Priscian, to shew the polite men of our age, that the language of their forefathers is neither so barren nor barbarous as they affirm, with equal ignorance and boldness. Since this is such an instance of its copiousness, as is not to be found in any of the polite modern languages; and the Latin itself is beholden to the Greek, not only for the terms, but even the names of arts and sciences, as is easily discerned in the words, *Philosophy, Grammar, Logick, Rhetorick, Geometry, Arithmetic, &c.* These gentlemen's ill treatment of our mother tongue has led me into a stile not so agreeable to the mildness of our sex, or the usual manner of my behaviour, to persons of your character; but the love and honour of one's country, hath in all ages been acknowledg'd such a virtue, as hath admitted of a zeal even somewhat extravagant. *Pro Patria mori*, used to be one of the great boasts of antiquity; and even the so celebrated magnanimity of Cato, and such others as have been called Patriots, had wanted their praise, and their admiration, had they wanted this plea. The justness and propriety of the language of any nation, hath been always rightly esteem'd a great ornament and test of the good sense of such a nation; and consequently to arraign the good sense or language of any nation, is to cast upon it a great reproach. Even private men are most jealous, of any wound, that can be given them in their intellectual accomplishments, which they are less able to endure, than poverty itself or any other kind of disgrace. This hath often occasioned my admiration, that those persons, who talk so much, of the honour of our country, of the correcting, improving and ascertaining of our language, should dress it up in a character so very strange and ridiculous: or to think of improving it to any degree of honour and advantage, by divesting it of the ornaments of antiquity, or separating it from the Saxon root, whose branches were so copious and numerous. But it is very remarkable how ignorance will make men bold, and presume to declare that unnecessary, which they will not be at the pains to render useful. Such kind of teachers are no new thing, the spirit of truth itself hath set a mark upon them; desiring to be teachers of the law, understanding neither what they say, nor whereof they affirm (I Tim. I.7). It had been well if those wise grammarians had understood this character, who have taken upon them to teach our ladies and young gentlemen, the whole system of an English education; they had not incurr'd those self-contradictions of which they are guilty; they had not mentioned your self, and you incomparable Treasury of Northern Literature in so cold and negligent a manner, as betrays too much of invidious pedantry: but in those terms of veneration and applause which are your just tribute, not only from the learned of your own country, but of most of the other Northern Nations, whether more or less polite: who would any of them have glory'd in having you their native, who have done so much honour to the original of almost all the languages in Europe....

But to leave these pedagogues to huff and swagger in the heighth of all their arrogance, I cannot but think it a great pity, that in our considerations, for refinement of the English Tongue, so little regard is had to antiquity, and the original of our present language, which is the Saxon. This indeed is allow'd by an ingenious person, who hath lately made some proposals for the refinement of the English tongue, that the old Saxon, except in some few variations in the orthography, is the same in most original words with our present English, as well as with the German and other Northern dialects; which makes it a little suprizing to me, to find the same gentleman not long after to say, "The other languages of Europe I know nothing of, neither is there any occasion to consider them": because, as I have before observ'd, it must be very difficult to imagine, how a man can judge of a thing he knoweth nothing of, whether there can be occasion or no to consider it.[11] I must confess I hope when ever such a project shall be taken in hand, for correcting, enlarging, and ascertaining our language, a competent number of such persons will be advised with, as are knowing, not only in Saxon, but in the other languages of Europe, and so be capable of judging how far those languages may be useful in such a project. The want of understanding this aright would very much injure the success of such an undertaking and the bringing of it to perfection; in denying that assistance toward adjusting the propriety of words, which can only be had from the knowledge of the original, and likewise in depriving us of the benefit of many useful and significant words, which might be revived and recalled, to the increase and ornament of our language, which wou'd be the more beautiful, and being more genuine and natural, by confessing a Saxon original for their native stock, or an affinity with those branches of the other northern tongues, which own the same original.

The want of knowing the Northern Languages, has occasion'd an unkind prejudice towards them: which some have introduc'd out of rashness, others have taken upon tradition. As if those languages were made up of nothing else but monosyllables, and harsh sounding consonants; than which nothing can be a greater mistake. I can speak for the Saxon, Gothick, and Francick, or old

Teutonick: which for aptness of compounded and well sounding words, and variety of numbers, are by those learned men that understand them, thought scarce inferior to the Greek itself. I never cou'd find my self shocked with the harshness of those languages, which grates so much in the ears of those that never heard them. I never perceiv'd in the consonants any hardness, but such as was necessary to afford strength, like the bones in a human body, which yield it firmness and support. So that the worst that can be said on this occasion of our forefathers is, that they spoke as they fought, like men.

The Author of the Proposal, may think this but an ill return, for the soft things he has said of the Ladies, but I think it gratitude at least to make the return, by doing justice to the gentlemen. I will not contradict the relation of the ingenious experiment of his with vocal ladies, tho' I could give him some instances to the contrary, in my experience of those, whose writings abound with consonants; where vowels must generally be understood, and appear but very rarely. Perhaps that gentleman may be told that I have a northern correspondence, and a northern ear, probably not so fine as he may think his own to be, yet a little musical.

And now for our monosyllables. In the controversy concerning which, it must be examin'd, first whether the charge which is exhibited against the Northern Languages is true, that they consist of nothing but monosyllables; and secondly, whether or no the copiousness and variety of monosyllables may be always justly reputed a fault, and may not sometimes as justly be thought to be very useful and ornamental.

And first I must assert, that the ancient Northern Languages, do not wholly nor mostly consist of monosyllables. I speak chiefly of the Gothick, Saxon, and Teutonick. It must be confest that in the Saxon, there are many primitive words of one syllable, and this to those who know the esteem that is due to simplicity and plainness in any language, will rather be judged a virtue than a vice: That is, that the first notions of things should be exprest in the plainest and simplest manner, and in the least compass: and the qualities and relations, by suitable additions, and composition of primitive words, for which the Saxon language is very remarkable, as has been before observed, and of which there are numerous examples, in the following Treatise of Saxon Grammar, and infinitely more might have been added.

The second enquiry is, whether or no the copiousness and variety of monosyllables may be always justly reputed a fault, and may not as justly be thought, to be very useful and ornamental? Were this a fault, it might as justly be charged upon the learned languages, the Latin and the Greek: for the Latin you have in Lilly's *Rules Concerning Nouns*, several verses, made up for the most part of monosyllables, I mention him not as a classick, but because the words are classical and monosyllables; and in the Greek there are several as it were, idle monosyllables, that have little significancy, except to make the numbers in verse complete, or to give fullness to their periods, as the verses of Homer and other Greek Poets plainly evidence: an instance or two may suffice;[12]

Ex hou dē ta prōta diastēt én erisante (*Iliad*, 1.6.)

Here are four monosyllables in this verse.

> Tén d'egō ou lusō, prin men kai géras epeisin (*Iliad*, 1. 29.)

Here are six monosyllables, and one cutting off.

> All' ithi, mé m'erethize, saōteros hōs ke neēai. (*Iliad*, 1.32.)
> Hos ēdē ta t'eonta, ta t'essomena, pro t'eonta (*Iliad*, 1. 70.)

Here are seven monosyllables; yet so far is Virgil from being angry with his master Homer on this account, that he in a manner transcribes his very words, imitating him as near as the Latin wou'd permit;

> Quae sint, quae fuerint, quae mox ventura trahantur.

Here is the whole sense of Homer exprest, and five monosyllables. But Mr. Dryden, who has exprest the sense of Virgil with no less accuracy, gives you the whole line in monosyllables;

> He sees what is, and was and is to come.

Mr. Pope is equally happy in the turn he has given to the original, who as he is an exact master of criticism, so has he all those accomplishments of an excellent poet, that give us just reason to hope he will make the father of the poets speak to us in our own language, with all the advantages he gave to his works in that wherein they were first written, and the modest opinion he prescribes to his own, and other men's poetical performances, is no discouragement to these hopes;

> Whoever thinks a faultless Piece to see,
> Thinks what ne'er was, nor is, nor e'er shall be.

And Horace, while he is teaching us the Beauties in the *Art of Poetry,* gives no less than nine monosyllables in the compass of a verse and a half;

> Sed numc non erat his locus: & fortasse cupressum
> Scis simulare. Quid hoc si, &c.

Now if these are beauties, as I doubt not but the politer criticks will allow, I cannot see why our language may not now and then be tolerated in using monosyllables, when it is done discreetly, and sparingly; and as I do not commend any of our moderns who contract words into monosyllables to botch up their verses, much less such as do it out of affectation; yet certainly the use of monosyllables may be made to produce a charming and harmonious effect, where they fall under a judgment that can rightly dispose and order them. And indeed, if a variety and copiousness of feet, and a latitude of shifting and transposing words either in prose or poetical compositions, be of any use, towards the rendering of such compositions sweet, or nervous, or harmonious, according to the exigencies of the several sorts of stile, one wou'd think monosyllables to be best accommodated to all these purposes, and according to the skill of those who know how to manage them, to answer all the ends, either of masculine force, or female tenderness; for being single you have a liberty of placing them where, and as you please; whereas in words of many syllables you are more confined, and must take them as you find them, or be put upon the cruel necessity of mangling and tearing them asunder. Mr. Dryden, it is true, wou'd make us believe he had a great aversion to monosyllables. Yet he cannot help making use of them sometimes in entire verses, nor conceal his having a sort of pride, even where he tells us he was forc'd to do it. For to have done otherwise would have been a force on nature, which would have been unworthy of so great a genius, whose care it was to study nature, and to imitate and copy it to the life; and it is not improbable, that there might be somewhat of a latent delicacy and niceness in this matter, which he chose rather to dissemble, than to expose, to the indiscreet management of meaner writers. For in the first line of his great work the *Æneis*, every word is a monosyllable; and tho' he makes a seeming kind of apology, yet he cannot forbear owning a secret pleasure in what he had done.

41

> My first line in the *Æneis*, says he, is not harsh.
> Arms and the Man I sing, who forc'd by Fate.

> But a much better instance may be given from the last line of
> *Manlius*, made English by our learned and judicious Mr. Creech;
> Nor could the World have born so fierce a Flame.

Where the many liquid consonants are placed so artfully, that they give a pleasing sound to the words, tho' they are all of one syllable.

It is plain from these last words, that the subject-matter, monosyllables, is not so much to be complained of; what is chiefly to be requir'd, is of the poet, that he be a good workman, in forming them aright, and that he place them artfully: and, however Mr. Dryden may desire to disguise himself, yet, as he somewhere says, nature will prevail. For see with how much passion he has exprest himself towards these two verses, in which the poet has not been sparing of monosyllables:

I am sure, says he, there are few who make verses, have observ'd the sweetness of these two lines in *Coopers Hill;*

> Tho deep, yet clear; tho gentle, yet not dull;
> Strong without Rage, without o'erflowing full.

And there are yet fewer that can find the reason of that sweetness, I have given it to some of my friends in conversation, and they have allow'd the criticism to be just.

You see, Sir, this great master had his reserves, and this was one of the arcana, to which every novice was not admitted to aspire; this was an entertainment only for his best friends, such as he thought worthy of his conversation; and I do not wonder a it, for he was acquainted not only with the Greek and Latin poets, but with the best of his own country, as well of ancient as of latter times, and knew their beauties and defects: and tho' he did not think himself obliged to be lavish, in dispersing the fruits of so much pains and labour at random, yet was he not wanting in his generosity to such as deserved his friendship, and in whom he discern'd a spirit capable of improving the hints of so great a master. To give greater probability to what I have said concerning monosyllables, I will give some instances, as well from such poets as have gone before him, as those which have succeeded him. [There follow examples from Chaucer, Gower, Lydgate, the Earl of Surrey, Drayton, Vallans, Spenser, Cowley, Waller, Lord Orrery, the Duke of Buckingham, Lord Halifax, Lord Landsdowne, Addison, Dr. Sacheverell, and Prior]....

And Michael Drayton, who had a talent fit to imitate, and to celebrate so great a genius, of all our English poets, seems best to have understood the sweet harmonious placing of monosyllables, and has practised it with so great a variety, as discovers in him a peculiar delight, even to fondness; for which however, I cannot blame him, notwithstanding this may be reputed the vice of our sex, and in him be thought effeminate. But let the reader judge for himself;

> Care draws on Care, Woe comforts Woe again,
> Sorrow breeds Sorrow, one Griefe brings forth twaine,
> If live or dye, as thou doost, so do I
> If live, I live, and if thou dye, I dye,
> One Hart, one Love, one Joy, one Grief, one Troth,
> One Good, one Ill, one Life, one Death to both.

Again,

> Where as thou cam'st unto the Word of Love,
> Even in thine Eyes I saw how Passion strove;
> That snowy Lawn which covered thy Bed,
> Me thought lookt white to see thy cheeke so red,
> Thy rosye cheeke oft changing in my sight,
> Yet still was red to see the Lawn so white:
> The little Taper which should give the Light,
> Me thought waxt dim, to see thy Eye so bright.

Again,

> Your Love and Hate is this, I now do prove you,
> You Love in Hate, by Hate to make me love you.

And to the Countess of Bedford, one of his great patronesses;

> Sweet Lady yet, grace this poore Muse of mine,
> Whose Faith, whose Zeal, whose Life, whose All is thine.

To these let me add the testimony of that darling of the muses, Mr. Prior, with whom all the poets of ancient and modern times of other nations, or our own, might seem to have intrusted the chief secrets, and greatest treasures of their art. I shall speak only concerning our own island, where his Imitation of Chaucer, of Spencer, and of the old Scotch Poem, inscribed the Nut-Brown Maid, shew how great a master he is, and how much every thing is to be valued which bears the stamp of his approbation. And we shall certainly find a great deal to countenance the use of monosyllables in his writings. Take these examples;

43

> Me all too mean for such a Task I weet.

Again,

> Grasps he the Bolt? we ask, when he has hurl'd the Flame.

And,

> Nor found they lagg'd too slow, nor flew too fast.

And again,

> With Fear and with Desire, with Joy and Pain
> She sees and runs to meet him on the Plain.

And,

> With all his Rage, and Dread, and Grief, and Care.

In his poem in answer to Mrs. Eliz. Singer, on her poem upon *Love and Friendship*,

> And dies in Woe, that thou may'st live in Peace.

The only farther Example of Monosyllabick verses I shall insert here, and which I cannot well omit, is what I wou'd desire the author [Jonathan Swift] to apply to his own censure of monosyllables, they are these which follow;

> Then since you now have done your worst,
> Pray leave me where you found me first.

Part of the seventh Epistle of the first Book of Horace imitated, and address' to a noble Peer, p. ult.

After so many authorities of the gentlemen, these few instances from some of our female poets, may I hope be permitted to take place. I will begin with Mrs. Philips on *The Death of the Queen of Bohemia*;

> Over all Hearts and her own Griefs she reign'd.

And on *The Marriage of the Lord Dungannon*,

> May the vast Sea for your sake quit his Pride,
> And grow so smooth, while on his Breast you ride,
> As may not only bring you to your Port,
> But shew how all things do your Virtues court.

To Gilbert Lord Archbishop of Canterbury,

> That the same Wing may over her be cast,
> Where the best Church of all the World is plac'd.

Mrs. Wharton upon the *Lamentations of Jeremiah*;

> Behold those Griefs which no one can repeat,
> Her Fall is steep, and all her Foes are great.

And my Lady Winchelsea in her poem entitled, The Poor Man's Lamb;

> Thus wash'd in Tears, thy Soul as fair does show
> As the first Fleece, which on the Lamb does grow.

Sir, from these numerous instances, out of the writings of our greatest and noblest poets, it is apparent, that had the enmity against monosyllables, with which there are some who make so great a clamour, been so great in all times, we must have been deprived of some of the best lines, and finest flowers, that are to be met with in the beautiful garden of our English posie. Perhaps this may put our countrymen upon studying with greater niceness the use of these kind of words, as well as the heroick compositions, as in the softer and more gentle strains. I speak not this, upon confidence of any judgment I have in poetry, but according to that skill, which is natural to the musick of a northern ear, which, if it be deficient, as I shall not be very obstinate in its defence, I beg leave it may at least be permitted the benefit of Mr. Dryden's *Apology for the Musick of old Father Chaucer's Numbers*, "That there is the rude sweetness of a Scotch tune in it, which is natural and pleasing, tho' not perfect."

Sir, I must beg your Pardon for this long digression, upon a subject which many will think does not deserve it: but if I have herein discover'd some of the greatest beauties of our English poets, it will be more excusable, at least for the respect that is intended to so noble an art as theirs. But to suspect the worst, considering that I am now writing a preface, I am provided with another apology from Mr. Dryden, who cautions his reader with this observation, *that the nature of a preface is rambling, never wholly out of the way, nor in it.* Yet I cannot end this preface, without desiring that such as shall be employ'd in refining and ascertaining our English tongue, may entertain better thoughts both of the Saxon tongue, and of the study of antiquities.[13] Methinks it is very hard, that those who labour and take so much pains to furnish others with materials, either for writing, or for discourse, who have not leisure, or skill, or industry enough to serve themselves, shou'd be allow'd no other instances of gratitude, than the reproachful title of Men of low Genius, of which low genius's it may be observed, that they carry some ballast, and some valuable loading in them, which may be despised, but is seldom to be exceeded in anything truly valuable, by light and fluttering wits. But it is not to be wonder'd, that men of worth are to be trampled upon, for otherwise they might stand in the way of these assumers; and indeed were it not for the modesty of their betters, and their own assurance, they wou'd not only be put out of the way of those expectations that they have, but out of all manner of countenance. There is a piece of history that I have met with in the *Life of Archbishop Spotswood,* that may not unfitly be remember'd on this occasion, shewing that studious men of a private character are not always to be reputed Men of low Genius:

> Nor were his Virtues (says the history) buried and confined within the boundaries of his parish, for having formerly had a relation to the noble family of Lenox, he was looked upon as the fittest person of his quality to attend Lodowic, Duke of Lenox, as his chaplain in that honourable embassy to Henry the Fourth of France, for confirming the ancient amity between both nations; wherein he so discreetly carried himself, as added much to his reputation, and made it appear that men bred up in the shade of learning might possibly endure the sun-shine, and when it came to their turns, might carry themselves as handsomely abroad, as they (whose education being in a more pragmatick way) usually undervalue them.

But that of low genius is not the worst charge which is brought against the antiquaries, for they are not allow'd to have so much as common sense, or to know how to express their minds intelligly. This I learn from a dissertation of reading the classicks, and forming a just stile; where it is said,

> It must be a great fault of judgment if where the thoughts are proper, the expressions are not so too: a disagreement between these seldom happen, but among men of more recondite studies, and what they call deep learning, especially among your antiquaries and schoolmen.

45

This is a good careless way of talking, it may pass well enough for the genteel negligence in short, such nonsense, as our antiquaries are seldom guilty of; for propriety of thoughts, without propriety of expression is such a discovery, as is not easily laid hold of, except by such hunters after spectres and meteors, as are forced to be content with the froth and scum of learning, but have indeed nothing to shew of that deep learning, which is the effect of recondite studies. And there was a gentleman, no less a friend to polite learning, but as good a judge of it as himself, and who is also a friend to antiquities, who was hugely pleased with the humour of his saying *your Antiquaries*, being very ready to disclaim an acquaintance with all such wits, and who told me the antiquaries, were the men in all the world who most contemn'd your men of sufficiency and self-conceit. But here his master Horace is quite slipt out of his mind, whose words are,

46

> Sribendi recte, sapere est & principium & fons.
> Rem tibi Socraticae poterunt ostendere chartae:
> Verbaque provisam rem non invita sequentur.

Thus translated by my Lord Roscommon,

> Sound judgement is the ground of writing well:
> And when Philosophy directs your Choice
> To proper Subjects rightly understood,
> Words from your Pen will naturally flow....

To conclude, if this preface is writ in a stile, that may be thought somewhat rough and too severe, it is not out of any natural inclination to take up a quarrel, but to do some justice to the study of antiquities, and even of our own language itself, against the severe censurers of both; whose behaviour in this controversy has been such, as cou'd not have the treatment it deserved in a more modest or civil manner. If I am mistaken herein, I beg pardon: I might allege that which might be admitted for an excuse, but that I will not involve the whole sex, by pleading woman's frailty. I confess I thought it should be to little purpose to write an [English Saxon Grammar] if there was nothing of worth in that language to invite any one to the study of it; so that I have only been upon the defensive. If any think fit to take up arms against me, I have great confidence in the protection of the learned, the candid, and the noble; amongst which, from as many as bear the ensigns of St. George, I cannot doubt of that help, that true chevalrie can afford, to any damsel in distress, by cutting off the heads of all those dragons that dare but to open their mouths, or begin to hiss against her.

Sir, I once more heartily beg your pardon for giving you so much trouble, and beg leave to give you my thanks for the great assistance I have receiv'd in the Saxon Studies from your learned works, and conversation; and in particular for your favourable recommendation of my endeavours, in a farther cultivating those studies, who with sincere wishes for your good health, and all imaginable respect for a person of your worth and learning, am,

> SIR,
> Your most obliged,
> Humble Servant,
> *Elizabeth Elstob*

ENDNOTES

1   23 May 1737, "Letters of Mr George Ballard to the Reverend Francis Wise," in John Nichols, *Illustrations of the Literary History of the Eighteenth Century*, vol. 4 (London: John Nichols and Son, 1822).

2   John Nichols, *Literary Anecdotes of the Eighteenth Century*, vol. 4 (London: Nichols, Son and Bentley, 1812), 128.

3   Nichols, *Literary Anecdotes*, vol. 4, 129.

4   Ruth Perry, *The Celebrated Mary Astell: An Early English Feminist* (Chicago and London: University of Chicago Press, 1986), 324–25.

5   Nichols, *Literary Anecdotes*, vol. 4, 115.

6   Nichols, *Literary Anecdotes*, vol. 4, 138.

7   See especially Elstob's re-evaluation by Mechthild Gretsch, "Elizabeth Elstob: A Scholar's Fight for Anglo-Saxon Studies, Part I," *Anglia: Zeitschrift für Englische Philologie* 117 (1999): 163–200.

8   Nichols, *Literary Anecdotes*, vol. 4, 131.

9   Mechthild Gretsch, "Elizabeth Elstob," *Oxford Dictionary of National Biography* (Oxford: Oxford University Press, 2004).

10 For the Greek text, the editors have transposed the characters into the Latin alphabet. Elstob printed them in the original Greek alphabet.

11 Elstob is referring here to Jonathan Swift's *Proposal for Correcting, Improving and Ascertaining the English Tongue* (1712).

12 The following verses from Homer's *Iliad* have been transposed into Latin script for the convenience of readers following Elstob's argument on monosyllables. She, however, used the Greek script.

13 This is a direct reference to Swift's *Proposal for Correcting, Improving and Ascertaining the English Tongue*.

Priscilla Wakefield (1750–1832)

Born in Tottenham, London, Priscilla Wakefield devoted much of her life to philanthropic activities. A Quaker, she enshrined the optimistic reformist views on human improvement of Enlightenment England. Her projects for social betterment included founding a savings or "frugality" bank for the poor of Tottenham and a hospice for lying-in women. In response to her husband's business difficulties, she turned her energies to writing in the 1790s and successfully captured the market for clear, accessible and inexpensive texts of instruction in botany and more general subjects for children and young people. The growing popular interest in science in the second half of the eighteenth century was particularly marked in the field of botany, a study, as Wakefield noted, accessible to almost anyone who took pleasure in nature and the outdoors. Her chosen format was either familial conversations or letters between family members. Between 1794 and 1816, she wrote sixteen natural history books, travelogues, and a treatise on women's education, *Reflections on the Present Condition of the Female Sex* (1798).

One of Wakefield's best-known educational texts was *Mental Improvement: Or, the Beauties and Wonders of Nature and Art* (1794–1797). Written in a conversational format, the book guides the children of the fictional Harcourt family through lessons lead by their parents, lessons on a series of diverse topics ranging from the whale-fishing industry to sugar production and slavery, to the habits of salmon, and to discoveries concerning shells, fossils, and glassmaking. The Harcourts (father, mother, and four children), as members of this nuclear family, share an ethos of improvement through which the children learn method, self-reliance, and industry, assumed to be an effective preparation for industrial and mercantilist society.

Priscilla Wakefield wrote within the convention of didactic domestic fiction as a way of reaching out to a wider audience. Her botanical handbook *Introduction to Botany, in a Series of Familiar Letters* (1796) was the first woman-authored, systematic botanical handbook and, by its price and format (conversation), was destined to appeal to the general public. Though not revolutionary in its scientific content, Wakefield's *Introduction to Botany* was original in bridging the gap between academic and polite culture.[1] It based its botanical method on the Linnaean system of classifying plants, which by its simplicity and clarity had made botanical studies generally accessible.

Linnaeus's taxonomy focused on the importance of the flower in the reproductive life of plants. His sexual system, as it was called, identified the male (stamens) and female (pistils) in plants and based classification on the numbers of each in different plants. Linnaeus drew analogies between plant and animal sexual reproduction. Plants were "read" as exhibiting animal or human characteristics. This tendency was exploited by Erasmus Darwin in his erotic paean to botanical sexuality, *The Loves of Plants* (1789), in which he attributed conventional human sexual roles to the plant kingdom.

Botany in the late eighteenth century developed as a study particularly accessible to women, but the sexual nomenclature to which Linnaeus gave such prominence created difficulties for popularisers of the science to a middle- or upper-class female audience.[2] The cult of pure womanhood and girlish innocence rendered a frank discussion of even plant sexuality problematic. Partly in response to this anxiety, William Withering, a member of the Lunar Society of Birmingham, published his *Botanical Arrangement of All the Vegetables Naturally Growing in Great Britain* (1776) in which he translated or transposed the Linnaean sexual vocabulary into English, denuding it of its explicitly sexual content: thus the stamen became threads or chives; the pistils, styles or pointals. Darwin, among others, objected to this anglicization, arguing that terms should be literally translated, and he taxed Withering with having failed to note the sexual distinctions of plants.

Sexual politics were, then, at the centre of botanical culture in the 1790s when Priscilla Wakefield published her botanical handbook. She was also writing in the aftermath of the French Revolution and conscious of the British cultural backlash against radical ideas.[3] As a woman writer, a Quaker Nonconformist, and as someone hoping that her book would reach a wide audience of middle-class and upper-middle-class young people, as well as being acceptable to their parents, she was certainly not prepared to take Erasmus Darwin's route of eroticising the lives of plants. Her account is strictly Linnaean, with all the correct terms (in brackets), but she employs Withering's vocabulary in tandem, and, like him, whilst faithfully describing the reproduction of plants, does not explicitly state that they are sexual at all.

REFLECTIONS ON THE PRESENT CONDITION OF THE FEMALE SEX (1798)

Wakefield bases her plea for greater female participation in education and the workforce on Adam Smith, whom she says argues that every member of society (every man) should contribute his share of productive labour to the whole. Therefore, idleness and cultivated incapacity are wrong. It follows, Wakefield suggests, that women too should contribute their share of usefulness, if not the same share as men.

She then enquires why women are deficient in their contribution to society. The explanation lies not in a lack of intellect but is a result of women's poor education, of custom, of false pride, and of being idolised for the wrong qualities. Gentlewomen spend their lives in "indolent indulgence and trifling pursuits."

Wakefield suggests that it is pointless to argue about equality. She assumes a different excellence for each sex and that different intellectual functions are adapted to each. Nevertheless, women's capacities are not genuinely tried or exerted to their utmost extent. Women's intellect is confined by a narrow education. Their mental powers are neglected. Women are either too highly praised or too strongly despised (the Madonna/whore syndrome). Their mental powers have been neglected. Women have been willing to forego reason for the empire of the senses. Where some women have achieved excellence in intellectual fields, they have found themselves the objects of envy and slander by other women.

Wakefield recommends the pursuit of "rational improvement" and better education. In addition, when they are not supported by male relatives or spouses, women need to have respectable work. She also raises the question of unequal pay for same or similar work. Women should be able to learn a trade. She blames women's recourse to prostitution on a lack of decent employment. Progress is possible and is occurring. There are many useful occupations for women to fill without encroaching upon those professions that are appropriate to men. Women can develop their talents for the public good without destroying their femininity or "exceeding the most exact limits of modesty and decorum."

Though Wakefield accepts the idea of gender stratification, she focuses on the corrupting effects of genteel idleness for women and especially on women's extreme economic vulnerability.

Reflections on the Present Condition of the Female Sex with Suggestions for Its Improvement (1798)

Priscilla Wakefield

Chapter I

It is asserted by Doctor Adam Smith, that every individual is a burden upon society to which he belongs, who does not contribute his share of productive labour for the good of the whole. The Doctor, when he lays down this principle, speaks in general terms of man, as a being capable of forming a social compact for mutual defence, and the advantage of the community at large. He does not absolutely specify, that both sexes, in order to render themselves beneficial members of society, are equally required to comply with these terms; but since the female sex is included in the idea of the species, and as women possess the same qualities as men, though perhaps in a different degree, their sex cannot free them from the claim of the public for their proportion of usefulness. That the major part of the sex, especially of those among the higher orders, neglect to fulfil this important obligation, is a fact that must be admitted, and points out the propriety of an enquiry into the causes of their deficiency.

The indolent indulgence and trifling pursuits in which those who are distinguished by the appellation of gentlewomen, often pass their lives, may be attributed, with greater probability, to a contracted education, custom, false pride, and idolizing adulation, than to any defect in their intellectual capacities. The contest for equality in the mental capacity of the sexes, has been maintained, on each side of the question, with ingenuity; but as a judgment only can be formed from facts, as they arise in the present state of things, if the experiments have been fairly tried, the rare instances of extraordinary talents, which have been brought forward to support the system of equality, must yield to the irresistible influence of corporeal powers. Which leads to a conclusion, that the intellectual faculties of each sex, are wisely adapted to their appropriate purposes, and that, laying aside the invidious terms of superiority and inferiority, the perfection of mind in man and in woman, consists in a power to maintain the distinguishing characteristics of excellence in each. But this concession by no means proves, that even in this enlightened age and country, the talents of women have ever been generally exerted to the utmost extent of their capacity, or that they have been turned towards the most useful objects; neither does it imply, that the cultivation they receive, is adequate to bring into action the full strength of those powers, which have been bestowed on them by nature. The intellectual faculties of the female mind have too long been confined by narrow and ill-directed modes of education, and thus have been concealed, not only from others, but from themselves, the energies of which they are capable. The exigence of circumstances in private life has called forth numberless examples of female prudence, magnanimity and fortitude, which demonstrated no less a clearness of conception, than a warmth of feeling, reflecting equal honour upon the heads, and upon the hearts of the sex. Neither has history been silent in recording memorable instances of female capacity, in all the various branches of human excellence. These united testimonies are surely sufficient to justify an opinion, that the imperfect contributions to the mass of public activity have not arisen from want of ability to be useful, but from some defect of another kind, which it is necessary to discover, that a remedy may be found, and applied to the evil.

In civilised nations it has ever been the misfortune of the sex to be too highly elevated, or too deeply depressed; now raised above the condition of mortals, upon the score of their personal attractions; and now debased below that of reasonable creatures, with respect to their intellectual endowments. The result of this improper treatment has been a neglect of the mental powers, which women really possess, but know not how to exercise; and they have been contented to barter the dignity of reason, for the imaginary privilege of an empire, of the existence of which they can entertain no reasonable hope beyond the duration of youth and beauty.

Of the few who have raised themselves to pre-eminence by daring to stray beyond the accustomed path, the envy of their own sex, and the jealousy or contempt of the other, have too often been the attendants; a fate which doubtless has deterred others from attempting to follow them, or emulate, even in an inferior degree, the distinction they have attained.

But notwithstanding these disadvantages, and others of less perceptible influence, the diffusion of Christianity, and the progress of civilization, have raised the importance of the female character; and it has become a branch of philosophy, not a little interesting, to ascertain the offices which the different ranks of women are required to fulfil. Their rights and their duties have lately occupied the pens of writers of eminence; the employments which may properly exercise their faculties, and fill up their time in a useful manner, without encroaching upon those professions, which are appropriate to men, remain to be defined. There are many branches of science, as well as useful occupations, in which women may employ their time and their talents, beneficially to themselves and to the community, without destroying the peculiar characteristic of their sex, or exceeding the most exact limits of modesty and decorum. Whatever obliges them to mix in the public haunts of men, or places the young in too familiar a situation with the other sex; whatever is obnoxious to the delicacy and reserve of the female character, or destructive, in the smallest degree, to the strictest moral purity, is inadmissible. The sphere of feminine action is contracted by numberless difficulties, that are no impediments to masculine exertions. Domestic privacy is the only sure asylum for the juvenile part of the sex; nor can the grave matron step far beyond that boundary with propriety. Unfitted, by their relative situation in society, for many honourable and lucrative employments, those only are suitable for them, which can be pursued without endangering their virtue, or corrupting their manners.

But, under these restrictions, there may be found a multitude of objects adapted to the useful exertions of female talents, which it will be the principal design of these *Reflections* to point out, after making some remarks upon the present state of female education, and suggesting some improvements towards its reformation.

And here the author may perhaps be allowed to express her hope, that among the numbers of the female world, who appear to be satisfied with inferiority, many require only to be awakened to a true sense of their own real consequence, to be induced to support it by a rational improvement of those hours, which they have hitherto wasted in the most frivolous occupations. The promotion of so useful a design, is the only apology for intruding her opinions upon the subject; and it will be esteemed her highest recompence, should her observations contribute to its accomplishment.

Chapter III

Remarks on the duties of a married and a single life. Maternal tuition, when practicable, recommended; with a sketch of the qualifications of a Governess. Plan suggested for a Female College, and Select Day Schools proposed. Ranks in society discriminated. The necessity of Women being for the exercise of lucrative employments shewn, and the absurdity of a Woman honourably earning a support, being excluded from Society, exposed.

The necessity of directing the attention of females to some certain occupation is not so apparent, because custom has rendered them dependant upon their fathers and husbands for support; but as some of every class experience the loss of those relations, without inheriting an adequate resource, there would be great propriety in preparing each of them, by an education of energy and useful attainments, to meet such disasters, and to be able, under such circumstances, to procure an independence for themselves. There is scarcely a more helpless object in the wide circle of misery which the vicissitudes of civilized society display, than a woman genteelly educated, whether single or married, who is deprived, by any unfortunate accident, of the protection and support of male relations;

53

unaccustomed to struggle with difficulty, unacquainted with any resource to supply an independent maintenance, she is reduced to the depths of wretchedness, and not unfrequently, if she be young and handsome, is driven by despair to those paths which lead to infamy. Is it not time to find a remedy for such evils, when the contention of nations has produced the most affecting transitions in private life, and transferred the affluent and the noble to the humiliating extremes of want and obscurity? When our streets teem with multitudes of unhappy women, many of whom might have been rescued from their present degradation, or who would perhaps never have fallen into it, had they been instructed in the exercise of some art or profession, which would have enabled them to procure for themselves a respectable support by their own industry.

54

This reasonable precaution against the accidents of life is resisted by prejudice, which rises like an insurmountable barrier against a woman, of any degree above the vulgar, employing her time and her abilities, towards the maintenance of herself and her family: degradation of rank immediately follows the virtuous attempt, as it did formerly, among the younger branches of the noble families in France. But the nature of truth is immutable, however it may be obscured by error: that which is a moral excellence in one rational being, deserves the same estimation in another; therefore, if it be really honourable in a man, to exert the utmost of his abilities, whether mental or corporal, in the acquisition of a competent support for himself, and for those who have a natural claim upon his protection; it must be equally so in a woman, nay, perhaps still more incumbent, as in many cases, there is nothing so inimical to the preservation of her virtue as a state of poverty, which leaves her dependant upon the generosity of others, to supply those accommodations, which use has rendered necessary to her comfort.

There appears then no moral impediment to prevent women from the application of their talents to purposes of utility; on the contrary, an improvement in public manners must infallibly result from it; as their influence over the other sex is universally acknowledged, it may be boldly asserted, that a conversion of their time from trifling and unproductive employments, to those that are both useful and profitable, would operate as a check upon luxury, dissipation, and prodigality, and retard the progress of that general dissoluteness, the offspring of idleness, which is deprecated by all political writers, as the sure forerunner of national decay.

Some alteration in the general turn of thinking among young women, must take place before they can be persuaded to render themselves capable of these useful exertions; and that can be produced only by the early impressions they imbibe; the manner in which they are received in society, after such application; and their finding no impediment arise from it to their settlement in marriage. It cannot be expected that young females will of choice apply themselves to serious studies, or be willing to become industrious members of the community, whilst they are impressed from infancy with a notion, that they are born only to create admiration, and that they are excluded from the necessity of any regular occupation, beyond that of domestic superintendance, or what conduces to the acquisition of elegant accomplishments. The correction of these errors depends upon the discretion of those, whose duty it is to form their opinions upon just principles. But their reception in society rests not upon the propriety of their sentiments, or the prudence of their conduct, in this respect; it can only be assured to them by persons of rank and consequence, whose countenance will be sufficient gradually to undermine the unreasonable prepossession against the exercise of female industry. Can it be accounted for on any other ground than that of prejudice, in a country like England, where commerce forms one of the principal sinews of national strength, where the character of the merchant is honourable, and no obstacle to a favourable reception in the highest circles, that degradation should attend the female who engages in the concerns of commerce, and that she whose good sense and resolution enable her to support herself, is banished from that line of company, of which she had perhaps previously formed a distinguished ornament? One of the effects of this ill-directed pride, is to deter young men of liberal prospects, from demeaning themselves, as it is erroneously termed, by marrying a girl who has been trained up to any profitable employment. How much more reasonable would it be to give them a preference on account of this mark of their superior judgment, which may fairly be estimated as an earnest of their becoming useful helpmates through the uncertain contingency of future events.

Were but these three barriers removed, of false notions, exclusion from society, or diminishing the chance of an advantageous marriage; the example of a few might influence others, and extend like a drop of oil spread upon the surface of the water. But where are the parents, who have sufficient independence of mind to encourage their daughters to lead the way, and to prepare them, by an improved plan of education, to succeed in it? To lay aside the fetters of prejudice, and adopt a practice contrary to established customs, requires a cool unbiased judgment, and unshaken resolution to comply with its dictates. The utility of the object would apologize for the innovation, and the difficulty of the attempt but enhances its merit. The word reform, has become the signal of a party, and the fear of change may render some averse from the very idea of introducing an alteration in female manners: But let such be informed, that it is not a novelty that is proposed; the Dutch adopted it in part a century ago, as we are told by Sir Joshua Child, in his discourse concerning trade, wherein he remarks that the education of the Dutch women prepared them to receive instruction from their husbands, in the different species of commerce in which they were engaged: He recommends the imitation of this example to the English, as one of the means that promoted the riches and prosperity of Holland; and contributed in no small degree to the happiness of individuals: And as he does not state that any inconvenience arose from this practice, it is candid to suppose that this useful knowledge had no ill effect upon the Dutch women, to render them independent of their husbands, or less submissive to their authority, than the wives of modern times.

The first step to be pursued towards this desirable improvement, is the adoption of a more energetic mode of education. Instruction has been bestowed upon

55

girls with a much greater liberality of late years than formerly; and it will scarcely be controverted, that the beneficial effects of it are apparent, in the improved state of female knowledge and conduct. But they are still taught, what they learn, too superficially, and the more solid acquirements are too often neglected. Music, dancing, dress, and works of fancy, engross a larger share of time and attention than is their due: they should be regarded as amusements, rather than as occupations, and be restrained with a proper subordination to those pursuits, which are superior in their nature and consequence. The importance of promoting health and vigour of constitution, has been already suggested as a suitable foundation for the attainment of strength of mind; with which may properly be combined, whatever is conducive to personal beauty or graceful deportment; for it is not asserted, that external appearance is unworthy of all regard, it certainly claims due attention; but it is advisable to temper that care with every possible precaution against exciting the emotions of self-complacency and personal vanity, the most dangerous of all qualities in a female mind, as they are the source of the most common errors in female conduct. One injurious consequence of a vain mind, is an extravagant taste for dress, and exhibiting the person in public places; a disposition subversive of domestic happiness, and that sobriety of character, which, in youth, is the presage of every thing useful and honourable.

ENDNOTES

1   For an illuminating discussion of the issues around the popularisation of scientific ideas, see Cheryce Kramer, "Introduction," *Literature and Science, 1660–1834*, vol. 1, *Science as Polite Culture, Literature and Science 1660–1834*, ed. Cheryce Kramer, Trea Martyn, and Michael Newton (London: Pickering and Chatto, 2003–2004) and Greg Myers, "Science for women and children: the dialogue of popular science in the nineteenth century," in *Nature Transfigured: Science and Literature, 1700–1900*, ed. John Christie and Sally Shuttleworth, 171–200 (Manchester: Manchester University Press, 1989).

2   See Ann B. Shteir, *Cultivating Women, Cultivating Science: Flora's Daughters and Botany in England, 1760–1860* (Baltimore: Johns Hopkins University Press, 1996).

3   See Maureen McNeil, *Under the Banner of Science: Erasmus Darwin and His Age* (Manchester: Manchester University Press, 1987), especially Chapter 3 for the backlash against radical ideas in science as well as in politics, and Ian Bewell, "'Jacobin Plants': Botany as Social Theory in the 1790s," *The Wordsworth Circle* 20, no. 3 (Summer 1989): 32–139.

Anna Lætitia Barbauld (née Aikin) (1743–1825)

Anna Lætitia Aikin Barbauld, poet, educationist, literary critic, and radical polemicist, was born into a Presbyterian family. Her father, the Reverend John Aikin, served for many years as tutor at the nonconformist Warrington Academy in Lancashire. Anna gave early evidence of her intelligence. Mr. and Mrs. Aikin seem, however, to have feared their daughter's precocity and that growing up in the company of boys at the Academy, she would lack feminine graces;

> Her education was entirely domestic and principally conducted by her excellent mother whose manners were polished by an early introduction to good company which her family connexions had procured her.... In the middle of the last century a strong prejudice still existed against imparting to females any tincture of classical learning; and the father of Miss Aikin, proud as he justly was of her uncommon capacity, long refused to gratify her earnest desire of being initiated in this kind of knowledge.[1]

In spite of her mother's efforts to rein in her intellectual appetite and her father's hesitations, Anna eventually persuaded him to tutor her in Latin and Greek.

Her mother set a standard of gentility (gentility in young women definitely did not include scholarship) that Anna felt she never could achieve. We hear a lifetime of maternal reproaches echoing in the counsels of Anna Barbauld when she wrote, "... young ladies ... ought only to have such a general tincture of knowledge as to make them agreeable companions to a man of sense" and "thefts of knowledge in our sex are only connived at while carefully concealed, and if displayed, punished with disgrace."[2]

Nevertheless, Anna passed her youth at Warrington in an intellectually stimulating environment. She was encouraged in her literary interests by her brother, John Aikin, became a close friend of the Priestleys, and, through them, was introduced to new discoveries in science and to radical ideas. In the 1760s, she began writing poems on scientific, political, and religious subjects, as well as showing a talent for burlesque. A collection of her poetry published in 1773 established her as a leading poet.

In 1774, at the age of thirty-one, Anna Aikin married the Reverend Rochemont Barbauld (1749–1808), who, while studying at Warrington Academy, had converted from the Anglican Church to Dissent, eventually becoming a Unitarian minister. Though Rochemont was a talented and high-minded man, he suffered throughout his adult life from bouts of serious mental illness, which made him prone to extreme violence. Lucy Aikin wrote of their marriage: "My father ascribed that ill-starred union in great part to the baleful influence of the 'Nouvelle Héloïse,' Mr B. impersonating St. Preux."[3] This romantic excess and the price she was to pay for it may go some way to explaining Anna Barbauld's later emphasis on didactic and utilitarian training for young children. The Barbauld's marriage, marred though it was by Rochement's periodic outbreaks of madness, endured for thirty-four years, until his suicide in 1808. Anna was devoted to her husband, and long resisted his incarceration in a private asylum, a step to which she only consented in the last year of his life after he had physically attacked her. She remembered him for "the kindness of his nature and his acts of benevolence."[4]

58

Believing in the hereditary nature of Rochemont's madness, the Barbauld's did not have children but adopted their nephew Charles Aikin. From 1774–1785, they ran a very successful boys school at Palgrave in Suffolk. Anna showed herself to be an imaginative teacher. She published a series of innovative children's early reading books, initially written to teach Charles. Designed in size, print size, and vocabulary for the very young, these were little volumes with big print and simple words, recounting short didactic stories. There had been nothing like them before. Though Charles Lamb and Coleridge were later to mock them as overly factual, Barbauld's tales were brilliantly adapted to her audience of two- to four-year-olds.[5]

In 1785, the Barbaulds travelled to France and absorbed much of the excitement of the approaching revolution. In the 1790s, following Edmund Burke's denunciation of the French Revolution, Anna Barbauld published four polemical works: *An Address to the Opposers of the Repeal of the Corporation and Test Acts* (1790); *An Epistle to William Wilberforce esq.* (1791); *Sins of the Government, Sins of the Nation* (1793); and *Remarks on Mr. Gilbert Wakefield's Enquiry into the Expediency and Propriety of Public or Social Worship* (1792). In the first three, she condemned Parliament for not abolishing discrimination against dissenters, for refusing to abolish the slave trade, and for attacking the French Revolution abroad while suppressing opposition at home. Her pamphlet on Wakefield's enquiry, which defended public worship against Wakefield's strictures, took a more consensual line.[6]

In 1802, the Barbaulds moved to Stoke Newington, then an eastern suburb of London. There they mixed with radical intellectuals such as the publisher Joseph Johnson (also Mary Wollstonecraft's publisher); the poets Joanna Baillie, George Dyer, and Henry Crabbe Robinson; the novelist Maria Edgeworth; and the philosopher William Godwin. In subsequent years, Barbauld wrote biography and literary criticism, edited Samuel Richardson's letters (1804), contributed to periodicals, and wrote prefaces for the fifty-volume publication, *The British Novelists* (1810) and reviews for the *Monthly Review*. Her last work was a satiric poem entitled "1811," describing a future Britain ruined by war. Though today the poem ranks as an important Romantic work, savage reviews in the patriotic press on its publication in 1812 effectually silenced her.

Anna Barbauld's last years were clouded by the melancholy occasioned by her husband's suicide and the death of her brother John Aikin in 1822. In her old age, she was a prey to asthma, the eventual cause of her death in 1825. She continued to be revered by many who kept alive hopes of a more liberal society.

AN ADDRESS TO THE OPPOSERS OF THE REPEAL OF THE CORPORATION AND TEST ACTS (1790)

The Corporation Act (1661) and the Test Act (1673), passed in the reign of Charles II, were intended to ensure that Catholics and Nonconformists, seen as potentially subversive to the restored monarchy, were excluded from public office and from positions of political power (See footnote 1, *Address*). Anna Barbauld's 1790 publication *Address to the Opposers of the Repeal of the Corporation and Test Acts* (published anonymously but soon identified as hers) formed part of a long campaign by British Nonconformists, Jews, and Catholics for the abolition of these laws. A petition to Parliament in that year had failed. Barbauld, writing in the early days of the French Revolution, compares the conservative response of Parliament and the Anglican Church unfavourably with the enormous strides towards liberty visible across the English Channel in France.

First, rejecting the idea of *toleration*, Barbauld demands equality under the law as a *right*, thereby explicitly allying herself with the sentiments of the French drafters of the *Déclaration des droits de l'homme et du citoyen* and the American Declaration of Independence. Secondly, Barbauld defends the French Revolution of 1789, attacking Edmund Burke, who had, in 1790, opposed the repeal of the Corporation and Test Acts. Further, Burke, who initially displayed a certain apprehensive enthusiasm for the French Revolution, soon denounced it and its English champions in his *Reflections on the Revolution in France, and on the proceedings in certain societies in London relative to that event* (1790). The *Reflections* would attract some notable replies: from Thomas Paine, in his *The Rights of Man* (1791–1792); Mary Wollstonecraft, in her *Vindication of the Rights of Men* (November, 1790); and Catharine Macaulay, in *Observations on Burke's Reflections on the French Revolution* (1790). Barbauld, however, was one of the first to join the fray, penning her *Address* on the third of March 1790, following the rejection of the attempt at repeal on the second of that month. Her *Address* was reprinted at least four times in the first year.[7]

Barbauld conveyed powerfully the excitement and sense of intellectual liberation at the outset of the Revolution. With hindsight, the Terror, the Napoleonic wars, France's eventual defeat, the restoration of the monarchy, and, in Britain, a long period of political reaction would not bear out Barbauld's enthusiastic hopes. Yet for her like-minded contemporaries, Barbauld communicated the optimism of the revolutionary moment, ironically echoing Burke, by bringing the language of romantic sensibility to the service of political argument. Like Macaulay, Paine, and Wollstonecraft, she responded powerfully to the challenge of Burke's emotive text. Barbauld's linking of the non-repeal of the Corporation and Test Acts with English attitudes towards the French Revolution demonstrated her ability convincingly to connect two contemporary dramas concerning human rights.

An Address to the Opposers of the Repeal of the Corporation and Test Acts (1790) [8]

Anna Lœtitia Barbauld

"A System of Toleration, attended with humiliating Distinctions, is so vicious in itself, that the Man who is forced to tolerate is as much dissatisfied with the Law as he that obtains such a Toleration."

Speech of Count Clermont Tonnerre.

Gentlemen,

Had the question of yesterday been decided in a manner more favourable to our wishes, which however the previous intimations of your temper in the business left us little room to expect, we should have addressed our thanks to you on the occasion. As it is, we address to you our thanks for much casual light thrown upon the subject, and for many incidental testimonies of your esteem (whether voluntary or involuntary we will not stop to examine) which in the course of this discussion you have favoured us with. We thank you for the compliment paid the Dissenters, when you suppose that the moment they are eligible to places of power and profit, all such places will at once be filled with them. Not content with confounding, by an artful sophism, the right of eligibility with the right to offices, you again confound that right with the probable fact, and then argue accordingly. Is then the Test Act, your boasted bulwark, of equal necessity with the dykes in Holland; and do we wait, like an impetuous sea, to rush in and overwhelm the land? Our pretensions, Gentlemen, are far humbler. *We* had not the presumption to imagine that, inconsiderable as we are in numbers, compared to the established Church; inferior too in fortune and influence; labouring, as we do, under the frown of the Court, and the anathema of the orthodox; we should make our way so readily into the secret recesses of royal favour; and, of a sudden, like the frogs of Egypt, swarm about your barns, and under your canopies, and in your kneading troughs, and in the chamber of the King. We rather wished this act as a removal

60

of a stigma than the possession of a certain advantage, and we might have been cheaply pleased with the acknowledgement of the right, though we had never been fortunate enough to enjoy the emolument.

Another compliment for which we offer our acknowledgements may be extracted from the great ferment, which has been raised by this business all over the country. What stir and movement has it occasioned among the different orders of men! How quick the alarm has been taken, and sounded from the Church to the Senate, and from the press to the people; while fears and forebodings were communicated like an electric shock! The old cry of, *the Church is in Danger*, has again been made to vibrate in our ears. Here too if we gave way to impressions of vanity, we might suppose ourselves of much greater importance in the political scale than our numbers and situation seem to indicate. It shews at least we are feared, which to some minds would be the next grateful thing to being beloved. We, indeed, should only wish for the latter; nor should we have ventured to suppose, but from the information you have given us, that your Church *was* so weak. What! fenced and guarded as she is with her exclusive privileges and rich emoluments, stately with her learned halls and endowed colleges, with all the attraction of her wealth, and the thunder of her censures; all that the orator calls *the majesty of the Church* about her, and does she, resting in security under the broad buckler of the State, does she tremble at the naked and unarmed sectary? he, whose early connections, and phrase uncouth, and unpopular opinions set him at a distance from the means of advancement; he, who in the intercourses of neighbourhood and common life, like new settlers, finds it necessary to clear the ground before him, and is ever obliged to root up a prejudice before he can plant affection. He is not of the world, Gentlemen, and the world loveth her own. All that distinguishes him from other men to common observation, operates in his disfavour. His very advocates, while they plead his cause, are ready to blush for their client; and in justice to their own character think it necessary to disclaim all knowledge of his obscure tenets. And is it from his hand you expect the demolition of so massy an edifice? Does the simple removal of the Test Act involve its destruction? These were not *our* thoughts. *We* had too much reverence for your establishment to imagine that the structure was so loosely put together, or so much shaken by the years, as that the removal of so slight a pin should endanger the whole fabric—or is the Test Act the *talisman* which holds it together, that, when it is broken, the whole must fall to pieces like the magic palace of an enchanter? Surely no species of regular architecture can depend upon so slight a support. —After all what is it we have asked?—to share in the rich benefices of the established church? to have the gates of her schools and universities thrown open to us? No, let her keep her golden prebends, her scarfs, her lawn, her mitres. Let her dignitaries be still associated to the honours of legislation; and, in our courts of executive justice, let her inquisitorial tribunals continue to thwart the spirit of a free constitution by a heterogeneous mixture of priestly jurisdiction. Let her still gather into barns, though she neither sows nor reaps. We desire not to share in her good things. We know it is the children's bread, which must not be given to dogs. But *having* these good things, we *could* wish to hear her say with the

61

generous spirit of Esau, *I have enough, my brother.* We could wish to be considered as children of the State, though we are not so of the Church. She must excuse us if we look upon the alliance between her and the State as an ill sorted union, and herself as a mother-in-law who, with the too frequent arts of that relation, is ever endeavouring to prejudice the State, the common parent of us all, against a part of his offspring, for the sake of appropriating a larger portion to her own children. We claim no share in the dowry of her who is not our mother, but we may be pardoned for thinking it hard to be deprived of the inheritance of our father.

But it is objected to us that we have sinned in the manner of making our request; we have brought it forward as a claim instead of asking it as a favour. We should have sued, and crept, and humbled ourselves. Our preachers and our writers should not have dared to express the warm glow of honest sentiment, or, even in a foreign country glance at the downfall of a haughty aristocracy. As we were suppliants, we should have behaved like suppliants, and then perhaps —No, Gentlemen, we wish to have it understood, that we *do* claim it as a right. It loses otherwise half its value. We claim it as men, we claim it as citizens, we claim it as good subjects. We are not conscious of having brought the disqualification upon ourselves by a failure in any of these characters.

But we already enjoy a complete toleration—It is time, so near the end of the eighteenth century, it is surely time to speak with precision, and to call things by their proper names. What you call toleration, we call the exercise of a natural and unalienable right. We do not conceive it to be toleration, first to strip a man of all his dearest rights, and then to give him back a part; or even if it were the whole. You tolerate us in worshipping God according to our consciences—and why not tolerate a man in the use of his limbs, in the disposal of his private property, the contracting of his domestic engagements, or any other [of] the most acknowledged privileges of humanity? It is not to these things that the word toleration is applied with propriety. It is applied, where from lenity or prudence we forbear doing all which in justice we might do. It is the bearing with what is confessedly an evil, for the sake of some good with which it is connected. It is the Christian virtue of long suffering; it is the political virtue of adapting measures to times and seasons and situations. *Abuses* are tolerated, when they are so interwoven with the texture of the piece, that the operation of removing them becomes too delicate and hazardous. *Unjust claims* are tolerated, when they are complied with for the sake of peace and conscience. The failings and imperfections of those characters in which there appears an evident preponderancy of virtue, are tolerated. These are the proper objects of toleration, these exercise the patience of the Christian and the prudence of the Statesman; but if there be a power that advances pretences which we think unfounded in reason or scripture, that exercises an empire within an empire, and claims submission from those naturally her equals; and if we, from a spirit of brotherly charity, and just deference to public opinion, and a salutary dread of innovation, acquiesce in these pretensions; let her at least be told that the virtue of forbearance should be transferred and that it is we who tolerate her, and not she who tolerates us.

Complete Toleration, though an expression often adverted to by both parties, is in truth a solecism in terms; for all that is tolerated ought to be done away whenever is found practicable and expedient. Complete Convalescence is no longer Convalescence, but Health; and complete Toleration is no longer Toleration, but Liberty. Let the term therefore be discarded; which, however softened, involves in it an insult with regard to us, and however extended, an absurdity with regard to yourselves. Sensible that a spirit of liberality requires the indulgence to be *complete*, and desirous at the same time to retain the idea of our holding it through sufferance and not of right, you have been betrayed into this incongruity of expression. Those are always liable to be betrayed into such, who have not the courage to embrace a system in its full extent, and to follow a principle wherever it may lead them. Hence the *progress* from Error to Truth, and from Bigotry to the most enlarged freedom of sentiment, is marked with greater *inconsistencies* than that state in which the mind quietly rests in the former position. It is only when we view objects by a dubious and uncertain twilight that we are apt to mistake their figure and distances, and to be disturbed by groundless terrors; in perfect darkness we form no judgment about them—It has ever been the untoward fate of your Church to partake largely of these inconsistencies. Placed between the Catholics on one side, and the Dissenters on the other, she has not been able to defend either her resistance or her restraints, and lies equally open to censure for her persecution and her dissent. Pressed by the difficulties of her peculiar situation, she is continually obliged in the course of her polemic warfare to change her ground, and alter her mode of defence; and like the poor Bat in the fable, to tell a different story upon every new attack; and thus it must be, till she shall have the magnanimity to make use of all her light, and follow her reason without reserve.

For Truth is of a nature strangely encroaching, and ought to be kept out entirely if we are not disposed to admit her with perfect freedom. You cannot say to her, Thus far shalt thou go, and no further. Give her the least entrance, and she will never be satisfied till she has gained entire possession. Allow her but a few plain axioms to work with, and step by step, syllogism after syllogism, she insensibly mines her way into the very heart of her enemy's entrenchments. Truth is of a very intolerant spirit. She will not make any compromise with Error, and if she be obliged to hold any fellowship with her, it is such fellowship as light has with darkness, a perpetual warfare and opposition. Every concession made by her antagonist is turned into a fresh weapon against her, and being herself invulnerable, she is sure to gain by each successive contest, till her adversary is driven from every shelter and lurking-hole, and fairly obliged to quit possession of the field.

But this, it is again imputed to us, is no contest for religious liberty, but a contest for power, and place, and influence. We want civil offices—And why should citizens *not* aspire to civil offices? Why should not the fair field of generous competition be freely opened to every one!—A contention for power—It is not a contention for power between Churchmen and Dissenters, nor is it as Dissenters we wish to enter the lists; we wish to bury every name of distinction

63

in the common appellation of Citizen. We wish not the name of Dissenter to be pronounced, except in our theological researches and religious assemblies. It is you, who by considering us as Aliens, make us so. It is you who force us to make our dissent a prominent feature in our character. It is you who give relief, and cause to come out upon the canvas what we modestly wished to have shaded over, and thrown into the back ground. If we are a party, remember it is you who force us to be so.—We should have sought places of trust—By no unfair, unconstitutional methods should we have sought them, but in the open and honourable rivalship of virtuous emulation; by trying to deserve well of our King and our Country. Our attachment to both is well known.

64

* * * * *

To return to ourselves, and our feelings on the business lately in agitation—You will excuse us if we do not appear with the air of men baffled and disappointed. Neither do we blush at our defeat; we may blush, indeed, but it is for our country; but we lay hold on the consoling persuasion, that reason, truth and liberality must finally prevail. We appeal from Philip intoxicated to Philip sober. We know you will refuse us while you are narrow minded, but you will not always be narrow minded. You have too much light and candour not to have more. We will no more attempt to pluck the green unripe fruit. We see in you our future friends and brethren, eager to confound and blend with ours your interests and affections. You will grant us all we ask. The only question between us is, whether you will do it to-day—To-morrow you certainly will. You will even intreat us, if need were, to allow you to remove from your country the stigma of illiberality. We appeal to the certain, sure operation of increasing light and knowledge, which it is no more in your power to stop, than to repel the tide with your naked hand, or to wither with your breath the genial influence of vegetation. The spread of that light is in general gradual and imperceptible; but there are periods when its progress is accelerated, when it seems with a sudden flash to open the firmament, and pour in day at once. Can ye not discern the signs of the times? The minds of men are in movement from the Borysthenes to the Atlantic. Agitated with new and strong emotions, they swell and heave beneath oppression, as the seas within the Polar Circle, when, at the approach of Spring, they grow impatient to burst their icy chains; when what, but an instant before, seemed so firm, spread for many a dreary league like a floor of solid marble, at once with a tremendous noise gives way, long fissures spread in every direction, and the air resounds with the clash of floating fragments, which every hour are broken from the mass. The genius of Philosophy is walking abroad, and with the touch of Ithuriel's spear is trying the establishments of the earth.[9] The various forms of Prejudice, Superstition and Servility start up in their true shapes, which had long imposed upon the world under the revered semblances of Honour, Faith, and Loyalty. Whatever is loose must be shaken, whatever is corrupted must be lopt away; whatever is not built on the broad basis of public utility must be thrown to the ground. Obscure murmurs gather, and swell into a tempest; the spirit of Enquiry, like a severe and searching wind, penetrates every part of the great body politic; and whatever is unsound, whatever is infirm, shrinks at the visitation. Liberty, here with the lifted crosier in hand, and the crucifix conspicuous on her breast; there led by Philosophy, and crowned with the civic wreath, animates men to assert their long forgotten rights. With a policy, far more liberal and comprehensive than the boasted establishments of Greece and Rome, she diffuses her blessings to every class of men; and even extends a smile of hope and promise to the poor African, the victim of hard, impenetrable avarice. Man, *as* man, becomes an object of respect. Tenets are transferred from theory to practice. The glowing sentiment and lofty speculation no longer serve "but to adorn the pages of a book;" they are brought home to men's business and bosoms; and, what some centuries ago was daring but to think, and dangerous to express, is now realized, and carried into effect. Systems are analysed into their first principles, and principles are fairly pursued to their legitimate consequences. The enemies of reformation, who palliate what they cannot defend, and defer what they dare not refuse; who, with Festus, put off to a more convenient season what, only because it is the present season is inconvenient, stand aghast; and find they have no power to put back the important hour, when nature is labouring with the birth of great events. Can ye not discern—But you do discern these signs; you discern them well, and your alarm is apparent. You see a mighty empire breaking from bondage, and exerting the energies of recovered freedom: and England—which was used to glory in being the assertor of liberty, and refuge of the oppressed—England, who with generous and respectful sympathy, in times not far remote from our own memory, has afforded an asylum to so many of the subjects of that very empire, when crushed beneath the iron rod of persecution; and, by so doing, circulated a livelier abhorrence of tyranny within her own veins—England, who has long reproached her with being a slave now censures her for daring to be free. England, who has held a torch to her, is mortified to see it blaze brighter in her hands. England, for whom, and for whose manners and habits of thinking, that empire has, for some time past, felt even an enthusiastic predilection; and to whom, as a model of laws and government, she looks up with affectionate reverence—England, nursed at the breast of liberty, and breathing the purest spirit of enlightened philosophy, views a sister nation with affected scorn and real jealousy, and presumes to ask whether she yet exists—Yes, all of her exists that is worthy to do so. Her dungeons indeed exist no longer, the iron doors are forced, the massy wall are thrown down; and the liberated spectres, trembling between joy and horror, may now blazon the infernal secrets of their prison house. Her cloistered Monks no longer exist, nor does the soft heart of sensibility beat behind the grate of a convent, but the best affections of the human mind permitted to flow in their natural channel, diffuse their friendly influence over the brightening prospect of domestic happiness. Nobles, the creatures of Kings, exist there no longer; but Man, the creature of God, exists there. Millions of men exist there who, only now, truly begin to exist, and hail with shouts of grateful acclamation

65

the better birth-day of their country. Go on, generous nation, set the world an example of virtues as you have of talents. Be our model, as we have been yours. May the spirit of wisdom, the spirit of moderation, the spirit of firmness, guide and bless your counsels. With intelligence to discern the best possible, may you have prudence to be content with the best practicable. Overcome our wayward perverseness by your steadiness and temper. Silence the scoff of your enemies, and the misgiving fears of your timorous well-wishers. Go on to destroy the empire of prejudices, that empire of gigantic shadows, which are only formidable while they are not attacked. Cause to succeed to the mad ambition of conquest the pacific industry of commerce, and the simple, useful toils of agriculture. While your corn springs up under the shade of your Olives, may bread and peace be the portion of the Husbandman; and when beneath your ardent sun, his brow is bathed in honest sweat, let no one dare any longer with hard and vexatious exactions to wring from him the bitter drop of anguish. Instructed by the experience of past centuries, and by many a sad and sanguine page in your own histories, may you no more attempt to blend what God has made separate; but may religion and civil polity, like the two necessary but opposite elements of fire and water, each in its province do service to mankind, but never again be forced into discordant union. Let the wandering pilgrims of every tribe and complexion, who in other lands find only an asylum, find with you a country, and may you never seek other proof of the purity of your faith than the largeness of your charity. In your manners, your language, and habits of life, let a manly simplicity, becoming the intercourse of equals with equals, take the place of overstrained refinement and adulation. Let public reformation prepare the way for private. May the abolition of domestic tyranny introduce the modest train of household virtues, and purer incense be burned upon the hallowed altar of conjugal fidelity. Exhibit to the world the rare phœnomenon of a patriot minister, of a philosophic senate. May a pure and perfect system of legislation proceed from their forming hands, free from those irregularities and abuses, the wear and tear of a constitution, which in the course of years are necessarily accumulated in the best formed States; and like the new creation in its first gloss and freshness, yet free from any taint of corruption, when its Maker blest and called it good. May you never lose sight of the great principle you have held forth, the natural equality of men. May you never forget that without public spirit there can be no liberty; that without virtue there may be a confederacy, but cannot be a community. May you, and may we, consigning to oblivion every less generous competition, only contest who shall set the brightest example to the nations, and may its healing influence be diffused, till the reign of Peace shall spread

> "from shore to shore,
> "Till *Wars* shall cease, and *Slavery* be no more."[10]

Amidst causes of such mighty operation, what are we, and what are our petty, peculiar interests! Triumph, or despondency, at the success or failure of our plans,

66

would be treason to the large, expanded, comprehensive wish which embraces the general interests of humanity. Here then we fix our foot with undoubting confidence, sure that all events are in the hands of him, who from seeming evil

> · " is still educing good;
> "And better thence again, and better still,
> "In infinite progression."[11]

In this hope we look forward to the period when the name of *Dissenter* shall no more be heard of, than that of *Romanist* or *Episcopalian*, when nothing shall be venerable but truth, and nothing valued but utility.

67

March 3, 1790   A DISSENTER

ENDNOTES

1   *The Works of Anna Laetitia Barbauld with a Memoir by Lucy Aikin* (London: Longman, Hurst, Rees, Orme Brown, and Green, 1825), 1: vi–vii. See also Betsy Rodgers, *A Georgian Chronicle: Mrs. Barbauld and her Family* (London: Methuen and Co. Ltd., 1958).

2   *The Works of Anna Laetitia Barbauld*, 1: xviii.

3   Lucy Aikin quoted in Anna Letitia Le Breton, *Memoir of Mrs. Barbauld* (London: George Bell and Sons, 1874), 42–43. *La Nouvelle Héloïse* (1761), a celebrated epistolary novel by Jean Jacques Rousseau, had for its hero a tutor to a young family, St. Preux, who falls in love with the wife of his employer. The novel is marked by a tone of emotional extravagance. It was an immensely popular and influential work.

4   Le Breton, *Memoir of Mrs. Barbauld*, xlix.

5   See Sarah Burton, *A Double Life: A Biography of Charles and Mary Lamb* (London: Viking, 2003), who discusses Charles Lamb's dislike of Mrs. Barbauld's tales as ruling out the imagination.

6   For a discussion of Anna Barbauld's religious position, see Daniel E. White, "'With Mrs Barbauld it is different': Dissenting Heritage and the Devotional Taste," in *Women, Gender and Enlightenment*, ed. Sarah Knott and Barbara Taylor (Basingstoke: Palgrave, 2005).

7   Betsy Rodgers, *A Georgian Chronicle*, 107–08.

8   The Corporation Act (1661) was passed by the first Parliament of Charles II with the intention of destroying the power of the Dissenters in the towns. By this statute it was enacted that all officers of corporations should take the sacrament according to the rites of the Church of England, within twelve months of their election to office; and, on their election, they should take the oaths of supremacy, allegiance, and non-resistance, as well as abjure the Solemn League and Covenant, a 1643 agreement that promised the preservation of the

reformed Church of Scotland and religious reform in England and Ireland. The Corporation Act was repealed in 1828.

The Test Act (1673), a measure passed in the reign of Charles II, intended to exclude from office the Catholic councillors of the king. It was passed at the instance of Shaftesbury and the country party after the king had been compelled to abandon his attempt to dispense with the penal laws against Dissenters. It required all persons holding any office of profit or trust under the Crown to take the oaths of allegiance and supremacy, receive the sacrament according to the rites of the Church of England, and subscribe to the declaration against transubstantiation. This Act was directed against the Catholics but was equally operative against Dissenters. It was repealed in 1829.

9   John Milton, *Paradise Lost*, Bk. 4, lines 790–810. Ithuriel was one of the cherubim sent by the Archangel Gabriel to keep guard over Adam and Eve. Ithuriel discovers Satan disguised as a toad, whispering into Eve's ear. When Ithuriel touches him with his spear, the toad appears in his true guise, namely that of Satan. Thus Ithuriel's spear destroys falsehood, hypocrisy, and dissembling.

10   Alexander Pope, *Windsor Forest* (1713), 408. Barbauld has substituted "Wars" for "Conquest." Pope, a Catholic, was also affected by the Corporation and Test Acts.

11   James Thomson, *A Hymn on the Seasons* (1730), lines 114–16. Though in the poem's context this quotation relates to Thomson's theological views on cosmic harmony, Barbauld may also have invoked him because she was in sympathy with Thomson's libertarian and Whig oppositional politics.

Catharine Macaulay Graham (née Sawbridge) (1731–1791)

Catharine Macaulay's career as a political thinker, pamphleteer, historian, and educational writer illustrates the possibilities and pitfalls for celebrated women in the mid-to-late eighteenth century. As an historian, Macaulay not only laid claim to authority in what was regarded as a masculine genre,[1] she participated actively in radical politics, wielding influence in England, France, and America. Lauded as the new "Muse of History" for her early volumes of the *History of England* (1763–1774), Macaulay saw her reputation subsequently plummet, thanks to an eminently mockable personality cult celebrated by her friend and patron the Reverend Thomas Wilson, followed by her "unsuitable" second marriage to a man twenty-six years her junior, but, more generally, because the political radicalism that she championed was eclipsed by the conservative English reaction to the French Revolution.

Born Catharine Sawbridge, she was one of four children of John Sawbridge, a wealthy landowner. Her brother John became a member of parliament and was a supporter of John Wilkes. Though taught by a governess, Catharine largely educated herself in her father's extensive library. She did not learn the classical languages, those eighteenth-century passports to erudition, but avidly devoured Greek and Roman histories. "I read with delight those histories that exhibit Liberty in its most exalted state."[2] Given her easy financial circumstances, she was able to pursue her intellectual enthusiasms throughout her twenties. Elizabeth Carter, meeting her in 1757, remarked ironically that Catharine was "much more deeply learned than becomes a fine lady."[3]

In 1760, at the age of twenty-nine, Catharine married a Scottish doctor, George Macaulay, fifteen years her senior. The marriage only lasted six years, until Dr. Macaulay's death in 1766, but it seems to have been happy. They had one daughter. With the doctor's encouragement, Catharine embarked on what was to become her eight-volume *History of England*, published over a twenty-year period. The first volume (1763) was welcomed by the Whigs as an antidote to David Hume's *History of Great Britain*, considered sympathetic to the Tory interest. However, her political radicalism, her republicanism, and her espousal of the cause of American independence, as well as her close links with prominent dissenters, lost her many Whig supporters. Nevertheless, Macaulay continued with a demanding publication schedule, producing four more volumes of her *History* by 1773.

Macaulay's militant republicanism won her a number of distinguished enemies, one of the most celebrated being Dr. Johnson. Johnson is reported dining at her house, where he suggested that if she really believed in equality she should ask her footman to sit down at table with her.[4] In 1764, after the publication of the first volume of the *History*, Boswell recounts how Johnson, at a Cambridge dinner, "stripped her to the skin," a curiously sexual metaphor for abusing her work.[5]

By 1774, the strain of researching and writing the first five volumes of her *History* had told on Macaulay's health. She moved to Bath where a fellow radical, the Reverend Thomas Wilson, invited her and her daughter to share his house. The relationship between her and Wilson (who was seventy-one), even in the world of eighteenth-century gossip, was never thought to be physical, but Macaulay's reputation suffered badly from her willingness to countenance Wilson's star-struck admiration. This culminated in the forty-sixth birthday celebration he organised for her, where Catharine, seated on a throne, was feted like the royalty she so despised in her political writings, an episode that, when publicised in the press, did her immense damage.

In 1777, Macaulay travelled to France, meeting many admirers of her *History* among the *philosophes*, *salonnières*, and liberal aristocrats. The following year, when she was forty-seven, she further stunned her public, and enraged the Reverend Wilson, by marrying William Graham, a twenty-one-year-old Scots apothecary. The age disparity between Macaulay and Graham, which would not have been shocking if the genders were reversed, added to the class disparity, ruined for a time her public image.

Macaulay returned to her *History* and, in 1778, brought out two further volumes, the eighth and final one appearing in 1783. More admired abroad than at home, she and her husband spent a year (1784) in America, welcomed by many of the founders of the republic, including Benjamin Franklin and George Washington. Macaulay's other historical work, her *History of England From the Revolution to the Present Time in a Series of Letters to a Friend* (1778), was intended as a popular history, but its poor reception ensured that only one volume was written. In 1790, the year before her death, she published her *Letters on Education* and her *Observations on the Reflections of the Right Hon. Edmund Burke on the Revolution in France*. She died after a long illness at Binfield in Berkshire, 22 June 1791.

Though only expressing explicit feminist views in her *Letters on Education*, Macaulay lived her life with the assumption of sexual equality. Her evident enjoyment of fame and adulation became a subject for ridicule, but it would not have been so to the same extent in a man. Macaulay's scholarship, her vivid and closely argued writing, her polemical flair and political passion testify to a remarkable mind. The unifying themes of her work were a love of liberty and a belief in natural rights, much-contested concepts in the eighteenth century. She decried the corruption so prevalent in English public life. The purpose of politics, she believed, should be to make society more moral. Writing history, for Macaulay, was a political act.

OBSERVATIONS ON THE REFLECTIONS OF THE RIGHT HON. EDMUND BURKE ON THE REVOLUTION IN FRANCE, IN A LETTER TO THE RIGHT HON. THE EARL OF STANHOPE (1790)

Macaulay's *Observations* were not her first encounter with Edmund Burke in print. Twenty years previously, in 1770, she had published her "Observations" on Burke's *Thoughts on the Cause of our Present Discontents* in which she had argued for a root and branch reform of parliament, an extension of the franchise, frequent elections, and a redistribution of seats.[6] Twenty years later, Burke had effectively torn up what remained of his Whig credentials by opposing the repeal of the Corporation and Test Acts and by publishing his *Reflections on the Revolution in France*, both in 1790. Macaulay's was one of at least 38 replies to Burke's polemic. (See the discussion of Barbauld's *Address to the Opposers of the Repeal of the Test and Corporation Acts* in this text). Macaulay's *Observations* of 1790 take up many of the themes of her earlier pamphlet.

Macaulay realised that Burke's *Reflections* appealed to the emotions through their overblown rhetoric. She therefore attacked them as weak on reasoned argument. "We find him [Burke] *obliged* to substitute a *warm* and *passionate declamation* to a *cool investigation*, and to address the *passions* instead of the *reason* of mankind." By contrast, her rebuttal, she promises, will be based on the sober and plain language of reason. Nevertheless, Macaulay was fully aware of the extent to which Burke's rhetorical exuberance could and did sway public opinion.

The first half of Macaulay's pamphlet concerns the question of the basis of sovereignty, whether it lies with the people or with the monarch. She defends Richard Price, whose sermon in 1789, "A Discourse on Love of our Country" congratulating the National Assembly in Paris, so infuriated Burke. Macaulay characterises Price as a genuine patriot.

The second half of the *Observations* defends the French Revolution as an instance of the people asserting their legitimate rights. She praises "the moderation with which the people used their complete victory." The members of the National Assembly who voluntarily relinquished their feudal privileges are especially commended. On the issue of extra-judicial executions, Macaulay admits that "The punishment of the lamp-post ... strikes terror to the mind." But the common people, who carried out these lynchings, she argues, had been brutalised by a regime that routinely practised torture.

Macaulay concludes that we cannot be certain which direction the revolution will take. Burke had given it a completely pessimistic interpretation, based on his conviction that popular sovereignty was contrary to order and good government. Macaulay agrees that it is possible that the French people could abandon their new constitution for a new form of tyranny. The salient issue, she believes, is that the only legitimate basis of government is the people's will.

THE HISTORY OF ENGLAND FROM THE ACCESSION OF JAMES I TO THE ELEVATION OF THE HOUSE OF HANOVER (1768)

The trial and execution of Charles I on 30 January 1649 is one of the most dramatic scenes in Macaulay's *History*.[7] This narrative, followed by her analysis of the king's character and the political implications of his execution, provides a telling example of her historical writing. Macaulay recounts her story with vividness but with sobriety. The reader has no need of visual imagery to see Charles standing before his judges, or awaiting the executioner's axe. The passage falls into two sections: first, a narration of events and second, their interpretation with ancillary questions about justice, morality, and political efficacy and judgements on Charles's character as the key to the political crisis.

Charles's arguments to the High Court of Justice, whose jurisdiction he refused to recognise, assert the divine authority underpinning kingship; these Macaulay gives in indirect speech. His character emerges in its negatives and positives, an attempt at even-handedness for which Macaulay was criticised by monarchists and republicans alike. The accusation of uxoriousness that she brings against the king seems, however, gratuitous.

Macaulay tackles the question of the legality of Charles's trial, conducted by those members of the House of Commons sympathetic to the rebellion and excluding members of the House of Lords, who might have supported the king. Rejecting biblical authority, invoked by monarchists and anti-monarchists alike, she argues that the central question is whether the people "have a right to depose and punish their sovereign." She believes that sovereignty originally lay with the people, whose rulers hold it in trust. If they violate that trust, her argument runs, the people have a right to reclaim their sovereignty and depose their leader. Legalistic hair-splitting, or what Macaulay terms "the narrow bottom of constitutional forms," does not constitute an adequate justification for the overthrow and execution of the king. The defence of this "eminent act of justice" must lie in the concept of liberty, which the people vest in the king and which he had betrayed. Concluding that "the people are with difficulty moved to assert their rights, even against the most obvious, the most oppressive tyrannies," Macaulay believed that the popular rebellion against the king was evidence of the justness of the cause.

72

Observations on the Reflections of the Right Hon. Edmund Burke on the Revolution in France, In a Letter to the Right Hon. The Earl of Stanhope (1790)

Catharine Macaulay Graham

OBSERVATIONS &c.

My Lord,

Your lordship's character as a patriot, a philosopher, and the firm friend of the general rights of man, encourages me to present to you the following Observations on Mr. Burke's famous *Reflections on the Revolution in France*. They claim no popular attention for the ornaments of stile in which they are delivered; they can attract no admiration from the fascinating charms of eloquence; they are directed, not to *captivate*, but to *convince*; and it is on the presumption that your lordship attends more to the *substance* and *end* of literary compositions, than to the *art* of their arrangement, which induces me to flatter myself with your approbation.

It is not suprizing that an event, the most *important* to the dearest interests of mankind, the most *singular* in its nature, and the most *astonishing* in its means, should not only have attracted the curiosity of all civilized nations, but that it should have engaged the passions of all *reflecting* men.

Two parties are already formed in this country, who behold the French Revolution with very opposite temper: to the one, it inspires the sentiments of *exultation* and *rapture*; and to the other, *indignation* and *scorn*. I shall not take upon me to consider what are the *secret* passions which have given birth to these last sentiments; and shall content myself with observing, that Mr. Burke has undertaken to be the oracle of this last party. The abilities of this gentleman have been fully acknowledged by the impatience with which the public have waited for his observations; and when we consider that he has been in a manner educated in the great school of Parliament, that he has assisted in the public councils of the English nation for the greater part of his life, we must suppose him fully competent to the task he has undertaken, of censuring the politics of our neighbour kingdom, and entering into an exact definition of those native rights which equally attach themselves to every description of men.

Is there a rational observation, or argument, in moral existence, which this gentleman (so highly favoured by nature and circumstances for political debate) could possibly have passed over, on a subject in which he appears so greatly interested, and of which he has taken a full leisure to consider. When we find him then *obliged* to substitute a *warm* and *passionate declamation* to a *cool investigation*, and to address the *passions* instead of the *reason* of mankind, we shall be induced to give a fuller credit to our judgment and our feelings, in the view we have taken of this interesting object, and the pleasure it has given us.

Mr. Burke sets out with throwing a *great deal* of contemptuous censure on two club societies in London, for a very harmless exertion of natural and constitutional liberty.[8] They certainly had a right to compliment the French National Assembly on a matter of domestic government, and to express an *approbation* of their conduct, with a freedom equal to that which Mr. Burke has taken in his letter to express his *abhorrence*.

The National Assembly of France have taken no such *supercilious state* upon them, as would render such a communication of sentiment ridiculous or presumptuous. As the patrons of *equal liberty*, they have not disdained the addresses of the *meanest* individual: consequently the Revolution Society then might rationally expect that their address would have met with a civil reception, though not clothed with the "dignity of the whole representative majesty of the whole English nation."

But Mr. Burke thinks that these gentlemen have so strong a predilection in favour of the democratic arrangements which have taken place in France, that they have been induced to wish, if not to indulge a hope, that some very important reformations may in the process of time also take place in this country; and these harmless operations of the mind in a *few obscure* individuals (for such are the members described who compose the offending clubs) have produced in Mr. Burke apprehensions no way consistent with the *high* opinion he has formed of the English constitution, or of the *strong* attachment which he supposes all that is *great* and *good* in the nation have to it.

Dr. Price, whose animated love for mankind and the spread of general happiness moved to express the effusion of his patriotic sentiment, in a sermon preached the 4th of Nov. 1789, at the dissenting meeting-house in the Old Jewry, is censured by Mr. Burke in *severe*, and even *acrimonious terms*.[9] Among other parts of the very offensive matter with which he charges this sermon, the having asserted that the *King of Great Britain owes his right to the Crown by the choice of the people*, is particularly selected, as worthy an historical and argumentative confutation.

The liberty that was taken in the year 1688, by a convention of Lords and Commons, to depose king James the reigning sovereign from the throne, and to vest the sovereignty of the realm in his daughter Mary, and her husband the Prince of Orange; and afterwards by the legislature, to pass an act to settle the succession in queen Anne and her issue, and in default of these, in the heirs of king William's body, and in default of these, in the house of Hanover, (the Protestant descendants of the house of Stuart in the female line;) and this to the prejudice not only of king James, but of his son, who had been acknowledged as the lawful heir of his throne; and also to the prejudice of the house of Savoy, who by lineal descent were the next in regular succession; are indeed facts, which *might warrant a plain thinking man* in the opinion, that the present reigning family owe their succession to the choice or assent of the people. But, in Mr. Burke's opinion, these facts are of no weight, "because the whole family of the Stuarts were not entirely left out of the succession, and a native of England advanced to the throne; and because it was declared in the act of succession, that the Protestant line drawn from James the first, was absolutely necessary for the security of the realm."

That those individuals of the family of the Stuarts, who had never committed an offence against the peace of the country, and whose mode of faith was not injurious to its welfare, should not be set aside in favour of an absolute stranger to the blood, was certainly a *just measure*; and it was certainly *wise* to leave as *few* competitors to the crown as possible, whether on grounds founded in justice, or in mere plausibility. But there was a reason still more forcible for the conduct of the two Houses of Convention, and afterwards for the Parliament in their constitutional capacity; and the reason is this, that *without the prince of Orange, and the assistance of his Dutch army, there could have been no Revolution.* For the English nation at large was so little convinced of the *severe and grave necessity* which Mr. Burke talks of, that the people of themselves would never have been roused to have deposed king James; and they regarded all his innovations with such a *constitutional phlegm*, that had this unfortunate monarch possessed the qualities of *firmness, perseverance,* or *patience,* he must either have been killed by the dark means of *assassination*, or he would have *continued on the throne.*

That the friends of the Revolution knew they could not do without the assistance of king William, is plain, by their laying aside the intention of vesting Mary *singly* with the sovereignty, on his declaring that if this event took place, he would return to Holland, and leave them to themselves.

However strongly the warm friends of freedom might wish that this abstract right of the people, of chusing their own magistrates, and deposing them for ill conduct, had been laid open to the public by a formal declaration of such a right in the acts of succession, this certainly was not a period of time for carrying these wishes into execution. The whole body of the people had swallowed deeply of the *poison* of church policy; *passive obedience*, by their means, had so entirely supplanted the *abstract notion* of the *rights of men*, which prevailed in the opposition to Charles the first; and so desirous were the triumphant party to prevent the revival of such a principle, by which their interests had been affected, that they took care to confound the *only just authority* they had for their conduct, in as great *a mist of words and terms as possible*. Besides, would William, who was the soul of the whole proceeding, have given way to a claim, by which, in the plainest terms, he was bound to his good behaviour?

Mr. Hume justly supposes, that if the revolution had happened one hundred years after it did, it would have been *materially different* in all its circumstances.[10] Instead of thinking with Mr. Burke, that such a plain declaration of the rights of men would have tended to disturb the quiet of the nation, I firmly believe that it would have had a contrary effect; for, in this case, those endless disputes between the *Nonjurors, Tories,* and *Whigs,* would soon have had an end. For the question not being involved in that *obscurity, contradiction,* and *absurdity,* in which it was enveloped by the revolutionists, *truth* and *reason* would have resumed their sway; *party jargon* would have been exploded; the people would have given a chearful obedience to the new government; and that dreadful *necessity* by which Sir Robert Walpole excused the introducing a settled *system of corruption* into the administration, would never have existed.[11]

When the succession to a crown in one family, or even the possession of private property, owes its origin to the people, most undoubtedly the authority from whence it's derived, attaches itself to the gift as equally in every individual of the family through the whole line of succession, as in the first possessor. And I can hardly believe, that there was *one* enlightened member who composed part of that legislative body who settled the succession to the throne, could possibly think that body possessed of such a plenitude of power, as should give them a right, not only to *set aside* the regulations of their ancestors, but to *bind their posterity*, to all succeeding generations, in the permanent chains of an unalterable law. Should we once admit of *a power so incompatible with the conditions of humanity,* and only reserved for the dictates of *divine wisdom,* we have not, in these enlightened days, improved on the politics of the fanatic atheist Hobbes:[12] *For he supposes an original right in the people to chuse their governors;* but, in exerting this right, the citizen and his posterity for ever lose their native privileges, and become bound through the whole series of generations to the service of a master's will.

We will now take into consideration the nature and tendency of the two different compliments which have been paid by Dr. Price and Mr. Burke to his Majesty and his successors. Dr. Price, I think, puts their right to government on the *most dignified,* and perhaps, in the event of things, on the *most permanent* footing. But Mr. Burke would have done well to consider, whether such a compliment as he is willing to pay to royalty is at all *proper,* either for the subject to make, or the King to receive. To a weak prince, it would be apt to cancel in his mind *all obligations* which he owes to the people, and, by flattering him in a *vain* conceit of a mere personal right, tempt him to break those sacred ties which ought to *bind* and *direct* his government. I am apt to believe, that almost *all the vices* of royal administration have principally been occasioned by a *slavish adulation* in the language of their subjects; and, to the *shame of the English people* it must be spoken, that none of the enslaved nations in the world address the throne in a more *fulsome* and *hyperbolical* stile of submissive flattery.

To a *wise* and *good* prince, compliments of the same complexion, made and recommended by Mr. Burke, would be *offensive*. He would consider it as taking away the *noblest* and *safest title* by which he possesses his power: he would consider it as acknowledging a kind of *latent* right in other families; and the liberality of his sentiment would incline him to triumph in the opinion, that he was *called* to government, and *continued* in it, by the *choice* and *confidence* of a free nation.

Mr. Burke seems to adopt *prejudice, opinion,* and the powers of the *imagination,* as the *safest grounds* on which *wise* and *good* statesmen can establish or continue the happiness of societies. These have always been imputed by philosophers (a tribe of men whom indeed Mr. Burke affects much to despise), as causes, which have produced all that is *vicious* and *foolish* in man, and consequently have been the fruitful source of human *misery.*

Mr. Burke has certainly a *fine* imagination; but I would not advise either *him,* or any of *his admirers,* to give *too much* way to such direction; for if from the virtue of our nature it does not lead us into *crimes,* it always involves us in *error.*

The being put into a situation clearly to understand and to obey the *principles of truth,* appears to be the basis of our happiness in this, and our perfection in another world; and the *more* truth is followed and pursued in this dark vale of human ignorance and misery, the *more,* we shall *encrease* our mundane felicity, and *secure* the blessings of a future existence. *Every opinion* which deviates from *truth,* must ever be a *treacherous* guide; and the more it deviates from it, it becomes the *more dangerous.*

Though a false opinion of the rights and powers of citizens may *enslave* the ductile mind into a state of passive obedience, and thus secure the peace of government; yet in the same degree does it inflate the *pride* and *arrogance* of princes, until all considerations of *rectitude* give way to *will,* the barriers of personal security are flung down, and thence arises that *tremendous necessity* which must be followed by a state of *violence* and *anarchy,* which Mr. Burke so *justly* dreads. That this is the case, the experience of all societies of men who acknowledge a *power* in their princes *paramount* to all resistance, fully evinces. These societies are obliged often to have recourse to violence and massacre; not indeed to establish any popular rights, but in the way of force, to wreck their vengeance on their tyrants.

As to the right of *cashiering* or *deposing* monarchs for misgovernment, I cannot possibly agree with Mr. Burke, that in England it only existed in that Convention of the two Houses in 1688, which exercised their power over King James and his legal successors. But I am clearly of opinion, that it is a right that ought *never* to be exercised by a people who are satisfied with their form of government, and have spirit enough to correct its abuse; and so far from *condemning* the French nation for not deposing or executing their king, even though the *strongest presumptions* of the *most atrocious guilt* should have appeared against him, I think, had they elected any other person to that high office, they would have thrown difficulties in the way of their liberty, instead of improving it. But it is the *wisdom,* and not the *folly* of the National Assembly, which gives *offence* to their *enemies;* and *forces even Mr. Burke* to contradict, in this instance, the rule which he has laid down, "That monarchs should not be deposed for misconduct, but only when its criminality is of a kind to render their government totally incompatible with the safety of the people"....

The French Revolution was attended with something so *new* in the history of human affairs; there was something so *singular* so *unique,* in that *perfect* unanimity in the people; in that *firm* spirit which baffled *every hope* in the *interested,* that they could possibly divide them into parties, and render them the instruments of a re-subjection to their old bondage; that it naturally excited the *surprise* and the *admiration* of all men. It appeared as a *sudden spread of an enlightened spirit,* which promised to act as an effectual and permanent barrier to the inlet of those usurpations, which from the very beginning of social life the *crafty* have imposed on *ignorance.*

This was a triumph of *sufficient importance* to call forth the exultation of individuals, and the approbation of societies. But the two clubs who have the *misfortune* to fall under Mr. Burke's severe censure, did not testify a formal approbation of the conduct of their neighbours, till the deputies they had chosen for the transaction of their affairs, had manifested a virtue *equal* to so high a trust; for no sooner was the power of the court *sufficiently* subdued to enable them to act with *freedom* and *effect,* than they gave an example of *disinterested magnanimity,* that has *no parallel* in the conduct of *any* preceding assembly of men, and which was *never surpassed by any individual.* That memorable day in which the members of the National Assembly, with a *virtuous enthusiasm,* vied with each other in the alacrity with which they surrendered to the people all their feudal privileges, will for ever stand in the records of time as a monument of their *singular greatness.* Such an instance of human virtue was surely a *proper subject of applause and congratulation.*

Men who have suffered in their personal interest by the new order of things in France, must naturally be inclined to *exaggerate* every blemish which appears in the conduct of a multitude, by whose spirit they have been deprived of many fond privileges. Their *petulant* observations, whilst their minds are *heated* by imaginary wrongs and injuries, is excusable; because it is a *weakness* almost inseparable from *human frailty.* It would, however, have become *Englishmen,* from whom might have been expected a *more sympathising* indulgence towards the *friends* and *promoters* of liberty, to have been more *candid* in their censures; but in no part of Europe perhaps, have the evils which must *necessarily* attend all Revolutions, and especially a Revolution so *complete* and *comprehensive* as that which has taken place in France, been *more exaggerated,* and *more affectedly* lamented.

Had this *great work* been effected without the shedding one drop of *innocent* or even *guilty* blood, without doubt it would have better pleased the *generous* and *benevolent* mind. But, was it *possible* that such a pleasing circumstance could ever have had an existence? If we take into consideration that *animosity* which subsisted between the *aristocratists* and *democratists* on the eve of the Revolution, an animosity which was greatly heightened by the imprudent *insults* which the *Tier* [sic] *État* had received from the first mentioned body, we shall rather *wonder at the moderation* with which the people used their *complete* victory, than lament their cruelty. After the successful storming the king's camp, and the flight or desertion of his Janizaries, instead of that *order* and voluntary *subjection* to discipline which appeared in an armed mob, and which prevented *all* infringement of the rights of property, had the subdued party been delivered over to the *outrage* and the *pillage* of the rabble, the *horrid* scene might have been *paralleled* by examples drawn from the guilty violence of *civilized* nations, without calling our attention to *Theban* and *Thracian orgies*, or a procession of American *savages* entering into *Onondaga*. I do not indeed exactly know how much blood has been spilled in France, or how many individuals have fallen a sacrifice in the public commotions; but by all the general accounts which have been transmitted to us, the history of monarchies will point out as many sufferers who have fallen in *one hour* to the *rage* and *outrageous pride* of kingly despots.

The punishment of the lamp-post, it must be owned, strikes terror to the mind, and calls forth an immediate effusion of *sympathy* to the sufferer. But when *candid reflection* supersedes the *first emotions* of human tenderness, this truth will force itself on our consideration, that a people who had been used to such *barbarous* spectacles as that of beholding wretches, whose *destitute poverty* had in a manner *compelled* to the forlorn course of highway robbery, broken on a wheel, and *lingering* out the last hours of life under the *agonising* strokes of a stern executioner, would naturally regard hanging as a *mild* punishment on men whom they considered as the worst of criminals. Let us rejoice, then, that such *dreadful legal executions,* which must from their nature tend to *barbarize* men, are happily put an end to by the Revolution....

The opinion which Mr. Burke endeavours to establish in his elaborate Reflections on the French Revolution, is the *incompatibility* of a truly popular government with the human constitution: And the subject which affords him the most ample scope for the display of his argumentative powers, is found in the investment of that military force which is necessary to the support of all governments; for if that force is trusted to the people at large, they may be tempted to act in their natural capacity, and, by destroying or weakening the energy of those organs by which regular councils are held and enforced, induce a state of anarchy. And if the support of the government is made to subsist in a regular standing disciplined body, under the controul of an individual, that individual will become the *master of the people*, and *violate* the government he was appointed to *defend*.

Either the establishment or the overthrow of an opinion so fatal to the proud hopes of man, must be left to time and experience; for I am sorry to say, that we have no notices on which we can attempt the construction of an opposite argument. We cannot venture to establish an opinion on the state of a country not yet recovered from the convulsive struggles which every important revolution must occasion. We can gain no light from history; for history furnishes *no example*

79

of any government in a large empire, which, in the strictest sense of the word, has secured to the citizen the *full* enjoyment of his rights. Some attempts indeed have been made of this kind; but they have hitherto failed, through the *treachery* of leaders, or by the *rash folly* of the multitude. But though these circumstances will prevent cautious persons from giving a *decided* opinion on what may be the event of things, yet they do not so *benight* the understanding as to deprive the mind of hope. They do not prevent it from seeing that the present complexion of things in France has something of a different aspect from what history, or the state of other countries, presents to our view. Instead of that *barbarous ignorance* or that *depravity* of *principle*, which are to be seen in other European States, and which might reasonably prevent the patriot from bestowing (if it were in his power) the full boon of liberty, we see a people *firm* and *united* in their efforts to *support* their rights, yet obedient to the dictates of that government which they have appointed to defend them.

From what can this difference which subsists between the French nation and other societies arise, but in a more *general* diffusion of *knowledge*, and in a principle of action which consults the *public* good, as well as the gratifications of *self*? It is the business of *knowledge* to teach men their *real interests*; and it is to be hoped it will so far prevail over that *mist* which *inordinate* affections cast over the mind, as to enable the French municipalities to see, that if they so far *abuse* the power with which they have been invested for the defence of their rights, as to gratify a *private* passion at the expence of the *public* peace, they will induce a *necessity* which will lead to their *utter* destruction. It is to be hoped also, that a *true* sense of interest will enable the army to perceive, that the *moment they fling off the character of the citizen, and assume a controuling power over their country,* from that moment they become *individually slaves*; for the very circumstance in their condition by which this power must subsist, is a discipline inseparable to the *strictest subordination*, and which in *all* respects must militate against their civil rights. When the Roman army was in the very height of their power; when it was enabled to depose and murder emperors, and raise private men to the imperial throne; when they were enabled to ravage the empire at their pleasure, and exact largesses from its spoils; they were, in an *individual* capacity, the *greatest* of slaves.

The patriot Frenchman has a prospect of hope which *never* yet offered itself to the view of society, and that is the *disinterestedness* of those councils to which he has confided his right. The republican parliament of England, by their *inordinate* thirst after public offices, and by using their power to their *own emolument*, gave *too much room* for the suspicions of a divided people to act in their disfavour; and it must be acknowledged, that the interests of self have been observed to act as much in popular councils as in courts. But the French legislature have set, in this point, an example *unparellelled* in the history of man. To a *bold* and *enterprising* spirit, they have united a *disinterestedness* of principle which has deprived their enemies of *every* means of opposition, but *vain* declamation, *groundless* accusation, and *impotent* hope. Long may they continue the *admiration* of the world in these important particulars! Long may they thus continue to *aggrandize* the character of man! And long may they continue to deserve a *monument of esteem* on the minds of their species, which neither *time*, nor *accident*, nor *adverse fortune, shall be able to efface!*

It cannot be denied that Mr. Burke has made a display of very *uncommon* abilities in his attack on the French Revolution; but why has he deigned to make use of the *mean arts* of abuse as an *auxiliary* in the contest. Why has he, by the most *invidious* comparisons, and *groundless* accusations, endeavoured to rouse all nations and all descriptions of men against them, and thus to *crush in their ruin all the rights of man*? Is the tendency of his publication a *recommendation* to the British government, to dragoon their neighbours into an adoption of their own system of policy? Would he recommend to the potentates of Europe, a renewal of that *wicked conspiracy* against the rights of men, which was planned by Henry the Fourth and his minister Sully, and which was only prevented from taking place by the timely death of that monarch?—a plan, by which, through the *combination* of power, modes of government were to be *arbitrarily* imposed and supported, and the rights of conscience *abolished*. If such *violent* councils were indeed to take place of that *moderation* and *equity* which has hitherto been shewn, it would *prove* that the *forming treaties* and directing the *force of nations* were but *ill* trusted to the *secrecy* of cabinets. When we reflect that such dreadful purposes can never be effected without the effusion of *oceans* of blood, of such an invidious intention we must certainly exculpate Mr. Burke; unless, by a *strange* modification of *sympathy*, the lives of plebeians, and those vulgar characters which compose the "*swinish multitude*," is held at *no value* in his account. Some of Mr. Burke's expressions, indeed, seem to warrant us in making such a supposition, though we *must acknowledge*, that, in others, he appears to have a *concern* for the *spiritual*, if not for the *temporal* happiness of those he despises "Whilst," says he, "the wealth and pride of individuals at every moment makes the man of humble rank and fortune sensible of his inferiority, and *degrades* and *vilifies* his condition;* it is for the man in humble life, and to raise his nature, and to put him in mind of a state in which the privileges of opulence will cease, when he will be equal by nature, and may be more than equal by virtue, that this portion of the general wealth of his country is employed, and sanctified."

If Mr. Burke, in the management of his argument, could have descended from the *lofty* strain of a *poetic* imagination, to the *drudgery* of close reasoning, he would have perceived the *error* of deviating from the line of *expediency* into the question of *right*; for when we once *give up* the point, that there is an *inherent* right attached to privileged persons to make laws for the community, we cannot fix on any other principle that will stand the test of argument, but the *native* and *unalienable* rights of man. For if we say that *lawful* governments are formed on the authority of conventions, it will be asked, *who gave these conventions their*

---

* This is a sad condition, indeed, for "*naked shivering nature:*" But what is the remedy? why, let them respect property, and seek "their consolation in the final proportions of eternal justice." *Vide* Reflections, 147, 351.

authority? If we grant that they derived their authority from the *assent of the people*, how came the people, it will be said, to exert such an authority at *one* period of society, and not *another*? If we say it was *necessity* that recovered to the social man the full rights of his nature, it will be asked, *who is to be the judge* of this necessity? Why *certainly* the people.

Thus, in *every* light in which we can place the argument, in every possible mode of reasoning, we shall be driven back to elect either the first or second of these propositions; either that an individual, or some privileged persons, have an inherent and indefeasible right to make laws for the community, or that this authority rests in the unalienable and indefeasible rights of man.

82

That the people have often abused their power, it must be granted; for they have often *sacrificed* themselves and their posterity to the *wanton will* of an individual, and *this* is the foundation of all the regal tyrannies which have subsisted in society; but *no abuse* of their power can *take away their right*, because their right *exists in the very constitution of things*. If the French people therefore should be so *capricious* as to fling off their new constitution, and subject themselves to more *unequal* forms of government, or even to *tyranny*, it will be agreeable to the course of past experience: but such an exertion of power *cannot injure their right*; and whatever form or complexion any future government in France may bear, it can have no *legitimate* source, *but in the will of the people*.

I am,
My Lord,

                                  With great esteem and respect,

Your Lordship's
Most obedient
Humble Servant,
The Author.

[Account of the trial and execution of Charles I and a sketch of his character]

The History of England From the Accession of James I to the Elevation of the House of Hanover (1768)

Catharine Macaulay Graham

From the second of January [1649] to the nineteenth of the same month the terms of the important trial had been adjusting. The special commission was composed of the prime officers of the army, several members of the lower house, and several citizens of London: It consisted of one hundred and thirty-three persons,* and was nominated the High-Court of Justice. Bradshaw, a lawyer of note, was by his fellow commissioners elected president; Coke was appointed solicitor for the people; Dorislaus Steele and Ask, assistants to the court; Westminster Hall was fitted up for their sitting; and the ceremony with which the whole transaction was conducted, corresponded in pomp and dignity to the singular, the great occasion: A sovereign prince brought before the tribunal of his own subjects, and tried by their delegates for his misgovernment and breach of trust. Dendy, the serjeant at arms to the house of Commons, by beat of drum and sound of trumpet, had, in the Palace-Yard, at the Old-Exchange, and in Cheapside, proclaimed to the people the time when the commissioners of the high-court of justice commenced their sitting; and that all those who had any thing to say against the King would be heard.

On the twentieth of January, the commissioners proceeded in state from the Painted Chamber to Westminster Hall. Colonel Humphrey carried the

---

* Though there were one hundred nominated to the high commission, there was not above fifty odd who had courage enough to engage personally in the daring office.

sword before the president, serjeant Dendy the mace, and twenty gentlemen (commanded by colonel Fox) attended as his guard of partizans. The royal prisoner, who, for the purpose of his trial, had been removed from Windsor to St. James's, was by a strong guard of musqueteers conveyed by water to Westminster Hall. A chair of crimson velvet was prepared for him within the bar, and thirty officers and gentlemen waited with halberts behind it. The solicitor of the Commons, in his charge against the King, represented, That Charles Stewart, being admitted King of England, and entrusted with a limited power, had, with the wicked design to erect an unlimited and tyrannical government, traitorously and maliciously levied war against the people and their representatives: That, on behalf of the people, he did, for this treasonable breach of trust, impeach him as a tyrant, a traitor, a murderer, and a public and implacable enemy to the commonwealth.

84

On the conclusion of the charge, the King demanded by what authority he was brought before the court.* He told the commissioners to remember he was their King, their lawful King, and to beware of the sins with which they were going to stain themselves and the land. He was answered by the president, that he was tried in the name and authority of the parliament assembled, and the good people of England. Charles objected, That both King and house of Lords were necessary to constitute a parliament: He had a trust, he said, committed to him by God, by old and lawful descent; and he would not betray it to answer to a new and unlawful authority: He again bade the commissioners remember he was their hereditary sovereign; and that the whole authority of the state, when free and united, was not entitled to try him, who derived his dignity from the supreme majesty of heaven: That, admitting those extravagant principles which place the origin of power in the people, the court could plead to no authority delegated by the people, unless the consent of every individual, down to the meanest, the most ignorant peasant, had been previously asked and obtained.[†] There was no jurisdiction on earth could try a King: The authority of obedience to Kings was clearly warranted and strictly commanded both in the Old and New Testaments: This, if denied, he was ready instantly to prove; "Where the word of a King was there was power, and who might say unto him, what dost thou?" He owned, he said, he was entrusted; a sacred trust had been committed to him by God, the liberties of his people, which he would not betray by recognizing a power founded on violence and usurpation: He had taken arms, and frequently exposed his life, in defence of public liberty, in defence of the constitution, in defence of the fundamental laws of the kingdom, and was now willing to seal with his blood those precious rights for which he had so long in vain contended. To the King's extravagant assertion, that he had taken up arms to defend the liberty of the constitution, and that he now pleaded for the rights and freedom of all his

---

* Ludlow says, That the King interrupted the clerk whilst he was reading, and exclaimed, "I am not entrusted by my people; they are mine by inheritance." *Ludlow*, 107.
† This argument is mere sophistry; since the sense of the people in their collective capacity, never can come to any determined conclusive point, unless the sense of the majority is binding to the whole.

subjects, the president returned, "How great a friend, Sir, you have been to the laws and liberties of the people, let all England and the world judge: Your actions have sufficiently declared it, and your meaning has been written in bloody characters throughout the kingdom." The court was reminded by the prisoner, that the laws of England determined the King could do no wrong; however, he was able, he said, by the most satisfactory reasons, to justify his conduct; but must forego the apology of his innocence, lest, by ratifying an authority no better founded than that of robbers and pirates, he should be justly branded as the betrayer, instead of applauded as the martyr, of the constitution.

Three several days the King was produced before the court, and as often urged to answer to his charge. The fourth, on his constantly persisting to decline its jurisdiction, the commissioners, after having examined witnesses, by whom it was proved that the King had appeared in arms against his people, proceeded to pronounce sentence against him. Before the passing sentence, Charles earnestly desired to be admitted to a conference with the two houses [House of Commons and House of Lords]: he had something to propose, he said, which he was sure would be for the welfare of the kingdom and the liberty of the subject. It was supposed that he intended to offer to resign the crown to his son; and some of the commissioners pressed that he might be heard. This was not the opinion of the majority; and the commissioners returning from the court of Wards, where they had adjourned to consult on the King's proposal, acquainted the prisoner, that his request was considered as a delay of justice. The president passed sentence of death, by severing the head from the body; and all the members of the court stood up in token of approbation.

An example of justice, from which they had ever regarded their rank to be totally exempt, awakened in every sovereign prince a sense of horror and indignation; whilst political reasons, of a different nature, inclined them to endeavor to prevent the change of government in England. The French court was now sincere in their interposition for favor to the King; and the Dutch employed very earnest intercessions for the preservation of his life. All solicitations were found vain. The Scots fruitlessly exclaimed and protested; the prince wrote an ineffectual letter to the army, and the queen to the parliament. Three days only were allowed the King between his sentence and his execution. This interval he passed in reading and devotion; and preserved, from the time when his intended fate was known to him, to his last moment, a perfect tranquillity and composure; or can his bitterest enemies deny, that in his conduct, under the dreadful apprehension of a violent death were united the magnanimity of heroism and the patience of martyrdom.

To mark to the gaping multitude the triumph of popular justice over royal rank, the scaffold for execution was erected before the palace at Whitehall; care was taken that it should be sufficiently surrounded with soldiers, to prevent disorder or interruption; and the King, finding himself shut out from the hearing of the people, addressed a speech to colonel Tomlinson, the commander of the guard, in which he attempted to justify his innocence in the war he had levied, termed it defensive, accused the parliament of having first enlisted forces, and averred that he had no other object in his military operations than to preserve entire that authority which had been transmitted to him by his ancestors; insisted on a perfect innocence towards his people; observed, that the unjust sentence now inflicted on him was an equitable return for that which he had suffered to be inflicted on Strafford; forgave his enemies; and exhorted the people to return to the paths of obedience, and submit to the government of their lawful sovereign, his son and successor. Bishop Juxon, whose attendance (though a cold inanimate speaker, and very incapable of raising the thoughts beyond their natural bounds) the King had very particularly and earnestly desired, remembered his master, that the people would expect him to make some declaration of the point of religion: On this the King very earnestly protested, that he had ever lived, and now died in the religion of the church of England. Whilst he was preparing for execution, the bishop poured out a few insipid lifeless exhortations: To these the King returned, "I go from corruptible to an incorruptible crown, where no disturbance can have place." Then laying his head upon the block, the executioner (whose face was concealed with a vizor) severed it with one stroke from the body: an assistant (in the like disguise) held it up to the spectators, streaming with blood and, after the usual manner observed in similar executions, cried aloud, "This is the head of a traitor."

Thus, by a fate unparalleled in the annals of princes, terminated the unfortunate life and turbulent reign of Charles Stewart; a monarch whose principles, conduct, fortune, and death, by powerfully engaging the opposite affections attending the different views and different interests of men, have given rise to bitter and irreconcilable contest. Regarded as the martyr to church and state, the patron of the clergy, the support of the nobility, we behold him, in the representations of a considerable party, adorned with every flower of panegyrick: By the bigots of a different persuasion, his memory, notwithstanding the tribute he paid to his crimes, is held in the highest detestation. The partizans of Liberty applaud his fate; the liberal and humane condemn and pity him: To a mind softened by habits of amusement, and intoxicated with ideas of self-importance, the transition from royal pomp to a prison, from easy, gay, and luxurious life to a premature and violent death by the hands of an executioner, are punishments so sharp and touching, that, in the suffering prince, we are apt to overlook the designing tyrant, to dwell on his hardships, and forget his crimes. Compassion is the constant attendant of liberal minds; and the commiseration of Charles's singular and unfortunate fate, but for the interests of truth and the violence of his partizans, would have inclined all such to have thrown the mantle of oblivion over the dark parts of his character, and only to have remembered that he bore his sufferings in a manner which would have done honor to the best cause. From such indulgence the ill-fated Charles is necessarily excluded: History is called upon to scrutinize with exactness his principles, conduct, and character; since, from the false colorings which by designing men have been thrown on these, and the rancor with which his opponents have been falsely aspersed, have been deduced consequences destructive to the security and welfare of man, and highly injurious to the reputation of patriot citizens.

In the character of Charles, as represented by his panegyrists, we find the qualities of temperance, chastity, regularity, piety, equity, humanity, dignity, condescension, and equanimity; some have gone so far as to allow him integrity; and many writers, who condemn his political principles, give him the title of a moral man. In the comparison of this representation with Charles's conduct, accurately and justly described, it is discernible that vices of the worst tendency, when shaded by a formal and plausible carriage, when concordant to the interests of a faction and the prejudices of the vulgar, assume the appearances of, and are imposed on the credulous world as, virtues of the first rank.—Passion for power was Charles's predominant vice; idolatry to his regal prerogatives his governing principle: The interests of his crown legitimated every measure, and sanctified in his eye the widest deviation from moral rule. His religion was to this a secondary and subordinate affection: The prelates of the church of England paid him an impious flattery; they inculcated a slavish dependence on the regal authority; the corruptions in their ecclesiastical discipline fostered superstition; superstition secured their influence over the people; and on these grounds, and to these ends, they kept an interest in the King's heart, which continued to the last period of his life. If Charles had an higher estimation of the faith in which he had been educated than of Popery, it was because the principles of Popery acknowledged a superior allegiance to their spiritual than their temporal prince; but regarding that superstition to be more favourable to the interests of monarchy, he preferred it to the religion of any differing sect, and publicly avowed his wish, that there never had been a schism in the church. Neither gratitude, clemency, humanity, equity nor generosity, have place in the fair part of Charles's character. Of the virtues of temperance, fortitude, and personal bravery, he was undeniably possessed. His manners partook of the dissipation, and his conversation of the indecency of a court. His chastity has been called in question by an author of the highest repute; and were it allowed, it was tainted by an excess of uxoriousness, which gave it the properties and the consequences of vice. The want of integrity is manifest in every part of his conduct; which, whether the corruption of his judgment or heart, lost him fair opportunities of reinstatement in the throne, and was the vice for which, above all others, he paid the tribute of his life. His intellectual powers were naturally good, and so improved by a continued exercise, that, though in the beginning of his reign he spoke with difficulty and hesitation, towards the close of his life he discovered in his writings purity of language and dignity of style, in his debates elocution and quickness of conception. The high opinion he entertained of regal dignity occasioned him to observe a stateliness and imperiousness of manner, which, to the rational and intelligent, was unamiable and offensive; by the weak and the formal, it was mistaken for dignity. In the exercise of horsemanship he excelled; had a good taste, and even skill in several of the polite arts; but, though a proficient in some branches of literature, was no encourager of useful learning, and only patronized adepts in the jargon of the divine right and utility of kings and bishops. His understanding in this point was so depraved by the prejudices of his education, the flattery of priests, and the affections of his heart, that he would never endure conversation which tended to inculcate the principles of equal rights in men; and notwithstanding that the particularity of his situation enforced his attention to doctrines of this kind, he went out of the world with the same fond prejudices with which he had been fostered in his nursery, and cajoled in the zenith of his power.

Charles was of middle stature; his body strong, healthy, and justly proportioned; his face was regular, handsome, and well complexioned; and his aspect melancholy, yet not unpleasing. His surviving issue were three sons and three daughters. He was executed in the forty-ninth year of his age, and buried, by the appointment of the parliament, at Windsor, decently, yet without pomp. The duke of Richmond, the marquis of Hertford, the earls of Southampton and Lindsay, at their express desire, were permitted to pay the last duty to their master, but were denied (by colonel Whitchcot, the governor of Windsor Castle) the use of the burial service, according to the book of Common Prayer.

88

A question whether the people, in any case, have a right to depose and punish their sovereign, became, on the death of Charles, the subject of earnest debate, and was pursued by the high-church and prerogative party with the utmost violence and acrimony. The sufferings of the royal martyr, for so the deceased monarch was termed, were compared to those of Christ the Redeemer: In the comparison, the hardships of the King's case (on account of his rank) were ridiculously and impiously preferred; and the crucifiers of their God, by churchmen and their adherents, were regarded with an inferior detestation to the murderers of their King. The corrupt doctrines which had been taught by the clergy were currently broached as standards of political and divine truths; and the utmost depravity of human reason appeared in the contest. Monarchy was represented as a form of government of God's immediate appointment; kings his sacred viceregents, whom to resist was impious, to depose was damnable, to punish was atrociously criminal beyond the hope of mercy; nor could the utmost height of depravity in the nature, or wickedness in the conduct of a monarch, excuse, in any degree, such an act of jurisdiction in revolted subjects. Systems, on the principles of fate and necessity, were written to support the doctrines of slavery: A paternal and legislative power in kings was attempted to be proved by succession from Adam; of whom it was absurdly asserted, that he was by God invested with the absolute power of life and death.

As the scriptures were wrested to authorize the doctrines of the adversary, so the partizans of Liberty, from the same source, argued, That the death of a bloodshedder was required by the Lord, who by his word cautions against the respect of persons, or the exempting individuals from judgement on account of their authority; that men of all ranks and orders were included in this command; and, in the case of the deficiency of the magistrate, were bound to see it fulfilled. On the rule of policy, they observed, That the constitution of a King did not take away that lawful defence against force and injury allowed by the law of nature: That even the civil laws which were imperial, declared, that we are not to obey a prince ruling above the limits of the power entrusted to him; for the commonwealth, by constituting a King, doth not rob or deprive itself of the power of its own preservation: That God having given the world to no one man, nor declared how it should be divided, left it to the will of man: That government and magistracy, whether supreme or subordinate, was a mere human ordinance:

That the laws of every nation were the measure of magistratical power: That Kings, the servants of the state, when they degenerated into tyrants, forfeited their right to government: That where there is a covenant and oath, there must be coactive power to enforce it: That the oaths of allegiance were to be understood as conditionally binding, according to the observance of the oaths kings made to their people: And that neither the laws of God nor nature were against the people's laying aside Kings and kingly government, and the adopting more convenient forms. To the opposition of the Presbyterians, it was objected, That he whom they had exclaimed against in the pulpits as a tyrant, as an enemy to God and saints, as laden with all the innocent blood spilt in the three kingdoms; that he whom they had devoted to perdition, with exhortation to curse, in the name of God, all those who did not make war against him; was without penitence or alteration in his first principles, a lawful magistrate, a sovereign lord, the Lord's anointed, his person sacred, though they had formally denied him his office, and every where resisted his power, but where it survived in their own faction. To their arguments of indefeasible right it was returned, that though a derivative power was committed in trust from the people to Kings and magistrates, yet it remained fundamentally in its source: That to say a King had as good a right to his crown and dignity as another man to his inheritance, was to make the subject no better than his slave; yet even on the supposition of hereditary right, there were crimes for which hereditary right was justly forfeitable: That to say a King was accountable to none but God, was neither founded on command, precept, nor reason; that it was the overthrow of all law, and the destruction of good policy: That the authority of the scripture, in the example of the Israelites, established the right of chusing and changing government: That God himself had given the preference to a republic, as a more perfect form than a monarchy, and more suitable to the conditions of mankind; and that Christ bore testimony against the absolute authority of the Gentile governors:* That to resist, depose, and kill weak and wicked princes, had been in part the conduct of the Reformed, and the favorite doctrine of Calvinistical divines: That even in the case in question, the King, by being deprived of his office, had been in a manner deposed by both the Scotch and English Presbyterians: That to war upon a King, that his instruments might be brought to condign punishment, to inflict sufferance on the instruments, and not only to spare but defend and honor the author, was the absurdest piece of justice to be called Christian, and of reason to be called human, which ever yet entered the heads of men of reverence and learning.

---

* Absolute monarchy (says Locke, that deep and accurate reasoner, on the principles of government and subjection) is inconsistent with civil society, and therefore no form of civil government. Where men have no standing rule to appeal to on earth, they are still in a state of nature, and under all the inconveniencies of it; but with this woeful difference to the subject of an absolute prince, that as, in an ordinary state of nature, he is at liberty to judge of, and maintain his right under such government, as if degraded from the common state of rational creatures, he is denied that privilege, and so exposed to all the miseries which a man has to fear from one, who, being in the unrestrained state of nature, is yet corrupted with flattery, and armed with power. *Locke on Civil Government*, oct. ed. 1764.

The positions to be found in these arguments, That government is the ordinance of man; that, being the mere creature of human invention, it may be changed or altered according to the dictates of experience, and the better judgment of men; that it was instituted for the protection of the people, for the end of securing not overthrowing the rights of nature; that it is a trust either formally admitted, or supposed; and that magistracy is consequently accountable; will meet with little contradiction in a country enlightened with the unobstructed ray of rational learning. Systems of slavery, condemned to oblivion by general neglect, are no where to be found but among the lumber of a university; nor, till the light of letters are again extinct, will another Filmer arise, to dispute the equal justice of God, and the natural freedom of mankind.[13]

90

On general grounds it must be indisputably acknowledged, that the partizans of Liberty gained a complete triumph over the adversary; on the particular circumstances of the case in question it must be allowed, they discovered error and fallacy. "The absence of twice so many members," says Goodwin[14] (on the argument that the parliament, by whose authority the high court of justice was erected, was no true parliament), "as were detained from the house by force doth not at all maim its legitimacy, nor disable its legal authority, in respect of any parliamentary end or purpose whatsoever. The detainment of some of their members from them by force doth not alter the case, in respect of nulling the authority or parliamentary power of those who did sit, especially they not consenting or being accessory to such their detainment. Suppose some of their members, employed by them in carrying messages or petitions to the King, during the time of the wars, had been forcibly detained by him, would such a restraint laid upon them by the King have dissolved the parliamentary authority of the house?" No, it would not; but if the house had been garbled of all those members who were engaged in an opposite interest to the King, and none but his creatures permitted to sit, it certainly would: assertions like these, without argument, disgrace the cause they were intended to defend. A parliament under any undue influence or force can do no constitutional act; and it is to be disputed whether, in a free capacity, the joint powers of both houses reach to the warring with or dethroning their King. The oaths of supremacy and allegiance, every form of law, are against it. Sovereignty and jurisdiction over sovereignty is a contradiction in terms; and in all the addresses of the two houses to the monarch, far from assuming superior or equal stations in the legislature, they acknowledge a subordinate inferiority.

To attempt the defence of that eminent act of justice, the King's death, on the narrow bottom of constitutional forms, is to betray the cause of Liberty, and confound both truth and reason. When a sovereign, by enlarging the limits of that power with which he is vested for the protection of the people, weakens the authority of laws, and consequently the security of the subject; when he acts in opposition to the just ends for which government was instituted, and from a protector of the commonwealth becomes an enemy; when, by breach of trust and non-performance of obligations, the good purposes of his institution are inverted; his trust and right to government from that period are forfeited,* the tie of allegiance is dissolved, and the law and the constitution being rendered incapable of affording the subject protection, he is no longer bound by their forms or dictates, and may justly, by the right of self-preservation, take every probable mean to secure himself from the lawless power and enterprizes of the tyrant. It is on these grounds the parliament are to be defended in the war they made on the King: It is on these grounds the army, as they profess in several declarations, supported their pretensions; not as servants to the dictates of a master, but as fellow-citizens in support of equal Liberty. The parliament, as watchmen for the commonwealth, were to represent to the people their danger: The parliament, as elected by the people for the purposes of guarding the Liberties of the constitution, though not formally invested with the power of opposing by the force of arms a tyrannical headstrong prince, yet this power being, by the nature of their office, rationally implied, it was a duty binding in conscience and in honor: The parliament, by the advantages which the possession of part of the authority of the government gave them, were entitled to lead in the undertaken war against the encroachments of power; but not, as masters of the community, to mould the constitution to their pleasure, and gain to themselves the sole benefits of the conquest: The parliament, on the principles of self-defence, on the principles of equity and reason, without respect to constitutional forms, had a right to oppose the tyrant to the utmost; so, upon the same principles, had the collective body of the people; so, upon the same principles, had any party or individual of the people. Exclude this position, and all governments are equal tyrannies; the destroyers, not the preservers of the rights of nature.

Never any prince who sat on the English throne had made greater innovations in the government than Charles; never any prince had laid deeper schemes against the freedom of the constitution; never any prince, even to the last period of his life, had manifested in his conduct less title to farther trust. The parliament, the majority of whom were Calvinists, against the sense of their fellow-associates, the army, who had borne the danger, the burthen, the heat of the day, neglecting or rather betraying the cause of equal Liberty, on the pretence of which they had began the contention, attempted by a coalition with the King to establish their own authority over, and coerce their religion upon, the people. The army, who had fought for Freedom, not for a change of tyranny, on the same grounds of equity on which the first quarrel was began, opposed their measures, and over-powered their authority.—Against the objection, That on these positions all government must be unstable, that good and just, as well as bad and tyrannical, would be liable to be shaken by the interested views and giddy enterprizes of a faction, it is to be observed, that these objections, though common, are weak and designing; the fears of the frail, the ignorant, and the wicked: Government never can stand on better, never on firmer, never on equitable grounds, than on

---

* "All power," says Locke, "is given with trust for the attaining an end; being limited by that end, whenever that end is manifestly neglected or opposed, the trust must necessarily be forfeited, and the power devolve into the hands of those who gave it; who may place it anew, where they shall think best for their safety and security." *Locke*, 82.

its good behavior. Just government will be felt, its advantages will be seen, its security will be fixed in the hearts of its subjects, not to be shaken by the fantastic or selfish ends of individuals. The experience of all times shews, that the people are with difficulty moved to assert their rights, even against the most obvious, the most oppressive tyrannies.

ENDNOTES

1   See Devoney Looser, *British Women Writers and the Writing of History,* 1670–1820 (London and Baltimore: John Hopkins University Press, 2000), 15: "Macaulay may well have been the first eminent British woman historian of England, but she was by no means the only woman of her day who wrote history."

2   Catharine Macaulay, introduction to *History of England* (London, 1763–1774).

3   Quoted in Bridget Hill, *The Republican Virago* (Oxford: Clarendon Press, 1992), 11.

4   James Boswell, entry for 21 July 1763 in *Boswell's Life of Johnson* (1791; repr., London: Oxford University Press, 1965), 316.

5   Boswell, 172.

6   Bridget Hill, *The Republican Virago,* 77.

7   Some of Macaulay's shorter footnotes have been included in our excerpt. The longer ones, usually quoting seventeenth-century sources, have been omitted for considerations of space.

8   Macaulay is referring to the London Revolution Society and the Society for Constitutional Information, attacked by Burke because sympathetic to the French Revolution. These clubs were suppressed by the government with the Treason Act (1795), the Sedition Act (1798), and the Combination Acts (1799–1800).

9   Dr. Richard Price (1723–91) was a philosopher, demographer, political radical, rationalist, and libertarian. A dissenting minister in East London (Poor Jewry Lane, Hackney, and Stoke Newington), he published *Observations on the Nature of Civil Liberty* (1776), supported the American rebels, and engaged in agitation for the repeal of the Corporation and Test Acts. He was a founding member of the Society for Constitutional Reform and a member of the Revolution Society. On 4 November 1789, he preached "A Discourse on Love of our Country" in which he argued that a true love of country was shown by citizens defending their natural rights. He also praised the French revolutionaries. Burke attacked him in his *Reflections on the Revolution in France* of 1790. Among those to reply in defence of Price were Catharine Macaulay, Joseph Priestley, Mary Wollstonecraft, Anna Barbauld, and Thomas Paine.

10   David Hume (1711–76), a philosopher and historian, published a *History of Great Britain* in which he traced from the reign of James I and Charles I the rise of commerce and protestant religious enthusiasm as fostering a love of liberty. His account was sympathetic to Charles I; he was consequently attacked by the Whigs.

11 Robert Walpole was Prime Minister of England from 1721–42.

12 Thomas Hobbes (1588–1679), the philosopher and author of *The Leviathan*, was a philosophical materialist; he believed in utilitarian morality and, in politics, championed strong rule.

13 Robert Filmer (d. 1653) was a political writer and the author of the *Patriarcha*, a defence of patriarchal theory in government. He attacked the social compact theories of Hobbes. Filmer was in his turn attacked by Locke in his *Two Treatises on Government* (1690), for his defence of absolutism.

14 John Goodwin (1594–1665), republican divine and theological controversialist, defended the army leaders in the Civil War. In 1648, the year of the execution of Charles I, he published "Might and Right Well Met," praising the purging of parliament for the king's trial.

Lucy Aikin (1781–1864)

Lucy Aikin was a talented member of the Jennings/Aikin/Barbauld family with roots, through her mother, in Presbyterianism and, through her father, in the intellectual life of religious dissent. An essayist and biographer of her father, John Aikin, MD, and her aunt, Anna Laetitia Barbauld, Lucy Aikin was most distinguished as a social historian. A liberal Unitarian, but less politically radical than Mary Hays or Mary Wollstonecraft, she nevertheless championed education for women. She herself had received an excellent education, being taught almost entirely at home, reading widely in English, French, Italian, and Latin history and literature. Living in a post-revolutionary age and gauging the temper of the times, Aikin held, but did not advertise, her feminist views.

Aikin is best known for her memoirs of court life, which she was careful not to call "histories":

> It has been the constant endeavour of the writer to preserve to her work the genuine character of Memoirs, by avoiding as much as possible all encroachments on the peculiar province of history;— that amusement of a not illiberal kind has been consulted at least equally with instruction; and that on subjects of graver moment, a correct sketch has alone been attempted.[1]

In spirited narrative, much of it based on archival research, she described the manners and morals of the reigns of Elizabeth I (1818), James I (1822), and Charles I (1833). The following extract, taken from her *Memoirs of the Court of Elizabeth*, makes it clear that, whilst she admired the queen, she did not applaud her more tyrannous actions. Aikin gives us a poignant sense of a monarch surrounded by enemies, obsessed with power, and most alone at those moments, such as the execution of her favourite, Essex, or her royal cousin, Mary Stewart, when her inclinations and conscience were in conflict with political expediency.

Aikin's nephew, Le Breton, while praising her scholarship, described her memoir of Queen Elizabeth in slightly patronising tones as an "animated picture of a reign which Englishmen [sic] have always contemplated with pride."[2] Aikin created much more than animation, and aimed at evoking more than patriotic pride. She exposed the dark side of ambition and the wider social and cultural currents informing the period. Her portrait of Elizabeth I reveals the moral cost of the pursuit of power.

"The Trial and Execution of Mary Queen of Scots," Memoirs of the Court of Elizabeth (1818)

Lucy Aikin

The Trial and Execution of Mary Queen of Scots

Soon after the arrival of Mary at Fotheringay, Elizabeth ... issued out a commission to forty noble-men and privy counsellors, empowering them to try and pass sentence upon Mary, daughter and heir of king James V and late queen of Scots;—for it was thus that she was designated, with a view of intimating to her that she was no longer to be regarded as possessing the rights of a sovereign princess. Thirty-six of the commissioners repaired immediately to Fotheringay, where they arrived on 9th Oct. 1586, and cited Mary to appear before them. This summons she refused to obey, on the double ground, that, as an absolute princess, she was free from all human jurisdiction, since kings only could be her peers; and that having been detained in England as a prisoner, she had not enjoyed the protection of the laws; and consequently ought not in equity to be regarded as amenable to their sentence. Whatever may be thought of these objections, the commissioners refused to admit them, and declared that they would proceed to judge her by default. This menace she at first disregarded; but soon after, overcome by the artful representations of Hatton on the inferences which must inevitably be drawn from her refusal to justify herself for the satisfaction of a princess who had declared that she desired nothing so much as the establishment of her innocence, she changed her mind and consented to plead ... it does not appear that, with respect to its forms and modes of proceeding, Mary had good cause to complain that her trial was other than a regular and legal one....

Intercepted letters, authenticated by the testimony of her secretaries, formed the chief evidence against Mary. From these the crown lawyers showed, and she did not attempt to deny, that she had suffered her correspondents to address her as queen of England; that she had endeavoured by means of English fugitives to incite the Spaniards to invade the country; and that she had been negotiating at

Rome the terms of a transfer of all her claims, present and future, to the king of Spain; disinheriting by this unnatural act her own schismatical son. The further charge of having concurred in the late plot for the assassination of Elizabeth, she strongly denied and attempted to disprove; but it stood on equally good evidence with all the rest; and in spite of some suggestions of which her modern partisans have endeavoured to give her the benefit, there appears no solid foundation on which an impartial enquirer can doubt the fact....

The deportment of Mary on this trying emergency exhibited somewhat of the dignity, but more of the spirit and adroitness, for which she has been famed. She justified her negotiations, or intrigues with foreign princes, on the ground of her inalienable right to employ all the means within her power for the recovery of that liberty of which she had been cruelly and unjustly deprived.... On the whole, her presence of mind was remarkable; though the quick sensibilities of her nature could not be withheld from breaking out at times, either in vehement sallies of anger or long fits of weeping; as the sense of past and present injuries, or of her forlorn and afflicted state, and the perils and sufferings which still menaced her, rose by turns upon her agitated and affrighted mind....

The commissioners, after a full hearing of the cause, quitted Fotheringay; and meeting again in the Star-chamber, summoned before them the two secretaries, who voluntarily confirmed on oath the whole of their former depositions; after this, they proceeded to an unanimous sentence of death against Mary, which was immediately transmitted to the queen for her approbation. On the same day a declaration was published on the part of the commissioners and judges, importing, that the sentence did in no manner derogate from the titles and honours of James, the king of Scotland....

Most of the subsequent steps taken by Elizabeth in this unhappy business are marked with the features of that intense selfishness which, scrupling nothing for the attainment of its own mean objects, seldom fails by exaggerated efforts and overstrained manoeuvres to expose itself to detection and merited contempt....

Never had she enjoyed a higher degree of popularity than at this juncture; the late discoveries had ópened to view a series of popish machinations which had fully justified in the eyes of an alarmed and irritated people, even those previous measures of severity on the part of her government which had most contributed to provoke these attempts of her catholic subjects....

It is manifest, therefore, that no deference for the opinions or feelings of her subjects compelled Elizabeth to hesitate or to dissemble at all in this matter.... But it was the weakness of Elizabeth to imagine, that an extraordinary parade of reluctance, and the interposition of some affected delays, would change in public opinion the whole character of the deed which she contemplated; and preserve to her the reputation of feminine mildness and sensibility, without the sacrifice of that great revenge on which she was secretly bent. The world, however, when it has no interest in deceiving itself, is too wise to accept the words instead of deeds, or in opposition to them; and the sole result of her artifices was to aggravate in the eyes of all mankind the criminality of the act, by giving it rather the air of a treacherous and cold-blooded murder, than of solemn execution done upon a formidable culprit by the sentence of offended laws. The parliament which Elizabeth had summoned to partake the odium of Mary's death, met four days after the judges had pronounced her doom, and was opened by commission. An unanimous ratification of the sentence by both houses was immediately carried; followed by an earnest address to her majesty for its publication and execution; to which she returned a long and laboured answer....

She began with the expression of her fervent gratitude to Providence for the affections of her people; adding protestations of her love towards them, and of her perfect willingness to have suffered her own life still to remain exposed as a mark to the aim of enemies and traitors, had she not perceived how intimately the safety and well-being of the nation was connected with her own. With regard to the queen of Scots, she said, so severe had been the grief which she had sustained from her recent conduct, that the fear of renewing this sentiment had been the cause, and the sole cause, of her withholding her personal appearance at the opening of that assembly; where she knew that the subject must of necessity become matter of discussion; and not, as had been suggested, the apprehension of any violence to be attempted against her person;—yet she might mention, that she had actually seen a bond by which the subscribers bound themselves to procure her death within a month....

So far was she from indulging any ill-will against one of the same sex, the same rank, the same race as herself;—in fact her nearest kinswoman;—that after having received full information of certain of her machinations, she had secretly written with her own hand to the queen of Scots, promising that, on a simple confession of her guilt in a private letter to herself, all should be buried in oblivion....

The statute, by requiring her to pronounce judgement upon her kinswoman, had involved her in anxiety and difficulties. Amid all her perils, however, she must remember with gratitude and affection the voluntary association into which her subjects had entered for her defence. It was never her practice to decide hastily on any matter; in a case so rare and important some interval of deliberation must be allowed her; and she would pray Heaven to enlighten her mind and guide it to the decision most beneficial to the church, to the state, and to the people....

Twelve days after the delivery of this speech, her majesty sent a message to both houses entreating that her parliament would carefully reconsider the matter; and endeavour to hit upon some device by which the life of the queen of Scots might be rendered consistent with her own safety and that of the country. Her faithful parliament, however, soon after acquainted her, that with their utmost diligence they had found it impracticable to form any satisfactory plan of the kind she desired; and the speakers of the two houses ended a long representation of the mischiefs to be expected from any arrangement by which Mary would be suffered to continue in life, with a most earnest and humble petition, that her majesty would not deny to the united wishes and entreaties of all England, what it would be iniquitous to refuse to the meanest individual; the execution of justice....

Elizabeth, after pronouncing a second long harangue designed to display her own clemency, to upbraid the malice of her libellers, and to refute the suspicion, which her conscience no doubt helped her to anticipate, that all this irresolution was but feigned; and the decisions of the two houses were influenced by a secret acquaintance with her wishes;—again dismissed their petitions without any positive answer. Soon after, however, she permitted herself to authorize the proclamation of the sentence; and sent lord Buckhurst and Beal, clerk of the council, to announce it to Mary herself.... [Interventions attempted by the kings of France and Scotland were unsuccessful.]

At length, on Feb. 1st, 1587, her majesty ordered secretary Davison[3] to bring her the warrant, which had remained ready drawn in his hands for some weeks; and having signed it, she told him to get it sealed with the great seal; and in this way to call on Walsingham and tell him what she had done; "though," she added smiling, "I fear he will die of grief when he hears of it;"—this minister being then sick. Davison obeyed her directions, and the warrant was sealed. The next day he received a message from her, purporting that he should forbear to carry the warrant to the lord-keeper till further orders. Surprised and perplexed, he immediately waited upon her to receive her further directions; when she chid him for the haste he had used in this matter; and talked in a fluctuating and undetermined manner respecting it, which greatly alarmed him. On leaving the queen, he immediately communicated the circumstances to Burleigh[4] and Hatton; and thinking it safest for himself to rid his hands of the warrant, he delivered it up to Burleigh, by whom it had been drawn and from whom he had at first received it. A council was now called consisting of such of the ministers as either the queen herself or Davison had made acquainted with the signing of the warrant; and it was proposed that, without any further communication with her majesty, it should be sent down for immediate execution to the four earls to whom it had been directed....

Davison appears to have expressed some fears that he should be made to bear the blame of this step; but all his fellow-councillors then present joined to assure him that they would share the responsibility; it was also said that her majesty had desired of several that she might not be troubled respecting any of the particulars of the last dismal scene; consequently it was impossible that she could complain of their proceeding without her privity. By these arguments Davison was seduced to give his concurrence; and Beal, a person noted for the vehemence of his attachment to the protestant cause ... was dispatched with the instrument; in obedience to which Mary underwent the fatal stroke of the executioner on February 8th....

The news of this event was received by Elizabeth with the most extraordinary demonstrations of astonishment, grief, and anger. Her countenance changed, her voice faltered, and she remained for some moments fixed and motionless; a violent burst of tears and lamentations succeeded, with which she mingled expressions of rage against her whole council. They had committed, she said, a crime never to be forgiven; they had put to death without her knowledge her dear kinswoman and sister, against whom they well knew that it was her fixed resolution never to proceed to the fatal extremity. She put on deep mourning; kept herself retired among her ladies abandoned to sighs and tears; and drove from her presence with the most furious reproaches such of her ministers as ventured to come near her. She caused several of the counsellors to be examined as to the share which they had taken in this transaction. Burleigh was of the number; and against him she expressed herself with such peculiar bitterness that he gave himself up for lost, and begged permission to retire with the loss of all his employments. This resignation was not accepted; and after a considerable interval, during which this great minister deprecated the wrath of his sovereign in letters of penitence and submission worthy only of an Oriental slave, she condescended to be reconciled to one whose services she felt to be indispensable....

But the blood of Mary, or the indignation of her son, could not be appeased, it was thought, without a sacrifice; and a fit victim was at hand. From some words dropped by lord Burleigh on his examination, either incautiously, or with design to shift the blame from himself, it had appeared that it was the declaration of Davison respecting the sentiments of the queen, as expressed to himself, which had finally decided the council to send down the warrant; and on this ground proceedings were instituted against the unfortunate secretary. He was stripped of his office, sent to the Tower in spite of the remonstrances of Burleigh, and after several examinations subjected to a process in the Star-chamber for a two-fold contempt. First, in revealing her majesty's counsels to others of her ministers;— secondly, in giving up to them an instrument which she had committed to him of special trust and secrecy, to be kept in case of any sudden emergency which might require its use....

Davison demanded that his own examination, which, with that of Burleigh, formed the whole evidence against him, should be read entire, instead of being picked and garbled by the crown lawyers; but this piece of justice the queen's counsel refused him, on the plea that they contained matter unfit to be divulged. He was found guilty, and sentenced to a fine of ten thousand marks and imprisonment during the queen's pleasure, by judges who at the same time expressed a high opinion both of his abilities and his integrity; and who certainly regarded his offence as nothing more than an error of judgment or a want of due caution. Elizabeth ordered a copy of his sentence to be immediately transmitted to the king of Scots, as triumphant evidence of that perfect innocence in the tragical *accident* of his mother's death, of which she had already made solemn protestation. James complied so far with obvious motives of policy as to accept her excuses without much enquiry; but posterity will not be disposed to dismiss so easily a curious investigation which it possesses abundant means of pursuing. The record of Burleigh's examination is still extant; and so likewise is Davison's apology; a piece which was composed by himself at the time, and addressed to Walsingham, who could best judge of its accuracy; and which, after being communicated to Camden, who inserted an extract from it in his annals, has at length been found entire among the original papers of Sir Amias Paulet....

[There follows an account of Davison's self-defence, analysing how he allowed himself to be entrapped by Elizabeth.]

Of this unaccountable imprudence the utmost advantage was taken against him by his cruel and crafty mistress; whose chief concern it had all along been to discover by what artifice she might throw the greatest possible portion of the blame from herself upon others. Davison underwent a long imprisonment; the fine, though it reduced him to beggary, was rigorously exacted; some scanty supplies for the relief of his immediate necessities, while in prison, were all that her majesty would vouchsafe him; and neither the zealous attestations of Burleigh, who must have felt that he owed him some reparation, to his merit and abilities and the importance of his public services, nor the subsequent earnest pleadings of her own beloved Essex for his restoration, could ever prevail with Elizabeth to lay aside the appearances of perpetual resentment which she thought good to preserve against him. She would neither reinstate him in office nor ever more admit him to her presence; unable perhaps to bear the pain of beholding a countenance which carried with it such an everlasting reproach to her conscience.... To relate again those melancholy details of Mary's closing scene on which the historians of England and of Scotland, as well as the numerous biographers of this ill-fated princess, have exhausted all the arts of eloquence, would be equally needless and presumptuous. It is, however, important to remark, that she died rather with the triumphant air of a martyr to her religion, than with the meekness of a victim or the penitence of a culprit. She bade Melvil tell her son that she had done nothing injurious to his rights or his honour;—though she was actually in treaty to disinherit him, and had also consented to a nefarious plot for carrying him off prisoner to Rome;—and she denied with obstinacy to the last, the charge of conspiring the death of Elizabeth, though by her will, written the day before her death, she rewarded as faithful servants the two secretaries who had borne this testimony against her. A spirit of self-justification so haughty and so unprincipled,—a perseverance in deliberate falsehood so resolute and so shameless, ought under no circumstances and in no personage, not even in a captive beauty and an injured queen, to be confounded, by any writer studious of the moral tendencies of history and capable of sound discrimination, with genuine religion, true fortitude, or the dignity which renders misfortune respectable....

Let such censure as is due be passed on the infringement of morality committed by Elizabeth, in detaining as a captive that rival kinswoman and pretender to her crown, whom the dread of still more formidable dangers had compelled to take refuge in her dominions:—let it be admitted, that the exercise of criminal jurisdiction over a person thus lawlessly detained in a foreign country, was another stretch of power, which none but a profligate politician will venture to defend;—and let the efforts of Mary to procure her own liberty, though with the destruction of her enemy and at the cost of a civil war to England, be held, if religion will permit, justifiable or venial;—but let not our resentment of the wrongs, or compassion for the long misfortunes of this unhappy woman, betray us into a blind concurrence in eulogiums lavished by prejudice or weakness on a character blemished by many foibles, stained by some enormous crimes, and never submitted to the guidance of the genuine principles of moral rectitude.

ENDNOTES

1   Lucy Aikin, "Preface," *Memoirs of the Court of Elizabeth* (London: Alex. Murray and Son, 1869), 1.

2   Philip Hemery Le Breton, ed., *Memoirs, Miscellanies and Letters of the late Lucy Aikin* (London: Longman, Roberts and Green, 1864), xix–xx.

3   William Davison (d. 1608) was a diplomat and administrator. He served as Secretary of State from 1586–1587. Contrary to Aikin's account, after his trial, he was released from the tower on October 23, 1588 and continued to be paid his salary until the end of his life. He never had to pay the fine imposed upon him. His trial was a device to vindicate Elizabeth following the execution of Mary Stewart.

4   William Cecil, 1st Baron Burghley (1520/21–1598), was Secretary of State and Lord Treasurer under Elizabeth I. He played a leading role in the trial and condemnation of Mary Stewart and helped draft the petition for her execution, taking the lead in expediting the warrant. He was briefly banished from the court after Mary's death.

Agnes Strickland (1796–1874)

Agnes Strickland (1796–1874) represented the public face of a successful partnership with her older sister Elizabeth (1794–1875). Sometimes separately, but mainly together, the Strickland sisters made groundbreaking efforts to write a new kind of history based on newly discovered documentary evidence. They wrote not as male historians, trained in history at university, who advanced the profession of historian, such as Edward Gibbon, Thomas Carlyle, or T.B. Macaulay, or as privileged amateurs. Rather, the Stricklands took advantage of the market for life-writing to make money by producing multiple biographies of public figures largely ignored by male writers, especially royal women and children. They extended the range of female biography to include notorious and exemplary women, opening commercial print possibilities to aspiring women writers.* They sought to validate their authority as female historians by their assiduous research, but the use of primary—even rare—sources did not provide immunity from charges of emotionalism and frivolity in their work. Macaulay was probably the critic in the *Edinburgh Review* (1847) who wrote of them, "ladies who assume masculine functions must learn to assume masculine gravity and impartiality."†

Their father, Thomas Strickland, educated his nine children in Latin, mathematics, and history at home, his seven daughters equally with his two sons. The family lived in London, East Anglia, Suffolk, and Norwich. Wide reading and ambitions to write for publication were important elements of the family culture. Agnes early demonstrated her enthusiasm for British history.

When Thomas Strickland's income and health failed, his children faced the necessity of earning their livings. Agnes and four of her sisters tried writing for the lucrative children's market. She had some success and, with Elizabeth, aspired to make a place for herself as a professional writer. During their visits to London, they met established authors, including Robert Southey, Charles Lamb, and William Jerdan, editor of the *Literary Gazette*. They made important

---

* See Anne Laurence's illuminating discussion in "Women Historians and Documentary Research: Lucy Aikin, Agnes Strickland, Mary Anne Everett Green and Lucy Toulmin Smith," in *Women, Scholarship, and Criticism: Gender and Knowledge, c. 1790–1900*, ed. Joan Bellamy, Anne Laurence, and Gillian Perry (Manchester: Manchester University Press, 2000), 125.

† The Stricklands were probably the target for Anthony Trollope's gently satiric figure Lady Matilda Carbury, in *The Way We Live Now* (1875), and her book on *Criminal Queens*. Trollope's narrator advises that Lady Carbury "could write after a glib, commonplace, sprightly fashion, and had already acquired the knack of spreading all she knew very thin, so that it might cover a vast surface. She had no ambition to write a good book, but was painfully anxious to write a book that the critics should say was good."

connections with women writers who introduced them to some of the publishing possibilities available to women: keepsake albums, annuals, poetry, and historical romances. Agnes greatly admired Sir Walter Scott, to whom she had been introduced, and she modelled her work on his.

Although Elizabeth avoided publicity, she became the editor of the *Court Journal* in 1830. Agnes, more gregarious than Elizabeth, enjoyed court and aristocratic circles, and, in the course of her work, she met Princess Victoria whose position as heir apparent to the British throne whetted the public's appetite for works about queens and princesses.[*] By the time Victoria became queen in 1837, the sisters had already decided to try their hands at the new genre of popular history, with plans to write biographies of "all the queens of England, whether consort or regnant," in 14 volumes.[†] Reclusive Elizabeth insisted on being the silent partner, although she proved to be an effective businesswoman in negotiating their contracts with publishers. They agreed that only Agnes's name would appear as author and she would assume responsibility for the social contacts necessary for their work with other scholars, journalists, reviewers, readers, British and foreign custodians of historical records, and government officials. Their ambitious 14-volume *Lives of the Queens of England*, published between 1840 and 1848, became one of the best-selling Victorian historical works. Agnes used her acquaintance with the new Queen to obtain permission to dedicate the work to her. In subsequent reissues, notable artists illustrated the volumes.[‡]

The sisters determined that "facts not opinions" would define their histories, though this statement needs to be qualified. They were committed to examining documentary evidence in archives but felt free to interpret their material in light of their own views. They read and transcribed historical manuscripts at the British Museum, Elizabeth learning palaeography (the study of ancient and medieval manuscripts), and sought out previously unexamined documents in far-flung locations and private hands. Agnes demonstrated their commitment to primary research by insisting in 1837 that she be given access to the State Papers that required the permission of the Prime Minister or Home Secretary. When she met with "an uncourteous repulse" at first, she called upon influential friends to gain admission to the archives. She was among the eighty-three signatories, including Lucy Aikin, of a petition presented to the Master of the Rolls in 1851 arguing that fees for consulting public documents be waived for those engaged in serious literary or historical work.[§]

The sisters traveled widely, both in England and the Continent, visiting historic private homes and public sites and researching archives. Agnes proposed that they write the lives of the Scottish queens. Elizabeth resisted: she feared that she would be responsible for the difficult medieval research because Agnes had

[*] Laurence, 126.
[†] Mary Delorme, "'Facts, not Opinions'—Agnes Strickland," *History Today* 38 (1988): 46.
[‡] Alison Booth discusses the "itinerant life" of certain illustrations that appeared in other books after the Stricklands; see *How to Make It as a Woman: Collective Biographical History from Victoria to the Present* (Chicago: University of Chicago Press, 2004), 34.
[§] The petition was successful. Among the other signatories were Carlyle, Charles Dickens, Macaulay, Lucy Aikin, and Mary Anne Everett; see Laurence, 125.

so many social commitments. They resolved their differences by agreeing to begin the new work with Margaret Tudor, wife of James IV. This allowed Agnes to research in Scotland for "the crowning labour of my life," her account of Mary, Queen of Scots. This, though prolix, was well received.

Although Agnes achieved rare public recognition for her original historical work, she refused to use her uncommon status to advance women's economic, legal, or social position, not signing a petition in favour of the Married Women's Property Act because she considered women's grievances unavoidable, "part and parcel of the penalties entailed by Eve's transgression."* Nevertheless as a highly successful female historian, Agnes Strickland participated in the transition to greater gender equality by "tutoring her readers in the proper work of both women in history and the history of women."[†]

Although Agnes and Elizabeth Strickland were constrained by the gender prejudices of their time to represent female figures chiefly in the private and domestic rather than the public aspects of their lives, yet, as the portrait of Elizabeth I makes clear, they showed the political world inextricably conjoined to their subjects' private concerns. The Strickland sisters presaged later women who would be trained as professional historians by their insistence, in Agnes's words, that "it is a [historian's] sacred duty to assert nothing lightly or without good evidence, of those who can no longer answer for themselves." Women of the past, Agnes wrote, "have left mute but irrefragable witnesses of what they were in their own deeds, for which they, and not their biographers, must stand accountable." Agnes in her painstaking documentary research attempted an empirical historical method: "Opinions," she instructed her readers, "have their date, and change with circumstances, but facts are immutable." Nevertheless, she tended to read many of her preferred opinions as facts, especially as, in the case of Elizabeth, they coincided with her feminine sympathies.[‡]

"ELIZABETH," *LIVES OF THE QUEENS OF ENGLAND* (1877)

Elizabeth Strickland wrote at least half the entries in *Queens of England*, while Agnes wrote the prefaces to each volume.[§] In her preface to the first volume, Agnes explains the sisters' method of "historical biography": "Truth," she writes, "lies not on the surface, but, as the wisdom of ages bears testimony, in a well, which only those who will take the trouble of digging deeply can find."[**]

---

* *Oxford Dictionary of National Biography*, vol. 7, s.v. "Strickland, Agnes" (by Rosemary Mitchell).
† Miriam Elizabeth Burstein, "From Good Looks to Good Thoughts: Popular Women's History and the Invention of Modernity, ca. 1830–1870," *Modern Philology* 97, no. 1 (August 1999): 66.
‡ See Rosemary Mitchell, "A Stitch in Time? Woman, Needlework and the Making of History in Victorian Britain," *Journal of Victorian Culture* 1 (1996): 105 for Agnes Strickland's holding to Queen Mathilda as creator of the Bayeux tapestries in the face of strong conflicting evidence.
§ Mary Delorme, "'Facts, Not Opinions'—Agnes Strickland," 46.
** Agnes Strickland, "Preface," *Lives of the Queens of England, From the Norman Conquest*, vol. 1 (London: George Bell & Sons, 1877), ix.

The following excerpt from Agnes's life of Elizabeth I illustrates the power of the Stricklands' zeal for primary research. Agnes explains that she, like other historians, assumed Elizabeth's responsibility for the death of Mary Queen of Scots, despite Elizabeth's disclaimers. Agnes's discovery of manuscript minutes from Elizabeth's Star Chamber in the Cottonian Library* changed her mind and her text after the first edition. The documents Agnes consulted allege that Sir Francis Walsingham, master of the Queen's espionage system, forged Elizabeth's signature on Mary's death warrant. In the words of Strickland's biographer, Pope-Hennessy, "We know that this belief is unsupported today by any historian, but as Jane Margaret [Agnes Strickland's sister] goes on to say, 'This female biographer was perfectly convinced later on of the innocence of the great queen."[†] Though the thesis of Elizabeth's forged signature no longer has support among historians—Strickland's documentary source could have been one of many attempts contemporary with Elizabeth's reign to absolve the queen of her cousin's death—her portrait of the queen is a challenging reinterpretation of the monarch.

105

We may appropriately at this juncture compare Lucy Aikin, Mary Hays, and Agnes Strickland's portraits of Mary Queen of Scots and Elizabeth I. Aikin seeks to show her subjects' strengths and their accompanying character weaknesses, examining those flaws that led Mary to her death and Elizabeth first to order her cousin's execution and then to deny culpability. Hays focuses on Elizabeth's classical education, by inference a clear contrast to that available to women in nineteenth-century Britain. She paints her as a woman of her time, with remarkable qualities of intellect, who was no more if not less autocratic than her predecessors. Born before the age of toleration (an Enlightenment agenda underlies Hays's text), Elizabeth demonstrates that a woman of extraordinary capacity could rule as well if not better than men. Strickland, on the other hand, seeks to exonerate both her queens morally and to pin their alleged crimes on others. In her version, Mary is the innocent victim of "unjust detention." It is Elizabeth's ministers, not she, who pursue "a systematic course of espionage and treachery." This argument has the effect of making both queens the pawns of courtiers and diminishing their influence. Nevertheless, Strickland powerfully evokes an atmosphere of conspiracy and revenge surrounding the two queens. Her discussion of the alleged forgery of Elizabeth's signature, if biased, is well argued and forceful.

* Robert Cotton (1571–1631) was an antiquarian and founder of the library whose collection of historical documents later formed the basis of the British Museum's manuscript collection.
† Una Pope-Hennessy, *Agnes Strickland, Biographer of the Queens of England 1796–1874* (London: Chatto and Windus, 1940), 115.

"Elizabeth," *Lives of the Queens of England, From the Norman Conquest* (1877)

Agnes Strickland

The unjust detention of Mary queen of Scots in an English prison had, for fifteen years, proved a source of personal misery to Elizabeth, and a perpetual incentive to crime. The worst passions of the human heart—jealousy, hatred, and revenge—were kept in a constant state of excitement by the confederacies that were formed in her dominions, in behalf of the captive heiress of the crown. Her ministers pursued a systematic course of espionage and treachery in order to discover the friends of the unfortunate Mary, and when discovered, omitted no means, however base, by which they might be brought under the penalty of treason.* The sacrifice of human life was appalling; the violation of all moral and divine restrictions of conscience more melancholy still. Scaffolds streamed with blood; the pestilential gaols were crowded with victims, the greater portion of whom died of fever or famine, unpitied and unrecorded, save in the annals of private families.†

Among the features of this agitating period, was the circumstance of persons of disordered intellects accusing themselves of designs against the life of their sovereign, and denouncing others as their accomplices. Such was the case with regard to Somerville, an insane Catholic gentleman, who attacked two persons with a drawn sword, and declared that he would murder every protestant in England, and the queen as their head. Somerville had, unfortunately, married the daughter of Edward Arden, a high-spirited gentleman of ancient descent in Warwickshire, and a kinsman of Shakespeare's mother. Arden had incurred the deadly malice of Leicester, not only for refusing to wear his livery, like the neighbouring squires, to swell his pomp during queen Elizabeth's visit to Kenilworth, "but chiefly," says Dugdale, "for galling him by certain strong expressions touching his private addresses to the countess of Essex before she was his wife." These offences had been

---

* See Camden. Bishop Goodman. Howell's State Trials.
† On the 17th of November, 1577, the attorney-general was directed to examine Thomas Sherwood on the rack, and orders were given to place him in the dungeon among the *rats*. This horrible place was a den in the Tower below high-water mark, entirely dark, and the resort of innumerable rats, which had been known to wound and maim the limbs of the wretched denizens of this dungeon.

duly noted down for vengeance; and the unfortunate turn which the madness of the lunatic son-in-law had taken, formed a ready pretext for the arrest of Arden, his wife, daughters, sister, and a missionary priest named Hall. Arden and Hall were subjected to the torture, and Hall admitted that Arden had once been heard to wish "that the queen were in heaven." This was sufficient to procure the condemnation and execution of Arden. Somerville was found strangled in his cell at Newgate. Hall and the ladies were pardoned. As the insanity of Somerville was notorious, it was generally considered that Arden fell a victim to the malice of Leicester, who parcelled out his lands among his own dependants.[*]

But while plots, real and pretended, threatening the life of the queen, agitated the public mind from day to day, it had become customary for groups of the populace to throw themselves on their knees in the dirt by the wayside, whenever she rode out, and pray for her preservation, invoking blessings on her head, and confusion to the papists, with the utmost power of their voices. A scene of this kind once interrupted an important political dialogue, which the maiden queen was holding with the French ambassador Mauvissière, as he rode by her side from Hampton-court to London, in November, 1583. She was in the act of discussing the plots of the Jesuits, "when," says he,[†] "just at this moment many people, in large companies, met her by the way, and kneeling on the ground, with divers sorts of prayers wished her a thousand blessings, and that the evil-disposed who meant to harm her might be discovered, and punished as they deserved. She frequently stopped to thank them for the affection they manifested for her. She and I being alone amidst her retinue, mounted on goodly horses, she observed to me 'that she saw clearly that she was not disliked by all.'"

The parsimony of Elizabeth in all affairs of state policy, where a certain expenditure was required, often embarrassed her ministers, and traversed the arrangements they had made, or were desirous of making, in her name with foreign princes. Walsingham was so greatly annoyed by her majesty's teasing minuteness and provoking interference in regard to money matters, that he took the liberty of penning a long letter of remonstrance to her, amounting to an absolute lecture on the subject. In the course of this epistle he uses the following expressions: —

"Heretofore your majesty's predecessors, in matters of peril, did never look into charges, though their treasure was neither so great as your majesty's is, nor their subjects so wealthy, nor so willing to contribute. I pray God that the abatement of the charges towards that nobleman that hath the custody of the *bosom serpent* [meaning Mary queen of Scots], hath not lessened his care in keeping of her. To think that a man of his birth and quality, after twelve years' travail in charge of such weight, to have an abatement of allowance, and no recompense otherwise made, should not breed discontentment, no man that hath reason can so judge; and, therefore, to have so special a charge committed to a person discontented, everybody seeth it standeth no way with policy."[‡]

---

[*] Camden.
[†] Reports of Mauvissière de Castelnau.
[‡] Complete Ambassador, p. 427.

Elizabeth had curtailed the allowance of fifty-two pounds per week, which had been, in the first instance, granted to the earl of Shrewsbury for the board and maintenance of the captive queen of Scots and her household, to thirty. The earl complained of being a great loser, and pinched the table of his luckless charge in so niggardly a fashion, that a serious complaint was made to queen Elizabeth by the French ambassador, of the badness and meanness of the diet provided for Mary. Elizabeth wrote a severe reprimand to Shrewsbury; on which he petitioned to be released from the odious office that had been thrust upon him. After a long delay his resignation was accepted, but he had to give up his gloomy castle of Tutbury for a prison for Mary, no other house in England, it was presumed, being so thoroughly distasteful to the royal captive as an abiding place.* Walsingham's term of "bosom serpent" appears peculiarly infelicitous as applied to Mary Stuart, who was never admitted to Elizabeth's presence, or vouchsafed the courtesies due to a royal lady and a guest; but, when crippled with chronic maladies, was denied the trifling indulgence of a coach, or an additional servant to carry her in a chair.

Mauvissière, in a letter to his own court, gives an amusing detail of an altercation which was carried on between Elizabeth and the Scottish ambassador, on account of the execution of Morton, in which she vituperated the queen of Scots and the young king James, and in the midst of her choler exclaimed, "I am more afraid of making a fault in my Latin, than of the kings of Spain, France, and Scotland, the whole house of Guise, and their confederates."† King James despatched his favourite minister, the duke of Lennox, with a letter and message to her explanatory of the late events in Scotland. Elizabeth at first refused to see him, and when she was at last induced to grant him an interview, she, according to the phrase of Calderwood, the historian of the kirk, "rattled him up" on the subject of his political conduct; but he replied with so much mildness and politeness, that her wrath was subdued, and she parted from him courteously. [....]

The junta by whom Elizabeth's resolves were at times influenced, and her better feelings smothered, had sinned too deeply against Mary Stuart to risk the possibility of her surviving their royal mistress. Elizabeth shrank from either incurring the odium, or establishing the dangerous precedent of bringing a sovereign princess to the block. The queens whose blood had been shed on the scaffold by her ruthless father, were subjects of his own, puppets whom he had raised and then degraded from the fatal dignity which his own caprice had bestowed upon them; but even he, tyrant as he was, had not ventured to slay either of his royally-born consorts, Katharine of Aragon or Anne of Cleves, though claiming the twofold authority of husband and sovereign over both. Mary Stuart was not only a king's daughter, but a crowned and anointed sovereign; and under no pretence could she legally be rendered amenable to Elizabeth's authority. Every species of quiet cruelty that might tend to sap the life of a delicately-organized and sensitive female, had been systematically practised

---

* Lodge's Illustrations.
† MS. Harl., folio 398.

on the royal captive by the leaders of Elizabeth's cabinet. Mary had been confined in damp, dilapidated apartments, exposed to malaria, deprived of exercise and recreation, and compelled occasionally, by way of variety, to rise from a sick bed and travel, through an inclement country, from one prison to another in the depth of winter.* These atrocities had entailed upon her a complication of chronic maladies of the most agonizing description; but she continued to exist, and it was evident that the vital principle in her constitution was sufficiently tenacious to enable her to endure many years of suffering. The contingencies of a day, an hour, meantime, might lay Elizabeth in the dust, and call Mary Stuart to the seat of empire. Could Burleigh, Walsingham, and Leicester expect, in that event, to escape the vengeance which their injurious treatment had provoked from that princess? It is just possible that Burleigh, rooted as he was to the helm of state, and skilled in every department of government, might, like Talleyrand, have made his defence good, and retained his office under any change. He had observed an outward show of civility to Mary, and was suspected by Walsingham of having entered into some secret pact with James of Scotland; but Walsingham and Leicester had committed themselves irrevocably, and for them there could be no other prospect than the block, if the Scottish queen, who was nine years younger than Elizabeth, outlived her.

From the moment that Elizabeth declared that "honour and conscience both forbade her to put Mary to death," it had been the great business of these statesmen to convince her, that it was incompatible with her own safety to permit her royal captive to live. Assertions to this effect were lightly regarded by Elizabeth, but the evidence of a series of conspiracies, real as well as feigned, began to take effect upon her mind, and slowly, but surely, brought her to the same conclusion. For many years it had been the practice of Walsingham to employ spies, not only for the purpose of watching the movements of those who were suspected of attachment to the Scottish queen, but to inveigle them into plots against the government and person of queen Elizabeth. One of these base agents, William Parry, after years of secret treachery in this abhorrent service, became himself a convert to the doctrines of the church of Rome, and conceived a design of assassinating queen Elizabeth. This he communicated to Neville, one of the English exiles, the claimant of the forfeit honours and estates of the last earl of Westmoreland. Neville, in the hope of propitiating the queen, gave prompt information of Parry's intentions against her majesty: but as Parry had formerly denounced Neville, Elizabeth, naturally imagining that he had been making a very bold attempt to draw Neville into an overt act of treason, directed Walsingham to inquire of the spy whether he had recently, by way of experiment, suggested to any one the idea of taking away her life? If Parry had replied in the affirmative, he would have been safe; but the earnest manner of his denial excited suspicion. He and Neville were confronted, and then avowed "that he had felt so strong an impulse to murder the queen, that he had, of late, always left his dagger at home when summoned to her presence, lest he should fall upon her and slay her."† This strange conflict of feeling appears like the reasoning

* See Life of Mary Queen of Scots, by Agnes Strickland. Blackwood.
† Hamilton's Annals. State Trials.

madness of a monomaniac, and suggests the idea that Parry's mind had become affected with the delirious excitement of the times. He was condemned to death, and on the scaffold cited his royal mistress to the tribunal of the all-seeing Judge in whose presence he was about to appear.*

The unhappy man expressly acquitted the queen of Scots of any knowledge of his designs. Mary herself, in her private letters, denies having the slightest connection with him. The plot, however, furnished an excuse for treating her with greater cruelty than before. Her comparatively humane keeper, Sir Ralph Sadler, was superseded by Sir Amias Paulet and Sir Drue Drury, two rigid puritans, who were selected by Leicester for the ungracious office of embittering the brief and evil remnant of her days. The last report made by Sadler of the state of bodily suffering to which the royal captive was reduced by her long and rigorous imprisonment, is very pitiable. "I find her," says he, " much altered from what she was when I was first acquainted with her. She is not yet able to strain her left foot to the ground, and to her very great grief, not without tears, findeth it wasted and shrunk of its natural measure."† In this deplorable state, the hapless invalid was removed to the damp and dilapidated apartments of her former hated gaol, Tutbury-castle.‡ A fresh access of illness was brought on by the inclemency of the situation, and the noxious quality of the air. She wrote a piteous appeal to Elizabeth, who did not vouchsafe a reply. Under these circumstances, the unfortunate captive caught, with feverish eagerness, at every visionary scheme that whispered to her in her doleful prison-house the flattering hope of escape. The zeal and self-devotion of her misjudging friends were the very means used by her foes to effect her destruction. Morgan, her agent in France, to whom allusion has already been made, was a fierce, wrong-headed Welshman, who had persuaded himself, with some others, that it was not only expedient but justifiable to destroy Elizabeth, as the sole means of rescuing his long-suffering mistress from the living death in which she was slowly pining away. So greatly had Elizabeth's animosity against Morgan been excited by the disclosures of Parry, that she declared "that she would give ten thousand pounds for his head." When she sent the order of the Garter to Henry III, she demanded that Morgan should be given up to her vengeance. Henry, who was doubtless aware that many disclosures might be forced from Morgan on the rack, that would have the effect of committing himself with his good sister of England, endeavoured to satisfy her by sending Morgan to the Bastile and forwarding his papers to Elizabeth. Morgan's friends were permitted to have access to him, and he employed himself in plotting a more daring design against the life of queen Elizabeth than any that had yet been devised. Mary's faithful ambassador at Paris, Beaton archbishop of Glasgow, and her kinsmen of the house of Guise, decidedly objected to the project.§ Intent

110

* Camden.
† Sadler Papers, 460.
‡ See Life of Mary Queen of Scots, by Agnes Strickland, vol. v. Blackwood.
§ Murdin's State Papers. Egerton Papers. Lingard.

on his vindictive scheme, Morgan paid no heed to the remonstrances of Mary's faithful counsellors, but took into his confidence two of Walsingham's most artful spies, in the disguise of Catholic priests—Gifford and Greatly by name, together with Poley and Maude, two other of the agents of that statesman. Easy enough would it have been for Walsingham, who had perfect information of the proceedings of the conspirators from the first, to have crushed the plot in its infancy; but it was his occult policy to nurse it till it became organized into a shape sufficiently formidable to Elizabeth, to bring her to the conclusion that her life would never be safe while the Scottish queen was in existence, and, above all, to furnish a plausible pretext for the execution of that unfortunate princess. [....]

The great point for which Burleigh, Leicester, Walsingham, and their colleagues had been labouring for the last eighteen years, was at length accomplished. They had succeeded in persuading Elizabeth that Mary Stuart, in her sternly-guarded prison, crippled with chronic and neuralgic maladies, surrounded by spies, and out of the reach of human aid, was so formidable to her person and government, that it was an imperative duty to herself and to her Protestant subjects to put her to death. Having once brought their long-irresolute mistress to this conclusion, all other difficulties became matters of minor importance to the master-spirits who ruled Elizabeth's council, since they had only to arrange a ceremonial process for taking away the life of their defenceless captive in as plausible and formal a manner as might be compatible with the circumstances of the case. It was determined that Mary should be tried by a commission of peers and privy councillors, under the great seal, the fatal innovations* which Henry VIII's despotic tyranny had made in the ancient laws of England on life and death having rendered the crown arbitrary on that point. The commissioners appointed for this business left London for Fotheringay-castle before the 8th of October, 1586; for on that day Davison dates a letter written to Burleigh by her majesty's command, containing various instruction, and informing him "that a Dutchman, newly arrived from Paris, who was familiar with the queen-mother's jeweller, had begged him to advise her majesty to beware of one who will present a petition to her on her way to chapel, or walking abroad." Davison then requests Burleigh to write to the queen, to pray her to be more circumspect of her person, and to avoid showing herself in public till the brunt of the business then in hand be overblown.† This mysterious hint of a new plot against the queen's life was in conformity with the policy of the cabinet, which referred all attempts of the kind to the evil influence of the captive, Mary Stuart. In conclusion, Davison informs Burleigh and Walsingham that he is especially commanded by her majesty to signify to them

---

* Namely, the practice of trying noble or royal victims by a commission selected from the house of lords, and such commoners as held great crown places and were lords of the council. The members of such committees were called *lords-triers*, and as the house of peers was, at the Tudor era, a very small body whose interests and prejudices were intimately known to the government, only those prepared to go all lengths with it were put into commission; neither was the victim allowed to protest against any enemy in the junta. This shameful precedent was first adopted for the judicial murder of Anne Boleyn.

† Sir Harris Nicolas' Life of Davison.

both, "how greatly she doth long to hear how her 'spirit' and her 'moon' do find themselves after so foul and wearisome a journey."* By the above pet names was the mighty Elizabeth accustomed, in moments of playfulness, to designate those grave and unbending statesmen, Burleigh and Walsingham; but playfulness in such a season was certainly not only in bad taste, but revolting to every feeling of humanity, when the object of that foul and weary journey on which her "spirit" and her " moon" had departed is considered. [....] With all Elizabeth's masculine powers of intellect, be it remembered that she must have been as dependent for information on the reports of her ministers and personal attendants as any other princess. If it suited the policy of those around her to withhold or mystify the truth, what channel was there through which it could reach her? The press was in its infancy, public journals detailing the events of the day were not in existence, and the struggles of certain independent members of the house of commons for liberty of speech had ceased. The spies of Walsingham, Burleigh, and Leicester were, it is true, perpetually at work, and there was no class of society into which they did not insinuate themselves. They were goers to and fro throughout the realm, and made reports to their employers of all they heard and saw; but were their reports faithfully conveyed to the queen by her ministers, ungarbled and uninterpolated? Assuredly not, unless it suited their own policy to do so; for have we not seen how long she was kept in ignorance by Leicester of so public an event as the fall of Rouen?—and does not the under-current of the transactions respecting Mary queen of Scots abound with evidence that the mighty Elizabeth was frequently the dupe, and at last the absolute tool, of her ministers?

They had drawn the death-warrant of the queen of Scots, but no persuasions could induce Elizabeth to sign it. It lay for six weeks in the hands of secretary Davison unheeded; and that Elizabeth ever did sign it rests on his unsupported testimony. [....] Such then is Davison's statement in his "apology," artfully dedicated to his colleague, Sir Francis Walsingham, who either was, or pretended to be, incapacitated by sickness from transacting business at this responsible crisis. Nevertheless the joint letter addressed to Paulet and Drury, as alleged by the queen's desire, was authenticated by his signature as well as that of Davison. The reproachful answer to the shrewd castellans† of Fotheringay, refusing "to make shipwreck of their consciences, by shedding blood without law or warrant," is addressed to Walsingham alone, without the slightest notice of his partner in the iniquitous suggestion, Davison, a Scotch adventurer, who was evidently regarded by them as a mere cipher. Davison was, in fact, an under-strapper of Leicester, having entered the court and cabinet of Elizabeth under his patronage. Leicester had always been a strenuous advocate for putting the queen of Scots to death, witness his letter, previously quoted, urging his colleagues to the deed "without waiting for the assembling of parliament, or delaying for temporizing solemnities, but all to be stout and resolute in speedy execution." And this before the

---

* Ibid.
† Wardens of the castle.

royal victim was either tried or sentenced. It will not be desirable to interrupt the current of Elizabeth's life and reign by relating the death-scene of Mary queen of Scots; full particulars of that heart-thrilling tragedy will be found in my life of that hapless sovereign, to which the reader is referred.[*]

The instant the axe had fallen on Mary, lord Talbot rode off with fiery speed to Greenwich, where he arrived early on the morning of the 9th of February, and communicated the news to Burleigh and his colleagues, who were anxiously awaiting it. Burleigh forbade him to announce it to their royal mistress, saying, "that it would be better for time to be allowed to break it cautiously to her by degrees." Lingard regards this extraordinary proceeding as indicative of a secret collusion between Elizabeth and her premier. It affords, on the contrary, a strong presumption that he had acted on his own responsibility, and feared to reveal what he had done, and corroborates Elizabeth's assertion, that she was neither consenting to, nor even cognizant of, the murder that had been perpetrated on her royal kinswoman at Fotheringay. The deed was concealed from her the whole of that day, which she passed as if nothing remarkable had occurred.[†] She rode out in the morning with her ladies and equerries to take the air; after her return she had a long interview with don Antonio, the claimant of the crown of Portugal,[‡] whose title she supported for the annoyance of her great political foe, Philip II of Spain. In the evening she observed the blaze of bonfires, and asked, "Why the bells rang out so merrily?" "Because of the death of the queen of Scots," replied one of her ladies. Elizabeth made no reply. Mary had long been in a state of health so infirm that her decease by natural means would have excited no surprise; but when Elizabeth learned the truth, which was not till the following morning, she heard it with transports of grief and indignation. Camden declares, that "her countenance altered, her speech faltered and failed her, and through excessive sorrow she stood in a manner astonished, insomuch that she gave herself over to passionate grief, putting herself into a mourning habit, and shedding abundance of tears. The council she sharply rebuked, and commanded them out of her sight." Elizabeth's tears and lamentations, and the reproaches with which she overwhelmed her ministers on this occasion, have hitherto been attributed to the most profound hypocrisy—an opinion in which I, in common with other historians, judging from existing evidences, very fully coincided.

The duty of an historian, which, as honest William of Malmesbury observes, "is never entirely performed," now requires me, in justice to the memory of Elizabeth, to declare frankly that since the publication of her biography in the preceding editions of "Lives of the Queens of England," my opinion of her conduct, in regard to the death of Mary queen of Scots, has been materially altered by the discovery of a contemporary document in the Cottonian library, transferring the stain of that murder from her to her ministers. This document is apparently

─────────────────────────────
[*] See Lives of the Queens of Scotland, by Agnes Strickland, vol. vii. pp. 468 to 492. Blackwood and Sons. Edinburgh.
[†] Lingard.
[‡] Bishop Goodman's Court of James I.

the minute of a Star-chamber investigation, containing the deposition of two persons named Mayer and Macaw, stating "that the late Thomas Harrison, a private and confidential secretary of the late Sir Francis Walsingham, secretary of state, did voluntarily acknowledge to them that he was employed by his said master, Sir Francis Walsingham, to forge the signature of queen Elizabeth to the death-warrant of the queen of Scots, which none of her council could ever induce her to sign, and that he did this with the knowledge and assent of four of her principal ministers of state."* [....] The position in which her ministers had placed Elizabeth, was the more painful because, unless she could have brought them to a public trial, convicted them of the treasonable crime of procuring her royal signature to be forged, she could not explain the offence of which they had been guilty. The impossibility of proclaiming the whole truth rendered her passionate protestations of her own innocence not only unsatisfactory, but apparently false and equivocating. While she denied the deed, she was in a manner compelled to act as if it were her own, being unable to inflict condign [appropriate] punishment on the subtle junta who had combined to make unauthorized use of her name for the immolation of the heiress-presumptive of the crown. It was to their interest that Mary should not survive Elizabeth, but Elizabeth had nothing to apprehend from the life of the powerless, impoverished, invalided captive of Fotheringay; nothing to gain by her death, except the execration of the world in general.

With regard to the joint letters written by Walsingham and Davison, urging Paulet and Drury to perpetrate a private murder on their royal prisoner, we will dispassionately ask, whether ministers who, by their own showing, rendered themselves accomplices in the projected crime by coolly urging the expediency of the assassination of a helpless woman in her prison, would have hesitated to use the name of their royal mistress for the purpose of inducing compliance with their suggestion? There is no other evidence than Davison's statements that Elizabeth ordered such application to be made, and we trust it was done unknown to her. At any rate, the men who deliberately set their hands to so nefarious a proposition are not trustworthy witnesses against her. It is credible, we would ask, that Elizabeth, if she had actually signed Mary's death-warrant, would have employed the secretary of state to whom she had delivered it, to tamper with the keepers of the royal prisoner, to destroy her by a private murder? And, above all, after their stern refusal to stain their consciences with so illegal a deed, that she should have ordered Davison to write a second time, to urge them to the commission of the crime, without offering the slightest inducement to overcome their inconvenient scruples? Davison, unless conscious of the forgery of her signature, by the secretary of his colleague Walsingham, would, of course, have taken that opportunity of informing her that there was no need for her majesty to disquiet herself, for her faithful ministers, out of tender care for her safety, had ordered her royal warrant to be executed, and the queen of Scots was

---

* Cottn. MS. Caligula C ix. F 463.

no more; but he pretends, as we have seen, that he said " there would be no occasion for the letter, the warrant being so general and sufficient as it was." To what purpose was the warrant mentioned, and its execution concealed?

Mary Hays (1759–1843)

Mary Hays was born into a Rational Dissent family in the shipping trade in South London.[1] Her earliest text, published after the sudden death in 1780 of her Baptist lover John Eccles, was the "book" of love letters she constructed from their correspondence. The letters express her early and abiding frustration at the gulf between the philosophies and practices of male and female education among even so enlightened a group as the radical Dissenters. She sought training from maverick Baptist minister Robert Robinson (1735–1790), proponent of "the right to private judgment," who encouraged her aspirations to become a learned woman. She read Robinson's publications that introduced Huguenot political and religious heterodoxy and the concept of "universal toleration." Hays quickly identified misogyny as a form of intolerance.

After Robinson's death in 1790, Hays's deep theological convictions prompted her to become a Unitarian. She participated at the periphery of dissenting pedagogy at New College Hackney (1786–96) where Joseph Priestley and other Enlightenment leaders were tutors. Hays attended sermons and, perhaps, fund-raising lectures, and she read and discussed tutors' publications with them at her mother's home in Southwark. When former New College classicist Gilbert Wakefield attacked the practices of his dissenting colleagues in 1791, Hays published the first defense of "public or social worship" in the pamphlet *Cursory Remarks*,[2] using the pen name "Eusebia," the pious widow with an interest in female education, drawn from William Law's influential *The Serious Call to a Devout and Holy Life* (1728). Anna Barbauld also responded to Wakefield who then counterattacked the "amazonian auxiliaries."

Hays read *A Vindication of the Rights of Woman* in 1792, met Wollstonecraft, and looked to Wollstonecraft to further her ambitions as one of "a new genus" of professional women writers.[3] Wollstonecraft issued stern advice to Hays to "rest on your own" in the manuscript of *Letters and Essays, Moral, and Miscellaneous* (1793) in which Hays broke new ground for a burgeoning female audience by interpreting Enlightenment concepts for them. After Wollstonecraft returned to London in autumn 1795, Hays proved her a staunch defender and famously reintroduced Wollstonecraft and William Godwin. Intellectually adventurous, Hays sought training in the new science of mind; her intense interactions with Godwin during 1794–97 anticipated "proto-psychoanalysis."[4] She was publicly excoriated for explicit expressions of female sexual and intellectual passion in her experimental "fiction" *Memoirs of Emma Courtney* (1796), which incorporated correspondence with Godwin and Unitarian mathematician William

Frend, the object of her desire. Frend was later tutor to Annabella Milbanke and her daughter Ada Byron.

Hays participated in the debates about female intellectual potential in the *Monthly Magazine* in 1796–97, reviewed novels for the *Analytical Review,* and participated in the "radical sociability" exercised by Wollstonecraft, Godwin, and their associates. Hays tried to keep feminist concerns alive in her next publications: *An Appeal to the Men of Great Britain in Behalf of Women* (1798, published anonymously) and *The Victim of Prejudice* (1799), her second novel, which portrayed Wollstonecraft. For these efforts, she became the female scapegoat in the repressive political climate in Britain at the end of the century.

Hays's "memoir" of Wollstonecraft after her death was the first of an imagined continuum of competent, powerful women represented in her *Female Biography; or, Memoirs of Illustrious and Celebrated Women, of All Ages and Countries,* in six volumes (1803). In *Memoirs of Queens* (1821), her last published work, Hays identified a unique historical moment when British women of all classes coalesced as a political force in public support for the uncrowned Queen Caroline of Brunswick during the spectacular "Queen's Trial" in which George IV tried and failed to divorce Caroline on charges of adultery.[5] With women's civic participation, Hays predicted, "all things will become new."

Hays's equivocal reputation as controversialist in her own time continued well into the twentieth century. The archive of letters, her own and others to her, that she purposefully preserved have allowed reassessments of her significant contributions to Enlightenment feminisms.

"CATHARINE MACAULAY GRAHAM," *FEMALE BIOGRAPHY* (1803)

Mary Hays offered an alternative to the history of "Great Men" in *Female Biography; or, Memoirs of Illustrious and Celebrated Women, of All Ages and Countries,* in six volumes, a compendium of the lives of 288 women. Most general biographical dictionaries before and after *Female Biography* dealt almost exclusively with men or with conventionally pious women. The first major work of specifically English female biography was George Ballard's celebratory *Memoirs of Several Ladies of Great Britain, who have been Celebrated for their Writings or Skill in the Learned Languages, Arts and Sciences* (1752). The feminist history of women Hays undertook to compile was important as a source of income, a vehicle for scholarship by and about women,[6] and a woman's contribution to the subspecies of history writing that was mainly the province of men.[7] Hays used personal memoirs, letters, and autobiographies to supplement more general, standard works.

Hays included women renowned for their erudition, their adventures, their political influence, their infamy, and their piety. Hays documents that women pursue the life of the mind despite the historical assertion that they are not mentally capable of the pursuit. The exceptional women whose stories she tells, by their very existence, refute the misogynist rule. Hays made an important con-tribution to women's history in the original research she provided in the 20-page entry for Catharine Macaulay Graham. Hays located and interviewed one of Macaulay's close female friends and reports Mrs. Arnold's intimate accounts of the historian. Hays makes no mention of the notoriety attending Macaulay's second marriage, but instead celebrates Macaulay's intellectual achievement and republicanism, and ends the memoir with a list of her publications.

Hays's representation of Elizabeth, Queen of England, expresses her convic-tion that, historically, female monarchs have been the only women to exercise real power. Hays emphasizes Elizabeth's education, her competence, and her complex persona.

Contemporary reviewers, whatever their political convictions, mostly treated *Female Biography* as a serious, but morally flawed, work because it exposed fe-male readers to impious women.

"Catharine Macaulay Graham," Female Biography (1803)

Mary Hays

This lady, who, by her writings, and the powers of her mind, has reflected so much credit on her sex and country, was born about the year 1733, at her father's seat at Ollantigh, near Ashford in Kent. Her paternal and maternal grandfathers were both concerned in the South-sea scheme, in which fatal speculation they had considerable fortunes engaged. The former, Mr. Jacob Sawbridge, was a banker in London, a director of the South-sea company, a member of parliament, and one of those who, on the breaking up of the scheme, was, to appease the clamours of the sufferers, deprived of his seat in the house, and fined to the amount of a great part of his property. With the wreck of his fortunes, and what had been settled on his son by marriage articles, he was enabled to purchase the estate of Ollantigh, which the family still possess. From a paragraph in his grand-daughter's History of England, it appears, that Mr. Sawbridge, though carried along with the tide of other men's iniquity in the South-sea scheme, was guiltless of any intentional defraud or wrong; he protested, both publicly and privately, against every unfair method taken by the directors to give an unnatural rise to the stock; and that it was generally acknowledged that government, in order to calm the people, confounded, on this occasion, the innocent with the guilty.

The maternal grandfather of Mrs. Macaulay was a Mr. Wanley, who, dying, left one daughter, heiress to a fortune of more than 30,000*l.* Mr. Sawbridge, her father, was, in his youth, an officer in the Guards, but retired early in his estate in the country, where he led an inactive life. Her mother, a beautiful woman, with a delicate and feeble constitution, died before she was twenty years of age, after having borne two sons and two daughters. The late alderman Sawbridge was the eldest of these sons. The younger entered into the church, and died in the year 1796. The eldest daughter married a gentleman of fortune in the county of Kent. The younger, Catharine, having lost her mother in the first period of infancy, was deprived of the benefit of maternal tenderness and care. Her father, who severely felt the loss of his wife, almost entirely secluded himself from society, though possessed of a fortune of 3000*l.* a-year. He paid no attention to the education of his daughters, who were left at the family seat, at Ollantigh, to the charge of an antiquated, well recommended, but ignorant, governess, ill qualified for the task she undertook. Mr. Sawbridge satisfied himself with occasional visits to his family, to assure himself of their health and safety.

Under the superintendence of this woman, they grew together, while their minds and characters, as directed by other circumstances, took a different turn. The eldest daughter, whose temper was placid and amiable, while she improved in health and strength, derived amusement from her baby-house, and from the customary avocations of her sex and age. The younger, Catharine, found nothing to interest her attention in her sister's pursuits; active and curious, she thirsted for knowledge, and her dolls could give her no information. The books which were put into her hands and entertained her for a time, while they interested her imagination, and gratified her taste for novelty: but at length she became satiated with fairy tales and romances, which afforded not aliment sufficiently substantial to satisfy the cravings of her enquiring mind. Having found her father's well-furnished library, she became her own purveyor, and rioted in intellectual luxury. Every hour in the day, which no longer hung heavy upon her hands, was now occupied and improved. She first made choice of the periodical writers, the Spectators, Guardian, &c. who, in treating of morals and manners, led her to reflection, while they opened and strengthened her mind. As she advanced in age, her studies took a wider range; she grew attached to history, and dwelt with delight and ardour on the annals of the Greek and Roman republics. Their laws and manners interested her understanding, the spirit of patriotism seized her, and she became an enthusiast in the cause of freedom. The heroic characters and actions with which this period of history is intermingled and enlivened, seldom fail to captivate the affections of a youthful and uncorrupted heart. All other books were thrown aside; history became her darling passion, and liberty the idol of her imagination. Rollin's Ancient History, and his Account of the Roman Republic, first lighted up that spark in her mind, which afterwards blazed with so much fervour and splendour, and which gave the tone to her sentiments and character through the subsequent periods of her life. To a spirit thus excited, retirement, by concentrating its force, added strength: the world, with its lax principles and vicious habits, had not yet broken in upon the gay mistakes of the just expanding heart, enamoured of truth and virtue, and ignorant of the difficulties which retard and obstruct their progress.—

Oh Youth! The lovely source of generous errors!

From early habits of seclusion, it became the choice of Catharine: ordinary amusements and occupations were tasteless to a spirit wrought to higher views and purposes: great delicacy, talents, and sensibility, united in the female mind, rarely fail to inspire a distaste for common intercourse. From the world of frivolity, flattery, and dissipation, she shrunk back to a more improving world of her own. In the course of her historical studies, the pictures of vice and turpitude which occasionally presented themselves, while they roused her indignation, excited the astonishment of her inexperienced heart; the feelings of which were called forth, exercised, and exalted. The history of the despotism and tyranny of a few individuals, and the slavish subjection of uncounted millions, their passive acquiescence, their sufferings, and their wrongs, appeared to her a moral problem, which she had no instruments to solve. She had yet to learn the force of prescription, of habits, and of association, the imitative and progressive nature of the human mind, and the complicated springs by which it is set in motion. She deeply reflected on the subject of government, with its influence on the happiness and virtue and mankind: she became anxious that the distance should be diminished that separates man from man; and to see extended over the whole human race those enlightened sentiments, equal laws, and equitable decisions, that might restore to its due proportion a balance so ill adjusted, and combine with the refinement of a more advanced age the simplicity and virtue of the earlier periods. Fraught with these ideas, and with a heart glowing with goodwill towards her species, she took up her pen, and gave to the most interesting portion of the history of her country a new spirit and interest.

A female historian, by its singularity, could not fail to excite attention: she seemed to have stepped out of the province of her sex; curiosity was sharpened, and malevolence provoked. The author was attacked by petty and personal scurrilities, to which it was believed her sex would render her vulnerable. Her talents and powers could not be denied; her beauty was therefore called in question, as if it was at all concerned with the subject; or that, to instruct our understandings, it was necessary at the same time to charm our senses. "'She is deformed (said her adversaries, wholly unacquainted with her person), she is unfortunately ugly, she despairs of distinction and admiration as a woman, she seeks, therefore, to encroach on the province of man.' These were the notions," said a lady* afterwards intimately connected with the historian, "that I was led to entertain of Mrs. Macaulay, previous to my introduction to her acquaintance. Judge then of my surprise, when I saw a woman elegant in her manners, delicate in her person, and with features, if not perfectly beautiful, so fascinating in their expression, as deservedly to rank her face among the higher order of human countenances. Her height was above the middle size, inclining to tall; her shape slender and elegant; the contour of her face, neck and shoulders, graceful. The form of her face was oval, her complexion delicate, and her skin fine; her hair was of a mild brown, long and profuse; her nose between the Roman and the Grecian, her mouth small, her chin round, as was the lower part of her face, which made it appear to more advantage in front than in profile. Her eyes were beautiful as imagination can conceive, full of penetration and fire, but their fire softened by the mildest beams of benevolence; their colour was a fine dark hazel, and their expression the indication of a superior soul. Infirm health, too

---

* The late Mrs. Arnold of Leicester, an excellent and amiable woman, to whom I am indebted for materials for this memoir, and whose lamented death will, I trust, plead with her friends in my excuse for the mention of her name and this tribute of respect to her memory.

often the attendant on an active and highly cultivated understanding, gave to her countenance an extreme delicacy, which was peculiarly interesting. To this delicacy of constitution was added a most amiable sensibility of temper, which rendered her feelingly alive to whatever concerned those with whom she was connected either by nature or by friendship."

In her friendships, we are told by this lady, Mrs. Macaulay was fervent, disinterested, and sincere; zealous for the prosperity, and for the moral improvement, of those whom she distinguished and loved. She was earnest, constant, and eloquent, in her efforts for rectifying the principles, and enlarging the minds, of her friends and connections. It was her favourite maxim, that universal benevolence, and a liberal way of thinking, were, not only essential to the freedom and welfare of society, but to individual virtue, enjoyment and happiness. There was no arrogance in her exhortations and counsels; her accents were not less mild and persuasive, than her reasoning was energetic and forcible. "In the course," says her friend, from whose communications the present account is extracted, "of my acquaintance with this most intelligent and amiable woman, I had an opportunity of studying every part of her character."

Towards the latter end of the year 1777, she was ordered by her physicians to the south of France, for the benefit of her health; in which journey Mrs. Arnold accompanied her. A low nervous fever, to which she was subject, had debilitated her frame, without deducting either from the force or activity of her mind. Nothing, during this excursion, escaped her observation; her conversations and remarks were at once acute and profound.

After crossing the sea, on which she was severely exhausted by sickness, she rested two days at Calais, where she soon experienced, from the change of air, and possibly from the sea sickness itself, a salutary effect. Her fever seemed to have left her, and she suffered in the remainder of her journey to Paris but little inconvenience. She was greatly struck with the different appearance of the inhabitants of the two countries, as also with the face of the country itself. Between Calais and Paris, she looked in vain for the healthy and well-fed peasant, the beautiful and luxuriant meadows, the cultivated farms, and comfortable farm-houses, of her native island. Despotism had palsied the hand of industry; an indigent and miserable people appeared thinly scattered over wild and dreary plains. The reflections which she made on this occasion, raised in her opinion the country which she had quitted; where in comparative freedom, commerce and the arts grew and flourished. She praised, and quoted, the sentiments and remarks of Dr. Smollet on the same subject. The travelers stopped one day at Chantilly, where they met with two of their friends, and where they had an opportunity of observing a royal residence,* and contrasting it with the wretchedness which they had so recently witnessed. Mrs. Macaulay was not in a state of health to bear the fatigue of inspecting the palace. To Dr. Nash, one of the gentlemen whom she met at Chantilly, who would, with apparent

---

* The palace of the prince of Condé.

satisfaction, have described to her the curiosities and magnificence of the prince's residence, she replied (after thanking him curiously for the trouble he was about to give himself), that she would spare him the repetition, since she could receive no pleasure in hearing of the splendour of one mortal, while the misery of thousands pressed upon her recollection.

As they proceeded towards the capital, the face of the country, and the looks of its inhabitants, gradually improved; but, at the first post-house at which they stopped to change horses, the feelings of the travellers were again excited by the objects, which crowding around their carriage, clamorously implored their charitable donations, while they exhibited in their persons and squalid appearance every variety of want and of human wretchedness. "My God! My god!" exclaimed Mrs. Macaulay, with a benevolent enthusiasm, bursting into tears, "have mercy on the works of thine own hand!" She made her servant distribute to them each three livres, and divided among them the provisions she had in the carriage. For some miles after this incident she preserved a profound silence; at length, taking the hand of her fellow-traveller in hers—"you, my dear friend," said she, "saw yesterday the habitation of the prince of Condé, and his family at dinner!"—She paused, unable to proceed, but by a look that conveyed her meaning more eloquently than words.*

123

The apartments provided for the travellers, near the Luxembourg palace, on their arrival at Paris, were commodious and elegant. Mrs. Macaulay found her health so much amended by the journey, that in a few days, she collected around her, by her letters of introduction, an agreeable society. Persons of the first rank and eminence were gratified with the opportunity of paying their respects to an Englishwoman, whose talents entitled her to distinction. Among the number of her visitors were the family of the count de Sarsfield; the dukes of Harcourt and Liancourt; the chevalier de Rigemont; the abbé Colbert, a descendant of the great financier of that name; madame Boccage, madame Grigson, &c. with lord Stormont, the English embassador. Dr. Franklin was at that time in Paris; Mrs. Macaulay met him several times, among the literati of Paris, at dinners given on her account, but she never received him at her hotel. During a day which she passed at monsieur Turgot's, with a large party, she was introduced to the celebrated Marmontel and to the widow of the philosopher Helvetius, a woman of extraordinary character. In these societies, so congenial to her disposition, she experienced a high gratification, and appeared with peculiar spirit and advantage. The pleasure which she inspired was equally lively with that which she received; the universal information which her conversation displayed, appeared to her auditors not less

---

* Alas! The people have but too severely retaliated on these princes and nobles!

admirable than her historical acquisitions, and the powers of her mind.* Her brilliant talents for conversation, with the variety of her knowledge, and the vivacity of her imagination, rendered her a most interesting and instructive companion.

With a mind too enlightened for bigotry, and an enemy to mere forms of devotion, often absurd, and always spiritless, the freedom with which she delivered her sentiments on these subjects, drew upon her the imputation of scepticism and infidelity. These assertions are declared, by her friend, to have been ill founded, as proved by some passages in her treatise on the "Immutability of Truth." "She confirmed the reality of her prepossession," says the lady already quoted, "in favour of the Christian revelation, by the most diligent cultivation of benevolence towards mankind, and the most exact moral rectitude in every action of her life." "She had those hopes, and that confident expectation of her own future happiness, which Christian faith and conscious rectitude only can inspire." In testimony of this opinion, Mrs. Arnold refers to a conversation which passed between herself and Mrs. Macaulay, when her health was in a languishing state, at Abbeville, in their way to Paris. After reproving her friend's too great sensibility and solicitude on her account, "I thought and hoped," said she, "that you viewed my death but as a short separation between virtuous friends, and that your assurance of a re-union with me, in a more perfect state, would have preserved you from being thus severely affected by the idea of my dissolution." She went on to console her companion and fellow traveller in the same strain—"Consider our parting," said she, "but as a short privation; for, be assured, the friendship of the good will not be dissolved by death: we shall again unite in another life." The feeble state of her frame, and consequent sufferings, she said, naturally led her to these reflections. She considered the present state of being but as the dawning of existence, nor did she shrink from its termination as a subject of terror, but was rather prepared to meet her change with confidence and satisfaction. Her researches, she observed into the nature of God and of man, and the relations subsisting between them, would have been in vain, had it not brought her to this conclusion; vain also would have been her convictions of truth of the Christian revelation, and the recompence which its author promises to his disciples. She trusted, she declared, in that Being, who had not given her capacities of enjoyment for no adequate end, that he would preserve and support her through the various stages of an everlasting existence. She lamented the prevalence of sense, and the pursuits by which the mind, capable of sublimer flights, was bound down

---

* "Hear her but reason on divinity" (says her friend from Shakespear),
 "And all admiring, with an inward wish,
 Would straight desire that she were made a prelate:
 Hear her debate of commonwealth affairs,
 You'd say it had been *all in all* her study:
 Turn her to any course of policy,
 The gordian knot of it she will unloose
 Familiar as her garter. When she speaks,
 The air, a charter'd libertine, is still,
 And the mute wonder lurketh in men's ears,
 To steal her sweet and honied sentences."

to earth and inferior gratifications. She called upon her friend to observe and to witness, that in her present enfeebled situation, her prospects grew brighter with her progress towards the grave: she anticipated the period when her spirit, disencumbered of its tenement, should no longer be impeded in its aspirations and researches, and when, in the presence of the Supreme Intelligence, it should find the sources of knowledge, of science, and of beauty, laid open to its view, while its capacities and powers should expand without bounds. In this exalted and visionary strain she continued, at intervals, through the day to expatiate; while she seemed to derive peculiar pleasure from the idea of the future re-union of the virtuous; a cheering and delightful notion to susceptible and tender minds!

Her visit to Paris was critically timed, at the period when Great Britain, at war with her colonies, beheld the French government with a jealous eye. The *habeas corpus* act was also at that time suspended in England. In these circumstances, Mrs. Macaulay was peculiarly cautious to give no offence to the administration of her country, by entering with too much fervor into the cause of the Americans; or by appearing to have any views in her excursion to France (by which the colonies were assisted and favoured), than for the benefit and restoration of her health. During the six weeks that she remained in Paris, her apartments were crowded with visitors, and her invitations to dinner daily multiplied. Among the Americans who were at that time numerous at Paris, those who were eminent for their learning or talents seized every opportunity of observing their fair historian, and mingling in the societies she was accustomed to frequent. Apprehensive, from these circumstances, lest her conduct be misconstrued, and finding her health much amended since she had quitted England, she determined to give up the idea of proceeding southward, and the rather as the season of the year was unfavourable to traveling, and to the accommodations indispensable to an invalid. The end of her journey was in part accomplished, and business rendered her presence necessary at home. These motives combined to influence her to bid adieu to the hospitable societies at Paris, and to return once more to her native land. In a letter to Dr. Franklin, before her departure, she informed him of the motives by which she had been induced to wave the satisfaction of seeing him and his American friends at her hotel. The circumstances of the times, and of her known republican principles, rendered her liable to suspicions; and the suspension of the *habeas corpus* act in England to consequences, which in the delicate state of her health, could not but prove fatal.—"The whole tenor of my conduct must have convinced you, sir," says she, towards the conclusion of her letter, "that I should with pleasure sacrifice my life, could it be of any *real service* to the cause of public freedom. I am now nursing my constitution, to enable me to treat at large, in the history in which I am at present engaged, on our fatal civil war. I am, sir, with profound respect for your great qualities, as a statesman, patriot, and philosopher, yours &c. &c."

Having been personally acquainted with the greater number of the celebrated Americans who had visited England, and in the habit of corresponding with those who had distinguished themselves on the other side of the Atlantic, Mrs. Macaulay was very desirous of making a visit to the transatlantic republic; a design which she executed in 1785. She visited nine of the thirteen united states, by whom she was received with kindness and hospitality. She terminated her journey to the south by paying her respects to general Washington, at his seat at Mount Vernon in Virginia. Under the roof of this illustrious man she remained three weeks; and continued to correspond with him during the remainder of her life.

It seemed to have been her intention, after her return to England, to have composed a history of the American contest; for which purpose she had been furnished by general Washington with many materials. It is to be regretted that, thus qualified, she was, by the infirm state of her health, for some years prior to her death, prevented from the execution of her plan. She resided during the greater part of the remainder of her life at Binfield in Berkshire; where, after a tedious illness, attended by much suffering, which she supported with exemplary patience and fortitude, she expired, June 22, 1791. She was interred in the chancel of Binfield church, under an elegant marble monument executed by Mr. Bacon.

She was twice married: the first time to Dr. George Macaulay, a physician of some eminence in London; and, after his death, to Mr. William Graham, who had also been educated to the profession of physic, but who afterwards entered into the church. A daughter was the fruit of her first marriage; who gave her hand to captain Gregory, many years a commander in the east-India service, in which he acquired ample fortune: his wife has since become a widow, with four children.

Dr. Wilson, whose enthusiastic admiration of the talents of Mrs. Macaulay was perhaps demonstrated rather extravagantly, was introduced to her by her brother, Mr. Sawbridge: they were both members of the Bill of Rights club; and had been united by their political sentiments.

After the marriage of Mrs. Macaulay with Mr. Graham, she retired with her husband to their house at Binfield, upon Windsor-forest; where, with congenial tastes and dispositions, they passed their time in literary avocations and pursuits.

Mrs. Macaulay, when in tolerable health, was accustomed to be in her library by six in the morning: she was tenacious of the value of time, and solicitous for its improvement.

The lady, from whose communications and the preceding account is extracted, adds an earnest and affectionate testimony to the domestic qualifications and virtues of her friend; who, as a wife, a mother, a friend, a neighbour, and the mistress of a family, was irreproachable and exemplary. "My sentiments," says she, "of this admirable woman are derived from a long and intimate acquaintance with her various excellences, and I have observed her in different points of view. I have seen her exalted on the dangerous pinnacle of worldly prosperity, surrounded by flattering friends, and an admiring world; I have seen her marked out by party prejudice as an object of dislike and ridicule; I have seen her bowed down by bodily pain and weakness: but never did I see her forget the urbanity of a gentlewoman, her conscious dignity as a rational creature, or a fervent aspiration after the highest degree of attainable perfection. I have seen her humble herself in the presence of her Almighty Father; and, with a contrite heart, acknowledging her weakness and imploring his protection; I have seen her languishing on the bed of sickness, enduring pain with the patience of a Christian, and with the firm belief, that the light afflictions of this life are but for a moment, and that the fashion of this world will pass away, and give place to a system of durable happiness."

Her works are:

> The History of England, from the Accession of James I to the Elevation of the House of Hanover; printed in successive volumes in quarto, making in all eight volumes. The first volume was printed before the year 1769. The eighth and last volume was published in the year 1783. This volume, ending with James II's reign, did not complete the design expressed in the title-page; the history, may however, be considered as continued in
>
> The History of England, from the Revolution to the present Time, in a Series of Letters to the Rev. Dr. Wilson, Rector of St. Stephen's, Walbrook, and Prebendary of Westminster; published in one volume in quarto in 1778.
>
> A Treatise on the Immutability of Truth, by Catharine Macaulay Graham, octavo, 1783.
>
> Letters on Education.
>
> Loose remarks on certain Positions to be found in Mr. Hobbie's Philosophical rudiments of a Government and Society, with a short Sketch of a Democratical Form of Government; in a Letter to Signior Paoli: octavo, 1767.
>
> Observations on a Pamphlet, entitled, Thoughts on the Causes of the present Discontent. The fifth edition, published in octavo, in the year 1770.
>
> An Address to the People of England, Scotland and Ireland, on the present important Crisis of Affairs; by Catharine Macaulay, octavo, second edition, 1775.
>
> A Modest Plea for the Property of Copy-right, quarto; by Catharine Macaulay.
>
> Observations on the Reflections of the Right Honourable Edmund Burke on the revolution in France, in a Letter to the right Honourable the Earl of Stanhope, 1790.

ENDNOTES

1   The information about Hays is drawn from Gina Luria Walker, *Mary Hays: The Growth of A Woman's Mind* (Aldershot: Ashgate Publishing, 2006). See also, Marilyn L. Brooks for information about the extended Hays family, "Introduction," *The Correspondence (1779–1843) of Mary Hays, British Novelist* (Lewiston: Edwin Mellen Press, 2004), 7–9.

2   See Gina Luria Walker, *The Idea of Being Free: A Mary Hays Reader.* (Peterborough, ON: Broadview Press, 2006).

3   Mary A. Waters, *British Women Writers and the Profession of Literary Criticism, 1789–1832* (Houndmills: Palgrave Macmillan, 2004).

4   Mary Jacobus, "Traces of an Accusing Spirit: Mary Hays and the Vehicular State," in *Psychoanalysis and the Scene of Reading* (Oxford: Oxford University Press, 1999), 202–34.

5   Anna Clark, *Scandal: The Sexual Politics of the British Constitution* (Princeton: Princeton University Press, 2004).

6   Although she views Hays as torn between revolutionary feminism and "conservative domestic feminism," Mary Spongberg describes *Female Biography* as "the first and perhaps the most important collection of women's lives." "'Heroines of Domestic Life': Women's History and Female Biography," in *Writing Women's History Since the Renaissance* (Houndmills: Palgrave Macmillan, 2002), 115–18.

7   Jane Rendall notes that, at about the same time, Elizabeth Hamilton was writing her historical work, *The Memoirs of Agrippina, the Wife of Germanicus* (1804). Rendall writes, "In her one work of history ... she was to explore the political dilemmas which faced those who sought to shape new roles for British women. In doing so, she also illustrated the difficulties which face women writers, who like Wollstonecraft herself, were ambitious to transcend the limits of genres judged appropriate for women." "Writing History for British Women: Elizabeth Hamilton and *The Memoirs of Agrippina*," in *Wollstonecraft's Daughters: Womanhood in England and France 1780–1920*, ed. Clarissa Campbell Orr (Manchester: Manchester University Press, 1996), 79.

Mary Wollstonecraft Shelley (1797–1851)

Mary Wollstonecraft Godwin was the daughter of Mary Wollstonecraft and William Godwin. She was born on 30 August 1797; her mother died on 10 September of the aftereffects of childbirth.[1] Godwin was left to care for the infant and his stepdaughter, Fanny Imlay (1794–1816), Wollstonecraft's child by her American lover, Gilbert Imlay. In 1801, Godwin married Mary Jane Clairmont, a widow with two illegitimate children, Charles and Clara Mary Jane (Claire). Mrs. Godwin gave birth to William Godwin junior in 1803. In this complex domestic environment, Mary Shelley read her mother's works and learned to venerate her[2]—"one of those beings who appear once in a generation perhaps to gild humanity." Her father, she believed, was "unequalled perhaps in the world for genius, single-heartedness, and nobleness of disposition."

Godwin was his daughter's most formative early teacher, although she attended a dame-school and a school for Dissenters' daughters. He impressed on her his high standards of mental discipline and intellectual achievement. Mary loved writing stories,[3] and was an apt pupil, studying ancient and modern history, mythology, literature, the Scriptures, Latin, and, from visiting teachers, French, Italian, and art. Godwin's stimulating friends—among them the poet Coleridge and American Aaron Burr—also influenced her. Relations with her stepmother were fraught, yet Mrs. Godwin kept the family solvent by publishing books for children with her husband through The Juvenile Library of M.J. Godwin & Co. New titles were tried out on the four children in the Godwin household. In her wide-ranging reading, Mary Wollstonecraft Shelley discovered a passion for the past and life-writing that continued through her life.

The story of 16-year-old Mary Wollstonecraft Shelley's romance and elopement with the 21-year-old poet Percy Bysshe Shelley (1792–1822), already married and father of two children, is well known, as is their flight from parental disapproval to the continent in July 1812, accompanied by Claire Claremont. The trio commenced a life that kept them in "a state of agitation."[4] The Shelleys' decade together was marked by creditors' demands, familial rebuffs, the deaths of four of their children by miscarriage and illness, the death of Claire's young daughter by Lord Byron, the suicides of Harriet Shelley, Percy Shelley's first wife, and of Fanny Imlay, Mary's half-sister, and, finally in 1822, P.B. Shelley's death by drowning. Less known are their mutual intellectual projects. They kept a common journal almost immediately after their elopement, which Mary Shelley continued until 1844. In 1817 she published anonymously her *History of a Six Weeks' Tour of France, Switzerland, and Germany*, based on their journal, which included letters and Percy Shelley's poem, "Mont Blanc." *Frankenstein* (1818), her most popular work, was the result of a ghost-story writing contest with Percy Shelley, Lord Byron, and others. The Shelly marriage was intellectually stimulating. Percy taught Mary Greek; she studied Latin[5] and did translations from Italian, including Dante's *Purgatorio* with her husband. Mary's novella, *Matilda*, on the taboo of incestuous love between father and daughter, was begun while Percy was working on *The Cenci*, a drama based on the Cenci family's tragic history of incest, which they both researched in Italian archives. *Matilda* was finally published in 1959. After her husband's death, Mary Shelley began his biography, a project that she never completed. At the insistence of her hostile father-in-law, Sir Timothy Shelley, she returned to England with her surviving son, Percy Florence, and undertook the work of gaining recognition for her husband by editing his works.

Widowed Mary Shelley found herself without funds: her father was chronically hard up; Sir Timothy provided only a pittance for his grandson, on the condition that she not write about her husband or publish any of his work. After she published Percy Shelley's *Posthumous Works* (1824), he temporarily stopped their allowance. The need to support herself and her son compelled Mary Shelley to become a hardworking professional writer. She published frequently in periodicals, submitting reviews, stories, poems, and pieces by her husband. She also wrote and published ambitious novels: historical fiction in *Valperga* (1823) and *Perkin Warbeck* (1830); *The Last Man* (1826) set in the twenty-first century; *Lodore* (1835) that treats the condition of women based on their gendered education;[6] and *Falkner* (1837), in part the psychological analysis of a stepfather and stepdaughter which critics trivialized as expressing Mary Wollstonecraft Shelley's radical political and social views.[7]

Early in her life, Mary Wollstonecraft Shelley evinced a strong interest in life-writing, influenced by the model provided in her father's account of her mother in *Memoirs of the Author of A Vindication of the Rights of Woman* (1798). She also subscribed to her parents' reformist beliefs in the ability of individuals to be shaped by and to shape events.[8] She combined the need to make money with her progressive convictions and her interest in writing lives in her extensive contributions to the Reverend Dionysius Lardner's *Cabinet of Biography* (1832–1839). Simultaneously, she carried on her plan to produce an authoritative edition of Percy Shelley's works. This involved painstaking transcriptions from manuscripts, letters, and fragments, accompanied by her contextual notes and comments.[9] In 1839, she published *The Poetical Works of Percy Bysshe Shelley* and *Letters from Abroad, Translations and Fragments by Percy Bysshe Shelley*, and she followed these with a one-volume edition of his poetry in 1840. Her last work was *Rambles in Germany and Italy in 1840, 1842, and 1843*, published in 1844 and based on her letters while she traveled with her son. Percy Florence inherited his grandfather's estate in 1844. Mary Shelley died in 1851, and, at her request, was buried with her parents.

"MADAME DE STAËL," *LIVES OF THE MOST EMINENT LITERARY AND SCIENTIFIC MEN OF FRANCE* (1838–1839)

Biography and autobiography were staples of Mary Shelley's reading and research.[10] Much of her literary production involved the stories of compelling figures, including that of her husband and, after his death and by his instructions, her father. Neither was completed. Several of her female fictional characters can be seen as composites of her mother and herself.[11] The many biographies she produced for Lardner's *Lives of the Most Eminent Literary and Scientific Men of Italy, Spain, and Portugal* and separate volumes of French *Lives*, display her erudition in several languages.

Lardner's *Cabinet Cyclopaedia* was one of the most successful collective biographies produced in the 1820s and 1830s, in response to general readers' demands for self-learning.[12] As one of Lardner's contributing writers, Mary Shelley was not expected to produce original research, although she did interview people who had known de Staël. Mary Shelley was assiduous in consulting multiple primary and secondary sources about her subjects and in interpreting these to convey her sense of the individual life. In the French *Lives*, she included Manon Roland, martyr of the French Revolution whom her mother may have met in Paris and whose prison memoir, *Appeal to Impartial Posterity* (1795) in English translation, greatly influenced Wollstonecraft, Godwin, Hays, and other English Jacobins. In the life of de Staël, Mary Shelley called attention to the unusual connection between father and daughter, perhaps with reference to her own experience but also representing her female subject as observer, critic, and vital public woman of letters. Nora Crook discerns her father's influence in Mary Shelley's literary *Lives* in the "uniting of biography, moral suasion and political and social history."[13]

The subject of this excerpt from Mary Shelley's life-writing, Anne Louise Germaine Necker, later Madame de Staël, was the only child of Jacques Necker, statesman and finance minister to Louis XVI, and his wife, the *salonnière* Suzanne Curchod. Mlle. Necker began writing as a girl and later published in several genres. Her marriage to an older Swedish diplomat without money gave her freedom from scandal; the couple had three children but little affection for each other, and she took many lovers. Personal experience of the French Revolution profoundly affected her; in her most influential published works, particularly on the Revolution and France, she proved herself a "genius at doing history."[14] When Napoleon came to power, their mutual dislike caused her to retire to her father's property at Coppet, on Lake Geneva, where she established a *salon*. She published a novel, *Delphine* (1802), which introduced the misunderstood woman as heroine. When Napoleon finally exiled her, she travelled in Germany, meeting artists and intellectuals. She published *Corrine* (1807), her most famous fiction, about the heroine's picaresque travels. After her husband's death, she made a second, happy marriage to a Swiss officer twenty-three years her junior. Among her important work was *De l'Allemagne* (1810; *Germany*, in English translation, 1813), in which she was the first to use the term "Romanticism" and represent appealingly the interest of German thinkers in personal liberty, aesthetics, and heightened subjectivity.

Some modern commentators see elements of Mary Wollstonecraft's radical feminism of subjectivity in Mary Shelley's life of de Staël.[15]

"Madame de Staël," Lives of the Most Eminent Literary and Scientific Men of France (1838–39)

Mary Wollstonecraft Shelley

She was born in Paris on the 22d April 1766. Her mother was desirous of bestowing on her a perfect education. Madame Necker[16] possessed great firmness of character, and a strong understanding. She submitted every feeling and action of her life to the control of reason. She carried her love of logical inference into the smallest as well as the most important events of life; and fulfilled to the letter every the slightest duty of daily and hourly occurrence. Finding her young daughter apt and willing to learn, she thought she could not teach her too much, nor store her mind with too many facts and words. This was not done as an English mother would have practised in the seclusion of the schoolroom, but in the midst of society, in which the young lady soon learnt to shine by her eloquent sallies and vivacious spirits. [....] [T]his extraordinary woman imbibed, as it were with her mother's milk, a taste for society and display. She learnt to take intense pleasure in the communication of ideas with intelligent men, and in sharing in the sparkling wit that gathered round her. She enjoyed the excitement of spirits that results from the sense of expressing her thoughts, and at the same time having the sphere enlarged by the instant interchange with others. The sensations of success in society, of praise and reputation, were familiar to her in childhood, and no wonder they became as necessary as her daily bread in after years.

It was her mother's plan to tax her intellects to their height. She was incited to study diligently, to listen to conversation on subjects beyond her years, to frequent the theatre; her pleasures and occupations alike were so many exertions of mind. She wrote a great deal. Her writings were read in society, and applauded. The praises she received developed also the feelings of her heart. She passionately loved her parents and her friends; she read with an enthusiasm and interest that made books a portion of her existence. She was accustomed to say, that the fate of Clarissa Harlowe[17] was one of the events of her youth. Susceptible to impression, serious in the midst of her vivacity, she rather loved what made her weep rather than laugh.

The species of perpetual excitement in which she lived, and the excessive application and attention required of her by her mother, had at length a bad effect on her health. At the age of fourteen it became apparent that she was declining. The advice of Tronchin[18] was asked; he was alarmed by the symptoms, and ordered her to be removed into the country, to spend her life in the open air, and to abandon all serious study. Madame Necker was deeply mortified. She saw all the materials for a prodigy of learning and knowledge in her daughter, and was almost angry that her frame was injured by the work she required from her to bring her to the perfection she meditated. Unable to continue to its height her system of education, she abandoned it altogether. Henceforth no longer looking on her own work, she ceased to take interest in her talents, which she regarded as superficial and slight; when she heard her praised, she replied, "Oh! it is nothing, absolutely nothing, in comparison to what I intended to make her."

The young lady meanwhile enjoyed the leisure she obtained: no longer called upon to store her mind with words and facts, she gave herself up to her imagination. She and her friend passed the summer at St. Ouen, a country-house of Necker, two leagues from Paris; they dressed themselves like muses; they composed poetry, and declaimed it; they wrote and acted plays. Giving the rein to her fancy, and impelled by natural vivacity, she became poetess, tragedian, actress, thus, almost in childhood. The carelessness that her mother showed, after her disappointment with regard to her education, had the effect of developing in the young girl the chief passion of her heart—filial affection towards her father: she had now leisure to seek his society; and his great goodness, his admiration of herself, and the perfect friendship and openness of communication that subsisted between them, gave rise to the passionate attachment towards him which she dwells upon in her writings with so much fervour. She seized every opportunity of enjoying his society; and he perceived and delighted in her talents, which displayed themselves with peculiar advantage when with him. She saw that, overwhelmed as he was by public cares and engrossing business, he needed to be amused in his moments of leisure. He adored his wife, but no one was ever less amusing; his daughter, on the other hand, exerted herself to divert him: she tried a thousand ways and risked any sally or pleasantry so to win him to smile, and smiles quickly came at her bidding. He was not prodigal of his approbation; his eyes were more flattering than his words; and he believed it to be more necessary and even more amusing to rally her for her defects, than to praise her for her excellences. She saw that his gay reproofs were just, and modelled herself by them. She often said to her friends, "I owe to the inconceivable penetration of my father the frankness of my character and the sincerity of my mind: he unmasked every affectation or pretension, and when near him I got into the habit of thinking that every feeling of my heart could be read." Madame Necker grew a little jealous of the superior power her daughter possessed of amusing her husband; besides, although she had ardently wished her to shine in society, yet she had desired her to be remarkable for her attainments and knowledge, not for her wit and imagination. She looked coldly therefore on the admiration she excited, and even protested against it. The young girl turned from her chilling and prim rebuffs to the encouragement she found in her father's sympathy and gladden-ing smiles. In the drawing-room she escaped from the side of Madame Necker, who regarded the mistakes which her giddiness and vivacity caused her to make with severe and correcting eyes. She listened with respect when reproved, but gladly sheltered herself behind her father's chair; at first silently, then throwing in a word, till at last, one after the other, the cleverest men in the room gathered round to listen to her sallies and to be charmed by her eloquence. [....] The young are apt to think their parents superior to the rest of the world. The claims which M. and Madame Necker possessed to real superiority, from their virtues and tal-ents, naturally added to the warmth of their daughter's affection. The distinction in which they were held made the path of her life bright; and even the first check that occurred in her father's career tended to excite still more her admiration for him, as opposition gives form and strength to every power exerted to overcome it. Necker was too conscientious and too firm in his schemes of reform not to have enemies: he was too vain also not to desire to have his plans universally known and approved. Publicity is indeed the proper aim of every honest public man; but it was in utter variance with the policy of the old French government. [...] In the retreat at Coppet he published a work on finance, of which 80,000 copies were sold in one day. Mdlle. Necker shared the triumph; she was his companion, his friend. On her part she was not idle; and, even at an early age, began the career of authorship in which in after life she became so distinguished. It was the custom in French society to meet to hear an author read his productions. In this country, such a style of amusement would be considered very dull and tiresome; but it was otherwise in Paris. The audience was easily pleased. The women wept at the right moment—the men were ready to start from their chairs: enthusiasm became contagious. If the subject were pathetic, the room resounded with sobs and suppressed cries; if comic, with bursts of laughter. Mediocre authors reaped easy but animating success; and many works, like the "Saisons" of St. Lambert, were vaunted to the skies by listening friends, which were acknowledged to be poor and wearisome when published. In the same way, the plays and tales of Mdlle. Necker were read by her in numerous companies. These productions were afterwards printed, and possess slight merit. The plays are flat, and what in common parlance is called maudlin; the tales inflated, and without originality: when read in society, they were applauded with transport. It cannot be doubted that this sort of encouragement must rouse to its height the power of an author of real genius. In this country, writers receive little praise except that which results from the number of copies that are sold; and must rely entirely on the spirit of inspiration to carry them through the toils of authorship. How seldom, how very seldom, does an English author hear one word of real sympathy or admiration! Over reserve, over fear of compromising our opinions, and being laughed at for being in the wrong, holds us in. Madame de Staël, animated by the fervour of her French friends, believed in her own genius, even before it was developed; and self-confidence gave it a strength of wing that enabled her to soar to the extreme height that her abilities permitted.

These were stirring days in which she lived. [....] We dwell upon these circumstances of Necker's life, as they were the events that chiefly interested his daughter. She had been struck with dismay at the moment of his exile. She was married at this time; but it is a singular circumstance that in her life her marriage is a very secondary event, and her husband's name seldom mentioned. As the only daughter of a millionaire, Mdlle. Necker's hand had been asked by many French nobles; but it was determined not to marry her to a Catholic, at the same time that she and her parents were anxious to make a marriage that should enable her to reside in France, and to appear at court. It is told of the childhood of madame de Staël, that, at the age of eleven, she offered to marry Gibbon. He being a favourite friend of her parents, she hoped to please them by giving them a son-in-law of whom they were fond, with little regard to his strange repulsive figure and ugly face. And now she thought of station and convenience, and not at all of finding a friend or companion—far less a lover—in her husband. The baron de Staël Holstein, chamberlain to the queen of Sweden, had resided in Paris for some years, first as counsellor to the Swedish embassy, and afterwards as ambassador. He frequented the society of the French liberals, was a friend of Necker, and entered the lists of his daughter's admirers. He was a protestant and a noble, and he was also an amiable honourable man. The only objection to the union was the likelihood of his being recalled to his own country. The king of Sweden, Gustavus III, with whom he was a favourite, favoured the match, and promised that he should continue for several years to be ambassador at the French court. In addition, M. de Staël promised never to take her to Sweden without her own consent. On these considerations the marriage took place in the year 1786, when she was just twenty. Madame de Staël appeared at court. It is related that, desirous as she had been of acquiring this privilege, yet Parisian society was ill-naturedly amused by the numerous mistakes in etiquette which the young ambassadress had made on her presentation. She gaily related them herself, so to disarm her enemies. At this time, also, she appeared as an authoress in print, publishing her letters on the writings of Rousseau. We find in this work all the traits that distinguished madame de Staël's writings to the end,—great enthusiasm and eloquence, a pleasure in divining the mysteries of existence, and dwelling on the melancholy that attends it,—considerable power of expressing her thoughts, and much beauty and delicacy in the thoughts themselves, but an absence of strength and of the highest elevation both of talent and moral feeling. [....] She stept, as on to a stage, in the first brilliancy of youth, to be admired and to enjoy; but public events were swelling and disturbing the stream of time, and it became a tempestuous flood, that wrecked her dearest hopes, and consigned her at last to that domestic retirement and peace, for which her outset in life had not formed her, and which, instead of being a haven of rest and enjoyment, was as a dead sea on which she weltered in misery and despair. [....] Madame de Staël witnessed nearly all the more deplorable events of the revolution. On the 5th October, when she heard of the march of the people to Versailles to bring the king and queen to Paris, she hastened to join her parents, who were in attendance at court. When she arrived, Necker hastened to the castle to join the council, and madame Necker and her daughter repaired to the hall preceding the one where the king remained, that they might share Necker's fate. The tumult, the inquietude, the various projects, and the trembling expectation of the hour agitated all, and augmented as night approached. A noble arrived from Paris with the latest news. He appeared in the royal presence in a common dress. It was the first time that any man had entered the king's apartment, except in court dress. His recital of the furious armed multitude, which was gathering and approaching, increased the general terror. On the morrow the storm burst. Murder assailed the gates of the palace, and the royal personages, for the first time, were attacked by those outrages, at once sanguinary and insulting, which, thus beginning, never stayed till their destruction was accomplished.

Madame de Staël was present during the whole scene. She stood near when the crowd forced the queen to appear before them, and when at their demand the royal family were carried to Paris. Such scenes could never be forgotten. When the king and queen set off to the capital, the family of Necker repaired by another route. "We crossed," madame de Staël writes, "the Bois de Boulogne; the weather was beautiful, the breeze scarcely stirred the trees, and the sun was bright enough to dispel all gloom from the scenery. No exterior object replied to our sadness." When they arrived at the Tuileries, the Parisian palace of the kings of France, which had not been inhabited for many years, they found that the beds of the royal children were put up in the room where the queen received them; Marie Antoinette apologised. "You know," she said, "that I did not expect to come here." Her beautiful face expressed anger as she spoke; and madame de Staël must have felt that her father, as popular minister, and herself, as a lover of liberty, were included in the sentiments of resentment which filled the queen's heart. [....] This period was checkered by the illness, and finally the death, of madame Necker. She died of a lingering nervous disorder. Her husband was unwearied in his attentions and watchful tenderness, and madame de Staël shared his fatigues, and sympathised with and consoled him in his grief. The warmer kindness testified by her father caused her to prefer him; and madame Necker herself, looking on her daughter as a rival in her husband's affections, had repelled her. But death obliterated these passions, and madame de Staël acknowledged her mother's talents and virtues; she lamented her death, and respected her memory. [....]

During the whole of the reign of the directory, the influence of Madame de Staël was great. The expectation of a civil war became more imminent as the royalists rested their hopes on the armies of la Vendée, and the victories of the republican troops on the eastern frontiers, supporting the new state of things, gave energy to the men in power. Moderate and enlightened lovers of freedom desired to reconcile the two parties, and prevent a struggle. Madame de Staël attempted to effect this reconciliation. She had no desire for the return of the Bourbons; for such a change could only have been operated through the subjugation of France by foreign troops, a circumstance to be looked upon as the lowest fall in its political greatness. She was the centre of a brilliant society, which, while it regarded the chiefs of the republic as vulgar, was attached to a form of government full of promise of distinction and power to able and daring men. In France the influence of women is one of the engines used by the other sex for their advancement. Madame de Staël had already placed one of her friends in an elevated post; she exerted herself for others. She was generous and active. No gall—no bad feelings of hatred, or love of mischief, mingled in her desire to be influential. But passionately loving glory, and eager to take a part in the busier scenes of life, she made her house the rendezvous of all parties, and sought her own elevation in trying to reconcile them all, and to diffuse abroad a spirit of moderation and mutual toleration, and was often exposed to the danger of imprisonment and exile from the preponderance of the more popular party. Her mind was active, her imagination lively; but she was without prudence. Her father said of her, that she was like the savages, who sell their cabin in the morning and find themselves without shelter at night. Ardent but without forethought, ambitious of distinction without selfishness, she looked on danger as a crown of laurel, and, as far as she was personally concerned, cared more for the excitement of the combat than the repose of success. Thus, though she failed in her attempts to reconcile contending factions, she felt neither despondency nor sorrow. Meanwhile, the struggle of parties—the violence of each occasioning the weakness of all—became the stepping-stone to the man who, raising himself by the sword, and establishing and increasing his power by the same method, fell, when his weapon failed to be able to deal with all the enemies from the extremities of the earth whom he challenged to the contest.

Bonaparte and madame de Staël were neither impressed favourably by the other when they first met. He saw in her a factitious but a not the less powerful influence with which he could only cope by trampling it in the dust; and she found in him a man unimpressible by words or sentiments, aiming at one goal, and wholly indifferent to the thousands to be mowed down or the one tortured by the methods he used for his success. In their encounter she felt her existence strike against a rock which, while it wrecked whole fleets, did not disdain to swamp a skiff which had every right to expect shelter beneath its shadow. When, after the treaty of Campo-Formio, Bonaparte arrived in Paris, he and madame de Staël often met in society. She declared that a feeling of fear always overcame her in his presence. She was struck by his superiority, but repelled by a certain coldness that remained as a wall between them. When, for the sake of amassing funds for his expedition to Egypt, Bonaparte proposed the invasion of Switzerland to the directory, madame de Staël regarded the cause of the independence of that country as so sacred, that she sought a conference with the general for the purpose of turning him from his design. Nothing can better show the difference of French manners from ours than this circumstance; and Bonaparte, a child of the army, little conversant with the spirit of French society, regarded a woman's interference on such a subject as impertinent and out of character with her sex; but, although he was not to be moved by her, such was her acknowledged influence that he did not disdain to discuss the question with her with an appearance of candour, till, having pronounced certain words which he considered sufficient to refute her arguments, declaring that men must have political rights, and advancing the falsehood that the Swiss would have more as a portion of France than as an independent insignificant state, he turned the conversation, and talked of his love of retirement,—of the country and the fine arts,—expressing himself as sharing many of the lady's own tastes. Madame de Staël felt the influence of his power of pleasing, but was mortified to be treated like a mere woman. He, on the other hand, perceiving that she had talents sufficient to persuade and influence men, and that she was likely to exert this power against himself, conceived a dislike, which he afterwards showed in a series of persecutions. [....]

Love for this father was the master passion of madame de Staël's life. She looked on him as the wisest and best of men; but, more than this, his kindness and sympathy gifted him with something angelic in her eyes. He was her dearest friend—the prop of her fortunes; her adviser, her shelter, her teacher, her approver—the seal of her prosperity and her glory. He was an old man, and this imparted unspeakable tenderness to her attachment. Her very love of Paris, and her consequent absences from him, added force to her feelings. While away she gathered anecdotes and knowledge for his amusement. Their correspondence was regular and full. [....]

She was, with all her vivacity, naturally melancholy. The *society of nature*, as she termed it, nursed her darkest reveries, and she turned from her own thoughts as from a spring of bitterness. As existence became stagnant, *ennui* generated a thousand imaginary monsters of mind; she felt lost and miserable. Death and solitude were, in her mind, closely allied. Take away the animation of conversation; the intercommunication of ideas among the many; the struggle, the applause, the stirring interest in events; the busy crowd that gave variety to every impression; and the rest of life was, in her eyes, a fearful vigil near the grave. It is beautifully said, that God tempers the wind to the shorn lamb. Sometimes, however, the exact contrary has place, and our weak and sore points are sought out to be roughly handled. Thus madame de Staël, brought up to act a foremost part on the brilliant theatre of the civilised world, was cast back on herself, and found there only discontent and misery. To us sober English, indeed, her life at Coppet seems busy enough. She assembled all travellers about her; her domestic circle was large; she acted plays; she declaimed; but it would not do: Paris was interdicted, and she was cut off from happiness. [....] She never saw the day return, she says, that she did not repine at being obliged to live to its end. She was married again at this time. This event, which was kept secret till after her death, is one of the most singular of her history.[19] [....] Her character softened as she advanced in life, and she appreciated its real blessings and disasters more rationally, at the same time that she acquired greater truth and energy in her writings. This may often be observed with women. When young, they are open to such cruel attacks, every step they take in public may bring with it irreparable injury to their private affections, to their delicacy, to their dearest prospects. As years are added they gather courage; they feel the earth grow steadier under their steps; they depend less on others, and their moral worth increases. She was an affectionate and constant friend, and the sentiments of her heart replaced the appetite she formerly had for the display of talent: she placed a true value on courage and resignation, when before she had reserved her esteem for sensibility. She grew calmer, and ceased to fabricate imaginary woes for herself, happy when she escaped real ones. She grew pious. From her earliest years she had strong feelings of religion, resulting from dependence on Providence, from adoration for the Supreme Being, and hope of a future life. The Christian principles mingled more entirely with these sentiments in her latter years. As her health declined, her sleepless hours were spent in prayer, and existence lost, as it often does to those about to leave it, its gay and deceptive colours. "Life," she said, "resembles Gobelin tapestry: you do not see the canvass on the right side; but when you turn it the threads are visible. The mystery of existence is in the connection between our faults and our misfortunes. I never committed an error that was not the cause of a disaster." And thus, while the idea of death was infinitely painful, the hope of another life sustained her. "My father waits for me on the other side," she said, and indulged the hope of hereafter being rejoined by her daughter.

She perished gradually: the use of opium, from which she could not wean herself, increased her danger; nor could medicine aid her. She died in Paris on the 14th July 1817, in her fifty-second year. Rocca[20] survived her but a few months.

She possessed too much merit not to have many enemies during her life, and these were increased by her passion for display, and the jealous spirit with which she competed with those whom she looked on as rivals. The eagerness with which during the days of the republic she mingled in politics, and her attempts to acquire influence over Napoleon, were arms that she put into the hands of her enemies to injure her. They accused her of an intriguing meddling disposition, saying of her, that to make a revolution she would throw all her friends into the river, content with fishing them out the next day, and so showing the kindness of her heart. But her faults were more than compensated among her friends by the truth and constancy of her attachment. Her temper was equable, though her mind was often tempest-tost, clouded by dark imaginations, torn by unreal but deeply felt anxieties and sorrows. "I am now," she said, in her last days, "what I have ever been,—sad, yet vivacious." To repair wrong, to impress on the minds of princes benevolence and justice, were in her latter years the scope of, so to speak, her public life. She loved France with passion. Lord Brougham records the alarm and indignation which caused her to pant for breath, as she exclaimed, "Quoi donc, cette belle France!" when lord Dudley, half in jest half seriously, wished the Cossacks, in revenge for Moscow burnt, to nail a horse-shoe on the gates of the Tuileries.

Our memoir has extended to so great a length that we can only avert cursorily to her writings. M. Anneé, a French critic, observes of her, that her understanding had more brilliance than profundity; and yet that no writer of her epoch had left such luminous ideas on her route. Chateaubriand, while he deplores the party spirit which gave irritation to her sentiments and bitterness to her style, pronounces her to be a woman of rare merit, and who would add another name to the list of those destined to become immortal. She wrote on a vast variety of subjects, and threw light on all. Yet she gathered her knowledge, not by profound study, but by rapid dipping into books and by conversation with learned men;

thus her opinions are often wrongly grounded, and her learning is superficial. Still her conclusions are often admirable; granting that the ground on which she founds them is true. She has great felicity of illustration, and her style is varied and eloquent, the fault being that it sometimes abounds in words, and wants the merit of concentration and conciseness; often, too, she is satisfied with a sentiment for a reason. Her wit is not pleasantry, but it is pointed and happy. She neither understood nor liked humour; but she enjoyed repartee: many are recorded as falling from her, and they are distinguished by their point and delicacy. Her "Dix Anneés d'Exil" is the most simple and interesting of her works; but her "Germany," perhaps, deserves the highest rank, from its research, and the great beauty of its concluding chapters. Of her novels we have already spoken. They do not teach the most needful lesson—moral courage; but they are admirable as pictures of life and vivid representations of character, for subtle remark and vivid detail of what in youth forms our joys and sorrows. She puts much of herself in all; and thus adds to the charm and truth of her sentiments and ideas. Her "Considerations on the French Revolution" is valuable, from its affording us a personal picture of the impressions made by that epoch; but the great preponderance of praise which she gives to Necker renders it a work of prejudice. Like him, she had no strong republican sentiments. She desired an English constitution; she disliked the girondists as well as the mountain, and attempted the impossible task of reconciling the interests of the nation as established by the revolution with that of the *ancienne régime*. Her feelings are praiseworthy, but her views are narrow.

Such is the defect of human nature that we have no right to demand perfection from any individual of the species. We may sum up by saying that, though the character and writings of madame de Staël, in some respects, display weaknesses, and though she committed errors, her virtues and genius raise her high; and the country that gave her birth, and which she truly loved, may, with honest pride, rank her among its most illustrious names.

THE END.

ENDNOTES

1   See Vivien Jones, "The Death of Mary Wollstonecraft," *British Journal for Eighteenth-Century Studies* 20, no. 2 (Autumn 1997): 187–205.

2   According to Emily Sunstein, Godwin taught his daughter to read and write by "tracing the inscriptions" on Wollstonecraft's gravestone. *Mary Shelley: Romance and Reality* (Baltimore, MD: Johns Hopkins University Press, 1991), 26.

3   Nora Crook, "General Editor's Introduction," in *Mary Shelley's Literary Lives and Other Writings*, vol. 1, *Italian Lives*, ed. Tilar J. Mazzeo (London: Pickering & Chatto, 2002), xiv.

4   *Oxford Dictionary of National Biography*, s.v. "Shelley [née Godwin], Mary Wollstonecraft," by Betty T. Bennett, 3.

5   Miranda Seymour, *Mary Shelley* (London: John Murray, 2000), 142.

6   Lisa Vargo, "Introduction," *Lodore* (Peterborough, ON: Broadview Press, 1997), 21–40.

7   Betty T. Bennett, "Introduction," in *Lives of the Great Romantics III: Mary Shelley*, ed. Betty T. Bennett (London: Pickering & Chatto, 1999), x.

8   Michael Rossington, "Sacred Monuments: Mary Shelley's Lives of William Godwin and Mary Wollstonecraft," in *Chamber Music: the Life-Writing of William Godwin, Mary Wollstonecraft, Mary Hays, and Mary Shelley*, ed. Gina Luria Walker, Romantic Circles Features & Events (College Park, MD: University of Maryland, April 2002), http://www.rc.umd.edu/features/features/chambermusic (accessed July 5, 2007).

9   Richard Allen comments that in Mary's edition Percy Shelley's poems "become a kind of narrative first of [Percy] Shelley's life but increasingly also of Mary Shelley's." "Mary Shelley as Editor of the Poems of Percy Shelley," in *Women, Scholarship and Criticism c. 1790–1900*, ed. J. Bellamy, A. Laurence, and G. Perry (Manchester: Manchester University Press, 2000), 85.

10   See Nora Crook's detailed account of Mary Shelley's reading, writing, and translating: "General Editor's Introduction," in *Mary Shelley's Literary Lives and Other Writings*, vol. 1, *Italian Lives*, ed. Tilar J. Mazzeo (London: Pickering & Chatto, 2002), xiii–xix.

11   For example, Anne K. Mellor argues that, in *Lodore*, the character of Fanny Derham "embodies a female potentiality that Mary Wollstonecraft had described, and her presence in the novel is Mary Shelley's homage to her mother's radical feminist convictions." *Mary Shelley: Her Life, Her Fiction, Her Monsters* (Oxford: Routledge, 1988), 208.

12   Crook, "General Editor's Introduction," xix–xxxii.

13   Crook, "General Editor's Introduction," xxviii.

14   Bonnie G. Smith, "History and Genius: The Narcotic, Erotic, and Baroque Life of Germaine de Staël," *French Historical Studies* 19, no. 4 (Fall 1996): 1059–91.

15   Julie A. Carlson, "Characters: Mary Wollstonecraft and Germaine de Staël," *Modern Philology*, Vol. 98, No. 2, Religion, Gender, and the Writing of Women: Historicist Essays in Honor of Janel Mueller. (Nov. 2000), 320-38.

16   De Staël's father was Jacques Necker (1732–1804), King Louis XVI's Finance Minister.

17   Clarissa Harlowe is the heroine of Samuel Richardson's influential epistolary novel *Clarissa: or The History of a Young Lady* (1748–49) in which the virtuous Clarissa dies after being persecuted and raped.

18   Théodore Tronchin (1709–81) was an eminent Swiss medical doctor.

19   Madame de Staël was known to have an affair with a younger Swiss officer, but there was uncertainty about whether or not they married during her life.

20   Albert Jean Michel de Rocca, a Swiss national who served as a lieutenant in the French army during the Napoleonic wars, was Madame de Staël's second husband. He published *Mémoires sur la guerre des Français en Espagne* (1814), in modern translation, *Hussar Rocca: A French Cavalry Officer's Experiences of the Napoleonic Wars and His Views on the Peninsular Campaigns Against the Spanish, British and Guerilla Armies* (2006).

Harriet Martineau (1802–1876)

Harriet Martineau was a phenomenon of the Victorian age. Hugely influential as a public educator and opinion former, through her journalism, didactic stories on economic and social issues, her historical writing, travel books, autobiography, and one novel, she held a uniquely authoritative position in the intellectual and political culture of her own day.

Martineau was one of eight children of a Unitarian family in Norwich and, like her brothers, was given a thorough grounding in Latin, English literature, modern languages, music, and mathematics. Her formal education, though desultory, was what was then called a boy's education.[1] A nervous child, she read voraciously and found solace in religion. By the age of sixteen, her deafness, which had been gradually increasing, became acute. Throughout her adult life, she communicated by the aid of an ear trumpet. Her disabilities also extended to lacking a sense of smell and taste. Nonetheless, her visual sense and her physical and mental energy largely compensated for these deprivations.

In her early twenties, during the financial crisis of 1825–26, her father's textile manufacturing business failed, and, on his death, Harriet and her mother and sisters were left with very little money. They were confronted by the classic plight of English middle-class girls without private means. The only career opportunities open to them were teaching as a governess in a private family or needlework. Harriet, who because of her deafness could not teach, took up needlework for a time, but knew that her real vocation lay in authorship. She was later to express her frustration at the limited opportunities open to educated women in her novel *Deerbrook*: "for such a woman there is in all England no chance of subsistence but by teaching."[2]

After attaining some success with didactic tales and winning three prizes in a Unitarian magazine for essays on the conversion of Catholics, Jews, and Muslims to Unitarianism, she decided on a major project, namely to publish a series of stories illustrating the "new science" of political economy. From her Norwich manufacturing roots, she was imbued with the principles of free trade and a belief, from her religious training, of individual duty. Philosophically, she embraced what was called "necessarianism," the view that, in social life as in the physical world, there was a cause for every effect and that freedom for individuals lay in understanding and acting upon the laws that govern society. She was a liberal, in the sense that she was committed to the idea of human freedom, both positive and negative. Her Unitarian background had given her a belief in intrinsic human goodness and in the potential perfectibility of human institutions. Perfectibility depended on the proper understanding of the laws governing society, which political economy purported to explain.

In the late 1820s, she read Adam Smith's *The Wealth of Nations* and Jane Marcet's *Conversations on Political Economy*. From the latter, she realised that she had been writing tales about the principles of political economy without realising it. With the backing of her family, though with very unfavourable terms to herself, she persuaded the publisher Charles Fox to print her *Illustrations of Political Economy*. The stories began publication in February 1832 and, in spite of Fox's forebodings, proved an immediate and runaway success. They established Martineau as an authority in the field and gave her financial security. She was "lionised" by politicians and London society, but kept to a severe work schedule, producing 25 stories in as many months.

In 1834, she went to America for two years, touring both the northern and southern states. Thanks to the explicitly anti-slavery views she had expressed in her story "Demerara," it was known that she opposed slavery, but politicians in the South welcomed her, hoping that lavish hospitality and a charm offensive would help change her views. They did not succeed. When in Boston, she appeared at an abolitionist meeting; she was excoriated by much of the American press and forced to curtail part of her visit. On her return to England, she published *Society in America* (1836), which has been hailed as an important early work of sociology. Her one novel, *Deerbrook*, followed in 1839.

At the end of that year, she fell seriously ill on a journey to Venice and, for eight years, remained in a state of almost complete invalidism. Martineau believed that she owed her seemingly miraculous cure in 1844 to mesmerism. In 1845, she moved to Westmoreland where she built a house, the Knoll, near Ambleside and lived there for a further thirty years, much of it in good health and always intellectually active. She undertook a journey with friends to the Near East in 1847, visiting Egypt, Syria, and Palestine. The book she wrote on her return, *Eastern Life* (1848), a study in comparative religions, made clear her repudiation of religious belief. Her frankness on this subject, as on many others, caused enormous offence, especially to her brother James, who severed relations with her. Charlotte Brontë, a friend and admirer, also broke off contact with Martineau over her atheism.

Martineau led a busy and productive life in the Lake District, writing articles for the *Daily News*, as well as guide books of the Lakes, giving public lectures to artisans, setting up a housing cooperative for farm labourers, and running her own small farm. She was an active promoter of women's emancipation, who championed divorce and campaigned against the Contagious Diseases Act. An admirer of August Comte's positive philosophy (in spite of his idealising and retrograde views on women), she published a two-volume adaptation of his *Positive Philosophy* (1852), a trenchant and accurate rendition of his views. When, in 1855, she was diagnosed as having heart disease and believed she would soon die, she wrote her *Autobiography*, but she lived for a further twenty years, intellectually vigorous until her death in 1876.

"PREFACE," *ILLUSTRATIONS OF POLITICAL ECONOMY* (1832)

Martineau aimed in her *Illustrations* to publicise the new "science" of political economy to as wide an audience as possible. The Preface does not merely justify the study of the subject; it makes an impassioned case for educational texts on economics to be available to the mass of the people. Properly presented in accessible form, political economy need not be any longer considered "dull, abstract and disagreeable." Defining her science as that which "treats of the Production, Distribution and Consumption of Wealth," she furnishes an analogy between the organization (economy) of a nation state and that of a well-run household. The modern state, she argues, while not feudal, is still in a feudal state of mind concerning social inequality and misery, which is visible on every hand. The cure for this disorder lies in understanding the laws that govern society, an understanding that must be extended to the majority, not only the learned minority. Labourers and Capitalists, she suggests, share the same interest in creating and sustaining wealth. Her fictional format will ensure that what is otherwise a dry and abstract subject will appeal to the masses, by showing social laws working themselves out in familiar human situations.

145

Each story in Martineau's *Illustrations* was designed to illustrate a particular point in political economy. A story that caused particular controversy, especially in the United States, was "Demerara," describing life on a West Indian slave plantation. Martineau's arguments against slavery demonstrate how she believed that the laissez-faire principles of political economy were, nevertheless, grounded in enlightened principles of human rights. Her attack on slavery is both economic and moral. Firstly, slavery and the sugar trade involve an acute form of protectionism and inefficient labour management. West Indian sugar producers, Martineau points out, opposed free trade and had a virtual monopoly in Britain, thus ensuring an artificially high price for sugar. With regard to labour management, slaves, unlike agricultural labourers, could not be dismissed when their labour was no longer required. The cost of their upkeep bore no relation to productivity. Capital and labour alike were wasted under this system. Second, and more important, slavery violated the fundamental premise of human freedom, of which the above noted freedom to trade was a part. No man could alienate from himself or legitimately have his freedom taken from him. Thus, slavery contravened the principles of human rights as well as of political economy.

Harriet Martineau's work shows a remarkable consistency. She championed laissez-faire economics, political radicalism, social progress, and liberalism. Any social evils arising from the application of laissez-faire principles would disappear given sufficient education of the masses and benevolent philanthropy. She believed that political economy was the social application of the scientific revolution and that social laws of necessity, when properly understood, would create a free but ordered society. Her authority and fame throughout her lifetime illustrate the Victorian fascination with scientific explanation as well as the possibility for women, as amateurs, to mould public opinion.

"Preface," *Illustrations of Political Economy* (1832)

Harriet Martineau

Preface

In an enlightened nation like our own, there are followers of every science which has been marked out for human pursuit. There is no study which has met with entire neglect from all classes of our countrymen. There are men of all ranks and every shade of opinion, who study the laws of Divine Providence and human duty. There are many more who inquire how the universe was formed and under what rules its movements proceed. Others look back to the records of society and study the history of their race. Others examine and compare the languages of many nations. Others study the principles on which civil laws are founded, and try to discover what there has been of good and what of evil in the governments under which men have lived from the time of the patriarchs till now. Others—but they are very few—inquire into the principles which regulate the production and distribution of the necessaries and comforts of life in society.

It is a common and true observation that every man is apt to think his own principal pursuit the most important in the world. It is a persuasion which we all smile at in one another and justify in ourselves. This is one of the least mischievous of human weaknesses; since, as nobody questions that some pursuits are really more important than others, there will always be a majority of testimonies in favour of those which are so, only subject to a reservation which acts equally upon all. If, for instance, votes were taken as to the comparative value of the study of medicine, the divine would say that nothing could be more important except theology; the lawyer the same, excepting law; the mathematician the same, excepting mathematics; the chemist the same, excepting chemistry; and so on. As long as every man can split his vote, and all are agreed to give half to themselves, the amount of the poll will be the same as if all gave whole votes. There is encouragement, therefore, to canvas, as we are about to do, in favour of a candidate whom we would fain see more popular than at present.

Can any thing more nearly concern all members of any society than the way in which the necessaries and comforts of life may be best procured and enjoyed by all? Is there any thing in any other study (which does not involve this) that can be compared with it in interest and importance? And yet Political Economy has been less studied than perhaps any other science whatever, and not at all by those whom it most concerns,—the mass of the people. This must be because its nature and its relation to other studies are not understood. It would not else be put away as dull, abstract, and disagreeable. It would be too absurd to complain of its being difficult in an age when the difficulties of science appear to operate as they should do, in stimulating to enterprise and improving patience.

Political Economy treats of the Production, Distribution and Consumption of Wealth; by which term is meant whatever material objects contribute to the support and enjoyment of life. Domestic economy is an interesting subject to those who view it as a whole; who observe how, by good management in every department, all the members of a family have their proper business appointed them, their portion of leisure secured to them, their wants supplied, their comforts promoted, their pleasures cared for; how harmony is preserved within doors by the absence of all causes of jealousy; how good will prevails towards all abroad through the absence of all causes of quarrel. It is interesting to observe by what regulations all are temperately fed with wholesome food, instead of some being pampered above-stairs while others are starving below; how all are clad as becomes their several stations, instead of some being brilliant in jewels and purple and fine linen, while others are shivering in nakedness; how all have something, be it much or little, in their purses, instead of some having more than they can use, while others are tempted to snatch from them in the day-time or purloin by night. Such extremes as these are seldom or never to be met with under the same roof in the present day, when domestic economy is so much better understood than in times when such sights were actually seen in rich men's castles: but in the larger family—the nation—every one of these abuses still exists, and many more. If it has been interesting to watch and assist the improvement of domestic economy from the days of feudal chiefs till now, can it be uninteresting to observe the corresponding changes of a state. If it has been an important service to equalize the lot of the hundred members of a great man's family, it must be incalculably more so to achieve the same benefit for the many millions of our population, and for other nations through them. This benefit cannot, of course, be achieved till the errors of our national management are traced to their source, and the principles of a better economy are established. It is the duty of the people to do this.

If a stranger had entered the castle of a nobleman, eight hundred years ago, and, grieved at what he saw, had endeavoured to put matters on a better footing, how ought he to set about it, and in what temper should he be listened to? If he had the opportunity of addressing the entire household at once, he would say, "I have been in your splendid halls, and I saw vast sums squandered in gaming, while hungry creditors were looking on from without with rage in the countenances. I have been in your banqueting room, and saw riot and drunkenness to-day where there will be disease and remorse tomorrow. I have been in your kitchens, and I saw as much waste below as there had been excess above, while the under servants were driven into a cold corner to eat the broken food which was not good enough for their masters' dogs. I have been in your dungeons, and I saw prisoners who would fain have laboured for themselves or their fellow-captives, condemned to converse in idleness with their own melancholy thoughts or with companions more criminal and miserable than themselves. I have been among the abodes of those who hew your wood, and draw your water, and till your fields, and weave your garments; and I find that they are not allowed to exchange the produce of their labour as they will, but that artificial prices are set upon it, and that gifts are added to the profits of some which are taken out of the earnings of others. I hear complaints from all in turn, from the highest to the lowest; complaints which I cannot call unreasonable, since it is equally true that the poor among you are oppressed, and that the rich are troubled; that the rulers are perplexed and the governed discontented. These things need not be. There are methods of governing a family which will secure the good of all. I invite you to join me in discovering what these methods are." What would be thought of the good sense of such a household if they should reject the invitation; —if the rulers should say, "We are much perplexed, it is true, to know how to govern; but it is very difficult to change the customs of a family, and so we will go on as we are;" if the sons and daughters of the house should reply, "It is true the servants threaten us with vengeance, and we have more trouble than enough with their complaints; but we should find the inquiry you propose very dull and disagreeable, so do not let us hear any more about it;" if the servants should say, "We have many grievances certainly, and we can easily tell what ought to be remedied; but as to what the remedies are, we are told we cannot understand the subject; so instead of trying to learn, we shall redress our troubles in our own way"? If this is folly, if this is neglect, if this is madness, it is no more than as many people are guilty of as refuse to hear any thing of Political Economy, because it is new, or because it is dull, or because it is difficult. No one could make any of these objections, if he knew the nature or saw any thing of the utility and beauty of the science.

Half-civilized states were like the half-civilized household we have described, eight centuries ago. We wish we could go on to say that civilized states are managed like civilized households, that Political Economy was nearly as well understood by governments as domestic economy is by the heads of families. That it is far otherwise, our national distresses too plainly shew. The fault lies, however, quite as much with the governed as with their rulers. Unless the people will take the pains to learn what it is that goes wrong, and how it should be rectified, they cannot petition intelligently or effectually, and government will regard their complaints as unreasonable and their afflictions as past help. However true it may be that governments ought to look over the world at large for the purpose of profiting by universal experience and improving their measures in proportion as knowledge advances, it is equally true that the people should look abroad also, and observe and compare and reflect and take to heart whatever concerns the common interests of the millions of their countrymen. If many of them occupy such a position as that they cannot do this, is it not at least their duty, should it not be their pleasure, to listen to those who have observed and compared and reflected and come to a certain knowledge of a few grand principles, which, if generally understood, would gradually remove all the obstructions, and remedy the distresses and equalize the lot of the population? Such ought to be the disposition of the people.

But the people complain, and justly, that no assistance has been offered them which they could make use of. They complain that all they can do is to pick up bits and scraps of knowledge of Political Economy, because the works which profess to teach it have been written for the learned, and can interest only the learned. This is very true, and it is the consequence of the science being new. All new sciences are for some time engrossed by the learned, both because preparation is required before they can be generally understood, and because it is some time before men perceive how close an interest the bulk of society has in every new truth. It is certain, however, that sciences are only valuable in as far as they involve the interests of mankind at large, and that nothing can prevent their sooner or later influencing general happiness. This is true with respect to the knowledge of the stars; to that of the formation and changes of the structure of the globe; to that of chemical elements and their combinations; and, above all, to that of the social condition of men. It is very natural that the first eminent book on this new science should be very long, in some parts very difficult, and, however wonderful and beautiful as a whole, not so clear and precise in its arrangement as it might be. This is the case with Smith's Wealth of Nations,—a book whose excellence is marvellous when all the circumstances are considered, but which is not fitted nor designed to teach the science to the great mass of the people. It has discharged and is discharging its proper office in engaging the learned to pursue the study, and in enabling them to place it in new lights according to the various needs of various learners. It is very natural, again, that the first followers of the science should differ among themselves, and that some should think certain points important which others think trifling; and it is a matter of course that their disputes must be tiresome to those who know little of the grounds of them. It is perfectly natural that the science should be supposed obscure and the study of it fruitless which could thus cause contradictions and perplexities at the very outset. It is perfectly natural that when certainty began to be obtained and regularity to come out of the confusion, formality should be the order of the day; that truths should be offered in a cold, dry form, and should be left bare of illustration, and made as abstract and unattractive as possible. This is a very hopeful state of things, however: for when truth is once laid hold of, it is easy to discover and display its beauty; and this, the last and easiest process, is what remains to be done for Political Economy. When it is done, nobody must again excuse himself from learning, out of discontent at the way in which it is taught.

The works already written on Political Economy almost all bear a reference to books which have preceded, or consist in part of discussions of disputed points. Such references and such discussions are very interesting to those whom they concern, but offer a poor introduction to those to whom the subject is new.

149

There are a few, a very few, which teach the science systematically as far as it is yet understood. These too are very valuable, but they do not give us what we want—the science in a familiar, practical form. They give us its history; they give us its philosophy; but we want its *picture*. They give us truths, and leave us to look about us, and go hither and thither in search of illustrations of those truths. Some who have a wide range in society and plenty of leisure, find this all-sufficient; but there are many more who have neither time nor opportunity for such an application of what they learn. We cannot see why the truth and its application should not go together,—why an explanation of the principles which regulate society should not be made more clear and interesting at the same time by pictures of what those principles are actually doing in communities.

150

For instance: if we want to teach that security of property is necessary to the prosperity of a people, and to shew how and in what proportion wealth increases where there is that security, and dwindles away where there is not, we may make the fact and the reasons very well understood by stating them in a dry, plain way: but the same thing will be quite as evident, and far more interesting and better remembered, if we confirm our doctrine by accounts of the hardships suffered by individuals, and the injuries by society, in such a country as Turkey, which remains in a state of barbarism chiefly through the insecurity of property. The story of a merchant in Turkey, in contrast with one of an English merchant, will convey as much truth as any set of propositions on the subject, and will impress the memory and engage the interest in a much greater degree. This method of teaching Political Economy has never yet been tried, except in the instances of a short story or separate passage here and there.

This is the method in which we propose to convey the leading truths of Political Economy, as soundly, as systematically, as clearly and faithfully, as the utmost pains-taking and the strongest attachment to the subject will enable us to do. We trust we shall not be supposed to countenance the practice of making use of narrative as a trap to catch idle readers, and make them learn something they are afraid of. We detest the practice and feel ourselves insulted whenever a book of the *trap* kind is put into our hands. It is many years since we grew sick of works that pretend to be stories, and turn out to be catechisms of some kind of knowledge which we had much rather become acquainted with in its genuine form. The reason why we choose the form of narrative is, that we really think it the best in which Political Economy can be taught, as we should say of nearly every kind of moral science. Once more we must apply the old proverb, "Example is better than precept." We take this proverb as the motto of our design. We declare frankly that our object is to teach Political Economy, and that we have chosen this method not only because it is new, not only because it is entertaining, but because we think it the most faithful and the most complete. There is no doubt that all that is true and important about any virtue,—integrity, for instance,—may be said in the form of a lecture, or written in a chapter of moral philosophy; but the faithful history of an upright man, his sayings and doings, his trials, his sorrows, his triumphs and rewards, teaches the same truths in a more effectual as well as more popular form. In like manner, the great principle of Freedom of Trade may be perfectly established by a very dry argument; but a tale of the troubles, and difficulties, and changes of good and evil fortune in a manufacturer and his operatives, or in the body of a manufacturing population, will display the same principle, and may be made very interesting besides; to say nothing of getting rid of the excuse that these subjects cannot be understood.

We do not dedicate our series to any particular class of society, because we are sure that all classes bear an equal relation to the science, and we much fear that it is as little familiar to the bulk of one as of another. We should not be so ready to suspect this ignorance if we did not hear so much of the difficulty of the subject. We trust it will be found that as the leading principles come out in order, one after another, they are so clear, so indisputable, so apparently familiar, that the wonder is when the difficulty is to come,—where the knotty points are to be encountered. We suspect that these far-famed difficulties arise, like the difficulties of mathematical and other sciences, from not beginning at the beginning and going regularly on. A student who should open Euclid in the middle, could no more proceed for want of knowing what came before, than a sawyer who should insert his saw in a hole in the middle of a plank could go on sawing while the wood was closed both behind and before. In like manner, any novice who wishes to learn in a hurry the philosophy of Wages, and dips into a treatise for the purpose, can make nothing of it for want of understanding the previous chapters on Labour and Capital. This is the only way in which we can account for the common notion of the difficulty of the science; and as this notion is very prevalent, we are constrained to believe that the ignorance we speak of is prevalent too. When, therefore, we dedicate our series to all to whom it may be of use, we conceive that we are addressing many of every class.

If we were to dedicate our work to all whom it may concern, it would be the same thing as appealing to the total population of the empire. We say this, of course, in reference to the subject, and not to our peculiar method of treating it. Is there anyone breathing to whom it is of no concern whether the production of food and clothing and the million articles of human consumption goes on or ceases? whether that production is proportioned to those who live? whether all obtain a fair proportion? whether the crimes of oppression and excess on the one hand, and violence and theft on the other, are encouraged or checked by the mode of distribution? Is there any one living to whom it matters not whether the improvement of the temporal condition of the race shall go on, or whether it shall relapse into barbarism? whether the supports of life, the comforts of home, and the pleasures of society, shall become more scanty or more abundant? whether there shall be increased facilities for the attainment of intellectual good, or whether the old times of slavery and hardship shall return? Is any one indifferent whether famine stalks through the land, laying low the helpless and humbling the proud; or whether, by a wise policy, the nations of the earth benefit one another, and secure peace and abundance at home by an exchange of advantages abroad? Is there any one living, in short, to whom it matters not whether the aggregate of human life is cheerful and virtuous or mournful and depraved? The question comes to this: for none will doubt whether a perpetuity of ease or hardship is the more favourable to virtue. If it concerns rulers that their measures should be wise, if it concerns the wealthy that their property should be secure, the middling classes that their industry should be rewarded, the poor that their hardships should be redressed, it concerns all that Political Economy should be understood. If it concerns all that the advantages of a social state should be preserved and improved, it concerns them likewise that Political Economy should be understood *by all*.

As society is in widely different states of advancement in various parts of the world, we have resolved to introduce as wide a diversity of scenery and characters as it might suit our object to employ. Each tale will therefore be usually, if not always complete in itself, as a tale, while the principles it exhibits form a part of the system which the whole are designed to convey. As an instance of what we mean: the scene of the first tale is laid in a distant land, because there is no such thing to be found in our own country as Labour uncombined with Capital, and proceeding through many stages to a perfect union with Capital. In the next volume, which treats of the operation and increase of Capital, the scene is laid in a more familiar region, because Capital can be seen in full activity only in a highly civilized country.

As the necessaries and comforts of life must be produced before they can be distributed, and distributed before they can be consumed, the order of subjects seemed to be determined by their nature.

We propose to shew what Labour can effect, and how it is to be encouraged and economized and rewarded: to treat of Capital, its nature and operation, and the proportions of its increase; and to exhibit the union of these two mighty agents of PRODUCTION. Under the second head, DISTRIBUTION, occur the great questions of Rent, Wages, and Population, the various modes of Interchange at home and abroad, including the consideration of all Monopolies, domestic and foreign. Under the third head, CONSUMPTION, are considered the modes of Demand and Supply and of Taxation. All these and many more will be exemplified in sketches of society, in narratives of those who labour and earn and spend, who are happy or otherwise according as the institutions under which they live are good or bad. There can be no lack of subjects for such tales in our own country, where the pauper and the prince, the beneficent landlord and the unreasonable tenant, the dissolute grandee and the industrious artizan, are to be found in the near neighbourhood of each other. If we look further abroad into lands where different institutions vary the interests of individuals, we are furnished with rich illustrations of every truth our science can furnish. If we could hope to supply the interest as abundantly as society does the subject-matter of our tales, we should reckon upon their success and usefulness as certain. We will do our best. But to enable us to do our best, the encouragement of the public is as necessary as our own efforts. Upon the degree of that encouragement afforded us it depends whether our plan be pursued, or stop short near the outset.

ENDNOTES

1   Fenwick Miller, *Harriet Martineau* (1884; repr., London: Kennikat Press, 1972).
2   Harriet Martineau, *Deerbrook* (London: Edward Moxon, 1839), 448.

PART 2
Education

Hester Chapone (née Mulso) (1727–1801)

The daughter of a gentleman farmer in Northamptonshire, Hester Mulso re-ceived an excellent education and was encouraged by her father and brothers to develop her abilities. Her mother, vain and frivolous, did not approve of advancing women's education. Hester learned French, Italian, and Latin and, endowed with a fine singing voice, was an enthusiastic performer of Handel's music. She began writing seriously at the age of eighteen, publishing four pieces in Dr. Johnson's *Rambler* (1750) and "The Story of Fidelia" in *The Adventurer* (1753). A friend of the novelist Samuel Richardson, her letters to him on "Filial Obedience" and "A Matrimonial Creed" were widely circulated and admired, though only published posthumously.[1] Her early work develops the themes of companionate marriage, the importance of female friendship, and women's right and duty to improve their minds, all in the context of strong religious faith. In 1760, after a six-year engagement, she married John Chapone, a lawyer, who died ten months later. Facing an uncertain economic future, Hester Chapone turned to writing as a source of income. She was encouraged by Elizabeth Montagu, who persuaded Chapone to publish letters written to her niece, the *Letters on the Improvement of the Mind* (1773). These were followed by *Miscellanies in Prose and Verse* (1775) and *Letter to a New-Married Lady* (1777). Relieved from financial distress by her writing and some small legacies, Chapone published nothing further.

A central figure in the first generation of the Bluestocking Circle, and as part of a group who made women's writing respectable, Chapone prized the opportunity to pursue learning, friendship, and a virtuous life. Her *Letters on Improvement of the Mind* form part of the body of conduct literature as exempli-fied by Dr. Gregory's *A Father's Legacy to His Daughters* (1774) or James Fordyce's *Sermons to a Young Woman* (1766). In this tradition, the decadence of aristocratic manners is opposed to the domestic virtues of the middle classes.

"A MATRIMONIAL CREED" (1750–1751) AND *LETTERS ON THE IMPROVEMENT OF THE MIND ADDRESSED TO A YOUNG LADY* (1773)

The excerpts chosen reflect the two major phases in Chapone's writing. Her "Matrimonial Creed," addressed to Richardson, represents the confident "little spitfire" attempting to establish ethical independence, while accepting women's divinely ordained subordination in marriage. She commends companionate marriage and friendship between partners as essential to happiness and virtue. The excerpt from *Letters on the Improvement of the Mind*, belonging to the later phase, is darker in tone, focusing on the pitfalls awaiting young women entering adulthood. Preserving them within middle-class respectability seems an arduous process, partly because, as Chapone points out, they are so protected from the world that they can form no adequate judgment of its temptations or deceptions. Reliance on paternal advice and strong religious faith are the best bulwarks against vice and provide consolation in misfortune. Chapone develops the role of female friendship before, within, and exclusive of marriage as being among the moral positives for young women, who are otherwise vulnerable to snares on every side.

"A Matrimonial Creed; addressed by Miss Mulso to Mr. Richardson in consequence of his questioning her strictly on what she believed to be the duties of the married state (1750–1751)," The Works of Mrs. Chapone (1807)

Hester Chapone (née Mulso)

Being told one evening that I could not be quite a good girl, whilst I retained some particular notions concerning the behaviour of husbands and wives: being told that I was intoxicated with false sentiments of dignity; that I was proud, rebellious, a little spitfire &c., I thought it behoved me to examine my own mind on these particulars, to distrust its rectitude, and endeavour to detect those erroneous principles and faulty passions, which could draw on me censures so severe from some of my best friends. Therefore, at the hour of retirement, when silence and solitude left my thoughts free, cool and sedate, and my reason unperplexed by the ambiguities of expression, the mutual misconstructions and exaggerations, the warmth of self-vindication, and the desire of converting others to our own way of thinking, which sometimes embarrass truth, and prevent conviction in argument, I endeavoured to recollect and re-consider my own sentiments on the subject. And that I might do so with more certainty and regularity, I collected them, and set them down in as good order as I could, in the manner of a creed, which, considering the importance of the subject, will not I hope be thought a profanation of the form. If the opinions here set down shall be found to vary from those I set out with, be it imputed, not to designed evasion, but to the gradual effects which the arguments I have since heard, and the reflections I have made, may have imperceptibly produced in a mind, which, however tenacious, is not disingenuous, and would have acknowledged those effects at the time, had it, at the time, been sensible of them.

I.

I believe that a husband has a divine right to the absolute obedience of his wife, in all cases where the first duties do not interfere: and that, as her appointed ruler and head, he is undoubtedly her superior. And I think it probable that the divine institution which gives him this right, and the customs and usages of all nations and ages in this respect, are founded on some natural advantages and superiority of the man, which make the law of obedience a wise, just, and merciful law, with respect to the woman. This I think probable in general, although, in many instances, the contrary is true of individuals, and in many matches, the natural superiority, in all mental excellences, is evidently on the woman's side.

II.

I believe it expedient that every woman should choose for her husband one whom she can heartily and willingly acknowledge her superior, and whose judgment and understanding she can prefer to her own; although in some points it may not be possible for her to adopt his opinions, or be convinced by his reasoning. Nor ought this (which must always be in some measure the case, even between the best paired minds that can be selected from the whole race of mankind) to interrupt or abate their felicity. Since such opinions as are general and speculative, may be retained on both sides without any inconvenience; and as to those which relate to action, the husband's will must ultimately determine, even though the wife should remain unconvinced; excepting such actions as are in themselves immoral, or which interest the wife's happiness greatly more than that of the husband. I do not know that this latter exception can stand of right, though with a generous man I think it must be allowed.

III.

Notwithstanding this acknowledged superiority of right of command, I believe it highly conducive, and, to delicate minds, absolutely necessary to conjugal happiness, that the husband have such an opinion of his wife's understanding, principles, and integrity of heart, as would induce him to exalt her to the rank of his *first* and *dearest friend*, and to endow her, by his own free gift, with all the privileges, rights, and freedoms of the most perfect friendship.

VII.

I cannot, on self-examination, convince myself that any of the above sentiments are founded in pride, or in aversion to being governed, or in jealousy of power. I would not marry a man, upon whose generosity I could not absolutely depend, and whose will and wishes would not be mine as soon as known. I have never yet been the mistress of myself, nor ever wished to be so; for I am convinced that it is generally a happiness, and often a relief to have some person to determine for us, either to point out our duty, or direct our choice. If I know myself in this respect, I should be a loyal subject, but a rebellious slave.

I have also examined myself on the article of tenaciousness, imputed to me so often by Mr. Richardson, and some others of my good friends, who probably know me better than I do myself. I am very far from denying the charge, which I think is very likely to be true, but what I wish is, to find the cause of this defect, and the remedy. That I am not insincere and disingenuous, I can boldly and safely determine; and if I felt myself convinced, I am certain I could own it freely. Whether my understanding or temper be in fault, I cannot tell. Perhaps I am still tenaciously persisting in the wrong, but I do not find that I *can*, from any argument I have yet heard, retract from, or concede any of the opinions contained in This Paper.

Letters on the Improvement of the Mind. Addressed to a Young Lady (1773)

Hester Chapone

Letter V

[On friendship, marriage, and the passions.]

I have hitherto spoken of a friend in the singular number, rather in compliance with the notions of most writers, who have treated of friendship, and who generally suppose it can have but one object, than from my own ideas.—The highest kind of friendship is indeed confined to one;—I mean the conjugal—which, in its perfection, is so entire and absolute an union, of interest, will, and affection, as no other connection can stand in competition with.—But, there are various degrees of friendship, which can admit of several objects, esteemed, and delighted in, for different qualities—and whose separate rights are perfectly compatible.—Perhaps it is not possible to love two persons exactly in the same degree; yet, the difference may be so small, that none of the parties can be certain on which side the scale preponderates.

It is a narrowness of mind to wish to confine your friend's affection solely to yourself; since you are conscious that however perfect your attachment may be, you cannot possibly supply to her all the blessings she may derive from several friends, who may each love her as well as you do, and may each contribute largely to her happiness.—If she depends on you alone for all the comforts and advantages of friendship, your absence or death may leave her desolate and forlorn.—If therefore you prefer her good to your own selfish gratification, you should rather strive to multiply her friends, and be ready to embrace in your affections all who love her, and deserve her love: this generosity will bring its own reward, by multiplying the sources of your pleasures and supports; and your first friend will love you the more for such an endearing proof of the extent of your affection, which can stretch to receive all who are dear to her. But if, on the contrary, every mark of esteem shewn to another excites uneasiness or resentment in you, the person you love must soon feel her connection with you a burden and restraint.—She can own no obligation to so selfish an attachment; nor can her tenderness be increased by that which lessens her esteem.—If she is

160

really fickle and ungrateful, she is not worth your reproaches: if not, she must be reasonably offended by such injurious imputations.

You do not want to be told, that the strictest fidelity is required in friendship: though possibly instances might be brought, in which even the secret of a friend must be sacrificed to the calls of justice and duty, yet these are rare and doubtful cases, and we may venture to pronounce that "*Whoso discovereth secrets, loseth his credit, and shall never find a friend to his mind.—Love thy friend, and be faithful unto him: but if thou betrayeth his secrets, follow no more after him.—For as a man that hath destroyed his enemy, so hast thou destroyed the love of thy friend.—As one that letteth a bird go out of his hand, so hast thou let they neighbour go.—Follow no more after him, for he is too far off; he is as a roe escaped out of the snare.—As for a wound it may be bound up; and after revilings there may be reconcilement; but he that betrayeth secrets, is without hope."

But in order to reconcile this inviolable fidelity with the duty you owe to yourself or others, you must carefully guard against being made the repository of such secrets as are not fit to be kept.—If your friend should engage in any unlawful pursuit—if, for instance, she should intend to carry on an affair of love, unknown to her parents—you must first use your utmost endeavours to dissuade her from it;—and, if she persists—positively and solemnly declare against being a confidant in such a case.—Suffer her not to speak to you on the subject, and warn her to forbear acquainting you with any step she may propose to take towards a marriage unsanctified by parental approbation.—Tell her, you would think it your duty to apprize her parents of the danger into which she was throwing herself.—However unkindly she may take this at the time, she will certainly esteem and love you the more for it, whenever she recovers a sense of her duty, or experiences the sad effects of swerving from it.

There is another case, which I should not choose to suppose possible, in addressing myself to so young a person, was it not that too many instances of it have of late been exposed to public animadversion: I mean the case of a married woman, who encourages or tolerates the addresses of a lover.—May no such person be ever called a friend of yours! but if ever one whom, when innocent, you had loved, should fall into so fatal an error, I can only say that, after proper remonstrances, you must immediately withdraw from all intimacy and confidence with her.—Nor let the absurd pretence of *innocent intentions*, in such circumstances, prevail with you to lend your countenance, a moment, to disgraceful conduct.—There cannot be innocence in any degree of indulgence to unlawful passion.—The sacred obligations of marriage are very ill understood by the wife, who can think herself innocent while she parleys with a lover, or with love—and who does not shut her heart and ears against the most distant approaches of either.—A virtuous wife—though she should be so unhappy as not to be secured by having her strongest affections fixed on her husband—will

161

---

* Ecclus. xxvii, 16.

never admit an idea of any other man, in the light of a lover:—but if such an idea should unawares intrude into her mind, she would instantly stifle it before it grew strong enough to give her much uneasiness.—Not to the most intimate friend—hardly to her own soul—would she venture to confess a weakness, she would so sincerely abhor:—Whenever therefore such infidelity of heart is made a subject of confidence, depend upon it the corruption has spread far, and has been faultily indulg'd.—Enter not into her counsels:—Shew her the danger she is in, and then, withdraw yourself from it, whilst you are yet unsullied by contagion.

It has been supposed a duty of friendship to lay open every thought and every feeling of the heart to our friend.—But I have just mentioned a case, in which this is not only unnecessary, but wrong.—A disgraceful inclination, which we resolve to conquer, should be concealed from every body; and is more easily subdued when denied the indulgence of talking of its object:—and, I think, there may be other instances, in which it would be most prudent to keep our thoughts concealed even from our dearest friend.—Some things I would communicate to one friend, and not to another, whom perhaps I loved better, because I might know that my first friend was not so well qualified as the other to counsel me on that particular subject: a natural bias on her mind, some prevailing opinion, or some connection with persons concerned, might make her an improper confidant with regard to one particular, though qualified to be so, on all other occasions.

The confidence of friendship is indeed one of its sweetest pleasures and greatest advantages.—The human heart often stands in need of some kind and faithful partner of its cares, in whom it may repose all its weaknesses, and with whom it is sure of finding the tenderest sympathy. Far be it from me to shut up the heart with cold distrust, and rigid caution, or to adopt the odious maxim, that "we should live with a friend, as if he were one day to become an enemy."—But we must not wholly abandon prudence in any sort of connection; since when every guard is laid aside, our unbounded openness may injure others as well as ourselves.—Secrets entrusted to us must be sacredly kept even from our nearest friend—for we have no right to dispose of the secrets of others.

If there is danger of making an improper choice of friends, my dear child, how much more fatal would it be to mistake in a stronger kind of attachment—in that which leads to an irrevocable engagement for life! yet so much more is the understanding blinded when once the fancy is captivated, that it seems a desperate undertaking, to convince a girl in love that she has mistaken the character of the man she prefers.

If the passions would wait for the decision of judgment, and if a young woman could have the same opportunities of examining into the real character of her lover, as into that of a female candidate for her friendship, the same rules might direct you in the choice of both;—for marriage being the highest state of friendship, the qualities requisite in a friend, are still more important in a husband.—But young women know so little of the world, especially of the other sex, and such pains are usually taken to deceive them, that they are in every way unqualified to choose for themselves, upon their own judgement.—Many a heart-ach shall I feel for you, my sweet girl, if I live a few years longer!—Since, not only all your happiness in this world, but your advancement in religion and virtue, or your apostacy from every good principle you have been taught, will probably depend on the companion you fix upon for life.—Happy will it be for you if you are wise and modest enough to withdraw from temptation, and preserve your heart free and open to receive the just recommendation of your parents: farther than a recommendation I dare say they never will go, in an affair, which, though it should be begun by them, ought never to be proceeded in, without your free concurrence.

Whatever romantic notions you may hear, or read of, depend upon it, those matches are almost always the happiest which are made on rational grounds— on suitableness of character, degree and fortune—on mutual esteem, and the prospect of a real and permanent friendship.—Far be it from me, to advise you to marry where you do not love;—a mercenary marriage is a detestable prostitution.—But, on the other hand, an union formed upon mere personal liking, without the requisite foundation of esteem, without the sanction of parental approbation, and consequently, without the blessing of God, can be productive of nothing but misery and shame.—The passion to which every consideration of duty and prudence is sacrificed, instead of supplying the loss of all other advantages, will soon itself be changed into mutual distrust— repentance—reproaches—and finally perhaps into hatred.—The distresses it brings will be void of every consolation:—you will have disgusted the friends who should be your support—debased yourself in the eyes of the world—and, what is much worse, in your own eyes; and even in those of your husband— above all, you will have offended that God, who alone can shield you from calamity.

From an act like this, I trust, your duty and gratitude to your kind parents— the first duties next to that we owe to God, and inseparably connected with it— will effectually preserve you.—But most young people think they have fulfilled their duty if they refrain from actually marrying against prohibition.—They suffer their affections, and even perhaps their word of honour to be engaged, without consulting their parents: yet satisfy themselves with resolving not to marry without their consent: not considering that, besides the wretched, useless, uncomfortable state they plunge *themselves* into, when they contract an hopeless engagement, they likewise involve a *parent* in the miserable dilemma of either giving a forced consent against his judgment, or of seeing his beloved child pine away her prime of life in fruitless anxiety—seeing her accuse him of tyranny, because he restrains her from certain ruin—seeing her affections alienated from her family—and all her thoughts engrossed by one object, to the destruction of her health and spirits, and of all her improvements and occupations.—What a cruel alternative for parents whose happiness is bound up with that of their child!—The time to consult them is before you have given a lover the least en- couragement; nor ought you to listen a moment to the man, who would wish to

163

keep his addresses secret; since he thereby shews himself conscious that they are not fit to be encouraged.

But perhaps I have said enough on this subject at present; though, if ever advice on such a topic can be of use, it must be before passion has got possession of the heart, and silenced both reason and principle.—Fix therefore in your mind as deeply as possible, those rules of duty and prudence, which now seem reasonable to you, that they may be at hand in the hour of trial, and save you from the miseries, in which strong affections, unguided by discretion, involve so many of our sex.

If you love virtue sincerely, you will be incapable of loving an openly vicious character.—But, alas!—your innocent heart may be easily ensnared by an artful one—and from this danger nothing can secure you but the experience of those, to whose guidance God has entrusted you: may you be wise enough to make use of it! So will you have the fairest chance of attaining the best blessings this world can afford, in a faithful and virtuous union with a worthy man, who may direct your steps in safety and honour thro' this life, and partake with you the rewards of virtue in that which is to come—But if this happy lot should be denied you, do not be afraid of a single life.—A worthy woman is never destitute of friends, who in a great measure supply to her the want of nearer connections.—She can never be slighted or disesteemed, while her good temper and benevolence render her a blessing to her companions.—Nay, she must be honoured by all persons of sense and virtue, for preferring the single state to a union unworthy of her.—The calamities of an unhappy marriage are so much greater than can befall a single person, that the unmarried woman may find abundant argument to be contented with her condition, when pointed out to her by Providence.—Whether married or single, if your first care be to please God, you will undoubtedly be a blessed creature; —"For that which he delights in *must be happy.*" How earnestly I wish you this happiness, you can never know, unless you could read the heart of Your truly affectionate.

ENDNOTE

1   *The Posthumous works of Mrs. Chapone, containing her correspondence with Mr. Richardson, a series of letters to Mrs. Elizabeth Carter, and some fugitive pieces,* 2 vols. (London: John Murray, 1807).

Hester Lynch Piozzi (1740–1821)

Hester Lynch Piozzi[1] was best known during her first marriage as Dr. Samuel Johnson's favorite Mrs. Thrale. She sustained a career as a learned woman, unrecognised for most of her life and criticized later. She was born to aristocratic Welsh cousins from landowning families: an educated but improvident father and an older, learned mother who used her dowry to pay her husband's debts. Learning, writing, and performing played important parts in Hester Lynch Salusbury's unconventional childhood. She demonstrated unusual mental and verbal aptitudes as a little girl and a particular talent for languages. Her parents quickly deployed these in unsuccessful attempts to persuade successive wealthy relatives to name the child as their heir.

At the age of seventeen, Mrs. Salusbury became concerned about her adolescent daughter's autodidactism, and arranged for her daughter to be tutored in Latin, rhetoric, and logic by Dr. Arthur Collier (1707–77), son of the philosopher Arthur Collier, when he was a bachelor of fifty-one and Hester was seventeen. Dr. Collier augmented his pupil's rigorous studies with informal correspondence in Latin about their daily lives. Mrs. Thrale later declared that Collier rather than Johnson was the primary intellectual influence on her.[2]

Through Collier, Salusbury came into contact with other learned people who applauded her scholarship, including Sarah Fielding (1710–68), and grammarian James Harris (1709–80) who supported the scholarship of Elizabeth Carter. Dr. William Parker, later Chaplain to George III, advanced Salusbury's study of French literature and supervised her free translation of Jansenist Louis Racine's "Épitre I sur l'homme" (1747) which she intended to publish. She studied Italian, Spanish, and Hebrew.[3]

Learning for Salusbury was not isolated from other aspects of her life. She kept her accounts in Latin, wrote poetry that imitated and parodied Pope and other British poets, and commenced a career as a diarist when she was seventeen. When she was twenty-three, she fantasized in a letter about being a writer, Collier reminded her that she must marry well. Continuing financial distress led Salusbury reluctantly to accept Henry Thrale, a rich, high-living brewer in Southwark, ten years older than Salusbury, whom her father and Collier despised and Mrs. Salusbury encouraged. Thrale is alleged to have favored the mother rather than the daughter. The couple was married in October 1763. Mrs. Thrale moved into her husband's country home, Streatham Park. Thrale and her mother were her only companions; soon after they met, Johnson admonished her that, while she fed the Streatham chickens, she was starving her mind.[4]

Mrs. Thrale produced a daughter, Queeney, in September 1764, the first of twelve children. She began a separate diary, "The Children's Book," in 1766, in which she recorded the births, illnesses, and deaths of her babies, amid multiple miscarriages, over the next decade, and, for the children who survived, their academic progress. In 1765, Dr. Johnson came to dinner at a Streatham. Almost immediately, Johnson became a part-time fixture in the Thrale home where he depended on Mrs. Thrale's attentions and Mr. Thrale's enjoyment of conversation at his abundant table. In return, Johnson stimulated and supported Mrs. Thrale's intellectual life. The two collaborated on a translation of Boethius's *The Consolations of Philosophy*.[5] Johnson's presence at Streatham "turned its mistress into a saloniere."[6] Johnson introduced Mrs. Thrale to other women whose friendship and scholarship he supported, especially the circle of Bluestockings.

Mrs. Thrale enjoyed a dazzling public life. At the same time, she suffered from annual pregnancies; the death at age nine of her only son; and her husband's infidelities, his efforts to remain as Member of Parliament for Southwark, and his business risks that threatened the lucrative brewery with bankruptcy. To avert failure, Mrs. Thrale and Johnson twice took over the financial mess Henry Thrale had created.

After one bout of what was ultimately diagnosed as venereal disease, Henry Thrale presented his wife with six calf-bound blank books, each labeled "Thraliana," stamped in gold on the cover.[7] The gift acknowledged Mrs. Thrale's fascination with the French genre of *ana*, defined by Johnson in his *Dictionary* as "loose thoughts, or casual hints, dropped by eminent men, and collected by their friends." Mrs. Thrale took as the model for her own *anas* the French philologist Gilles Ménage's *Ménagiana* (1693) or table talk.[8] *Thraliana* became and remained the record of her most intimate life over the next three decades.[9]

Mrs. Thrale now tracked her growing gift for exchanging ideas with others in conversation and correspondence. Among the documents she produced, *Three Dialogues on the Death of Hester Lynch Thrale* (1779) reveal her perspective on the Streatham circle. She composed these in the midst of Henry Thrale's declining health and financial worries, using as inspiration Swift's comic poem on his own death in which he envisions the members of his club discussing him afterwards. *Three Dialogues* caricatures several of Mrs. Thrale's close associates, including Johnson, Boswell, and the Bluestockings, Mrs. Vesey and Mrs. Montagu.[10]

Henry Thrale died by gluttony in 1781. Mrs. Thrale was by this time in love with her daughters' music teacher, Gabriel Piozzi, a year younger, handsome, cultivated, and an Italian Catholic. Mrs. Thrale now wrestled with her dubious passion, the legal complications produced by her husband's will, her four daughters' defiance, and Johnson's ill health and increasing demands on her.

Love won out. Mrs. Piozzi, as she became, was publicly represented as disloyal to Johnson, irresponsible as a mother, and sexually aggressive. The Bluestocking Mrs. Chapone considered the remarriage insane.[11] Mrs. Montagu opined, "I respected Mrs. Thrale, & was proud of the honour she did to ye human and female character in fulfilling all ye domestick duties & cultivating her mind with whatever might adorn it. I wd. give much to make every one think of her as mad.... If she is not considered in that light she must throw a disgrace at her Sex."[12] Mrs. Piozzi was blamed for Johnson's death 5 months after her marriage, and this slander permanently compromised her reputation.

The Piozzis left England in September 1784 to get away from their critics. They traveled through France and Germany and spent nearly two years in Italy. Here, for the first time, Mrs. Piozzi felt able to express all her passions, including her love of romantic scenery and painting. Virginia Woolf advises, "When her husband's dead weight was lifted off her, up she sprang." Once again, "her appetite for life was prodigious."[13] During the honeymoon, she made travel notes and recorded her impressions in *Thraliana*, which she used as sources for several of her subsequent works. Returned to England in 1787, the Piozzis lived first in London, then at Streatham. They traveled frequently to Wales where they built a house.

Ambitious to make a career as a writer independently of her connection with Johnson, Mrs. Piozzi published *Observations and Reflections Made in the Course of a Journey Through France, Italy, and Germany* (1789) and *British Synonymy; or, An attempt at Regulating the Choice of Words in Familiar Conversation* (1794). She challenged Boswell's accounts of Johnson with *Anecdotes of the late Samuel Johnson, LL.D. during the Last Twenty Years of his Life* (1786) and *Letters to and from the Late Samuel Johnson, LL.D.: To which Are Added Some Poems Never Before Printed, Published from the Original MSS. in Her Possession by Hester Lynch Piozzi* (1788). Gabriel Piozzi died in 1809. Mrs. Thrale continued to write and to socialise. She moved to Bath where she attracted yet another social circle. She produced a spectacular party to celebrate her eightieth birthday. She died in May 1821.

OBSERVATIONS AND REFLECTIONS MADE IN THE COURSE OF A JOURNEY THROUGH FRANCE, ITALY, AND GERMANY (1789)

Italy intrigued Mrs. Piozzi as her new husband's country, as a romantic landscape reminiscent of Wales, and as the place Johnson longed to see, but never did.[14] The Piozzis' extended tour through Italy followed many of the traditional stages of the Grand Tour. Piozzi intentionally distinguishes her book from those written by predecessors—classically trained male travelers, such as Addison in *Remarks on Several Parts of Italy* (1705), and earlier women travelers, such as Lady Mary Wortley Montagu in *Turkish Embassy Letters* (1763) and Lady Anna Miller in *Letters from Italy* (1776). Piozzi resists the epistolary form because "A work of which truth is the best recommendation, should not above all others begin with lies."[15] The "truth" of her book is its self-writing, not its temporality: the primary theme is an encounter with herself as the arbiter of experience for her reader as subject, observer, narrator, traveler, and emblem of British womanhood.

Piozzi conveys the appearance of spontaneity, although her accounts were fashioned from travel notes, entries in *Thraliana*, and descriptions from a trip to Paris thirteen years earlier.[16] She aspires to rid her authorial perspective of national, religious, and gender prejudices, but expresses few qualms about social class, race, or political persuasion. Piozzi is intrigued by the public presence of Italian women that coincides with her own rebellion against English male authority.[17] The material evidence of the past inspires her scholarly curiosity; she responds to the varieties of Italian culture in a proto-journalist style, continually comparing English and Italian *mores*.[18]

The published accounts are in praise of Italy and the Italians. She rarely alludes to the discomforts of travel or her uneasiness with the Italian language. Piozzi's informal style and freewheeling associations express her liberty from even linguistic proprieties. Reviewers assessed *Observations and Reflections* according to their responses to Piozzi's second marriage. Wollstonecraft disparaged the work, particularly Piozzi's colloquial, effusive style. Perhaps Piozzi's apparent disregard for textual distinctions between public and private prose influenced Wollstonecraft to adopt the more controlled style of her own *Letters* (1796). Nonetheless, readers continued to enjoy Piozzi's conversational tone, and despite criticisms of the extreme *"womanliness"* of her text, she was sufficiently buoyed to undertake another bold effort in *British Synonymy*.

The excerpt reflects Piozzi's scholarly responses to Italian history, astute observations on the status of Italian women for her female readers, a sense of her own upper class Englishness, her heightened reactions to Italian art, and her feelings of dislocation in an unfamiliar culture where she, not her husband, is regarded as the heretic.

BRITISH SYNONYMY; OR, AN ATTEMPT AT REGULATING THE CHOICE OF WORDS IN FAMILIAR CONVERSATION (1794)

Piozzi announces herself a student of philology by taking the epigraph for *British Synonymy* from *Minerva, seu de causis linguae Latinae commentaries* (1578) by the Spanish humanist philologist and theorist Franciscus Sanctius (1523–1600). The choice of epigraph wittily aligns Piozzi with "Minerva," the Roman goddess of Wisdom, in her bold ambition to provide a first original guide to English synonyms. She professes a less ambitious rationale in the "Preface" itself, crediting her ability to tackle the enterprise to the gendered stereotype that women are "accomplished talkers," while men are trained to be more proficient writers.[19] Piozzi also knew the work of Abbé Girard (1677–1748) in *La Justesse de la langue française* (1718), the first work in French to demonstrate that perfect synonyms do not and cannot exist in any language.

Piozzi declares her intention to make English accessible to other, less privileged people, especially foreign speakers, not only in public discourse but also in daily conversation. Languages were one of her abiding interests, perhaps from her early exposure to Welsh in her native Wales, a study encouraged by Dr. Johnson. She instructs using examples from her wide knowledge of others' texts, particularly Johnson's, drawing, as well, on her own in *Thraliana*.

Privately, Piozzi equivocated about the undertaking, confiding to her diary, the "Project is a two Volume Book of *Synonymes* in English ... for the use of Foreigners, and other Children of six feet high: such a Business well manag'd would be useful, but I have not depth of Literature to do it as one ought.—A good parlour-Window Book is however quite within *my* Compass."[20] Some reviewers took her at her apologetic word in the "Preface": the *British Critic* approved the author's modesty in aspiring to produce a work rather "entertaining than profound." Other readers judged her more harshly. William Gifford remarking in 1797 that Mrs. Piozzi regrettably "brought to the task, a jargon long since become proverbial for its vulgarity, and utter incapability of defining a single term in the language, and just as much Latin from a child's Syntax, as sufficed to expose the ignorance which she so anxiously labours to conceal."

Piozzi later described *British Synonymy* as a "Book of Knowledge."[21] Piozzi, like Girard, produces miniature essays and dramas to demonstrate the shades of meaning between and among words in her time. She cites Johnson fifty times in the book, frequently reporting new anecdotes about him, sometimes referring to his *Dictionary* and his other works. She quotes poetry, by others and her own, as well as her original translations, to illustrate the differences between and among words.

The narrator of *British Synonymy* is informal, entertaining, and erudite. She is also serious, troubled by present social, political, and religious turbulence in the wake of the French Revolution. She is the *salonnière* of Streatham, welcoming new friends to her table, her language, and her bountiful life.

Observations and Reflections Made in the Course of a Journey Through France, Italy, and Germany (1789)

Hester Lynch Piozzi

PREFACE

I was made to observe at Rome some vestiges of an ancient custom very proper in those days—it was the parading of the streets by a set of people call *Preciæ*, who went some minutes before the *Flamen Dialis* to bid the inhabitants leave work or play, and attend wholly to the procession; but if ill omens prevented the pageants from passing, or if the occasion of the show was deemed scarcely worthy its celebration, these *Preciæ* stood a chance of being ill-treated by the spectators. A Prefatory introduction to a work like this, can hope little better usage from the Public than they had; it proclaims the approach of what has often passed by before, adorned most certainly with greater splendour, perhaps conducted too with greater regularity and skill: Yet will I not despair of giving at least a momentary amusement to my countrymen in general, while their entertainment shall serve as a vehicle for conveying expressions of particular kindness to those foreign individuals, whose tenderness softened the sorrows of absence, and who eagerly endeavoured by unmerited attentions to supply the loss of their company on whom nature and habit had given me stronger claims.

That I should make some reflections, or write down some observations, in the course of a long journey, is not strange; that I should present them before the Public is I hope not too daring: the presumption grew up out of their acknowledged favour, and if too kind culture has encouraged a coarse plant till it runs to seed, a little coldness from the same quarter will soon prove sufficient to kill it. The flattering partiality of private partisans sometimes induces authors to venture forth, and stand a public decision; but it is often found to betray them too; not to be tossed by waves of perpetual contention, but rather to sink in the silence of total neglect. What wonder! He who swims in oil must be buoyant indeed, if he escapes falling certainly, though gently, to the bottom; while he who commits his safety to the bosom of the wide-embracing ocean, is sure to be strongly supported, or at worst thrown upon the shore.

On this principle it has been still my study to obtain from a human and generous Public that shelter their protection best affords from the poisoned arrows of private malignity; for though it is not difficult to despise the attempts of petty malice, I will not say with the Philosopher, that I mean to build a monument to my fame with the stones thrown at me to break my bones; nor yet pretend to the art of Swift's German Wonder-doer, who promised to make them fall about his head like so many pillows. Ink, as it resembles Styx in its colour should resemble it a little in its operation too; whoever has been once *dipt* should become *invulnerable*: But it is not so; the irritability of authors has long been enrolled among the comforts of ill-nature, and the triumphs of stupidity; such let it long remain! Let me at least take care in the worst storms that may arise in public or in private life, to say with Lear,

> —I'm one
> More sinn'd against, than sinning.

For the book—I have not thrown my thoughts into the form of private letters; because a work of which truth is the best recommendation, should not above all others begin with a lie. My old acquaintance rather chose to amuse themselves with conjectures, than to flatter me with tender inquiries during my absence; our correspondence then would not have been any amusement to the Public, whose treatment of me deserves every possible acknowledgment; and more than those acknowledgements will I not add—to a work, which, such as it is, I submit to their candour, resolving to think as little of the event as I can help; for the labours of the press resemble those of the toilette, both should be attended to, and finished with care; but once complete, should take up no more of our attention; unless we are disposed at evening to destroy all effect of our morning's study. [...]

FLORENCE

Poets, as well as jesters, do oft prove prophets:

Prior's happy prediction for the female wits in one of his epilogues is come true already, when he says,

> Your time, poor souls! We'll take your very money,
> Female *third nights* shall come so thick upon ye, &c.

and every hour gives one reason to hope that Mr. Pope's glorious prophecy in favour of the Negroes will not now remain long unaccomplished, but that liberty will extend her happy influence over the world;

> Till the *freed Indians,* in their native groves,
> Reap their own fruits, and woo their sable loves.

I will not extend myself in describing the heaps of splendid ruin in which the rich chapel of St. Lorenzo now lies: since the elegant Lord Corke's letters were written, little can be said about Florence not better said by him; who has been particularly copious in describing a city which every body wishes to see copiously described.

The libraries here are exceedingly magnificent; and we were called just now to that which goes under Magliabechi's name, to hear an eulogium finely pronounced upon our circumnavigator Captain Cook; whose character has attracted the attention, and extorted the esteem of every European nation: far less the wonder that it forced my tears; they flowed from a thousand causes: my distance from England! my pleasure in hearing an Englishman thus lamented in a language with which he had no acquaintance!

> By strangers honour'd, and by strangers mourn'd!

Every thing contributed to soften my heart, though not to lower my spirits. For when a Florentine asked me, how I came to cry so? I answered, in the words of their divine Mestastasio:

> "Che questo pianto mio
> Tutto non è dolor;
> È meravigila, è amore,
> È riverenza, è speme,
> Son mille affetti assieme
> Tutti raccolti al cor."

> 'Tis not grief alone, or fear,
> Swells the heart, or prompts the tear;
> Reverence, wonder, hope, and joy,
> Thousand thoughts my soul employ,
> Struggling images, which less
> Than falling tears can ne'er express.

Giannetti, who pronounced the panegyric, is the justly-celebrated improvisatore, so famous for making Latin verses *impromptu,* as others do Italian ones: the speech has been translated into English by Mr. Merry, with whom I had the honour here first to make acquaintance, having met him at Mr. Greatheed's, who is our fellow-lodger, and with whom and his amiable family the time passes in reciprocations of confidential friendship and mutual esteem.

Lord and Lady Cowper too contribute to make the society at this place more pleasing than can be imagined; while English hospitality softens down the stateliness of Tuscan manners.

172

Sir Horace Mann is sick and old; but there are conversations at his house of a Saturday evening, and sometimes a dinner, to which we have been almost always asked.

The fruits in this place begin to astonish me; such cherries did I never yet see, or even hear tell of, as when I caught the Laquais de Place weighing two of them in a scale to see if they came to an ounce. These are, in the London street phrase, *cherries like plums*, in size at least, but in flavour they far exceed them, being exactly of the kind that we call bleeding-hearts, hard to the bite, and parting easily from the stone, which is proportionately small. Figs too are here in such perfection, that it is not easy for an English gardener to guess at their excellence; for it is not by superior size, but taste and colour, that *they* are distinguished; small, and green on the outside, a bright full crimson within, and we eat them with raw ham, and truly delicious is the dainty. By raw ham, I mean ham cured, not boiled or roasted. It is no wonder though that fruits should mature in such a sun as this is; which, to give a just notion of its penetrating fire, I will take leave to tell countrywomen is so violent, that I use no other method of heating the pinching-irons to curl my hair, than that of poking them out at a south window, with the handles shut in, and the glasses darkened to keep us from being actually fired in his beams. Before I leave off speaking about the fruit, I must add, that both fig and cherry are produced by standards; that the strawberries here are small and high-flavoured, like our *woods*, and that there are not other. England affords greater variety in *that* kind of fruit than any nation; and as to peaches, nectarines, or green-gage plums, I have seen none yet. Lady Cowper has made us a present of a small pine-apple, but the Italians have no taste to it. Here is sun enough to ripen them without hot-houses I am sure, thought they repeatedly told us at Milan and Venice, that *this* was the coolest place to pass the summer in, because of the Appenine mountains shading us from the heat, which they confessed to be intolerable with *them*.

Here however, they inform us, that it is madness to retire into the country as English people do during the hot season; for as there is no shade from high timber trees, one is bit to death by animals, gnats in particular, which here are excessively troublesome, even in the town, notwithstanding we scatter vinegar, and use all the arts in our power; but the ground-floor is coolest, and every body struggles to get themselves a *terreno* as they call it.

Florence is full just now, and Mr. Jean Figliazzi, an intelligent gentleman who lives here, and is well acquainted with both nations, says, that all the genteel people come to take refuge *from* the country to Florence in July and August, as the subjects of Great Britain run *to* the country from the heats of London or Bath.

The flowers too! how rich they are in scent here! how brilliant in colour! how magnificent in size! Wallflowers perfuming every street, and even every passage; while pinks and single carnations grow beside them, with no more soil than they require themselves; and from the tops of houses, where you least expect it, an aromatic flavour highly gratifying is diffused. The jessamine is large, broad-leaved, and beautiful as an orange-flower; but I have seen no roses equal to those at Lichfield, where on one tree I recollect counting eighty-four within my own reach; it grew against the house of Doctor Darwin. Such a profusion of sweets made me enquire yesterday morning for some scented pomatum, and they brought me accordingly one pot smelling strong of garden mint, the other of rue and tansy.

Thus do the inhabitants of every place forfeit or fling away those pleasures, which the inhabitants of another place think *they* would use in a much wiser manner, had Providence bestowed the blessing upon *them*.

A young Milanese once, whom I met in London, saw me treat a hatter that lives in Pallmall with the respect due to his merit; when the man was gone, "Pray, madam," says the Italian, "is this a *gran riccone?*"* "He is perhaps," replied I, "worth twenty or thirty thousand pounds; I do not know what ideas you annex to a *gran riccone.*" "*Oh Santissima Vergine!*" exclaims the youth, "*s'avess' io mai settanta mila zecchini! non so pur troppo cosa ne farei; ma questo è chairo non venderei mai cappelli.*" "Oh dear me! had I once seventy thousand sequins in my pocket, I would dear I cannot think myself *what* I should do with them all: but this at least is certain, I would not *sell hats.*"

I have been carried to the Laurentian library, where the librarian Bandi shewed me all possible, and many unmerited civilities; which, for want of deeper erudition, I could not make the use I wished of. We asked however to see some famous manuscripts. The Virgil has had a *fac simile* made of it, and a printed copy besides; so that it cannot now escape being known all over Europe. The Bible in Chaldaic characters, spoken of by Langius as inestimable, and brought hither, with many other valuable treasures of the same nature, by Lascaris, after the death of Lorenzo de' Medici, who had sent him for the second time to Constantinople for the purpose of collecting Greek and Oriental books, but died before his return, is in admirable preservation. The old geographical maps, made out in a very early age, afforded me much amusement; and the Latin letters of Petrarch, with the portrait of his Laura, were interesting to me perhaps more than many other things rated much higher by the learned, among those rarities which adorn a library so comprehensive.

Every great nation except ours, which was immersed in barbarism, and engaged in civil broils, seems to have courted the residence of Lascaris, but the university of Paris fixed his regard: and though Leo X treated with favour, and even friendship, the man whom he had encouraged to intimacy when Cardinal John of Medicis; though he made him superintendant of a Greek college at Rome; it is said he always wished to die in France, whither he returned in the reign of Francis the First; and wrote his Latin epigrams, which I have heard Doctor Johnson prefer even to the Greek ones preserved in Anthologia; and of which our Queen Elizabeth, inspired by Roger Ascham, desired to see the author; but he was then upon a visit to Rome, where he died of the gout at ninety-three years old.

* * *

---

* Heavy-pursed fellow.

June 24, 1785

St. John the Baptist is the tutelary Saint of this city, and upon this day of course all possible rejoicings are made. After attending divine service in the morning, we were carried to a house whence we could conveniently see the procession pass by. It was not solemn and stately as that I saw at Bologna, neither was it gaudy and jocund like the show made at Venice upon St. George's day; but consisted chiefly in vast heavy pageants, or a sort of temporary building set on wheels, and drawn by oxen some, and some by horses; others carried upon things made not unlike a chairman's horse in London, and supported by men, while priests, in various coloured dresses, according to their several stations in the church, and to distinguish the parishes, &c. to which they belong, follow singing in praise of the saint.

Here is much emulation shewed too, I am told, in these countries, where religion makes the great and almost the sole amusement of men's lives, who shall make most figure on St. John the Baptist's day, produce most music, and go to most expence. For all these purposes subscriptions are set on foot, for ornamenting and venerating such a picture, statue, &c. which are then added to the procession by the managers and called a Confraternity, in honour of the Blessed Virgin Mary, the Angel Raphael, or who comes in their heads.

The lady of the house where we went to partake the diversion, was not wanting in her part; there could not be fewer than a hundred and fifty people assembled in her rooms, but not crowded as we should have been in England; for the apartments in Italy are all high and large, and run in suits like Wanstead house in Essex or Devonshire house in London exactly, but larger still: and with immense balconies and windows, not sashes, which move all away, and give good room and air. The ices, refreshments, &c. were all excellent in their kinds, and liberally dispensed. The lady seemed to do the honours of her house with perfect good-humour; and every body being full-dressed, though so early in a morning, added much to the general effect of the whole.

Here I had the honour of being introduced to Cardinal Carsini,[22] who put me a little out of countenance by saying suddenly, "*Well, madam! you never saw one of us red-legged partridges before I believe; but you are going to Rome I hear, where you will find such fellows as me no rarities.*" The truth is, I had seen the amiable Prince d'Orini at Milan, who was a Cardinal; and who had taken delight in showing me prodigious civilities: nothing ever struck me more than his abrupt entrance one night at our house, when we had a little music, and every body stood up the moment he appeared: the Prince however walked forward to the harpsichord, and blessed my husband in a manner the most graceful and affecting: then sate the amusement out, and returned the next morning to breakfast us, when he indulged us with two hours conversation at least; adding the kindest and most pressing invitations to his country-seat among the mountains of Briana, when we should return from our tour of Italy in spring 1786. Florence therefore was not the first place that shewed me a Cardinal.

British Synonymy; or, An Attempt at Regulating the Choice of Words in Familiar Conversation (1794)

Hester Lynch Piozzi

ACUTENESS, SHARPNESS, QUICKNESS, KEENNESS.

IF applied to intellect, a man is said popularly to reason with the first of these qualities, I think—to converse, if such be his custom, with the second—to conceive with the third—and to dispute or argue with the fourth. When turned into adverbs, and applied to objects of mere sensation, we say, The student learns QUICKLY; his sister discerns distances ACUTELY; and the razor shaves KEENLY. Coarse people have meantime, by the too frequent use of their favourite figure Aphæresis, rendered it vulgar to call any one an ACUTE fellow by the way of saying he is a sharp-witted one; it having been a practice lately, among low Londoners, to say, when they like a boy—how 'CUTE he is! so that the word would now shock a polished circle from its grossness.—A nation like ours, where reception depends less on established rank, than that gained by talents and manner, has a natural tendency to keep the language of high people apart from that of the low—and while the senator of Venice hears his gondolier talk just like himself, without being surprised or offended, nor thinks of desiring his son to avoid mean phrases used by the coffeehouse boy; our parents and school teachers wear out their lives in keeping the confines of conversation free from all touch of vicinity with ordinary people, who are known to be such _here_, the moment they open their mouths. Whole sentences are often dismissed the drawing-room, only because they are familiar in a shop. _He is a rough diamond,_ says the upper journey man at his club, when speaking of the apprentice, whom he conceives to be a person of intrinsic worth, but wanting polish. Now 'tis impossible to find a better phrase for such a character; yet no gentleman or lady uses the expression, because it is a favourite with the vulgar. A thousand such others might be found. Let not my foreign readers, however, hastily condemn the word ACUTE, and say I taught them so; for, in a serious sense, 'tis still a good one; nor will any Englishman accuse them of impropriety, for saying Mr. Burke is an ACUTE reasoner, or that the feeling of Mrs. Siddons must be singularly ACUTE, or she could not so SHARPEN distress in representation.

FREEDOM, LIBERTY, INDEPENDENCE, UNRESTRAINT.

OF these so fashionable words 'twere good at least to know the meaning, while their sound is ever in our ears. They are not I think strictly and actually synonymous, because FREEDOM seems always to require, and often even in conversation takes an ablative case after it, as FREEDOM *from* sorrow, *from* guilt, or punishment, &c. while LIBERTY claims a more positive signification, and seems to imply an original grant given by God alone—a semi-barbarous, semi-social state, like that of the Tartar nations who live by rapine, and subsist in wandering hordes—*their band against every man, and every man's band against them,* as was promised to their progenitor Ishmael. Yet even these as cranes obey a leader, and reject not subordination, which is paid to him who best remembers and can most readily repeat his long traced genealogy. This is rational: for superiority of wisdom may be disputed; superiority of strength may fail by age or sickness; while superiority of descent is least obnoxious to acknowledge, and most easy to ascertain, of any pretension to preeminence. How different however are these notions of LIBERTY to those of modern democrats! who seem to mean only childish desire of total UNRESTRAINT, like that enjoyed by boys at a barring out; where blustering rebellion however grew so noisy, that the world would no longer look on upon that folly. Yet is that now the conduct of a once enlightened, polished nation; for not even Frenchmen I trust do yet seriously desire a return to solitary, savage, unconnected INDEPENDENCE, such as can be only possessed by wild Americans, who hunt the woods and fish the rivers singly for support, dying at last of hunger in their caverns, as do in the deserts disabled beasts of prey. Complete LIBERTY, in the present acceptation of the word, though will soon in such a state as France finish by fresh tyrannies. Aristocracy quickly forms to herself a second-hand canopy from the fragments of kingly power; and 'tis nothing after all but such ill-judged UNRESTRAINT that makes the Baron of Transilvania so hateful and so formidable, the dread of his vassals, the abhorrence of human-kind. When the Roman *empire* was *destroyed,* these Gothic governments and feudal systems first were formed; let the votaries of airy INDEPENDENCE, or of FREEDOM armed by Phrensy against herself, keep this fact full in view.

MONEY, CASH, COLE, ASSETS, READY RINO, CHINK, CORIANDERS;

FORM a string of hateful words—synonymous enough, however, or nearly so, in the vulgar and despicable dialect of coarse traders in the hour of merriment; but to be ever sedulously avoided by those who mean to be thought eminent for choice of phrase and elegance of conversation. The first is, after all these heavy denunciations, a necessary and proper term, when business comes to be seriously spoken upon: the second is always pert and pedantic, unless used in its native foil, the banker's shop, where it means coin, opposed to notes; such MONEY as may be kept in a CAISSE or strong-box, is properly and from that derivation justly denominated CASH. The fourth word on this unpleasing list is likewise of French etymology, and belongs rather to the cant of lawyers than of merchants. When a man dies, his executors and their attorney begin to enquire if he has left ASSETS (meaning ASSEZ) sufficient for payment of legacies, debts, dues, &c.: The others are nothing better than a mere jargon of school-boys, prentices, &c. and so surely are these terms excluded civil society, and so attentive must foreigners be never to pronounce them, that I am confident a nobleman would scruple to introduce the best recommended son of his own best friend in England, to Sir William Hamilton or Sir Robert Murray Keith at Naples or Vienna, should the youth in his fist visit give my lord to understand that he "took care not to set out from home without having the touched the *COLE*, provided the *READY RINO*, and tipt Old Squaretoes for the *CORIANDERS*."

178

Nothing is so certain a brand of beggary in our country as coarse and vulgar language. We know almost the street a man resides in here at London—at least the company he has kept—by a peculiar train of discourse, which though endurable enough so long as the talk is serious, relapses into wretchedness the moment a jest is attempted. I have heard Dr. Johnson say there was such a thing as a city voice—a city laugh there is, that's certain, different from that of the people who inhabit, and have from their youth inhabited, the court end of the town.

It appears from some of Martial's epigrams, meantime, and there are corroborating reasons to believe, that in old times as well as now some waggish way was always adopted by low people, when speaking of pecuniary concerns: and *NUMMI* was certainly a cant word at Rome, because *Numa* first coined silver, which he substituted for the scrapes of leather then in use; and when a fellow filled his bag with *NUMMI*, he was I trust talking no higher language than he who in our country wishes for the *CHINK*, or boasts his familiarity with KING GEORGE'S PICTURE.

It may be worth observation, and has I think been hinted at in the First Volume, that to describe any thing by its causes is less likely to please or be right in conversation than describing the fame by its adjuncts; and perhaps the Milanese patois owes much of its grossness to the contrary practice. They call a chair *quadrega* or *four-legs*; a fan *crespin* or *crackling-thing*; the door *l'uscio* or *the going out place*. No wonder, say my English readers, that this dialect is reckoned a coarse one: while 'tis notoriously a mean phrase here to ask a gentleman—"Well, Sir, how goes your *Tompion*?" meaning—"Pray what is the time o' day by your watch?" made possibly by that artist; or—"So, my lady, how does your *mouser*?" to a woman of quality if she is fond of a favourite cat. I know not whether vice and folly are half as attentively avoided by elegant people in Grate Britain as such expressions; but this I know, that 'tis difficult to endure even virtue and wisdom combined with so much grossness.

ENDNOTES

1   Lisa Berglund points out that this is the only name Mrs. Piozzi published under, although she has continued to be referred to as "Mrs. Thrale." Lisa Berglund,

"'Familiar talk': Hester Lynch Piozzi and Female Synonymy," (presentation, Dictionary Society of North America 15th Biennial Meeting, Boston, June 8–11, 2005,).

2 William McCarthy, *Hester Thrale Piozzi: Portrait of a Literary Woman* (Chapel Hill: University of North Carolina Press, 1985), 7–8.

3 McCarthy, 11.

4 McCarthy, 66.

5 McCarthy, 23.

6 Jaclyn Geller, "The Unnarrated Life: Samuel Johnson, Female Friendship, and the Rise of the Novel Revisited," in *Johnson Re-Visioned: Looking Before and After,*" ed. Philip Smallwood (Lewisburg, PA: Bucknell University Press, 2001), 82.

7 Mary Hyde, *The Thrales of Streatham Park* (Cambridge, MA: Harvard University Press, 1977), 167–68.

8 Hyde, 10, 30–32.

9 McCarthy, 31.

10 M. Zamick, "Three Dialogues by Hester Lynch Thrale," *Bulletin of the John Rylands Library* 16 (1932): 101.

11 Clifford, 230–31.

12 McCarthy, 39 [Clifford, 229].

13 Virginia Woolf, "Mrs. Thrale," *The Moment and Other Essays* (New York: Harcourt, Brace and Company, 1945), 52–53.

14 James Boswell, *Life of Johnson* 3: 458, quoted in Danielle Insalaco, "Thinking of Italy, Making History," in *Johnson Re-Visioned: Looking Before and After,* ed. Philip Smallwood (Lewisburg: Bucknell University Press, 2001), 105.

15 Hester Lynch Piozzi, "Preface," *Observations and Reflections made in a journey through France, Italy, and Germany (1789),* ed. Herbert Barrows (Ann Arbor: University of Michigan Press, 1967), 2.

16 Brian Dolan, *Ladies of the Grand Tour* (Hammersmith: HarperCollins, 2001), 281.

17 Jane Stabler, "Taking Liberties: The Italian Picturesque in Women's Travel Writing," *European Romantic Review* 13 (2002): 16.

18 Lu Ann Marrs, "Hester Thrale Piozzi and the Art of Travel," (unpublished doctoral dissertation, University of North Carolina at Chapel Hill, 1997), 38.

19 Dennis Baron, *Grammar and Gender* (New Haven: Yale University Press, 1986), 143.

20 *Thraliana,* quoted in McCarthy, 182.

21 McCarthy, 196.

22 Piozzi refers here to Cardinal Corsini, who had an impressive art collection.

Elizabeth Hamilton (1758–1816)

Elizabeth Hamilton came from an ancient Saxon family. After the death of her father when she was six, she went to live with an aunt and uncle in Stirling who taught her "frugality, morality, meritocracy and tolerance."[1] Hamilton described her childhood in Scotland as happy, secure, and relatively unrestricted, exemplifying the philosophy of Dugald Stewart, who advocated that nature be "allowed free scope ... during early youth" to influence the formation of a strong character.[2] She disdained playing with dolls and preferred reading Shakespeare, identifying with heroes, particularly Achilles and William Wallace.[3]

From the age of eight, Hamilton attended a co-educational boarding school where masters trained her in rhetoric, geography, dancing, singing, music, and French, but not Latin or Greek, an omission which she afterwards regretted.[4] Although Mrs. Marshall, her aunt, encouraged her independence, she also cautioned her niece against "any display of superior knowledge." Hamilton experienced a moral turning point at thirteen. Mrs. Marshall was an Episcopalian, her husband a Presbyterian, and they were tolerant of Protestants who held differing sectarian views. Confronted with a family friend's attempt to shake her religious principles with ridicule, Hamilton secretly examined the scriptures to decide the issue for herself. She emerged convinced of Christianity's truth.[5] Thereafter, she remained an evangelical Christian, though she resisted sectarianism and opposed the imposition of religious dogma on children.[6]

From 1780–88, following her aunt's death, Hamilton kept house for her uncle. Her first foray into print was an anonymous essay on "Anticipation" in Henry Mackenzie's short-lived periodical *The Lounger* (1785). After her uncle's death, her brother, on his return from India, introduced her into London literary circles. She met Dr. George Gregory, editor of the *Critical Review*, and his wife, who became close friends and supporters. Her brother's sudden death from tuberculosis in 1792 devastated Hamilton. She expressed her grief, respect, and desire to continue his work in Oriental studies in a satiric fiction, *Translation of the Letters of a Hindoo Rajah* (1796).[7] The book was well received by the critics, except for an unsigned review in the *Analytical*, apparently by Mary Hays.[8]

The tensions between Hays and Hamilton reflected their mutual insecurity as new female authors in the republic of letters. They shared a consciousness that they lacked the rigorous training of their male contemporaries.[9] Hamilton had advantages of birth, class, and social connections that Hays did not. Yet Hamilton feared that, as a female author, she risked the glare of exposure because a "woman, who has once been brought before the public, can never be restored to the security of a private station."[10]

In the late 1790s, Hamilton began to suffer from gout and took the waters at Bath to restore the use of her limbs. In 1800, she published anonymously her *Memoirs of Modern Philosophers*, which ridicules both ideology and ideologues.[11] In the book, Hamilton represented Hays as the self-proclaimed heroine Bridgetina Botherim and combined conservative criticism of Jacobin ideas and personalities with a savage parody of Hays's personal and professional behavior and her private morality.[12]

Memoirs was wildly popular. Hamilton became famous and socially successful. She was admired by many notables of the day, including Sir Walter Scott and Maria Edgeworth. Although suffering from debilitating illness, she continued to publish regularly. She published *Letters on Education* (1801). Her later works display a range of subjects. In *Memoirs of the life of Agrippina, the wife of Germanicus* (1804) she drew on her reading, in translation, of Tacitus's *Annals of the Roman Empire* to represent a female historical figure that expressed universal philosophical ideas. At the same time, she offered a "conjectural history" of women that merged national and Christian aspirations. In the same year, Hamilton settled in Edinburgh where she served as tutor to the daughters of a Scottish aristocrat, an experience that became the basis for her next work, *Letters addressed to the Daughters of a Nobleman on the Formation of the Religious and the Moral Principle* (1806), and resulted in a royal pension for promoting "religious sentiment."

In 1808, Hamilton published her most popular book, *The Cottagers of Glenburnie: A Tale for the Farmer's Ingle-nook*. Maria Edgeworth praised its realistic portrayal of human nature and local customs, and its benevolent satire. Although written in Scottish dialect, it sold widely. This was followed by *Exercises in Religious Knowledge* (1809), *A Series of Popular Essays Illustrative of Principles Connected with the Improvement of the Understanding, the Imagination and the Heart* (1813), and *Hints addressed to Patrons and Directors of Schools* (1815). When Hamilton died in 1816, Maria Edgeworth, it is thought, wrote her obituary for *The Gentleman's Magazine*. She lauded Hamilton's character and principles, particularly where these benefited "the cause of female literature ... by setting the example ... of that uniform propriety of conduct, and of all those domestic virtues ... which ought to characterize her sex."

LETTERS ON THE ELEMENTARY PRINCIPLES OF EDUCATION (1801; REPRINTED 1818)

In the cultural debate following the French Revolution, Hamilton positioned herself as a conservative loyalist. *Letters on the Elementary Principles of Education* followed *Memoirs of Modern Philosophers* in 1801. *Letters* condemned the intellectual pretensions and unseemly public ambitions of Wollstonecraft, Hays, and their female associates. Hamilton argued that "By far the greater part of those, who have hitherto taken upon them to stand forth as champions for sexual equality, have done it upon grounds that to me appear indefensible, if not absurd."[13]

Nevertheless, Hamilton's position on women's mental competence is more nuanced than her critique might suggest. She argues against "Contempt for the Female Character" and against "sexual prejudice." She agrees with Hays and Wollstonecraft about the dire condition of women's education. Although Hamilton pointedly attacks Hays, she endorses Wollstonecraft's critique of Rousseau, published in Wollstonecraft's *A Vindication of the Rights of Woman* (1792). Hamilton concurs with Wollstonecraft about the social benefits of training women "for self-sufficiency and usefulness" and of employing single women. Nonetheless, she does not look to improvements in female education to make revolutionary changes in gender relations or society in general. She is intent on equipping women better to fulfil their Christian roles.

Letters on the Elementary Principles of Education (1801)

Elizabeth Hamilton

LETTER IX
ASSOCIATIONS DESTRUCTIVE OF BENEVOLENCE

Pernicious Effects of Partiality.—Of Ridicule.—Of Contempt for the Female Character.

The disposition to benevolence is sown and nourished in the grateful soil of family affection. Where children are educated upon sensible principles, so that their wills are not perpetually clashing with each other, mutual affection must naturally spring from sympathy in each other's joys, and the pleasure derived from each other's society. But this affection is too often nipped in the bud by the canker of parental partiality.

Children are so far conscious of their *rights,* as to feel they have an equal claim to the parent's tenderness and affection. Where this claim is not allowed, and capricious fondness singles out some particular objects on which to lavish its regards, it never fails to produce the worst consequences both on the favoured and neglected parties. In the former it engenders pride and arrogance, in the latter it brings forth indignation and hatred; and destroys the sense of justice in both. It too often happens, that personal defects, or personal charms, occasion this unfortunate bias in the mother's mind. Sometimes that briskness which is so frequently mistaken for genius, or that slowness which is confounded with stupidity, becomes an excuse for partiality or dislike; and sometimes no excuse is attempted, but the sensible one, that "it is a feeling which cannot be helped!"

Whatever may be the motive assigned for partiality to a favourite, or for dislike to an unfavoured child, the mother who indulges her feeling with regard to either, may be assured she is guilty of a crime of no light dye. She, in the first place, breaks the bonds of family affection and sows the seeds of discord among her children, which, as they grow up, produce envy, jealousy, and perpetual recurrence of strife. Home is thus made a scene of displacency and discontent; than which nothing can be more inimical to the feelings of benevolence.

If the injury done to the rest of her offspring make a slight impression on the mother's heart, the injury done to the favourite by her ill-judged partiality is surely worthy her attention. Let the partial mother consider, that she is not only perverting the heart of her beloved darling by the introduction of all the passions connected with pride and arrogance, but, by rendering him an object of jealousy and envy, is begetting towards him the hatred and aversion of those, to whom in after life he ought naturally to look for solace and support; that she may be the means of depriving his youth of the blessing of fraternal affection, and his old age of the consolations of fraternal sympathy.

184

Nor is it the affection and good-will of his own family alone of which she robs him. No one can regard a spoiled child but with feelings of dislike. The faults which good-nature would overlook, the blemishes which compassion would regard with tenderness, become odious and revolting, when seen in the object of blind and doting partiality. Can a mother compensate by her endearments for thus depriving her child of the good-will of brothers, sisters, relations, and friends?

The child who finds itself the object of dislike to every one besides, will, it is true, be induced to cling to her whom alone it perceives itself an object of affection; and this exclusive preference is so pleasing to self-love, that a weak mother is sufficiently gratified by the expression of it, without troubling herself to examine the principles from which it flows.

In families where connubial harmony has not survived the honey-moon, wherein mutual esteem and mutual complacency have given place to the little jealousies of prerogative and the splenetic humours of contradiction, it is no uncommon thing to see the well-being and happiness of children sacrificed to the spirit of contention. In such families whatever incurs reproof or reprehension from one of the parties, is excused or applauded by the other. Whenever this species of counteraction takes place, we may bid adieu to all improvement, and, alas, how few are the number of families in which it does not in some degree take place! Even where the sentiments of father and mother completely harmonize, the children may still experience the baneful effects of the counteractions alluded to, in the extenuation of the faults complained of by the governess or master. Every attempt at such extenuation is matter of triumph to the faulty child, increases the strength of pride in its little bosom, and produces a feeling of malignity towards the accuser, which may easily degenerate into habitual malice. No association can be more injurious than that which connects the ideas of malignant intention with every discovery of our faults, and leads us to attribute to goodness of heart every instance of blindness to our imperfections. To prevent the formation of this fatal association, children ought to be made sensible, that a perception of their faults does not diminish the love or regard of those by whom they are most clearly seen.

The feelings of benevolence will neither be uniform nor extensive in their operation, unless they are supported by a strong sense of justice. For this end, the necessity and propriety of practising the rule of "doing as they would be done by," ought to be early and forcibly inculcated on the minds of children; and as opportunities of inculcating it daily and hourly occur, they ought never to be passed in silence.

When a child has received pleasure from the complaisance of a companion, or been gratified by an act of kindness or generosity, an appeal ought instantly be made to his feelings, and the duty of contributing in a similar manner to the happiness of others, enforced at the moment when the mind is in a proper tone for the exercise of the sympathetic affections. When he has received any hurt or injury, instead of soothing his angry passions by taking part in his quarrel, the opportunity ought to be seized for recalling to his mind the petty injuries he may have inflicted on a companion on some former occasion, and thus inspiring him with a regard for the feelings of others.

An early and deep-founded sense of justice, is the proper soil wherein to nourish every moral virtue. Nor is it more essential towards the culture of the heart, than of the understanding. When we come to investigate the faculty of judgment, we shall have a fuller view of its important consequences. At present I shall only urge the necessity of paying a strict attention to those early habits and associations, by which the sense of justice is diminished or destroyed.

I have already endeavoured to point out the danger of permitting young persons to attach ideas of contempt to any person, on account of involuntary defects, peculiar manners, or peculiar sentiments. Wherever contempt is felt, it must be accompanied with a consciousness of superiority; and if this consciousness of superiority be built on a bad foundation, pride and arrogance are the inevitable consequences.

What, then, shall we say for those parents, who encourage their children in a practice by which all the feelings of contempt, pride, and arrogance, are inspired and cherished? You will here anticipate my mention of mimicry and ridicule, which is often applauded in children as a proof of wit, while in reality it is the worst of folly.

Ridicule is a sacred weapon, which ought never to be lightly wielded. When applied to as the means of exposing sophistry, it is sanctioned by truth and justice; though, even then, the person who dares to use it ought to be assuredly purified from every sinister motive.

By children it can never be applied to any useful purpose; while, from the particular light in which it places the object of it to their imaginations, the judgment is perverted, and the nice feelings of moral justice completely destroyed.

Children who are brought up at great schools, seldom, I believe, escape this vice. The under-teachers at such seminaries are, in general, considered as butts, at which the darts of ridicule may be lawfully shot. Thus the infant wit is whetted by malignity; the mind is corrupted, and rendered callous to every generous sentiment, while obstinacy and self-conceit lead to all the errors of presumption.

Would we implant the sense of justice in the heart, we must vigilantly guard it against those prejudices, which effectually check its growth, and prevent its ever coming to maturity. Of this nature, in my opinion, are those which originate in the early distinction that is made between the sexes, from which boys acquire ideas of an inherent superiority, grafted on pride, and supported by selfishness.

The foolish partiality, which some mothers evince toward their male offspring, is sometimes such as would induce a spectator to think they have embraced the opinion vulgarly attributed to Mahommed, and have been taught to believe that men only have souls; and that the female children, whom God has sent them, have been brought into the world for no other purpose than to contribute to the pleasure, and submit to the authority, of the lords of creation. Were this, indeed, the case, it would still behoove the tender mother to consider, that, till the age when this decided and incontrovertible superiority in every natural endowment was unequivocally displayed, a boy might be taught to respect the feelings of the companion in the sister, without injury to his inherent dignity; and that the early sense of justice thus acquired, would produce habits of urbanity highly favourable to his happiness as well as to his virtue.

Christian mothers cannot, for their partiality, plead the same excuse that may be offered in favour of the Mahommedan. She who believes her daughters and her sons to be equally born heirs of immortality, equally favoured in the sight of the Most High, equally endowed with all that can exalt and ennoble human nature—the means of grace, and the hope of glory; she who considers eternal misery as the consequence of vice, and eternal happiness as the reward of virtue, cannot show the preference of superior regard and affection on account of sex, independently of mental qualification, without a manifest dereliction of religious principle. Yet so powerful are first impressions, so strongly rooted are the prejudices of our education, that not even religion itself, no, not in minds where it is deeply cherished, can prevail against them. These are the tares which the enemy has sown while we slept; and which will continue to grow up with the wheat till the great and general harvest. Alas! who can tell how many of the opinions, we now so fondly cherish, may then be found in the number? "By far the greater part of the opinions, on which we act in life, are not (says Stewart) the result of our own investigations; but are adopted implicitly in infancy and youth, upon the authority of others. When a child hears either a speculative absurdity, or an erroneous principle of action, recommended and enforced daily by the same voice which first conveyed to it those simple and sublime lessons of morality and religion, which are congenial to its nature, is it to be wondered at, that in future life it should find it so difficult to eradicate prejudices, which have twined their roots with all the essential principles of the human frame?" That a contempt of the female nature, and an overweening conceit of the essential superiority of that of the male, are of the number of these hereditary prejudices, will, I imagine, be no difficult matter to prove. Though as it is a prejudice that has "twined its roots," not only with the essential principles, but with the strongest passions of his nature, the hopes of eradicating it must be faint and remote.

The obstinacy of prejudices received from early association, is commonly in proportion to the mixture of truth with error. Had nature, indeed, made no distinction in the mental endowments of the sexes, the prejudice alluded to would long since have yielded to conviction; but the distinction made by nature, which is merely such as to render each sex most fit and capable to fulfil the duties of its peculiar sphere, confers neither superiority on the one, nor degradation on the other. Of all that is truly worthy, of all that is truly estimable, in the sight of God and man, both sexes are capable alike. Excited to similar virtue by similar motives, exposed to similar temptations by similar passions and frailties, would it not be wise, if, instead of strengthening these passions by mutual jealousy concerning objects of comparatively small importance, they endeavoured to be mutually instrumental in the support of each other's virtue? This, I am convinced, would be much more commonly the case, were it not for the prevalence of that prejudice, which teaches even boys to regard females with contempt, as being of an inferior order.

187

All the prejudices which originate in early association, are for a time deemed obvious and incontrovertible truths, discovered by the light of nature. Thus, while the West-Indian planter judges the jetty skin of the negro a mark of inferiority inscribed by the hand of the Great Creator, to point out the immensity of the distance between him and his sable brethren; the African, seated under the bentang tree of his native village, and listening to the tale of the stranger, regards the white skin of the European with disgust and horror, as the signet of nature stamped with the character of cruelty and cunning. Thus too does man, in every nation, and in every stage of society, from the associations of his infancy, attach to the weakness arising from the more delicate structure of the female frame, ideas of contempt and inferiority.

In order to analyze this prejudice, it is necessary to trace it to its source, that is to say, to the *savage state*, in which it evidently originated; for in the savage state bodily strength gives an indisputable title to superiority. Man is, in this state, distinguished from the brute, chiefly by the possession of improvable faculties: but this is a latent treasure, of which he is long insensible; and while he remains in ignorance, he is, in some respects, beneath his brothers of the field. The lion brings not his weaker mate into a state of slavish subjection, but, inspired by instinct, lays at her feet the spoils his strength and courage have procured; while the savage, his inferior in all but pride and cruelty, treats the miserable partner of his hut with contumelious disdain and rigorous oppression. The poor female, subdued by habitual wretchedness to habitual submission, acquiesces in her miserable destiny; and while she teaches her daughters to submit with cheerfulness to the doom of slavery, she inspires her sons with savage notions of their own comparative importance, and glories in the first indications of their haughtiness and ferocity; dispositions with which she associates the ideas of strength and valour, which comprise all that is in her view great and honourable.

As society advances in its progress toward civilization, the mental powers begin to rise into importance; but the associations of contempt, which the inferiority, with regard to physical strength, had originally generated, continue to operate, and debar females from those opportunities of improvement, which gradually open on the other sex. Thus we still find in many nations of Asia, where society is advanced to a considerable degree of refinement, this refinement entirely confined to the men; the women being still destined to all the miseries of ignorance and slavery. Thus throughout the world, while man advanced in knowledge and science, from merely physical to rational life, women were doomed to remain stationary; till the distance between the sexes was deemed as great with regard to mental endowments in the civilized state, as it had been with respect to personal strength in the savage.

A lively picture is given by the Easter writers, of the consequences of this continued degradation of the female character. It is, however, worthy of remark, that the vices of which they uniformly accuse women are the vices of slaves; and that while innate depravity is by them constantly attributed to the sex, the cause of this depravity is never once hinted at, though it must be sufficiently obvious to every unprejudiced mind.

A more enlightened policy than was ever known to Oriental wisdom elevated the European nations of antiquity to nobler sentiments, and more enlarged views; but so deeply rooted are the prejudices of early association, nourished by habit, and strengthened by the pride of power, that neither legislator, philosopher, priest, or poet, appears to have been superior to their control. The prejudices of the savage state, with regard to women, continued to operate on the enlightened sages of the Grecian and Roman world, even while, in the intercourse of social life, the minds of the females of Greece and Rome acquired a degree of improvement, which elevated their sentiments to high notions of honour and virtue. The improvement was casual, the effect transient. The virtue, that is merely the effect of imitation, cannot be expected to survive its model. Never taught to consider themselves as having an inherent interest in the cultivation of their faculties, they learned to value their virtues and accomplishments, not as intrinsically their own, but as shedding a lustre on the house from which they sprung, or on that to which they were allied. Virtues built on such a shallow foundation might be brilliant, but could not be comprehensive or durable. It was, however, the only foundation, which the pride of man, in the most advanced state of human knowledge, allowed for female virtue; nor did it ever enter in the heart of the most philanthropic sage, to place it on the same foundation as his own.

That to which human philanthropy and human wisdom were unequal, was accomplished by Divine.

Were there no other proofs of the superiority of our blessed Saviour to the wisest of the sons of men, his superiority to all the prejudices of his age, and country, and sex, and situation, would, I think, be sufficient to prove him more than human.

By making the purification of the heart, and the subjugation of the passions, alike the duty of all, he broke down the barrier which pride and prejudice had placed between the sexes. He elevated the weaker, not by the pride of intellect, but by the dignity of virtue. He changed the associations of honour and esteem from the *nature of the duty* to its due performance; and promised eternal life as the reward, not of great talents or elegant accomplishments, not of valour, or of renown, or of worldly wisdom, but of a pure faith, producing a pure heart and undefiled conscience.

So far did this doctrine operate, that wherever it was embraced, it procured for women, as heirs of immortality, a degree of respect to which the philosophy of Greece and Rome had never elevated them.

But the doctrine of Christ was embraced nominally by millions, who remained strangers to the spirit of its precepts. It was made to bend to human passions and human prejudices, with which it was so blended, as to become distorted and disgraced. The instructions which our Saviour and his Apostles addressed indiscriminately to the poor and to the rich, to the learned and the ignorant, to *men* and to *women*, were supposed, in process of time, to be incomprehensible to all but the priesthood, which arrogated to itself the privilege of explaining them. The explanations being generally tinctured by prejudice, and not unfrequently by prejudices of the impurest sort, originating in the selfish passions, were opposed, contested, censured, till the passions were inflamed into resentment; and both parties became infinitely more zealous for the establishment of their own particular explanations, than for the diffusion of the spirit of the Gospel. Had that spirit continued to preserve its influence on the human heart, great is the alteration which would have undoubtedly been produced on the human character. But instead of subduing the passions that opposed it, these passions were enlisted in support of what was called by its name. Prejudices, which the example and doctrines of our Divine Master would have completely overthrown, became thus in a manner sanctified by their alliance with superstition; and selfishness continued to justify injustice. That the prejudices of the savage state should continue to prevail in the ages of barbarism, when the light shed by the Christian dispensation was veiled in impenetrable darkness, is not surprising; but that these prejudices should continue to prevail after this veil was removed, appears a little extraordinary, though the cause may easily be ascertained.

When the light of science began to illumine our long-benighted hemisphere, and the art of printing diffused those treasures of knowledge, which had been a useless deposit in the hands of ignorance and superstition, an enthusiastic admiration of the writings of the ancients was generally inspired. Devoted to the study of heathen wisdom, men forgot, or lightly esteemed, the fountain of truth; they beheld it agitated by theological controversy, and polluted by theological prejudice, and turned from it with disgust; not permitting themselves to examine, whether a stream so polluted could have its source in Divine perfection.—The consequence has long been, still is, and may long continue, fatal to the cause of sound morality and virtue.

However the study of the classics may have opened the understanding, enlarged the views, and elevated the sentiments of men, it is to be feared, that many prejudices have flowed from the same source, which are inconsistent with the spirit of the religion we profess; prejudices that are inimical to that spirit, at variance with the whole tenor of our Saviour's precepts, and the cause of a

189

perpetual and manifest inconsistency between the practice and profession of Christians. These prejudices have thrown a shade of ignominy over the mild glories of humility, meekness, and mercy; and exalted pride and revenge into the rank of virtues: They have substituted the love of glory for the love of truth, emblazoned the crimes of ambition with the lustre of renown, and taught man to prefer the applause of a giddy multitude to the approbation of his God. By introducing false associations of regard and preference, with adventitious circumstances, altogether foreign to the moral character, as learning, strength, valour, power, &c. they have destroyed the just criterion of human worth, and given to situation, which marks the nature of the duty to be performed, that respect which is morally due to the just performance of duty. These prejudices have all an evident tendency to continue and perpetuate the ideas of sexual superiority, which would infallibly have been destroyed by the pure morality of the Gospel. They have gratified the pride of man at the expense of his virtue.

With a contempt for the female sex, on account of this fancied inferiority, has been associated a contempt for those moral qualities, which are allowed to constitute the perfection of the female character. Meekness, gentleness, temperance, and chastity; that command over the passions which is obtained by frequent self-denial; and that willingness to sacrifice every selfish wish, and every selfish feeling, to the happiness of others, which is the consequence of subdued self-will, and the cultivation of the social and benevolent affections; are considered as feminine virtues, derogatory to the dignity of the manly character. Nay, further. By this unfortunate association has religion itself come into disgrace; devotional sentiment is considered as a mere adjunct of female virtue, suitable to the weakness of the female mind, *and for that reason* disgraceful to the superior wisdom of man. At the thought of *judgment* to *come,* women, like Felix, may learn to tremble; and, in order to avert the consequences of Divine displeasure, may study the practice of that righteousness and temperance recommended by the Apostle to his royal auditor: but while the Christian graces are associated with that contempt which the idea of inferiority inspires, neither righteousness, nor temperance, nor judgment to come, will be considered as worthy of consideration in the mind of man.

This unhappy prejudice is in some respects far less injurious to the female than to the male. The obedience which they are taught to pay to authority, the submission with which they are made to bow to arrogance and injustice, produce habits of self-denial favourable to disinterestedness, meekness, and humility; dispositions which are allied to every species of moral excellence. And so seldom do these amiable dispositions fail to be produced by the subjugation of self-will, in females who have been properly educated, that in combating the prejudice which throws contempt upon the female character, I shall be found to plead the cause of the other sex rather than of my own.—Every prejudice founded in selfishness and injustice inevitably corrupts the mind, and every act of tyranny resulting from it debases the human character; but submission "for conscience sake," even to the highest degree of tyranny and injustice, is an act, not of meanness, but of magnanimity. Instead of murmuring at the circumstances under which they are placed, women ought early to be taught to turn those very circumstances to their advantage, by rendering them conducive to the cultivation of all the milder virtues. And this they would not fail to do, unless they were made to participate in those prejudices which I have humbly attempted to explain, and to expose.

By far the greater part of those, who have hitherto taken upon them to stand forth as champions for sexual equality, have done it upon grounds that to me appear indefensible, if not absurd. It is not an equality of moral worth for which they contend, and which is the only true object of regard; not for an equality of rights, with respect to the Divine favour, which alone elevates the human character into dignity and importance; but for an equality of employments and avocations, founded upon the erroneous idea of a perfect similarity of powers. Infected by the prejudices which associate ideas of honour and esteem with knowledge and science, independent of moral virtue, and envious of the short-lived glories of ambition, they desire for their sex an admission into the theatre of public life, and wish to qualify them for it by an education in every respect similar to that of men. Men scoff at their pretences, and hold their presumption in abhorrence; but men do not consider, that these pretences, and that presumption, have been caught from the false notions of importance which they have themselves affixed to their own particular avocations. Taught, from earliest infancy, to arrogate to themselves a claim of inherent superiority, this idea attaches itself to all the studies and pursuits which custom has exclusively assigned them. These prejudices operating likewise on the minds of women, it is not surprising, that those who perceive in themselves a capacity for attaining a high degree of intellectual eminence, should aspire to be sharers in those honours, which they have been taught by the pride of men to regard as supreme distinction. Were both sexes guarded from the admission of early prejudice, and taught to value themselves on no superiority but that of virtue, these vain and idle jealousies would cease; man would become more worthy, and woman more respectable. Were these prejudices annihilated, the virtues of temperance and chastity would not in the mind of man be associated with ideas of contempt, as merely proper to be observed by the inferior part of the species; nor would habits of licentiousness be considered as a light and venial evil, but regarded with the same horror which is happily still attached to female depravity.

Of the licentiousness of one sex, however, the depravity of the other is the natural and certain consequence. Accustomed to acquiesce in the idea of man's superiority in all wisdom and perfection, women cease to respect those laws of decency and reserve, which they perceive it the glory of the other sex to set at defiance. They learn to consider the restrictions of chastity as the fetters of worldly prudence; and as those, to whom they are accustomed to look up, as beings of a superior order, scoff at that religion which teaches purity of heart, as well as manners, they likewise learn to regard it with contempt. The *believing wife* is, from the prejudices of early association, considered as too much inferior, in point of intellect and intelligence, to have any chance of converting the *unbelieving husband;* while a thousand to one are in favour of the unbelieving husband's perverting the believing wife!

If such are the consequences of sexual prejudice, it becomes the duty of every parent, who is anxious for the temporal and eternal happiness of the beings intrusted to her care, to guard against its introduction into the infant mind. For this end, she must carefully and conscientiously maintain a strict impartiality in the distribution of favour and affection. There must be no separate rules of discipline; no system of individual and partial indulgence, nor partial restriction, nor partial exemption; but one law of propriety, decency, modesty, and simplicity; one rule of humble submission and cheerful obedience. Boys and girls must equally be made to perceive, that there is but one path to approbation and esteem, *the path of duty;* and made to feel that they are approved of and esteemed on no other principle.

I can see no good reason why, in early life, their tasks and instructions should not be the same. Is it because the superior portion of reason supposed to be inherent in man is so very evidently equal to the government of his passions, that we think we may safely neglect in infancy the culture of his heart? Or has the instinctive faculty of imitation proved so efficient a guide to the other sex; has it always so certainly led to the performance of the important duties assigned to females in civilized society, as to justify us in withholding from them the advantages of mental cultivation? Such seems to have been the opinions on which the common practice has been founded. But before we implicitly adopt them, it is surely proper to ascertain, whether they have originated in prejudice, or have been justified by long and ample experience.

The pride and arrogance, which boys acquire from early ideas of inherent superiority, are greatly increased by the premature distinction that is made between their pursuits and avocations, and those of girls. The trifling accomplishments, to which the girls are devoted, they despise as irrational; while consciousness of the superior dignity of that species of knowledge into which they are early initiated, augments their supercilious disdain, and increases the idea of the distance that is placed between them. They soon cease to tolerate them as companions, but regard them as incumbrances, at once troublesome and despicable.

In men of little minds this early-acquired contempt for the female character takes deep and lasting root. It is an everlasting source of consolation to their pride, and a happy excuse for the exercise of a selfish tyranny over the unfortunate females of their families. Where the mind is enlightened and the heart is generous, this early prejudice will cease to operate; but its strength is not always in proportion to the weakness of the character. To what but to this early prejudice, can we ascribe the conduct of some men of sense, in the most important concern of life? Having never experienced any pleasure in female society but through the medium of passion, by passion only are they guided in the choice of a connexion sacred and indissoluble. Passion is short-lived; but when passion is no more, a sense of common interest, habit, and necessity, happily unite their forces to keep off wretchedness. Without their powerful aid, how miserable must existence drag on in the society of a person, with whom there is no intercourse of intellect, no interchange of sentiment, no similarity of taste, no common object of pursuit, no common subject of conversation! To be tied to one week of such society would be misery. What, then, shall we say to those, who voluntarily tie themselves to it for life? To the children of such marriages the contempt for the female character is inevitable. It is with them an hereditary sentiment, confirmed by the father's conduct, and the mother's folly. In such families, it may easily be supposed, that a distinction will soon be made between the boys and girls; a distinction, which if it prove injurious to the male, is no less fatal to the female mind.

By the early association above described, girls learn to place the virtues recommended to their practice on an improper basis; not founded on immutable truth, but on worldly notions of prudence and propriety. It is in reality *manners,* not *morals,* which they thus acquire. Opinion is the idol they are taught to worship. Opinion is their rule of life, their law of virtue; and fashion, their only test of propriety. Hence we behold decency outraged in the dress and behaviour of women, who assume the appellation of virtuous! We behold modesty depending on the caprice of fashion; and by the ease with which it is plucked up by the roots at her decree, we may judge of the lightness of the soil in which it was planted.

By these early associations, which render opinion the test of truth, the female mind is so much perverted, as to render it in some degree dangerous for us to rise above the prejudices of education. For want of proper notions of the immutability of moral truth, females, who have had sufficient strength of mind to emancipate themselves from the dominion of opinion, have sometimes been seen to despise the virtues they had in early life learned to associate with it, and to pique themselves on a dereliction of the peculiar duties of their sex and station. From these examples, plausible arguments have been formed against the cultivation of the female mind. But a more enlarged view of the subject would afford different conclusions. Where judicious care has been exercised in the cultivation of the moral and intellectual faculties in early life, the respect for virtue is placed on a more permanent foundation. The female who is taught an early and habitual respect to the laws of God, and has acquired just notions of moral obligation, will, by every step in the cultivation of her reason, acquire fresh motives to the practice of her duties, and will, at the same time, be preserved from the vanity which is so prone to over-rate the value of every attainment.

By the early distinction that is made between the sexes, the idea of a distinct and separate code of morality is inevitably inspired; and if the consequences of this idea be such as I have represented them, it is incumbent on parents to consider how the evil may be avoided. Far am I from considering the preservation of female delicacy as a matter of slight importance; but it is in the purity of the heart, and not in a deference to public opinion, that I would fix its basis. To guard the purity of the heart from spot or blemish, is, in a private family, brought up under the eye of a judicious parent, no difficult task.*

193

---

* There is no point in which the conduct of servants toward children ought to be more severely scrutinized, than in that to which I now allude; for in none do I believe it more generally reprehensible. Would we have delicacy fixed in the heart, infancy itself must be treated with decency and respect.

But the purity that depends solely on innocent ignorance, is liable to be soiled on the slightest exposure. It may be contaminated by chance, and receive a lasting stain through the medium of a natural curiosity. It is not by mere ignorance of evil, that genuine delicacy can be inspired. If pains be not taken, at an early period of life, firmly to associate the ideas of personal delicacy and personal decency with the ideas of propriety and virtue, and to attach ideas of shame and remorse to the smallest breach of the laws of decorum, our pupils may remain personally unpolluted from principle, but they will have little chance of being numbered with the "pure of heart."

194

It is, I am well convinced, only by attaching ideas of disgust and abhorrence to every sentiment, every circumstance, and every idea, which can tend to soil the purity of the imagination, that we can hope to inspire that species of delicacy, which, like the beautiful armour that nature has bestowed upon some plants and flowers, is at once a guard and ornament. Let it be firmly fixed in the mind, by the methods I have mentioned, let it be strengthened by frequent communication with the Author of all purity and all perfection, and we need entertain no apprehension, that it will be injured by learning, or contaminated by science. Often, I fear, is this delicacy a stranger to the hearts of those, who nevertheless assume its appearance. But where it is only assumed, it will, like other parts of dress, obey the decrees of fashion, and be reserved for particular occasions; whereas the sensibility arising from unsoiled purity is seen

> "In all the thousand decencies that flow
> From ev'ry word and action."

The delicacy that is produced by association, and confirmed by religious principle will be found as superior to the spurious sort born of affectation and sentiment, (which is often only another word for affection,) as reality is to fiction. The former is unalterable and undeviating, while the latter is ever liable to be contaminated by the contagion of example, and to vary with situation and circumstances.

Modesty has been with much truth and propriety represented as the first ornament of the female mind; but it may be questioned, whether both sexes have not been injured by considering it as a *sexual* virtue. Why should not boys be inspired with the feelings of delicacy as well as girls? Why should the early corruption of their imagination be deemed a matter of light importance? What do we gain by attaching ideas of manliness and spirit to depravity of heart and manners? Alas, many and fatal are the errors, which may be traced to this unfortunate association! Let it be the endeavour of my friends to guard their sons from its pernicious effects; and may they in their future lives evince, that dignity of conduct, elevation of sentiment, and refinement of taste, are connected with modesty, purity, and virtue! Adieu.

ENDNOTES

1 Claire Grogan, "Introduction," in *Memoirs of Modern Philosophers*, by Elizabeth Hamilton, ed. Claire Grogan (1800; repr., Peterborough, ON: Broadview Press, 2000), 12.

2 Elizabeth Benger, *Memoirs of the Late Mrs. Elizabeth Hamilton with a Selection from Her Correspondence, and Other Unpublished Writings* (London: Longman, Hurst, Rees, Orme, and Brown, 1818), 1: 32–33.

3 Pamela Perkins and Shannon Russell, "Introduction," in *Translations of the Letters of a Hindoo Rajah*, by Elizabeth Hamilton (Peterborough, ON: Broadview Press, 1999), 8.

4 Benger took the occasion at this point in her memoir to urge that "day-schools on a similar plan be established under female supervision." Benger, *Memoirs*, 1: 37.

5 Benger, *Memoirs*, 1: 44–45.

6 Jane Rendall, "'Writing History for British Women': Elizabeth Hamilton and *The Memoirs of Agrippina*," in *Wollstonecraft's Daughter: Womanhood in England and France 1780–1920*, ed. Clarissa Campbell Orr (Manchester: Manchester University Press, 1996).

7 Perkins writes, "*Translations of the Letters of a Hindoo Rajah* (1796), is in part a tribute to Charles." Pamela Perkins, "Elizabeth Hamilton," *The Literary Encyclopedia*, first published online July 17, 2001 by The Literary Dictionary Company, http://www.litencyc.com/php/speople.php?rec=true&UID=1957 (accessed October 24, 2005).

8 Five editions of the novel were published between 1796 and 1811. An American edition appeared in 1819 (see Perkins and Russell, 51). For the unfavourable review, see [Mary Hays], "Art. XL," Review of *Translation of the Letters of a Hindoo Rajah; written previous to, and during the Period of his Residence in England*, by Elizabeth Hamilton, *Analytical Review* (October 1796): 429.

9 Rendall, "Writing History."

10 Benger, *Memoirs*, 1: 129–30.

11 Jane Rendall, "'Women that would plague me with rational conversation': Aspiring Women and Scottish Wigs, c. 1790–1830," in Women, *Gender and Enlightenment*, ed. Barbara Taylor and Sarah Knott (Basingstoke, Hampshire: Palgrave Macmillan, 2005), 338–39.

12 Grogan, "Introduction," 15. Readers responded so enthusiastically that a second edition appeared later the same year, a third edition in early 1801, and a fourth edition in 1804.

13 Elizabeth Hamilton, *Letters on the Elementary Principles of Education* (1801; repr., London: Baldwin, Cradock, and Joy, 1818), 171–73.

Catharine Macaulay Graham (1731–1791)

Catharine Macaulay Graham (1731–91) contributed to scholarship in a variety of fields. Her main biographical profile can be found in Part 1.

LETTERS ON EDUCATION WITH OBSERVATIONS ON RELIGIOUS AND METAPHYSICAL SUBJECTS (1790)

Macaulay's book *Letters on Education* articulates her views on the formation of responsible citizens through an educational training in ethics. Many of her prescriptions in terms of method follow the sensationalist views of John Locke and Jean-Jacques Rousseau. Children should learn from experience and according to their various stages of development. However in Letters XXI–XXIII, Macaulay, like Mary Wollstonecraft in her *A Vindication of the Rights of Woman* (1792), attacks Rousseau's views on the innate intellectual and moral differences of the sexes. What Janet Todd has termed "the extraordinary education in narcissistic passivity and cultural sexualization given to Sophie" (Rousseau's heroine) constituted a flagrant contradiction in his educational theory, otherwise based on a Lockean rejection of innate ideas.[1] In Book V of *Émile*, Rousseau argued that, while nature had decreed that women were created to please and serve men, they nonetheless required a rigorous training in submission to fulfil this predestined role. Macaulay condemns the moral assumptions in Rousseau's argument as absurd, illogical, and evidence of a warped eroticism. "It is pride and sensuality that speaks in Rousseau, and, in this instance, has lowered the man of genius to the licentious pedant" (Letter XXII).

Letter XXI concerns the ethical imperatives she believes should inform educational theory and practice. Since, in Macaulay's view, virtue is immutable, both sexes should be educated equally, according to the same principles, in order to attain the greatest possible moral perfectibility. Because Rousseau had posited radically different natures for male and female, he was driven to posit different moral universes for them. Macaulay, like Poulain de la Barre a century earlier, agreed that "the soul/mind has no sex nor does virtue."[2]

Letters XXII and XXIII concern the "vices and imperfections, that have been regarded as inseparable from the female character," but which Macaulay argues are the result of acculturation. In this cultural critique, Macaulay, like Rousseau, Kant, Wollstonecraft, and most writers on "woman," conflated gender with class or status. The idle, vain, frivolous, physically fragile women of whom she writes are predominately women of the leisured and moneyed classes. The mass of the female population, who performed heavy physical labour in all sectors of the workforce, thereby giving the lie to the myth of female weakness, would have had neither the time nor the means for the frivolities Macaulay enumerates. Yet the alleged social failings and physical weaknesses of wealthy women continued to figure as innate female qualities in discussions about women's education and potential. Macaulay's contribution to feminist thinking in these letters was to make a powerful case for women's emancipation both through legal and educational reform. Women, if liberated from their debasing subservience to men, a subservience based on a toxic mixture of fear and vanity, could become moral persons and responsibly free citizens.

Letters on Education with Observations on Religious and Metaphysical Subjects (1790)

Catharine Macaulay Graham

LETTER XXI

Morals must be taught on immutable Principles.

It is one thing, Hortensia, to educate a citizen, and another to educate a philosopher. The mere citizen will have learnt to obey the laws of his country, but he will never understand those principles on which all laws ought to be established; and without such an understanding, he can never be religious on rational principles, or truly moral; nor will he ever have any of that active wisdom which is necessary for co-operating in any plan of reformation. But to teach morals on an immutable fitness, has never been the practice of any system of education yet extant. Hence all our notions of right and wrong are loose, unconnected, and inconsistent. Hence the murderer, in one situation, is extolled to the skies; and, in another, is followed with reproach even beyond the grave. For it is not only the man of the world who idolises power, though in the garb of villainy, and persecutes dishonesty when united to weakness, but even those who bear the specious title of philosophers are apt to be dazzled with the brilliancy of success, and to treat qualities and characters differently, according to the smiles or frowns of fortune.

As an instance, to illustrate this observation, I will select out of the huge mass of human inconsistencies, the praises bestowed by Xenophon on Cyrus; who, whether a real or fictitious character, is set up by this philosopher as a model of princely perfection.

Cyrus, it is true, is represented as moderate in the gratification of his appetites, liberal to his followers, and just, when he found justice correspond with his interest; but, as himself confesses, he never practised any virtue on other principles but those of personal utility; and he animates his countrymen to exertions, which he dignifies with this title, on motives of obtaining means, by the spoils of others, for future enjoyment. In short, Cyrus was neither liberal from generosity, just from honesty, nor merciful from benevolence; and the address he made use of to enslave the minds of his subjects, is of the same kind as that used by a courtezan to extend and preserve her influence over the hearts of those she has trepanned into her snares. Cyrus was master of all those arts which are necessary to obtain and preserve to himself and successors an unjust measure of power; he enflamed with this lust all his warlike followers, in order to eradicate from their minds the love of freedom and independence. His system of policy, of which many parts are atrocious outrages on the rights of Nature, established the firmest and most extensive despotism that was ever established in the East, and has, on these reasons, prevailed more or less in the Persian dynasty, and in all the governments which have been built on its ruins; yet Xenophon and Cicero, who were both republicans and philosophers, extol Cyrus to the skies. But had these men understood rectitude on the principles of truth, they must have perceived, that power never can be justly obtained but by conquest over those by whom we are first unlawfully attacked, or by such a fair influence over the mind as shall convince men that they will be safe and happy under our authority.

Cyrus is one of those plausible knaves who have been set up as models for example; and, on these reasons, he imposes on all those who do not reflect deeply. But I am convinced, that a Caesar Borgia, or a Cataline, had their characters been united with a brilliant success, would have equally imposed on the vulgar; for as Helvetius very justly observes, it is only the weakness of the poor rogue which men despise, not his dishonesty.

In order to take from public sentiment a reproach which leaves a deep stain on the human character, and to correct many irregularities, and even enormities, which arise from incorrect systems of ethics, it ought to be the first aim of education to teach virtue on immutable principles and to avoid that confusion which must arise from confounding the laws and customs of society with those obligations which are founded on correct principles of equity. But as you have had patience to go through my whole plan of education, from infancy to manhood, it is but fair that I should attend to your objections, and examine whether my plan is founded on error, or on the principles of reason and truth. Know then, good Hortensia, that I have given similar rules for male and female education, on the following grounds of reasoning.

First, That there is but one rule of right for the conduct of all rational beings; consequently that true virtue in one sex must be equally so in the other, whenever a proper opportunity calls for its exertion; and, *vice versa*, what is vice in one sex, cannot have a different property when found in the other.

Secondly, That true wisdom, which is never found at variance with rectitude, is as useful to women as to men; because it is necessary to the highest degree of happiness, which can never exist with ignorance.

Lastly, That as on our first entrance into another world, our state of happiness may possibly depend on the degree of perfection we have attained in this, we cannot justly lessen, in one sex or the other, the means by which perfection, that is another word for wisdom, is acquired.

It would be paying you a bad compliment, Hortensia, were I to answer all the frivolous objections which prejudice has framed against the giving a learned education to women; for I know of no learning, worth having, that does not tend to free the mind from error, and enlarge our stock of useful knowledge. Thus much it may be proper to observe, that those hours which are spent in studious retirement by learned women, will not in all probability intrude so much on the time for useful avocation, as the wild and spreading dissipations of the present day; that levity and ignorance will always be found in opposition to what is useful and graceful in life; and that the contrary may be expected from a truly enlightened understanding. However, Hortensia, to throw some illustration on what I have advanced on this subject, it may be necessary to shew you, that all those vices and imperfections which have been generally regarded as inseparable from the female character, do not in any manner proceed from sexual causes, but are entirely the effects of situation and education. But these observations must be left to further discussion.

200

LETTER XXII

No characteristic Difference in Sex.

The great difference that is observable in the characters of the sexes, Hortensia, as they display themselves in the scenes of social life, has given rise to much false speculation on the natural qualities of the female mind.—For though the doctrine of innate ideas, and innate affections, are in a great measure exploded by the learned, yet few persons reason so closely and so accurately on abstract subjects as, through a long chain of deductions, to bring forth a conclusion which in no respect militates with their premises.

It is a long time before the crowd give up opinions they have been taught to look upon with respect; and I know many persons who will follow you willingly through the course of your argument, till they perceive it tends to the overthrow of some fond prejudice; and then they will either sound a retreat, or begin a contest in which the contender for truth, though he cannot be overcome, is effectually silenced, from the mere weariness of answering positive assertions, reiterated without end. It is from such causes that the notion of sexual difference in the human character has, with very few exceptions, universally prevailed from the earliest times, and the pride of one sex, and the ignorance and vanity of the other, have helped to support an opinion which a close observation of Nature, and a more accurate way of reasoning, would disprove.

It must be confessed, that the virtues of the males among the human species, though mixed and blended with a variety of vices and errors, have displayed a bolder and more consistent picture of excellence than female nature has hitherto done. It is on these reasons that, when we compliment the appearance of a more than ordinary energy in the female mind, we call it masculine; and hence it is, that Pope has elegantly said *a perfect woman's but a softer man.* And if we take in the consideration, that there can be but one rule of moral excellence for beings made of the same materials, organized after the same manner, and subjected to similar laws of Nature, we must either agree with Mr. Pope, or we must reverse the proposition, and say, that *a perfect man is a woman formed after a coarser mold.* The difference that actually does subsist between the sexes, is too flattering for men to be willingly imputed to accident; for what accident occasions, wisdom might correct; and it is better, says Pride, to give up the advantages we might derive from the perfection of our fellow associates, than to own that Nature has been just in the equal distribution of her favours. These are the sentiments of the men; but mark how readily they are yielded to by the women; not from humility I assure you, but merely to preserve with character those fond vanities on which they set their hearts. No; suffer them to idolize their persons, to throw away their life in pursuit of trifles, and to indulge in the gratification of the meaner passions, and they will heartily join in the sentence of their degradation.

Among the most strenuous asserters of a sexual difference in character, Rousseau is the most conspicuous, both on account of that warmth of sentiment which distinguishes all his writings, and the eloquence of his compositions: but never did enthusiasm and the love of paradox, those enemies of philosophical disquisition, appear in more strong opposition to plain sense than in Rousseau's definition of this difference. He sets out with a supposition, that Nature intended the subjection of the one sex to the other; that consequently there must be an inferiority of intellect in the subjected party; but as man is a very imperfect being, and apt to play the capricious tyrant, Nature, to bring things nearer to an equality, bestowed on the woman such attractive graces, and such an insinuating address, as to turn the balance on the other scale. Thus Nature, in a giddy mood, recedes from her purposes, and subjects prerogative to an influence which must produce confusion and disorder in the system of human affairs. Rousseau saw this objection; and in order to obviate it, he has made up a moral person of the union of the two sexes, which, for contradiction and absurdity, outdoes every metaphysical riddle that was ever formed in the schools. In short, it is not reason, it is not wit; it is pride and sensuality that speak in Rousseau, and, in this instance, has lowered the man of genius to the licentious pedant.

But whatever might be the wise purpose intended by Providence in such a disposition of things, certain it is, that some degree of inferiority, in point of corporal strength, seems always to have existed between the two sexes; and this advantage in the barbarous ages of mankind, was abused to such a degree, as to destroy all the natural rights of the female species, and reduce them to a state of abject slavery. What accidents have contributed in Europe to better their condition, would not be in my purpose to relate; for I do not intend to give you a history of women; I mean only to trace the sources of their peculiar foibles and vices; and these I firmly believe to originate in situation and education only: for so little did a wise and just Providence intend to make the condition of slavery an unalterable law of female nature, that in the same proportion as the male sex have consulted the interest of their own happiness, they have relaxed in their tyranny over women; and such is their use in the system of mundane creation, and such their natural influence over the male mind, that were these advantages properly exerted, they might carry every point of any importance to their honour and happiness. However, till that period arrives in which women will act wisely, we will amuse ourselves in talking of their follies.

The situation and education of women, Hortensia, is precisely that which must necessarily tend to corrupt and debilitate both the powers of mind and body. From a false notion of beauty and delicacy, their system of nerves is depraved before they come out of their nursery; and this kind of depravity has more influence over the mind, and consequently over morals, than is commonly apprehended. But it would be well if such causes only acted towards the debasement of the sex; their moral education is, if possible, more absurd than their physical. The principles and nature of virtue, which is never properly explained to boys, is kept quite a mystery to girls. They are told indeed, that they must abstain from those vices which are contrary to their personal happiness, or they will be regarded as criminals, both by God and man; but all the higher parts of rectitude, every thing that ennobles our being, and that renders us both innoxious and useful, is either not taught, or is taught in such a manner as to leave no proper impression on the mind. This is so obvious a truth, that the defects of female education have ever been a fruitful topic of declamation for the moralist; but not one of this class of writers have laid down any judicious rules for amendment. Whilst we still retain the absurd notion of a sexual excellence, it will militate against the perfecting a plan of education for either sex. The judicious Addison animadverts on the absurdity of bringing a young lady up with no higher idea of the end of education than to make her agreeable to a husband, and confining the necessary excellence for this happy acquisition to the mere graces of person.

Every parent and tutor may not express himself in the same manner as is marked out by Addison; yet certain it is, that the admiration of the other sex is held out to women as the highest honour they can attain; and whilst this is considered as their *summum bonum*, and the beauty of their persons the chief *desideratum* of men, Vanity, and its companion Envy, must taint, in their characters, every native and every acquired excellence. Nor can you, Hortensia, deny, that these qualities, when united to ignorance, are fully equal to the engendering and rivetting all those vices and foibles which are peculiar to the female sex; vices and foibles which have caused them to be considered, in ancient times, as beneath cultivation, and in modern days have subjected them to the censure and ridicule of writers of all descriptions, from the deep thinking philosopher to the man of *ton* and gallantry, who, by the bye, sometimes distinguishes himself by qualities which are not greatly superior to those he despises in women. Nor can I better illustrate the truth of this observation than by the following picture, to be found in the polite and gallant Chesterfield. "Women," says his Lordship, "are only children of a larger growth. They have an entertaining tattle, sometimes wit; but for solid reasoning, and good sense, I never in my life knew one that had it, or who acted or reasoned in consequence of it for four and twenty hours together. A man of sense only trifles with them, plays with them, humours and flatters them, as he does an engaging child; but he neither consults them, nor trusts them in serious matters."

LETTER XXIII

Coquettry

Though the situation of women in modern Europe, Hortensia, when compared with that condition of abject slavery in which they have always been held in the east, may be considered as brilliant; yet if we withhold comparison, and take the matter in a positive sense, we shall have no great reason to boast of our privileges, or of the candour and indulgence of the men towards us. For with the total and absolute exclusion of every political right to the sex in general, married women, whose situation demand a particular indulgence, have hardly a civil right to save them from the grossest injuries; and though the gallantry of some of the European societies have necessarily produced indulgence, yet in others the faults of women are treated with a severity and rancour which militates against every principle of religion and common sense. Faults, my friend, I hear you say; you take the matter in too general a sense; you know there is but one fault which a woman of honour may not commit with impunity; let her only take care that she is not caught in a love intrigue, and she may lie, she may deceive, she may defame, she may ruin her own family with gaming, and the peace of twenty others with her coquettry, and yet preserve both her reputation and her peace. These are glorious privileges indeed, Hortensia; but whilst plays and novels are the favourite study of the fair, whilst the admiration of men continues to be set forth as the chief honour of woman, whilst power is only acquired by personal charms, whilst continual dissipation banishes the hour of reflection, Nature and flattery will too often prevail; and when this is the case, self preservation will suggest to conscious weakness those methods which are the most likely to conceal the ruinous trespass, however base and criminal they may be in their nature. The crimes that women have committed, both to conceal and to indulge their natural failings, shock the feelings of moral sense; but indeed every love intrigue, though it does not terminate in such horrid catastrophes, must naturally tend to debase the female mind, from its violence to educational impression, from the secrecy with which it must be conducted, and the debasing dependancy to which the intriguer, if she is a woman of reputation, is subjected. Lying, flattery, hypocrisy, bribery, and a long catalogue of the meanest of the human vices, must all be employed to preserve necessary appearances. Hence delicacy of sentiment gradually decreases; the warnings of virtue are no longer felt; the mind becomes corrupted, and lies open to every solicitation which appetite or passion presents. This must be the natural course of things in every being formed after the human plan; but it gives rise to the trite and foolish observation, that the first fault against chastity in woman has a radical power to deprave the character. But no such frail beings come out of the hands of Nature. The human mind is built of nobler materials than to be so easily corrupted; and with all the disadvantages of situation and education, women seldom become entirely abandoned till they are thrown into a state of desperation by the venomous rancour of their own sex.

The superiority of address peculiar to the female sex, says Rousseau, is a very equitable indemnification for their inferiority in point of strength. Without this, woman would not be the companion of man, but his slave; it is by her superior art and ingenuity that she preserves her equality, and governs him, whilst she affects to obey. Woman has every thing against her; as well our faults, as her own timidity and weakness. She has nothing in her favour but her subtlety and her beauty; is it not very reasonable therefore that she should cultivate both?

I am persuaded that Rousseau's understanding was too good to have led him into this error, had he not been blinded by his pride and his sensuality. The first was soothed by the opinion of superiority, lulled into acquiescence by cajolement; and the second was attracted by the idea of women playing off all the arts of coquettry to raise the passions of the sex. Indeed the author fully avows his sentiments, by acknowledging that he would have a young French woman cultivate her agreeable talents, in order to please her future husband, with as much care and assiduity as a young Circassian cultivates hers to fit her for the harem of an eastern bashaw.[3]

These agreeable talents, as the author expresses it, are played off to great advantage by women in all the courts of Europe; who, for the arts of female allurement, do not give place to the Circassian. But it is the practice of these very arts, directed to enthral the men, which act in a peculiar manner to corrupting the female mind. Envy, malice, jealousy, a cruel delight in inspiring sentiments which at first perhaps were never intended to be reciprocal, are leading features in the character of the coquet, whose aim is to subject the whole world to her own humour; but in this vain attempt she commonly sacrifices both her decency and her virtue.

By the intrigues of women, and their rage for personal power and importance, the whole world has been filled with violence and injury; and their levity and influence have proved so hostile to the existence or permanence of rational manners, that it fully justifies the keeness of Mr. Pope's satire on the sex.[4]

But I hear my Hortensia say, whither will this fit of moral anger carry you? I expected an apology, instead of a libel, on women; according to your description of the sex, the philosopher has more reason to regret the indulgence, than what you have sometimes termed the injustice of the men; and to look with greater complacency on the surly manners of the ancient Greeks, and the selfishness of Asiatic luxury, than on the gallantry of modern Europe.

Though you have often heard me express myself with warmth in the vindication of female nature, Hortensia, yet I never was an apologist for the conduct of women. But I cannot think the surliness of the Greek manners, or the selfishness of Asiatic luxury, a proper remedy to apply to the evil. If we could inspect narrowly into the domestic concerns of ancient and modern Asia, I dare say we should perceive that the first springs of the vast machine of society were set a going by women; and as to the Greeks, though it might be supposed that the peculiarity of their manners would have rendered them indifferent to the sex, yet they were avowedly governed by them. They only transferred that confidence which they ought to have given their wives, to their courtezans, in the same manner as our English husbands do their tenderness and complaisance. They

204

will sacrifice a wife of fortune and family to resentment, or the love of change, provided she give them opportunity, and bear with much Christian patience to be supplanted by their footman in the person of their mistress.

No; as Rousseau observes, it was ordained by Providence that women should govern some way or another; and all that reformation can do, is to take power out of the hands of vice and folly, and place it where it will not be liable to be abused.

To do the sex justice, it must be confessed that history does not set forth more instances of positive power abused by women, than by men; and when the sex have been taught wisdom by education, they will be glad to give up indirect influence for rational privileges: and the precarious sovereignty of an hour enjoyed with the meanest and most infamous of the species, for those established rights which, independent of accidental circumstances, may afford protection to the whole sex.

205

ENDNOTES

1   Janet Todd, *Mary Wollstonecraft: A Revolutionary Life* (London: Weidenfeld and Nicholson, 2000), 181.

2   "L'esprit n'a point de sexe, non plus que la vertu." François Poulain de la Barre, *De l'égalité des deux sexes, discours physique et morale où l'on voit l'importance de se défaire des préjuges* (Paris 1673), 109.

3   A bashaw or pascha is a Turkish nobleman.

4   Alexander Pope, "Of the Characters of Women: An Epistle to a Lady," *Moral Essay* II (London, 1735).

Hannah More (1745–1833)

Hannah More was a figure of authority and controversy throughout her life. Her father trained for the Church but was forced to become a teacher. He married a much younger, uneducated farmer's daughter who was determined that her children should learn. The Mores had five daughters and a son who died young.

Hannah showed early aptitude for learning. Her father was her first teacher.[1] He tutored her in Latin and mathematics, but stopped, alarmed at her precocity and fearing she would become a pedant. Mrs. More protested, and the lessons resumed, cautiously. Hannah More later commented, "I, a girl, was educated at random."[2]

The More sisters trained to be schoolteachers. The eldest was sent to boarding school in Bristol to study French and returned home each week to teach her younger sisters what she had learned. In 1758, the sisters opened a girls' school, also in Bristol, where Hannah was first a student and then a popular teacher. She studied French, Italian, Spanish, and Latin with visiting masters. At this time, she met Dr. Johnson, Edmund Burke, and William Turner, twenty years older and a wealthy bachelor. More accepted Turner's proposal of marriage, but he postponed the wedding three times in six years, effectively jilting her. James Stonhouse, a minister and physician, secretly intervened on Hannah's behalf with Turner, who agreed to pay her a yearly annuity of £200. When More learned of the negotiations, she was furious, but Stonhouse convinced her to accept Turner's money as compensation for time and opportunity lost. More reacted to Bristol gossips' criticism of her "calculating prudence"[3] with a nervous collapse. She never again considered marriage, although several other men proposed to her. Instead, she directed her energies to gain public eminence.[4]

More's first play, *The Search After Happiness*, became a staple of girls' boarding school performances. It announces More's persistent concerns with moral reform, particularly of the aristocratic and wealthy, and with women's education, as well as her ambivalence about women's quest for an energetic and pious life. More received public acclaim and some money for the play. She resolved to earn her living as a playwright.

Stonhouse introduced More to the great world of London, where she met David Garrick, the celebrated Shakespearean actor and manager at the Drury Lane Theatre, and the Bluestocking Circle. More expressed her enthusiasm for the women's society in her poem "The Bas Bleu, or, Conversation" (written in 1782, published in 1784), in which she celebrated female talents for intellectual conversation.

More's commercial plays, *The Inflexible Captive* (1775) and *Percy* (1777), high-light the battle of wills between fathers and daughters. In *Captives,* the warrior father declares that his daughter should "set a bright example of submission."[5] *Percy* was a critical success, earning More £600.

More anonymously published *Essays on Various Subjects, Principally Designed for Young Ladies* (1777). Dedicated to Elizabeth Montagu, the work reveals her ambivalence about women's public prominence, which was perhaps triggered by republican Catharine Macaulay's ostentatious celebration of her forty-sixth birthday. More quotes the Athenian general Pericles that woman's "greatest commendation [is] not to be talked of one way or the other." She counseled that men rather than women were suited to be poets, satirists, and playwrights. Montagu, she argued, was the "exception that proved the rule."[6]

In 1784, More took up the cause of Ann Yearsley (1752–1806), the "Bristol Milkwoman" and poet. More's friends bought subscriptions for Yearsley's *Poems, on Several Occasions* (1785) that yielded £600. With Elizabeth Montagu, More put the money in a trust to keep it away from Yearsley's husband, whom More distrusted. Yearsley publicly accused her two benefactors of stealing her money.

In the 1780s, More experienced a spiritual crisis in reaction to her successes and failures in the fashionable world. She turned to Evangelism and quickly became one of the leaders of the second Evangelical revival within the Church of England, joining William Wilberforce and the Clapham Sect. Like them, she advocated the abolition of slavery and the reform of manners.[7] In 1787–88, she published *Slavery: A Poem* (1787) contributing to the unprecedented national pressure on Parliament to end the slave trade.

She also published *Thoughts on the Importance of the Manners of the Great to General Society*—anonymously—in which she pointed to the Evangelical conviction that "Reformation must begin with the GREAT, or it will never be effectual." More's authorship was soon known, and the work went through seven editions in three months. She followed with *An Estimate of the Religion of the Fashionable World* (1791) that attacked polite society and articulated her vision of a culture regenerated by Christian values.[8]

In 1789, More and her sister Patty established "an empire of charity schools"[9] in the southeast of Bristol that eventually served 1,000 children, financed by their own and others' money. More promoted Evangelical morals in opposition to radical texts, like Thomas Paine's *Rights of Man* (1791–92). She spearheaded publication, distribution, and funding for Cheap Repository Tracts (1795–98), Christian tales for the working poor. She emerged as a national force, selling two million tracts in a year.[10]

More's criticisms of clergymen's neglect of their pastoral responsibilities stirred up the "Blagdon controversy" (1800–03), pitting More against powerful Anglican leaders who accused her of preaching "schism, Methodism, and Jacobinism at her schools."[11] She was dubbed the "She-Bishop," and the reactionary *Anti-Jacobin Review* linked Napoleon's threat of invasion with More's menace to the established Church. More suffered symptoms similar to her illness when she broke with William Turner. Her efforts, however, produced public acceptance of Sunday schools.

More lobbied against Catholic emancipation and parliamentary reform. She published *Hints towards Forming the Character of a Young Princess* (1805) to bolster support for the monarchy and the Anglican Church. Though she railed against the effects of novels on female readers as "a complicated drug," she wrote Evangelical fiction, of which *Coelebs in Search of a Wife* (1808) was the most popular. She left an estate of £27,500, an enormous sum for a woman to accumulate. Debate continues about Hannah More's contributions to the advancement of women.

208

STRICTURES ON THE MODERN SYSTEM OF FEMALE EDUCATION (1799)

Strictures on the Modern System of Female Education is Hannah More's contribution to the debate over female education in the wake of the French Revolution. In 1799, More was under increasing attack by male Anglican leaders for setting up a network of Sunday schools. Perhaps *Strictures* is meant to reassert her role as defender of establishment religious and political values. More argues against the radical implications of the proto-feminism of Macaulay, Wollstonecraft, and Hays. Yet she shares with them more assumptions than she concedes, as astute readers recognised. Mary Berry (1763–1852), self-educated minor Bluestocking, bitter about her lack of formal training, wrote to a friend after reading *Strictures* that she found it "amazing, or rather ... not amazing, but impossible ... [that Hannah More and Mary Wollstonecraft] agree on all the great points of female education." Berry predicted that "H. More will ... be very angry when she hears this, though I would lay a wager that she never read ... [Wollstonecraft.]" [12]

Like her non-Evangelical female contemporaries, More argues from Locke's associationist theory that the human "mind has no sex," that women possess the same faculties for reason and study as men, and that, therefore, "female education" must be reformed to produce the kind of woman that a sensible man wants to marry. More argues that, as women have "equal [intellectual] parts" as men, like men, they should be deliberately trained for their appropriate "profession" to exert their influence as "daughters, wives, mothers, and mistresses of families." [13]

More distances herself from Wollstonecraft and Godwin's *Memoirs*, published the previous year, by attacking foreign influences with socially destabilizing messages. She compares novel reading to a "complicated drug" capable of arousing erotic fantasies and the neglect of Christian duties. Ladies who take the lead in society, More instructs, must "act as the guardians of public taste as well as public virtue" to stem revolutionary tides washing across the Channel from France and Germany.

More also responds to Hays's Unitarian revision of the conduct book for women, *Letters and Essays, Moral and Miscellaneous* (1793). Chapter VII of

Strictures, "On female study, and initiation into knowledge," refutes specifics of Hays's recommendations for the female reader, given in her Chapter VII of *Letters*, "On reading Romances, &c." More emphasizes her differences with Macaulay, Wollstonecraft, and Hays: the ladies who learn according to More's plan are first Christian reformers subscribing to the view that "education be a school to fit us for life, and life be a school to fit us for eternity." Here is the great divide between More and her Enlightenment peers: she wants women disciplined for earthly, individual atonement; they envision female education for active republican citizenship.

Strictures went into a seventh edition within seven months. More's Evangelicalism quickly aroused criticism. Hester Piozzi noted that the male students at Westminster School burnt More in effigy for her *Strictures* "against the Dissipation of Youth." [14]

Strictures on the Modern System of Female Education. With a View of the Principles and Conduct Prevalent Among Women of Rank and Fortune (1799)

Hannah More

On female study, and initiation into knowledge.—Error of cultivating the imagination to the neglect of the judgment.—Books of reasoning recommended.

As this little work by no means assumes the character of a general scheme of education, the author has purposely avoided expatiating largely on any kind of instruction; but so far as it is connected, either immediately or remotely, with objects of a moral or religious nature. Of course she has been so far from thinking it necessary to enter into the enumeration of those books which are useful in general instruction, that she has forborne to mention any. With such books the rising generation is far more copiously and ably furnished than any preceding period has been; and out of an excellent variety the judicious instructor can hardly fail to make such a selection as shall be beneficial to the pupil.

But while due praise ought not to be withheld from the improved methods of communicating the elements of general knowledge; yet is there not some danger that our very advantages may lead us into error, by causing us to repose so confidently on the multiplied helps which facilitate the entrance into learning, as to render our pupils superficial through the very facility of acquirement? Where so much is done for them, may they not be led to do too little for themselves? May there not be a moral disadvantage in possessing them with the notion that learning may be acquired without diligence and labour? Sound education never *can* be made a "primrose path of dalliance." Do what we will we cannot *cheat* children into learning or *play* them into knowledge; according to the smoothness of the modern creed. There is no idle way to any acquisition which really deserve the name. And as Euclid, in order to repress the impetuous vanity of greatness, told his Sovereign that there was no royal way to geometry, so the fond mother may be assured that there is no short cut to any other kind of learning. The tree of knowledge, as a punishment perhaps, for its having been at first unfairly tasted, cannot now be climbed without difficulty; and this very circumstance serves afterwards to furnish not only literary pleasures, but moral advantages: for the knowledge which is acquired by unwearied assiduity is lasting in the possession, and sweet to the possessor; both perhaps in proportion to the cost and labour of the acquisition. And though an able teacher ought to endeavour, by improving the communication faculty in himself, (for many know what they cannot teach,) to soften every difficulty; yet in spite of the kindness and ability with which he will smooth every obstruction, it is probably, among the wise institution of Providence, that great difficulties should still remain. For education is but an initiation into that life of trial to which we are introduced on our entrance into this world. It is the first breaking-in to that state of toil and labour to which we are born; and in this view of the subject the acquisition of learning may be converted to higher uses than such as are purely literary.

211

Will it not be ascribed to a captious singularity if I venture to remark that real knowledge and real piety, though they have gained in many instances, have suffered in others from that profusion of little, amusing, sentimental books with which the youthful library overflows? Abundance has its dangers as well as scarcity. In the first place may not the multiplicity of these alluring little works increase the natural reluctance to those more dry and uninteresting studies, of which after all, the rudiments of every part of learning must consist? And, secondly, is there not some danger (though there are many honourable exceptions) that some of those engaging narratives may serve to infuse into the youthful heart a sort of spurious goodness, and confidence of virtue? And that the benevolent actions with the recital of which they abound, when they are not made to flow from any source but feeling, may tend to inspire a self-complacency, a self-gratulation, a "stand by, for I am holier than thou?" [Isaiah 65:5] May they not help to infuse a love of popularity and an anxiety for praise, in the place of that simple and unostentatious rule of doing whatever good we do, *because it is the will of God?* The universal substitution of this principle would tend to purify the worldly morality of many a popular little story. And there are few dangers which good parents will more carefully guard against than that of giving their children a mere political piety;* that sort of religion which just goes to make people more respectable, and to stand well with the world.

There is a certain precocity of mind which is much helped on by these superficial modes of instruction; for frivolous reading will produce its correspondent effect, in much less time than books of solid instruction; the imagination being liable to be worked upon, and the feelings to be set a going, much faster than

---

* An ingenious (and in many respects useful) French Treatise on Education, has too much encouraged this political piety; by sometimes considering religion as a thing of human convention; as a thing creditable rather than commanded: by erecting the doctrine of expediency in the place of Christian simplicity; and wearing away the spirit of truth, by the substitution of occasional deceit, equivocation, subterfuge, and mental reservation. [More refers to Rousseau's *Émile* (1761).]

the understanding can be opened and the judgment enlightened. A talent for conversation should be the result of education, not its precursor; it is a golden fruit when suffered to ripen gradually on the tree of knowledge; but if forced in the hot-bed of a circulating library, it will turn out worthless and vapid in proportion as it was artificial and premature. Girls who have been accustomed to devour frivolous books, will converse and write with far greater appearance of skill as to style and sentiment at twelve or fourteen years old, than those of a more advanced age who are under the discipline of fewer studies; but the former having early attained to that low standard which had been held out to them, became stationary; while the latter, quietly progressive, are passing through just gradations to a higher strain of mind; and those who early begin with talking and writing like women, commonly end with thinking and acting like children.

The swarms of *Abridgments, Beauties,* and *Compendiums,* which form too considerable a part of a young lady's library, may be considered in many instances as an infallible receipt of making a superficial mind. The *names* of the renowned characters in history thus become familiar in the mouth of those who can neither attach to the idea of the person, the series of his actions, nor the peculiarities of his character. A few fine passages from the poets (passages perhaps which derived their chief beauty from their position and connection) are huddled together by some extract-maker, whose brief and disconnected patches of broken and discordant materials, while they inflame young readers with the vanity of reciting, neither fill the mind nor form the taste: and it is not difficult to trace back to their shallow sources the hackney'd quotations of certain *accomplished* young ladies, who will be frequently found not to have come legitimately by any thing they know: I mean, not to have drawn it from its true spring, the original works of the author from which some *beauty-monger* has severed it. Human inconsistency in this, as in other cases, wants to combine two irreconcileable things; it strives to unite the reputation of knowledge with the pleasure of idleness, forgetting that nothing that is valuable can be obtained without sacrifices and that if we would purchase knowledge we must pay for it the fair and lawful price of time and industry.

This remark is by no means of general application; there are many valuable works which from their bulk would be almost inaccessible to a great number of readers, and a considerable part of which may not be generally useful. Even in the best written books there is often superfluous matter; authors are apt to get enamoured of their subject, and to dwell too long on it: every person cannot find time to read a longer work on any subject, and yet it may be well for them to know something on almost every subject; those therefore, who abridge voluminous works judiciously, render service to the community. But there seems, if I may venture the remark, to be a mistake in the *use* of abridgments. They are put systematically into the hands of youth, who have, or ought to have leisure for the works at large; while abridgments seem more immediately calculated for persons in more advanced life, who wish to recall something they had forgotten; who want to restore old ideas rather than acquire new ones; or they are useful for persons immersed in the business of the world who have little leisure for voluminous reading. They are excellent to refresh the mind, but not competent to form it.

Perhaps there is some analogy between the mental and bodily conformation of women. The instructor therefore should imitate the physician. If the latter prescribe bracing medicines for a body of which delicacy is the disease, the former would do well to prohibit relaxing reading for a mind which is already of too soft a texture, and should strengthen its feeble tone by invigorating reading.

By softness, I cannot be supposed to mean imbecility of understanding, but natural softness of heart, with that indolence of spirit which is fostered by indulging in seducing books and in the general habits of fashionable life.

I mean not here to recommend books which are immediately religious, but such as exercise the reasoning faculties, teach the mind to get acquainted with its own nature, and to stir up its own powers. Let not a timid young lady start if I should venture to recommend to her, after a proper course of preparation, to swallow and digest such strong meat, as Watt's or Duncan's little book of Logic, some parts of Mr. Locke's Essay on the Human Understanding, and Bishop Butler's Analogy. Where there is leisure, and capacity, and an able counsellor, works of this nature might be profitably substituted in the place of so much English Sentiment, French Philosophy, Italian Poetry, and fantastic German imagery and magic wonders. While such enervating or absurd books sadly disqualify the reader for solid pursuit or vigorous thinking, the studies here recommended would act upon the constitution of the mind as a kind of alternative, and, if I may be allowed the expression, would help to brace the intellectual stamina.

213

This is however by no means intended to exclude works of taste and imagination, which must always make the ornamental part, and [of] course a very considerable part of female studies. It is only suggested that they should not form them entirely. For what is called dry tough reading, independent of the knowledge it conveys, is useful as an habit and wholesome as an exercise. Serious study serves to harden the mind for more trying conflicts; it lifts the reader from sensation to intellect; it abstracts her from the world and its vanities; it fixes a wandering spirit, and fortifies a weak one; it divorces her from matter; it corrects that spirit of trifling which she naturally contracts from the frivolous turn of female conversation, and the petty nature of female employments; it concentrates her attention, assists her in a habit of excluding trivial thoughts, and thus even helps to qualify her for religious pursuits. Yes; I repeat it, there is to woman a Christian use to be made of sober studies; while books of an opposite cast, however unexceptionable they may be sometimes found in point of expression; however free from evil in its more gross and palpable shapes, yet by their very nature and constitution they excite a spirit of relaxation, by exhibiting scenes and ideas which soften the mind; they impair its general powers of resistance, and at best feed habits of improper indulgence, which lays the mind open to error and the heart to seduction.

Women are little accustomed to close reasoning on any subject; still less do they inure their minds to consider particular parts of a subject; they are not habituated to turn a truth round and view it in all its varied aspects and positions; and this perhaps is one cause (as will be observed in another place) of the too great confidence they are disposed to place in their opinions. Though their imagination is already too lively, and their judgment naturally incorrect; in educating them we go on to stimulate the imagination, while we neglect the regulation of the judgment. They already want ballast, and we make their education consist in continually crowding more sail than they can carry. Their intellectual powers being so little strengthened by exercise, makes every little business appear a hardship to them; whereas serious study would be useful, were it only that it leads the mind to the habit of conquering difficulties. But it is peculiarly hard to turn at once from the indolent repose of light reading, from the concerns of mere animal life, the objects of sense, or the frivolousness of chit chat; it is peculiarly hard, I say; to a mind so softened, to rescue itself from the dominion of self-indulgence, to resume its powers, to call home its scattered strength, to shut out every foreign intrusion, to force back a spring so unnaturally bent, and to devote itself to religious reading, reflection, or self-examination: whereas to an intellect accustomed to think at all the difficulty of thinking seriously is obviously lessened.

Far be it from me to desire to make scholastic ladies or female dialecticians; but there is little fear that the kind of books here recommended, if thoroughly studied, and not superficially skimmed, will make them pedants or induce conceit; for by shewing them the possible powers of the human mind, you will bring them to see the littleness of their own, and to get acquainted with the mind and to regulate it, does not seem the way to puff it up. But let her who is disposed to be elated with her literary acquisitions, check her vanity by calling to mind the just remark of Swift, "that after all her boasted acquirements, a woman will, generally speaking, be found to possess less of what is called learning than a common school-boy."

Neither is there any fear that this sort of reading will convert ladies into authors. The direct contrary effect will be likely to be produced by the perusal of writers who throw the generality of readers at such an unapproachable distance. Who are those ever multiplying authors, that with unparalleled fecundity are overstocking the world with their quick succeeding progeny? They are novel writers; the easiness of whose productions is at once the cause of their own fruitfulness, and of the almost infinitely numerous race of imitators to whom they give birth. Such is the frightful facility of this species of composition, that every raw girl while she reads, is tempted to fancy that she can also write. And as Alexander, on perusing the Iliad found by congenial sympathy the image of Achilles in his own ardent soul, and felt himself the hero he was studying; and as Corregio, on first beholding a picture which exhibited the perfection of the Graphic art, prophetically felt all his own future greatness, and cried out in rapture, "And I too am a painter!" so a thorough paced novel reading Miss, at the close of every tissue of hackney'd adventures, feels within herself the stirring impulse of corresponding genius, and triumphantly exclaims, "And I too am an author!" The glutted imagination soon overflows with the redundance of cheap sentiment and plentiful incident, and by a sort of arithmetical proportion, is enabled by the perusal of any three novels to produce a fourth; till every fresh production, like the progeny of Banquo, is followed by

> Another, and another, and another!*

Is a lady, however destitute of talents, education, or knowledge of the world whose studies have been completed by a circulating library, in any distress of mind? writing a novel suggests itself as the best soother of her sorrows! Does she labour under any depression of circumstances? writing a novel occurs as the readiest receipt for mending them! And she solaces herself with conviction that the subscription which has been given to her importunity or her necessities, has been given to her genius. And this confidence instantly levies a fresh contribution for a succeeding work. Capacity and cultivation are so little taken into the account, that writing a book seems to be now considered as the only sure resource which the idle and the illiterate have always in their power.

215

May I be indulged in a short digression to remark, though rather out of its place, that the corruption occasioned by these books has spread so wide, and descended so low, that not only among milleners, mantua-makers, and other trades where numbers work together, the labour of one girl is frequently sacrificed that she may be spared to read those mischievous books to the other; but the Author has been assured by clergymen, who have witnessed the fact, that they are procured and greedily read in the wards of our Hospitals! an awful hint, that those who teach the poor to read, should not only take care to furnish them with principles which will lead them to abhor corrupt books, but should also furnish them with such books as shall strengthen and confirm their principles.† And let every Christian remember, that there is no other way of entering truly into the spirit of that divine prayer, which petitions that the name of God may be "hallowed," that "his kingdom (of grace) may come," and that "his will may be done on earth as it is in heaven," than by each individual contributing according to his measure to accomplish the work for which he prays; for to pray that these great objects may be promoted, without contributing to their promotion, is a palpable inconsistency.

---

* It is surely not necessary to state, that no disrespect can be here intended to those females of real genius and correct character, some of whose justly admired writings in this kind, are accurate histories of life and manners, and striking delineations of character. It is not *their fault* if their works have been attended with the consequences which usually attend good originals, that of giving birth to a multitude of miserable imitations.

† The above facts furnish no argument on the side of those who would keep the poor in ignorance. Those who cannot *read* can *hear*, and are likely to hear a worse purpose than those who have been better taught. And that ignorance furnishes no security for integrity either in morals or politics, the late revolts in more than one country, remarkable for the ignorance of the poor, fully illustrates. It is earnestly hoped that the above facts may tend to impress ladies with the importance of superintending the instruction of the poor, and of making it an indispensable part of their charity to give them moral and religious books.

ENDNOTES

1 Patricia Demers, *The World of Hannah More* (Lexington: The University Press of Kentucky, 1996), 3.

2 Anne Stott, *Hannah More: The First Victorian* (Oxford: Oxford University Press, 2003), 6.

3 Charles Howard Ford, *Hannah More: A Critical Biography* (New York: Peter Lang, 1996), 16.

4 Norma Clark, *Dr Johnson's Women* (London: Hambledon and London, 2000), 155.

5 Ford, 20–26.

6 Ford, 36–37.

7 Ford, 80–102.

8 Ford, 132.

9 Anna Clark, "Women in Eighteenth-Century British Politics," in *Women, Gender and Enlightenment*, ed. Barbara Taylor and Sarah Knott (Basingstoke, Hampshire: Palgrave Macmillan, 2005), 579.

10 Stott, 182–86.

11 *Oxford Dictionary of National Biography*, s.v. "More, Hannah (1745–1833)" (by S.J. Skedd).

12 Quoted in Ford, *Hannah More: A Critical Biography*, 223. For Berry, see Brian Dolan, *Ladies of the Grand Tour* (New York: HarperCollins, 2001), 18–21.

13 Ford, 90.

14 Ford, 90.

Mary Hays (1759–1843)

Mary Hays, who also distinguised herself in writing history is profiled in Part 1.

"LETTER IV," LETTERS AND ESSAYS, MORAL, AND MISCELLANEOUS (1793)

Letters and Essays, Moral, and Miscellaneous was intended for a friendly female audience. Hays capitalized on historian Catharine Macaulay's *Letters on Education* (1790) and Wollstonecraft's *A Vindication of the Rights of Woman* (1792) to break new ground by appropriating the female conduct book that hectored women and transforming it into a vehicle for instructional curricula for them, curricula adapted from the male education at New College, the Dissenting academy in Hackney. *Letters and Essays* functions as a primer of enlightened Dissent for female readers. Hays identifies the rights of woman, "founded on nature, reason, and justice," as the basis of her personal feminism.

The book reveals the breadth of Hays's autodidactism and her purposeful intellectual genealogy. She combines the psycho-perceptual dynamics described by Locke and Hartley and Rousseau's ethical pedagogy to convince women that their first responsibility is to educate themselves and their daughters. In contrast to Wollstonecraft and Hannah More, Hays endorses novel reading for women where enthusiasm can foster associations that strengthen the mind. Hays resists the historical imperative of women's handwork, the insistence that all women in every culture produce textiles.

In "Letter IV," Hays situates her narrator in the privacy of the domestic enclosure where the tedium of women's work stifles aspirations to pursue the life of the mind. In the story of Sempronia and her family of daughters, Hays connects female education and political theory. Sempronia inculcates her daughters conventionally by "early train[ing] with unrelenting rigour to the duties of non-resistance and passive obedience." Such training makes companionate marriage impossible for women because they seek to manipulate their husbands rather than attempt to be their rational equals. Hays proposes that enlightenment should change women's traditional work, which is the justification for keeping them ignorant of anything else and, with vanity as their socially sanctioned pursuit, interested only in pleasing men. For women, too, earthly existence is preparation for the divine.

The conservative critic for the *English Review* merged the person of the unattractive author and her thinning hair with her nasty ideas, identifying Hays as "the baldest disciple of Mrs. Wollstonecraft" in his review of *Letters and Essays*.[1] The wretched literary performance, the critic asserted, was consistent with the unnatural ambitions of the female author and, like all abominations against nature, produced an "abortion." The reviewer was particularly contemptuous of Hays's pretensions to knowledge and disparaging of woman's handwork, opposing this with the argument that "even to manage her needle with dexterity (though there be no sewing in the next world) may be as rational a mode preparing herself for hereafter, as to weave the web of sophistry, in attempting to disprove the existence of an immortal soul!"

"Letter IV," Letters and Essays, Moral, and Miscellaneous (1793)

Mary Hays

No. IV.

To Mrs.——.

My dear Madam,

YOUR eldest daughter you inform me is now entering her fifteenth year, and discovers a love of books, which gives you great pleasure, as you justly consider a taste for reading as the best foundation for moral as well as speculative improvement. Books contain the best parts of the finest human minds, in them you perceive only the excellencies of genius without those shades that must unavoidably discolour the purest human virtues. I am aware that book-knowledge has been ridiculed by many, as useless in the common intercourses of life; but these sarcasms I fancy have generally been the refuge of ignorance, glorying in its shame; and that knowledge of the world which they recommend as a substitute, when analysed, I believe frequently consists in an acquaintance with chicanery and turpitude, and "to touch pitch and not be defiled," is very difficult. It certainly is not necessary for every individual to apply himself to abstract and scientific pursuits, as this would be defeating the purposes of society, which requires hands as well as heads. "And what is above us (said Socrates) doth not concern us"; but there are few situations in the least degree superior to the lowest ranks of life, that do not allow of some leisure, and to fill up that leisure in a manner that may not only afford present entertainment, but also lay in stores for future improvement, is certainly highly laudable. Nothing is so much to be avoided in the education of young people, as the leaving too many hours of vacuity; by habits of indolence, the body, the mind, and the morals are endangered. Lavater justly observes, that "idleness is the crying sin of human nature." It is an ancient and a true maxim, "That nothing can be accomplished without labour, and every thing with it." Those to whom the care of youth is intrusted, should be particularly sedulous to

219

guard them from this canker of every virtue, by exciting them to exercise their fancy and ingenuity, their faculties and their limbs.

I confess I am no advocate for cramping the minds and bodies of young girls, by keeping them for ever poring over needlework (and when I see the tapestry and tent stitch of former times, I sigh at the waste of eyes, spirits, and time); nor do I think it so very important a part of female education as has generally been supposed. In well-regulated families, where nothing is left till to-morrow, which can be done today, where every department is conducted with order and economy, where the business of the day is planned in the morning, and one thing concluded before another is begun; where the day is lengthened by early hours, and short temperate meals, "eating to live, and not living only to eat;" I am well assured there cannot be any occasion for this laborious and seamstress-like application: surely the covering of the body ought not to be the sole business of life. I doubt whether there will be any sewing in the next world, how then will those employ themselves who have done nothing else in this?

Sempronia had a large family of daughters, whom she early trained with unrelenting rigour to the duties of non-resistance and passive obedience. All attention to literature, she considered as a mere waste of time, and valued herself upon being unacquainted with any other book than the Bible. The sole accomplishments which this notable lady deemed necessary to constitute a good wife and mother, were to scold and half starve her servants, to oblige her children to say their prayers, and go stately to church, and to make clothes and household furniture from morning till night; while to supply them with constant employment of this nature, more money was expended, and materials wasted, than would have paid for having the work done from home, and have purchased a handsome collection of books beside. The unfortunate girls submitted to this severe discipline from hard necessity, but not without murmuring; till at length, from close confinement, and the dull uniformity of one tedious pursuit, the bloom faded from their cheeks, and the lustre from their eyes, their health its vigor. Their mother who really loved them, and who thought that while she was blighting the tender blossom in its spring, she was performing the duties of a prudent and good parent, was alarmed at the change she perceived; and after vainly trying the efficacy of various quack medicines recommended as infallible restoratives, accompanied the young ladies to one of the fashionable watering places, in the hope of their receiving benefit from the salubrious effects of the sea air.

During their residence at Brighthelmstone, the languid charms of the elder daughter attracted the notice of the son of a wealthy citizen, who having received a liberal, though mercantile education, had been accustomed to amuse himself in the intervals of commercial business, with the study of the Belle-Letters. His imagination had acquired by these pursuits a tincture of what is commonly called romance by the generality of the trading part of mankind; he had been disgusted with the venal daughters of fashion, and the really sweet, though fading countenance of our young lady (whom I shall call Serena) the bashfulness of her manners, and the meekness of her deportment, awakened his tenderness, and flattered his vanity. The vulgar and confined notions of the mother he dignified with the name of simplicity; and as his Serena seldom ventured to converse freely in his presence, her silence he construed into the effect of a delicate timidity. He could not but perceive that her mind had been greatly neglected, but he consoled himself with the hope of giving it improvement and polish, and exclaimed with Rousseau, "Lovely ignorance! Happy will he be who is destined to instruct her." Full of these ideas he hastened their union, that he might remove his charming mistress out of a family where he conceived she was degraded, and transplant her into—

> "A richer soil, where vernal suns and showers,
> Diffuse their warmest, largest influence."

Serena, by sea-bathing, recreation, and the attentions of her lover, which gave her thoughts a new turn, in some measure recovered her health and beauty, and in a few weeks became the wife of Melville, who now believed himself at the summit of human felicity. After the first congratulations and compliments were over, he conducted his bride to a pleasant villa, situated on the banks of the Thames, a few miles from the metropolis, intending before he introduced her to his connections (many of whom were among the polite and the literary) to devote his leisure hours to the cultivation and enlargement of her understanding.

For this purpose he furnished a commodious library with an elegant assortment of books, and when after the business of the day he returned from town, he would endeavour to entertain his Serena, by reading select passages from the best English authors, particularly the works of the Poets, and moral Essayists. But to his great mortification, when after repeating with enthusiasm some of the finest passages in Shakespear, he glanced his eyes on his lady to perceive the effect it produced; the settled vacuity of her features announced the blank within. She seemed to listen, and faintly smiled, but it was the forced smile of lassitude; she had no associations that could make her feel any interest in the glowing pictures of genius, and would interrupt the soul-harrowing scene between Hamlet and his guilty mother, to observe upon a phaeton that passed the window, or return the caresses of a favourite lap-dog. Poor Melville shuddered! the visionary scene of bliss began to fade from his imagination, he threw down his book, and to hide his chagrin, proposed to his wife a walk, as she had yet seen but little of the adjacent country. She readily agreed to accompany him, happy to be relieved from the irksome task, of giving a feigned attention to what she could not comprehend. Melville endeavoured to direct her view as they passed to every sublime and beautiful feature in nature, the wood and the water, the hill and the valley, the wild heath and cultivated garden—

> "The sun-shine gleaming as through amber clouds,
> O'er all the western sky."

But alas! the varied "shews and forms"* of nature were lost on the sterile fancy that had never received—"fair culture's kind enlivening aid." She entreated that they might return to the high road, for she was sure the path they had taken must be equally unsafe as dull and difficult, and she was every moment in terror, lest a robber should start out of the thicket. Her disgusted companion sighed as he silently acceded to her proposal, and began unwillingly to be convinced that true beauty must depend upon moral sentiment, and that the mere varnish of a fair complexion could make no amends for a weak and empty mind.

Vain was every subsequent attempt to give fire to this breathing clay, early habits had rendered the mental organs callous; the pretty insipid Serena would smile when he smiled, and weep when he frowned, but her tenderness flattered not; for there was no distinction in it. She had no will of her own (for the little energy she inherited from nature, had been quenched by the despotic discipline of the good lady her mother) and Melville wearied of the uniformity of her compliances, which gratified neither his judgement nor his heart, vainly exhorted her sometimes to have a taste of her own; for he would even have preferred opposition to the dead calm in which their days languished, and he dreaded to enliven them by society; for the gross inaccuracies, and frivolity of his lady's conversation, exposed him to the ridicule of his acquaintance, and covered him with confusion.

Nor did the domestic management of his affairs afford him any consolation. His wife sought amusement in the company of her servants, she preserved no dignity of character, and acted not upon any plan; consequently her authority was despised, nothing was conducted with regularity, and while she sat whole days in loose dishabille to supernumerary needle-work, which turned to little account, her house was filled with litter and disorder, her children ran wild, and her domestics quarrelled among themselves, and defrauded their master, as amid frequent changes, the certain consequence of mismanagement, it could not be expected that they would all be honest.

The unfortunate Melville, whose mind was formed for elegant and domestic tenderness, execrated his fate in the bitterness of his soul, and desperately sought to forget his disappointment in the scenes of dissipation and extravagance; and in a few years his expences abroad, and the want of order and economy at home, involved them in the miseries of insolvency.

This little history requires no comment; your Elizabeth, for whose entertainment it is intended, will perhaps be stimulated by it to new ardor in mental pursuits. That I interest myself in her happiness, you need not now be informed, and that I am affectionately, &c. yours.

ENDNOTE

1   *The English Review*, 2nd ser., 22 (October 1793): 253–57.

---

* Oh! nature, all they shews and forms,
For pensive feeling hearts have charms.
Burn's Poems.

Maria Edgeworth (1767–1849)

Maria Edgeworth (born 1 January 1767) was the third child and first daughter of Richard Lovell Edgeworth (1744–1817), an Irish inventor, member of the Lunar Society, and educational reformer, and of his first wife Anna Maria Elers, an Englishwoman, who died when Maria was 6. Richard Edgeworth remarried Honora Sneyd soon after, the next of his four wives. Neglected by her father, Maria was educated at a boarding school in Derby and then, at her father's instance, at a fashionable school in London. However, her most important influences were her father's reformist friends, some of whom supported women's education. They included Joseph Priestley, Unitarian *philosophe* and chemist; Erasmus Darwin, medical doctor and researcher and poet; and, most important, Thomas Day, author of the popular *The History of Sandford and Merton* (1789), a novel based on Rousseau's pedagogical principles.

Though Richard Edgeworth disapproved of novels, he interested himself in her reading, especially when in 1781 Maria's eyesight became compromised.[1] When she was fifteen, her father set her the task of translating *Adèle et Théodore ou Lettres sur l'éducation*, published that year by Stéphanie Félicité de Genlis, a work consistent with the Edgeworths' subsequent approach to landowning and education.[2] In a departure from Rousseau's theories, Genlis's epistolary fiction applied his educational methods to both girls as well as boys.[3] Thomas Day, alarmed by the radical gender implications of Genlis's novel, pressured Richard Edgeworth to withdraw the translation from publication in 1783 because "female authorship," Day believed, was unacceptable.

In June 1782, a propitious year in Irish politics, Maria moved with her father and his growing family to the hereditary estate at Edgeworthstown. Richard Edgeworth had decided to turn his property into a "'moral school,' in which experiments in agriculture, engineering, and education could be pioneered."[4] Maria quickly assumed responsibilities as her father's "heir apparent,"[5] responsibilities that set the course of her future life. She played an active role in managing their tenants; tutored her step-siblings, thirteen of whom were educated at home, out of a total of twenty-two; and she collaborated with her father on book projects, especially on *Essays on Practical Education* (1798), and, after his death in 1817, completed his *Memoirs* (1820). Maria Edgeworth went on to become a wealthy and successful novelist and an innovator in juvenile literature, but, in spite of her growing fame, she continued to make Edgeworthstown her principal residence. While visiting Paris in 1802 with her father, she had one offer of marriage from a Swedish courtier, but refused him. She made frequent visits to London and Paris where she met prominent figures in the world of letters. Her publications were widely reviewed, and praised by Jeremy Bentham, Sir Humphrey Davy, David Ricardo, Jane Austen, and, especially, by Sir Walter Scott, who gave credit to her influence for his Waverly novels.[6]

Family and community life in Ireland provided Maria Edgeworth with her literary material. She was a partner with her father in developing innovative pedagogical principles, assessing and recording the intellectual progress of the younger Edgeworths, and devising new teaching methods and texts, all in the interests of applying Lockean psychology and Rousseauean principles to prepare real children for active life. She also recorded her father's stories about a fictional Irish Freeman family, eventually published as *Patronage* under her own name in 1814.[7] Her novel *Castle Rackrent* (1800), published by Unitarian Joseph Johnson, reflected the changing Irish political situation as it had shifted from hopes for reform to subsequent disillusionment. Between 1800 and 1817, she published fifteen works that revealed her intimate knowledge of Irish class conflict. She debated amicably with the political economist David Ricardo about his theory of rising rents and whether potatoes were a sufficiently "risk adverse" crop compared with wheat to sustain the Irish population, all part of her determination to demonstrate enlightened land ownership.[8]

Maria Edgeworth experimented in her writings with multiple concerns—national identity, gender, and literary form. She published a series of moral tales promoting traditional values in *The Parents' Assistant* (1800), *Early Lessons* (1801), and *Moral Tales for Young People* (1801). She joined the current debate about women's status in successive novels, devising strong female characters but taking a moderate position between radicals like Wollstonecraft and Hays and conservatives like Hannah More and even Elizabeth Hamilton. In "The good Aunt Angelina, or, L'amie inconnue," the heroine, a parody of Hays's Emma Courtney, after reading a new circulating library novel, *The Woman of Genius*, sets out to find its author. Angelina eventually acquires "good sense" rather than genius. Edgeworth privately noted what she considered to be the absurdity of the idea of female lawyers, yet she also declared, "facts are of no sex." She was the second woman elected as an honorary member of the Royal Irish Academy in 1842.[9]

LETTERS FOR LITERARY LADIES (1795)

Letters for Literary Ladies, published by Joseph Johnson in 1795, was Maria Edgeworth's first printed work. It includes "Letter to a Gentleman on the birth of a Daughter, with a Reply," "Letters of Julia and Caroline," and "An Essay on the Noble Science of Self-Justification." The excerpts that follow are between two male correspondents, modelled on Thomas Day and Richard Edgeworth, and, in these selections, Maria Edgeworth reconstructs the interchanges between her father and Day that prevented her from publishing her translation of de Genlis's *Adèle et Théodore ou Lettres sur l'éducation* (1782) when she was sixteen.[10] Though

Literary Ladies is her most explicitly feminist work, a modern critic traces "a striking continuity" from this to her last novel, *Helen* (1834).[11] Maria Edgeworth at 27 vividly recreates Day's arguments that had swayed her father "to dread for his daughter the name of authoress." Day, like Richard Edgeworth, was concerned about women exerting a public influence, a concern derived from Rousseau's view that women were too much the prisoners of their bodies to be the equals of men in society. In 1760, Day had written Edgeworth from France about French women's dominance "over their husbands, not because they are their husbands, but because they are men."[12] In 1795, Maria Edgeworth argues, as she could not as an adolescent, for women's right to education on the basis of their equal intellectual potential with men and their competence to express their views in the republic of letters. She refers to the intensifying print wars over gender in which Edmund Burke and Mary Wollstonecraft, among others, staked out conflicting positions. Maria Edgeworth represents Day's positions with more force than her father's rebuttals. The father figure suggests that women with literary aspirations and ability may find their place as authors rather in smaller print networks than in the great public arena.[13]

Maria Edgeworth revised and republished *Letters to Literary Ladies* in 1798. The changes she made emphasized the revolution in female manners galvanized by the surging print culture: "It is absolutely out of our power," says the Richard Edgeworth character, "to drive the fair sex back to their former state of darkness: the art of printing has totally changed their situation: their eyes are opened,—the class page is unrolled, they *will* read"—and, as his daughter ably demonstrated, write.

Letters for Literary Ladies (1795)

Maria Edgeworth

LETTER FROM A GENTLEMAN TO HIS FRIEND UPON THE BIRTH OF A DAUGHTER

I Congratulate you, my dear Sir, upon the birth of your daughter; and I wish that some of the Fairies of ancient times were at hand to endow the damsel with health, wealth, wit, and beauty—Wit?——I should make a long pause before I accepted of this gift for a daughter—you would make none.

As I know it to be your opinion, that it is in the power of education, more certainly than it was ever believed to be in the power of Fairies, to bestow all mental gifts; and as I have heard you say that education should begin as early as possible, I am in haste to offer you my sentiments, lest my advice should come too late.

Your general ideas of the habits and virtues essential to the perfection of the female character nearly agree with mine; but we differ materially as to the cultivation, which it is necessary or expedient to bestow upon the understandings of women: you are a champion for the rights of woman, and insist upon the equality of the sexes. But since the days of chivalry are past, and since modern gallantry permits men to speak, at least to one another, in less sublime language of the fair, I may confess to you that I see neither in experience or analogy much reason to believe that, in the human species alone, there are no marks of inferiority in the female;—curious and admirable exceptions there may be, but many such have not fallen within my observation. I cannot say that I have been much enraptured either on a first view or on a closer inspection with female prodigies. Prodigies are scarcely less offensive to my taste than monsters; humanity makes us refrain from expressing disgust at the awkward shame of the one, whilst the intemperate vanity of the other justly provokes ridicule and indignation. I have always observed in the understandings of women who have been too much cultivated, some disproportion between the different faculties of their minds. I have seen women vain of exhibiting mental deformities, which to me appeared no less disgusting. In the course of my life it has never been my good fortune to meet with a female whose mind, in strength, just proportion, and activity, I could compare to that of a sensible man [...] It is not possible that women should ever be our equals in knowledge, unless you assert that they are far our superiors in natural capacity.—Not only time but opportunity must be wanting to complete female studies—we mix with the world without restraint, we converse freely with all classes of people, with men of wit, of science, of learning, with the artist, the mechanic, the labourer; every scene of life is open to our view;—every assistance, that foreign or domestic ingenuity can invent, to encourage literary studies, is ours almost exclusively. From academies, colleges, public libraries, private associations of literary men, women are excluded, if not by law, at least by custom, which cannot easily be conquered——Whenever women appear, even when we seem to admit them as our equals in understanding, every thing assumes a different form; our politeness, delicacy, habits towards the sex forbid us to argue, or to converse with them as we do with one another—we see things as they are, but women must always see things through a veil, or cease to be women.—With these insuperable difficulties in their education and in their passage through life, it seems impossible that their minds should ever acquire that vigour and *efficiency*, which accurate knowledge and various experience of life and manners can bestow.

Much attention has lately been paid to the education of the female sex, and you will say, that we have been amply repaid for our care—That ladies have lately exhibited such brilliant proofs of genius as must dazzle and confound their critics. I do not ask for proofs of genius,—I ask for solid proofs of utility. In which of the useful arts, in which of the exact sciences have we been assisted by female sagacity or penetration?—I should be glad to see a list of discoveries, of inventions, of observations, evincing patient research, of truths established upon actual experiment, or deduced by just reasoning from previous principles—If these or any of these can be presented by a female champion for her sex, I shall be the first to clear the way for her to the Temple of Fame.

I must not speak of my contemporaries, else candor might oblige me to allow, that there are some few instances of great talents applied to useful purposes— But, except these, what have been the literary productions of women?—In poetry, plays and romances, in the art of imposing upon the understanding by means of the imagination, they have excelled—but to useful literature they have scarcely turned their thoughts—I have never heard of any female proficients in science—few have pretended to science till within these few years.—I know of none of their inventions, and few of their discoveries.

You will tell me, that in the most difficult and most extensive science of politics women have succeeded—you will cite the names of some illustrious queens—I am inclined to think, with the Duke of Burgundy, that "queens who reigned well were governed by men, and kings who reigned ill were governed by women."

The isolated examples of a few heroines cannot convince me that it is safe or expedient to trust the sex with power—their power over themselves has regularly been found to diminish, in proportion as their power over others has been encreased.—I should not refer you to the scandalous chronicles of modern times, to volumes of private anecdotes, or to the abominable secret histories of courts, where female influences, and female depravity are synonymous terms, but I appeal to the open equitable page of history, to a body of evidence collected from the testimony of ages, for experiments tried upon the grandest scale of which nature admits, registered by various hands without the possibility of collusion and without a view to any particular system—from these you must be convinced, that similar consequences have uniformly resulted from the same causes in nations the most unlike, and at periods the most distant. [...] You will assert, that the fatal consequences which have resulted from our trusting the sex with liberty and power, have been originally occasioned by the subjection and ignorance in which they had previously been held, and of our subsequent folly and imprudence in *throwing the reins of dominion into hands unprepared and uneducated to guide them.* I am at a loss to conceive any system of education that can properly prepare women for the exercise of power:—Cultivate their understandings, "cleanse the visual orb with Euphrasy" and Rue,[14] till they can with one comprehensive glance take in "one half at least of round eternity," still you have no security that their reason shall govern their conduct. The moral character seems, even amongst men of superior strength of mind, to have no certain dependence upon the reasoning faculty; ... No one can feel more strongly than you do the necessity and the value of female integrity; no one can more clearly perceive how much in society depends upon the honour of women, and how much it is the interest of every individual, as well as of every state, to guard their virtue, and to preserve inviolate the purity of their manners. Allow me, then, to warn you of the danger of talking in loud strains to the sex of the noble contempt of prejudice. You would look with horrour at one who should go to sap the foundations of the building; beware then how you venture to tear away the ivy which clings to the walls, and braces the loose stones together.

I am by no means disposed to indulge in the fashionable ridicule of prejudice. There is a sentimental, metaphysical argument, which, independently of all others, has lately been used to prevail upon us to relinquish that superiority which strength of body in savage, and strength of mind in civilized, nations secures to man. We are told, that as women are reasonable creatures, they should be governed only by reason; and that we *disgrace* ourselves, and *enslave* them when we instil even the most useful truths as prejudices.—Morality should, we are told, be founded upon demonstration, not upon sentiment; and we should not require human beings to submit to any laws or customs, without convincing their understandings of the universal utility of these political conventions. When are we to expect this conviction? .... What could we expect from that woman whose moral education was to begin at the moment when she was called upon to *act*; and who without having imbibed in her early years any of the salutary prejudices of her sex, or without having been educated in the amiable acquiescence to well-established maxims of female prudence, should boldly venture to conduct herself by the immediate conviction of her understanding? I care not for the names or titles of my guides; all that I shall enquire is, which is best acquainted with the road. Provided women be conducted quietly to their good, it is scarcely worth their while to dispute about the pompous, metaphysical names or precedency of their motives. Why should they deem it disgraceful to be induced to pursue their interest by what some philosophers are pleased to call *weak* motives? [....] Reason in its highest perfection seems just to arrive at the certainty of instinct; and truth, impressed upon the mind in early youth by the united voice of affection and authority, gives all the real advantages of the most investigating spirit of philosophy. If the result of the thought, experience, and sufferings of one race of beings is (when inculcated upon the belief of the next) to be stigmatised as prejudice, there is an end to all the benefits of history and of education. The mutual intercourse of individuals and of nations must be only for the traffic of amusement of the day. Every age must repeat the same experiments; every man and every nation must make the same mistakes, and suffer the same miseries, whilst the civilization and happiness of the world, if not retrograde in their course, must for ever be stationary.

Let us not, then, despise or teach the other sex to despise the traditional maxims of experience, or those of early possessions, which may be termed prejudices, but which in reality serve as their moral instinct. I can see neither tyranny on our part, nor slavery on theirs, in this system of education. This sentimental or metaphysical appeal to our candour and generosity has then no real force, and every other argument for the *literary* and *philosophical* education of women, and for the extraordinary cultivation of their understandings, I have examined.

You probably imagine, that, by the superior ingenuity and care you propose to bestow on your daughter's education, you shall make her an exception to general maxims, you shall give her all the blessings of a literary cultivation, and at the same time preserve her from all the follies and faults, and evils which have been found to attend the character of a literary lady. [...] Women of literature are much more numerous of late than they were a few years ago. They make a class in society, they fill the public eye, and have acquired a degree of consequence and an appropriate character. The esteem of private friends, and the admiration of the public for their talents, are circumstances highly flattering to their vanity, and as such I will allow them to be substantial pleasures. I am also ready to acknowledge that a taste for literature adds much to the happiness of life, and women may enjoy to a certain degree this happiness as well as men. But with literary women this silent happiness seems at best but a subordinate consideration; it is not by the treasures they possess, but by those which they have an opportunity of displaying, that they estimate their wealth. To obtain public applause, they are betrayed too often into a miserable ostentation of their learning. [...] Allowing, however, that you could combine all these virtues—that you could form a perfect whole, a female wonder from every creature's best, dangers still threaten you. How will you preserve your daughter from that desire of universal admiration, which will ruin all your work? How will you, along with all the pride of knowledge, give her that "retiring modesty" which is supposed to have more charms for our sex than the fullest display of wit and beauty.[...]

Modern ladies, by frequenting public places so regularly, declare their approbation of the wholesome regulations of these prudent magistrates. Very different was the crafty policy of the Prophet Mahomet, who forbad his worshippers even to paint his picture. The Turks have pictures of the hand, the foot, the features, of Mahomet, but no representation of the whole face or person is allowed. The portraits of our beauties, in our exhibition-room, shew a proper contempt of this insidious policy; and those learned and ingenious ladies, who publish their private letters, select maxims, secret anecdotes, and family memoirs, are entitled to our thanks for thus presenting us with full lengths of their minds.

230

Can you expect, my dear Sir, that your daughter, with all the genius and learning which you intend to give her, should refrain from these imprudent exhibitions? Will she "yield her charms of mind with sweet delay?" will she, in every moment of her life, recollect that the fatal desire for universal admiration always defeats its own purpose, especially if the purpose be to win love as well as admiration? It is in vain to tell me that more enlarged ideas in our sex would alter our tastes, and alter even the associations which now influence our passions. The captive who has numbered the links of his chains, and who has even discovered how those chains are constructed, is not therefore nearer to the recovery of his liberty.

Besides, it must take a length of time to alter associations and opinions, which, if not *just*, are at least *common* in our sex. You cannot expect even that conviction should operate immediately upon the public taste. You will, in a few years, have educated your daughter; and if the world be not educated exactly at the right time to judge of her perfections, to admire and love them, you will have wasted your labour, and you will have sacrificed your daughter's happiness: that happiness, analyse it as a man of the world or as a philosopher, must depend on friendship, love, the exercise of her virtues, the just performance of all the duties of life, and the self-approbation arising from the consciousness of good conduct.
I am, my dear friend,
Yours sincerely.

AN-
[...]
ANSWER TO THE PRECEDING LETTER
[...]

Do not, my dear Sir, call me "*a champion for the rights of women*"; I am more intent upon their happiness than ambitious to enter into a metaphysical discussion of their rights. Their happiness is so nearly connected with ours, that it seems to me absurd to manage any argument so as to set the two sexes at variance by vain contention for superiority. It is not our object to make an invidious division of rights and privileges, but to determine what is most for our general advantage.

I shall not, therefore, examine with much anxiety how far women are naturally inferior to us either in strength of mind or body. The strength of the one has no necessary connection with the other, I may observe; and intellectual ability has ever conquered mere bodily strength, from the times of Ajax and Ulysses to the present day. In civilized society, that species of superiority which belongs to superior force, is reduced to little in the lowest classes, to less in the higher classes of life.

The invention of fire-arms renders address and presence of mind more than a match for force, or at least reduces to an affair of chance the pretensions of the feeble and the strong. The art of printing has extended the dominion of the mind, as much by facilitating the intercourse and combination of persons of literature, as by the rapid and universal circulation of knowledge. Both these inventions have tended to alter the relative situation of women in modern society.

I acknowledge that, with respect to the opportunities of acquiring knowledge, institution and manners are much in favour of our sex; but your argument concerning *time* appears to me to be inaccurate. Whilst the knowledge of the learned languages continues to form an indispensable part of a gentleman's education, many years of childhood and youth must be devoted to their attainment. During these studies, the general cultivation of the understanding is in some degree retarded. All the intellectual powers are cramped, except the memory, which is sufficiently exercised, but which is overloaded with words, and with words which are seldom understood. The genius of living and of dead languages differs so much, that the pains which are taken to write elegant Latin, frequently spoil the English style. Girls usually write much better than boys: they think and express their thoughts clearly at an age when young men can scarcely write an easy letter upon any common occasion. Women do not read the best authors of antiquity as school books; but they can have excellent translations of most of them, when they are capable of tasting their beauties. I know that it is supposed no one can judge of the classics by translations; and I am sensible that much of the merit of the originals may be lost; but I think the difference in pleasure is more than overbalanced to women, by the *time* they save, and by the labour and misapplication of abilities which is spared. If they do not acquire a classic taste, neither do they acquire classic prejudices: nor are they early disgusted with literature, by pedagogues, lexicons, grammars, and all the melancholy apparatus of learning. Field-sports, travelling, gaming, lounging, and what is called pleasure in various shapes, usually fill the interval between quitting the college and settling for life: this period is not lost by the other sex. Women begin to taste the real pleasures of reading just at the age when young men, disgusted with their studies, begin to be ashamed amongst their companions of alluding to literature. When this period is past, business, the necessity of pursuing a profession, the ambition of shining in parliament, or of rising in public life, occupy a large portion of their lives. The understanding is but partially cultivated for these purposes; men of genius must contract their enquiries, and concentrate their powers; they must pursue *the expedient*, even when they distinguish that it is not *the right*, and they are degraded to "*literary artisans*".* The other sex have no such constraint upon their

---

* Stuart. [Edgeworth refers to Dugald Stewart, Scottish Enlightenment philosopher.]

understandings; neither the necessity of earning their bread, nor the ambition to shine in public life, hurry or prejudice their minds; in domestic life, "they have leisure to be wise." Women, who do not love dissipation, must have more time for the cultivation of their understandings, than men can have if you compute the whole of life.

You apprehend that knowledge must be hurtful to the sex, because it will be the means of their acquiring power. It seems to me impossible that women can acquire the species of direct power which you dread: the manners of society must totally change before women can mingle with men in the busy and public scenes of life. They must become Amazons before they can effect this change; they must cease to be women before they can desire it. The happiness of neither sex could be increased by this metamorphosis: the object cannot be worth the price. Power, supposing it to be a certain good to its possessor, is like all our other pleasures, capable of being appreciated; and if women are taught to estimate their pleasures, they will be governed in their choice by the real, not by the imaginary, value. They will be convinced, not by the voice of the moralist alone, but by their own observation and experience, that power is an evil in most cases; and to those who really wish to do good to their fellow-creatures, it is at best but a painful trust. If, my dear Sir, it be your object to monopolize power for our sex, you cannot possibly better secure it from the wishes of the other, than by enlightening their minds, and enlarging their view of human affairs. The common fault of ignorant and ill-educated women is a love for domination: this they shew in every petty struggle where they are permitted to act in private life. You are afraid that the same disposition should have a larger field for its display; and you believe this temper to be inherent in the sex. I doubt whether any temper be *natural*, as it is called: certainly this disposition need not be attributed to any innate cause; it is the consequence of their erroneous education. The belief that pleasure is neces- sarily connected with the mere exercise of free-will, is a false and pernicious asso- ciation of ideas, arising from the tyranny of those who have had the management of their childhood, from their having frequently discovered that they have been more happy in chusing about trifles, when they have acted in opposition to the maxims of those who govern them, than when they have followed their advice. I shall endeavour to prevent this from happening in my daughter's early educa- tion, and shall thus, I hope, prevent her acquiring any unconquerable prejudice in favour of her own wishes, or any unreasonable desire to influence the opinions of others. People, who have reasons for their preferences and aversions, are never so zealous in the support of their own tastes, as those are who have no arguments either to convince themselves or others that they are in the right. *Power* over the minds of others will not, therefore, in domestic, any more than in public life, be an object of ambition to women of enlarged understandings.

You appeal to history to prove to me that great calamities have ensued whenever the female sex has been indulged with liberty, yet you acknowledge that we cannot be certain whether these evils have been the effects of our trusting them with liberty, or of our not having previously instructed them in the use of it: upon the decision of this rests your whole argument. Women have not erred from having knowledge, but from not having had experience: they may have grown vain and presumptuous when they have learned but little, they will be sobered into good sense when they shall have learned more.

But you fear that knowledge should injure the delicacy of female manners, that truth would not keep so firm a hold upon the mind as prejudice, and that the conviction of the understanding will never have a permanent, good effect upon the conduct. I agree with you in thinking, that the strength of mind, which makes people govern themselves by reason, is not always connected with abilities in their most cultivated state. I deplore the instances I have seen of this truth; but I do not despair: I am, on the contrary, excited to examine into the causes of this phaenomenon in the human mind: nor, because I see some evil, would I sacrifice the good on a motive of bare suspicion. It is a contradiction to say, that to give the power of discerning what is good, is to give a disposition to prefer what is bad. All that you prove when you say that prejudice, passion, habit, often impel us to act in opposition to our reason, is, that there exist enemies to reason, which have not yet been subdued. Would you destroy her power because she has not been always victorious? rather think on the means by which you may extend her dominion, and secure to her in future the permanent advantages of victory [...] You dislike in the female sex that daring spirit which despises the common forms of society, and which breaks through the delicacy and reserve of female manners. So do I. And the best method to make my pupil respect these things, is to shew her how they are indispensably connected with the largest interests of society, and with their highest pleasures. Surely this perception, this view of the utility of forms, apparently trifling, must be a strong security to the sex, and far superior to the automatic habits of those who submit to the conventions of the world, without consideration or conviction. Habit, improved by reason, assumes the rank of virtue. The motives which restrain from vice must be encreased, by the clear conviction that vice and wretchedness are inseparably united.

It is too true that women, who have been but half instructed, who have seen only superficially the relations of moral and political ideas, and who have obtained but an imperfect knowledge of the human heart, have conducted themselves so as to disgrace their talents and their sex: these are conspicuous and melancholy examples, cited oftener with malice than with pity. The benevolent and the wise point out the errors of genius with more care than those of folly, because there is more danger from the example.

I appeal to examples, which every man of literature will immediately recollect amongst our contemporaries, to prove, that where the female understanding has been properly cultivated, women have not only obtained admiration by their useful abilities, but respect by their exemplary conduct.

You very prudently avoid alluding to your contemporaries, but you must excuse me if I cannot omit instances essential to my cause. Modern education has been improved; the fruits of these improvements appear, and you must not forbid me to point them out.

233

Instead of being ashamed that so little has been hitherto done by female abilities, in science and in useful literature, I am surprised that so much has been effected. Till of late, women were kept in Turkish ignorance; every means of acquiring knowledge was discountenanced by fashion, and impracticable even to those who despised fashion. Our books of science were full of unintelligible jargon, and mystery veiled pompous ignorance from public contempt; but now, writers must offer their discoveries to the public in distinct terms, which every body may understand; technical language will no longer supply the place of knowledge, and the art of teaching has been carried to great perfection by the demand for learning: all this is in favour of women. Many things, which were thought to be above their comprehension, or unsuited to their sex, have now been found to be perfectly within the compass of their abilities, and peculiarly suited to their situation. Botany has become *fashionable*; in time it may become useful, if it be not so already. Science has "*been enlisted under the banners of imagination*," by the irresistible charms of genius; by the same power her votaries will be led *from the looser analogies which dress out the imagery of poetry, to the stricter ones which form the ratiocination of philosophy.**

Chemistry will follow botany; chemistry is a science particularly suited to women, suited to their talents and to their situation. Chemistry is not a science of parade, it affords occupation and infinite variety; it demands no bodily strength, it can be pursued in retirement, it applies immediately to useful and domestic purposes; and whilst the ingenuity of the most inventive mind may be exercised, there is no danger of inflaming the imagination; the judgment is improved, the mind is intent upon realities, the knowledge that is acquired is exact, and the pleasure of the pursuit is a sufficient reward for the labour. [...] far from despising domestic duties, women, who have been well educated, will hold them in high respect, because they will see that the whole happiness of life is made up of the happiness of each particular day and hour, and that the enjoyment of these must depend upon the punctual practice of those virtues which are more valuable than splendid. Taste, ingenuity, judgment, are all applicable to the arts of domestic life; and domestic life will be most preferred by those who have within their own minds a perpetual flow of fresh ideas, who cannot be tempted to dissipation, and who are most capable of enjoying all the real pleasures of friendship and of love. [...] The elegant Lord Lyttleton, the benevolent Haller, the amiable Dr. Gregory,[15] have all, in the language of affection, poetry, and truth, described the pleasures which men of genius and literature enjoy in a union with women who can sympathise in all their thoughts and feelings; who can converse with them as equals, live with them as friends; who can assist them in the important and delightful duty of educating their children; who can make their family their most agreeable society, and their home the attractive centre of happiness.

Can women of uncultivated understandings make such wives?

Women have not the privilege of choice as we have; but they have the power to determine. Women cannot precisely force the tastes of the person with whom

---

* Preface to Dr. Darwin's Botanic Garden.

they may be connected, yet their happiness will greatly depend upon their being able to conform their tastes to his. For this reason, I should rather, in female education, cultivate the general powers of the mind than any particular faculty. I do not desire to make my daughter a musician, a painter, or a poetess; I do not desire to make her a botanist, a mathematician, or a chemist; but I wish to give her the habit of industry and attention, the love of knowledge and the power of reasoning: these will enable her to attain excellence in any pursuit of science or of literature. Her tastes and her occupations will, I hope, be determined by her situation, and by the wishes of her friends: she will consider all accomplishments and all knowledge as subordinate to her first object, and the contributing to their happiness and her own.

I am, my dear friend,

Yours sincerely.

ENDNOTES

1   W.J. McCormack, "Edgeworth, Maria (1768–1849), novelist and educationist," in *Oxford Dictionary of National Biography* (Oxford: Oxford University Press, 2004–05), 2.

2   Marilyn Butler, *Maria Edgeworth: A Literary Biography* (Oxford: Clarendon Press, 1972), 149.

3   Jean Bloch, "Discourses of Female Education in the Writings of Eighteenth-Century French Women," in *Women, Gender and Enlightenment*, ed. Sarah Knott and Barbara Taylor (Houndmills: Palgrave Macmillan, 2005), 252.

4   Clíona Ó Gallchoir, "Gender, Nation and Revolution: Maria Edgeworth and Stéphanie-Félicité de Genlis," *Women, Writing and the Public Sphere 1700–1830*, ed. Elizabeth Eger, Charlotte Grant, Clíona Ó Gallchoir, and Penny Warburton (Cambridge: Cambridge University Press, 2001), 202–03.

5   McCormack, 2.

6   W.J. McCormack comments, "Indirectly Edgeworth helped to launch the historical novel across Europe.... What she demonstrated was a means of relating one cultural tradition to another." McCormack, 5.

7   McCormack, 3.

8   William Kern, "Maria Edgeworth and Classical Political Economy," *CSWEP: Committee on the Status of Women in the Economics Profession*, http://www.cswep.org/edgeworth.html (accessed July 16, 2007).

9   McCormack, 57.

10   Marilyn Butler, *Maria Edgeworth: A Literary Biography* (Oxford: Clarendon Press, 1972), 148–49.

11   Clíona Ó Gallchoir, "Gender, Nation and Revolution: Maria Edgeworth and Stéphanie-Félicité de Genlis," in *Women, Writing and the Public Sphere 1700–1830*, ed. Elizabeth Eger, Charlotte Grant, Clíona Ó Gallchoir, and Penny Warburton (Cambridge: Cambridge University Press, 2001), 201.

12   Thomas Day to R.L. Edgeworth, 1769, quoted in Ó Gallchoir, 205.

13   Thomas Day to R.L. Edgeworth, 1769, quoted in Ó Gallchoir, 209–10.

14   These are medicinal herbs.

15   Dr. John Gregory (1724–73), Scottish physician and philosopher, wrote the hugely popular *A Father's Legacy for his Daughters* (1774); Albrecht von Haller (1708–77), Swiss anatomist and physiologist, was known for his theory of "irritability"; George Lyttelton (1709–73), British politician and statesman, wrote *Advice to a Lady* (1733).

PART 3

Philosophy and Religion

Catharine Trotter (1674–1749)

Catharine Trotter (born 29 August 1674) was the daughter of David Trotter, a Scots naval captain, and Sarah Bellenden, connected to the earls of Perth and Lauderdale. Following her father's death in 1684, the family struggled in financially reduced circumstances for much of Catharine's youth. She received an excellent education, nevertheless, studying French, Latin, Greek, and logic. While still in her twenties, in order to improve her family's fortunes, she launched herself in the literary marketplace, publishing poetry; a novella, *The Adventures of a Young Lady* (1693); and *Letters of Love and Gallantry and Several Other Subjects, All Written by Ladies* in two volumes (1693–94). Her greatest success, however, occurred with the five plays she wrote, four tragedies and a comedy, all staged in London between 1695 and 1706.

In the midst of her career as a recognised dramatist, Trotter published anonymously a philosophical treatise, *A Vindication of an Essay Concerning Human Understanding Written by Mr. Locke* (1702). This shift from successful playwright to respected philosopher has puzzled biographers and critics, who have tended to focus either on the plays or on her philosophical writing as representing her most significant work. Yet, as Anne Kelley has convincingly demonstrated, the themes of her plays depicting ethical struggle are entirely congruent with her later philosophical writing.[1]

In 1708, Catharine Trotter married the Reverend Patrick Cockburn, who, though holding various Church of England livings, did not rise to eminence or affluence in the Church. Catharine Cockburn, as she became, continued to write philosophical pieces and was recognised, by such eminent figures as Locke and Leibniz, to be a powerful logician. John Locke expressed himself as indebted to her for her demolition of his critics, praising her in a heartfelt letter of thanks for "the strength and clearness of your reasoning."[2]

Trotter's philosophical work took the form of commentaries on, or responses to, central theological and philosophical questions of the day. The practice of philosophy has always involved ongoing debates between philosophers, so the fact that Trotter did not found her own philosophical system does not detract from her acuity as a philosophical mind. She believed that ethical conduct was founded on reason, which explains her attraction to John Locke's concept of knowledge founded on sense experience and rational reflection. She also admired Samuel Clarke's theological writings.[3] Both Locke and Clarke argued that natural religion (or natural law) was accessible to human reason but that revealed religion (e.g., the Gospels) confirmed and enforced natural religion. The view that Trotter confused or misunderstood the theories of Clarke and Locke has been ably refuted by Bolton and Kelley.[4] From Trotter's perspective, the essential point was to found social and political action on rational morality. Like both Clarke and Locke, she believed in immutable moral laws and opposed moral relativism.

Catharine Trotter's correspondence shows her to have been a fully rounded individual, combining family duties and affections with her intellectual pursuits. She was painfully aware of the time-wasting frivolity in which many well-born women spent their lives. In one of her poems, she described the difficulties faced by gifted women in educating themselves, showing how "partial custom checks the soaring mind" and how women pursue "unbeaten paths, that late to knowledge lead." "By secret steps," they may "break thro' the obstructed way," yet must take care never to show too much learning: "Nor dare acquirements gain'd by stealth display." She notes that attaining a public reputation for learning is likely to harm a woman's reputation:

> If some advent'rous genius rare arise,
> Who on exalted themes her talent tries
> She fears to give the work, tho' praised, a name,
> And flies not more from infamy than fame.[5]

It was such inhibitions that led Trotter to publish her *Vindication* anonymously, although intelligent detective work soon allowed Locke to discover its author's name. As the poem above demonstrates, she evidently feared censure or ridicule as a woman attempting philosophical disputation, yet, in fact, her work was acknowledged by her contemporaries to be authoritative and brilliantly argued. John Duncombe's eulogy of her in his poem *The Feminiad* reminds us how she was venerated, even if he dwells on her poverty and her relative lack of recognition. Her achievements in philosophy are described as a cause for wonder, injecting an unfortunately patronising note. Nonetheless she figures as a pre-eminent intellect:

> Hail, COCKBURN, hail! ev'n now from Reason's bow'rs
> Thy Locke delighted culls the choicest flow'rs
> To deck, his great successful champion's head,
> And Clarke expects thee in the laurel shade.
> Tho' long, to dark, oblivious want a prey,
> Thy aged worth past unperceiv'd away,
> Yet Scotland now shall ever boast thy fame,
> While England mourns thy undistinguish'd name,
> And views with wonder, in a female mind,
> Philosopher, Divine, and Poet join'd.[6]

A VINDICATION OF AN ESSAY CONCERNING HUMAN UNDERSTANDING (1702)

Catharine Trotter was involved in complex philosophical and theological debates. In her *Vindication*, she wrote to defend Locke, responding to a critique of Locke by Thomas Burnet, *Remarks upon an Essay Concerning Humane Understanding* (1697). Burnet had attacked Locke on the basis of the implications of Locke's *Essay Concerning Human Understanding* for morality and the conception of God that he saw in it. Briefly, Locke had argued that human knowledge of God and thus of good and evil, like all knowledge, is not innate but derived from experience. According to Locke, the basis for human knowledge is sensation (sense perception) coupled with rational reflection, by which means we derive ideas from sense impressions. The universe and God conform to the laws of reason, goodness, and probity, of which God is the guarantor.

Locke also argued a necessary connection between moral duty (which we discover by our reason) and God as law giver and law enforcer—e.g., one who distributes rewards and punishments. This position, Burnet thought, made Locke's moral scheme suspect, as one would only act virtuously out of self-interest in order to escape punishment or to win reward. Virtue, in other words, was little more than selfishness, and so, not virtuous at all. Further, in Locke's concept of God, Burnet saw the implication of what was termed an extreme voluntarist position. Voluntarism implied that God, being all powerful, could arbitrarily change the basis of morality—that he could, for example, make evil good and good evil. Burnet could therefore charge Locke with undermining moral absolutes. It was principally against these charges that Trotter directed her rebuttal.

The following excerpts from Trotter's *Vindication* develop three main arguments: first, that knowledge of morality can be derived from experience and reflection and is not innate; second, that Locke's principles of knowledge offer a basis for natural religion and right action; and third, that the view of God as divine lawmaker does not mean that he can make good actions bad, for example, but merely that morality has the force of law as well as of reason.[7] Thus, in a general sense, Trotter defends the rule of reason over the idea of arbitrary judgements and grounds all moral action in lived experience. Like Locke, she rejects the concept of innate ideas. She praises the moral courage of philosophers, who dare to upset traditional ways of viewing the world, evoking the difficulty of overthrowing authoritarian political rule as a metaphor to illustrate our difficulty in re-examining received or fixed ideas: "He who dares attempt against this established monarchy over men's judgments, must be looked on as a troublesome and dangerous innovator, and needs a mighty force of reason and generous courage, to break through the prejudices of men and free them from a willing slavery." For Trotter, justified rebellion against arbitrary and unreasonable ideas can be applied in areas other than pure philosophy. Her indignation at the arbitrary rule of men over women's minds lay behind much of her admiration for Locke, where an emphasis on experience and the need to use our rational capacities could, she believed, have positive implications for women's intellectual development.

A Vindication of an Essay Concerning Human Understanding (1702)

Catharine Trotter

Tis happy for mankind, when men of an elevated genius, and uncommon penetration, have too a truly noble and beneficent nature, above any low particular ends, and resolute enough to encounter all the oppositions they must meet in an unbiassed search of truth, form those, who having with much pains imbibed the opinions of reverenced authors, are unwilling to unlearn all their former knowledge, to examine what they have been taught for first principles, not to be questioned, and lay aside their sacred *ipse dixit*. He, who dares attempt against this established monarchy over men's judgments, must be looked on as a troublesome and dangerous innovator, and needs a mighty force of reason and generous courage, to break through all the prejudices of men, and free them from a willing slavery. To that united force we owe the excellent *Essay on Human Understanding;* and to these prejudices, all the cavils against it.

When the light of truth shines too clear and strong to be directly faced, the only shelter for those, who would not feel its force, is to seek for far fetched danger-ous consequences, supposed inconsistencies with revealed truths, and mysteries of faith, deduced by a long train of arguments, which engaging in an intricate dispute shades them with some pretence, for not confessing the splendour of that truth, they cannot encounter; inconsistencies with revealed truths, when the real necessary consequence of any principles being sufficient proofs against them, how plausible soever they appear. But Mr. *Locke* has so well vindicated his *Essay* from those imputed to it by the most considerable of his opposers, that the rest could only hope to triumph in his neglect of their attempts, who by the help of some suppositions, and many mistakes, have endeavoured to draw an odium on that excellent *Essay*.

The Remarker, whom I have now under consideration, in his first letter,* desires to be informed how far all the principles of that ingenious *Essay*, taken together, will give us a sure foundation for morality, revealed religion, and a future life, which

---

* Page 4.

he does not find that they do. What his reasons, or rather difficulties (as he terms them) are, is my design to consider, and endeavour to satisfy. In his second remarks, he mentions an answer of Mr. *Locke's*, which I have not read, but suppose, by what he quotes out of it, that it was rather designed to shew the weakness of his objections, than to give a full answer to them, Mr. *Locke*, perhaps, thinking it sufficient to shew they required none. But I find they are still of weight with the Remarker, his second and third remarks being only enlargements upon the same heads.

I shall therefore examine them in their order, taking on each head the substance of what I find relating to it in all the three remarks, that the answer, lying together, may be the more clear, and the better considered, which, I hope, will be done by the Remarker without prejudice, as it was writ, with a design to satisfy him, and in a sincere love of truth, to do justice to a book, which, I think, removes the obstacles to it, and shews the method of attaining it, clearer and more effectually, and is writ in an exacter method, than any before it, to vindicate it from a defect in the foundation of certainty, in those things, which are of the greatest concern to us: which I doubt not to do; it being clear to me, that whatever we can know at all, must be discoverable by Mr. *Locke's* principles; for I cannot find any other way to knowledge, or that we have any one idea not derived from sensation and reflection. But let us see, how those points may be established on them, for which the Remarker doubts their force; and first of morality, or natural religion. Of which, he thus begins:

> As to morality, we think the great foundation of it is the distinction of good and evil, virtue and vice.—And I do not find, that my eyes, ears, nostrils, or any other outward senses, make any distinction of these things, as they do of colours, sounds, &c.— Nor from any ideas taken in from them, or from their reports, am I conscious, that I do, or can conclude, that there is such a distinction in the nature of things.*

In which words,† he says, he thought he had taken in enough to comprehend both Mr. *Locke's* principles of knowledge, *sensation and reflection*, which I should not have thought; but since he owns he designed them to do so, we will suppose both expressed and proceed with him. "I allow, that we may infer from observation and reason, that such a distinction is useful to society, but both philosophers and divines, you know, make a more immutable and intrinsic distinction, which is that I cannot make out from your principles.—This I am sure of, that the distinction, suppose of gratitude and ingratitude, fidelity and infidelity, justice and injustice, and such others, is as sudden without any ratiocination, and as sensible and piercing, as the difference I feel from the scent of a rose and *affa foetida*."[8] One would think here, he were doubting, whether upon Mr. *Locke's* principles we can distinguish *gratitude* from *ingratitude*, *fidelity* from *infidelity*, &c. that is,

---

* 1sft Rem. p. 4.
† 2nd Rem. p. 8.

know that breaking a trust is not keeping a trust, &c. which (as all other moral virtues, as Mr. *Locke* has shewn)* are a collection of simple ideas, received from sensation and reflection. But since he allowed above, that *we can from observation and reason, infer such a distinction to be useful to society*, and by consequence, that we can by them perceive such a distinction, we will guess his meaning here, to be, that the perception of the *morality* and *immorality* of these things is as sudden, &c. *as the difference he feels from the scent of a rose, and* affa foetida; though I do not know what it is, to perceive the *morality and immorality* of these things *without any ratiocination. Justice and injustice*, I think, depend upon the rights of men, whether natural, or established by particular societies; and therefore to know what they are, it is necessary to know what right is, which sure requires some *reflection*. But to know, that *injustice* is *evil*, without any *reflection*, seems to me no more than to know, that the term *injustice* stands for something that we do not know, which is evil; unless it will be said, that we may know it to be a detaining any one's right, without knowing what right is, which will be a very insignificant knowledge. But if the Remarker means, that as soon as he knows what it is to have a right to a thing, he perceives, that to detain from a man what he has such a right to, is evil, without any farther reflection, I understand him, but see not how it can be objected against the force of Mr. *Locke's* principles, being only a perception of the disagreement of these two ideas, of one man's having a right to a thing, and another's having a right to take it away: but this only by the way.

243

Let us now consider that, for which this sudden perception without ratiocination is brought as a proof, *viz.* that the ground of the distinction of moral good and evil is in the *nature of the things themselves*, abstract from the good of society; which is that he cannot make out from Mr. *Locke's* principles. By which distinction in the nature of things, if he means, that without respect to men, or to society, though mankind had never been, or never been designed, justice, gratitude, fidelity, &c. had been good, and their contraries evil; I confess myself incapable of having a notion of these virtues abstract from any subject to conceive: For example, that it would have been good to be faithful to a trust, though there had never been any one to trust, or be trusted: nor do I find, that the assertors of this distinction in the nature of things have any real idea of them more abstracted than I have, which will appear in examining their particular instances. I will take that, which the Remarker gives,† being one of the most incontested principles in morality, *That it is a wicked thing, for a man maliciously to kill his friend, or his father, or any other innocent person. The truth of this,* he says, *seems to him as clear and eternal, as any proposition in mathematics;* and it seems to me as clear, that it cannot possibly be conceived at all, either *true* or *false*, in itself, i.e. without any relation to man. I desire any one, to try, whether he can conceive it to be an eternal truth, that it is a wicked thing, for a man to kill his father, or his friend, though there had never been or designed to be, such a thing as friend, father, or man. But whether he can or not, it will still be a truth as

* Es. p. 195. § 14.
† Rem. p. 26.

certain and immutable, as any proposition in mathematics. No mathematician, that I know of, thinks it necessary to establish the immutability of this truth, that the three angles of a triangle are equal to two right ones; to affirm, that it is true, without any relation to angles or triangles. Either of these propositions are sufficiently established, if it is, and always must be true, supposing those things, to which it relates to exist.*

But here the Remarker's[†] question will be made, upon what grounds must it be so? If *good* and *evil*, virtue and vice, áre not such in their own nature, *they must be so from the arbitrary will of God; and all things are indifferent, till he declare this, or that, to be sin, according to his pleasure*: that is, he might, if he had so pleased, have made *virtue vice*; and *vice, virtue*: To which, I answer, that God having made man such a creature as he is, it is as impossible, that good and evil should change their respects to him, as that *pleasure* can be *pain*, and *pain pleasure*, which no one in his sense will affirm; and yet, I think, no body has supposed them to be real existences, independent of any subject. And if the relation, which moral good and evil has to natural good and evil, were sufficiently observed, there would be as little dispute about the nature and reality of *virtue* and *vice*. Those, who think they are only notions in the mind, would be convinced they are as real as natural good and evil; all *moral good* consisting in doing, willing, or chusing, for one's self or others, whatever is a *natural good*; and all *moral evil*, in doing, willing, or chusing whatever is a *natural evil*, to one's self or others. This, I doubt not, will appear a full definition, when tried by every instance of *moral good* and *evil*, to all, who reflect on it; unless there are any, who do not place the perfection and imperfection, the advantages and disadvantages of the *mind*, in their account of *natural good* or *evil*; which I believe no rational man will own.

And as this unalterable relation makes the real and immutable nature of virtue and vice undeniable; so also from thence it is plain, *that the nature of man is the ground or reason of the law of nature*; i.e. of moral good and evil. But if the Remarker will rather have it, that the nature of these things is the reason of the nature of man, that they are essentially in the nature of God, which is the rule of his will, and according to which he formed man; let it be so, as it is unquestionable, that he cannot will any thing contrary to his nature. But however the moral attributes of God, goodness, justice, &c. are in him (who is infinitely beyond the reach of our narrow capacities) this I say (which Mr. *Locke* has observed of our idea of their infinity) that we have no idea of them, but what carries with it a respect to their objects, *the natural good or evil of his creatures*; and we could have no idea of them at all without reflection upon ourselves; for whatever is

___

* This whole paragraph is a partial and temporary consideration of moral truths (as the opposers of Dr. *Clarke* do now consider them) with relation only to the present constitution of things, not to their original ground, as they exist eternally in the divine mind. An error, the author is now sensible of, and that there was no need of this for the defence of Mr. *Locke's* principles. If his plan led him only to speak of the immediate origin of our ideas, or how we come by our ideas of moral relations, his principles are sufficient by the reflections we make on the operations of our own minds, to lead us to the supreme mind, where all truth, and the abstract nature of all possible things, must eternally and immutably exist.

† 2 Rem p. 22.

the original standard of good and evil, it is plain, we have no notion of them but by their conformity, or repugnancy to our reason, and with relation to our nature; and that what according to it we perceive to be good, we ascribe to the Supreme Being; for we cannot know, that the nature of God is good, before we have a notion of good. It must be then by reflecting upon our own nature, and the operations of our minds, that we come to know the nature of God; which therefore cannot *be to us* the rule of good and evil; unless we will argue in a circle, that by our notion of good, we know the nature of God, and by the nature of God, we know what is good.

From whence it will follow, that the nature of man, and the good of society, *are to us* the reason and rule of moral good and evil; and there is no danger of their being less immutable on this foundation than any other, whilst man continues *a rational and sociable creature*. If the law of nature is the product of human nature itself (as the great *Grotius* speaks) it must subsist as long as human nature; nor will this foundation make it the less sacred, since it cannot be doubted, that it is originally the will of God, whilst we own him the author of that nature, of which this law is a consequence.

If then, in Mr. *Locke's* way, we can perceive what is conformable, or not, to our own nature, which cannot be doubted; if by reflecting on ourselves, we can come to know there must be a Supreme Being, the source of all others, which he has admirably shewn;* we have a sacred and immutable foundation for natural religion, on his principles; this being a plain and infallible inference, that the Author of our being does require those things of us, to which he has suited our nature, and visibly annexed our happiness, which he has made the necessary motive of all our actions. For it is inconsistent with that divine wisdom, which we see has fitted all other things to their proper and certain end, to have formed us after such a manner, that if we employ those faculties, which he has given us, we cannot but judge, that such things are fit to be done, and others to be avoided, and this is no end at all. Much less can we suppose he has designed us to act contrary to the necessary motives of our actions, and judgment of our minds; it being a flat contradiction, that infinite wisdom and power should form any of his works so disproportionate to their end.

It will not be much from the purpose here, to take notice of the folly of those men, who think to weaken the authority of religion, by calling it a politic contrivance, established for the good of government or society; which is as much as to say, it is the less obligatory, because it is necessary. Whereas that very thing shews it to be our indispensable duty, and of divine authority, without any revelation; since the divine workmanship, *human nature*, could not subsist without it. If they could prove it unpolitic or destructive to society, it would be much more for their purpose; for such a religion must necessarily be false; nothing can be a *law to nature*, which of direct consequence would *destroy nature*.

But if any one thinks it better established on the nature of God, I have shewn how we come to the knowledge of it in Mr. *Locke's* way, by ascribing to him

---

* Es. B. iv. c.x.

245

whatever by its conformity to our nature we perceive to be good; because we see, that we cannot admit any imperfection in the Supreme Being, without a contradiction (which I shall shew in Mr. *Locke's* way, when I come to the next head) and having by the *effect* found out the *cause*, we may then conclude the nature of God to be the arch-type of ours, because we cannot suppose the most perfect Being can will anything contrary to his own nature; for if he could, the rule of that will must be something less perfect than himself, (for whatever is most perfect is God) and therefore to will any thing contrary to his own nature, would be an imperfection in him, which to admit in the most perfect being, is a contradiction. Thus (when I have more fully shewn, how we come by the idea of perfection in the Supreme Being) the Remarker may perceive, that we can, in Mr. *Locke's* way, arrive to the original notion of intrinsic holiness,* into which 'tis ultimately resolved, which he is so much concerned to find; and that I hope will reconcile him to Mr. *Locke's* principles.

And if he will attentively examine his own without prepossession, if he will trace his idea of God, and of moral good and evil, to their first source, I believe he will find he has no other principle of knowledge than Mr. *Locke*; and that the mistake lies, in that being taught truths after they are discovered, and finding them agreeable to our reason, we immediately assent to them, without reflecting, how they were first found out, and are apt to conclude those things, which we find first in our knowledge, to be the first principles of knowledge; tho' they were proceeded to by many steps and degrees, and were the last established in the discovery.

But the Remarker will object, that Mr. *Locke* does not establish morality upon the nature of man, and the nature of God,[†] but *seems to ground his demonstration upon future punishments and rewards, and upon the arbitrary will of the law-giver; and he does not think these the first grounds of good and evil.* To which I answer, first, supposing it were so, the question is not what Mr. *Locke* thinks, but what may be proved from his principles.[‡] But secondly, I say, that Mr. *Locke* does ground his demonstration upon the *nature of God and man*, as will plainly appear by his express words, which are these.[§] "The idea of a Supreme Being, infinite in power, goodness, and wisdom, whose workmanship we are, and on whom we depend, and the idea of ourselves, as understanding rational creatures, being such, as are clear in us, would, I suppose, if duly considered and pursued, afford such foundations of our duty and rules of action, as might place morality among the sciences capable of demonstration." Nothing can be clearer than this; and in all those places, which the Remarker quotes out of Mr. *Locke*, where he seems to establish morality upon *the will of God, and rewards and punishments*, he is speaking of it, as it has the force of a law; and the Remarker cannot deny, whatever he thinks, *the first grounds of good and evil*; or however clearly we may

246

---

* 2 Rem p. 2.
† 2 R. p. 2.
‡ 2 R. p. 4.
§ Ess. B. iv. c.3. § 18.

see the *nature of these things*, we may approve or condemn them; but they can only have the force of a *law* to us, considered as *the will of the Supreme Being*, who can, and certainly will, reward the compliance with, and punish the deviation from that rule, which he has made knowable to us by the light of nature.*

But that we can only know these things to be his will by their conformity to our nature, and that therefore they cannot be arbitrary, I have before shewn; and that he will punish or reward us according to our obedience or disobedience to it, is a consequence of his nature. So that, tho' Mr. *Locke* says, that the will of God, rewards and punishments, can only give morality the force of a law; that does not make them the *first grounds* of good and evil, since by his principles, to know what the will of God is (antecedently to revelation) we must know what is good by the conformity it has to our nature, by which we come to know the nature of God, which therefore may be to him the first ground or rule of good; tho' *the will of God, &c.* can only enforce it as a *law*.

247

I cannot here omit to take notice of a question the Remarker asks on this subject:[†] How, pray you, upon these principles, do you preserve the distinction (that good old distinction, which it may be you despise) of *Bonum Utile*, and *Honestum*? In your way, either the parts are coincident, or *Bonum Utile* is superior to *Bonum Honestum*. I'm afraid the Remarker will have hard thoughts of me, if I should say I do not like his good old distinction, and that I think the parts are coincident. I know not whether he will have a better opinion of me, when I tell him, I do not mean it in the way, which he injuriously insinuates to be Mr. *Locke's*; but that nothing can be truly profitable, that is not honest. However, not to cavil about words, this am I sure of, that there is no ground for the Remarker's reflection on those principles, which he is dissatisfied with, *viz.* "That morally good and evil is the conformity or disagreement of our actions to the divine law; which [‡]Mr. *Locke* says is the only true touch-stone of moral rectitude; and that by comparing them to this law, men judge of the most considerable moral good or evil of their actions, that is, whether as duties or sins, they are like to procure them happiness

---

* Some, who had lately read this defence, have thought, that the author's sentiments, on *the grounds of moral obligation*, were different when this was wrote, from what they now appear to be in some late pieces. But the author thinks there is no real difference: the grounds of moral obligation are not here discussed at all; the notion of founding morality on arbitrary will is carefully rejected; and the nature of God, or the divine understanding, and the nature of man, all along supposed to be the true grounds of it. New terms have been since introduced into these subjects; we talk now of essential differences, nature, relation, truth, and fitness of things: but the meaning is the very same; for all these are to be sought for in the nature of God, or of man. But Mr. *Locke* is here defended in establishing morality on *the will of God, and rewards and punishments considered, as if it has the force of a law*; there I suppose lies the *apparent* difference, tho' there is none in reality. The author still agrees to that proposition; for strictly and properly speaking a law implies authority and sanctions; and though we say the *law of reason*, and the *law of nature*, is in a less proper sense, importing, that they are as effectual grounds of obligation, as if they were real laws, but they oblige us, not as *dependent*, but as *reasonable* beings; in the same manner as the Supreme Being, who is subject to no laws, and accountable to none, obliges himself to do always what he perceives to be right and fit to be done. In this light the author has all along considered the grounds of moral obligation; and this I presume is not inconsistent with allowing, that the will of God, rewards and punishments, can only give morality the force of a law.

† 2 Rem. p. 25.

‡ Ess. B. ii. c. 28.

or misery from the hands of the Almighty." Upon these principles _Bonum Utile_ can never be superior to _Bonum Honestum_, in Mr. _Locke's_ way, till the Remarker can shew him some moral evil, that is not contrary to the divine law; or a way to escape the hands of the Almighty when we disobey him.

What has been said, will be sufficient to answer all that the Remarker has said directly on this point: but what further concerns it, _of natural conscience_, and the proofs of the _moral attributes of God_, will be considered in their order; which leads us to the second head, of which the Remarker.

*_As to revealed religion, my difficulty is only this, how it can be proved from your principles, that the author of the revelation is veracious;_ and p.7. _to establish the certainty of revealed religion, we must know the moral attributes of the divine nature, such as goodness, justice, holiness, and particularly veracity. Now these I am not able to deduce from your principles. You have proved very well an eternal all-powerful and all-knowing being: but, &c._ The Remarker, it seems, does not find what Mr. _Locke_ says, after he has _very well proved_ an eternal, most powerful, and most knowing being; †That _from this idea, duly considered, will easily be deduced all those other attributes we ought to ascribe to this eternal Being._ The Remarker is _not able to do it,_ tho', to help him, Mr. _Locke_ says, _he may be ashamed to have raised such a doubt as this,_ viz. _whether an infinitely powerful and wise being be veracious, or no, unless he concludes lying to be no mark of weakness, and folly._‡ As I find in his words repeated by the Remarker, which he complains of, _as misrepresenting, and perverting his sense; the question is not_ (says he) _whether God be veracious, but whether, according to your principles, he can be proved to be so._ Answ. But the question is, _whether an infinitely powerful and wise being is veracious or no;_ for such a being Mr. _Locke_ has _very well proved,_ as the Remarker owns: so that the doubt must be, whether, as such, he must be _veracious;_ for the Remarker allows _veracity_ to be a consequence of _infinite power and wisdom._ The veracity of God is proved by Mr. _Locke's_ principles; and this is an absurd question, whether the veracity of God can be proved from his principles, if _falsehood_ is allowed to be _a mark of weakness and folly;_ for then it cannot possibly be admitted in a being, which he has proved of _infinite wisdom and power_; and I know no better way of proving any thing, than by proving principles, upon which it cannot be denied without a contradiction; so that Mr. _Locke_ has not _perverted_ the Remarker's sense; for he cannot avoid this dilemma, either he concludes falsehood to be _a mark of weakness and folly,_ or he does not: if not, then Mr. _Locke_ has rightly represented his sense; if he does, then this is an absurd question, whether one, who has proved an infinitely powerful and wise Being, can prove he is not false.

But this is not sufficient for the Remarker: he is _not able to deduce_ one attribute from another. Let us see then what is his way to know the moral attributes of God, which, he tells us, is this, he _ascribes veracity to God, because it is a perfection._

248

---

* 1 ft. Rem. p. 6.
† Ess. B. iv. c. 10 § 6.
‡ 2nd. Rem. p. 3.

But from what grounds does he conclude, that whatever is a perfection must be in God? Will he say, that it is a principle imprinted on the mind, without any reflection; that is, we clearly see, that God must be perfect, we don't know why: or will he not rather say, that the want of any perfection would imply either that he does not know what is best, or cannot attain it, and therefore is inconsistent with infinite wisdom and power? Or that to suppose there may be a being of greater perfection than the supreme source of all being, is a gross contradiction? I believe, if he reflects attentively on the progress of the mind in the knowledge of God, he will find perfection is not first in our notion of him, (as an ingenious author has shewn*) but that having discovered a first being, the source of all others, and what attributes we must necessarily ascribe to him, as such, we perceive, that to admit any imperfection in him would be a contradiction to our first necessary conceptions of him; which Mr. *Locke* has established in his way, and tells us, that from them all his other attributes will easily be deduced.

249

But this will not satisfy the Remarker, unless Mr. *Locke* tells us, *what is to be understood by perfection in his way; how it is derived from the* senses; *and how it includes veracity.*† The Remarker is very apt to forget, that Mr. *Locke* has another principle of knowledge, which he calls *reflection*; or he thinks it insignificant. Perhaps it may be so as to his purpose; but happening to be serviceable in the present enquiry, I take leave to remind him of it, that we may consider how far it will help us to the idea of perfection.

But first, I observe, that we have no adequate idea of perfection; but perceiving in ourselves some *powers and faculties*, as of *knowing, willing, moving*, &c. and of particular actions, and general abstract ideas; that some are congruous, and others repugnant to each other, and to our reason; we know, that some things are better than others; and from every thing about us, and within us, we may learn, that the vastly greater part of them escape the extent of our power, knowledge, and goodness; from whence we conclude, these things may be far more extensive, even to all that can exist. And the highest possible degree of these, which we find it better to have, than to be without, that we call perfection; which to have an adequate idea of, we must comprehend the existence of an infinite spirit. But we cannot add any thing to make up this idea, which we do to find in ourselves; only the degrees, which we perceive must be ascribed, far beyond our measures, to that Being, from which we received all our powers and faculties, and by whose wisdom, power, and goodness, all things exist; for perfection is only the highest degree, or the best manner of possible existence; and that the eternal source of all being must exist in the most perfect manner possible, cannot be doubted; for there cannot be a greater absurdity, than to suppose there may be a more perfect being, than the eternal source of all Being. Thus we see how the idea of perfection, such as we have, may be derived from *sensation and reflection*; and any one, who considers it, will find that he has no positive idea of it, and that there is nothing in that idea, which he has, but what the objects without him, or

---

* Norris, Reason and Religion, Vol. I. E.
† 1ft. Rem. p. 8.

the faculties he perceives in himself, have furnished him with; and that therefore it is needless to seek for any other original of it.

Having now got the idea of perfection, in Mr. *Locke's* way, and found, that it must necessarily be ascribed to the eternal source of all being, we must next consider the other part of the Remarker's question, *how it includes veracity,* which he is the more concerned to know, because he says, *not only the truth of revelation, but also of our faculties in other things, depends upon the veracity of their author.** And here he must give me leave to ask him, upon what grounds veracity is to him a perfection? He will not say, because God is veracious (tho' the nature of God is to him the rule of good) for he ascribes veracity to God, because it is a perfection, and he does not approve of arguing in a circle. He must then know, that veracity is a perfection from some other rule; and here I am afraid he will be involved in a great difficulty; for *the truth of our faculties* he says, *depends upon the veracity of their author*: but before he can know the veracity of their author, he must be sure, that veracity is a perfection, since it is only as such he does, or it can be ascribed to him. Now by whatsoever means he perceives it to be so, how can he be certain, that the faculty, by which he receives that information, does not deceive him? For unless he is certain, that veracity is a perfection, he cannot be certain, that God is veracious, nor therefore the truth of his faculties. He must then remain in doubt, whether God is veracious, unless he can know it without the help of his faculties, that is, without the power or capacity of knowing it; or he must suppose the truth of his faculties without any proof. If that is not a first principle not to be doubted of, I see no defence against an incurable scepticism: we cannot argue for, or against any thing, and the Remarker cannot know, that his position is true, *viz.* That the truth of our faculties depends upon the veracity of their author, since he must take it upon the credit of those faculties. Let him doubt the truth of his faculties as much as he will, if he affirms any one thing, in that one he must believe them upon their own evidence; and since he could not trust them in other things, till he was certain of the veracity of their author; whatever principle he establishes that certainty upon, he must rely upon the evidence of his faculties for the truth of that principle, which he tells us is this, *that veracity is a perfection, and consequently must belong to the nature of God.*† For which propositions we may therefore conclude, he was contented to suppose the truth of his faculties; and he cannot deny Mr. *Locke* the same privilege, till he can show him some way to knowledge without their help.

In the mean time there can be but two ways of knowing, that veracity is a perfection: either it is an innate principle, originally imprinted on the mind; (which I shall not endeavour to confute, Mr. *Locke* having done it sufficiently, nor is it needful to my purpose.) Let that be the Remarker's way of knowledge, if he pleases, since he must no less rely upon the truth of his faculties in that way than any other, it being impossible for God himself to make any impression on us, without giving us a faculty whereby to receive it. But let us see, whether it is

---

* 1 ft. Rem. p. 8.
† 1 ft. Rem. p. 7. 2nd Rem. p. 18.

discoverable in the other way, which must be Mr. *Locke's* of *sensation and reflection.* I suppose the Remarker does not doubt, that in this way we can distinguish truth from falsehood, i.e. know, that things are as they are; appear, as they appear, and that doing a thing differs from not doing it; that an apple, for example, is not a horse; that pain is not pleasure; and that performing our promise is not breaking it; or that representing things as they are, or as they appear to us, and performing our promise, *i.e.* veracity, is more agreeable to our nature, and beneficial to mankind, than the contrary; which how far *to* us the rule of good and evil, I have before shewn, and shall only add here, that if in Mr. *Locke's* way we can know, that what is beneficial to mankind, is better than what is destructive to it; that happiness is better than misery, that power and knowledge is better than impotence and ignorance; if we may trust our faculties in discerning truths; as sensible to us as our own existence; it cannot be doubted that in his way we can be assured, that veracity is a perfection, till some other reason of falsehood can be imagined, than ignorance, impotence or willing evil for its own sake, which cannot be conceived possible; to chuse to prefer evil, as evil, being no less a contradiction, than to judge that to be best, which we know to be worst.

And the Remarker could not have been at a loss how to deduce this, and all the other moral attributes of God, from Mr. *Locke's* principles, if he had carefully considered his discourse of our idea of God, where he shews, that it is *made up of the simple idea we have received from sensation and reflection, by putting together all the qualities and powers, which we experiment in ourselves, and find it better to have, than to be without, and enlarging every one of them with our idea of infinity;* to which place I refer the Remarker. And if he can by *reflection* find veracity, justice, and goodness, among the things, that *it is better to have than to be without,* I hope (with what I have said) it will help him to deduce those attributes of God from Mr. *Locke's* principles; which will satisfy him, that they give us a sure foundation for natural and revealed religion; by which we have a full assurance of a future state; the Remarker's third head of enquiries, which we are next to consider.

That the immortality of the soul is only highly probable by the light of nature, none can deny, who believes that Apostle, by whom we are told, *that life and immortality is brought to light by* Jesus Christ *through the gospel.* Why then is it objected against Mr. *Locke's* principles, that they give us no certainty of the immortality of the soul without revelation? By what other way can we be certain of anything, that is only highly probable by the light of nature? Which is all that can be proved by any principles; and so far Mr. *Locke* will go, as I doubt not to make appear. But farther I shall shew, that there is nothing in his principles, which at all weakens the main proofs of the future state; so that if they are thought to amount to demonstration, they have no less force and evidence, upon his principles, which will leave no pretence on this account against them; as will plainly appear in examining the Remarker's objections.

251

---

* B. ii. C.23, § 33, 34.

ENDNOTES

1   Anne Kelley, *Catharine Trotter: An Early Modern Writer in the Vanguard of* *Feminism* (Aldershot and Burlington: Ashgate, 2002).

2   John Locke to Catharine Trotter, 30 December 1702, quoted in Mary Ellen Waithe, "Catharine Trotter Cockburn," *A History of Women Philosophers*, vol. 3, 1600–1900 (London: Kluwer Academic Publishers, 1991), 106.

3   Samuel Clarke (1675–1729) was a theologian and philosopher.

4   Kelley, *Catharine Trotter*, 140–46; Martha Brandt Bolton, "Some Aspects of the Philosophical Work of Catharine Trotter," in *Hypatia's Daughters, Fifteen Hundred Years of Women Philosophers*, ed. Linda Lopez McAllister (Bloomington: Indiana University Press, 1996), 139–68.

5   "A Poem, occasioned by the busts set up in the Queen's Hermitage," quoted in Kelley, *Catharine Trotter*, 213.

6   John Duncombe, *The Feminiad*; A Poem (London: 1754; Los Angeles, CA: The Augustan Reprint Society, no. 207, 1981), 14.

7   See Bolton, "Some Aspects of the Philosophical Work of Catharine Trotter," 143–45.

8   *Assa fœtida* is a concreted resinous gum with a strong odour of onions or garlic; it is used in medicine as an anti-spasmodic.

Elizabeth Carter (1717–1806)

Elizabeth Carter, recognised during her own lifetime as a leading classical scholar, combined learning and domesticity with intellectual conviviality. Successfully balancing scholarship and sociability, she was devoted to her extended family, her friends, and her studies. She was greatly admired by Dr. Johnson, whose comment—that she could make puddings as well as translate Greek—encapsulated the two roles Carter cultivated, the scholarly and the domestic, roles that enabled her to lead a remarkably independent life.

Elizabeth Carter was born in Deal on the Kentish coast. Her father, the Reverend Nicholas Carter, curate of Deal Chapel and a man of advanced views on education, believed that equal training should be given to his sons and daughters, including a solid grounding in Latin, Greek, and Hebrew. Elizabeth, the eldest child, was an enthusiastic pupil, learning in addition to the three languages above, French, Italian Spanish, German, Portuguese, and Arabic. To become proficient in foreign languages also required the study of the literature, history, and philosophy of the cultures that produced them. Carter attained an assured command in all these areas.

From an early age, Elizabeth knew that she wanted to make her mark in the Republic of Letters, in the literary world of London. In 1734, at the age of seventeen, she had already had a poetic riddle composed by her published in the *Gentleman's Magazine*. With her father's agreement, she settled in London and, from 1735–39, resided there for the greater part of the year, making the acquaintance of literary circles. She published poetry and translations from the French and Italian, the first a critique of Pope's *An Essay on Man* by Crousaz, and Algarotti's *Sir Isaac Newton's Philosophy Explain'd for the Use of Ladies.*[1] She met Dr. Johnson who became a life-long friend. In the 1750s, she would publish two prose pieces in Johnson's *Rambler*.

Four years of stimulating but exhausting work in Grub Street, as the world of aspiring authors and literary drudges was called, left Elizabeth Carter with a desire to establish an independent and less pressured existence away from London. She seems to have made a conscious decision not to marry, refusing at least four suitors. In 1740, she returned to Deal to reside with her father and his children by his second marriage (his first wife, Elizabeth's mother, died when she was ten). There, she established a mode of living that suited her ideas of freedom, combined with family duties and affections.

The central passion of Elizabeth Carter's life was intellectual enquiry. She pursued her studies somewhat to the detriment of her health. As an adult, she suffered from severe migraines. She habitually rose at four a.m., worked for two or three hours, embarked on a long and vigorous walk with a sister or close friend, and, on returning, plunged into family sociability and domestic tasks. Outside her family, she played a central role in the Bluestocking Circle. Carter's relations with Mrs. Montagu, Catherine Talbot, and Hester Chapone set the tone of friendship, learning, and virtue that defined the next bluestocking generation as well.[2] By the 1780s Carter was virtually a national institution, renowned for her affability, piety, and philanthropy, attributes that made her scholarship seem palatable to a society sometimes distrustful of female intellect.[3]

254

In 1749, Carter was encouraged by Catherine Talbot and Archbishop Secker to embark on a translation of all the extant works of Epictetus, the first-century, Greek Stoic philosopher. She had already established her name as perhaps the most learned woman in England and now proved her unchallenged command of ancient Greek and her understanding of Stoic philosophy. Not only did her translation, which took ten years to complete, consolidate her reputation as a classical scholar, its publication by subscription netted her a profit of £1,000, ensuring her financial independence.

Elizabeth Carter was conservative in her political and social views. She believed that women's abilities were underrated but deprecated radical ideas for reform. She was committed to the established order and to preserving distinctions of rank. She was able to negotiate her personal agenda of developing her exceptional talents by not challenging other gender norms. Belonging to the middle class, she had wealthy and aristocratic friends (notably Mrs. Montagu and Catherine Talbot), but she was careful to maintain herself in a position of independence with regard to them. A person of great physical vitality (she described herself as "fidgety"), she knew that exercise was necessary to her well-being, though she was under some pressure from family members to curtail her energetic walks as not befitting her sex and status. Carter constructed a life for herself that included sociability, loyalty to family, and intellectual enrichment, recorded in her witty and ironic letters.

Twentieth-century historians have tended to imply that Carter did not publish a major work after translating the works of Epictetus partly because, as a woman, she feared further exposure in the public sphere and that leaving London for Deal marked a retreat from professional writing.[4] Such a view may reflect our ideas of what constitutes scholarly activity and reputation, a view based largely on publishing output. Carter, in fact, "managed" her reputation with great skill, as her female friendships and participation in the Bluestocking Circle attest. She continued to be an honoured and admired figure in literary and scholarly circles into old age. She structured her life on what Norma Clarke called "an older, aristocratic or courtly style of conducting a writing life which valued scholarship for its own sake, and circulated ideas, books, and manuscripts among a carefully selected coterie."[5]

THE WORKS OF EPICTETUS (1758)

Pre-eminently for Elizabeth Carter, religion, in her case Anglicanism, provided the moral framework for action. She was attracted to the writings of Epictetus, a pre-Christian philosopher, by his emphasis on "establishing a correct ratio between contemplation, comfort, and active duties."[6] The fact that he was a "pagan" and thus not cognisant of the revelations of Christianity did not detract, in her view, from his teaching, though it alarmed her friend Catherine Talbot and Archbishop Secker, her advisors on the project, who feared that the very attractions of Stoic philosophy might lead unwary readers of Epictetus to abandon Christianity for pure rationalism. Though not convinced by this argument, Carter agreed to point out in her Introduction the extent to which Epictetus's teachings contradicted or omitted important Christian doctrine. Her letter to Catherine Talbot (1755), reproduced below, lays out her defence of Epictetus. Her *Rambler* piece "On Religion" (1750) and excerpts from her translation of Epictetus reveal her concept of the duties and pleasures compatible with the moral life. Epictetus's philosophy and her Christian faith were, for Elizabeth Carter, mutually re-enforcing.

The passages chosen from Carter's Introduction and Chapter XII of *The Works of Epictetus*, "On Contentment," illustrate the conflicts Carter experienced between offering a clear translation and analysis of a work of philosophy, and the pressure to underline Epictetus's inadequacies in relation to Christianity. Thus, Carter suggests, his teaching is characterised as elitist and ignores the problem of theodicy—why evil and imperfection exist in a world created by a just, benevolent, and perfect God. Epictetus's answer was that individuals should not agitate themselves about the necessary evils of life that they cannot change but seek to perfect themselves in virtue, the only means to contentment. For the Stoics, freedom lay in acquiescence to the divine rule.

From the Christian perspective, the answer to the problem of evil lay in the concept of original sin, arising, as Milton phrased it, from "Man's first disobedience" in Eden and passed on to all subsequent generations. Carter, like many eighteenth-century philosophers, may have had difficulty reconciling the concept of original sin with that of divine justice. She avoids that aspect of the debate and focuses instead on Epictetus's failure to hold out an afterlife of rewards and punishments as a spur to the virtuous life. Since he made no mention of the afterlife, he failed to account, Carter argues, for our human need for consolation for the ills all must encounter in the world. Stoic philosophy, unlike Christianity, was fit not for the mass of mankind, but only for a few intellectuals, and even they found that indifference to life's miseries was not always possible. Suicide, on the one hand, or a retreat into the pursuit of pleasure, on the other (see reference to the gardens of Epicurus), was proof that Epictetus's teaching did not respond to the human condition. Nevertheless, Carter was imbued with his concept of the balanced life. Her sympathy for his work shines through her conscientious critique and her praise of the superiority of Christianity.

"ON RELIGION," *THE RAMBLER* (1750)

Epictetus's doctrines that counselled his followers not to fasten their desires on earthly appetites but on God, yet not to despise the life of the body either, seem reflected in Carter's *Rambler* piece on religion. The narrator recounts a dream in which an allegorical figure, identified as Superstition and representing extremes of punitive and ascetic religious doctrine, lays waste to life and inspires the dreamer with thoughts of suicide. In the dream, Superstition is routed by true Religion, who reveals a proper understanding of the beauties and limitations of earthly life and seems a recreation of Epictetus in modern Christian dress. Philosophy and religion allowed Carter to reconcile the paradoxes of her position as a woman intellectual. She recognised the moral and psychological value of what she termed in her *Rambler* essay "those Chains of Benevolence and social Affection, that link the Welfare of every Particular with that of the Whole." These were the "chains" that Epictetus recognised as offering the prospect of genuine freedom.

"Introduction," All the Works of Epictetus which are now extant consisting of his discourses preserved by Arrian, in Four Books, the Enchiridion, and Fragments (1758)

Elizabeth Carter

1. THE Stoic Sect was founded by *Zeno*, about three hundred Years before the Christian Æra: and flourished in great Reputation, till the Declension of the *Roman* Empire. A complete History of this Philosophy would be the Work of a large Volume: and nothing further is intended here, than such a summary View of it, as may be of Use to give a clearer Notion of those Passage in *Epictetus*, a strict Professor of it, which allude to some of its peculiar Doctrines.

2. That the End of Man is to live conformably to Nature, was universally agreed on amongst all the Philosophers: but, in what that Conformity to Nature consists, was the Point in Dispute. The *Epicureans* maintained, that it consisted in Pleasure; of which they constituted sense the Judge.* The Stoics, on the contrary, placed it in an absolute Perfection of the Soul. Neither of them seem to have understood Man in his mixed Capacity; but while the first debased him to a mere Animal, the last exalted him to a pure Intelligence; and both considered him as independent, uncorrupted, and sufficient, either by Height of Virtue, or by well-regulated Indulgence, to his own Happiness. The stoical Excess was more useful to the Public, as it often produced great and noble Efforts towards that Perfection, to which it was supposed possible for human Nature to arrive. Yet, at the same time, by flattering Man with false and presumptuous Ideas of his own Power and Excellence, it tempted even

---

* Sensib*uts ipsis judicari voluptates.* Cic. De F9n. L. II. By Pleasure the *Epicureans* sometimes explained themselves to mean, only Freedom from Uneasiness: but the Philosophers of other Sects in general, as well as *Cicero*, insist, producing their own Expressions for it, that they meant sensual delights. This, indeed, was more explicitly the Doctrine of *Aristippus*, the Father of the *Cyrenaics*: a Sect, however, which sunk into the *Epicureans*; whose Notions plainly led to the Dissoluteness so remarkable in the lives of most of them.

the Best to Pride: a Vice not only dreadfully mischievous in human Society, but, perhaps of all others, the most insuperable Bar to real inward Improvement.

3. *Epictetus* often mentions Three Topics, or Classes, under which the Whole of Moral Philosophy is comprehended. These are, the *Desires* and *Aversions*, the *Pursuits* and *Avoidances*, or the Exercise of the active Powers, and the *Assents* of the Understanding.

4. The *Desires* and *Aversions* were considered as simple Affections of the Mind, arising from the Apprehension, that any thing was conducive to Happiness, or the contrary. The first Care of a Proficient in Philosophy was, to regulate these in such a manner, as never to be disappointed of the one, or incur the other: a Point not otherwise attainable, than by regarding all Externals as absolutely indifferent. *Good* must always be the Object of Desire, and *Evil* of Aversion. The Person then, who considers Life, Health, Ease, Friends, Reputation, &c. as *Good*; and their Contraries as *Evil*, must necessarily *desire* the one, and be *averse* to the other: and, consequently, must often find his *Desire* disappointed, and his *Aversion* incurred. The Stoics, therefore, restrained *Good* and *Evil* to *Virtue* and *Vice* alone: and excluded all Externals from any Share in human Happiness, which they made entirely dependent on a right Choice. From this Regulation of the *Desires* and *Aversions* follows that Freedom from Perturbation, Grief, Anger, Pity, &c. and in short, that universal Apathy, which they every-where strongly inculcate.

5. The next Step to Stoical Perfection was, the Class of *Pursuits* and *Avoidances*.* As the *Desires* and *Aversions* are simple Affections, the *Pursuits* and *Avoidances* are exertions of the active Powers towards the procuring or declining any thing. Under this Head was comprehended the whole System of moral Duties, according to Their incomplete Ideas of them: and a due Regard to it was supposed to ensure a proper Behaviour in all the social Relations. The constant Performance of what these point out, naturally followed from a Regulation of the *Desires* and *Aversions* in the first Topic: for where the Inclinations are exerted and restrained as they ought, there will be nothing to mislead us in Action.

6. The last Topic, and the Completion of the Stoic Character, was that of the *Assents.*† As the second was to produce a Security from Failure in Practice, *this* was to secure an Infallibility in Judgement, and to guard the Mind from ever either admitting a Falsehood, or dissenting from Truth. A wise Man, in the Stoic Scheme, was never to be mistaken, or to form any Opinion. Where Evidence could not be obtained, he was to continue in Suspense. His Understanding was never to be misled, even in Sleep, or under the Influence of Wine, or in a

---

* The Stoics define these Terms: the one, a Motion, by which we are carried toward some Object; the other, a Motion by which we strive to shun it. The original Words, by a Happiness in the *Greek* language, are properly opposed to each other; which the *English* will not admit. I have chosen the best I could find, and wish they were better.

† It seems strange, that the stoics generally put the *Assents* last: since both the Affections and Will should be governed by the Understanding; which, therefore should be rectified, in order to do its Office well. *Epictetus* seems to be of this Opinion in B. I. c.17. But, perhaps, they thought common sense, or natural Logic, sufficient for this Purpose; and artificial Logic, which they meant, but did not express clearly, by the Word *Assents*, necessary as a Guard only against Sophistry. Yet their mentioning it as a Guard also against being misled, when they were in Drink, and even in their Dreams, leaves but little Room for this Conjecture.

Delirium. In this last Particular, however, there is not a perfect Agreement: and some Authors are so very reasonable, as to admit it possible for a Philosopher to be mistaken in his Judgment, after he hath lost his Senses.

7. The Subjects of these several classes of philosophic Exercise are, the *Appearances* of Things. By these *Appearances* the Stoics understood the Impressions made on the Soul, by any Objects, presented either to the Senses, or to the Understanding. Thus a House, an Estate, Life, Death, Pain, Reputation, &c. (considered in the View, under which they are presented to the perceptive Faculties) in the Stoical Sense are, *Appearances*. The Use of Appearances is common to Brutes, and Men; an *intelligent* Use of them belongs only to the latter: a Distinction, which is carefully to be observed in reading these Discourses.

* * *

21. The Stoics thought, that every single Person had a tutelary Genius assigned him by God, as a Guardian of his Soul, and a Superintendent of his Conduct: and that all Virtue and Happiness consist in acting in concert with this Genius, with Reference to the Will of the supreme Director of the Whole. Sometimes, however, they make the Genius to be only the ruling Faculty of every one's own Mind.

22. A very slight examination of their Writings is sufficient to convince any impartial Reader, how little the Doctrines of this Sect were fitted to influence the Generality of Mankind. But indeed, about the Generality of Mankind, the Stoics do not appear to have given themselves any kind of Trouble. They seemed to consider All (except the Few, who were Students in the Intricacies of a philosophic System) as very little superior to Beasts: and, with great Tranquillity, left them to follow the Devices of their own ungoverned Appetites and Passions. How unlike was this to the diffusive Benevolence of the divine Author of the Christian Religion, who adapted his Discourses to the Comprehension, and extended the Means of Happiness to the Attainment, of all Mankind!

23. There seem to be only two Methods, by which the present Appearances of Things are capable of being reconciled to our Ideas of the Justice, Wisdom, and Goodness of God: the one is the Doctrine of a *future* State; the other, the Position, that Virtue alone is sufficient to human Happiness in *this*. The first, which was the method chosen by *Socrates*, solves every Difficulty, without contradicting either Sense or Reason: the latter, which was unfortunately maintained by the Stoics, is repugnant to both.

24. That there is an intrinsic Beauty and Excellency in moral Goodness; that it is the Ornament and Perfection of all rational Beings; and that, till Conscience is stifled by repeated Guilt, we feel an Obligation to prefer and follow, so far as we perceive it, in all Cases; and find an inward Satisfaction, and generally receive outward Advantages from so doing, are Positions, which no thinking Person can contradict: but it doth not follow from hence, that in such a Mixture, as Mankind, it is its own sufficient reward. God alone, infinitely perfect, is happy

in, and from Himself. The Virtue of *finite* Beings must be defective: and the Happiness of *created* Beings must be dependent. It is undeniable Fact, that the natural Consequences of Virtue in some, may be interrupted by the Vices of others. How much are the best Persons liable to suffer from the Follies of the Unthinking; from the Ill-nature, the Rage, the Scorn of the Malevolent; from the cold and penurious Hardheartedness of the Unfeeling; from Persecutions, for the sake both of Religion and Honesty; from ill Returns to conjugal, to parental, to friendly Affection; and from an innumerable Train of other Evils, to which the most amiable Dispositions are usually the most sensible. It is no less undeniable, that the natural Consequences of Virtue are interrupted by the Struggles of our own Passions; (which we may overcome rewardably, though very imperfectly; or, if we live to overcome more perfectly, we may not live to enjoy the Victory;) by Sickness, Pain, Languor, Want; and by what we feel from the Death, or the Sufferings of those, with whom we are most nearly connected. We are often indeed afflicted by many of these Things, more than we ought to be. But Concern for some, at least our own Failings for Instance, is directly a Duty; for others, it is visibly the Instrument of moral Improvement; for more still, it is the unavoidable Result of our Frame: and they who carry it too far, may, on the whole, be good Characters; and even they who do not, in any considerable Degree, may however be extremely wretched. How then can Virtue be its own Reward to Mankind in general, or indeed a proportionable Reward to almost any Man? Or how, unless the View be extended beyond such a Scene of things, the certain Means of Happiness? The originally *appointed* Means of Happiness it undoubtedly is: but that it should be an effectual and infallible Means to Creatures so imperfect, passing through such a disordered World, is impossible, without a State of future Reward; and of this the Gospel alone gives us full Assurance.

25. By rejecting the Doctrine of Recompences in another Life, the Stoics were reduced to the Extravagance of supposing Felicity to be enjoyed in Circumstances, which are incapable of it. That a good Man stretched on a Rack, or reposing on a Bed of Roses, should enjoy himself equally, was a Notion which could gain but few Proselytes: and a sad Experience, that Pain was an Evil, sometimes drove their own Disciples from the thorny Asperities of the Portico, to the flowery Gardens of *Epicurus*.

"Chapter XII: of Conetentment," All the Works of Epictetus which are now extant consisting of his discourses preserved by Arrian, in Four Books, the Enchiridion, and Fragments (1758)

Elizabeth Carter

Chapter XII: Of Contentment

1. CONCERNING the Gods, some affirm, that there is no Deity: others, that he indeed exists; but slothful, negligent, and without a Providence: a third Sort admits both his Being and Providence, but only in great and heavenly Objects, and in nothing upon Earth: a fourth, both in Heaven and Earth; but only in general, not Individuals: a fifth, like *Ulysses* and *Socrates**):

O Thou, who, ever present in my Way,
Dost all my Motions, all my Toils Survey.
POPE'S Homer.

It is, before all things, necessary to examine each of these; which is, and which is not, rightly said. Now, if there are no Gods, how is it our End to follow them? If there are, but they take no Care of any thing; how will it be right, in this Case, to follow them? Or, if they both are, and take Care; yet, if there is nothing communicated from them to Men, nor indeed to myself in particular, how can it be right even in this Case? A wise and good Man, after examining these Things, submits his Mind to him who administers the Whole, as good Citizens do to the Laws of the Commonwealth.

2. He, then, who comes to be instructed, ought to come with this Intention: "How may I in every thing follow the Gods? How may I acquiesce in the divine

---

* It was the Opinion of *Socrates*, That the Gods know all Things that are either said or done, or silently thought on: that they are everywhere present and give Significations to Mankind concerning all human Affairs. XEN. MEM. L. 1.

Administration? And how may I be free?" For He is free, to whom all happens agreeably to his Choice, and whom no one can restrain.

What! then, is Freedom, Distraction?

By no means: for Madness and Freedom are incompatible.

But I would have whatever appears to me to be right, happen; however it comes to appear so. You are mad: you have lost your Senses. Do not you know, that Freedom is a very beautiful and valuable Thing? But for me to chuse at random, and for things to happen agreeably to such a Choice, may be so far from a beautiful Thing, as to be, of all others, the most shocking. For how do we proceed in Writing? Do I chuse to write the Name of *Dion* [for Instance] as I will? No: but I am taught to be willing to write it, as it ought to be writ. And what is the Case in Music? The same. And what in every other Art or Science? Otherwise, it would be to no Purpose to learn any thing; if it was to be adapted to each one's particular Humour. Is it then only in the greatest and principal Point, that of Freedom, permitted me to will at random? By no means: but true Instruction is this: learning to will, that Things should happen as they do. And how do they happen? As the Appointer of them hath appointed. He hath appointed, that there should be Summer and Winter; Plenty and Dearth; Virtue and Vice; and all such Contrarieties, for the Harmony of the Whole.* To each of us he hath given a Body, and its Parts, and our several Properties, and Companions. Mindful of this Appointment, we should enter upon a Course of Education and Instruction, not to change the Constitutions of Things; which is neither put within our Reach, nor for our Good: but that, being as they are, and as their Nature is with regard to us, we may have our Mind accommodated to what exists. Can we, for Instance, fly Mankind? And how is that possible? Can we, by conversing with them, change them? Who hath given us such a Power? What then remains, or what Method is there to be found for such a Commerce with them, that while *they* act agreeably to the Appearances in their own Minds, *we* may nevertheless be affected conformably to Nature? But you are wretched and discontented. If you are alone, you term it a Desart;† and if with Men, you call them Cheats and Robbers. You find fault too with your Parents, and Children, and Brothers, and Neighbours. Whereas you ought, when you live alone, to call *that* a Repose and Freedom; and to esteem yourself as resembling the Gods: and when you are in Company, not to call it a Crowd and a Tumult, and a Trouble; but an Assembly, and a Festival: and thus to take all things contentedly. What, then, is the Punishment of those who do not? To be just as they are. Is any one discontented with being alone? Let him be in a Desart. Discontented with his Parents? Let him be a bad Son; and let him mourn. Discontented with his Children? Let him be a bad Father. Throw him into Prison. What Prison? Where he already is: for he is in a Situation against his Will; and where-ever any one is against his Will, that is to him a Prison: just as *Socrates* was *not* in Prison; for he was willingly there. "What then must my Leg be lame?"—And it is for one paultry Leg, Wretch, that you accuse the World?

---

* See *Enchiridion*, c. xxvii.
† See Introduction, 20.

Why will you not give it up to the Whole? Why will you not withdraw yourself from it? Why will you not gladly yield it to him who gave it? And will you be angry and discontented with the Decrees of *Jupiter*, which he, with the *Fates*, who spun in his Presence the Thread of your Birth, ordained and appointed? Do not you know how very small a Part you are of the Whole? That is, as to Body: for, as to Reason, you are neither worse, nor less, than the Gods. For Reason is not measured by Length or Height; but by Principles. Will you not therefore place your Good there, where you are equal to the Gods*? "How wretched am I in such a Father and Mother!"—What, then, was it granted you to come before-hand, and make your own Terms, and say, "Let such and such Persons, at this Hour, be the Authors of my Birth?" It was not granted: for it was necessary that your Parents should exist before you, and so you be born afterwards.—Of whom?—Of just such as they were. What, then, since they are such is there no Remedy afforded you? Now, surely, if you were ignorant to what Purpose you possess the Faculty of Sight, you would be wretched and miserable, in shutting your Eyes at the Approach of Colours: and are not you more wretched and miserable, in being ignorant, that you have a Greatness of Soul, and a manly Spirit, answerable to each of the above-mentioned Accidents? Occurrences proportioned to your Faculty [of Discernment] are brought before you: but you turn it away, at the very Time when you ought to have it the most open, and quick-sighted. Why do you not rather thank the Gods, that they have made you superior to whatever they have not placed in your own Power; and have rendered you accountable for that only, which is in your own Power? Of your Parents they acquit you; as not accountable: of your Brothers they acquit you: of Body, Possessions, Death, Life, they acquit you. For what, then have they made you accountable? For that which is alone in your own Power; a right Use of the Appearances of Objects. Why, then should you draw those Things upon yourself, for which you are not accountable? This is giving one's self Trouble, without need.

---

* One of the Stoic Extravagances; arising from the notion, that human Souls were literally Parts of the Deity.

A Series of Letters between Mrs. Elizabeth Carter and Miss Catherine Talbot, from the year 1741 to 1770 to which are added Letters from Mrs. Elizabeth Carter to Mrs. Vesey, between the years 1763 and 1787

Elizabeth Carter

What shall I say to you, my dear Miss Talbot upon the subject of Epictetus? Though I cannot help, in some instances, entertaining a more favourable opinion of him than you do, the probability which the Bishop of Oxford* and you seem to think there may be of his doing mischief, fill me with uneasiness and scruples. You say, indeed, that with proper notes and animadversions, the translation may be an excellent work. But it is surely a dangerous experiment to administer poison to try the force of an antidote. For my own part, I never had the least apprehension that an author who enjoins so strict a morality, who censures even the fashionable vices which fine gentlemen at present consider as mere trifles, and who discovers so deep a sense of religion, could be studied by bad people; or if he was, that the effect would be any other than the convincing them that there was nothing to be gained, though an infinite deal to be lost, by their turning Heathens. At present I know not what to think. The Bishop of Oxford and you, I hope, will think for me. The point which gives me the most uneasiness is that detestable "The door is open" [thought to indicate an approval of suicide]. And yet how very inconsistent in this article is Epictetus with himself! In an address to his scholars he expressly bids them wait for God, and not to depart unless they had a signal of retreat like Socrates: now Socrates

---

* The Reverend Thomas Secker (1693–1768) had a distinguished ecclesiastical career. First Rector of Houghton-le-Spring, Durham, then Bishop of Bristol, then Bishop of Oxford, he finally became Archbishop of Canterbury.

did not kill himself. And in several places I think "the door" &c. means only a natural departure out of life, or a violent death inflicted by others. In passages where the permission seems most plainly given, it is sometimes (if not always) in some ironical way: "Go and hang yourself like a grumbling mean-spirited wretch as you are; God has no need of such discontented querulous people as you." But however impossible it may be to vindicate Epictetus in this particular, do not you treat him a little too severely in some others? Is, "Remember God, invoke him for your aid and protector," and more to the same purpose, the language of one who bids us root out every passion, &c. by our own strength? The Bishop of Oxford has particularly taken notice, that Epictetus asserts the doctrine of grace, and the duty of prayer and thanksgiving to God for his assistance in moral improvement.

The Rambler, Number XLIV (1750)

Elizabeth Carter

To the RAMBLER.

SIR,

I had lately a very extraordinary Dream, which made so strong an Impression on me, that I remember it every Word: and if you are not better employed, you may read the Relation of it, as follows:

Methought I was in the Midst of a very agreeable Set of Company, and extremely delighted in attending to a lively Conversation; when on a sudden I perceived one of the most shocking Figures, Imagination can frame, advancing towards me. She was dressed in black: her Skin was contracted into a thousand Wrinkles, her Eyes deep sunk in her Head, and her Complexion pale and livid as the countenance of Death. Her Looks were filled with Terror and unrelenting Severity; and her Hands were armed with Whips and Scorpions. As soon as she came near, with a horrid Frown, and a Voice that chilled my very Blood, she bade me follow her: I obeyed; and she led me through rugged Paths beset with Briars and Thorns, into a deep solitary Valley. Whereever she past, the fading Verdure withered beneath her Steps: her pestilential Breath infected the Air with malignant Vapours, obscured the Lustre of the Sun, and involved the fair Face of Heaven in an universal Gloom. Dismal Howlings resounded through the Forest: from every baleful Tree the Night Raven uttered his dreadful Note; and the whole Prospect was filled with Desolation and Horror. In the Midst of this tremendous Scene, my execrable Guide addressed me in the following Manner:

"Retire with me, O rash unthinking Mortal, from the vain Allurements of a deceitful World; and learn, that Pleasure was not designed the Portion of human Life. Man was born to mourn, and to be wretched. This is the Condition of all below the Stars, and whoever endeavours to oppose it, acts in Contradiction to the Will of Heaven. Fly then from the fatal Enchantments of Youth and social Delight: and here consecrate thy solitary Hours to Lamentation and Woe. Misery is the Duty of all sublunary Beings; and every Enjoyment is an Offence to the Deity, who is to be worshipped only by the Mortification of every Sense of Pleasure, and by the everlasting Exercise of Sighs and Tears."

This melancholy Picture of Life quite sunk my Spirits, and seemed to annihilate every Principle of Joy within me. I threw myself beneath a blasted Yew, where the Winds blew cold and dismal round my Head, and dreadful Apprehensions chilled my Heart. Here I resolved to lie till the Hand of Death, which I impatiently invoked, should put an End to the Miseries of a Life so deplorably wretched. In this sad Situation I spied on one Hand of me, a deep muddy River, whose heavy Waves rolled on, in slow sullen Murmurs. Here I determined to plunge; and was just upon the Brink, when I found myself suddenly drawn back: I turned about and was surprised by the Sight of the most lovely Object I had ever beheld. The most engaging Charms of Youth and Beauty appeared in all her Form: effulgent Glories sparkled in her Eyes, and their awful Splendours were softened by the gentlest Looks of Compassion and Peace. At her Approach the frightful Spectre, who had before tormented me, vanished away, and with her all the Horrors which she had caused. The gloomy Clouds brightened into cheerful Sunshine; the Groves recovered their Verdure, and the whole Region looked gay and blooming as the Garden of *Eden*. I was quite transported at this unexpected Change, and reviving Pleasure began to gladden my Thoughts: when, with a Look of inexpressible Sweetness, my Deliverer thus uttered her divine Instructions.

267

"My Name is *Religion* I am the Offspring of *Truth*, and the Parent of *Benevolence, Hope*, and *Joy*. That Monster, from whose Power I have freed you, is called *Superstition*. She is the Child of *Discontent*, and her Followers are *Fear* and *Sorrow*. Thus different as we are, she has often the Insolence to assume my Name and Character, and seduces unhappy Mortals to think us the same, till she, at length, drives them to the Borders of Despair; that dreadful Abyss, into which you were just going to sink.

"Look round, and survey the various Beauties of this Globe, which Heaven has destined for the Seat of the Human Race, and consider, whether a World thus exquisitely framed, could be meant for the Abode of Misery and Pain! For what End has the lavish Hand of Providence diffused such innumerable Objects of Delight, but that all might rejoice in the Privilege of Existence, and be filled with Gratitude to the beneficent Author of it? Thus to enjoy the Blessings he has sent, is Virtue and Obedience; and to reject them, merely as the Means of Pleasure, is pitiable Ignorance, or absurd Perverseness. Infinite Goodness is the Source of created Existence. The proper Tendency of every rational Being, from the highest Order of raptured Seraphs to the meanest Rank of Men, is to rise incessantly from lower Degrees of Happiness to higher; and each have Faculties assigned them for various orders of Delight."

"What," cried I, "is this the Language of *Religion*? Does she lead her Votaries through flowery Paths, and bid them pass an unlaborious Life of gay Amusement? Where are the painful Toils of Virtue? The Mortification of Penitents, and the self-denying Exercises of Saints and Heroes? Are these only the gloomy Conceits of visionary Devotees? Are there no Difficulties to be encountered? No Restraints to be endured? Does the Whole of Human Duty consist in the chearful Enjoyment of a beautiful World, and a constant Indulgence of the soft Transports of Pleasure?"

"Not such a Kind of Pleasure," answered she, "as arises from the thoughtless Gaiety of a useless Life. The Enjoyments of a reasonable Being cannot consist in unbounded Indulgence, or luxurious Ease; in the Tumult of licentious Passion, the Languor of indolent Repose, or the Flutter of light Amusements. Yielding to immoral Pleasures corrupts the Mind; living to animal and trifling ones debases it; both, in their Degree, disqualify it for its genuine Good, and consign it over to Wretchedness. Whoever would be really happy, must make the diligent and regular Exercise of his superior Powers his chief Attention, adoring the Perfections of his Maker, expressing Good-will to his Fellow-creatures, and cultivating inward Rectitude. To his lower Faculties he must allow such Gratifications as will, by refreshing him, invigorate his nobler Pursuits. In the Regions inhabited by Angelic Natures, unmingled Felicity for ever blooms: Joy flows there with a perpetual and unbounded Stream; nor needs there any Mound to check its Course. Beings conscious of a Frame of Mind originally diseased, as all the Human Race has Reason to be, must use the Regiment of a stricter Self-Government. Whoever has been guilty of voluntary Excesses, must patiently submit both to the painful Workings of Nature, and needful Severities of Medicine, in order to his Cure. Still he is intitled to a moderate Share of whatever alleviating Accommodations this fair Mansion of his merciful Parent affords, consistent with his Recovery; and, in Proportion as this Recovery advances, the liveliest Joy will spring from his secret Sense of an amended and improving Heart.—So far from the Horrors of Despair is the condition even of the Guilty.—Shudder, poor Mortal, at the Thought of that Gulph into which thou was going to plunge."

"While the more Faulty have every Encouragement to amend, the more innocent Soul will be supported with still sweeter Consolations, under all its Experience of Human Infirmities: Supported by the gladdening Assurances, that every sincere Endeavour to out-grow them shall be assisted, accepted, and rewarded. To such a one, the lowliest Self-Abasement is but a deep laid Foundation for the most elevated Hopes: since they, who faithfully examine, and acknowledge what they are, shall be enabled, under my Conduct, to become what they desire. The Christian and the Hero are inseparable: and to the Aspirings of unassuming Trust, and filial Confidence, are set no Bounds. To him, who is animated with a View of obtaining Approbation from the Sovereign of the Universe, no Difficulty is unsurmountable. Secure in this Pursuit of every needful Aid, his Conflict with the severest Pains and Trials, is little more than the vigorous Exercise of a Mind in Health. His patient Dependence on that Providence which looks through all Eternity, his silent Resignation, his ready Accommodation of his Thoughts and Behaviour to its inscrutable Ways, is at once the most excellent source of Self-denial, and a Source of the most exalted Transports. Society is the true Sphere of human Virtue. In social active Life, Difficulties will perpetually occur; Restraints of many Kinds will be necessary: and studying to behave right in Respect of these, is a Discipline of the human Heart useful to others, and improving to itself. Suffering is no Duty, but where it is necessary to avoid Guilt, or to do Good; nor is Pleasure a crime, but where it strengthens the Influence of bad

Inclinations, or lessens the generous Activity of Virtue. The Happiness allotted to Man in his present State, is indeed faint and low, compared with his immortal Prospects and noble Capacities: but yet, whatever Portion of it the distributing Hand of Heaven offers to each Individual, is a needful support and refreshment for the present Moment, so far as it may not hinder the Attainment of his final Destination."

"Return then, with me, from continual Misery, to moderate Enjoyment, and grateful Alacrity. Return from the contracted Views of Solitude, to the proper Duties of a relative and dependent Being. Religion is not confined to Cells and Closets, nor restrained to sullen Retirement: these are the gloomy doctrines of Superstition, by which she endeavours to break those Chains of Benevolence and social Affection, that link the Welfare of every Particular with that of the Whole. Remember that the greatest Honour you can pay to the Author of your Being, is by such chearful Behaviour, as discovers a Mind satisfied with his Dispensations."

Here my Preceptress paused: and I was going to express my Acknowledgements for her Discourse, when a Ring of Bells from the neighbouring Village, and a new-risen Sun darting his Beams through my Windows, awaked me.

ENDNOTES

1   For a detailed analysis of Algarotti's importance, see Massimo Mazzotti, "Newton for Ladies: Gentility, Gender and Radical Culture," *British Journal of the History of Science* 37, no. 2 (June 2004): 119–46.

2   Sylvia Harcstark Myers, *The Bluestocking Circle: Women, Friendship, and the Life of the Mind in Eighteenth-Century England* (Oxford: Clarendon Press, 1990), 11.

3   Norma Clarke, *Dr Johnson's Women* (London: Habledon and London), 25.

4   Myers, 176 and Carolyn D. Williams, "Poetry, Pudding, and Epictetus: The Consistency of Elizabeth Carter" in *Tradition in Transition: Women Writers, Marginal Texts and the Eighteenth-Century Canon*, ed. Alvaro Ribeiro and James G. Basker (Oxford: Clarendon Press, 1996), 24.

5   Clarke, *Dr Johnson's Women*, 26.

6   Carolyn D. Williams, "Poetry, Pudding, and Epictetus: The Consistency of Elizabeth Carter," 17.

Anna Lætitia Barbauld (née Aikin) (1743–1825)

Anna Lætitia Barbauld contributed to scholarship in a variety of contexts. Her main biographical profile can be found in Part 1.

REMARKS ON MR. GILBERT WAKEFIELD'S ENQUIRY INTO THE EXPEDIENCY AND PROPRIETY OF PUBLIC OR SOCIAL WORSHIP (1792)

Anna Lætitia Barbauld responds to Gilbert Wakefield's *An Inquiry into the Expediency and Propriety of Public or Social Worship* (1791), his attack on Dissenting practices of public and social worship at New College Hackney. Barbauld's answer is not only a spirited defense of her colleagues; it also outlines some of the principles that made the Rational Dissenters (as the more heterodox were known) such a vibrant force in Britain at the end of the eighteenth century. Barbauld's voice is important because, as she was an established writer and critic, all sides respected her authority. On the level of religious history, "Dissent" is the blanket term that covers the groups excluded from various civic and business opportunities by the laws established when William of Orange became king in the Glorious Revolution of 1688. Technically, Dissenters included Catholics, Calvinists, and Presbyterians, who would not swear allegiance to the Anglican articles of faith codified during Elizabeth's reign. Barbauld represents the most outspoken and politically active branch of "Enlightened Dissent" which evolved into the Unitarian faith.

Barbauld was among the Dissenting leaders who engaged in public debate with Wakefield in what became a referendum over the heart and soul of the politicized Dissenting movement for religious toleration, parliamentary reform, and male suffrage.[1] In his blast against Dissenters, Wakefield suggested that public worship is not only unnecessary and pretentious but also a dangerous interference with personal faith. This is a purist form of Protestantism at the other end of the spectrum from Roman Catholicism and Anglicanism, which emphasize the role of saintly mediators and priests. Barbauld has the delicate theological task of defending public worship without moving too far away from the founding Protestant impulse of the individual's direct access to God. She does this by pointing to those aspects of Dissenting practice that make it useful to worship together: toleration of a wide spectrum of beliefs, the mixing of economic classes, and the benefits of listening to an intellectual preacher, who is educating the congregation. Barbauld's criticism of Calvinism is an important part of this text. It distinguishes the radical Dissenters from other such sects, but it also demonstrates their powerful blend of political, religious, and psychological ideas. Barbauld astutely comments that, if we imagine a God who is terrible, judgmental, and unforgiving, we are just projecting the image of earthly rulers, dictatorial tyrants such as Louis XIV, onto our conception of the deity. She also emphasizes the Dissenters' enlightened commitment to learning and progress.

Remarks on Mr. Gilbert Wakefield's Enquiry into the Expediency and Propriety of Public or Social Worship (1792)

Anna Lætitia Barbauld

REMARKS
ON
MR. GILBERT WAKEFIELD'S
ENQUIRY
INTO THE
EXPEDIENCY AND PROPRIETY
OF
PUBLIC OR SOCIAL WORSHIP (1792)
.................in swarming cities vast,
Assembled men, to the deep organ join
The long resounding voice, oft breaking clear,
At solemn pauses, through the swelling base;
And, as each mingling flame increases each,
In one united ardour rise to heaven.
THOMPSON.

REMARKS

ON

MR. WAKEFIELD'S ENQUIRY.

There are some practices which have not been defended because they have never been attacked. Of this number is public or social worship. It has been recommended, urged, enforced, but never vindicated. Through worldliness, scepticism, indolence, dissatisfaction with the manner of conducting it, it has been often neglected;

but it is a new thing to hear it condemned. The pious and the good have lamented its insufficiency in the reformation of the world, but they were yet to learn that it was unfriendly to it. Satisfied with silent and solitary desertion, those who did not concur in the homage paid by their fellow-citizens were content to acquiesce in its propriety, and had not hitherto assumed the dignity of a sect. A late pamphlet of Mr. Wakefield's has therefore excited the attention of the public, partly, no doubt, from the known abilities of the author, but still more from the novelty and strangeness of the doctrine. If intended as an apology, no publication can be more seasonable; but if meant as an exhortation, or rather a dehortation, it is a labour which many will think, from the complexion of the times and the tendencies of increasing habits, might well have been spared. It is an awkward circumstance for the apostle of such a persuasion, that he will have many practical disciples whom he will hardly care to own; and that if he succeeds in making proselytes, he must take them from the more sober and orderly part of the community; and class them, as far as this circumstance affords a distinction, along with the uneducated, the profligate, and the unprincipled. The negative tenet he inculcates does not mark his converts with sufficient precision: their scrupulosity will be in danger of being confounded with the carelessness of their neighbours; and it will be always necessary to ask, Do you abstain because you are of this religion, or because you are of no religion at all?

It would be unfair, however, to endeavour to render Mr. Wakefield's opinions invidious; they, as well as every other opinion, must be submitted to the test of argument; and public worship, as well as every other practice, must stand on the basis of utility and good sense, or it must not stand at all: and in the latter case, it is immaterial whether it is left to moulder like the neglected ruin, or battered down like the formidable tower.

[....]

The author of the Enquiry chooses to expatiate,—it is not difficult to do it,—on the discordant variety of the different modes of worship practised amongst men, and concludes it with characterizing this alarming schism by the comparison of the poet:

> One likes the pheasant's wing, and one the leg;
> The vulgar boil, the learned roast an egg.[2]

But might we not venture to ask,—Where, pray, is the harm of all this? unless indeed I will not allow my neighbour to boil his egg because I roast mine. Eggs are good and nutritious food either way; and in the manner of dressing them, fancy and taste, nay caprice, if you will, may fairly be consulted. If I prefer the leg of a pheasant, and my neighbour finds it dry, let each take what he likes. It would be a conclusion singularly absurd, that eggs and pheasants were not to be eaten. All the harm is in having but one table for guests of every description; and yet even there, were I at a public ordinary, good in other respects, I would rather conform my taste in some measure to that of my neighbour, than be reduced to the melancholy necessity of eating my morsel by myself alone.

The dissenters cannot be supposed to pass over in silence Mr. Wakefield's strictures upon the manner in which they have chosen to conduct their public and social worship. They are surprised and sorry to find themselves treated with such a mixture of bitterness and levity by a man whose abilities they respect, and whom they have shown themselves ready to embrace as a brother. They have their prejudices, they acknowledge—and he perhaps has his. Many forms and observances may to them be dear and venerable, through the force of early habit and association, which to a stranger in their Israel may appear uncouth, unnecessary, or even marked with a shade of ridicule. They pity Mr. Wakefield's peculiar and insulated situation. Separating through the purest motives from one church, he has not found another with which he is inclined to associate; divided by difference of opinions from one class of Christians, and by dissonance of taste from another, he finds the transition too violent from the college to the conventicle: he worships alone because he stands alone; and is, naturally perhaps, led to undervalue that fellowship which has been lost to him between his early predilections and his later opinions. If, however, the dissenters are not so happy as to gain his affection, they must be allowed to urge their claims upon his esteem. They wish him to reflect, that neither his classical knowledge, nor his critical acumen, nor his acknowledged talents, set him so high in the esteem of good men, as that integrity which he possesses in common with those whom he despises; they believe further consideration would suggest to him, that it were more candid to pass over those peculiarities which have originated in a delicate conscience and the fervour of devotion; and they cannot help asking, Whether they had reason to expect the severity of sarcastic ridicule from him, whose best praise it is that he has imitated their virtues and shared their sacrifices?

The dissenters, however, do not make it their boast that they have nothing to reform. They have, perhaps, always been more conspicuous for principle than for taste; their practices are founded upon a prevalence of religious fervour, an animation and warmth of piety, which, if it no longer exists, it is vain to simulate. But what they do make their boast is, that they acknowledge no principle which forbids them to reform; that they have no leave to ask of bishops, synods, or parliaments, in order to lay aside forms which have become vapid. They are open to conviction; they are ready to receive with thankfulness every sober and liberal remark which may assist them to improve their religious addresses, and model them to the temper of the public mind. But, with regard to those practices of superabundant devotion which have drawn down upon them the indignation of the critic, it is the opinion of those who best know the dissenters of the present day, that they might have been suffered to fall quietly of themselves: they are supported by no authority, defrayed by no impost. If they make long prayers, it is at the expense only of their own breath and spirits; no widows' houses are devoured by it. If the present generation yawn and slumber over the exercises which their fathers attended with pious alacrity, the sons will of course learn to shorten them. If the disposition of their public services wants animation, as per-

274

haps it does, the silent pews will be deserted one by one, and they will be obliged to seek some other mode of engaging the attention of their audience. But modes and forms affect not the essence of public worship; that may be performed with a form or without one; by words alone, or by symbolical expressions, combined with or separated from instruction; with or without the assistance of a particular order appointed to officiate in leading the devotions: it may be celebrated one day in seven, or in eight, or in ten. In many of these particulars a certain deference should be had to the sentiments of that society with which, upon the whole, we think it best to connect ourselves, and as times and manners change, these circumstances will vary; but the root of the practice is too strongly interwoven with the texture of the human frame ever to be abandoned. While man has wants, he will pray; while he is sensible of blessings, he will offer praise; while he has common wants and common blessings, he will pray and praise in company with his fellows; and while he feels himself a social being, he will not be persuaded to lay aside social worship.

It must, however, be acknowledged, that, in order to give public worship all the grace and efficacy of which it is susceptible, much alteration is necessary. It is necessary here, as in every other concern, that timely reformation should prevent neglect. Much might be done by judgement, taste, and a devotional spirit united, to improve the plan of our religious assemblies. Should a genius arise amongst us qualified for such a task, and in circumstances favourable to his being listened to, he would probably remark first, on the construction of our churches, so ill adapted are a great part of them to the purposes either of hearing or seeing. He would reprobate those little gloomy solitary cells, planned by the spirit of aristocracy, which deform the building no less to the eye of taste than to the eye of benevolence, and insulating each family within its separate inclosure, favour at once the pride of rank and the laziness of indulgence. He might choose for these structures something of the amphitheatrical form, where the minister, on a raised platform, should be beheld with ease by the whole wave of people, at once bending together in deep humiliation, or spreading forth their hands in the earnestness of petition. It would certainly be found desirable that the people should themselves have a large share in the performance of the service, as the intermixture of their voices would both introduce more variety and greater animation; provided pains were taken by proper teaching to enable them to bear their part with a decorum and propriety, which, it must be confessed, we do not see at present amongst those whose public services possess the advantage of responses. The explaining, and teaching them to recite, such hymns and collects as it might be thought proper they should bear a part in, would form a pleasing and useful branch of the instruction of young people, and of the lower classes; it would give them an interest in the public service, and might fill up agreeably a vacant hour either on the Sunday or on some other leisure day, especially if they were likewise regularly instructed in singing for the same purpose. As we have never seen, perhaps we can hardly conceive, the effect which the united voices of a whole congregation, all in the lively expression of one feeling, would have upon the mind. We should then perceive not only that we were doing the same thing in the same place, but that we were doing it with one accord. The deep silence of listening expectation, the burst of united praises, the solemn pauses that invite reflection, the varied tones of humiliation, gratitude, or persuasion, would swell and melt the heart by turns; nor would there be any reason to guard against the wandering eye, when every object it rested on must forcibly recall it to the duties of the place.—Possibly it might be found expedient to separate worship from instruction; the learned teacher from the leader of the public devotions, in whom voice, and popular talents, might perhaps be allowed to supersede a more deep and critical acquaintance with the doctrines of theology. One consequence, at least, would follow such a separation, that instruction would be given more systematically.—Nothing that is taught at all is taught in so vague and desultory a manner as the doctrines of religion. A congregation may attend for years, even a good preacher, and never hear the evidences of either natural or revealed religion regularly explained to them: they may attend for years, and never hear a connected system of moral duties extending to the different situations and relations of life: they may attend for years, and not even gain any clear idea of the history and chronology of the Old and New Testament, which are read to them every Sunday. They will hear abundance of excellent doctrine, and will often feel their hearts warmed and their minds edified; but their ideas upon these subjects will be confused and imperfect, because they are treated on in a manner so totally different from every thing else which bears the name of instruction. This is probably owing, in great measure, to the custom of prefixing to every pulpit-discourse a sentence, taken indiscriminately from any part of the Scriptures, under the name of a text, which at first implying an exposition, was afterwards used to suggest a subject; and is now, by degrees, dwindling into a motto.—Still, however, the custom subsists; and while it serves to supersede a more methodical course of instruction, tends to keep up in the minds of the generality of hearers a very superstitious idea,—not now entertained, it is to be presumed, by the generality of those who teach,—of the equal sacredness and importance of every part of so miscellaneous a collection.

If these insulated discourses, of which each is complete in itself, and therefore can have but little compass, were digested into a regular plan of lectures, supported by a course of reading, to which the audience might be directed, it would have the further advantage of rousing the inattentive and restraining the rambling hearer by the interest which would be created by such a connected series of information. They would occupy a larger space in the mind, they would more frequently be the subject of recollection and meditation; there would be a fear of missing one link in such a chain of truths; and the more intelligent part of a congregation might find a useful and interesting employment in assisting the teacher in the instruction of those who were not able to comprehend instruction with the same facility as themselves. When such a course of instruction had been delivered, it would not be expected that discourses, into which men of genius and learning had digested their best thoughts, should be thrown by, or brought forward again, as it were, by stealth; but they would be regularly and avowedly repeated at proper intervals. It is usual upon the continent for a set of sermons

276

to be delivered in several churches, each of which has its officiating minister for the stated public worship; and thus a whole district partakes the advantage of the labours of a man eminent for composition. Perhaps it might be desirable to join to religious information some instruction in the laws of our country, which are, or ought to be, founded upon morals; and which, by a strange solecism, are obligatory upon all, and scarcely promulgated, much less explained.—Many ideas will offer themselves to a thinking man, who wishes not to abolish, but to improve the public worship of his country. These are only hints, offered with diffidence and respect, to those who are able to judge of and carry them into effect.

Above all, it would be desirable to separate from religion the idea of gloom which in this country has but too generally accompanied it. The fact cannot be denied; the cause must be sought, partly in our national character, which I am afraid is not naturally either very cheerful or very social, and which we shall do well to meliorate by every possible attention to our habits of life;—and partly to the colour of our religious systems. No one who embraces the common idea of future torments, together with the doctrine of election and reprobation, the insufficiency of virtue to escape the wrath of God, and the strange absurdity which, it should seem, through similarity of sound alone has been admitted as an axiom, that sins committed against an infinite being do therefore deserve infinite punishment—no one, I will venture to assert, can believe such tenets, and have them often in his thoughts, and yet be cheerful. Whence a system has arisen so incompatible with that justice and benevolence, which in the discourses of our Saviour are represented as the most essential attributes of the Divine Being, is not easy to trace. It is probable, however, that power, being the most prominent feature in our conceptions of the Creator, and that of which we see the most striking image here on earth (there being a greater portion of uncontrouled power than of unmixed wisdom or goodness to be found amongst human beings), the Deity would naturally be likened to an absolute monarch;—and most absolute monarchs having been tyrants, jealous of their sovereignty, averse to freedom of investigation, ordering affairs, not with a view to the happiness of their subjects, but to the advancement of their own glory; not to be approached but with rich gifts and offerings; bestowing favours, not in proportion to merit, but from the pure influence of caprice and blind partiality; to those who have offended them severe, and unforgiving, except induced to pardon by the importunate intercession of some favourite; confining their enemies, when they had overcome them, after a contest, in deep dark dungeons under ground, or putting them to death in the prolonged misery of excruciating tortures—these features of human depravity have been most faithfully transferred to the Supreme Being; and men have imaged to themselves how a Nero or a Domitian would have acted, if from the extent of their dominion there had been no escape, and to the duration of it no period.

These ideas of the vulgar belief, terrible, but as yet vague and undefined, passed into the speculations of the schoolmen, by whom they were combined with the metaphysical idea of eternity, arranged in specific propositions, fixed in creeds, and elaborated into systems, till at length they have been sublimed into all the tremendous horrors of the Calvinistic faith. These doctrines, it is true, among thinking people, are losing ground; but there is still apparent, in that class called serious christians, a tenderness in exposing them; a sort of leaning towards them,—as in walking over a precipice one should lean to the safest side; an idea that they are, if not true, at least good to be believed, and that a salutary error is better than a dangerous truth. But that error can neither be salutary nor harmless, which attributes to the Deity injustice and cruelty; and that religion must have the worst tendencies, which renders it dangerous for man to imitate the being whom he worships. Let those who hold such tenets consider, that the invisible Creator has no name, and is identified only by his character; and they will tremble to think what being they are worshiping, when they invoke a power capable of producing existence, in order to continue it in never-ending torments. The God of the Assembly's Catechism is not the same God with the deity of Thomson's Seasons, and of Hutcheson's Ethics. Unity of character in what we adore is much more essential than unity of person. We often boast, and with reason, of the purity of our religion, as opposed to the grossness of the theology of the Greeks and Romans; but we should remember, that cruelty is as much worse than licentiousness, as a Moloch is worse than a satyr.—When will christians permit themselves to believe that the same conduct which gains them the approbation of good men here, will secure the favour of Heaven hereafter? When will they cease making their court to their Maker by the same servile debasement and affectation of lowliness by which the vain potentates of the earth are flattered? When a harmless and well-meaning man, in the exaggerated figures of theological rhetoric, calls himself the vilest of sinners, it is in precisely the same spirit of false humility in which the courtier uses degrading and disqualifying expressions, when he speaks of himself in his adulatory addresses to his sovereign. When a good man draws near the close of a life, not free indeed from faults, but pure from crime, a life spent in the habitual exercise of all those virtues which adorn and dignify human nature, and in the uniform approach to that perfection which is confessedly unattainable in this imperfect state; when a man—perhaps like Dr. Price, whose name will be ever pronounced with affectionate veneration and deep regard by all the friends of philosophy, virtue, and mankind—is about to resign his soul into the hands of his Maker, he ought to do it, not only with a reliance on his mercy, but his justice; a generous confidence and pious resignation should be blended in his deportment. It does not become him to pay the blasphemous homage of deprecating the wrath of God, when he ought to throw himself into the arms of his love. He is not to think that virtue is one thing here, and another in heaven; or that he on whom blessings and eulogiums are ready to burst from all honest tongues, can be an object of punishment with Him who is infinitely more benevolent than any of his creatures.

These remarks may be thought foreign to the subject in question; but in fact they are not so. Public worship will be tinctured with gloom while our ideas of its object are darkened by superstition; it will be infected with hypocrisy while its professions and tenets run counter to the genuine unperverted moral sense of mankind; it will not meet the countenance of philosophers so long as we are obliged to unlearn our ethics, in order to learn divinity. Let it be considered that these opinions greatly favour immorality. The doctrine that all are vile, and equally merit a state of punishment, is an idea as consolatory to the profligate, as it is humiliating to the saint; and that is one reason why it has always been a favourite doctrine. The indecent confidence of a Dodd, and the debasing terrors of a Johnson, or of more blameless men than he, spring from one and the same source. It prevents the genuine workings of real penitence, by enjoining confessions of imaginary demerit; it quenches religious gratitude, because conceiving only of two states of retribution, both in the extreme; and feeling that our crimes, whatever they may be, cannot have deserved the one, we are not sufficiently thankful for the prospect of the other, which we look upon as only a necessary alternative. Lastly, it dissolves the connexion between religion and common life, by introducing a set of phrases and a standard of moral feeling, totally different from those ideas of praise and blame, merit and demerit, upon which we do and must act in our commerce with our fellow-creatures.

279

There are periods in which the human mind seems to slumber, but this is not one of them. A keen spirit of research is now abroad, and demands reform. Perhaps in none of the nations of Europe will their articles of faith, or their church establishments, or their modes of worship, be able to maintain their ground for many years in exactly the same position in which they stand at present. Religion and manners reciprocally act upon one another. As religion, well understood, is a most powerful agent in meliorating and softening our manners; so, on the other hand, manners, as they advance in cultivation, tend to correct and refine our religion. Thus, to a nation in any degree acquainted with the social feelings, human sacrifices and sanguinary rites could never long appear obligatory. The mild spirit of christianity has, no doubt, had its influence in softening the ferocity of the Gothic times; and the increasing humanity of the present period will, in its turn, produce juster ideas of christianity, and diffuse through the solemnities of our worship, the celebration of our sabbaths, and every observance connected with religion, that air of amenity and sweetness, which is the offspring of literature and the peaceful intercourses of society. The age which has demolished dungeons, rejected torture, and given so fair a prospect of abolishing the iniquity of the slave-trade, cannot long retain among its articles of belief the gloomy perplexities of Calvinism, and the heart-withering perspective of cruel and never-ending punishments.

THE END.

ENDNOTES

1. Although not a leader, Mary Hays was the first Rational Dissenter to respond to Wakefield's polemic in her pamphlet "Cursory Remarks on an Enquiry into the Expediency and Propriety of Public or Social Worship: Inscribed to Gilbert Wakefield, B.A. Late Fellow of Jesus-College, Cambridge. By Eusebia" (1791). Hays took her pen name from William Law's "good Eusebia," a character in *The Serious Call to a Devout and Holy Life* (1728) who was a devout widow with a strong interest in female education.

2. Alexander Pope, *The Second Epistle of The Second Book of Horace*, 2. 84–85.

Harriet Martineau (1802–1876)

Harriet Martineau wrote stories, history, travel books, autobiography, and one novel, as well as contributing to journals and to philosophical scholarship. Her biographical profile is in Part 1.

THE POSITIVE PHILOSOPHY OF AUGUSTE COMTE (1853; REPRINTED 1875)

Harriet Martineau's two-volume translation, adaptation, and abridgement of Auguste Comte's six-volume *Cours de Philosophie Positive* (1830–42) was a tribute to her skills as a writer, thinker, and populariser, first displayed in a different format in her *Illustrations of Political Economy* (1832). Comte (1798–1857), a major political and social theorist, was the founder of sociology and of positivism. A thorough empiricist, he saw all human knowledge deriving from observation and experience. Positivism studied only what can be observed; it did not enquire into first or final causes, the "why" of things. According to Comte, we can describe phenomena but not explain them. Comte saw his role as charting the laws of human progress, arguing that all branches of knowledge passed through three historical stages (though not at the same rate): the theological, the metaphysical, and the positive. Once the science of social physics or sociology had been fully developed in the final positive stage, the causes of and remedies for social disorder would be understood and overcome.

Since Comte's writing was diffuse and rambling, Martineau's curtailment of his six volumes into two, couched in clear prose, was welcomed both in England and France. Comte's English admirers included George Henry Lewes and John Stuart Mill. Karl Marx adapted Comte's ideas of historical inevitability. Martineau was attracted to Comte by his scientific outlook and his rejection of religion; though to the dismay of many, he went on to found his own lay religion. The excerpts printed below from Martineau's Preface and the opening of *Positive Philosophy* develop Martineau's reasons for undertaking the work and, in the section on the law of the three stages, show her ability to convey complex ideas in a clear style.

"Preface," The Positive Philosophy of Auguste Comte (1853)

Harriet Martineau

Preface

....

During the whole course of my long task [of translation], it has appeared to me that Comte's work is the strongest embodied rebuke ever given to that form of theological intolerance which censures Positive Philosophy for pride of reason and lowness of morals. The imputation will not be dropped, and the enmity of the religious world to the book will not slacken for its appearing among us in an English version. It cannot be otherwise. The theological world cannot but hate a book which treats of theological belief as a transient state of the human mind. And again, the preachers and teachers, of all sects and schools, who keep to the ancient practice, one inevitable, of contemplating and judging of the universe from the point of view of their own minds, instead of having learned to take their stand out of themselves, investigating from the universe inwards, and not from within outwards, must necessarily think ill of a work which exposes the futility of their method, and the worthlessness of the results to which it leads. As M. Comte treats of theology and metaphysics as destined to pass away, theologians and metaphysicians must necessarily abhor, dread, and despise his work. They merely express their own natural feelings on behalf of the objects of their reverence and the purpose of their lives, when they charge Positive Philosophy with irreverence, lack of aspiration, hardness, deficiency of grace and beauty, and so on. They are no judges of the case. Those who are—those who have passed through theology and metaphysics, and, finding what they are now worth, have risen above them—will pronounce a very different judgment on the contents of this book, though no appeal for such a judgment is made in it, and this kind of discussion is nowhere expressly provided for. To those who have learned the difficult task of postponing dreams to realities till the beauty of reality is seen in its full disclosure, while that of dreams melts into darkness, the moral charm of this work will be as impressive as its intellectual satisfactions. The aspect in which it presents Man is as favourable to his moral discipline, as it is fresh and stimulating to his intellectual taste. We find ourselves suddenly living and moving in the midst of the universe,—as a part of it, and not as its aim and object. We find ourselves living, not under capricious and arbitrary conditions, unconnected with the constitution and movements of the whole, but under great, general, invariable laws, which operate on us as part of the whole. Certainly, I can conceive of no instruction so favourable to aspiration as that which shows us how great our faculties, how small our knowledge, how sublime the heights which we may hope to attain, and how boundless an infinity may be assumed to spread out beyond. We find here indications in passing of the evils we suffer from our low aims, our selfish passions, and our proud ignorance; and in contrast with them, animating displays of the beauty and glory of the everlasting laws, and of the sweet serenity, lofty courage, and noble resignation that are the natural consequence of pursuits so pure, and aims so true, as those of Positive Philosophy. Pride of intellect surely abides with those who insist on belief without evidence and on a philosophy derived from their own intellectual action, without material and corroboration from without, and not with those who are too scrupulous and too humble to transcend evidence, and to add, out of their own imaginations, to that which is, and may be, referred to other judgments. If it be desired to extinguish presumption, to draw away from low aims, to fill life with worthy occupations and elevating pleasures, and to raise human hope and human effort to the highest attainable point, it seems to me that the best resource is the pursuit of Positive Philosophy, with its train of noble truths and irresistible inducements. The prospects it opens are boundless; for among the laws it establishes that of human progress is conspicuous. The virtues it fosters are all those of which Man is capable; and the noblest are those which are more eminently fostered. The habit of truth-seeking and truth-speaking, and of true dealing with self and with all things, is evidently a primary requisite; and this habit once perfected, the natural conscience, thus disciplined, will train up all other moral attributes to some equality with it. To all who know what the study of philosophy really is,—which means the study of Positive Philosophy,—its effect on human aspiration and human discipline is so plain that any doubt can be explained only on the supposition that accusers do not know what it is that they are calling in question. My hope is that this book may achieve, besides the purposes entertained by its Author, the one more that he did not intend, of conveying a sufficient rebuke to those who, in theological selfishness or metaphysical pride, speak evil of a philosophy which is too lofty and too simple, too humble and too generous, for the habit of their minds. The case is clear. The law of progress is conspicuously at work throughout human history. The only field of progress is now Positive Philosophy, under whatever name it may be known to the real students of every sect; and therefore must that philosophy be favourable to those virtues whose repression would be incompatible with progress.

Autumn, 1853

"Chapter 1," The Positive Philosophy of Auguste Comte (1853)

Harriet Martineau

Chapter I

In order to understand the true value and character of the Positive Philosophy, we must take a brief general view of the progressive course of the human mind, regarded as a whole; for no conception can be understood otherwise than through its history.

From the study of the development of human intelligence, in all directions, and through all times, the discovery arises of a great fundamental law, to which it is necessarily subject, and which has a solid foundation of proof, both in the facts of our organization and in our historical experience. The law is this:—that each of our leading conceptions,—each branch of our knowledge,—passes successively through three different theoretical conditions: the Theological, or fictitious; the Metaphysical, or abstract; and the Scientific, or positive. In other words, the human mind, by its nature, employs in its progress three methods of philosophizing, the character of which is essentially different, and even radically opposed: viz, the theological method, the metaphysical, and the positive. Hence arise three philosophies, or general systems of conceptions on the aggregate of phenomena, each of which excludes the others. The first is the necessary point of departure of the human understanding; and the third is its fixed and definitive state. The second is merely a state of transition.

First stage.

In the theological state, the human mind, seeking the essential nature of beings, the first and final causes (the origin and purpose) of all effects,—in short, Absolute knowledge,—supposes all phenomena to be produced by the immediate action of supernatural beings.

Second stage.

In the metaphysical state, which is only a modification of the first, the mind supposes, instead of supernatural beings, abstract forces, veritable entities (that is, personified abstractions) inherent in all beings, and capable of producing all phenomena. What is called the explanation of phenomena is, in this stage, a mere reference of each to its proper entity.

Third stage.

In the final, the positive state, the mind has given over the vain search after Absolute notions, the origin and destination of the universe, and the causes of phenomena, and applies itself to the study of their laws,—that is, their invariable relations of succession and resemblance. Reasoning and observation, duly combined, are the means of this knowledge. What is now understood when we speak of an explanation of facts is simply the establishment of a connection between single phenomena and some general facts, the number of which continually diminishes with the progress of science.

The Theological system arrived at the highest perfection of which it is capable when it substituted the providential action of a single Being for the varied operations of the numerous divinities which had been before imagined. In the same way, in the last stage of the Metaphysical system, men substitute one great entity (Nature) as the cause of all phenomena, instead of the multitude of entities at first supposed. In the same way, again, the ultimate perfection of the Positive system would be (if such perfection could be hoped for) to represent all phenomena as particular aspects of a single general fact;—such as Gravitation, for instance....

Evidences of the law.
There is no science which, having attained the positive stage, does not bear marks of having passed through the others. Some time since it was (whatever it might be) composed, as we can now perceive, of metaphysical abstractions; and, further back in the course of time, it took its form from theological conceptions. We shall have only too much occasion to see, as we proceed, that our most advanced sciences still bear very evident marks of the two earlier periods through which they have passed....

The progress of the individual mind is not only an illustration but an indirect evidence of that of the general mind. The point of departure of the individual and of the race being the same, the phases of the mind of a man correspond to the epochs of the mind of the race. Now, each of us is aware, if he looks back upon his own history, that he was a theologian in his childhood, a metaphysician in his youth, and a natural philosopher in his manhood. All men who are up to their age can verify this for themselves....

Besides the observation of facts, we have theoretical reasons in support of this law. The most important of these reasons arises from the necessity that always exists for some theory to which to refer our facts, combined with the clear impossibility that, at the outset of human knowledge, men could have formed theories out of the observation of facts. All good intellects have repeated, since Bacon's time, that there can be no real knowledge but that which is based on observed facts. This is incontestable, in our present advanced stage; but, if we look back to the primitive stage of human knowledge, we shall see that it must have been otherwise then. If it is true that every theory must be based upon observed facts, it is equally true that facts cannot be observed without the guidance of some theory. Without such guidance, our facts would be desultory and fruitless; we could not retain them: for the most part we could not even perceive them....

Thus, between the necessity of observing facts in order to form a theory, and having a theory in order to observe facts, the human mind would have been entangled in a vicious circle, but for the natural opening afforded by Theological conceptions. This is the fundamental reason for the theological character of the primitive philosophy. This necessity is confirmed by the perfect suitability of the theological philosophy to the earliest researches of the human mind. It is remarkable that the most inaccessible questions,—those of the nature of beings, and the origin and purpose of phenomena,—should be the first to occur in a primitive state, while those which are really within our reach are regarded as almost unworthy of serious study. The reason is evident enough:—that experience alone can teach us the measure of our powers; and if men had not begun by an exaggerated estimate of what they can do, they would never have done all that they are capable of. Our organization requires this. At such a period there could have been no reception of a positive philosophy, whose function is to discover the laws of phenomena, and whose leading characteristic is to regard as interdicted to human reason those sublime mysteries which theology explains, even to their minutest details, with the most attractive facility. It is just so under a practical view of the nature of the researches with which men first occupied themselves. Such inquiries offered the powerful charm of unlimited empire over the external world,—a world destined wholly for our use, and involved in every way with our existence. The theological philosophy, presenting this view, administered exactly the stimulus necessary to incite the human mind to the irksome labour without which it could make no progress. We can now scarcely conceive of such a state of things, our reason having become sufficiently mature to enter upon laborious scientific researches, without needing any such stimulus as wrought upon the imaginations of astrologers and alchemists. We have motive enough in the hope of discovering the laws of phenomena, with a view to the confirmation or rejection of a theory. But it could not be so in the earliest days; and it is to the chimeras of astrology and alchemy that we owe the long series of observations and experiments on which our positive science is based. Kepler felt this on behalf of astronomy, and Bertollet on behalf of chemistry. Thus was a spontaneous philosophy, the theological, the only possible beginning, method, and provisional system, out of which the Positive philosophy could grow. It is easy, after this, to perceive how Metaphysical methods and doctrines must have afforded the means of transition from the one to the other....

As we have seen, the first characteristic of the Positive Philosophy is that it regards all phenomena as subjected to invariable natural *Laws*. Our business is,—seeing how vain is any research into what are called *Causes*, whether first or final,—to pursue an accurate discovery of these Laws, with a view to reducing them to the smallest possible number. By speculating upon causes, we could solve no difficulty about origin and purpose. Our real business is to analyse accurately the circumstances of phenomena, and to connect them by the natural relations of succession and resemblance. The best illustration of this is in the case of the doctrine of Gravitation. We say that the general phenomena of the universe are *explained* by

285

it, because it connects under one head the whole immense variety of astronomical facts; exhibiting the constant tendency of atoms towards each other in direct proportion to their masses, and in inverse proportion to the squares of their distances; whilst the general fact itself is a mere extension of one which is perfectly familiar to us, and which we therefore say that we know;—the weight of bodies on the surface of the earth. As to what weigh and attraction are, we have nothing to do with that, for it is not a matter of knowledge at all ... When any attempt has been made to explain them, it has ended only in saying that attraction is universal weight, and that weight is terrestrial attraction: that is, that the two orders of phenomena are identical; which is the point from which the question set out....

286   Before ascertaining the stage which Positive Philosophy has reached, we must bear in mind that the different kinds of our knowledge have passed through the three stages of progress at different rates, and have not therefore arrived at the same time. The rate of advance depends on the nature of the knowledge in question, so distinctly that, as we shall see hereafter, this consideration constitutes an accessory to the fundamental law of progress. Any kind of knowledge reaches the positive stage early in proportion to its generality, simplicity, and independence of other departments. Astronomical science, which is above all made up of facts that are general, simple, and independent of other sciences, arrived first; then terrestrial Physics; then Chemistry; and, at length, Physiology....

In mentioning the four principal categories of phenomena,—astronomical, physical, chemical, and physiological,—there was an omission which will have been noticed. Nothing was said of Social phenomena. Though involved with the physiological, Social phenomena demand a distinct classification, both on account of their importance and of their difficulty. They are the most individual, the most complicated, the most dependent on all others; and therefore they must be the latest,—even if they had no special obstacle to encounter. This branch of science has not hitherto entered into the domain of Positive philosophy. Theological and metaphysical methods, exploded in other departments, are as yet exclusively applied, both in the way of inquiry and discussion, in all treatment of Social subjects, though the best minds are heartily weary of eternal disputes about divine right and the sovereignty of the people. This is the great, while it is evidently the only gap which has to be filled, to constitute, solid and entire, the Positive Philosophy. Now that the human mind has grasped celestial and terrestrial physics,—mechanical and chemical; organic physics, both vegetable and animal,—there remains one science, to fill up the series of sciences of observation,—Social physics. This is what men have now most need of: and this it is the principal aim of this study to accomplish.

PART 4

Art and Literary Criticism

Elizabeth Montagu (1718–1800)

Elizabeth Robinson Montagu was an exemplar of female erudition, sociability, and solidarity in her time. Her parents, Elizabeth (Drake)[1] and Matthew Robinson, came from landed gentry. Their family included seven sons and two daughters, of whom Elizabeth was the elder. As a girl, she spent time with her maternal step-grandfather, classicist Dr. Conyers Middleton, who recognised her unusual potential. She seems to have been encouraged to learn by her brothers, but discerned that she could not share their freedom in play and travel: "I wish I could metamorphosis myself into a Brother from a Sister," she commented.[2] She became friends and maintained a lively correspondence with Lady Margaret Cavendish Harley who married the Duke of Portland and at whose country estate Elizabeth spent halcyon days. She met important people, perused the Duke's library, read aloud with other guests, and corresponded about what she was learning. She recognised her intellectual passions, but also the proscriptions against serious female education. "There is a Mahometan Error crept even into the Christian Church that Women have no Souls," she wrote a male friend, "& it is thought very absurd for us to pretend to read or think like Reasonable Creatures." Lady Portland subsequently hired Elizabeth Elstob to tutor her children.

At twenty-two, Elizabeth married Edward Montagu, nephew of the renowned Lady Mary Wortley Montagu. He was twenty-nine years older than Elizabeth, a Member of Parliament, rich, and willing to accept a wife with a small dowry. Edward took his wife to live in the country, and she assisted in managing their real estate in London, Berkshire, and several northern collieries with entrepreneurial skill.[3] She gave birth to a son the next year and was devastated by his sudden death. When the deaths of her mother and a brother followed soon after, she sought solace at Tunbridge Wells, a rural watering place, where she made important friendships over the next years, especially with Elizabeth Vesey, Frances Boscawen, George Lyttelton, who mentored her, and Gilbert West, a pious man with whom she discussed her religious doubts and desire for certitude. Montagu's group read together and corresponded about recent publications when apart. West encouraged her astute critical responses. The Montagu marriage foundered because of spiritual and intellectual incompatibilities. Elizabeth Montagu turned to study, correspondence, and social life in London where she entertained splendidly and, eventually, after her husband's death in 1775, built magnificent Montagu House for which Angelica Kauffmann created interior designs.[4]

Elizabeth Montagu used her money, competence, and belief in benevolent community to promote female learning, publication, and prominence in the contemporary republic of letters.[5] She emerged as a grand *salonniere* who advocated a meritocracy of talented men and women of various economic ranks.[6] Her social skills were notable—Hannah More, a younger bluestocking, celebrated them in her poem "Bas Bleu"—and she achieved iconic status as "Queen of the Blues" in paintings, ceramics, and several literary forms, including satire. Montagu used the term "bluestocking" to refer to Benjamin Stillingfleet, a learned guest at her gatherings who pointedly chose to wear common blue worsted stockings rather than the white or black silk hose. Gradually, the expression signified Montagu herself and the group of gifted female intellectuals she gathered around her. Their sophisticated conversations, mutual support, and incontrovertible proof of female competence contributed to the emergence of "bluestocking feminism."[7]

Bluestocking Elizabeth Carter proved to be Elizabeth Montagu's most important friend. The two met as girls; Montagu renewed contact after publication of Carter's edition of *Epictetus*. Their extensive correspondence reveals the care they took with each other to achieve and sustain both intellectual intimacy and autonomy. Carter was an accomplished scholar who published. Montagu expressed trepidations about becoming a "female Author." She published anonymously three pieces drawing on the classics in Lyttelton's *Dialogues of the Dead* (1760); Edmund Burke, who was in on the secret, copied over Montagu's manuscript so her handwriting would not be recognised. Emboldened by reactions to her work, and supported by Carter, Montagu decided to risk authorship on her own. In addition, her younger sister, Sarah Scott (1723–1795), now divorced, published anonymously a Utopian novel, *Millenium Hall* (1762), that depicted a feminist community. Montagu set to work studying Shakespeare in her bedroom because visitors, she remarked to her sister, "are not so used to see ye pen as ye needle in the hands of a Woman."[8] The completed work, *An Essay on the Writings & Genius of Shakespear* was published anonymously in 1769; her name was added in 1777 to the fourth edition. She subsequently considered writing about Voltaire, and a comparison of Queen Elizabeth and Catherine de' Medici, but she never produced another publication. She attempted to establish both a retreat for unmarried gentlewomen and a female college, but, after Anna Barbauld refused the offer of college superintendent, she renounced the effort.

ESSAY ON THE WRITINGS AND GENIUS OF SHAKESPEAR, COMPARED WITH THE GREEK AND FRENCH DRAMATIC POETS: WITH SOME REMARKS UPON THE MISREPRESENTATIONS OF MONS. DE VOLTAIRE (1769)

Publication of Elizabeth Montagu's *Essay on the Writings and Genius of Shakespear* coincided with Shakespeare's Jubilee in 1769. Although the work argued passionately for recognition of Shakespeare as a national, if neglected, treasure, Montagu withheld her name from the title page out of concern about prejudices against learned women appearing in print. She recognised that the work was innovative, even audacious, the result of long study of and attendance at productions of Shakespeare's plays performed by leading actors, including David Garrick. Montagu's work engaged with existing Shakespeare criticism by powerful men in her own country, particularly Samuel Johnson[9] and Alexander Pope, and among the French, specifically Voltaire as translator and Corneille as playwright. She rejected Voltaire's insistence on the Aristotelian unities of time, place, and action, which were sacred to French drama. Her detailed commentary on Greek culture displayed an uncommon erudition. Her authorial authority, albeit nameless until the fourth edition in 1777, contributed to what Elizabeth Eger characterizes as the remarkable effort by learned British women in the eighteenth century to "rescu[e] a male writer from oblivion—a writer who is now the most famous of England's history."[10]

290

The enterprise to enshrine Shakespeare had national and gendered elements. In her work, Montagu argues for British cultural supremacy through Shakespeare's claims to originality, his realistic portrayal of characters drawn from all social classes, his superiority to Greek dramatists in deploying "Praeternatural Beings" that are part of Britain's mythic past, and his ability to convey complex, enduring moral principles to ordinary people. Montagu's *Essay* set a new standard of critical accuracy for translations and interpretations of Shakespeare. Her detailed analyses of language, characters, and historical sources called attention to Shakespeare's unique psychological insights, particularly demonstrated in his female figures like Lady Macbeth. Montagu's work initiated a tradition of "more naturalistic and particularly feminine"[11] Shakespearean criticism by women that was continued by Elizabeth Griffith (1775), Joanna Baillie (1798–1812), Mary Cowden-Clarke, Mary Lamb, and Anna Jameson through the nineteenth century.[12]

Montagu was quickly discovered as Shakespeare's advocate, and her book received praise and success because of its appeal to British patriotism and her courage as a "critical Amazon" in defending Shakespeare against foreign and obtuse critics. The text went through multiple editions and was translated into German, Italian, and French. Samuel Johnson remained unimpressed. His champion, James Boswell, already sparring with Hester Piozzi, wrote that she had "been unable to get through Mrs. Montagu's Essay on Shakespear." Piozzi denied the charge, but the feud continued.[13] The sixth and last edition of Montagu's work was published in 1810.

"Introduction," Essay on the Writings and Genius of Shakespear, Compared with the Greek and French Dramatic Poets. With Some Remarks Upon the Misrepresentations of Mons. De Voltaire (1769)

Elizabeth Montagu

INTRODUCTION

MR. Pope, in the preface to his edition of Shakespear, sets out by declaring, that, of all English poets, this tragedian offers the fullest and fairest subject for criticism. Animated by an opinion of such authority, some of the most learned and ingenious of our critics have made correct editions of his works, and enriched them with notes. The superiority of talents and learning, which I acknowledge in these editors, leaves me no room to entertain the vain presumption of attempting to correct any passages of this celebrated author; but the whole, as corrected and elucidated by them, lies open to a thorough enquiry into the genius of our great English classic. Unprejudiced and candid judgment will be the surest basis of his fame. He is now in danger of incurring the fate of the heroes of the fabulous ages, on whom the vanity of their country, and the superstition of the times, bestowed an apotheosis founded on pretensions to achievements beyond human capacity, by which they lost in a more sceptical and critical age, the glory that was due to them for what they had really done; and all the veneration they had obtained, was ascribed to ignorant credulity, and national prepossession—Our Shakespear, whose very faults pass here unquestioned, or are perhaps consecrated through the enthusiasm of his admirers, and the veneration paid to long-established fame, is by a great wit, a great critic, and a great poet of a neighbouring nation, treated as the writer of monstrous farces, called by him tragedies; and barbarism and ignorance are attributed to the nation by which he is admired. Yet if wits, poets, critics, could ever be charged with presumption, one might say there was some degree of it in pronouncing, that, in a country where Sophocles and Euripides are as well understood as in any in Europe, the perfections of dramatic poetry should be as little comprehended as among the Chinese.

Learning here is not confined to ecclesiastics, or a few lettered sages and academics: every English gentleman has an education, which gives him an early acquaintance with the writings of the ancients. His knowledge of polite literature does not begin with that period which Mr. de Voltaire calls Le Siecle de Louis quatorze. Before he is admitted as a spectator at the theatre at London, it is probable he has heard the tragic muse as she spoke at Athens, and as she now speaks at Paris, or in Italy; and he can discern between the natural language in which she addressed the human heart, and artificial dialect which she has acquired from the prejudices of a particular nation, or the jargon caught from the tone of a court. To please upon the French stage, every person of every age and nation was made to adopt their manners. [....] Great indulgence is due to the errors of original writers, who, quitting the beaten track which others have travelled, make daring incursions into unexplored regions of invention, and boldly strike into the pathless sublime: it is no wonder if they are often bewildered, sometimes benighted; yet surely it is more eligible to partake the pleasure and the toil of their adventures, than still to follow the cautious steps of timid imitators through trite and common roads. Genius is of a bold enterprizing nature, ill adapted to the formal restraints of critic institutions, or indeed to lay down to itself rules of nice discretion. If perfect and faultless composition is ever to be expected from human faculties, it must be at some happy period when a noble and graceful simplicity, the result of well regulated and sober magnanimity, reigns through the general manners. Then the muses and the arts, neither effeminately delicate nor audaciously bold, assume their highest character, and in all their compositions seem to respect the chastity of the public taste, which would equally disdain quaintness of ornament, or the rude neglect of elegance and decorum. Such periods had Greece, had Rome! Then were produced immortal works of every kind! But, when the living manners degenerated, in vain did an Aristotle and a Quintilian endeavour to restore by doctrine what had been inspired by sentiments, and fashioned by manners.

If the severer muses, whose sphere is the library and the senate, are obliged in compliance to this degeneracy, to trick themselves out with meretricious and frivolous ornaments, as is too apparent from the compositions of the historians and orators in declining empires, can we wonder that a dramatic poet, whose chief interest it is to please the people, should, more than any other writer, conform himself to their humour; and appear most strongly infected with the faults of the times, whether they be such as belong to unpolished, or corrupted taste.

Shakespear wrote at a time when learning was tinctured with pedantry; wit was unpolished, and mirth ill-bred. The court of Elizabeth spoke a scientific jargon, and a certain obscurity of style was universally affected. James brought an addition of pedantry, accompanied by indecent and indelicate manners and language. By contagion, or from complaisance to the taste of the public, Shakespear falls sometimes into the fashionable mode of writing: but this is only by fits; for many parts of all his plays are written with the most noble, elegant, and uncorrupted simplicity. Such is his merit, that the more just and refined the taste of the nation has become, the more he has encreased in reputation. He was approved by his own age, admired by the next, and is revered, and almost adored by the present. His merit is disputed by little wits, and his errors are the jests of little critics; but there has not been a great poet, or great critic, since his time, who has not spoken of him with the highest veneration, Mr. Voltaire excepted. His translations often, his criticism still oftener, prove he did not perfectly understand the words of the author; and therefore it is certain he could not enter into his meaning. He comprehended enough to perceive he was unobservant of some established rules of composition; the felicity with which he performs what no rules can teach escapes him. Will not an intelligent spectator admire the prodigious structures of Stone-Henge, because he does not know by what law of mechanics they were raised? Like them, our author's works will remain for ever the greatest monuments of the amazing force of nature, which we ought to view as we do other prodigies, with an attention to, and admiration of their stupendous parts, and proud irregularity of greatness.

293

It has been already declared that Shakespear is not to be tried by any code of critic laws; nor is it more equitable to judge him entirely by the practice of any particular theatre. Yet some criterion must be established by which we may determine his merits. First, we must take into consideration what is proposed to be done by the means of dramatic imitation. Every species of poetry has its distinct offices. The effecting certain moral purposes, by the representation of a fable, seems to have been the universal intention, from the first institution of the drama to this time; and to have prevailed, not only in Europe, but in all countries where the dramatic art has been attempted. It has indeed been the common aim of all poetry to please and instruct; but by means as various as the kinds of composition. We are pleased with the ode, the elegy, the eclogue; not only for having invention, spirit, elegance, and such perfections as are necessary to recommend any sort of poetry, but we also require that each should have its specific merit; the ode, that which constitutes the perfection of an ode, &c. In these views, then, our author is to be examined. First, if his fables answer to the noblest end of fable, moral instruction; next, whether his dramatic imitation has its proper dramatic excellence. In the latter of these articles, perhaps, there is not any thing will more assist our judgment than a candid comparison (where the nature of the subjects well bear it) between his and some other celebrated dramatic compositions. It is idle to refer to a vague, unrealized idea of perfection: we may safely pronounce that to be well executed, in any art, which after the repeated efforts of great geniuses is equal to any thing that has been produced. We may securely applaud what the ancients have crowned; therefore should not withhold our approbation wherever we find our countryman has equalled the most admired passages in the Greek tragedians: but we shall not do justice to his native talents, when they are the object of consideration, if we do not remember the different circumstances under which these writers were composed. Shakespear's plays were to be acted in a paltry tavern, to an unlettered audience, just emerging from barbarity: the Greek tragedies were to be exhibited at the public charge, under the care and auspices of the magistrates at Athens; where the very populace were critics in wit, and connoisseurs in public spectacles. The period when Sophocles and Euripides wrote, was that in which the fine arts, and polite literature, were in a degree of perfection which succeeding ages have emulated in vain.

It happened in the literary as in the moral world; a few sages, from the veneration which they had obtained by extraordinary wisdom and a faultless conduct, rose to the authority of legislators. The practice and manner of the three celebrated Greek tragedians were by succeeding critics established as dramatic laws: happily for Shakespear, Mr. Johnson, whose genius and learning render him superior to a servile awe of pedantic institutions, in his ingenious preface to his edition of Shakespear has greatly obviated all that can be objected to our author's neglect of the unities of time and place.

Shakespear's felicity has been rendered compleat in this age. His genius produced works that time could not destroy: but some of the lighter characters were become illegible; these have been restored by critics whose learning and penetration traced back the vestiges of superannuated opinions and customs. They are now no longer in danger of being effaced, and the testimonies of these learned commentators to his merit, will guard our author's great monument of human wit from the presumptuous invasions of our rash critics, and the squibs of our witlings; so that the bays will flourish unwithered and inviolate round his tomb; and his very spirit seems to come forth and to animate his characters, as often as Mr. Garrick, who acts with the same inspiration with which he wrote, assumes them on the stage.

After our poet had received such important services from the united efforts of talents and learning in his behalf, some apology seems necessary for this work. Let it be remembered that the most superb and lasting monument that ever was consecrated to beauty, was that to which every lover carried a tribute. I dare hope to do him honour only by augmenting the heap of volumes given by his admirers to his memory; I will own I was incited to this undertaking by great admiration of his genius, and still greater indignation at the treatment he had received from a French wit, who seems to think he has made prodigious concessions to our prejudices in favour of the works of our countryman in allowing them the credit of a few splendid passages, while he speaks of every entire piece as a monstrous and ill-constructed farce.—Ridiculously has our poet, and ridiculously has our taste been represented, by a writer of universal fame; and through the medium of an almost universal language. Superficial criticisms hit the level of shallow minds, to whom a bon mot will ever appear reason, and an epigrammatic turn argument; so that many of our countrymen have hastily adopted this lively writer's opinion of the extravagance and total want of design in Shakespear's dramas. With the more learned, deep, and sober critics he lies under one considerable disadvantage. For copying nature as he found it in the busy walks of human life, he drew from an original, with which the literati are seldom well acquainted. They perceive his portraits are not of the Grecian or of the Roman school: after finding them unlike to the celebrated forms preserved in learned museums they do not deign to enquire whether they resemble the living persons they were intended to represent. Among these connoisseurs, whose acquaintance with the characters of men is formed in the library, not in the street, the camp, or village, whatever is unpolished and uncouth passes for fantastic and absurd, though, in fact, it is a faithful representation of a really exciting character.

But it must be acknowledged, that, when this objection is obviated there will yet remain another cause of censure; for though our author, from want of delicacy or from a desire to please the popular taste, thought he had done well when he faithfully copied nature, or represented customs, it will appear to politer times the error of an untutored mind; which the example of judicious artists, and the admonitions of delicate connoisseurs had not taught, that only graceful nature and decent customs give proper subjects for imitation. It may be said in mitigation of his fault that the vulgar here had not, as at Athens, been used to behold,

> Gorgeous tragedy
> In scepter'd pall come sweeping by,
> Presenting Thebes or Pelops' line,
> Or the tale of Troy divine.

Homer's works alone were sufficient to teach the Greek poets how to write, and their audience how to judge. The songs sung by our bards at feasts and merrymakings were of a very coarse kind: as the people were totally illiterate, and only the better sort could read even their mother tongue, their taste was formed on these compositions. As yet our stage had exhibited only those palpable allegories by which rude unlettered moralists instruct and please the gross and ignorant multitude. Nothing can more plainly evince the opinion the poets of those times had of the ignorance of the people, than the condescension shewn to it by the learned Earl of Dorset in his tragedy of Gorboduc; in which the moral of each act is represented on the stage in dumb shew. It is strange that Mr. de Voltaire who affects an impartial and philosophic spirit, should not rather speak with admiration than contempt of an author, who by the force of genius rose so much above the age and circumstances in which he was born, and who, even when he deviates most from rules, can rise to faults true critics dare not mend. In delineating characters he must be allowed far to surpass all dramatic writers, and even Homer himself; he gives an air of reality to every thing, and, in spite of many and great faults, effects, better than any one has done, the chief purposes of the theatrical representation. It avails little to prove that the means by which he effects them are not those prescribed in any art of poetry. While we feel the power and energy of his predominant genius, shall we not be apt to treat the cold formal precepts of the critic, with the same peevish contempt that the good lady in the Guardian, smarting in the anguish of a burn, does her son's pedantic intrusion of Mr. Locke doctrine, to prove that there is no heat in fire. Nature and sentiment will pronounce our Shakespear a mighty genius; judgment and taste will confess that as a writer he is far from being faultless. [....]

On the HISTORICAL DRAMA

[....]

Nothing great is to be expected from any set of artists, who are to give only copies of copies. The treasures of nature are inexhaustible, as well in moral as in physical subjects. The talents of Shakespear were universal, his penetrating mind saw through all characters; and, as Mr. Pope says of him, he was not more a master of our strongest emotions than of our idealist sensations.

One cannot wonder, that endued with so great and various powers, he broke down the barriers that had before confined the dramatic writers to the regions of comedy, or tragedy. He perceived the fertility of the subjects that lay between the two extreams; he saw, that in the historical play he could represent the manners of the whole people, give the general temper of the times, and bring in view the incidents that affected the common fate of his country. The Gothic muse had a rude spirit of liberty, and delighted in painting popular tumults, the progress of civil wars, and the revolutions of government, rather than a catastrophe within the walls of a palace. At the time he wrote, the wars of the Houses of York and Lancaster were fresh in mens [sic] minds. They had received the tale from some Nestor in their family, or neighbourhood, who had fought in the battle he related. Every spectator's affections were ranged under the white or red Rose, in whose contentions some had lost their parents and friends; others had gained establishments and honours.

All the inducements which the Greek tragedians had to chuse their heroes from the works of the poets who had sung the wars of Troy, and the Argonautic expedition, were still in greater force with our countryman to take his subjects from the history and traditions of those more recent transactions, in which the spectator was informed and interested more personally and locally. There was not a family so low, that had not had some of its branches torn off in the storms of these intestine commotions: nor a valley so happily retired, that at some time, the foot of hostile paces had not bruis'd her flow'rets. In these characters the rudest peasant read the sad history of his country, while the better sort were informed of the most minute circumstances by our chronicles. The tragedians who took their subjects from Homer, had all the advantage a painter would have, who was to draw a picture from a statue of Phidias or Praxiteles. Poor Shakespear from the wooden images in our mean chronicles was to form his portraits. What judgment was there in discovering, that by moulding them to an exact resemblance he should engage and please! And what discernment and penetration into characters, and what amazing skill in moral painting, to be able, from such uncouth models, to bring forth not only a perfect, but, when occasion required, a graceful likeness! [....]

Upon the Death of JULIUS CÆSAR

[....]

Mr. Voltaire formerly understood the English language tolerably well. His translation of part of Antony's speech to the people, in his own play of the death of Julius Cæsar, though far inferior to the original, is pretty good; and in his tragedy of Junius Brutus he has improved upon the Brutus of our old poet Lee: he has followed the English poet in making the daughter of Tarquin seduce the son of Junius Brutus into a scheme for the restoration of her father; but with great judgment has imitated only what was worthy of imitation; and by the strength of his own genius has rendered his piece much more excellent than that of Mr. Lee.

[....]

ON THE PRÆTERNATURAL BEINGS

AS the genius of Shakespear, through the whole extent of the poet's province, is the object of our enquiry, we should do him great injustice, if we did not attend to his peculiar felicity, in those fictions and inventions, from which poetry derives its highest distinction, and from whence it first assumed its pretensions to divine inspiration, and appeared the associate of religion.

The ancient poet was admitted into the synod of the Gods: he discoursed of their natures, he repeated their counsels, and, without the charge of impiety or presumption, disclosed their dissensions, and published their vices. He peopled the woods with nymphs, the rivers with deities; and, that he might still have some being within call to his assistance, he placed responsive echo in the vacant regions of air.

In the infant ages of the world, the credulity of ignorance greedily received every marvellous tale: but, as mankind increased in knowledge, and a long series of traditions had established a certain mythology and history, the poet was no longer permitted to range, uncontrolled, through the boundless dominions of fancy, but became restrained, in some measure, to things believed or known— Though the duty of poetry to please and to surprise still subsisted, the means varied with the state of the world, and it soon grew necessary to make the new inventions lean on the old traditions—the human mind delights in novelty, and is captivated by the marvellous, but even in fable itself requires the credible.— the poet, who can give to splendid inventions, and to fictions new and bold, the air and authority of reality and truth, is master of the genuine sources of the Castalian spring, and may justly be said to draw his inspiration from the well-head of pure poesy.

Shakespear saw how useful the popular superstitions had been to the ancient poets: he felt that they were necessary to poetry itself. One needs only to read some modern French heroic poems to be convinced how poorly epic poetry subsists on the pure elements of history and philosophy: Tasso, though he had a subject so popular, at the time he wrote, as the deliverance of Jerusalem, was obliged to employ the operations of magic, and the interposition of angels and dæmons, to give the marvellous, the sublime, and, I may add, that religious air to his work, which ennobles the enthusiasm, and sanctifies the fiction of the poet.

Ariosto's excursive muse wanders through the regions of romance, attended by all the superb train of chivalry, giants, dwarfs, and enchanters; and however these poets, by the severe and frigid critics may have been condemned for giving ornaments not purely classical, to their works; I believe every reader of taste admirers, not only the fertility of their imagination, but the judgment with which they availed themselves of the superstition of the times, and of the customs and modes of the country, in which they laid their scenes of action.

To recur, as the learned sometimes do, to the mythology and fables of other ages, and other countries, has ever a poor effect: Jupiter, Minerva, and Apollo, only embellish a modern story, as a print from their statues adorns the frontispiece.—We admire indeed the art of the sculptors who give their images with grace and majesty; but no devotion is excited, no enthusiasm kindled, by the representations of characters whose divinity we do not acknowledge.

When the Pagan temples ceased to be revered, and the Parnassian mount existed no longer, it would have been difficult for the poet of later times to have preserved the divinity of his muse inviolate, if the western world too had not had its sacred fables. While there is any national superstition which credulity has consecrated, any hallowed tradition long revered by vulgar faith; to that sanctuary, that asylum, may the poet resort.—Let him tread the holy ground with reverence; respect the established doctrine; exactly observe the accustomed rites, and the attributes of the object of veneration; then shall he not vainly invoke an inexorable or absent deity. Ghosts, fairies, goblins, elves, were as propitious, were as assistant to Shakespear, and gave as much of the sublime, and of the marvellous, to his fictions, as nymphs, satyrs, fawns, and even the triple Geryon, to the works of ancient bards. Our poet never carries his præternatural beings beyond the limits of the popular tradition. It is true, that he boldly exerts his poetic genius and fascinating powers in that magic circle, in which none e'er durst walk but he: but as judicious as bold, he contains himself within it. He calls up all the stately phantoms in the regions of superstition, which our faith will receive with reverence. He throws into their manners and language a mysterious solemnity, favorable to superstition in general, with something highly characteristic of each particular being which he exhibits. His witches, his ghosts, and his fairies, seem spirits of health or goblins damn'd; bring with them airs from heaven, or blasts from hell. His ghosts are sullen, melancholy, and terrible. Every sentence, utter'd by the witches, is a prophecy or a charm; their manners are malignant, their phrases ambiguous, their promises delusive.—The witches cauldron is a horrid collection of what is most horrid in their supposed incantations. Ariel is a spirit, mild, gentle, and sweet, possess'd of supernatural powers, but subject to the command of a great magician.

The fairies are sportive and gay; the innocent artificers of harmless frauds, and mirthful delusion. Puck's enumeration of the feats of a fairy is the most agreeable recital of their supposed gambols.

To all these beings our poet has assigned tasks, and appropriated manners adapted to their imputed dispositions and characters; which are continually developing through the whole piece, in a series of operations conductive to the catastrophe. They are not brought in as subordinate or casual agents, but lead the action, and govern the fable; in which respect our countryman has entered more into theatrical propriety than the Greek tragedians.

ENDNOTES

1   Elizabeth Drake may have studied at the rigorous school for girls run by Bathsua Makin (1600–75?), learned author of *An Essay to Revive the Ancient Education of Gentlewomen* (1673). See Gary Kelly, "Introduction: Sarah Scott, Bluestocking Feminism, and *Millenium Hall*," in *Millenium Hall*, ed. Gary Kelly (Peterborough, ON: Broadview Press, 1995), 14, 19.

2   See Sylvia Harcstark Myers's account of Elizabeth Robinson's formative years and her important friendships in *The Bluestocking Circle: Women, Friendship, and the Life of the Mind in Eighteenth-Century England* (Oxford: Clarendon Press, 1990), 21–44.

3   Elizabeth Child, "Elizabeth Montagu, Bluestocking Businesswoman," in "Reconsidering the Bluestockings," ed. Nicole Pohl and Betty A. Schellenberg, special issue, *Huntington Library Quarterly*, 65, no. 1–2 (2002): 153–73.

4   Ann Thompson and Sasha Roberts, "Elizabeth Montagu (née Robinson), 1720–1800," in *Women Reading Shakespeare 1660–1900* (Manchester: Manchester University Press, 1997), 22.

5   Elizabeth Eger, editor's introduction to *Elizabeth Montagu*, vol. 1 of *Bluestocking Feminism*, ed. Gary Kelly (London: Pickering & Chatto, 1999), lv–lxxxvii.

6   Montagu promoted the "washer woman" poet Ann Yearsley with Hannah More to everyone's eventual discomfort.

7   Myers explains that "the history of the origin and changes in the use of the term 'bluestocking' illuminates both the dissatisfactions of women with the state of their opportunities to have an intellectual life at all, and the underlying attitudes of those who resisted change"(p. 6), and see the more recent analysis by Gary Kelly, general introduction to *Bluestocking Feminism*, ix–xi.

8   Myers, 195.

9   Norma Clarke discusses the intense competition between Montagu and Johnson in *Dr. Johnson's Women* (London: Hambledon, 2000), 138–53.

10 Elizabeth Eger, editor's introduction to *Elizabeth Montagu*, vol. 1 of *Bluestocking Feminism*, ed. Gary Kelly (London: Pickering & Chatto, 1999), lxvi.

11 Elizabeth Eger, "The Bluestocking Defense of Shakespeare," in "Reconsidering the Bluestockings," ed. Nicole Pohl and Betty A. Schellenberg, special issue, *Huntington Library Quarterly* 65, no.1–2 (2002), 135.

12 See *Women Reading Shakespeare 1660-1900: An Anthology of Criticism*, ed. Ann Thompson and Sasha Roberts (Manchester: Manchester University Press, 1997).

13 Clarke, 138.

Mary Wollstonecraft (1759–1797)

Mary Wollstonecraft was one of the leading British female intellectuals at the end of the eighteenth century. She provoked controversy during her lifetime and continues to be controversial. We focus on her production as book review editor for the progressive *Analytical Review* from 1788 to 1797,[1] an important, if under appreciated, aspect of Wollstonecraft's writing.[2] In this capacity, Wollstonecraft identified herself as "the first of a new genus," a professional woman writer, aware that she was making women's history by functioning as a member of Joseph Johnson's (1738–1809) editorial staff with predictably assigned work and steady remuneration. Extensive book reviewing gave her the opportunity to broaden her knowledge and devise a critical model of reviewing and authorial behavior that she communicated to other women attempting to make the transition from female reader to professional writer, especially to Mary Hays.

Wollstonecraft was the second child and eldest daughter of Edward Wollstonecraft. Edward was heir to his family's silk-weaving business, but he squandered his inheritance and abused his wife as he deteriorated into alcoholism. Mary Wollstonecraft's childhood experiences of her father's brutality and her mother's passivity had profound and continuing effects on her adult beliefs. Her learning was almost all self-acquired and pursued in the face of great difficulty. Among the important influences on her was the father of her early friend Jane Arden, a self-styled itinerant "philosopher" whose lectures on experimental science Wollstonecraft attended.[3] Her subsequent friendship and correspondence with an older, more accomplished girl, Fanny Blood, started Wollstonecraft on the path of intellectual self-improvement that continued for the rest of her life. William Godwin, her husband and first biographer, commented, "she had read to gratify the ardour of an inextinguishable thirst of knowledge."[4]

Lacking independent means of support, Wollstonecraft struggled to earn a living through the limited occupations open to women. She worked as a paid companion, a schoolteacher, and a governess. For a brief period, she ran a school with her sisters, first in Islington, then at Newington Green. There, within the Dissenting community, Wollstonecraft encountered Dr. Richard Price, a leading radical thinker, who saw her potential and encouraged her ambitions. Lyndall Gordon describes Price's ideas that influenced Wollstonecraft as an "eighteenth-century trust in continuing enlightenment ... compassion for victims and ... commitment to liberty—all qualities she could share.[5] Urged to contribute to the growing literature on female education, Wollstonecraft wrote *Thoughts on the Education of Daughters* (1787) where she argued that girls should be trained to be independent, robust, and rational. The Unitarian publisher, Joseph Johnson, published *Thoughts* and became one of Wollstonecraft's most important advocates. When Wollstonecraft lost her post as governess (1787), she returned to London bringing the manuscript of her first novel, *Mary; A Fiction*, which Johnson also published (1788). He also engaged her as a translator, reader, and reviewer for his new periodical, the *Analytical Review*. Wollstonecraft thereby joined Johnson's intellectual circle where she met some of the most significant radicals of the day, whose works Johnson published and Wollstonecraft reviewed: Anna Barbauld, William Blake, Henry Fuseli, William Godwin, and Thomas Paine.

The outbreak of the French Revolution in 1789 had a cataclysmic effect on Wollstonecraft's understanding and future. Edmund Burke (1729–97), a conservative Whig, responded to events with his polarizing *Reflections on the Revolution in France* (1790), singling out for condemnation Richard Price's "Discourse on the Love of Our Country" (1789, 1790) that joined celebration of the Glorious Revolution and the French Revolution with Dissenting agitation for parliamentary reform.[6] Wollstonecraft shot back with *A Vindication of the Rights of Men*, published anonymously 28 days after Burke's polemic, which mounted a stirring defense of Price and his principles, which also "called into question the political status of women."[7] The success of this work emboldened Wollstonecraft to develop her radical analysis of gender in *A Vindication of the Rights of Woman* (1792), written in six weeks and published under her own name. Mary Hays in her "Memoirs" of Wollstonecraft (1800) remarked, "It is little wonderful that the magnanimous advocate of freedom ... should throw down the gauntlet, challenge her arrogant oppressors, and ... deny the existence of a sexual character."[8] The story of Wollstonecraft's subsequent contributions and struggles are integral to feminist history, most notably her attempts to integrate in her own life "theory and practice ... the sentiments of passion, and the resolves of reason."[9]

ANALYTICAL REVIEW (1790)

The excerpts from the *Analytical Review* illustrate Wollstonecraft's development from opinionated reader to authoritative reviewer. She began as an apprentice to publisher Joseph Johnson, advancing to editorial assistant and then review editor, commissioning others to review particular titles. Wollstonecraft reviewed many kinds of books in addition to her usual fare of novels and educational texts: travel literature, sermons, scientific treatises, poetry, drama, and "miscellaneous 'trash' as she termed it."[10] Johnson and his partner Thomas Christie initially intended reviews to be objective summaries of the works discussed rather than partisan advocacy, as in other periodicals. They planned to include excerpts from the text under discussion, varying from snippets to extended portions, for an audience of educated readers who expected straightforward accounts of books.[11] The publishers modified their approach when Christie intimated that the reading audience demanded more plainspoken assessment. In her reviews, Wollstonecraft both reflected and promoted this cultural shift.[12]

Wollstonecraft learned on the job—reading, translating, and reviewing. She devoured nearly four hundred works to produce dozens of reviews. Some of these were brief, merely an occasion for her to deplore the moral effects of circulating library novels. Others, like the two below, served as important vehicles for Wollstonecraft to test out her own reformist agenda, which she developed more fully in *A Vindication of the Rights of Woman* and later works. Wollstonecraft's review of Hester Lynch Piozzi's *Observations and Reflections, made in the Course of a Journey through France, Italy and Germany* (1789) attests to her ambivalence about other female writers:[13] She criticized Piozzi's "childish feminine" style, expecting better thinking and writing from a woman who had the privileges of education, money, social status, and who was the protégée of Samuel Johnson. The review of Catharine Macaulay's groundbreaking *Letters on Education* (1790) reveals Wollstonecraft as "an engaged critic,"[14] wide-ranging, analytic, and philosophical. Wollstonecraft explores Macaulay's political and theological positions while insisting on fuller female agency. Wollstonecraft addresses Macaulay within the context of the wider historical debates on liberty and authority.

302

Review of Letters on Education: with Observations on Religious and Metaphysical Subjects, by Catharine Macaulay Graham, Analytical Review (1790)

Mary Wollstonecraft

November, 1790

ARTICLE I. *Letters on Education: with Observations on Religious and Metaphysical Subjects.* By Catharine Macaulay Graham. 8vo. 507 pages. Price 6s. in boards. Dilly. 1790.

This masculine and fervid writer has turned the very superior powers of her mind to the consideration of a subject, which perhaps, embraces a wider circle of unsettled opinions, than most of those disputed points that have exercised the argumentative talents of ancient philosophers and modern theologians.

"Of all the arts of life," Mrs M. observes, "that of giving useful instruction to the human mind, and of rendering it the master of its affections, is the most important:"—and, she adds, "Every work published on education, that affords one new idea which may be found useful in practice is worthy the attention of the public. Nor does the author of these letters aspire to any other merit, than that of offering a few new hints on the subject, and throwing some illustration on those which have been already given. If the novelty of these should be made an objection to the work, let it be remembered, that every thing new is alarming to the ignorant and the prejudiced; and that morals taught on immutable principles, must carry a very different appearance from those founded on the discordant sentiments of selfish man."

Perfectly coinciding in opinion with this sagacious writer, not only respecting the importance of the subject, considered in an uncircumscribed view; but also with the tendency of her instruction, which she has intimated in the preface, by asserting that morals must be taught on immutable principles, we shall proceed to analyze a work that displays a store of knowledge, arranged by a sound understanding.

The Introductory Letter, though at the first glance it may appear desultory, contains many observations strictly connected with the main subject:—The author particularly dwells on the arguments which may be produced in favour of the future existence of brutes; and treating a moral objection to the goodness of God, involved in tenfold darkness, she agrees with Dr Jortin, who has cursorily dipped into this mysterious subject, in his sermon on the Goodness of God.

"The uniform voice of revelation," says Mrs M. "every where proclaims God the universal parent of the creation. By this appellation, Hortensia, I would describe a relation more tender than what we commonly annex to our ideas of the author of nature. Almost every sect of Christians, in order to spur on the lazy virtue of their votaries, have represented the rigorous justice of God, in a light which confines his benevolence to a narrow sphere of action; and whilst he is represented as devoting to an eternity of torments the far greater number of the human race, the gates of Paradise are barred to all but the elect. Tremendous thought! It is thus indeed that the gift of eternal life is a dangerous pre-eminence, and the balance becomes more than equal between us and the brute creation.

"These are the melancholy visions of, perhaps, the greater part of the religious world, whilst to the eye of the modern philosopher, God is infinite only in his natural attributes; and because they cannot find a more satisfactory reason for the introduction of moral and natural evil, they limit the power and the benevolence of God, to a size which exactly squares with all the objects of sense. The philosopher contemplates the monster Nature, who is continually devouring and regorging itself, with rapture and delight. He views with a complacent sentiment, myriads of being brought forth to animated and feeling life, merely to serve for the support of creatures, who in their turn must pay to the stern law of Nature, a tribute equally painful."

The question of public and private education is next considered. This is one of the disputed points, which affords continual fuel for controversial writers, though many of them, seeing the subject in different lights, do not dispute on fair ground. Before the discussion of this question, it is necessary to ask parents a few previous ones. What object have you principally in view, when you deliberate whether you shall give your son a public or private education? Do you wish to render him, supposing him to be a boy with a quick comprehension and a daring spirit, a man of shrewd abilities, calculated to rise in the world? Do you wish him to mix with his superiors, and form early connections, that may possibly be useful to him life? Do you wish him soon to become acquainted with the vices and weaknesses of human nature, and learn adroitly to turn them to his own advantage—send him to a public school. But, if you are more anxious to fix just principles in his mind, on a grand scale, than to see him dazzle by the brilliancy of his acquirements: if you wish him to have a sound mind in a sound body; and have sufficient resolution not to make a *little* gentleman of him; or allow the visitors and servants to vitiate his mind by false respect and flattery: if by example you can teach him to respect himself, on account of intrinsic worth; and are so situated as to be able to let him feel the comfort flowing from the exercise of domestic affections and duties—in the name of God keep him at home. For, to use the words of our author, "A public education may be formed on the very best plan; and yet, in many points, it may fall short of what may be effected by domestic instruction. The one cannot, in the nature of things, be so elaborate as the other: besides, what tutorage can equal that which proceeds from the attentive zeal of an enlightened parent? what affection less warm and intense will prescribe and follow such rules of self-denial, as is necessary to preserve the pupil from receiving any impression which may be mischievous to his future innocence and peace?"

305

We cannot agree with Mrs M. that it is easy for people of fortune to place their children under the care of governors and governesses in whose sobriety, discretion, and wisdom, they can put a full confidence; on the contrary, it is, perhaps, the most difficult of all tasks to procure, even when the expence is not considered, a person in whose discretion and abilities a discerning parent could rely without great anxiety.

Some judicious remarks occur in the two following letters respecting the management of both mind and body during infancy—and particular stress is judiciously laid on the necessity of acquiring hardy habits. Mrs M. directs that the amusements of boys and girls should be the same.—*The subject of amusements and innocent employments pursued.* The great advantage of inducing habits of independence is forcibly represented. *Happiness more likely to be found in the gentler satisfactions than in the higher enjoyments—filling the imagination of young people with prospects of enjoyment, improper.* The following remark appears just. p. 81.

"In the mind of man, Hortensia, we may observe propensities which are of such opposite qualities that the inattentive observer would be apt to accuse nature of caprice, in separating from simplicity, in order to produce confusion. But how far different are the conclusions of the philosopher! He acknowledges the necessity for every seeming contrariety. He perceives, that if the force and power which habit acquires over the mind were less strong, virtue would be cultivated without success, and education be of no avail. He allows that there is wisdom in imitating the empire of habit, by the appetites of curiosity, and the love of novelty. And he discovers that nature, in sowing the seeds of such discordant passions, and planting in the human mind such opposite inclinations, left it to the care of experience to perfect her work by cultivation, and by fixing the degrees of either as best sits the great end and purpose of education."

On the vice of lying–religion.—The Bible and New Testament totally excluded by Mrs M. from the religious study of children.

Severity in the education of children improper.—Common faults. Punishment. Benevolence. p. 11.

"Rousseau is right," says Mrs M. "in the opinion, that the virtues of children are of the negative kind; and that in endeavouring to produce the fruits of reason and experience at too early a season, we are deprived of the harvest of a riper age.

Let it be then the principal care of tutors to preserve the infant mind free from the malignant passions, and the benign affections will grow of themselves. Let it be their care to make their pupils feel the utility of benevolence, by being themselves the objects of it. Let no capricious partialities, no ill founded preference, growing from personal charms or accomplishments, or from the gifts of genius, set them the example of a departure from the strict principles of equity, and give them reason to complain both of the injustice of nature and man.

"But it is not through the medium of self only, that children should be taught lessons of benevolence; they should see it dispersed to every object around them with such a constancy, as should keep them in perfect ignorance that the views of injustice and inhumanity have any existence. They ought not to be suffered to ridicule others unreproved. Should they once take a pleasure in the pain they give the human mind, benevolence will never be the leading feature in their character. As children are not able to enter into any nice examination on the different claims of wretchedness, it might be proper to avoid carrying them much in the way of objects of charity; but whenever accident presented such, they should never see them go away unrelieved.

"You will perhaps say, that this indiscriminate liberality might lead them into enthusiasm or prodigality, and use them to bellow their alms without judgment or preference; but, neither of these consequences would ensue. Enthusiasm is the offspring of speculation, never of habitual practice; and as I have said before, children are not able to enter into distinctions, which experience alone can teach; it is sufficient for them, if their principles and habits are of a right kind: rules of prudence are to be left to after instruction, when a larger intercourse with the world sets forth a variety of examples to view. Prodigality is a vice that either owes its rise to the little value we see put on money by those about us, or it proceeds from having our pockets loaded with coin before we can attain any knowledge of its worth. But to avoid giving my pupils habits of avarice or prodigality, or teazing them with precepts, which would undoubtedly be misunderstood, I would never put them into possession of any money, till they were of an age to be taught its value by the use they would be able to make of it.

"If brutes were to draw a character of man, Hortensia, do you think they would call him a benevolent being? No; their representations would be somewhat of the same kind as the fabled furies, and other infernals in ancient mythology. Fortunately for the reputation of the species, the brute can neither talk nor write; and being our own panegyrists, we can give ourselves what attributes we please, and call our confined and partial sympathy, the sublime virtue of benevolence. Goodness to man, and mercy to brutes, is all that is taught by the moralist; and this mercy is of a nature, which if properly defined, can only be distinguished by the inferiority of its degree from the vice cruelty."

Literary education of young persons.—A series of books are here recommended, calculated to open the mind;—yet, we should be almost afraid that the number mentioned are more than could be digested, unless by a youth of uncommon abilities, during the period specified, (one and twenty years); and though we think with Mrs M. that the bible is not a book in which children should be taught

306

to read—we should, however, rather advise a parent to let some parts, at least, be interwoven with the first youthful impressions.

The remarks on some celebrated novels are just; but still we are of opinion, that we should not so widely deviate from nature, as not to allow the imagination to forage a little for the judgment.—It may be made a question, whether the understanding has sufficient strength before it arrives at maturity to investigate such important projects? It may be necessary for the passions to be felt before their operations can be understood, or observed to any useful or moral purpose.—The man, indeed, who at thirty, has read with attention the books here recommended, has made good use of his time. This course of reading is equally designed for girls and boys.

307

"I must tell you, Hortensia," says Mrs M. addressing her correspondent, "lest you should mistake my plan, that though I have been obliged (in order to avoid confusion) to speak commonly in the masculine character, that the same rules of education in all respects are to be observed to the female as well as to the male children, only to conform as much as rationally can be done to the customs of Europe; for we must make some difference in the sports of our pupils, after they have passed the period of mere childhood."

Influence of impressions.—Example should coincide with instruction. True, O moralist!—But then thou shouldst educate two generations:—this is the stumbling-block of education. Some observations on physical prudence, deserve to be considered.

Indiscretion. The difficulty in common life of preventing improper conversations to be started before young people, must have been felt by every person who has paid any attention to the subject before us.

Sophistry. Alluding to a well known and degrading feature in Dr Johnson's character, Mrs M. observes:

"Had the Doctor not unfortunately taken it into his head, that he could with innocence play the sophist for victory in conversation, he would have been a much more useful member of society than he really was, and his fame might perhaps have been greater: for truth, when defended with skill and vigour, throws a lustre on the combatant, which error cannot do. Had the niceness of his conscience led him to guard against these breaches of integrity, had he only used his great abilities in the investigating and illustrating of truth, instead of confounding the reason of others, he might, perhaps, in the course of his enquires, have corrected in himself, and in those who enjoyed the happiness of his conversation, many errors taken up in haste, and defended from motives of vanity."

Politeness.—Fashion.—Sobriety.—Personal Beauty.—Secrecy.—Flattery.—Modesty.—Selfishness. If we were to animadvert on some sentiments contained in this letter, we might be led beyond our limits, and out of our province; we therefore forbear.

Sympathy. If rectitude is, for a moment, allowed to be only founded on a principle of utility, and that utility confined to the human species, it does not authorize cruelty to the brute creation, for in doing violence to our sympathies, to the sympathies the brutes excite, we blunt our benevolence, and are not as useful to our fellow creatures, not to mention ourselves, as we should be if we acted more consistently. "Morals must be taught on immutable principles." From which position Mrs M. infers—"That true wisdom, which is never found at variance with rectitude, is as useful to women as to men; because it is necessary to the highest degree of happiness, which can never exist in ignorance." Again, "it would be paying you a bad compliment, were I to answer all the frivolous objections which prejudice has framed against the giving a learned education to women; for I know of no learning, worth having, that does not tend to free the mind from error, and enlarge our stock of useful knowledge."

308

No characteristic difference in sex. The observations on this subject might have been carried much farther, if Mrs M.'s object had not been a general system of education. p. 207.

"The situation and education of women," she observes, "is precisely that which must necessarily tend to corrupt and debilitate both powers of mind and body. From a false notion of beauty and delicacy, their system of nerves is depraved before they come out of their nursery; and this kind of depravity has more influence over the mind, and consequently over morals, than is commonly apprehended. But it would be well if such causes only acted towards the debasement of the sex; their moral education is, if possible, more absurd than their physical. The principles and nature of virtue, which is never properly explained to boys, is kept quite a mystery to girls. They are told indeed, that they must abstain from those vices which are contrary to their personal happiness, or they will be regarded as criminals, both by God and man; but all the higher parts of rectitude, every thing that ennobles our being, and that renders us innoxious and useful, is either not taught, or is taught in such a manner as to leave no proper impression on the mind. This is so obvious a truth, that the defects of female education have ever been a fruitful topic of declamation for the moralist; but not one of this class of writers have laid down any judicious rules for amendment."

Coquetry. Its baneful effects on the moral character of women, are explained with great perspicuity.

Flattery.—Chastity.—Male Rakes. The reflections on female chastity are just; but they required further explanation; for till the minds of women are more enlarged, we should not weaken the salutary prejudices which serve as a substitute, a weak one we own, for rational principles.

Hints towards the education of a Prince, conclude this division of the subject.

Part II. *Influences of domestic and national education.—Athens.—Sparta.—* Rome.—Observations on the state of the Romans after the subversion of the Commonwealth. Causes which may have hitherto prevented Christianity from having its full effect on the manners of society.

"Much has been said," she concludes, "of the progress of civilization, but it certainly has so little tended to bring us back to classic simplicity, that we are every day departing more and more from it; and vanity, with the extension of our ideas on the article of luxury, bids fair to extinguish some of the most useful of the moral virtues out of the human character."—However, as several good men have, notwithstanding these untoward appearances, promised to themselves a return of the golden age, as depictured by the poets, it may not be an unentertaining specu-lation, to examine the utility of such means as shall appear to us the most likely to conduce to the highest degree, and the most universal extent of possible good."

Accordingly she considers *The duty of governments towards producing a general civilization.*—She proceeds to enquire into the nature of those high and important obligations which, in the reason of things, must be annexed to the office of government.

"It is well known, that a great part of the ancient, and even of the modern world, have made a deity of their government, in whose high prerogative, they have buried all their natural rights. The monstrous faith of millions made for one, has been at different times adopted by the greater part of civilized societies; and even those enlightened nations who have been the most famed for asserting and defending their liberties, ran into another species of idolatry, which is almost as much at war with the happiness of individuals. Instead of making a deity of the government, they made a deity of the society in its aggregate capacity; and to the real or imagined interests of this idol, they sacrificed the dearest interests of those individuals who formed the aggregate. Thus they reversed a very plain and reasonable preposition. Society with them was not formed for the happiness of its citizens, but the life and happiness of every citizen was to be devoted to the glory and welfare of the society.

/ 309

"When the happiness of an individual is properly considered, his interest will be found so intimately connected with the interests of the society of which he is a member, that he cannot act in conformity to the one, without having a proper consideration for the other. But reason will revolt against a service for which it finds no adequate return; and when we admire the virtue of the ancients, we admire on that inflexible conduct, which carried them to sacrifice every personal interest to principle."

Sympathy.—*Equity.* The pernicious effects which public executions and slaughterhouses have on the manners of the people at large, as equally incom-patible with benevolence and equity, are very cogently and forcibly insisted.— Indeed it must be granted that the frequent sight of wanton cruelty on brutes, has a direct tendency to weaken every social affection; and as the mass of men are undoubtedly only guided by feeling and habit, it is not necessary to point out the consequences which must naturally ensue. p. 278.

"Oh! then let all slaughter-houses be treated as nuisance; let them be se-questered from the haunts of men; let premiums be given to those who can find out the least painful manner of taking away the lives of those animals which are necessary of sustenance; let every other manner of depriving them of life be forbidden, under severe penalties; let the privation of life, by way of sport and amusement, be discouraged by example and precept; and it is more than probable, that such a spirit of benevolence will be diffused over the minds of the public, as may tend to the general practice of those virtues, which reason approves, and which Christianity ordains.

"It has been a question lately much agitated, whether any such necessity exists, as is pretended, of depriving those delinquents of their lives, who act against the public peace, by reasonable offenses, and by injuring a fellow citizen's life or property. Those who take the benevolent side of the question, maintain, that the depriving a citizen of his life, is a breach of one of the fundamental obligations of government, and that there may be found a variety of punishments more fully adequate to the preservation of the public peace, than acts of violence which shook the sensibility of the feeling mind, and harden to a state of barbarism the unfeeling one. Those who take the adverse side of the question, oppose these positions with many plausible arguments; but whether the necessity contended for, really exists in the nature of things, or whether it exists only in the indolence of government, and their inattention to the happiness of the community in their individual capacity, certain it is, that the interests of humanity and the dictates of good policy, require that the examples of taking away life should be as few as the nature of things will admit. That all the ceremonies which attend this melancholy act, should be made as awful as possible; and that to prevent the public from receiving any impression which may shock the compassionate part of society, or contribute to steel the hearts of the more insensible, all executions should be performed in private."

Observations on Penal Laws.—Houses of Correction.—Charity. The abuse of public charities has long been a subject of complaint, and we perfectly agree with Mrs M. that "no law can possibly answer the benevolent purposes of the legislature, but one that entirely takes the executive part out of the hands of those who have an interest in abusing the trust, and whose mean situations in life, and low education, render them deaf to the voice of sympathy, and callous to the strings of remorse." Could the rich be induced to employ themselves in softening the distress of the poor, what good effects would result to both!*

"But the habits adopted by the gay and rich," observes the author, "and the common received notion, that a pleasurable life is the only way in which the advantages of fortune can be enjoyed, will raise insurmountable obstacles and objections to this opinion on the real duties of charity. To these objections, there is but one answer to be given, but that is a strong one, viz. That those who prize

---

* In our public hospitals the poor are shamefully left a prey to the ignorant and the interested. The medical gentlemen who superintend them, visit the sick at certain hours, when they are expected, and, of course, find every thing in order; but, if some benevolent person, with a sound understanding, who had the power of entering at any time, would attend to the complaints of the poor wretches, and lay them before the committee—how many comforts might be procured them, and they would be effectually shielded from the rapacity of nurses, etc. who feed on their very vitals. A friend of the writer of this article, has frequently visited the public hospitals, and seen the state of the sick. The meat, in summer, is often putrid, and never served up in a decent manner, though in this desolate condition, the only comforts within the reach of these poor creatures, is a wholesome meal. Many who enter are, of course, friendless; yet they must lose the benefit of the charity, or pawn their clothes to keep themselves decent, for the charity does not provide them with clean linen. I must be allowed to mention a fact:—A widow woman, who had long been unable to work on account of a disorder which had fallen into her leg, at last consented to have it amputated, and the few shillings, allowed by the charity to procure her some indulgencies, at that juncture, were all demanded by the nurse for washing an extraordinary number of sheets. Silence is absolutely necessary for the sick, yet when some poor neglected wretches were breathing their last, the most infernal noise has been made by servants employed to clean the ward, in a hurry, that the committee might find every thing in order.

pleasure beyond satisfaction, have never experienced the superiority of the latter in the scale of happiness."

Hints towards a more general civilization, by an attention to the objects of sense. The ingenious remarks contained in this and the three following letters, do equal honour to the author's discernment and benevolence.

"But it is not only habits of personal cleanliness which nations should be zealous of adopting, who pretend to any high degree of civilization, or who are ambitious of attaining it; cleanliness in every possible mode, is a luxury which ought to meet with all the encouragement which example and power can give: for we may find among the inhabitants of a neat cottage, sentiments which would grace the exalted ranks of life: but never did a filthy hovel send forth a civilized citizen."

Gardening.—Architecture.—Domestics.—Drama. The salutary effects which might be produced by such an attention to objects of sense as would refine the pleasures they procure us, are traced with philosophic eye.

Religious sentiments universal among the ancients. Hints towards rendering the fine arts subservient to religion. It may be made a question whether society will ever be in such a cultivated state, that the fine arts, instead of pampering vice, and destroying simplicity of manners, may be rendered subservient to religion and virtue. That true taste is subservient to religion cannot be doubted—for a love of order and beauty, leads directly to admiration of their author.

Part III. *On the Origin of Evil.* An examination of the different solutions of this important difficulty in morals, particularly Dr King's, the basis of Pope's Essay on Man, is first entered on. p. 342.

"Dr King," Mrs M. observes, "sets out with a denial of that catholic opinion in the creed of the moralist, a moral beauty and a moral deformity, necessarily independent of the will of every being created or uncreated. It is explained by Plato, under the form of everlasting ideas or moral entities, coeval with eternity, and residing in the divine mind, from whence by irradiating rays, like the emitting of the sun beams, they enlighten the understanding of all those intellectual beings, who, disregarding the objects of sense, give themselves up to the contemplation of the deity. The modern philosopher in a lower strain of reasoning asserts, that there is an abstract fitness of things perceived by the mind of God, and so interwoven in the nature of contemplative objects, as to be traced, like abstract truths, by those faculties of the mind, which enable us to compare and perceive the agreement and disagreement of our sensitive and reflex ideas."

Some of the difficulties respecting the origin of evil perhaps arise from a blind kind of respect to the power of God.—It has been thought disrespectful even to limit his power by supposing it dependent on, or directed, by his wisdom—and some well-disposed persons might almost think it blasphemy to repeat the sentiments of a German writer on this subject; that probably God *could not* instantly render an intelligent creature virtuous—it *must* be an acquirement.—The perfection of power is its consistency with wisdom: choosing the wisest (the right way) of producing the intended effect. They would possibly answer in my uncle Toby's

311

words, "God can do any thing." The existence of evil may be denied, when, what we call by that name, is considered as the surest means of procuring the greatest good for the individual, and that it could not exist without the permission of God, who foresaw it, when he called us into being; but who that has attentively surveyed the world can deny the existence of *present* evil?—But to return to our author, who would not, perhaps, perfectly coincide with these opinions, though it does not appear to us clear that we weaken the notion of the irresistible power of God, when we suppose it guided by wisdom.—His power is superior to every obstacle, yet no contradiction is implied by saying, that he *can* only do what his wisdom points out as the best. The grandest idea which we can form of God's is, that his motives are always right, and his Will wisdom. From her eagerness to defend revelation, Mrs M. has not treated this part of the subject with sufficient precision—for she, notwithstanding, thinks, philosophically, that moral necessity extends to God.

On the unlimited Power of God. Mrs M. very justly concludes, that that system of philosophy must be obnoxious to morality that "sets out with introducing an uncertainty respecting the nature of virtue; and by taking away the essential and eternal discriminations of moral good and evil, of just and unjust, and reducing these to arbitrary productions of the divine will, or rules and modifications of human prudence and sagacity, it takes away one regular, simple, and universal rule of action for all intelligent nature." Surely it is, as she intimates, entertaining a very derogatory idea of the Supreme Being, to suppose that power, and independent existence, is the only determinate attributes to be ascribed to him; and the humility appears equally false that fixes the origin of right and wrong, in the arbitrary determinations of the divine will, or rules and modifications of human prudence and sagacity, it takes way one regular, simple and universal rule of action for all intelligent nature." Surely it is, as she intimates, entertaining a very derogatory idea of the Supreme Being, to suppose that power, and independent existence, is the only determinate attributes to be ascribed to him; and the humility appears equally false that fixes the origin of right and wrong, in the arbitrary determinations of the divine will, denying the existence of an abstract fitness of things.

That the injudicious Defenders of Religion, have given means of triumph to the Infidel. She means the injudicious defenders of the Christian religion.—For a glimpse of immortality was caught before the promulgation of the Gospel, and all the hopes of futurity, founded on the attributes of God, are not clouded at least do not vanish, when a firm belief in revelation is shaken; and God may be reverenced, as perfectly good and benevolent, by those who do not call themselves believers.

Perfect Benevolence of God.—Observations on Lord Bolingbroke's Philosophy. The reflections here introduced are just, as far as they go; but we must restrain ourselves, and not pursue a train of reason not consistent with our character.—It is sufficient to remark, that Lord Bolingbroke's superficial philosophy would sink, or perhaps has sunk, into oblivion, without the luminating light of this able pen.

The same subject continued—a Revelation in the Person of Christ, worthy of Divine Wisdom.—Arguments for the belief of a future state. To believe that all things are ordered by a perfect being, and not to believe in a future state, is a manifest contraction.—From the many sensible arguments for a future state, which are forcibly expressed, if they are not new, we shall extract one. p. 385.

"Had man been only created for the purpose of filling a rank on this terrestrial globe, the system of his oeconomy would never have been constituted in such a manner, as to have made this life a state of trial, and his short day would never have been chequered with so large a portion of misery, as to render it a doubtful question, whether existence is worth having on such severe terms. That high privilege, reason, which raises him to so painful a superiority above his fellow animals, might have been well spared for a more useful instinctive principle, which would have necessarily led him to avoid every object of such a quality as to bring on him pain and misery, and to persue every one necessary to the pleasure and support of his existence. Had he been endued with reason, it might have been of that commanding kind, as to subdue every hostile impression, and to be superior to all the seductive excitements of appetite and passion. Or the appetites and passions might have been balanced by so strong and over-ruling a sympathy, as to counteract, on a principle of universal benevolence, all those mischiefs which he draws on himself and others, by an inordinate and injudicious selfishness. The short space of time allotted for his existence, might in such circumstances, have been spent with the enjoyment of health and tranquillity, and in an uninterrupted series of pleasing sensations; neither rising to the tumults of pleasure, nor changing into the anguish of pain. And when he had to finish his course, he might have quitted his existence with all that soft tranquillity which attends the state of the body, when it resigns itself to the peaceful empire of sleep.

"By such oeconomy of nature, existence, however short, must have been esteemed a gift worthy of perfect benevolence to bestow. But in regard to those faculties of the mind, which on a state of positive mortality, seem to have been given as a curse, rather than a blessing, their ever growing and improving powers form another very strong conjecture in favor of their perpetuity."

Some of the contradictions to be found in Lord B.'s works pointed out—No miraculous interposition necessary to confirm or strengthen the evidence of Gospel revelation. Or rather Mrs M. meant to say, that such an interposition would interfere with the design of providence, and prevent those trials deserving the name of trials which evidently produce virtue. We shall close our account of this part of the subject, which an analysis cannot do justice to, with a sensible observation. p. 423.

"It has often been said, that some of the most devout people, are the most addicted to the grossest interest of self. This, if true must undoubtedly arise from the sordid nature of that allegiance which they pay to the Deity, and from the false conceptions they have entertained of the general principles of his service. I must acknowledge that I have often heard with regret some very moral and religious people declare, that if they had been assured of the positive mortality of their nature, their lives would have been directed by a contrary rule. Thus, if by such a persuasion they had gained a liberty from the restraints of religion, they would have followed every perverse motion of their will; and found to their

313

cost, that their liberty consisted in being kept in a continual subjection to their passions, and the like being imposed in their most important choice."

On the philosophy and doctrines of the Stoics. The doctrines of the Stoics are clearly stated by Mrs M. and some unjust aspersions wiped off, which bigotry and ignorance have industriously propagated, to render doctrines ridiculous or odious, which deserve respect.

The question of Free-will and Necessity, involved in the study of the human mind.—Statement of the opinions entertained by the Free-Willers. Though this is an impartial statement of the opinions of the Free-Willers, yet very few of them, in direct terms, assert, what their first position, that man has an independent will, and can choose either good or evil, without being influenced by any motive, leads to:—they have not sufficiently considered the subject, or argue more vaguely to parry off some home questions.—But it is probable, that the principle difficulty amongst superficial reasoners, turns on the different meanings which the disputants affix to the same words, confounding physical and moral necessity.

Observations on the opinion of the Free-Willers.—Moral Necessity defended. These acute observations on moral necessity, are a very judicious conclusion to a book on education, for the influence of motive on human conduct, and the necessity of informing the understanding, that it may regulate the will, is the grand spur to industry, in every attempt to promote domestic and national education. So that she rationally draws the following inferences. p. 484.

"By the explanation of those different circumstances in the course of human life, which give rise to the two opposite necessities of doing good, or doing evil, it will appear, that bad governors, bad tutors, and bad company, are the primary authors of all the evil volitions of the species; and that ignorance is a foil in which no uniform virtue can take root and flourish. It will also appear by the invariable experience of mankind on the principle of philosophical liberty, as on the principle of philosophical necessity. For will any of the abettors of this doctrine say, that a child born of wicked parents, well educated, and who has been taught the proper distinctions between virtue and vice, and their influences on the rational interest of the species, who has also kept bad company, and acquired bad habits from its early infancy, can be in so likely a way of attaining to the perfection of virtue, as one born of good parents, well educated, and whose conversation has been among people from whom he has received the best impressions."

It is not easy to give a clear general view of argumentative discussions, not to cite passages which would enable those who do not see their connexion, and how they illustrate what has gone before, to comprehend the full force of the reasoning:—we must therefore refer our readers to the book itself, if they wish to read a clear and able statement of a question, which metaphysicians have not yet brought to an issue, though in the conduct of both parties there appears more similarity than in their opinions.—The virtuous Free-Willer still continues to cultivate his mind with as much care, that he may discern good from evil, and choose accordingly, as if he believed that the understanding was *quite* independent of the will; and in the education of his appetite may not lead the will astray; or, if the impulse of passion should have led them into errour, that the understanding might have motives at hand to bring them back to virtue and regulate their choice.—The vicious necessitarian, on the contrary, suffers himself to grow as vain when he is flattered, and as angry when he is injured, as if his views were more confined:—and after neglecting the education of his children, seems as much surprised at their disobedience, as he could be, if he believed that good motives had no effect on the will, or that the parent who has not given a substantial proof of parental affection by instilling motives sufficiently strong to produce rational, filial love and respect, has no right to expect it.—But to close our review:—This work, which we warmly recommend to parents, adds new lustre to Mrs M.'s character as a historian and a moralist, and displays a degree of sound reason and profound thought which either through defective organs, or a mistaken education, seldom appears in female productions.

M.

Review of *Observations and Reflections, made in the Course of a Journey through France, Italy and Germany, by* Hester Lynch Piozzi, *Analytical Review* (1789)

Mary Wollstonecraft

ARTICLE III. *Observations and Reflections, made in the Course of a Journey through France, Italy and Germany.* By Hester Lynch Piozzi. In two Volumes. 8vo. 778 p. pr. 12s. in boards. (Cadell. 1789).

These travels are very desultory, and have all the lax freedom of letters without that kind of insinuating interest, which slightly binds a nosegay of unconnected remarks, and throws a thin, but graceful veil over egotism; the substitution of *one* for *I*, is a mere cobweb.

In her anecdotes of Dr Johnson, Mrs P. informed us that she kept a day book; the present observations may be reckoned a continuance of it in the same style. The journey through France is very short, her face was set towards Italy. The account of the passage over the Alps first presents itself, and is one of her best descriptions.

"We have at length passed the Alps, and are safely arrived at this lovely little city, when I look back on the majestic boundaries of Italy, with amazement at his courage who first profaned them: surely the immediate sensation conveyed to the mind by the sight of such tremendous appearances must be in every traveller the same, a sensation of fulness never experienced before, a satisfaction that there is something great to be seen on earth—some objects capable of contenting even fancy.

[describes the beauties of the Alpine landscape and its fauna]

Here are many goats, but neither white nor large, like those which browze upon the steeps of Snowdon, or clamber among the cliffs of Plinlimmon."

Many amusing anecdotes, collected in Italy, or recalled to her mind by new objects, are related in a lively manner, and observations occur, which, if not profound, are often just and entertaining.

The shade of Dr Johnson frequently flitted before us, when we perceived a reflection of his narrow superstitious notions distorted by a new medium; but Mrs P. evidently did not catch his growling petulance or propensity to contradict, for she is ever in the highest good humour, and inclined to turn her eyes on the smooth and fairest side of things. It is indeed to be lamented, that lately we have only had the descriptions of good-humoured travellers; and, when novelty and civility gave a dazzling charm to each scene, we must of course expect to hear frivolous superficial remarks. Those who can readily gather flowers, will not laboriously turn up the earth for the most valuable minerals; and, they who are very scrupulous not to say any thing the world at large will not approve of, seldom think for themselves, or attain simple dignity of diction. We shall now select some anecdotes and descriptions ...

(To be continued.)

July 1789

ARTICLE VIII. *Observations and Reflections made in the course of a Journey through France, Italy, and Germany.* By Hester Lynch Piozzi. In two Volumes.

(Concluded from p. 146.)

.... Colloquial expressions, and a playful familiarity of style, contracts every moment as strangely with laboured thoughts, and far-fetched reflections, as do inaccurate, and even vulgar phrases, with classical allusions and quotations. From a lady who has had so many advantages, and whose knowledge of a dead language is so frequently displayed, we naturally expected more purity of style; yet we find in her journey all the childish feminine terms, which occur in common novels and thoughtless chat, *sweet, lovely,* dear dear, and many other pretty epithets and exclamations.* Notwithstanding these defects, which we mention that they be avoided in a future edition, the reader will find some information and much amusement in these *Observations and Reflections.*

/M.

ENDNOTES

1   Janet Todd advises that there were several extended periods when Wollstonecraft did not contribute: while she was living in France from late 1792 to spring 1795

---

* The word *though*, which so frequently occurs, is a vulgarism we were surprised to see: *to be sure, so, vastly, exactly, talk,* and many other expressions, are only a degree better.

and during her journey to Scandinavia from June to September 1795, which was followed by a second suicide attempt in October. (Wollstonecraft's first suicide attempt, in May of 1795, was half-hearted when compared to her second.) Wollstonecraft probably began contributing reviews again in March 1796 and continued until May 1797, after her marriage to William Godwin but before the birth of their child in late August and her death on September 10 from the aftereffects. Janet Todd, prefatory note to "Contributions to the *Analytical Review 1788–1797*," in *The Works of Mary Wollstonecraft*, ed. Marilyn Butler and Janet Todd (New York: New York University Press, 1989), 7: 14.

2   Mary Waters discusses the ways in which women's "hack" writing, like reviewing, was a vehicle for professional development and profoundly influential in the rapidly evolving British reading culture, in the introduction to *British Women Writers and the Profession of Literary Criticism, 1789–1832* (Houndmills: Palgrave Macmillan, 2004), 6–23.

3   Janet Todd, *Mary Wollstonecraft: A Revolutionary Life* (London: Weidenfeld & Nicolson, 2000), 14–15.

4   William Godwin, *Memoirs of the Author of a Vindication of the Rights of Woman* (1799), ed. Pamela Clemit and Gina Luria Walker (Peterborough, ON: Broadview Press, 1991), 51.

5   Lyndall Gordon, *Mary Wollstonecraft: A New Genus* (London: Little Brown, 2005), 58.

6   Helen Braithwaite, *Romanticism, Publishing and Dissent: Joseph Johnson and the Cause of Liberty* (Houndmills: Palgrave Macmillan, 2003), 95–114.

7   Wendy Gunter-Canada, *Rebel Writer: Mary Wollstonecraft and Enlightenment Politics* (DeKalb: Northern Illinois University Press, 2001), 79.

8   [Mary Hays], "Memoirs of Mary Wollstonecraft," in *The Annual Necrology for 1797-98; Including, also, Various Articles of Neglected Biography* (London: R. Phillips, 1800), 422.

9   *The Works of Mary Wollstonecraft*, ed. Marilyn Butler and Janet Todd (London: Pickering and Chatto, 1989), 6: 402.

10   Janet Todd, prefatory note to "Contributions to the *Analytical Review* 1788–1796," in *The Works of Mary Wollstonecraft*, 7: 15. See Todd's discussion of the attribution to Wollstonecraft of specific reviews.

11   Marilyn Butler, "Culture's Medium: The Role of the Review," *The Cambridge Companion to British Romanticism*, ed. Stuart Curran (Cambridge: Cambridge University Press, 1993), 126–27.

12   Mary Waters, "Mary Wollstonecraft, Mary Hays, and *The Analytical Review*," in *British Women Writers and the Profession of Literary Criticism, 1789–1832* (Houndmills: Palgrave Macmillan, 2004), 92.

13   Barbara Taylor, "The Female Philosopher," in *Mary Wollstonecraft and the Feminist Imagination* (Cambridge: Cambridge University Press, 2003), 37.

14   Mitzi Meyers, "Mary Wollstonecraft's Literary Reviews," in *The Cambridge Companion to Mary Wollstonecraft*, ed. Claudia Johnson (Cambridge: Cambridge University Press, 2002), 88.

Anna Lætitia Barbauld (née Aikin) (1743–1825)

A biographical profile of Anna Barbauld appears in Part 1 of this reader.

"MISS BURNEY," *THE BRITISH NOVELISTS* (1810)

Thirty-seven booksellers from London, Edinburgh, and York recognised Anna Barbauld's unique cultural authority when they chose her to oversee "a selection of English Novels, with biographical notices and critical remarks, by Mrs. Barbauld."[1] The fifty-volume series published in 1810 became known simply as "Mrs. Barbauld's Novelists." Barbauld's imprimatur established the importance of the publishers' undertaking: for the first time, the novel was presented as an English literary genre with its own history, evolution, and critical standards. Barbauld provided a preface to the series in "The Origin and Progress of Novel-Writing" that differed from previous accounts in its historical breadth and insistence that, like other genres, the novel contributed significantly to moral and social progress.

Barbauld knew that novel writing and reading continued to be controversial. Parents and moral guardians worried about the effects on women of novels by Rousseau and other fashioners of passionate romances. In 1774, Dr. John Gregory was perplexed about what to advise his daughters to read, other than history, art, or science—he never mentioned novels. Mary Wollstonecraft disapproved too, and tried her hand at reforming the genre. Hannah More warned that novel reading was "a complicated drug." Aware of these concerns, Barbauld began her preface by acknowledging, "A Collection of Novels has a better chance of giving pleasure than of commanding respect." But she pointed out that people keep reading novels because they entertain, instruct, inspire. "When the range of this kind of writing is so extensive, and its effects so great, it seems evident that it ought to hold a respectable place among the productions of genius."[2] She established the genre's respectability by tracing its origins in "the earliest accounts of the literature of every country," drawing upon a wide variety of ancient and modern sources and languages. In her preface, individual selections, life-writing about the novelists, and critical commentary, Barbauld established a canon. Importantly, that canon included women writers, which had the effect of "establish[ing] a canon of British women novelists."[3]

Barbauld's comments on Fanny Burney and her novels reflect the belief that the turn of the century was a particularly rich time for good novelists writing good novels, and that many of these were women. Barbauld includes Elizabeth Hamilton's *Memoirs of Modern Philosophers* in her list with Maria Edgeworth and Burney, among others. Barbauld identifies Fanny Burney as the daughter of the musician and writer Dr. Charles Burney and wife of the French *émigré* Monsieur D'Arblay. She describes Fanny Burney's progress as an artist, noting critical high and low points in her novels themselves. Barbauld endorses Burney's work in glowing terms: "Mrs. D'Arblay has observed human nature ... with the quick and penetrating eye of genius."[4] Barbauld commends Burney's deployment of the genre to explore the moral dimensions of everyday life.

As increasing numbers of women became professional writers out of ambition, economic need, or both,[5] they found themselves called upon to judge each other's work. Some, like Barbauld, joined gendered concerns about female reputation with their critical assessments. Others, like Hays, based her estimate of Elizabeth Hamilton's fiction on political and doctrinal intent. Some, like George Eliot, simply refused to opine about other women's texts, not wanting to be considered a member of what she described as "a genus" of "silly novels by women novelists."[6]

"Miss Burney," The British Novelists (1810)

Anna Lætitia Barbauld

[Frances Burney] (1752–1840) achieved fame at the age of 26 with the publication of her first novel, *Evelina* (1778). Although the work was published anonymously, with cloak-and-dagger secrecy, its success guaranteed the revelation of the author and her subsequent elevation into the literary beau monde. Burney's father, musicologist Charles Burney, saw to it that his talented daughter come to the attention of Hester Thrale, who entertained writers and other artists at her home in Streatham Place where reigning literary lion Samuel Johnson was a frequent houseguest. For several years, Frances Burney enjoyed the intimacy of this group, but with the publication of her second novel, *Celilia* (1782), her father's aspirations for her rose even higher, and she found herself an appointee of the court—Second Keeper of the Robes to Queen Charlotte, an employment that Burney found stressful and distasteful. She resigned from this post, ill, and, in 1793, married French émigré General Alexandre d'Arblay. After her marriage she published two more novels—*Camilla* (1796) and *The Wanderer* (1814), the latter unmentioned by Barbauld as it appeared after the first edition of *The British Novelists*.

MISS BURNEY

Scarcely any name, if any, stands higher in the list of novel-writers than that of Miss BURNEY, now Mrs. D'ARBLAY, daughter of the ingenious Dr. Burney. She has given to the world three productions of this kind; *Evelina*, in three vols., *Cecilia*, in five vols., and, after a long interval, in which, however honourable her employment might be deemed, she was completely lost to the literary world, *Camilla*, also in five vols. This latter was published by subscription in 1796.

It is necessary to speak of living authors with that temperance of praise which may not offend their delicacy; and though this lady by marriage was a foreigner, and her residence abroad, is in a manner lost to this her native country, the writer of these remarks does not feel herself at liberty to search for anecdotes which might gratify curiosity, or endeavour to detail the events of a life which every admirer of genius will wish prolonged to many succeeding years. One anecdote, however, may be mentioned, which is current, and she believes has never been contradicted. Miss Burney composed her *Evelina* when she was in the early bloom of youth, about seventeen. She wrote it without the knowledge of any of her friends. With the modesty of a young woman, and the diffidence of a young author, she contrived to throw it into the press anonymously, and, when published, laid the volumes in the way of her friends, whose impartial plaudits soon encouraged her to confess to whom they were obliged for their entertainment. There is perhaps no purer or higher pleasure than the young mind enjoys in the first burst of praise and admiration which attends a successful performance. To be lifted up at once into the favourite of the public; to be sensible that the name, hitherto pronounced only in the circle of family connexions, is become familiar to all that read, through every province of a large kingdom; to feel in the glow of genius and freshness of invention powers to continue that admiration to future years;—to feel all this, and at the same time to be happily ignorant of all the chills and mortifications, the impossibility not to flag in a long work, the ridicule and censure which fasten on vulnerable parts, and the apathy or diffidence which generally seizes an author before his literary race is run;—this is happiness for youth, and youth alone.

Evelina became at once a fashionable novel: there are even those who still prefer it to *Cecilia*, though that preference is probably owing to the partiality inspired by a first performance. Evelina is a young lady, amiable and inexperienced, who is continually getting into difficulties from not knowing or not observing the established etiquettes of society, and from being unluckily connected with a number of vulgar characters, by whom she is involved in a series of adventures both ludicrous and mortifying. Some of these are certainly carried to a very extravagant excess, particularly the tricks played upon the poor Frenchwoman; but the fondness for humour, and low humour, which Miss Burney discovered in this piece, runs through all her subsequent works, and strongly characterizes, sometimes perhaps blemishes, her genius. Lord Orville is a generous and pleasing lover; and the conclusion is so wrought, as to leave upon the mind that glow of happiness which is not found in her subsequent works. The meeting between Evelina and her father is pathetic. The agonizing remorse and perturbation of the man who is about to see, for the first time, his child whom he had deserted, and whose mother had fallen a sacrifice to his unkindness; the struggles between the affection which impels him towards her, and the dread he feels of seeing in her the image of his injured wife; are described with many touches of nature and strong effect.—Other characters in the piece are, Mrs. Selwyn, a wit and an oddity; a gay insolent baronet; a group of vulgar cits; a number of young bucks, whose coldness, carelessness, rudeness, and impertinent gallantry, serve as a foil to the delicate attentions of Lord Orville.

Upon the whole, *Evelina* greatly pleased; and the interest the public took in the young writer was rewarded with fresh pleasure by the publication of *Cecilia*, than which it would be difficult to find a novel with more various and striking beauties. Among these may be reckoned the style, which is so varied, according to the characters introduced, that, without any information from the names, the reader would readily distinguish the witty loquacity of Lady Honoria Pemberton, the unmeaning volubility of Miss Larolles, the jargon of the captain, the affected indifference of Meadows, the stiff pomposity of Delville senior, the flighty hero-ics of Albany, the innocent simplicity of Miss Belfield, the coarse vulgarity of her mother, the familiar address and low comic of Briggs, and the cool finesse of the artful attorney, with many others,—all expressed in language appropriate to the character, and all pointedly distinguished from the elegant and dignified style of the author herself. The character of the miser Briggs is pushed, perhaps, to a degree of extravagance, though certainly not more so than Moliere's Harpagon; but it is highly comic, and it is not the common idea of a miser half-starved, sullen and morose; an originality is given to it by making him jocose, good-humoured, and not averse to enjoyment when he can have it for nothing. All the characters are well discriminated, from the skipping Morrice, to the artful Monckton, and the high-toned feeling of Mrs. Delville. The least natural character is Albany. An idea prevailed at the time, but probably without the least foundation, that Dr. Johnson had supplied the part.

323

Cecilia herself is an amiable and dignified character. She is brought into situ-ations distressful and humiliating, by the peculiarity of her circumstances, and a flexibility and easiness readily pardoned in a young female. The restriction she is laid under of not marrying any one who will not submit to assume her name is a new circumstance, and forms, very happily, the plot of the piece. Love appears with dignity in Cecilia; with fervour, but strongly combated by pride as well as duty, in young Delville; with all the helplessness of unrestrained affection in Miss Belfield, whose character of simplicity and tenderness much resembles that of Emily in *Sir Charles Grandison*. If resemblances are sought for, it may also be observed that the situation of Cecilia with Mrs. Delville is similar to that of Marivaux's Marianne with the mother of Valville.

Miss Burney possesses equal powers of pathos and of humour. The terrifying voice of the unknown person who forbids the banns has an electrifying effect upon the reader; and the distress of Cecilia seeking her husband about the streets, in agony for his life, till her reason suddenly fails, is almost too much to bear. Indeed we lay down the volumes with rather a melancholy impression upon our minds; there has been so much of distress that the heart feels exhausted, and there are so many deductions from the happiness of the lovers, that the reader is scarcely able to say whether the story ends happily or unhappily. It is true that in human life things are generally so balanced; but in fictitious writings it is more agreeable, if they are not meant to end tragically, to leave on the mind the rainbow colours of delight in their full glow and beauty.

But the finest part of these volumes is the very moral and instructive story of the *Harrels*. It is the high praise of Miss Burney, that she has not contented herself with fostering the delicacies of sentiment, and painting in vivid colours those passions which nature has made sufficiently strong. She has shown the value of economy, the hard-heartedness of gaiety, the mean rapacity of the fashionable spendthrift. She has exhibited a couple, not naturally bad, with no other inlet to vice, that appears on the face of the story, than the inordinate desire of show and splendour, withholding his hard-earned pittance from the poor labourer, and lavishing it on every expensive trifle. She has shown the wife trifling and helpless, vain, incapable of serious thought or strong feeling; and has beautifully delineated the gradual extinction of an early friendship between two young women whom youth and cheerfulness alone had assimilated, as the two characters diverged in the afterlife,—a circumstance that frequently happens. She has shown the husband fleecing his guest and his ward by working on the virtuous feelings of a young mind, and has conducted him by natural steps to the awful catastrophe. The last scene at Vauxhall is uncommonly animated; every thing seems to pass before the reader's eyes. The forced gaiety, the starts of remorse, the despair, the bustle and glare of the place, the situation of the unprotected females in such a scene of horror, are all most forcibly described. We almost hear and feel the report of the pistol.—In the uncommon variety of characters which this novel affords, there are many others deserving of notice; that, for instance, of the high-minded romantic Belfield may give a salutary lesson to many a youth who fancies his part in life *ill cast*, who wastes life in projects, and does nothing because he thinks every thing beneath his ambition and his talents.

Such are the various merits of *Cecilia*, through the whole of which it is evident that the author draws from life, and exhibits not only the passions of human nature, but the manners of the age and the affectation of the day.

The celebrity which Miss Burney had now attained awakened the idea of extending that patronage to her which, in most countries, it has been usual in one way or other to hold out to literary merit; and it was thought, we must presume, the most appropriate reward of her exertions, and the happiest method of fostering her genius, that she was made *dresser* to Her Majesty. She held this post for several years, during which the duties of her situation seem to have engrossed her whole time. Her state of health at length obliged her to resign it, and she was soon after married to M. D'Arblay, a French emigrant.

She now again resumed her pen, and gave to the world her third publication, entitled *Camilla*. This work is somewhat too much protracted, and is inferior to *Cecilia* as a whole, but it certainly exhibits beauties of as high an order. The character of Sir Hugh is new and striking. There is such an unconscious shrewdness in his remarks, that they have all the effect of the sharpest satire without his intending any malice; while, at the same time, his complaints are so meek, his self-humiliation so touching, his benevolence so genuine and overflowing, that the reader must have a bad heart who does not love while he laughs at him. The incidents of the piece show much invention, particularly that which induces Sir Hugh to adopt Eugenia instead of his favourite. How charmingly is Camilla described! "Every look was a smile, every step was a spring, every thought was a hope, and the early felicity of her mind was without alloy."

Camilla, in the course of the work, falls, like Cecilia, into pecuniary difficulties. They are brought on partly by milliners' bills, which unawares and through the persuasion of others she has suffered to run up, but chiefly from being drawn in to assist an extravagant and unprincipled brother. The character of the brother, Lionel, is drawn with great truth and spirit, and presents but too just a picture of the manner in which many deserving females have been sacrificed to the worthless part of the family. The author appears to have viewed with a very discerning eye the manners of those young men who aspire to lead the fashion; and in all three of her novels has bestowed a good deal of her satire upon the affected apathy, studied negligence, coarse slang, avowed selfishness, or mischievous frolic, by which they often distinguish themselves, and through which they contrive to be vulgar with the advantages of rank, mean with those of fortune, and disagreeable with those of youth.

A very original character in this work is that of Eugenia. Her surprise and sorrow when, at the age of fifteen, she first discovers her deformity, and her deep, gentle, dignified sorrow for the irremediable misfortune, it is impossible to peruse without sympathy; and in the incident which follows, when her father, after a discourse the most rational and soothing, brings her to the sight of a beautiful idiot, the scene is one of the most striking and sublimely moral any where to be met with.

As well as great beauties there are great faults in *Camilla*. It is blemished by the propensity which the author has shown in all her novels, betrayed into it by her love of humour, to involve her heroines not only in difficult but in degrading adventures. The mind may recover from distress, but not from disgrace; and the situations Camilla is continually placed in with the Dubsters and Mrs. Mittin are of a nature to degrade, still more, the overwhelming circumstance of her father's being sent to prison for her debts seems to preclude the possibility of her ever raising her head again. It conveys a striking lesson; and no doubt Mrs. D'Arblay, in her large acquaintance with life, must have often seen the necessity of inculcating, even upon *young* ladies, the danger of running up bills on credit; but the distress becomes too deep, too humiliating, to admit of a happy conclusion. The mind has been harassed and worn with excess of painful feeling. At the conclusion of *Clarissa*, we are dismissed in calm and not unpleasing sorrow; but on the winding up of *Cecilia* and *Camilla* we are somewhat tantalized with imperfect happiness. It must be added, that the interest is more divided in *Camilla* than in the author's former work, and the adventures of Eugenia become at length too improbable.

Among the new characters in this piece is Mrs. Arlberry, a woman of fashion, with good sense and taste, but fond of frivolity through *désoeuvrement*, and amusing herself with a little court about her of fashionable young men, whom she at the same time entertains and despises. .

In short, Mrs. D'Arblay has observed human nature, both in high and low life, with the quick and penetrating eye of genius. Equally happy in seizing the ridiculous, and in entering into the finer feelings, her pictures of manners are just and interesting, and the highest value is given to them by the moral feelings they exercise, and the excellent principles they inculcate.

325

Mrs. D'Arblay lived some years after her marriage at a sweet retirement in the shade of Norbury park, in a house built under Mr. D'Arblay's direction, which went by the name of Camilla Lodge; but at the time when the greatest part of the emigrants returned to their native country, she followed her husband to France, in which country she now resides.

A writer who has published three novels of so much merit may be allowed to repose her pen; yet the English public cannot but regret an expatriation which so much lessens the chance of their being again entertained by her.

ENDNOTES

1   William McCarthy and Elizabeth Kraft, "From the British Novelists," in *Anna Letitia Barbauld: Selected Poetry and Prose* (Peterborough, ON: Broadview Press, 2002), 375.

2   Anna Barbauld, "On the Origin and Progress of Novel-Writing," in *Anna Letitia Barbauld: Selected Poetry and Prose*, ed. William McCarthy and Elizabeth Kraft (Peterborough, ON: Broadview Press, 2002), 377.

3   Mary A. Waters, "The British Common Reader: Critical Prefaces by Anna Letitia Barbauld," in *British Women Writers and the Profession of Literary Criticism, 1789–1832* (Houndsmill: Palgrave, 2004), 52.

4   Anna Barbauld, "Miss Burney," in *Anna Letitia Barbauld: Selected Poetry and Prose*, 449.

5   Betty A. Schellenberg, *The Professionalization of Women Writers in Eighteenth-Century Britain* (Cambridge: Cambridge University Press, 2005).

6   George Eliot, "Silly Novels by Lady Novelists," *Westminster Review*, 66 (October 1856): 442–61.

Mary Cowden Clarke (1809–1898)

Mary Cowden Clarke was born into the large family and distinguished circle of musician Vincent Novello and Mary Sabilla Hehl. Her parents were her principal teachers; their friend Mary Lamb instructed her in Latin. Mary Novello's "affectionate veneration" for Shakespeare began when she was a child and her father gave her Charles and Mary Lamb's *Tales from Shakespeare* (1806), a lively retelling of the plays that incorporated his language. At nineteen, she married Charles Cowden Clarke, 22 years her senior, a drama critic, and a lecturer on Shakespeare. During their nearly 50-year marriage, she became one of the first women to devote herself to Shakespeare studies.[1]

Cowden Clarke produced the first comprehensive *Concordance* (1845) to Shakespeare's plays. She spent twelve years constructing the verbal index, and four more years supervising publication.[2] The work was initially published in eighteen monthly installments (1844–45), met with great acclaim, and made Cowden Clark famous. She followed with *The Girlhood of Shakespeare's Heroines* (1852), fifteen fictional accounts of Shakespeare's major female characters from childhood and early life to their appearance in his plays. These, Cowden Clarke explained, were intended to suggest "such situations as should naturally lead up to, and account for, the known conclusion of their subsequent confirmed character and afterlife,"[3] and included sensational sex, violence, and death. Critics and readers applauded the approach.

Cowden Clarke published an edition of *Shakespeare's Works* in 1860. She expressed satisfaction in her preface at being "the first of [Shakespeare's] female subjects who has been selected to edit his works." In fact, Henrietta (Harriet) Bowdler (1754–1830) had previously published *The Family Shakespeare* in 1807 in which she cut or "bowdlerized" passages she considered revealing of "Shakespeare's obscenity."[4] Together, the Cowden Clarkes published an annotated edition of the *Works* (1865), followed by *The Shakespeare Key* (1879) that provided lists of and essays on specific subjects: "Oaths," "Soliloquies," and "Power in Writing Silence."

On her own, Mary Cowden Clarke continued to publish shorter pieces on Shakespeare: *Shakespeare's Proverbs* (1848), "On Shakespeare's Individuality in his Characters" (1848–51), a series on "Shakespeare–Studies of Women" (1849–54) in *The Ladies Companion* in which she praised the playwright for providing "a mental looking-glass [in which] we women may contemplate ourselves," and a series in *Sharpe's London Magazine* on "Shakespeare's Lovers" (1850), treating his male characters. She included some of Shakespeare's female characters in

World-Noted Women, or, Types of Womanly Attributes of All Lands and Ages (1858). Cowden Clarke became a leading figure in the international community of Shakespeare scholars. In her last years, she expressed her gratitude "for the liberal way in which distinguished Shakespearians have treated me with a cordial *fraternity* as one of their brotherhood."[5]

The Cowden Clarkes moved to Nice in 1856 and then to Genoa, where they lived in "Villa Novello." After Charles died in 1877, Mary Cowden Clarke returned to England where she published *Recollections of Writers* (1878), originally a series of articles for *Gentleman's Magazine* written with her husband, including letters and memoirs of figures in the Novello and Cowden Clarke circles—John Keats, Mary Lamb, Charles Lamb, Charles Dickens, Mary Shelley, and Percy Shelley. She also published a collection of poetry, a *Centennial Biographic Sketch* of her husband, and *My Long Life* (1896). She died at Villa Novello.

THE COMPLETE CONCORDANCE TO SHAKESPEARE (1845; 1881)

Mary Cowden Clarke conceived the idea to construct a concordance to Shakespeare's works at breakfast with her husband and friends on 15 July 1829. When the group went for a walk later that day, she remembered that she "took a volume of the Poet and a pencil with me, and jotted down the first lines of my book under B—

"Boatswain, have care, *Temp. I, I, &c.*"[6]

She later acknowledged that she knew nothing about Shakespeare studies. She invented her own system for creating the *Concordance*. She used her father's copy of Shakespeare's works as her source. Working with 26 portfolios marked for each letter of the alphabet and a stack of paper slips, she wrote each word that appeared in Shakespeare's text on a slip and copied the line that contained it. She examined two pages of Shakespeare's text at a time, copying each use of the word she was working on through the entirety of his dramas. Her daily schedule was to work four to six hours, "side by side" with her husband who was writing lectures on Shakespeare. "Happy—supremely happy—were the hours then!" she recalled. The *Concordance* ultimately included over 300,000 entries. Even that did not complete the job: Cowden Clarke purposely did not include line numbers. She explained in her preface to a subsequent edition that she chose to omit references to common words such as "let" and "well" and prepositions, pronouns, conjunctions, adjectives, and adverbs. Later scholars provided these. Helen Kate Rogers Furness (1837–83) completed *The Concordance to Shakespeare's Poems: an index to every word therein contained* (1872).

Twelve years into her labours, Cowden Clarke realised that the many editions of Shakespeare's works contained "various variousnesses," textual differences that represented scholarly disputes among Shakespeare scholars. She felt compelled to spend the next four years comparing editions, including several that appeared as she was at her work and one in manuscript. She later calculated that she had read through Shakespeare's plays seven times.

The first edition of the *Concordance* was sold by subscription to wealthy, aristocratic, and distinguished individuals. Cowden Clarke wanted to dedicate the *Concordance* to Queen Victoria, but was refused. Instead, she dedicated the work to the memory of Shakespeare. It became the standard reference work and appeared in successive editions. The work was superseded during Cowden Clarke's lifetime by Bartlett's *New and Complete Concordance* (1894).

Some modern commentators suggest that Cowden Clarke's representations of Shakespearean heroines serve as vehicles for her commentary on women's complex social status and as criticism of the paucity of women's education.[7]

The Complete Concordance to Shakespeare (1845; 1881)

Mary Cowden Clarke

1881

PREFACE TO NEW AND REVISED EDITION

It is now more than half a century ago, when, on the 15th July, 1829, sitting at the breakfast-table of some friends in pleasant Somersetshire, regret was expressed that there existed no Concordance to Shakespeare; whose works formed the Bible of the Intellectual World. Eager in everything, I resolved there and then that *I* would write this desired concordance; and that very forenoon, while joining my friends in their walk through the fields, I took a volume of the Poet and a pencil with me, and jotted down the first lines of my book under B:—

"Boatswain, have care." *Temp.* i. 1, &c.

Sixteen years of hard work, but delightful work, sufficed to complete the manuscript.

In deference to the wishes of Mr. Charles Knight, its original publisher, I allowed the name on the Title-page to be printed "Shakespere;" but now, in this new and perfected Edition, I substitute the spelling "Shakespeare" as that which was given in the First Folio Edition of his Plays and in the First Edition of his Sonnets, and as that which my beloved husband and I have adopted in all our works upon the unrivalled Dramatist, including our latest, "The Shakespeare Key," which forms the Companion Volume to the "Concordance."

The "Concordance" made its earliest appearance in Monthly Parts (the list of subscribers to which was headed by the King of Prussia); but when it was completed, the work obtained distinguished notice from various reviewers, among whom were John Forster and the Rev. N.J. Halpin; the latter writing two elaborate and long critiques in a leading Dublin paper. Leigh Hunt gave kind and fanciful prediction that his young friend "Victorinella's"[8] name would go down to the future on the same page with her great Master's; Douglas Jerrold playfully assuring her that she must "expect a kiss from Shakespeare" when she should meet him in Paradise; Professor Craik making handsome mention of the book in the Preface to his "English of Shakespeare;" and Dr. Ingleby writing: "It is now fifteen years since I first began to use systematically your 'Concordance to Shakespeare.' I have, in my time, been astonished by many marvels of literature; but the *completeness* and *accuracy* of your book still seem to me to place it on an eminence by itself, to which no triumph of mere labour and care can approach."

Other evidences of general estimation—public as well as private—attended the progress of the book. A Testimonial Chair was presented by several Ladies and Gentlemen of the United States of America (among other honoured names, those of Austin Allibone, William Cullen Bryant, Charlotte Cushman, Washington Irving, H. W. Longfellow, George Ticknor, R. Grant White, and Daniel Webster; who, in his letter on the occasion, sportively said: "She has treasured up every word of Shakespeare as if he were her lover, and she were his") through the Honourable Abbott Lawrence, then American Ambassador in England; while the sixth annual report of the Shakespeare Society (1846?) printed the following minute:—"The Chairman then announced that the Council had evinced their admiration and appreciation of Mrs. Cowden-Clarke, whose 'Concordance to Shakespeare' had rendered such service to the cause, by presenting to that lady a complete set of the works published by that Society from its commencement."

Such were some of the tokens of approval given during past years; and even quite lately, a periodical of the present day, in its "Echoes of the Week," has made frequent allusions to the use and excellence of the "Complete Concordance to Shakespeare."

Letters still flow over the Atlantic, telling me that a copy of the book holds place on shelves of noble libraries, while a second is kept for daily thumbing on library-tables by good Shakespearians and true. Perhaps no work of reference, for the last nearly fifty years, has been in such constant and such affectionate use; because no writer is so constantly and so affectionately in all men's thoughts as Shakespeare.

I have been asked to record these honours awarded to the work; and on this bright morning of Valentine's Day—an Italian sun shining upon me—it is with gratitude and happy pride that I find myself permitted thus to celebrate The Golden Wedding of my readers with

Their faithful servant,
Mary Cowden=Clarke
VILLA NOVELLO, GENOA,
14*th Feb.*, 1881.

PREFACE

SHAKESPEARE, the most frequently quoted, because the most universal-minded Genius that ever lived, of all Authors best deserves a complete Concordance to his Works. To what subject may we not with felicity apply a motto from this greatest of Poets? The Divine, commending the efficacy and "twofold force of prayer—to be forestalled, ere we come to fall, or pardoned being down;" the Astronomer, supporting his theory by allusions to "the moist star, upon whose influence Neptune's empire stands;" the Naturalist, striving to elucidate a fact respecting the habits of "the singing masons," or "heavy-gaited toads"; the Botanist, lecturing on the various properties of the "small flower within whose infant rind poison hath residence, and med'cine power," or on the growth of "summer grass, fastest by night, unseen, yet crescive in his faculty;" the Philosopher, speculating upon "the respect that makes calamity of so long life," "the dread of something after death, the undiscovered country, from whose bourn no traveller returns;" the Lover, telling his "whispering tale in a fair lady's ear," and vowing the "winnowed purity" and "persistive constancy" of his "heart's dear love;" the Lawyer, discussing some "nice sharp quillet of the law;" the Musician, descanting on the "touches of sweet harmony;" the Painter, describing his art, that "pretty mocking of the life;" the Novel-writer, seeking an illustrative heading to a fresh chapter, "the baby figure of the giant mass to come at large;" the Orator, labouring an emphatic point in an appeal to the passions of assembled multitudes, "to stir men's blood;" the Soldier, endeavouring to vindicate his profession, by "the quality of mercy," urging that, "to revenge is no valour, but to bear;" and maintaining that "the earth is wronged by man's oppression,"—may all equally adorn their page or emblazon their speech with gems from Shakespeare's works.

332

To furnish a faithful guide to this rich mine of intellectual treasure, superadding what was defective in my predecessors, Twiss and Ayscough, has been the ambition of a life; and it was hoped that the sixteen years' assiduous labour devoted to the work, during the twelve years' writing,* and the four more bestowed on collating with recent editions and correcting the press, may be found to have accomplished that ambition, and at length produced the great desideratum—a complete Concordance to Shakespeare.

The appearance of a Preface with the concluding number of a periodically published work, though it possesses the advantage of affording an opportunity of commenting upon any thing that may have occurred in the course of printing; yet on the other hand, it involves a degree of disadvantage to the author, more especially in the present case, where there was judgment to be exercised in the admission or omission of certain words, and the right of that judgment to be vindicated and explained. The apparent inconsistency of omitting particular words when used in one sense, while they were retained in other instances, could only be accounted for by that discretionary power, which the author must claim in the Preface; where good and sufficient reason could be advanced why that power was not merely exercised for the sake of condensation, but likewise for perspicuity, and the especial benefit of the quoter. For instance, it might at first excite surprise to find so few examples of the word *let*; but by omitting it as an auxiliary verb (where the simple fact of its being universally joined

---

* I cannot refuse myself the pleasure of mentioning that the day which witnessed the conclusion of this task, was the [bi]rth-day of the best of mothers—Mary Sabilla Novello; she who forms the glory and happiness of her children; she who [mo]st inspired me with a love for all that is good and beautiful, and who therefore may well be said to have originated my devotion to Shakespeare.

to another verb of more importance, renders it less likely to suggest itself as a means of reference, as—"*let* me remember thee what thou has promised,") and retaining it merely in its most singular sense, the space gained is the enormous difference between 17 lines and 2184, or six printed pages of three columns each; while at the same time the few important instances in which the word occurs are thus rendered far more clearly apparent and easy of reference.

This was felt to be so valuable an arrangement, that, even during the course of printing several thousand lines of MS. were cancelled—thus: *well*, omitted as an adverb, saves about 1550 lines, and leaves clearer the word as a noun, and where it indicates health; it is also retained where a pun is involved, as— "would not this *ill* do *well?*"

It must be borne in mind that these omitted references are so frequent, as well as of such insignificance, that their retention would but have encumbered, and (so to say) hidden the other references to the same word of more distinct and unquestionable importance: as an example of this, "my lord," as a mere title, occurs in the play of Hamlet alone, no fewer than 192 times!

Come, look, marry, pray, truth, truly, and *well,* when used merely interjectionally, a[nd] *still* and *well,* as adverbs, are omitted. *Like,* as an adverb merely conveying a simile, as—"he receives comfort *like* cold porridge," from the multiplicity of examples, and because such passages invariably contain words more striking—is omitted. *Toward* and *towards* are only retained when used peculiarly.

Titles: as *master, mistress, lord, lady, king, count, don, signior,* etc., when joined to proper names, are omitted; as are also *lord* and *lady,* when used merely as *sir* and *madam.* A few verbs and adverbs, as, *to be, to have, to do,* and *beyond, some, never,* etc., are omitted, on account of their insignificance, and frequent recurrence; also, oaths and exclamations of small importance, a few peculiar ones only, such as *aroint, avaunt,* etc., being retained.

All nouns and verbs spelt alike are placed under one heading; and all plural nouns will be found under the same headings with their respective singulars. A few words, such as *naught* and *nought, sallad* and *sallet,* spelt indiscriminately in various editions, are placed under one heading.

When a word recurs on the same subject, and with but little variation of context, in the course of a scene, or stands so closely repeated as inevitably to catch the eye in looking out the [ ] sage in the Play, as—"my poverty but not my will consents. I pay thy poverty, and not will;" the repetition is merely indicated by the word (*rep.*) in the Concordance.

The size of the Work has been selected with a view to its ranging with Mr. Charles Knight's popular and beautiful Pictorial Edition of Shakespeare; but it will admit of being [cut] down so as to conform with the usual octavo volumes.

In Mr. Payne Collier's edition of Shakespeare,[9] he divides the second act of the *Midsummer Night's Dream,* into two scenes only; but as in most editions it is divided into three, I have adopted the latter mode of reference, merely pointing out the variation here, to avoid any confusion. I avail myself of the present opportunity to offer my thanks publicly to the above-named gentleman, for the kind and handsome manner in which he entrusted me with the then unpublished MS. of his concluding volume, when I took the liberty of applying to him, though unknown, for the purpose of collating his edition with the others, in order to complete my Concordance. Such a mark of confidence was a worthy type of the fraternity of feeling inspired by a close study of our immortal Poet; and it is one of the not least agreeable con[co]mitants of my task, that it has been the means of my receiving generous testimonies of sympathy and encouragement from many of the cleverest men of our age, between whom and myself I could never have hoped for any assimilation, had it not been for the mutual existence of profound veneration and love for the genius of Shakespeare.

Let me not likewise omit to acknowledge (after the fashion of dramatic authors in the preface to their Plays, towards the actors who embody their conceptions) my obligations to my "co-mates and brothers in 'labour'"—the Printers; for though the public can judge of the typographical beauty and accuracy of the pages of the Concordance which they have produced, no one but myself can appreciate their care, minute correctness, and patient assiduity.

Shakespeare himself says: "Most poor matters point to rich ends,"—I trust my humble labour may tend to the "rich end" of furthering a universal study and appreciation of his genius;—in this hope, it only remains for me to take leave of those for whom I have been working so many years (I cannot call them my readers) with an assurance that it has been a labour of love, and that it has been productive of many happy thoughts and aspirations to
Their faithful and obedient servant,
Mary Cowden–Clarke

[Entries for the word "women" from pp. 842–43]

WOMEN—four or five women once......	*Tempest,*	i. 2
all men idle, all; and women too......	—	ii. 1
have I liked several women..........	—	iii. 1
women highly hold in hate ..	*Two Gen. of Ver.*	iii. 2
on silly women, or poor passengers..	—	iv. 1
how many women would do	—	iv. 4
when women cannot love...........	—	v. 4
the women have so cried...........	*Merry Wives,*	i. 1
but women indeed cannot abide 'em	—	i.1
praised women's modesty............	—	ii. 1
we are the sons of women, master Page	—	ii. 3
that come like women in men's apparel	—	iii. 3
in women's waxen hearts to set..	*Twelfth Night,*	ii. 2
sooner lost and worn, than women's are	—	ii. 4
for women are as roses	—	ii. 4
what love women to men may owe ..	—	ii. 4

nay, women are frail too ..	*Measure for Measure,*	ii. 4
women! help heaven! Men their	—	ii. 4
buy and sell men and women like beasts	—	iii. 2
much detected for women	—	iii. 2
WOMEN were all dead ...	*Measure for Measure,*	iv. 3
these poor informal women are no more	—	v. 1
hath set the women on to (*rep.*)......	—	v. 1
that's the way; for women are light	—	v. 1
thou hast suborned these women	—	v. 1
a dear happiness to women	*Much Ado,*	i. 1
all women shall pardon me..........	—	i. 1
look with your eyes as other women do	—	iii. 4
more than ever women spoke ..	*Mid. N.'s Dream,*	i. 1
women's eyes this doctrine (*rep.*).	*Love's L. Lost,*	iv. 3
these women to forswear	—	iv. 3
the authors of these women (*rep.*)....	—	iv. 3
lay two earthly women	*Merchant of Venice,*	iii. 3
mistake in her gifts to women	*As you Like it,*	i. 7
and all the men and women merely	—	ii. 7
he laid to the charge of women?	—	iii. 2
in the which women still give	—	iii. 2
as boys and women are for the most	—	iii. 2
there be some women, Silvus, had ..	—	iii. 3
the women. I charge you (*rep.*)..	—	(epilogue)
for the love you bear to women..	—	(epilogue)
between you and the women	—	(epilogue)
where but women were that had	*All's Well,*	iv. 3
do you know these women?..........	—	v. 3
women are made to bear......	*Taming of Shrew,*	ii. 1
when men and women are alone	—	ii. 1
kindness in women, not their beauteous	—	iv. 2
tell these headstrong women what ..	—	v. 3
that women are so simple to offer....	—	v. 3
when women are forward............	—	v. 2
women say so, that will say any ..	*Winter's Tale,*	i. 2
become some women best............	—	ii. 1
I learned it out of women's faces	—	ii. 1
my women may be with me (*rep.*) ..	—	ii. 1
to see her women? any of them......	—	ii. 2
which 'longs to women of all fashion	—	iii. 2
not women? Women will love her..	—	v. 1
alas, poor women! make us..	*Comedy of Errors,*	iii. 2
you should be women; and yet your..	*Macbeth,*	i. 3
as the weird women promised	—	iii. 1

make our women fight, to doff	—	iv. 3
it is the cry of women my good lord	—	v. 5
women and fools, break off your	*King John,*	ii. 1
boys, with women's voices, strive ..	*Richard II.*	iii. 2
yea, distaff women manage rusty	—	iii. 2
sup any women with him?..........	2 *Henry IV.*	Ii. 2
for the women,—for one of them	—	ii. 4
for women are shrews, both short	—	v. 3 (song)
in disdain the German women	*Henry V.* i. 2	
as ever you came of women, come in	—	ii. 1
and of women. Nay, that a' did not	—	ii. 3
the devil would have him about women	—	ii. 3
handle women; but then he was	—	ii. 5
grandsires, babies, and old women	—	iii. (chorus)
and none but women left to wail	1 *Henry VI.*	i. 1
these women are shrewd tempters..	—	i. 2
tush! women have been captivate..	—	v. 3
more than in women commonly	—	v. 5
these are no women's matters	2 *Henry*	VI. i. 3
that doth oft make women proud....	3 *Henry*	VI. i. 4
women are soft, mild, pitiful	—	i. 4
like soft-hearted women here........	—	ii. 3
Edward will use women honourably	—	iii. 2
women and children of so high......	—	v. 4
and the women cried, O Jesus	—	v. 6
when men are ruled by women	*Richard III.*	i. 1
these tell-tale women rail on the Lord's	—	iv. 4
two women placed together makes..	*Henry VIII.*	i. 4
the action of good women: there is hope	—	ii. 3
all other women could speak this with	—	iii. 1
virtues with these weak women's fears	—	iii. 1
and fears than wars or women have	—	iii. 2
great-bellied women, that had not ..	—	iv. 1
some pity upon my wretched women	—	iv. 2
call in more women; when I am	—	iv. 2
come to court, the women so besiege us?	—	v. 3
merciful construction of good women ..	—	(epil.)
comparison between the women .	*Troilus & Cress.*	i. 1
women are angels, wooing	—	i. 2
or that we women had men's	—	iii. 2
all false women Cressids	—	iii. 2
they dance! they are mad women .	*Timon of Ath.*	i. 2
why then! women are more valiant	—	iii. 5
if there sit twelve women at the	—	iii. 6 (grace)

336

women nearest; but men, men are ..	—	iv. 3
both too; and women's sons	—	iv. 3
tell these sad women, 'tis fond	*Coriolanus,*	iv. 1
the easy groans of old women........	—	v. 2
more unfortunate than all living women	—	v. 3
at a few drops of women's rheum	—	v. 5
tradesman's matters, nor women's.	*Julius Cæsar,*	i. 1
a hundred ghastly women transformed	—	i. 3
the melting spirits of women	—	ii. 1
how hard it is for women to keep....	—	ii. 4
then, we kill all our women .	*Antony & Cleopatra,*	i. 2
compelling occasion, let women die..	—	i. 2
no more women but Fulvia, then....	—	i. 2
might go to wars with the women! ..	—	ii. 2
other women cloy the' appetites they feed	—	ii. 2
leader's led, and we are women's men	—	iii. 7
women are not, in their best fortunes	—	iii. 10
see, my women! against the blown rose	—	iii. 11
and by a gem of women, to be	—	iii. 11
transformed us not to women	—	iv. 2
help me, my women (*rep.* iv. 13)	—	iv. 11
see, my women, the crown o' the	—	iv. 13
ah, women, women! look (*rep.*)	—	iv. 13
or women, tell their dreams..........	—	v. 2
show me, my women, like a queen ..	—	v. 2
very many, men and women too	—	v. 2
do the gods great harm in their women	—	v. 2
bear her women from the monument	—	v. 2
call my women: think on my words.	*Cymbeline,*	i. 6
I know her women are about her	—	ii. 3
one of her women (*rep.* ii. 4)	—	ii. 3
the vows of women of no more bondage	—	ii. 4
but women must be half-workers? ..	—	ii. 5
men's vows are women's traitors! ..	—	iii. 4
the handmaids of all women	—	iii. 4
these her women can trip me, if I err	—	v. 5
WOMEN—all this, her women?	*Cymbeline,*	v. 5
how many women saw this child.	*Titus Andron.*	iv. 2
take women's gifts for impudence	*Pericles,*	ii. 3
which even women have cast off	—	iv. 1
but, amongst honest women?	—	iv. 6
let not women's weapons	*Lear,*	ii. 4
betray thy poor heart to women	—	iii. 4
women will all turn monsters	—	iii. 7

centaurs, though women all above	—	iv. 6
therefore women, being the weaker...	*Romeo & Jul.*	i. 1
women grow by men	—	i. 3
making them women of good carriage	—	i. 4
women may fall, when there's	—	ii. 3
women fear too much	*Hamlet,*	iii. 2
framed to make women false............	*Othello,*	i. 3
if I court no women, you'll couch	—	iv. 3 (song)
that there be women do abuse their......	—	iv. 3

338

ENDNOTES

1   Ann Thompson and Sasha Roberts, eds., "Mary Cowden Clarke (née Novello)," in *Women Reading Shakespeare 1660–1900: An Anthology of Criticism* (Manchester: Manchester University Press, 1997), 81.

2   *Oxford Dictionary of National Biography*, s.v. "Clarke, Mary Victoria Cowden," by Betty T. Bennett, revised by C.E. Hughes.

3   *Women Reading Shakespeare*, 82.

4   *Women Reading Shakespeare*, 46.

5   *Women Reading Shakespeare*, 83.

6   Quoted in Richard D. Altick, *The Cowden Clarkes* (Oxford: Oxford University Press, 1948), 116.

7   Mary Cowden Clarke's middle name was Victoria after her father's friend the Reverend Victor Fryer.

8   John Payne Collier's new edition appeared in 1841.

9   Jennifer M. Lloyd, "Raising Lilies: Ruskin and Women," *The Journal of British Studies*, 34, no. 3 (July 1995), 325–50. In a footnote (pp. 332–33), Lloyd cites Susan Johnston, "Family Values? Education and Domestic Ideology in Mary Cowden Clarke's *The Girlhood of Shakespeare's Heroines*," an unpublished paper given at the Midwest Conference on British Studies, Toronto 1994.

Anna Jameson (1794–1860)

Anna Jameson was a hardworking, versatile woman of letters, the first professional female art critic in English,[1] and an advocate for women's rights to education, employment, and property.[2] She was born in Dublin in 1794, the eldest
of five daughters of Denis Murphy, a painter, and his English wife, Minnie.
Her parents moved from Ireland to England in 1798. They were able to afford a
governess to educate their daughters until Anna was about twelve. After that,
Anna taught her sisters. At sixteen, she became a governess to alleviate her
family's chronic lack of money. She wrote an account of the European travels
she took with her employers and published it in the popular autobiographical
novel, *Diary of an Ennuyée* (1826), originally issued anonymously as *A Lady's
Diary*. This was her only attempt at fiction. She also began contributing essays
to London periodicals about the art she observed in Europe, and continued to
do so throughout her life.

Anna Murphy worked as a governess until 1825 when she married Robert
Jameson, a lawyer. The marriage proved unsuccessful; the experience determined the directions of Anna Jameson's feminism.[3] When Robert Jameson was
appointed to a judicial position in Dominica in 1829, and subsequently as attorney-general of Upper Canada, Anna Jameson did not go with him. The couple
lived together again for a brief period when Anna spent 1836–37 in Canada to
promote Robert's advancement to vice-chancellor. On her return to England in
1838, she signed the formal separation her husband proposed in which he agreed
to pay her a yearly allowance of £300, although the payments proved unreliable.
For the remainder of her life, she continued writing and publishing to support
her family, including her sisters and a niece. Always concerned about her reputation, given her anomalous marital position and financial uncertainties, she
nonetheless expressed her ideas with great freedom and lived expansively.

Anna Jameson's major intellectual interest was to represent for a female audience women's "anomalous" position in a hypocritical culture. Woman, she commented, lived the contradiction between "a state of opinion, a license of custom,
which makes a home and a protection necessary to her, and a state of things
which throws her into the midst of the world, to struggle and toil for her daily
bread."[4] She used life-writing to explore the conditions of women's lives in the
present and the past, commenting on the diversity of experience among women
who were unmarried, divorced, and in unconventional marriages like her own.[5]
She capitalized on the market for collective biographies in *Memoirs of the Loves
of the Poets* (1829) and *Memoirs of Celebrated Female Sovereigns* (1831). She wrote

the narrative to accompany her father's etchings in *Beauties of the Court of King Charles* (1831). In 1832, she published her most popular work, *Characteristics of Women: Moral, Poetical, and Historical*, commonly called *Shakespeare's Heroines*, which modern critics describe as a "a hybrid"—simultaneously "an early Victorian conduct manual"[6] and "the first book to examine Shakespeare's female characters at length and to consider 'women' as a legitimate category of Shakespeare criticism."[7] More than twenty editions of the work were published by 1905.

Jameson was peripatetic. Her texts convey her complex responses to what she saw in her extensive travels in Germany and Italy, as well as her experiences with a wide circle of friends. She knew the novelist William Makepeace Thackeray, publisher John Murray III, writers Mary Ann Evans (who later wrote as "George Eliot") and Elizabeth Gaskell, actresses Frances Anne Kemble and Sarah Siddons, reformer Basil Montagu and his wife (née Benson), Elizabeth Jesser Reid, Harriet Martineau, Jane and Thomas Carlyle, Charles Dickens, and, in Italy, the art critic John Ruskin. Anna Jameson counted among her intimates ailing Elizabeth Barrett and Robert Browning. At their request, she accompanied them when they eloped in 1846 and remained with them in Italy while Barrett Browning regained her health. She formed mostly supportive friendships with Lady Byron and Lady Byron's daughter, Ada Byron Lovelace, and with Ottilie von Goethe (the writer's daughter-in-law) through whom she met German and Austrian writers, intellectuals, and actresses. She published well-received accounts of her travels in *Visits and Sketches at Home and Abroad* (1834) and *Winter Studies and Summer Rambles in Canada* (1838). Reviewers of her work included Mary Wollstonecraft Shelley and Geraldine Jewsbury.

Anna Jameson established her reputation as a serious art critic in guidebooks to public and private galleries in London, *Memoirs of the early Italian Painters* (1845), and her groundbreaking five-volume series, *Sacred and Legendary Art* (1848–64; the last volume published posthumously). As she gained eminence, she exercised her authority to support women's activities. She was mentor to younger feminist activists, later known as "The Langham Place Circle," particularly Barbara Bodichon, Adelaide Procter, and Bessie Rayner Parkes. Jameson lectured and published influential social commentary on *The Relative Position of Mothers and Governesses* (1846), *Sisters of Charity, Catholic and Protestant, Abroad and at Home* (1855), and *The Communion of Labour: Two Lectures on the Social Employments of Women* (1856). She is credited with the idea for *The Englishwoman's Journal*.[8] Her status as a public woman was recognised in 1851 when she was nominated for Her Majesty's Pension List for an annuity of £100. She discovered at her husband's death in 1854 that he had left her out of his will. In response, her numerous friends raised funds to provide her with an additional £100 annually.

Anna Jameson died in March 1860 of influenza caught after working at the British Library all day on *The History of Our Lord*, the fifth volume of *Sacred and Legendary Art*, and then walking home in a snowstorm. Harriet Martineau eulogized her as "restless, expatiating, fervent, unreasoning, generous, accomplished ... a great benefit to her time from her zeal for her sex and for Art."[9]

SACRED AND LEGENDARY ART (1848)

In *Sacred and Legendary Art*, Anna Jameson approached her vast subject from a similarly radical perspective as in *Shakespeare's Heroines*. Here she is the egalitarian autodidact who has studied the traditional commentaries and now invites her readers on a tour of the great icons of the past. In the preface to the first edition, Jameson confronts a maze of religious, national, and sexual prejudices. Despite her tempered apologies for what her book is not, she urges the reader to learn from it. She recognises the prevailing anti-Catholic bias among her British readers and assures them that she elucidates "Art," not faith, in her volumes. But subjectivity, she comments, has been integral to the production of the great works of art she will consider. In her introduction to the same edition, another path-breaking effort, she revises the historical continuum of the Western canon to locate the genesis of Catholic iconography not in "the brains of dreaming monks," but rather in "the intense expression" of common people in earlier times yearning for transcendence.

Jameson posits Christ's teachings as the progressive engine of civilization. She rejects the sectarian disputes and repressive practices of any church, including those of her own Church of England. She is ironic about the contemporary fashion for mindlessly collecting works of art and "running" through museums, galleries, and churches. She argues that to understand and appreciate art it is necessary "to bring [a] work to the test of truth ... and how can we do this, unless we know what to look for, what was *intended* as to incident, expression, character?" In response, she provides a lexicon of appropriate historical signifiers that includes specific, recurring stories, figures, themes, and motifs for viewers to use. She demonstrates how to do so. She is attentive to the feelings that these symbols are meant to evoke. She seeks to inform the reader's emotions and understanding by offering accurate historical, not devotional, contexts in which to assess art of cultures other than one's own.

The constructed image of woman is central to Jameson's interests. Alison Booth comments, "Powerful icons endorsed by history ... become, in Jameson's collections, means of restoring an apocryphal countermemory that inverts if it does not level hierarchy."[10] The passages selected below are from the section on "St. Mary Magdalene," a contested figure in Victorian England that represented competing cultural demands: woman must be the chaste angel in the house, or, if fallen, romantically penitent. Jameson traces the historical sources for the sinner/saint and concludes that most images of Mary Magdalene are wanting, embodied without reference to the wider social forces against which she struggled that gave her humanity, integrity, and power.[11]

Sacred and Legendary Art (1848)

Anna Jameson

PREFACE TO THE FIRST EDITION

THIS book was begun six years ago, in 1842. It has since been often laid aside, and again resumed. In this long interval, many useful and delightful works have been written on the same subject, but still the particular ground I had chosen remained unoccupied; and, amid many difficulties, and the consciousness of many deficiencies, I was encouraged to proceed, partly by the pleasure I took in a task so congenial,—partly by the conviction that such a work has long been wanted by those who are not contented with a mere manual of reference, or a mere catalogue of names. This book is intended not only to be consulted, but to be read,—if it be found worth reading. It has been written for those who are, like myself, unlearned; yet less, certainly, with the idea of instructing, than from a wish to share with others those pleasurable associations, those ever new and ever various aspects of character and sentiment, as exhibited in Art, which have been a source of such vivid enjoyment to myself.

This is the utmost limit of my ambition; and, knowing that I cannot escape criticism, I am at least anxious that there should be no mistake as to purpose and intention. I hope it will be clearly understood that I have taken throughout the æsthetic and not the religious view of those productions of Art which, in as far as they are informed with a true and earnest feeling, and steeped in that beauty which emanates from genius inspired by faith, may cease to be Religion, but cannot cease to be Poetry; and as poetry only I have considered them.

The difficulty of selection and compression has been the greatest of all my difficulties; there is not a chapter in this book which might not have been more easily extended to a volume than compressed into a few pages. Every reader, however, who is interested in the subject, may supply the omissions, follow out the suggestions, and enjoy the pleasure of discovering new exceptions, new analogies, for himself. With regard to the arrangement, I am afraid it will be found liable to objections; but it is the best that, after long consideration and many changes, I could fix upon. It is not formal, nor technical, like that of a catalogue or a calendar, but intended to lead the fancy naturally from subject to subject as one opened upon another, with just sufficient order to keep the

342

mind unperplexed and the attention unfatigued amid a great diversity of objects, scenes, stories, and characters. [....]

INTRODUCTION
I. OF THE ORIGIN AND GENERAL SIGNIFICANCE OF THE LEGENDS REPRESENTED IN ART

WE cannot look round a picture gallery, we cannot turn over a portfolio of prints after the old masters, nor even the modern engravings which pour upon us daily, from Paris, Munich, or Berlin, without perceiving how many of the most celebrated productions of Art, more particularly those which have descended to us from the early Italian and German schools, represent incidents and characters taken from the once popular legends of the Catholic Church. This form of "*Hero-Worship*" has become, since the Reformation, strange to us,—as far removed from our sympathies and associations as if it were antecedent to the fall of Babylon and related to the religion of Zoroaster, instead of being left but two or three centuries behind us and closely connected with the faith of our forefathers and the history of civilization and Christianity. Of late years, with a growing passion for the works of Art of the Middle Ages, there has arisen among us a desire to comprehend the state of feeling which produced them, and the legends and traditions on which they are founded;—a desire to understand, and to bring to some surer critical test, representations which have become familiar without being intelligible. To enable us to do this, we must pause for a moment at the outset; and, before we plunge into the midst of things, ascend to higher ground, and command a far wider range of illustration than has yet been attempted, in order to take cognizance of principles and results which, if not new, must be contemplated in a new relation to each other.

The Legendary Art of the Middle Ages sprang out of the legendary literature of the preceding ages. For three centuries at least this literature, the only literature which existed at the time, formed the sole mental and moral nourishment of the *people* of Europe. The romances of Chivalry, which long afterwards succeeded, were confined to particular classes, and left no impress on Art, beyond the miniature illuminations of a few manuscripts. This legendary literature, on the contrary, which had worked itself into the life of the people, became, like the antique mythology, as a living soul diffused through the loveliest forms of Art, still vivid and vivifying, even when the old faith in its mystical significance was lost or forgotten. And it is a mistake to suppose that these legends had their sole origin in the brains of dreaming monks. The wildest of them had some basis of truth to rest on, and the forms which they gradually assumed were but the necessary result of the age which produced them. They became the intense expression of that inner life, which revolted against the desolation and emptiness of the outward existence; of those crushed and outraged sympathies which cried aloud for rest, and refuge, and solace, and could nowhere find them. It will be said, "In the purer doctrine of the GOSPEL." But where was that to be found? The Gospel was not then the heritage of the poor: Christ, as a comforter, walked not among

343

men. His own blessed teaching was inaccessible except to the learned: it was shut up in rare manuscripts; it was perverted and sophisticated by the passions and the blindness of those few to whom it *was* accessible. The bitter disputes in the early Church relative to the nature of the Godhead, the subtle distinctions and incomprehensible arguments of the theologians, the dread entertained by the predominant church of any heterodox opinions concerning the divinity of the Redeemer, had all conspired to remove *Him*, in his personal character of Teacher and Saviour, far away from the hearts of the benighted and miserable people,— far, far away into regions speculative, mysterious, spiritual, whither they could not, dared not, follow Him. In this state of things, as it has been remarked by a distinguished writer, "Christ became the object of a remoter, a more awful adoration. The mind began, therefore, to seek out, or eagerly to seize, some other more material beings in closer alliance with human sympathies." [....] Now, if we go back to the *authentic* histories of the sufferings and heroism of the early martyrs, we shall find enough there, both of the wonderful and the affecting, to justify the credulity and enthusiasm of the unlettered people, who saw no reason why they should not believe in one miracle as well as in another. In these universally diffused legends, we may recognize the means, at least one of the means, by which a merciful Providence, working through its own immutable laws, had provided against the utter depravation, almost extinction, of society. Of the "Dark Ages," emphatically so called, the period to which I allude was perhaps the darkest; it was "of Night's black arch the key-stone." At a time when men were given over to the direst evils that can afflict humanity,—ignorance, idleness, wickedness, misery; at a time when the every-day incidents of life were a violation of all the moral instincts of mankind; at a time when all things seemed abandoned to a blind chance, or the brutal law of force; when there was no repose, no refuge, no safety anywhere; when the powerful inflicted, and the weak endured, whatever we can conceive of most revolting and intolerable; when slavery was recognized by law throughout Europe; when men fled to cloisters, to shut themselves from oppression, and women to shield themselves from outrage; when the manners were harsh, the language gross; when all the softer social sentiments, as piety, reverence, tenderness, found no resting-place in the actual relations of life; when for the higher ranks there was only the fierce excitement of war, and on the humbler classes lay the weary, dreary monotony of a stagnant existence, poor in pleasures of every kind, without aim, without hope; *then*—wondrous reaction of the ineffaceable instincts of good implanted within us!—arose a literature which reversed the outward order of things, which asserted and kept alive in the hearts of men those pure principles of Christianity which were outraged in their daily actions; a literature in which peace was represented as better than war, and sufferance more dignified than resistance; which exhibited poverty and toil as honorable, and charity as the first of virtues; which held up to imitation and emulation, self-sacrifice in the cause of good and contempt of death for conscience' sake: a literature, in which the tenderness, the chastity, the heroism of woman, played a conspicuous part; which distinctly protested against slavery, against violence, against impurity in word and deed; which refreshed the fevered and darkened spirit with images of moral beauty and truth; revealed bright glimpses of a better land, where "the wicked cease from troubling," and brought down the angels of God with shining wings and bearing crowns of glory, to do battle with the demons of darkness, to catch the fleeting soul of the triumphant martyr, and carry it at once into a paradise of eternal blessedness and peace!

Now the Legendary Art of the three centuries which comprise the revival of learning was, as I have said, the reflection of this literature, of this teaching. Considered in this point of view, can we easily overrate its interest and importance?

When, after the long period of darkness which followed upon the decline of the Roman Empire, the Fine Arts began to revive, the first, and for several ages the only, impress they received was that of the religious spirit of the time. Painting, Sculpture, Music, and Architecture, as they emerged one after another from the "formless void," were pressed into the service of the Church. But it is a mistake to suppose that in adroitly adapting the reviving Arts to her purposes, in that magnificent spirit of calculation which at all times characterized her, the Church from the beginning selected the subjects, or dictated the use that was to be made of them. We find, on the contrary, edicts and councils *repressing* the popular extravagances in this respect, and denouncing those apocryphal versions of sacred events and traditions which had become the delight of the people. But vain were councils and edicts; the tide was too strong to be so checked. The Church found herself obliged to accept and mould to her own objects the exotic elements she could not eradicate. She *absorbed*, so to speak, the evils and errors she could not expel. There seems to have been at this time a sort of compromise between the popular legends, with all their wild mixture of northern and classical superstitions, and the Church legends properly so called. The first great object to which reviving Art was destined, was to render the Christian places of worship a theatre of instruction and improvement for the people, to attract and to interest them by representations of scenes, events, and personages, already so familiar as to require no explanation, appealing at once to their intelligence and their sympathies; embodying in beautiful shapes (beautiful at least in their eyes) associations and feelings and memories deep-rooted in their very hearts, and which had influenced, in no slight degree, the progress of civilization, the development of mind. Upon these creations of ancient Art we cannot look as *those* did for whom they were created; we cannot annihilate the centuries which lie between us and them; we cannot, in simplicity of heart, forget the artist in the image he has placed before us, nor supply what may be deficient in his work, through a reverentially excited fancy. We are critical, not credulous. We no longer accept this polytheistic form of Christianity; and there is little danger, I suppose, of our falling again into strange excesses of superstition to which it led. But if we have not much sympathy with modern imitations of Mediæval Art, still less should we sympathize with that narrow puritanical jealousy which holds the monuments of a real and earnest faith in contempt. All that God has permitted

345

once to exist in the past should be considered as the possession of the present; sacred for example or warning, and held as the foundation on which to build up what is better and purer. It should seem an established fact, that all revolutions in religion, in government, and in art, which begin in the spirit of scorn, and in a sweeping destruction of the antecedent condition, only tend to a reaction. Our puritanical ancestors chopped off the heads of Madonnas and Saints, and paid vagabonds to smash the storied windows of our cathedrals;—*now*, are these rejected and outraged shapes of beauty coming back to us, or are we not rather going back to them? As a Protestant, I might fear lest in doing so we confound the eternal spirit of Christianity with the mutable forms in which it has deigned to speak to the hearts of men, forms which must of necessity vary with the degree of social civilization, and bear the impress of the feelings and fashions of the age which produced them; but I must also feel that we ought to comprehend, and to hold in due reverence, that which has once been consecrated to holiest aims, which has shown us what a magnificent use has been made of Art, and how it may still be adapted to good and glorious purposes, if, while we respect these time-consecrated images and types, we do not allow them to fetter us, but trust in the progressive spirit of Christianity to furnish us with new impersonations of the good, new combinations of the beautiful. I hate the destructive as I revere the progressive spirit. We must laugh if any one were to try and persuade us that the sun was guided along his blazing path by "a fair-haired god who touched a golden lyre"; but shall we therefore cease to adore in the Apollo Belvedere the majestic symbol of light, the most divine impersonation of intellectual power and beauty? So of the corresponding Christian symbols:—may that time never come, when we shall look up to the effigy of the winged and radiant angel trampling down the brute-fiend, without a glow of faith in the perpetual supremacy and final triumph of good over evil!

It is about a hundred years since the passion, or the fashion, for collecting works of Art, began to be generally diffused among the rich and the noble of this land; and it is amusing to look back and to consider the perversions and affectations of the would-be connoisseurship during this period;—the very small stock of ideas on which people set up a pretension to taste,—the false notions, the mixture of pedantry and ignorance, which everywhere prevailed. The publication of Richardson's book, and Sir Joshua Reynolds's Discourses, had this advantage,—that they, to a certain degree, diffused a more elevated idea of Art as *Art*, and that they placed connoisseurship on a better and truer basis. In those days we had Inquiries into the Principles of Taste, Treatises on the Sublime and Beautiful, Anecdotes of Painting; and we abounded in Antiquarian Essays on disputed Pictures and mutilated Statues: but then, and up to a late period, any inquiry into the true spirit and significance of works of Art, as connected with the history of Religion and Civilization, would have appeared ridiculous—or perhaps dangerous:—we should have had another cry of "No Popery," and acts of Parliament forbidding the importation of Saints and Madonnas. It was fortunate, perhaps, that connoisseurs meddled not with such high matters. They talked volubly and harmlessly of "hands," and "masters," and "schools,"—of "draperies," of "tints," of "handling,"—of "fine heads," "fine compositions"; of the "grace of Raphael," and of the "Correggiosity of Correggio." The very manner in which the names of the painters were pedantically used, instead of the name of the subject, is indicative of this factitious feeling; the only question at issue was, whether such a picture was a genuine "Raphael"? such another a genuine "Titian"? The spirit of the work—whether *that* was genuine; how far it was influenced by the faith and the condition of the age which produced it; whether the conception was properly characteristic, and of *what* it was characteristic—of the subject? or of the school? or of the time?—whether the treatment corresponded to the idea within our own souls, or was modified by the individuality of the artist, or by received conventionalisms of all kinds?—these were questions which had not then occurred to any one; and I am not sure that we are much wiser even now: yet, setting aside all higher considerations, how can we do common justice to the artist, unless we can bring his work to the test of truth? and how can we do this, unless we know what to look for, what was *intended* as to incident, expression, character? One result of our ignorance has been the admiration wasted on the flimsy mannerists of the later ages of Art; men who apparently had no definite *intention* in anything they did, except a dashing outline, or a delicate finish, or a striking and attractive management of color.

It is curious, this general ignorance with regard to the subjects of Mediæval Art, more particularly now that it has become a reigning fashion among us. We find no such ignorance with regard to the subjects of Classical Art, because the associations connected with them form a part of every liberal education. Do we hear any one say, in looking at Annibal Caracci's picture in the National Gallery, "Which is Silenus, and which is Apollo?" Who ever confounds a Venus with a Minerva, or a Vestal with an Amazon; or would endure an undraped Juno, or a beardless Jupiter? Even the gardener in Zeluco knew Neptune by his "fork," and Vulcan by his "lame leg." We are indeed so accustomed, in visiting the churches and the galleries abroad, and the collections at home, to the predominance of sacred subjects, that it has become a mere matter of course, and excites no particular interest and attention. We have heard it all accounted for by the fact that the Church and churchmen were the first, and for a long time the only, patrons of art. In every sacred edifice, and in every public or private collection enriched from the plunder of sacred edifices, we look for the usual proportion of melancholy martyrdoms and fictitious miracles,—for the predominance of Madonnas and Magdalenes, St. Catherines and St. Jeromes: but why these should predominate, why certain events and characters from the Old and the New Testament should be continually repeated, and others comparatively neglected; whence the predilection for certain legendary personages, who seemed to be multiplied to infinity, and the rarity of others;—of this we know nothing.

We have learned, perhaps, after running through half the galleries and churches in Europe, to distinguish a few of the attributes and characteristic figures which meet us at every turn, yet without any clear idea of their meaning,

347

derivation, or relative propriety. The palm of victory, we know, designates the martyr triumphant in death. We so far emulate the critical sagacity of the gardener in Zeluco that we have learned to distinguish St. Laurence by his gridiron, and St. Catherine by her well. We are not at a loss to recognize the Magdalene's "loose hair and lifted eye," even when without her skull and her vase of ointment. We learn to know St. Francis by his brown habit and shaven crown and wasted, ardent features; but how do we distinguish him from St. Anthony, or St. Dominick? As for St. George and the dragon,—from the St. George of the Louvre,—Raphael's,—who sits his horse with the elegant tranquillity of one assured of celestial aid, down to him "who swings on a sign-post at mine hostess's door,"—he is our familiar acquaintance. But who is that lovely being in the first blush of youth, who, bearing aloft the symbolic cross, stands with one foot on the vanquished dragon? "That is a copy after Raphael." And who is that majestic creature holding her palm-branch, while the unicorn crouches at her feet? "That is the famous Moretto at Vienna." Are we satisfied?—not in the least! but we try to look wiser, and pass on.

348

In the old times the painters of these legendary scenes and subjects could always reckon securely on certain associations and certain sympathies in the minds of the spectators. We have outgrown these associations, we repudiate these sympathies. We have taken these works from their consecrated localities, in which they once held each their dedicated place, and we have hung them in our drawing-rooms and our dressing-rooms, over our pianos and our sideboards,—and now what do they say to us? That Magdalene, weeping amid her hair, who once spoke comfort to the soul of the fallen sinner,—that Sebastian, arrow-pierced, whose upward, ardent glance spoke of courage and hope to the tyrant-ridden serf,—that poor tortured slave, to whose aid St. Mark comes sweeping down from above, can they speak to *us* of nothing save flowing lines and correct drawing and gorgeous color? must we be told that one is a Titian, the other a Guido, the third a Tintoret, before we dare to melt in compassion or admiration?—or the moment we refer to their ancient religious signification and influence, must it be with disdain or with pity? This, as it appears to me, is to take not a rational, but rather a most irrational as well as a most irreverent, view of the question; it is to confine the pleasure and improvement to be derived from works of Art within very narrow bounds; it is to seal up a fountain of the richest poetry, and to shut out a thousand ennobling and inspiring thoughts. Happily there is a growing appreciation of these larger principles of criticism as applied to the study of Art. People look at the pictures which hang round their walls, and have an awakening suspicion that there is more in them than meets the eye,—more than mere connoisseurship can interpret; and that they have another, a deeper, significance than has been dreamed of by picture dealers and picture collectors, or even picture critics. [....] These introductory observations and explanations will be found illustrated in a variety of forms as we proceed; and readers will be led to make comparisons, and discover analogies and exceptions, for themselves. I must stop here;—yet one word more.—

All the productions of Art, from the time it has been directed and developed by Christian influences, may be regarded under three different aspects. 1. The purely religious aspect, which belongs to one mode of faith; 2. The poetical aspect, which belongs to all; 3. The artistic, which is the individual point of view, and has reference only to the action of the intellect on the means and material employed. There is pleasure, intense pleasure, merely in the consideration of Art as *Art*; in the faculties of comparison and nice discrimination, brought to bear on objects of beauty; in the exercise of a cultivated and refined taste on the productions of mind in any form whatever. But a threefold, or rather a thousand-fold, pleasure is theirs who to a sense of the poetical unite a sympathy with the spiritual in Art, and who combine with delicacy of perception, and technical knowledge, more elevated sources of pleasure, more variety of association, habits of more excursive thought. Let none imagine, however, that, in placing before the uninitiated these unpretending volumes, I assume any such superiority as is here implied. Like a child that has sprung on a little way before its playmates, and caught a glimpse through an opening portal of some varied Eden within, all gay with flowers, and musical with birds, and haunted by divine shapes which beckon onward; and, after one rapturous survey, runs back and catches its companions by the hand and hurries them forwards to share the new-found pleasure, the yet unexplored reign of delight; even so it is with me:—I am on the outside, not the inside, of the door I open. [....]

349

ST. MARY MAGDALENE.

The penance of the Magdalene is a subject which has become, like the penance of St. Jerome, a symbol of Christian penitence, but still more endeared to the popular imagination by more affecting and attractive associations, and even more eminently picturesque,—so tempting to the artists, that by their own predilection for it they have assisted in making it universal. In the display of luxuriant female forms, shadowed (not hidden) by redundant fair hair, and flung in all the *abandon* of solitude, amid the depth of leafy recesses, or relieved by the dark umbrageous rocks; in the association of love and beauty with the symbols of death and sorrow and utter humiliation; the painters had ample scope, ample material, for the exercise of their imagination and the display of their skill: and what has been the result? They have abused these capabilities even to license; they have exhausted the resources of Art in the attempt to vary the delineation; and yet how seldom has the ideal of this most exquisite subject been—I will not say realized—but even approached? We have Magdalenes who look as if they never could have sinned, and others who look as if they never could have repented; we have Venetian Magdalenes with the air of courtesans, and Florentine Magdalenes with the air of Ariadnes; and Bolognese Magdalenes like sentimental Niobes; and French Magdalenes, *moitié galantes, moitié dévotes*; and Dutch Magdalenes, who wring their hands like repentant washerwomen. The Magdalenes of Van Dyck are fine ladies who have turned Methodists. But Mary Magdalene, such as we have conceived her, mournful yet hopeful,—tender yet dignified,—worn with grief and fasting, yet radiant with the glow of love and faith, and clothed with the beauty of holiness,—is an ideal which painting has not yet realized. Is it beyond the reach of Art? We might have answered this question, had Raphael attempted it;—but he has not. His Magdalene at the feet of Christ is yet unforgiven,—the forlorn castaway, not the devout penitent. [....] On reviewing generally the infinite variety which has been given to these favorite subjects, the life and penance of the Magdalene, I must end where I began;—in how few instances has the result been satisfactory to mind or heart, or soul or sense! Many have well represented the particular situation, the appropriate sentiment, the sorrow, the hope, the devotion: but who has given us the *character*? A noble creature, with strong sympathies, and a strong will, with powerful faculties of every kind, working for good or evil,—such a woman Mary Magdalene must have been, even in her humiliation; and the feeble, girlish, commonplace, and even vulgar women who appear to have been usually selected as models by the artists, turned into Magdalenes by throwing up their eyes and letting down their hair, ill represent the enthusiastic convert or the majestic patroness.

350

I must not quit the subject of the Magdalene without some allusion to those wild legends which suppose a tender attachment (but of course wholly pure and Platonic) to have existed between her and St. John the Evangelist. In the enthusiasm which Mary Magdalene excited in the thirteenth century, no supposition that tended to exalt her was deemed too extravagant: some of her panegyrists go so far as to insist that the marriage at Cana, which our Saviour and his mother honored by their presence, was the marriage of St. John with the Magdalene; and that Christ repaired to the wedding-feast on purpose to prevent the accomplishment of the marriage, having destined both to a state of greater perfection. This fable was never accepted by the Church; and among the works of art consecrated to religious purposes I have never met with any which placed St. John and the Magdalene in particular relation to each other, except when they are seen together at the foot of the cross, or lamenting with the Virgin over the body of the Saviour: but such was the popularity of these extraordinary legends towards the end of the thirteenth and in the beginning of the fourteenth century, that I think it possible such may exist, and, for want of this key, may appear hopelessly enigmatical.

In a series of eight subjects which exhibit the life of St. John prefixed to a copy of the Revelations, there is one which I think admits of this interpretation. The scene is the interior of a splendid building sustained by pillars. St. John is baptizing a beautiful woman, who is sitting in a tub; she has long golden hair. On the outside of the building seven men are endeavoring to see what is going forward: one peeps through the key-hole; one has thrown himself flat on the ground, and has his eye to an aperture; a third, mounted on the shoulders of another, is trying to look in at a window; a fifth, who cannot get near enough, tears his hair in agony of impatience; and another is bawling into the ear of a deaf and blind comrade a description of what he has seen. The execution is French, of the fourteenth century; the taste, it will be said, is also *French;* the figures are drawn with a pen and slightly tinted; the design is incorrect; but the vivacity of gesture and expression, though verging on caricature, is so true, and so comically dramatic, and the whole composition so absurd, that it is impossible to look at it without a smile.

ENDNOTES

1   *Oxford Dictionary of National Biography*, s.v. "Jameson [née Murphy], Anna Brownwell (1794–1860), writer and art historian," by Judith Johnston, 2004-05.

2   Judith Johnston, *Anna Jameson: Victorian, Feminist, Woman of Letters* (Aldershot: Scolar Press, 1997).

3   Sally Alexander, "Women, Class and Sexual Difference in the 1830s and 1840s: Some Reflections on the Writing of a Feminist History," *History Workshop Journal*, 17–18 (1984): 130–49.

4   [Mrs. Jameson], "Condition of the Women and the Female Children," *The Athenaeum* 16 (March 18, 1843): 258, quoted in Beth Harris, introduction to *Famine and Fashion: Needlewomen in the Nineteenth Century*, ed. Beth Harris (Aldershot: Ashgate, 2005), 7.

5   Cheri L. Larsen Hoeckley, introduction to *Shakespeare's Heroines: Characteristics of Women: Moral, Poetical, and Historical*, by Anna Murphy Jameson, ed. Cheri L. Larsen Hoeckley (Peterborough, ON: Broadview Press, 2005), 10.

6   Cheri L. Larsen Hoeckley, 9.

7   Ann Thompson and Sasha Roberts, eds., "Anna Brownwell Jameson (née Murphy), 1764–1860," in *Women Reading Shakespeare 1660–1900: An Anthology of Criticism* (Manchester: Manchester University Press, 1997), 66–67.

8   Hoeckley, 12.

9   Quoted in Johnston, ODNB.

10 Alison Booth, "The Lessons of the Medusa: Anna Jameson and Mutual Multibiography," in *How to Make It as a Woman* (Chicago: Cambridge University Press, 2004), 189.

11 See Judith Johnston's discussion in "Alien Aesthetics and Representation," in *Anna Jameson: Victorian, Feminist, Woman of Letters* (Aldershot: Scolar Press, 1997), 190–200, in which she points to Jameson's analysis as "coming in the vanguard of [an] historical shift in attitude towards the Magdalene," 193.

PART 5

Science and Mathematics

Priscilla Wakefield (1750–1832)

Priscilla Wakefield, who also wrote the treatise on women's education entitled *Reflections on the Present Condition of the Female Sex* (1798), is profiled in Part 1.

INTRODUCTION TO BOTANY (1796)

Wakefield's "Preface" is of interest in explaining the basis of her pedagogical theory, her justification for studying botany. Her target audience is "young persons," but both her protagonists and her explicit argument show that she is particularly interested in promoting botany as a study for young women because, although the Latin nomenclature of botany once made the subject inaccessible to most girls, now translations (such as Withering's) have overcome this difficulty. Further, Wakefield suggests that the order and method of botany can serve as a welcome antidote to the frivolous occupations of many women. We hear an echo of Mary Wollstonecraft's and Mary Robinson's strictures on the idle pursuits of so many genteel women of their age. Botany, as a rational pastime, can substitute for the "trifling not to say pernicious objects that occupy female leisure." Wakefield's pedagogical method, via the encompassing fiction of letters between sisters, is based on the principle that learning should be pleasurable. Children and young people, she believes, possess a natural curiosity, which should be encouraged not thwarted. All have the capacity to enlarge their intellectual powers. Botany, a healthy pursuit for mind and body, providing air and exercise at minimal expense, should be attainable to every rank of life. Wakefield does not believe that rank or gender distinctions could or should disappear, but her pedagogical programme is implicitly democratic in its scope. Finally, like many other scientific popularisers of the period, she concludes that the justification for scientific study lies in the way it reveals the workings of God in nature.

Letters I and III, reproduced here, reveal two key aspects of Wakefield's writing. First, the epistolary format, a favourite tool of informal didactic literature, ensures a familiar and familial context. The framing fiction of two sisters, Felicia and Constance, the former depressed by her separation from the latter, assumes the primary but desexualised bond of sisterly affection. Thanks to the care of maternal figures, the mother and governess, the study of botany will provide a means of tempering sentiment with rational occupation. Fresh air, exercise, and mental stimulus will assist in overcoming depression. Finally, Felicia, communicating her newfound knowledge to her sister, becomes an authoress as well as an authority. Communication is a way out of the cul-de-sac of loneliness.

In Letter III, Wakefield lays out the Linnaean sexual system, explaining the naming of parts of the flower. As noted above (see pages 48–49), the fact that the entire discussion concerns sexual reproduction is not mentioned directly. The text is clearly and helpfully linked to the accompanying illustration. Constance, after studying her sister's letters, will be in an excellent position to go out herself to identify and name the flower parts she finds. Learning and teaching in this text become an indivisible activity.

354

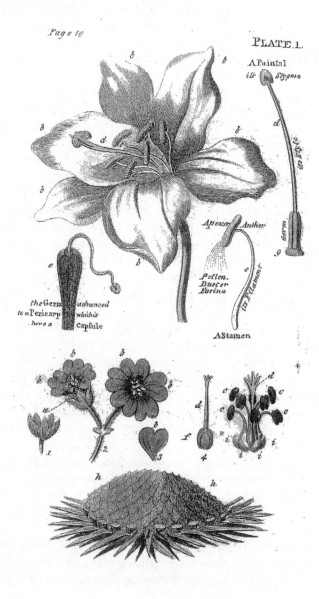

Introduction to Botany, in a series of familiar letters (1796)

Priscilla Wakefield

PREFACE

The design of the following *Introduction to Botany* is to cultivate a taste in young persons for the study of nature, which is the most familiar means of introducing suitable ideas of the attributes of the Divine Being, by exemplifying them in the order and harmony of the visible creation. Children are endowed with curiosity and activity, for the purpose of acquiring knowledge. Let us avail ourselves of these natural propensities, and direct them to the pursuit of the most judicious objects: none can be better adapted to instruct, and at the same time amuse, than the beauties of nature, by which they are continually surrounded. The structure of a feather or a flower is more likely to impress their minds with a just notion of the Infinite Power and Wisdom, than the most profound discourses on such abstract subjects, as are beyond the limits of their capacity to comprehend. In the important business of forming the human mind, the inclination and plea- sure of the pupil should be consulted; in order to render lessons effectual, they should please, and be sought rather as indulgencies, than avoided as laborious toils. Botany is a branch of Natural History that possesses many advantages; it contributes to health of body and cheerfulness of disposition, by presenting an inducement to take air and exercise; it is adapted to the simplest capacity, and the objects of its investigation offer themselves without expense or difficulty, which renders them attainable to every rank in life; but with all these allurements, till of late years, it has been confined to the circle of the learned, which may be at- tributed to those books that treated of it, being principally written in Latin; a difficulty that deterred many, particularly of the female sex, from attempting to obtain the knowledge of a science, thus defended, as it were, from their approach. Much is due to those of our own countrymen, who first introduced this delight- ful volume of nature to popular notice, by presenting it in our native language; their labours have been a means of rendering it very generally studied, and it is now considered as a necessary addition to an accomplished education. May it become a substitute for some of the trifling, not to say pernicious, objects, that too frequently occupy the leisure of young ladies of fashionable manners, and, by employing their faculties rationally, act as an antidote to levity and idleness. As there are many admirable English books now extant upon the subject, it may require some apology for obtruding the present work upon the public. It appeared that every thing hitherto published, was too expensive, as well as too diffuse and scientific, for the purpose of teaching the elementary parts to children or young persons; it was therefore thought, that a book of moderate price, and divested as much as possible of technical terms, introduced in an easy familiar form, might be acceptable.

356

Letter I. Felicia to Constance. Shrubbery, February 1

As it is an unusual thing for us to be separated, I do not doubt, but we equally feel the pain of being at a distance from each other; when I consider, that you are really gone to pass the whole summer with my aunt, and that I have parted with the beloved companion of my walks and amusements, I think I shall but half enjoy either, during the fine season that is approaching. With you, indeed, the case will be rather different; new scenes will present themselves, which will entertain by their novelty and variety, and the kind attentions of my aunt and cousins will compensate in degree for the absence of those friends you have left at home. Every place here looks solitary, especially our own apartment, and our favourite haunts in the garden. Even the approach of spring, which is marked by the appearance of snow drops and crocuses, affords me but little pleasure; my kind mother, ever attentive to my happiness, concurs with my governess in checking this depression of spirits, and insists upon my having recourse to some interesting employment that shall amuse me, and pass away the time while you are absent; my fondness for flowers has induced my mother to propose Botany, as she thinks it will be beneficial to my health, as well as agreeable, by exciting me to use more air and exercise than I should do, without such a motive; because books should not be depended upon alone, recourse must be had to the natural specimens growing in fields and gardens; how should I enjoy this pursuit in your company, my dear sister! But as that is impossible at present, I will adopt the nearest substitute I can obtain by communicating to you the result of every lesson. You may compare my descriptions with the flowers themselves, and, by thus mutually pursuing the same object, we may reciprocally improve each other. I am impatient to make a beginning, but am full of apprehension of the number of hard words at the entrance. However, I am resolved not to be deterred by this difficulty; perseverance and patience will overcome it; and as I know the easy method of instruction adopted by my dear governess in other sciences, I confide in her skill to render this easy and pleasant. Farewell.

FELICIA

Letter III. Shrubbery, February 18

The approbation you express, my dear Constance, of my endeavours to amuse you with an account of my botanical lectures, encourages me to proceed, though with great diffidence, as I find the subject becomes more intricate as I advance The fructification includes the flower and fruit, and contains the whole process of perfecting the seeds. It consists of seven parts; and, to illustrate them, I have sketched some particulars from the lily, &c. (See illustration on page 354.)

The (calyx) cup or empalement, *a*.
The (corolla) blossom, petals, or flower-leaves, *b*.
The (stamina) threads or chives, *c*.
The (pistillum) style or pointal, *d*.
The (pericarpium) seed vessel, *e*.
The seed or fruit, *f*.
The (receptaculum) receptacle or base, *g*.

357

Some flowers possess all these parts, others are deficient in some of them; but the chives or pointals, or both, are essential, and to be found in all, either in flowers on the same plant, or in different individual flowers of the same species, on separate plants. I shall give you as clear a description of these several parts as I possibly can, to enable you to distinguish them at first sight. The cup, empalement, or calyx (a) is that outer part of the flower, formed of one or more green or yellowish green leaves, sustaining the corolla at the bottom, and enclosing it entirely, before it expands, as you may remark in the Rose and Geranium, that latter of which I have sketched for an illustration. The empalement is either

A cup, as in the polyanthus,
A fence, as in the hemlock or carrot,
A catkin, as in the willow or hazel,
A sheath, as in the narcissus,
A husk, as in oats, wheat, or grasses,
A veil, as in mosses,
A cap, as in mushrooms.

The blossom, petals, or corolla (b), is that beautiful coloured part of a flower, which first draws the attention, and is regarded by common eyes as the flower itself; but botanists, more strict in their definitions, appropriate that term to the composition of the whole of the fructification of which the corolla is only a part.

The threads, or chives, are composed of two parts; one long and thin, by which they are fastened to the bottom of the corolla, called the filament; the other thicker, placed at the top of the filament, called anthera, or anther. Each anther is a kind of box, which opens when it is ripe, and throws out a yellow dust, that has a strong smell; this is termed pollen or farina, and is the substance of which bees are supposed to make their wax. The progress of the seed to maturity is deserving the most curious attention. First the calyx opens, then the corolla expands and discovers the stamens, which generally form a circle within the petals, surrounding the pointal. The pollen or dust, which bursts from the anthers, is absorbed by the pointal, and passing through the style, reaches the germ, and vivifies the seed, which, without this process, would be imperfect and barren. The stamens, pointal, and corolla, having performed their respective offices, decline and wither, making room for the seed-bud, which daily increases, till it attain its perfect state. Many curious experiments have been made by attentive naturalists, that prove the necessity of this communication between the stamens and pointals of the same flower, in order to render its seeds productive. The stamens and pointal being sometimes disposed on different plants, the trial may be made by shutting up a pot of those which have pointals only, in some place where they cannot be reached by the pollen of the stamens of other individual plants, and experiment has constantly shown, that no seed is produced in this situation; but how shall we account for the conveyance of the pollen from one plant to another, growing at a distance from it? They are both fixed, and cannot approach each other; yet nature, ever abounding in resources, has provided sufficient means for the purpose. It is probable that there is an attraction between them, which we may imagine, but cannot perceive; that this attractive quality may draw the pollen, floating about in the air, as it is wafted by the winds, to the pointals of its own species; or, in many cases, the numerous tribes of minute winged insects, which we observe so busily employed in a warm day, basking and hovering upon the flowers, may soon convey this fertilizing dust from one to another, and, whilst they are feasting upon the delicious honey afforded by these flowers, return the favour, by rendering them an essential service.

The style, pointal, or pistil is composed of three parts (Plate I.): the germen, the style, and the stigma. The germen varies, as to its form in different plants, but is always placed below the style; its office is to contain the embryo seeds. The style is placed on the germen, and is of a variety of figures and lengths, and sometimes seems wholly wanting. The stigma also appears of different forms, but always retains the same situation, being invariably placed at the top of the style; or, if that be wanting, it is fixed on the germen.

The seed vessel, or pericarpium, is the germen of the pistil enlarged, as the seeds increase in size, and approach nearer perfection. (Plate I.) The seed vessel is divided into seven kinds:

Capsule, as in poppy and convolvulus,
Pod, as in wallflower and honesty,
Shell, as in pea and broom,
Berry, as in elder and gooseberry,
Fleshy, as in apple and pear,
Pulpy, as in cherry and peach,
Cone, as in fir and pine.

The seeds, or fruit, resemble the eggs of animals, and are the essence of the fruit, containing the rudiments of a new vegetable. The formation of the seed is variously adapted to its purpose, and is composed of several parts: 1st, The heart; this is the principle of life in the future plant, contained within the lobes; it consists of two parts, the plume, which ascends, and forms the future stem; and the beak which descends and becomes the root. 2ndly, The side lobes; these supply the heart of the seed with nourishment, till it is capable of extracting support from the earth. In most plants the lobes ascend in the form of leaves, and are called seed or radical leaves; but, in some, they perish beneath the surface, without appearing above ground. 3dly, The Scar; is an external mark, where the seed was fastened within the seed vessel. 4thly, The seed-coat is a proper cover to some seeds. It is of various texture and consistence in different individuals. Sometimes the seed is crowned with the cup of the flower, and sometimes it is winged with a feather, or with a thin expanded membrane, which assists the wind to waft or disperse it to a distance. The seed contains the perfect plant in embryo, though in most instances, too minute to be discerned by our organs of sight; but if the seed of a bean or an acorn be sufficiently soaked in warm water, the form of the future plant may be plainly perceived.

359

The base, or receptacle (g), is that part by which the whole fructification is supported; in many flowers it is not very striking, but in others it is large and remarkable, as in the cotton thistle (h). The artichoke will also furnish us with an example: take away the empalement, blossoms, and bristly substances, and the part remaining is the receptacle, which we eat, and call the bottom.

It remains for me to describe the nectarium; nectary, or honey cup, an appendage with which some flowers are furnished, containing a small quantity of sweet honey-like juice, from which the bees collect their rich treasures. It is very conspicuous in some flowers, as the nasturtium, crown imperial, columbine, and larkspur; but less visible in others, and in some, appears to be entirely wanting. In the dove-footed cranesbill, there are five yellowish glands (i), which serve as a nectary. The use is supposed to be that of a reservoir, for the nourishment of the tender seed-bud.

I am fearful, my dear sister, that you are fatigued with these tedious definitions and descriptions of parts; to me they have been rendered more agreeable, as I have become acquainted with them from visible objects. I hope to participate this pleasure with you in degree, by exemplifying them in some individual flowers, which you may examine by yourself; but I shall defer this till my next letter and conclude affectionately yours

FELICIA

Jane Marcet (1769–1858)

Jane Haldimand Marcet was the eldest daughter of a wealthy Swiss émigré merchant banker, who believed in an equal education and inheritance for all his children, male and female. Jane's financial independence was an important factor in allowing her to pursue her scientific interests. When she was sixteen, her mother died of puerperal fever, leaving her daughter in charge of the household. Jane early became both her father's hostess for the wide circle of intellectual friends he habitually entertained, and the tutor for her younger siblings. At the same time, she studied mathematics, astronomy, philosophy, music, dancing, painting, and modern languages.

In 1799, aged thirty, she married Alexander Marcet, a Swiss refugee doctor from Geneva who specialised in the study and treatment of diabetes. He was also an enthusiast for the rapidly developing science of chemistry. Sharing his scientific interests, Jane Marcet found herself enthralled by chemistry, which seemed to open up a new way of seeing the world and understanding the composition of all matter.

Living in London, in a household comprising her husband, father, brothers, and a growing number of her own children, Jane Marcet was fortunate to participate in the still largely amateur but vital intellectual world of British science at the beginning of the nineteenth century. She attended Sir Humphrey Davy's chemistry lectures at the Royal Institution, which were open to the general public, including women. Alexander Marcet tutored her in chemistry with a course of practical experiments. In 1805, she turned this chemical education to good use by publishing *Conversations on Chemistry*, a beginner's guide, which became one of the most popular scientific works of the nineteenth century. It ran to sixteen British, two French, and sixteen American editions, each new edition updated with new discoveries taking place in chemistry.

In 1816, Marcet published *Conversations on Political Economy*, an attempt to make "the dismal science" of economics accessible to a wider public. She continued her scientific popularisations with *Conversations on Natural Philosophy* [physics] (1819), *Conversations on Mineralogy* (1822) and *Conversations on Vegetable Physiology* [biology] (1829). After her husband Alexander's death, she published *Conversations on the Evidences of Christianity* (1826), which affirmed her strong religious belief. She also wrote a series of works for children on a variety of subjects ranging from history to science. She was, by any standards, a gifted teacher and populariser.

Jane Marcet's role as a woman in the developing British scientific community is of particular interest. In a period when science, though becoming more professionalised, was still largely an amateur pursuit, Jane Marcet, as an intelligent and cultivated woman, found herself able to participate fully in a milieu where scientific discussion was the breath of intellectual life. Thanks to her own education, her intellectual curiosity, her husband's encouragement, and the wealth which made the pursuit of scientific enthusiasm possible, she developed a thorough understanding of the new and complex field of chemistry. Sensitive to gender norms, she was eager to refute any suggestion that, by studying science herself or by encouraging other women to do so, she was deviating from acceptable femininity.

If her *Conversations on Chemistry* text was really aimed, as she claims, "at the female sex," what was her justification for attempting to educate women in a science? It was certainly not to turn them into scientific professionals or independent researchers. Rather, Marcet argued, scientific knowledge for women would be a source of pleasure in itself—what she described as "the impression made upon her mind by the wonders of Nature, studied in this new point of view." Second, knowledge of the intricate laws governing the composition of matter pointed in a religious direction and could be read as evidence of God's grand design. Increased knowledge of God's creation would enhance ethical understanding. Potential critics of educating women in scientific subjects would, she hoped, be disarmed by this moral argument.

As is clear from the many re-editions of *Conversations on Chemistry*, the book fulfilled a public appetite for up-to-date scientific knowledge—and not just among young ladies. Michael Faraday (1791–1867), discoverer of electromagnetic induction and one of the leading scientists of his day, wrote glowingly of the effect the *Conversations* had on him when he was a struggling bookbinder's apprentice: "Mrs. Marcet was a good friend to me as she must have been to many in the human race."[1] Jane Marcet was also admired by Mme de Staël, Edward Jenner, Maria Edgeworth (who credited information gleaned from the *Conversations* with saving a younger sister's life, after she had accidentally swallowed poison), and Sir Humphry Davy, whose discoveries she publicised. One of Marcet's most important female friendships was with Mary Somerville, whom she and Alexander Marcet met in 1816. The Marcets introduced Mary Somerville to a distinguished scientific circle and helped launch her scientific career.

Jane Marcet was fortunate in studying science at a time when the scientific community was still largely a group of amateur enthusiasts. Marcet, herself, did not challenge gender boundaries. According to Harriet Martineau she was "sensible ... unaffected ... plain ... and under the strongest conventional influences and with no pretensions to scientific knowledge." The "conventional influences" of which Martineau speaks were Marcet's devotion to her extended family and the firmness of her religious belief. For Jane Marcet, the latter was not in conflict with scientific discoveries. The crisis of faith that was so marked an issue of Victorian intellectual and religious life did not assail her. Martineau's testimony reflects the way in which Jane Marcet played down her accomplishments, while achieving an authoritative position in the scientific community as an educator and a populariser in the best sense. She was a remarkable instance of a woman who accepted the limitations of contemporary gender roles and, in important ways, transcended them. Her personal wealth, her secure marriage to a doctor/scientist, her access to the burgeoning scientific establishment in early nineteenth-century England, and especially her intellectual curiosity were all in her favour.

CONVERSATIONS ON CHEMISTRY (5TH EDITION, 1817)

Jane Marcet was one of the early and great proponents of adult education, and her instructional method in the *Conversations* was both original and pedagogically sound. The conversations take place between a Mrs. B(rian), the instructress, and two "young ladies," Caroline and Emily. It is important that the latter are imagined as enquiring and intelligent, but certainly not "bluestockings" (already a term of opprobrium). Caroline, in particular, is more interested in fashion than learning. Mrs. B. seeks to broaden their interests, first by linking chemistry to what they already imperfectly know. Chemistry will begin as the science of ordinary things. Her first example concerns bread making. As the dialogues develop, we see that Caroline is the more flighty and Emily the more serious, but they are both charmed by the discoveries Mrs. B. unveils to their astonished gaze. Though the convention of these conversations may appear contrived to present-day readers (for example Mrs. B. almost invariably extracts a "right" answer from at least one of her pupils), her teaching method, grounded on Jane Marcet's own experience with her brothers and children, illustrates the value of genuine intercommunication between teacher and taught. The *Conversations* aimed to publicise the groundbreaking work of such men as Volta, Rumford, Lavoisier (who isolated oxygen), Cavendish, Black, and Davy, hence the importance of updating her editions. (The first edition of 1805 was rapidly succeeded by newer editions, and, by 1817, the fifth edition, reproduced here, was published.) Chemistry was not just about making pills or lavender water. It was one of the newest and most exciting areas of scientific discovery.

Mrs. B. begins by disabusing her pupils of false notions: namely, the idea, dating from ancient Greece, that matter consists of four elements—earth, air, fire, and water. She reveals that these can be decomposed into their integral parts. She structures her lessons by moving from the simple to the complex and by asking her pupils at each stage to confirm that they have understood the distinctions previously made, for example, the definition of *constituent* and *integrant* parts. Finally, Mrs. B. illustrates her points with concrete demonstrations, such as showing the effects of acid on copper, as an example of chemical attraction. Although rote learning is also part of her method (Caroline and Emily are instructed, to their alarm, to memorise the list of "simple bodies" for the next lesson), her pedagogic principle is based on moving the learner from one comprehensible step to the next by means of logical and demonstrable methods. Mrs. B's pupils are shown increasingly enthralled by the new vistas of knowledge opening up to them, proof that learning for its own sake was a deeply satisfying activity.

Conversations on Chemistry in which the Elements of that Science are Familiarly Explained and Illustrated by Experiments, in two volumes (1817)

Jane Marcet

[Updated to include new applications of chemical science such as gas-lights and the miner's lamp.]

VOL. I. ON SIMPLE BODIES
PREFACE
In venturing to offer to the public, and more particularly to the female sex, an Introduction to Chemistry, the author, herself a woman, conceives that some explanation may be required; and she feels it the more necessary to apologise for the present undertaking, as her knowledge of the subject is but recent, and as she can have no real claims to the title of chemist.

On attending for the first time experimental lectures, the author found it almost impossible to derive any clear or satisfactory information from the rapid demonstrations which are usually, and perhaps necessarily, crowded into popular courses of this kind. But frequent opportunities having afterwards occurred of conversing with a friend on the subject of chemistry, and of repeating a variety of experiments, she became better acquainted with the principles of that science, and began to feel highly interested in its pursuit. It was then that she perceived, in attending the excellent lectures delivered at the Royal Institution, by the present Professor of Chemistry, the great advantage which her previous knowledge of the subject, slight as it was, gave her over others who had not enjoyed the same means of private instruction. Every fact or experiment attracted her attention, and served to explain some theory to which she was not a total stranger; and she had the gratification to find that the numerous and elegant illustrations, for which that school is so much distinguished, seldom failed to produce on her mind the effect for which the were intended.

Hence it was natural to infer, that familiar conversation was, in studies of this kind, a most useful auxiliary source of information; and more especially to the female sex, whose education is seldom calculated to prepare their minds for abstract ideas, or scientific language.

As, however, there are but few women who have access to this mode of instruction; and as the author was not acquainted with any book that could prove a substitute for it, she thought it might be useful for beginners, as well as satisfactory to herself, to trace the steps by which she had acquired her little stock of chemical knowledge, and to record, in the form of dialogue, those ideas which she had first derived from conversation.

But to do this with sufficient method, and to fix upon a mode of arrangement, was an object of some difficulty. After much hesitation, and a degree of embarrassment, which, probably, the most competent chemical writers have often felt in common with the most superficial, a mode of division was adopted, which, though the most natural, does not always admit of being strictly pursued—it is that of treating of first the simplest bodies, and then gradually rising to the most intricate compounds.

It is not the author's intention to enter into a minute vindication of this plan. But whatever may be its advantages of inconveniences, the method adopted in this work is such, that a young pupil, who should occasionally recur to it, with a view to procure information on particular subjects, might often find it obscure or unintelligible; for its various parts are so connected with each other as to form an uninterrupted chain of facts and reasonings, which will appear sufficiently clear and consistent to those only who may have patience to go through the whole work or have previously devoted some attention to the subject.

It will, no doubt, be observed, that in the course of these Conversations, remarks are often introduced, which appear much too acute for the young pupils, by whom they are supposed to be made. Of this fault the Author is fully aware. But in order to avoid it, it would have been necessary either to omit a variety of useful illustrations, or to submit such minute explanations and frequent repetitions, as would have rendered the work tedious, and therefore less suited to its intended purpose.

In writing these pages, the author was more than once checked in her progress by the apprehension that such an attempt might be considered by some, either as unsuited to the ordinary pursuits of her sex, or ill-justified by her own recent and imperfect knowledge of the subject. But, on the one hand, she felt encouraged by the establishment of those public institutions, open to both sexes, for the dissemination of philosophical knowledge, which clearly prove that the general opinion no longer excludes women from an acquaintance with the elements of science; and, on the other, she flattered herself that whilst the impression made upon her mind, by the wonders of Nature, studied in this new point of view, were still fresh and strong, she might perhaps succeed the better in communicating to others the sentiments she herself experienced.

Conversation I. On the General Principles of Chemistry

Mrs. B.

As you have now acquired some elementary notions of NATURAL PHILOSOPHY, I am going to propose to you another branch of science, to which I am particularly anxious that you should devote a share of your attention. This is CHEMISTRY, which is so closely connected with Natural Philosophy, that the study of the one must be incomplete without some knowledge of the other; for, it is obvious that we can derive but a very imperfect idea of bodies from the study of the general laws by which they are governed, if we remain totally ignorant of their intimate nature.

CAROLINE.

To confess the truth, Mrs. B., I am not disposed to form a very favourable idea of chemistry, nor do I expect to derive much entertainment from it. I prefer the sciences, which exhibit nature on a grand scale, to those that are confined to the minutiae of petty details. Can the studies which we have lately pursued, the general properties of matter, or the revolutions of the heavenly bodies, be compared to the mixing up of a few insignificant drugs? I grant, however, there may be entertaining experiments in chemistry, and should not dislike to try some of them: the distilling, for instance, of lavender, or rose water....

MRS. B.

I rather imagine, my dear Caroline, that your want of taste for chemistry proceeds from the very limited idea you entertain of its object. You confine the chemist's laboratory to the narrow precincts of the apothecary's and the perfumer's shops, whilst it is subservient to an immense variety of other useful purposes. Besides, my dear, chemistry is by no means confined to works of art. Nature also has her laboratory, which is the universe, and there she is incessantly employed in chemical operations. You are surprised, Caroline; but I assure you that the most wonderful and the most interesting phenomena of nature are almost all of them produced by chemical powers. What Bergman, in the introduction to his history of chemistry, has said of this science will give you a more just and enlarged idea of it. The knowledge of nature may be divided, he observes, into three periods. The first was that in which the attention of men was occupied in learning the external forms and characters of objects, and this is called *Natural History*. In the second, they considered the effects of bodies acting on each other by their mechanical power, as their weight and motion, and this constitutes the science of *Natural Philosophy*. The third period is that in which the properties and mutual action of the elementary parts of bodies was investigated. This last is the science of CHEMISTRY, and I have no doubt you will soon agree with me in thinking it the most interesting.

You may easily conceive, therefore, that without entering into the minute details of practical chemistry, a woman may obtain such a knowledge of the science as will not only throw an interest on the common occurrences of life, but will enlarge the sphere of her ideas, and render the contemplation of nature a source of delightful instruction.

CAROLINE.
If this is the case, I have certainly been much mistaken in the notion I had formed of chemistry. I own that I thought it was chiefly confined to the knowledge and preparation of medicines.

MRS. B.
That is only a branch of chemistry, which is called Pharmacy; and, though the study of it is certainly of great importance to the world at large, it belongs exclusively to professional men, and is therefore the last that I should advise you to pursue.

EMILY.
But, did not the chemists formerly employ themselves in search of the philosopher's stone, or the secret of making gold?

MRS. B.
These were a particular set of misguided philosophers, who dignified themselves with the name of Alchemists, to distinguish their pursuits from those of the common chemists, whose studies were confined to the knowledge of medicines.

But since that period, chemistry has undergone so complete a revolution, that, from an obscure and mysterious art, it is now become a regular and beautiful science, to which art is entirely subservient. It is true, however, that we are indebted to the alchemists for many very useful discoveries, which sprung from their fruitless attempts to make gold, and which, undoubtedly, have proved of infinitely greater advantage to mankind than all their chimerical pursuits.

The modern chemists, instead of directing their ambition to the vain attempt of producing any of the original substances in nature, rather aim at analysing and imitating her operations, and have sometimes succeeded in forming combinations, or effecting decompositions, no instances of which occur in the chemistry of Nature. They have little reason to regret their inability to make gold, whilst, by their innumerable inventions and discoveries, they have so greatly stimulated industry and facilitated labour, as prodigiously to increase the luxuries as well as the necessaries of life.

EMILY.
But, I do not understand by what means chemistry can facilitate labour; is not that rather the province of the mechanic?

MRS. B.
There are many ways by which labour may be rendered more easy, independently of mechanics; but even the machine, the most wonderful in its effects, the Steam-

engine, cannot be understood without the assistance of chemistry. In agriculture, a chemical knowledge of the nature of soils, and of vegetation, is highly useful; and, in those arts which relate to the comforts and conveniences of life, it would be endless to enumerate the advantages which result from the study of this science.

CAROLINE.
But, pray, tell us more precisely in what manner the discoveries of chemists have proved so beneficial to society?

MRS. B.
That would be an injudicious anticipation; for you would not comprehend the nature of such discoveries and useful applications, as well as you will do hereafter. Without a due regard to method, we cannot expect to make any progress in chemistry. I wish to direct your observations chiefly to the chemical operations of Nature; but those of Art are certainly of too high importance to pass unnoticed. We shall therefore allow them also some share of our attention.

EMILY.
Well, then, let us now set to work regularly. I am very anxious to begin.

MRS. B.
   The object of chemistry is to obtain a knowledge of the intimate nature of bodies, and of their mutual action on each other. You find therefore, Caroline, that this is no narrow or confined science, which comprehends every thing material within our sphere.

CAROLINE.
On the contrary, it must be inexhaustible; and I am at a loss to conceive how any proficiency can be made in a science whose objects are so numerous.

MRS. B.
If every individual substance were formed of different materials, the study of chemistry would, indeed, be endless; but you must observe that the various bodies in nature are composed of certain elementary principles, which are not very numerous.

CAROLINE.
Yes; I know that all bodies are composed of fire, air, earth, and water; I learnt that many years ago.

MRS. B.
But you must now endeavour to forget it. I have already informed you what a great change chemistry has undergone since it has become a regular science. Within these thirty years especially, it has experienced an entire revolution, and

it is now proved, that neither fire, air, earth, nor water, can be called elementary bodies. For an elementary body is one that has never been decomposed, that is to say, separated into other substances; and fire, air, earth, and water, are all of them susceptible of decomposition.

EMILY.

I thought that decomposing a body was dividing it into its minutest parts. And if so, I do not understand why an elementary substance is not capable of being decomposed, as well as any other.

MRS. B.

You have misconceived the idea of *decomposition*; it is very different from mere *division*. The latter simply reduces a body into parts, but the former separates it into the various ingredients, or materials, of which it is composed. If we were to take a loaf of bread, and separate the several ingredients of which it is made, the flour, the yeast, the salt, and the water, it would be very different from cutting or crumbling the loaf into pieces.

EMILY.

I understand you now very well. To decompose a body is to separate from each other the various elementary substances of which it consists.

CAROLINE.

But flour, water, and other materials of bread, according to our definition, are not elementary substances?

MRS. B.

No, my dear; I mentioned bread rather as a familiar comparison, to illustrate the idea, than as an example.

The elementary substances of which a body is composed are called the *constituent* parts of that body; in decomposing it, therefore, we separate its constituent parts. If, on the contrary, we divide a body by chopping it to pieces, or even by grinding or pounding it to the finest powder, each of these small particles will still consist of a portion of the several constituent parts of the whole body: these are called the *integrant* parts; do you understand the difference?

EMILY.

Yes, I think, perfectly. We *decompose* a body into its *constituent* parts; and *divide* it into its *integrant* parts.

MRS. B.

Exactly so. If therefore a body consists of only one kind of substance, though it may be divided into its integrant parts, it is not possible to decompose it. Such bodies are therefore called *simple* or *elementary*, as they are the elements of which all other bodies are composed. *Compound bodies* are such as consist of more than one of these elementary principles.

CAROLINE.
But do not fire, air, earth, and water, consist, each of them, but of one kind of substance?

MRS. B.
No, my dear; they are every one of them susceptible of being separated into various simple bodies. Instead of four, chemists now reckon upwards of forty elementary substances. The existence of most of these is established by the clearest experiments; but, in regard to a few of them, particularly the most subtle agents of nature, *heat, light,* and *electricity,* there is yet much uncertainty, and I can only give you the opinion which seems most probably deduced from the latest discoveries. After I have given you a list of the elementary bodies, classed according to their properties, we shall proceed to examine each of them separately, and then consider them in their combinations with each other.

369

Excepting the more general agents of nature, heat, light, and electricity, it would seem that the simple form of bodies is that of a metal.

CAROLINE.
You astonish me! I thought the metals were only one class of minerals, and that there were besides, earths, stones, rocks, acids, alkalies, vapours, fluids, and the whole of the animal and vegetable kingdoms.

MRS. B.
You have made a tolerably good enumeration, though I fear not arranged in the most scientific order. All these bodies, however, it is now strongly believed, may be ultimately resolved into metallic substances. Your surprise at this circumstance is not singular, as the decomposition of some of them, which has been but lately accomplished, has excited the wonder of the whole philosophical world.

But to return to the list of simple bodies—these being usually found in combination with oxygen, I shall class them according to their properties when so combined. This will, I think, facilitate their future investigation.

EMILY
Pray what is oxygen?

MRS. B.
A simple body; at least one that is supposed to be so, as it has never been decomposed. It is always found united with the negative electricity. It will be one of the first elementary bodies whose properties I shall explain to you, and, as you will soon perceive, it is one of the most important in nature; but it would be irrelevant to enter upon this subject at present. We must now confine our attention

to the enumeration and classification of the simple bodies in general. They may be arranged as follows:

CLASS I

Comprehending the imponderable agents, viz;
HEAT or CALORIC
LIGHT
ELECTRICITY.

CLASS II

Comprehending agents capable of uniting with inflammable bodies, and in most instances of effecting their combustion.
OXYGEN
CHLORINE
IODINE*

CLASS III

Comprehending bodies capable of uniting with oxygen, and forming with it various compounds. This class may be divided as follows:
DIVISION 1.
HYDROGEN, *forming* water.
DIVISION 2.
Bodies forming acids.
NITROGEN,...*forming* nitric acid.
SULPHUR,.... *forming* sulphuric acid.
PHOSPHORUS,....*forming* phosphoric acid.
CARBON,....*forming* carbonic acid.
BORACIUM,...*forming* boracic acid.
MURIATIUM,....*forming* muriatic acid.
DIVISION 3.
Metallic bodies forming alkalies.
POTASSIUM,... *forming* potash.
SODIUM,....*forming* soda.
AMMONIUM,....*forming* ammonia.
DIVISION 4.
Metallic bodies forming earths.

CALCIUM, *or metal forming* lime.
MAGNIUM,....*forming* magnesia.
BARIUM,....*forming* barytes.
STRONTIUM,....*forming* strontites.
SILICIUM,.....*forming* silex.
ALUMIUM,....*forming* alumine.

---

* It has been questioned by some eminent chemists whether these two last agents should not be classed among the inflammable bodies, as they are capable of combining with oxygen, as well as with inflammable bodies. But they seem to be more distinctly characterised by their property of supporting combustion than by any other quality. .

YTTRIUM,....*forming* yttria.
GLUCIUM,....*forming* glucina.
ZIRCONIUM,....*forming* zirconi.*

DIVISION 5.

Metals, either naturally metallic, or yielding their oxygen to carbon or to heat alone.

Subdivision 1.

Malleable Metals.

GOLD,	COPPER,
PLATINA,	IRON,
PALLADIUM,	LEAD,
SILVER†	NICKEL,
MERCURY‡	ZINC,
TIN	

Subdivision 2.

Brittle Metals.

ARSENIC,	ANTIMONY,
BISMUTH,	MANGANESE,
TELLURIUM,	URANIUM,
COBALT,	COLUMBIUM *or*
TUNGSTEN,	TANTALIUM,
MOLYBDENUM,	IRIDIUM,
TITANIUM,	OSMIUM,
CHROME,	RHODIUM.§

371

CAROLINE.

Oh, what a formidable list! You will have much to do to explain it, Mrs. B.; for I assure you it is perfectly unintelligible to me, and I think rather perplexes than assists me.

MRS. B.

Do not let that alarm you, my dear; I hope that hereafter this classification will appear quite clear, and, so far from perplexing you, will assist you in arranging your ideas. It would be in vain to attempt forming a division that would appear perfectly clear to a beginner: for you may easily conceive that a chemical division being necessarily founded on properties with which you are almost wholly

---

* Of all these earths, three or four only have as yet been distinctly decomposed.
† These first four metals have commonly been distinguished by the appellation of *perfect* or *noble* metals, on account of their possessing the characteristic properties of ductility, malleability, inalterability, and great specific gravity, in an eminent degree.
‡ Mercury, in its liquid state, cannot, of course, be called a malleable metal. But when frozen, it possesses a considerable degree of malleability.
§ These last four or five metallic bodies are placed under this class for the sake of arrangement, though some of their properties have not been yet fully investigated.

unacquainted, it is impossible that you should at once be able to understand its meaning or appreciate its utility.

But, before we proceed further, it will be necessary to give you some idea of chemical attraction, a power on which the whole science depends.

Chemical Attraction, or the *Attraction of Composition,* consists in the peculiar tendency which bodies of a different nature have to unite with each other. It is by this force that all the compositions and decompositions are effected.

EMILY.

What is the difference between chemical attraction, and the attraction of cohesion, or of aggregation, which you often mentioned to us, in former conversations?

MRS. B.

The attraction of cohesion exists only between particles of the *same* nature, whether simple of compound; thus it unites the particles of a piece of metal which is a simple substance, and likewise the particles of a loaf of bread which is a compound. The attraction of composition, on the contrary, unites and maintains, in a state of combination, particles of a *dissimilar* nature; it is this power that forms each of the compound particles of which bread consists; and it is by the attraction of cohesion that all these particles are connected into a single mass.

EMILY.

The attraction of cohesion, then, is the power which unites the integrant particles of a body: the attraction of composition that which combines the constituent particles. Is it not so?

MRS. B.

Precisely: and observe that the attraction of cohesion unites particles of a similar nature, without changing their original properties; the result of such an union, therefore, is a body of the same kind as the particles of which it is formed; whilst the attraction of composition, by combining particles of a dissimilar nature, produces compound bodies, quite different from any of their constituents. If, for instance, I pour on the piece of copper, contained in this glass, some of this liquid (which is called nitric acid), for which it has a strong attraction, every particle of the copper will combine with a particle of acid, and together they will form a new body, totally different from either the copper or the acid.

Do you observe the internal commotion that already begins to take place? It is produced by the combination of these two substances; and yet the acid has in this case to overcome not only the resistance which the strong cohesion of the particles of copper opposes to their combination with it, but also to overcome the weight of the copper, which makes it sink to the bottom of the glass, and prevents the acid from having such free access to it as it would if the metal were suspended in the liquid.

EMILY.

The acid seems, however, to overcome both these obstacles without difficulty, and appears to be very rapidly dissolving the copper.

MRS. B.

By this means it reduces the copper into more minute parts than could possibly be done by any mechanical power. But as the acid can act only on the surface of the metal, it will be some time before the union of these two bodies will be completed.

You may, however, already see how totally different this compound is from either of its ingredients. It is neither colourless, like the acid, nor hard, heavy, and yellow like the copper. If you tasted it, you would no longer perceive the sourness of the acid. It has at present the appearance of a blue liquid; but when the union is completed, and the water with which the acid is diluted is evaporated, the compound will assume the form of regular crystals, of a fine blue colour, and perfectly transparent* Of these I can shew you a specimen, as I have prepared some for that purpose.

373

CAROLINE.

How very beautiful they are, in colour, form, and transparency!

EMILY.

Nothing can be more striking than this example of chemical attraction.

MRS. B.

The term *attraction* has been lately introduced into chemistry as a substitute for the word *affinity*, to which some chemists have objected, because it originated in the vague notion that chemical combinations depended upon a certain resemblance or relationship, between particles that are disposed to unite; and this idea is not only imperfect, but most erroneous, as it is generally particles of the most dissimilar nature, that have the greatest tendency to combine.

CAROLINE.

Besides, there seems to be no advantage in using a variety of terms to express the same meaning; on the contrary it creates confusion; and as we are well acquainted with the term Attraction in natural philosophy, we had better adopt it in chemistry likewise.

MRS. B.

If you have a clear idea of the meaning, I shall leave you at liberty to express it in the terms you prefer. For myself, I confess that I think the word Attraction best suited to the general law that unites the integrant particles of bodies; and

* These crystals are more easily obtained from a mixture of sulphuric with a little nitric acid.

Affinity better adapted to that which combines the constituent particles, as it may convey an idea of the preference which some bodies have for others, which the term *attraction of composition* does not so well express.

EMILY.
So I think; for though that preference may not result from any relationship, or similitude, between the particles (as you say was once supposed), yet, as it really exists, it ought to be expressed.

MRS. B.
Well, let it be agreed that you may use the terms *affinity, chemical attraction,* and *attraction of composition,* indifferently, provided you recollect that they all have the same meaning.

374

EMILY.
I do not conceive how bodies can be decomposed by chemical attraction. That this power should be the means of composing them, is very obvious; but that it should, at the same time, produce exactly the contrary effect, appears to me very singular.

MRS. B.
To decompose a body is, you know, to separate its constituent parts, which, as we have just observed, cannot be done by mechanical means.

EMILY.
No: because mechanical means separate only the integrant particles; they act merely against the attraction of cohesion, and only divide a compound into smaller parts.

MRS. B.
The decomposition of a body is performed by chemical powers. If you present to a body composed of two principles, a third, which has a greater affinity for one of them than the two first have for each other, it will be decomposed, that is, its two principles will be separated by means of the third body. Let us call two ingredients, of which the body is composed, A and B. If we present to it another ingredient C, which has a greater affinity for B than that which unites A and B, it necessarily follows that B will quit A to combine with C. The new ingredient, therefore, has effected a decomposition of the original body A B; A has been left alone, and a new compound, B C, has been formed.

EMILY.
We might, I think, use the comparison of two friends, who were very happy in each other's society, till a third disunited them by the preference which one of them gave to the new-comer.

MRS. B.

Very well. I shall now show you how this takes place in chemistry.

Let us suppose that we wish to decompose the compound we have just formed by the combination of the two ingredients, copper and nitric acid; we may do this by presenting to it a piece of iron, for which the acid has a stronger attraction than for copper; the acid will, consequently, quit the copper to combine with the iron, and the copper will be what the chemists call *precipitated,* that is to say, it will be thrown down in its separate state, and reappear in its simple form.

In order to produce this effect, I shall dip the blade of this knife into the fluid, and, when I take it out, you will observe, that, instead of being wetted with a bluish liquid, like that contained in the glass, it will be covered with a thin coat of copper.

375

CAROLINE.

So it is really! But then is it not the copper, instead of the acid, that has combined with the iron blade?

MRS. B.

No; you are deceived by appearances: it is the acid which combines with the iron, and, in so doing, deposits or precipitates the copper on the surface of the blade.

EMILY.

But, cannot three or more substances combine together, without any of them being precipitated?

MRS. B.

That is sometimes the case; but, in general, the stronger affinity destroys the weaker; and it seldom happens that the attraction of several substances for each other is so equally balanced as to produce such complicated compounds.

CAROLINE.

But, pray, Mrs. B., what is the cause of the chemical attraction of bodies for each other? It appears to me more extraordinary or unnatural, if I may use the expression, than the attraction of cohesion, which unites particles of a similar nature.

MRS. B.

Chemical attraction may, like that of cohesion or gravitation, be one of the powers inherent in matter which, in our present state of knowledge, admits of no other satisfactory explanation than an immediate reference to a divine cause. Sir H. Davy, however, whose important discoveries have opened such improved views in chemistry, has suggested an hypothesis which may throw great light upon that science. He supposes that there are two kinds of electricity, with one or other of which all bodies are united. These we distinguish by the names of *positive* or *negative* electricity; those bodies are disposed to combine, which possess opposite electricities, as they are brought together by the attraction which these electricities have for each other. But, whether this hypothesis be altogether founded on truth or not, it is impossible to question the great influence of electricity in chemical combinations.

EMILY.
So, that we must suppose that the two electricities always attract each other, and thus compel the bodies in which they exist to combine?

CAROLINE.
And may not this be also the cause of the attraction of cohesion?

MRS. B.
No, for in particles of the same nature the same electricities must prevail, and it is only the different or opposite electric fluids that attract each other.

CAROLINE.
These electricities seem to me to be a kind of chemical spirit, which animates the particles of bodies, and draws them together.

EMILY.
If it is known, then, with which of the electricities bodies are united, it can be inferred which will, and which will not, combine together?

MRS. B.
Certainly.—I should not omit to mention, that some doubts have been entertained whether electricity be really a material agent, or whether it might not be a power inherent in bodies, similar to, or, perhaps identical with, attraction.

EMILY.
But what then would be the electric spark which is visible, and must therefore be really material?

MRS. B.
What we call the electric spark, may, Sir H. Davy says, be merely the heat and light, or fire produced by the chemical combinations with which these phenomena are always connected. We will not, however, enter more fully on this important subject at present, but reserve the principal facts which relate to it to a future conversation.

Before we part, however, I must recommend you to fix in your memory the names of the simple bodies, against our next interview.

***

CONVERSATION XXVI
ON ANIMAL HEAT

....

But all that we enjoy, whether produced by the spontaneous operations of nature, or the ingenious efforts of art, proceed alike from the goodness of Providence.— To God alone man owes the admirable faculties which enable him to improve and modify the productions of nature, no less than those productions themselves. In contemplating the works of the creation, or studying the inventions of art; let us, therefore, never forget the Divine Source from which they proceed; and thus every acquisition of knowledge will prove a lesson of piety and virtue.

377

ENDNOTE

1   Quoted in Bette Polkinghorn, *Jane Marcet: An Uncommon Woman* (Aldermaston: Forestwood Publications, 1993), 29–30.

Ada (Augusta) Byron, married name Ada King, Countess of Lovelace (1815–1852)

Ada Byron, Countess of Lovelace, is an intriguing figure both for her place in the history of mathematics and for her personal history. Born in 1815, the only child of George Gordon, Lord Byron, and Annabella Milbanke's disastrous marriage, she was, like her mother, liberally and scientifically educated. She studied history, poetry, French, Italian, Latin, Greek, philosophy, mathematics, and science. Her mother, Annabella, Lady Byron, who devoted much of her life to blackening her estranged husband's reputation, ensured that Ada's education should consist of rigorous intellectual discipline to combat her alleged inheritance of Byronic waywardness. Mathematical studies were to this end enlisted as a rational discipline to curb imaginative excess.

As the daughter of wealthy aristocrats, Ada Byron had every educational advantage. She was tutored, or advised, by some of the most respected scientists and mathematicians of the day: William King, William Frend, and Augustus de Morgan. Frend, who had also been tutor to her mother, was a political radical, although a conservative on mathematical questions. A firm rationalist, he rejected the idea of negative and imaginary numbers and symbolic algebra as irrational. De Morgan, Frend's son-in-law, on the other hand, was a proponent of symbolical algebra. He took over as Ada's mathematical tutor in 1842 and guided her through the complexities of functional equations and trigonometry. She was thrilled by the concept of imaginary numbers (a number which when squared results in a negative number, though all negative numbers when squared produce positive numbers—hence imaginary).[1] For Byron's daughter, fed on a mathematical diet that had stressed the real over the fanciful, reason over the imagination, the notion of imaginary numbers seems to have released her suppressed romanticism.

Though Ada's education was unusual in its intellectual rigour, it did not disqualify her for her assumed role in society or from marriage. In 1835, she married the Earl of Lovelace, who, proud of his wife's intellectual, and especially mathematical, attainments, encouraged her in her studies. She had, the previous year, made the acquaintance of Charles Babbage, the famous and eccentric mathematician and creator of the "Difference Engine," an arithmetical calculating machine. She was helped in her studies at this period by Mary Somerville (1780–1872), universally respected as a scientific and mathematical expositor. Unlike Mrs. Somerville, Ada Byron did not seek greater rights for women in general. As she wrote with reference to Harriet Martineau, "I lament some of her theories, and none more than her female emancipation tenets." In 1843, she published a translation and annotation of L.F. Menabrea's "Sketch of the Analytical Engine invented by Charles Babbage esq." (1840). In spite of the brilliant exposition in these "Notes," Ada's mathematical promise, noted especially by de Morgan, was never entirely fulfilled. Throughout her short adulthood, her studies were interrupted by bouts of illness and impeded by her increasing dependence on laudanum as well as her gambling mania. She died of cancer, after prolonged suffering, in 1852.

Ada's "Notes," like Babbage's unrealised plans, sank into obscurity and remained unrecognised for 100 years.[2] The computer revolution rediscovered her in the 1950s. B.V. Bowden (1953) praised her "Notes" as the first sequence of coded instructions written for a computer. Alan Turing, the code breaker at Bletchley Park, spoke of her "prophetic insight."[3] Other historians, biographers, or mathematicians have been cooler in their appreciation, notably Dorothy Stein who felt Ada's mathematical abilities had been overrated.[4] Joan Baum has sought to balance Ada's imaginative originality with the limitations of her mathematical knowledge. More general biographies have also appeared placing Ada Lovelace in the wider context of post–Romantic and early Victorian culture and focussing on her role as an unwilling pawn in the Lord and Lady Byron quarrels and scandals.[5] Her gambling and opium addictions and her early death meant that she never fully developed her undoubted scientific and mathematical potential. In this, her fate was not dissimilar to that of Babbage's Analytical Engine. Nevertheless, her place in the history of computing was recognised in 1980 when the programming language of US military systems was named after her.

NOTES ON MENABREA'S MEMOIR ON BABBAGE'S CALCULATING ENGINES (1843)

Though Ada Byron King bore three children, the "child" of whom she said she was most proud was the "Notes," which she appended to her translation of L.F. Menabrea's French version of Babbage's lectures on his Analytical Engine, given at Turin in 1840. Her translation and notes were published in Richard Taylor's *Scientific Memoirs* in 1843. They describe and analyse the potential of Babbage's Analytic Engine, a machine that, unlike the Difference Engine, was never built and existed only in Babbage's plans. In writing her "Notes," she attempted two tasks: first, to explain the superior potential of the Analytical Engine over the Difference Engine in order to gain public support for the former and, second, to describe the amazing possibilities inherent in the Analytical Engine. Here Ada ranged beyond what some critics feel was her mathematical competence to imagine new processes. The "Notes" became the first published account of what can be called a computer program, though some 100 years in advance of the technology necessary to implement it.

The extracts from "Note A," reprinted here, establish distinctions between Babbage's Difference Engine, an ingenious calculator, and the possibilities of the Analytical Engine. The salient point about the latter was its capacity to be programmed, that is to say, to act on general instructions and to be capable of responding to symbols, not numbers. Ada had understood the conception of the first computer program. We see also in "Note A," Ada expressing her metaphysical or imaginative side, so repressed by Lady Byron, in a passionate eulogy on the meaning of numbers. She saw in mathematics evidence of a grand design, a way of supporting religious faith. "Those who think on mathematical truth as the instrument through which the weak mind of man can most effectually read his Creator's work, will regard with especial interest all that can tend to facilitate the translation of its principles into explicit forms." This was a task that she believed the Analytical Engine could help to accomplish.

Reception of the "Notes" was muted. Babbage, though he quarrelled with Ada on some points, approved of "Note A" strongly. As he said in his autobiography, "Their author has entered fully into almost all the very difficult and abstract questions connected with the subject."[6] The lack of impact of Ada's mathematical work had less to do with its author, or her mathematical competence, than with the non-success of Babbage's scheme. The Analytical Engine, an idea before its technological moment, was never built.

Notes on Menabrea's *Memoir on Babbage's Calculating Engines* (1843)

Ada Byron

In studying the action of the Analytical Engine, we find that the peculiar and independent nature of the considerations which in all mathematical analysis belong to *operations*, as distinguished from *the objects operated upon* and from the *results* of the operations performed upon those objects, is very strikingly defined and separated.

It is well to draw attention to this point, not only because its full appreciation is essential to the attainment of any very just and adequate general comprehension of the powers and mode of action of the Analytical Engine, but also because it is one which is perhaps too little kept in view in the study of mathematical science in general. It is, however, impossible to confound it with other considerations, either when we trace the manner in which that engine attains its results, or when we prepare the data for its attainment of those results. It were much to be desired, that when mathematical processes pass through the human brain instead of through the medium of inanimate mechanism, it were equally a necessity of things that the reasonings connected with the *operations* should hold the same just place as a clear and well-defined branch of the subject of analysis, a fundamental but yet independent ingredient in the science, which they must do in studying the engine. The confusion, the difficulties, the contradictions which, in consequence of a want of accurate distinctions in this particular, have up to even a recent period encumbered mathematics in all those branches involving the consideration of negative and impossible quantities, will at once occur to the reader who is at all versed in this science, and would alone suffice to justify dwelling somewhat on the point, in connexion with any subject so peculiarly fitted to give forcible illustration of it as the Analytical Engine. It may be desirable to explain, that by the word *operation*, we mean *any process which alters the mutual relation of two or more things*, be this relation of what kind it may. This is the most general definition, and would include all subjects in the universe. In abstract mathematics, of course, operations alter those particular relations which are involved in the considerations of number and space, and the *results* of operations are those peculiar results which correspond to the nature of the subjects of operation. But the science of operations, as derived from mathematics more especially, is a science of itself, and has its own abstract truth and value; just as logic has its own peculiar truth and value, independently of the subjects to which we may apply its reasonings and processes. Those who are accustomed to some of the more modern views of the above subject, will know that a few fundamental relations being true, certain other combinations of relations must of necessity follow; combinations unlimited in variety and extent if the deductions from the primary relations be carried on far enough. They will also be aware that one main reason why the separate nature of the science of operations has been little felt, and in general little dwelt on, is the *shifting* meaning of many of the symbols used in mathematical notation. First, the symbols of *operation* are frequently *also* the symbols of the results of operations. We may say that these symbols are apt to have both a *retrospective* and a *prospective* signification. They may signify either relations that are the consequences of a series of processes already performed, or relations that are yet to be effected through certain processes. Secondly, figures, the symbols of *numerical magnitude*, are frequently *also* the symbols of *operations*, as when they are the indices of powers. Wherever terms have a shifting meaning, independent sets of considerations are liable to become complicated together, and reasonings and results are frequently falsified. Now in the Analytical Engine, the operations which come under the first of the above heads are ordered and combined by means of a notation and of a train of mechanism which belong exclusively to themselves; and with respect to the second head, whenever numbers meaning *operations* and not *quantities* (such as the indices of powers) are inscribed on any column or set of columns, those columns immediately act in a wholly separate and independent manner, becoming connected with the *operating mechanism* exclusively, and re-acting upon this. They never come into combination with numbers upon any other columns meaning *quantities*; though, of course, if there are numbers meaning *operations* upon *n* columns, these may *combine amongst each other*, and will often be required to do so, just as numbers meaning *quantities* combine with each other in any variety. It might have been arranged that all numbers meaning *operations* should have appeared on some separate portion of the engine from that which presents numerical *quantities*; but the present mode is in some cases more simple, and offers in reality quite as much distinctness when understood.

The operating mechanism can even be thrown into action independently of any object to operate upon (although of course no *result* could then be developed). Again, it might act upon other things besides *number*, were objects found whose mutual fundamental relations could be expressed by those of the abstract science of operations, and which should also be susceptible of adaptations to the action of the operating notation and mechanism of the engine. Supposing, for instance, that the fundamental relations of pitched sounds in the science of harmony and of musical composition were susceptible of such expression and adaptations, the engine might compose elaborate and scientific pieces of music of any degree of complexity or extent.

The Analytical Engine is an *embodying of the science of operations*, constructed with peculiar reference to abstract number as the subject of those operations. The Difference Engine is the embodying of *one particular and very limited set of operations*, which may be expressed thus (+, +, +, +, +, +), or thus, 6 (+). Six repetitions of the one operation, +, is, in fact, the whole sum and object of that engine. It has seven columns, and a number on any column can add itself to a number on the next column to its *right-hand*. So that, beginning with the column furthest to the left, six additions can be effected, and the result appears on the seventh column, which is the last on the right-hand. The *operating* mechanism of this engine acts in as separate and independent a manner as that of the Analytical Engine; but being susceptible of only one unvarying and restricted combination, it has little force or interest in illustration of the distinct nature of the *science of operations*. The importance of regarding the Analytical Engine under this point of view will, we think, become more and more obvious as the reader proceeds with M. Menabrea's clear and masterly article. The calculus of operations is likewise in itself a topic of so much interest, and has of late years been so much more written on and thought on than formerly, that any bearing which that engine, from its mode of constitution, may possess upon the illustration of this branch of mathematical science should not be overlooked. Whether the inventor of this engine had any such views in his mind while working out the invention, or whether he may subsequently ever have regarded it under this phase, we do not know; but it is one that forcibly occurred to ourselves on becoming acquainted with the means through which analytical combinations are actually attained by the mechanism. We cannot forbear suggesting one practical result, which it appears to us, must be greatly facilitated by the independent manner in which the engine orders and combines its *operations:* we allude to the attainment of those combinations into which *imaginary quantities* enter. This is a branch of its processes into which we have not had the opportunity of inquiring, and our conjecture therefore as to the principle on which we conceive the accomplishment of such results may have been made to depend, is very probably not in accordance with the fact, and less subservient for the purpose than some other principles, or at least requiring the co-operation of others. It seems to us obvious, however, that where operations are so independent in their mode of acting, it must be easy, by means of a few simple provisions, and additions in arranging the mechanism, to bring out a *double* set of *results*, viz.—1st, the *numerical magnitudes* which are the results of operations performed on *numerical data*. (These results are the *primary* object of the engine.) 2ndly, the *symbolical results* to be attached to those numerical results, which symbolical results are not less the necessary and logical consequences of operations performed upon *symbolical data*, than are numerical results when the data are numerical.*

If we compare together the powers and the principles of construction of the Difference and of the Analytical Engines, we shall perceive that the capabilities

383

---

* In fact, such an extension as we allude to would merely constitute a further and more perfected development of any system introduced for making the proper combinations of the signs *plus* and *minus*. How ably M. Menabrea has touched on this restricted case is pointed out in Note B.

of the latter are immeasurably more extensive than those of the former, and that they in fact hold to each other the same relationship as that of analysis to arithmetic. The Difference Engine can in reality (as has been already partly explained) do nothing but *add*; and any other processes, not excepting those of simple subtraction, multiplication, and division, can be performed by it only just to that extent in which it is possible, by judicious mathematical arrangement and artifices, to reduce them to a series of additions. The method of differences is, in fact, a method of additions; and as it includes within its means a larger number of results attainable by *addition* simply, than any other mathematical principle, it was very appropriately selected as the basis on which to construct *an Adding Machine*, so as to give the powers of such a machine the widest possible range. The Analytical Engine, on the contrary, can either add, subtract, multiply or divide with equal facility; and performs each of these four operations in a direct manner, without the aid of any of the other three. This one fact implies everything; and it is scarcely necessary to point out, for instance, that while the Difference Engine can merely *tabulate,* and is incapable of *developing,* The Analytical Engine can *either tabulate or develop.*

The former engine is in its nature strictly *arithmetical,* and the results it can arrive at lie within a very clearly defined and restricted range, while there is no finite line of demarcation which limits the powers of the Analytical Engine. These powers are co-extensive with our knowledge of the laws of analysis itself, and need be bounded only by our acquaintance with the latter. Indeed we may consider the engine as the *material and mechanical representative* of analysis, and that our actual working powers in this department of human study will be enabled more effectually than heretofore to keep pace with our theoretical knowledge of its principles and laws, through the complete control which the engine gives us over the *executive manipulation* of algebraical and numerical symbols.

Those who view mathematical science, not merely as a vast body of abstract and immutable truths, whose intrinsic beauty, symmetry and logical completeness, when regarded in their connexion together as a whole, entitle them to a prominent place in the interest of all profound and logical minds, but as possessing a yet deeper interest for the human race, when it is remembered that this science constitutes the language through which alone we can adequately express the great facts of the natural world, and those unceasing changes of mutual relationship which, visibly or invisibly, consciously or unconsciously to our immediate physical perceptions, are interminably going on in the agencies of the creation we live amidst: those who thus think on mathematical truth as the instrument through which the weak mind of man can most effectually read his Creator's works, will regard with especial interest all that can tend to facilitate the translation of its principles into explicit practical forms.

The distinctive characteristic of the Analytical Engine, and that which has rendered it possible to endow mechanism with such extensive faculties as bid fair to make this engine the executive right-hand of abstract algebra, is the introduction into it of the principle which Jacquard devised for regulating, by means of punched cards, the most complicated patterns in the fabrication of brocaded stuffs. It is in this that the distinction between the two engines lies. Nothing of the sort exists in the Difference Engine. We may say most aptly, that the Analytical Engine *weaves algebraical patterns* just as the Jacquard-loom weaves flowers and leaves. Here, it seems to us, resides much more of originality than the Difference Engine can be fairly entitled to claim. We do no wish to deny to this latter all such claims. We believe that it is the only proposal or attempt ever made to construct a calculating machine *founded on the principle of successive orders of differences,* and capable of *printing off its own results*; and that this engine surpasses its predecessors, both in the extent of the calculations which it can perform, in the facility, certainty, and accuracy with which it can effect them, and in the absence of all necessity for the intervention of human intelligence *during the performance of its calculations.* Its nature is, however, limited to the strictly arithmetical, and it is far from being the first or only scheme for constructing *arithmetical* calculating machines with more or less of success.

385

The bounds of *arithmetic* were however outstepped the moment the idea of applying the cards had occurred; and the Analytical Engine does not occupy common ground with mere "calculating machines." It holds a position wholly its own; and the considerations it suggests are most interesting in their nature. In enabling mechanism to combine together *general* symbols in successions of unlimited variety and extent, a uniting link is established between the operations of matter and the abstract mental processes of the *most abstract* branch of mathematical science. A new, a vast, and a powerful language is developed for the future use of analysis, in which to wield its truths so that these may become of more speedy and accurate practical application for the purposes of mankind than the means hitherto in our possession have rendered possible. Thus not only the mental and the material, but the theoretical and the practical in the mathematical world, are brought into more intimate and effective connexion with each other. We are not aware of its being on record that anything partaking in the nature of what is so well designated the *Analytical* Engine has been hitherto proposed, or even thought of, as a practical possibility, any more than the idea of a thinking or of a reasoning machine.

We will touch on another point which constitutes an important distinction in the modes of operating of the Difference and Analytical Engines. In order to enable the former to do its business, it is necessary to put into its columns the series of numbers constituting the first terms of the several orders of differences for whatever is the particular table under consideration. The machine then works *upon* these as its data. But these data must themselves have been already computed through a series of calculations by a human head. Therefore that engine can only produce results depending on data which have been arrived at by the explicit and actual working out of processes that are in their nature different from any that come within the sphere of its own powers. In other words, an *analysing* process must have been gone through by the human mind in order to obtain the data upon which the engine then *synthetically* builds its results. The

Difference Engine is in its character exclusively *synthetical*, while the Analytical Engine is equally capable of analysis or of synthesis.

It is true that the Difference Engine can calculate to a much greater extent with these few preliminary data, than the data themselves required for their own determination. The table of squares, for instance, can be calculated to any extent whatever, when the numbers *one* and *two* are furnished; and a very few differences computed at any part of a table of logarithms would enable the engine to calculate many hundreds or even thousands of logarithms. Still the circumstance of its requiring, as a previous condition, that any function whatever shall have been numerically worked out, makes it very inferior in its nature and advantages to an engine which, like the Analytical Engine, requires merely that we should know the *succession and distribution of the operations to be performed;* without there being any occasion, in order to obtain data on which it can work, for our ever having gone through either the same particular operations which it is itself to effect, or any others. Numerical data must of course be given it, but they are mere arbitrary ones; not data that could only be arrived at through a systematic and necessary series of previous numerical calculations, which is quite a different thing.

To this it may be replied, that an analysing process must equally have been performed in order to furnish the Analytical Engine with the necessary *operative* data; and that herein may also lie a possible source of error. Granted that the actual mechanism is unerring in its processes, the *cards* may give it the wrong orders. This is unquestionably the case; but there is much less chance of error, and likewise far less expenditure of time and labour, where operations only, and the distribution of these operations, have to be made out, than where explicit numerical results are to be attained. In the case of the Analytical Engine we have undoubtedly to lay out a certain capital of analytical labour in one particular line; but this is in order that the engine may bring us in a much larger return in another line. It should be remembered also that the cards, when once made out for any formula, have all the generality of algebra, and include an infinite number of particular cases.

We have dwelt considerably on the distinctive peculiarities of each of these engines, because we think it essential to place their respective attributes in strong relief before the apprehension of the public; and to define with clearness and accuracy the wholly different nature of the principles on which each is based, so as to make it self-evident to the reader (the mathematical reader at least) in what manner and degree the powers of the Analytical Engine transcend those of an engine, which, like the Difference Engine can only work out such results as may be derived from *one restricted and particular series of processes.* We think this of importance because we know that there exists considerable vagueness and inaccuracy in the mind of persons in general on the subject. There is a misty notion amongst most of those who have attended at all to it that *two* "calculating machines" have been successively invented by the same person within the last few years; while others again have never heard but of the one original "calculating machine," and are not aware of there being any extension upon this. For either of these two classes of persons the above considerations are appropriate. While the latter require a knowledge of the fact that there *are two* such inventions, the former are not less in want of accurate and well-defined information on the subject. No very clear or correct ideas prevail as to the characteristics of each engine, or their respective advantages or disadvantages; and in meeting with those incidental allusions, of a more or less direct kind, which occur in so many publications of the day, to these machines, it must frequently be a matter of doubt *which* "*calculating* machine" is referred to, or whether *both* are included in the general allusion.

We are desirous likewise of removing two misapprehensions which we know obtain, to some extent, respecting these engines. In the first place it is very generally supposed that the Difference Engine, after it had been completed up to a certain point, *suggested* the idea of the Analytical Engine; and that the second is in fact the improved offspring of the first, and *grew out* of the existence of its predecessor, through some natural or else accidental combination of ideas suggested by this one. Such a supposition is in this instance contrary to the facts; although it seems to be almost an obvious inference, wherever two inventions, similar in their nature and objects, succeed each other closely in order of *time*, and strikingly in order of *value*; more especially when the same individual is the author of both. Nevertheless the ideas which led to the Analytical Engine occurred in a manner wholly independent of any that were connected with the Difference Engine. These ideas are indeed in their own intrinsic nature independent of the latter engine, and might equally have occurred had it never existed nor been thought of at all.

387

The second of the misapprehensions above alluded to relates to the well-known suspension, during some years past, of all progress in the construction of the Difference Engine. Respecting the circumstances which have interfered with the actual completion of either invention, we offer no opinion; and in fact are not possessed of the data for doing so, had we the inclination. But we know that some persons suppose these obstacles (be they what they may) to have arisen *in consequence* of the subsequent invention of the Analytical Engine while the former was in progress. We have ourselves heard it even *lamented* that an idea should ever have occurred at all, which had turned out to be merely the means of arresting what was already in a course of successful execution, without substituting the superior invention in its stead. This notion we can contradict in the most unqualified manner. The progress of the Difference Engine had long been suspended, before there were even the least crude glimmerings of any invention superior to it. Such glimmerings, therefore, and their subsequent development, were in no way the original *cause* of that suspension; although, where difficulties of some kind or other evidently already existed, it was not perhaps calculated to remove or lessen them that an invention should have been meanwhile thought of which, while including all that the first was capable of, possesses powers so extended as to eclipse it altogether.

We leave it for the decision of each individual (*after he has possessed himself* of competent information as to the characteristics of each engine) to determine how far it ought to be a matter of regret that such an accession has been made to the powers of human science, even if it *has* (which we greatly doubt) increased to a certain limited extent some already existing difficulties that had arisen in the way of completing a valuable but lesser work. We leave it for each to satisfy himself as to the wisdom of desiring the obliteration (were that now possible) of all records of the more perfect invention, in order that the comparatively limited one might be finished. The Difference Engine would doubtless fulfil all those practical objects which it was originally destined for. It would certainly calculate all the tables that are more directly necessary for the physical purposes of life, such as nautical and other computations. Those who incline to very strictly utilitarian views may perhaps feel that the peculiar powers of the Analytical Engine bear upon questions of abstract and speculative science, rather than upon those involving every-day and ordinary human interests. These persons being likely to possess but little sympathy, or possibly acquaintance, with any branches of science which they do not find to be *useful* (according to *their* definition of that word), may conceive that the undertaking of that engine, now that the other one is already in progress, would be a barren and unproductive laying out of yet more money and labour; in fact, a work of supererogation. Even in the utilitarian aspect, however, we do not doubt that very valuable practical results would be developed by the extended faculties of the Analytical Engine; some of which results we think we could now hint at, had we the space; and others, which it may not yet be possible to foresee, but which would be brought forth by the daily increasing requirements of science, and by a more intimate practical acquaintance with the powers of the engine, were it in actual existence.

On general grounds, both of an *a priori* description as well as those founded on the scientific history and experience of mankind, we see strong presumptions that such would be the case. Nevertheless all will probably concur in feeling that the completion of the Difference Engine would be far preferable to the non-completion of any calculating engine at all. With whomsoever or wheresoever may rest the present causes of difficulty that apparently exist towards either the completion of the old engine, or the commencement of the new one, we trust they will not ultimately result in this generation's being acquainted with these inventions through the medium of pen, ink and paper merely; and still more do we hope, that for the honour of our country's reputation in the future pages of history, these causes will not lead to the completion of the undertaking by some *other* nation or government. This could not but be a matter of just regret; and equally so, whether the obstacles may have originated in private interests and feelings, in considerations of a more public description, or in causes combining the nature of both such solutions.

We refer the reader to the "Edinburgh Review" of July 1834, for a very able account of the Difference Engine. The writer of the article we allude to has selected as his prominent matter for exposition a wholly different view of the subject from that which M. Menabrea has chosen. The former chiefly treats it under its mechanical aspect, entering but slightly into the mathematical principles of which that engine is the representative, but giving, in considerable length, many details of the mechanism and contrivances by means of which it tabulates the various orders of differences. M. Menabrea, on the contrary, exclusively develops the analytical view; taking it for granted that mechanism is able to perform certain processes, but without attempting to explain *how*; and devoting his whole attention to explanations and illustrations of the manner in which analytical laws can be so arranged and combined as to bring every branch of that vast subject within the grasp of the assumed powers of mechanism. It is obvious that, in the invention of a calculating engine, these two branches of the subject are equally essential fields of investigation, and that on their mutual adjustment, one to the other, must depend all success. They must be made to meet each other, so that the weak points in the powers of either department may be compensated by the strong points in those of the other. They are indissolubly connected, though so different in their intrinsic nature, that perhaps the same mind might not be likely to prove equally profound or successful in both. We know those who doubt whether the powers of mechanism will in practice prove adequate in all respects to the demands made upon them in the working of such complicated trains of machinery as those of the above engines, and who apprehend that unforeseen practical difficulties and disturbances will arise in the way of accuracy and of facility of operation. The Difference Engine, however, appears to us to be in a great measure an answer to these doubts. It is complete as far as it goes, and it does work with all the anticipated success. The Analytical Engine, far from being more complicated, will in many respects be of simpler construction; and it is a remarkable circumstance attending it, that with very *simplified* means it is so much more powerful.

A.A.L.

389

ENDNOTES

1   We are most grateful to Professor Lockwood Morris for his help on the mathematical issues arising from Ada Byron's work and especially for his exposition of imaginary numbers.

2   For analyses of Ada Byron's "Notes," see Philip Morrison and Emily Morrison, *Charles Babbage and his Calculating Engines* (New York: Dover Publications, 1961); Velma R. Huskey and Harry D. Huskey, "Lady Lovelace and Charles Babbage," *Annals of the History of Computing* 2, no. 4 (1980): 299–327; Judith S. Lewis, "Princess of Parallelograms and Her Daughter: Math and Gender in the Nineteenth Century English Aristocracy," *Women's Studies International Forum* 18, no. 4 (1995): 387–94.

3   Quoted in Joan Baum, *The Calculating Passion of Ada Byron* (Hamden, CT: Shoestring Press, 1986), 1.

4   Dorothy Stein, *Ada, A Life and Legacy* (Cambridge, MA: MIT Press, 1985).

5   Doris Lagley Moore, *Ada, Countess of Lovelace: Byron's Legitimate Daughter* (London: John Murray, 1977); Benjamin Woolley, *The Bride of Science: Romance, Reason and Byron's daughter* (London: Pan, 2000).

6   Charles Babbage, *Passages from the Life of a Philosopher* (London: Longmans, 1864), quoted in Philip and Emily Morrison, *Charles Babbage and His Calculating Engine* (New York: Dover Publications, 1961), 68.

Mary Fairfax Somerville (1780–1872)

Mary Somerville, writer and polymath, enjoyed an authoritative position in the intellectual and scientific circles of her age. The daughter of Vice-Admiral Sir William George Fairfax and Margaret Charters, she grew up at Burntisland, on the Firth of Forth, opposite Edinburgh. Neither parent was particularly well educated or interested in book learning. Apart from a deeply unhappy year from ten to eleven when Mary was sent to a fashionable academy for young ladies at Musselburgh, her childhood was remarkably unconstrained. She was left free to explore the shore and meadows near her parents' home; her formal education was sketchy. Nevertheless, she early demonstrated hunger for serious instruction, though discouraged by her father and mother, who saw no need for girls to learn anything beyond household management. In her *Personal Recollections*, Mary commented, "I thought it unjust that women should have been given a desire for knowledge if it were wrong to acquire it." She read Hester Chapone's *Letters on the Improvement of the Mind*, which further motivated her to study, even though Mrs. Chapone cautioned that women "should not be remarkable for learning."[1]

Mary Somerfield's daughter wrote of these early educational struggles:

> Few thoughtful minds will read without emotion my mother's own account of the wonderful energy and indomitable perseverance by which, in her ardent thirst for knowledge, she overcame obstacles apparently insurmountable, at a time when women were well-nigh totally debarred from education: and the almost intuitive way in which she entered upon studies of which she had scarcely heard the names.[2]

Her extraordinary mathematical bent revealed itself in her teens by an accidental encounter with an algebraic puzzle in a ladies' magazine. Thereafter, she manoeuvred to gain access to appropriate mathematical texts, teaching herself from John Bonnycastle's *Introduction to Algebra* (London, J. Johnson, 1796) and Euclid's *Elements of Geometry*. Her parents, fearing the possible effects of over-intellection for the female brain, encouraged her to pursue lady-like accomplishments (the piano, painting, and needlework). She was enabled to study Latin with a sympathetic uncle, Dr. Somerville, minister of Jedburgh. She also taught herself Greek and French, though she never felt herself fluent in modern languages.

Mary Fairfax married twice; first, in 1804, she wed a cousin, Sir Samuel Grieg, by whom she had two sons. The couple moved to London, and, while her husband did not prevent her from pursuing her studies, "he had," as Mary Somerville later commented, "a very low opinion of the capacity of my sex, and had neither knowledge of, nor interest in, science of any kind."[3] Grieg's death after three years of marriage left Mary with two small children but a good income. On returning to Edinburgh, she put her new-found financial and social independence to use by pursing her studies with renewed zeal, meeting with eminent Edinburgh intellectuals, who soon recognised her remarkable mathematical gifts.

In 1812, she married another cousin, Dr. William Somerville, a man of liberal views and scientific interests who fully supported Mary's intellectual ambitions. The couple moved to London in 1816, where they joined a growing circle of scientific amateurs and intellectuals. Mary's social skills, her gentle birth, and her remarkable abilities opened the scientific community to her. She met and was a friend of some of the major scientists and politicians of the day: Brougham, Melbourne, the Herschels, Lyell, and Whewell. In 1826, she presented a paper on "The Magnetic Properties of the Violet Rays of the Solar Spectrum" to the Royal Society, which attracted great interest.

In 1827, Mary Somerville was requested by Lord Brougham to write an account of Laplace's five-volume *Mécanique céleste* (1799–1825) for the Society for the Diffusion of Useful Knowledge. Brougham asserted that she was the only person in Britain qualified to do so, a remarkable claim about a woman who was entirely self-taught in mathematics. *The Mechanism of the Heavens*, which she published in 1831, was praised by such mathematical luminaries as Sir John Herschel and Dr. William Whewell, later Master of Trinity College, Cambridge. Following its publication, she visited France and Switzerland where she was welcomed by the principal savants. In 1834, she published her first work of scientific synthesis, *On the Connexion of the Physical Sciences*. It enjoyed immediate commercial and scholarly success. In 1838, the Somervilles moved permanently to Italy. Aside from providing new, updated editions of the *Connexion*, Mary subsequently published *Physical Geography* (1848) and *On Molecular and Microscopic Science* (1869). Her studies and expertise extended from the macrocosm to the microcosm.

Mary Somerville never forgot her own early struggles for learning. Throughout her career, she was active in promoting women's education and political rights. She greatly admired John Stuart Mill, praising his *On the Subjection of Women*: "The British laws are adverse to women; and we are deeply indebted to Mr. John Stuart Mill for daring to show their iniquity and injustice." She signed Mill's 1868 petition to Parliament for the extension of the suffrage to women.[4] In her memoirs, Mary Somerville, who rarely vaunted her accomplishments, took great pride in her commitment to feminism: "Age has not abated my zeal for the emancipation of my sex from the unreasonable prejudice too prevalent in Great Britain against a literary and scientific education for women."[5]

Many other honours came her way as she received national and international recognition for her work. She was elected an honorary member of the Royal

Astronomical Society, the Royal Academy, Dublin, and of a number of continental societies. Nevertheless, as a woman, she could not hold an academic post nor become a full member of the Royal Society. Though Mary Somerville succeeded in her intellectual ambitions, she knew that her extraordinary capacities might easily have been thwarted. Her commitment to women's higher education was commemorated when Somerville Hall, later Somerville College, Oxford, was named after her in 1876. At her death on 29 November 1872, she left her scientific library to Girton College, Cambridge (then the Ladies College at Hitchin).

The religious crisis that marked so much of the Victorian period does not seem to have affected Mary Somerville. Though she retained her early faith in a beneficent deity, she accepted the findings of geology that the earth was very much older than suggested by the creation stories of the Bible; yet, in her view, there was no contradiction between science and religion. In old age, she remained as enamoured of the beauty of the visible world as she had been as a child at Burntisland and convinced that the invisible but beautiful laws that regulated the heavens and earth were all part of a divine order.

ON THE CONNEXION OF THE PHYSICAL SCIENCES (1834)

The passages reproduced below (the Introduction, parts of Section I, Section XXXVII, and the Conclusion) illustrate central themes of Mary Somerville's thought. Two principal concerns emerge here: the first, relating to the audience for and purpose of her work, is her aim to make scientific discoveries comprehensible to an intellectual community that includes women, and the second is her portrait of the sciences, which stresses their interrelatedness as mirroring the coherence of a universe controlled by God under natural law.

Somerville speaks in her dedication to Queen Victoria of "my endeavour to make the laws by which the material world is governed more familiar to my countrywomen." Clearly, the book was aimed at men as well as women, but that she emphasised a female audience reflects both her feminism and the purpose of her scientific writing. She was not a popularising writer in the sense of Jane Marcet and Pricilla Wakefield, but she made accessible the newest scientific ideas of her age to a wide educated audience. Scientific discoveries require a level of expertise not available to all, she argues, but scientific knowledge can be widely understood and shared. She assumes an intimate connection between the pursuit of advanced knowledge and moral improvement. In this, she resembles many Enlightenment and post–Enlightenment thinkers. Her quotation from Sir James Mackintosh, with which she opens the Introduction, declares that the "object of all study ... is to inspire the love of truth, of wisdom, or beauty,—especially of goodness, the highest beauty."

The discussion on gravity focuses on Newton and Kepler, whose theories form the core of Section I. Gravity, she demonstrates, is not just a force; it is a principle operating throughout the known universe. She evokes powerfully the vastness of a cosmos of which human beings form an infinitesimal part. "... not only man, but the globe he inhabits,—nay, the whole system of which it forms so small a part,—might be annihilated, and its extinction be unperceived in the immensity of creation."

Gravitation, the law governing celestial and terrestrial objects, she argues, "must have been selected by Divine Wisdom out of an infinity of others, as being the most simple, and that which gives the greatest stability to the celestial motions." God is everywhere present in Somerville's universe. While celebrating the scientific knowledge attained in her own day, she recognises that human knowledge is always partial, but that science looks for the most universal, elegant, and all embracing solutions. "Perhaps the day may come, when even gravitation, no longer regarded as an ultimate principle, may be resolved into a yet more general cause, embracing every law that regulates the material world."

On the Connexion of the Physical Sciences (1834)

Mary Fairfax Somerville

DEDICATION TO THE QUEEN, 1 JANUARY 1834

If I have succeeded in my endeavour to make the laws by which the material world is governed more familiar to my countrywomen, I shall have the gratification of thinking that the gracious permission to dedicate my book to your Majesty has not been misplaced.

INTRODUCTION

Science, regarded as the pursuit of truth, must ever afford occupation of consummate interest, and subject of elevated meditation. The contemplation of the works of creation elevates the mind to the admiration of whatever is great and noble; accomplishing the object of all study,—which, in the elegant language of Sir James Mackintosh, "is to inspire the love of truth, of wisdom, or beauty,—especially of goodness, the highest beauty,—and of that supreme and eternal Mind, which contains all truth and wisdom, all beauty and goodness. By the love or delightful contemplation and pursuit of these transcendent aims, for their own sake only, the mind of man is raised from low and perishable objects, and prepared for those high destinies which are appointed for all those who are capable of them."

In tracing the connection of the physical sciences, astronomy affords the most extensive example of their union. In it are combined the sciences of number and quantity, of rest and motion. In it we perceive the operation of a force which is mixed up with everything that exists in the heavens or on earth; which pervades every atom, rules the motions of animate and inanimate beings, and is as sensible in the descent of a rain drop as in the falls of Niagara, in the weight of the air as in the periods of the moon. Gravitation not only binds satellites to their planet, and planets to the sun, but it connects sun with sun throughout the wide extent of creation, and is the cause of the disturbances, as well as of the order, of nature: since every tremour it excites in any one planet is immediately transmitted to the farthest limits of the system, in oscillations, which correspond in their periods with the cause producing them, like sympathetic notes in music, or vibrations from the deep tones of an organ.

The heavens afford the most sublime subject of study which can be derived from science. The magnitude and splendour of the objects, the inconceivable rapidity with which they move, and the enormous distances between them, impress the mind with some notion of the energy that maintains them in their motions, with a durability to which we can see no limit. Equally conspicuous is the goodness of the great First Cause, in having endowed man with faculties, by which he can not only appreciate the magnificence of his works, but trace, with precision, the operation of his laws, use the globe he inhabits as a base wherewith to measure the magnitude and distance of the sun and planets, and make the diameter of the earth's orbit the first step of a scale by which he may ascend to the starry firmament. Such pursuits, while they ennoble the mind, at the same time inculcate humility, by showing that there is a barrier which no energy, mental or physical, can ever enable us to pass: that, however profoundly we may penetrate the depths of space, there still remain innumerable systems, compared with which, those apparently so vast must dwindle into insignificance, or even become invisible; and that not only man, but the globe he inhabits,—nay, the whole system of which it forms so small a part,—might be annihilated, and its extinction be unperceived in the immensity of creation.

396

It must be acknowledged, that a complete acquaintance with physical astronomy can be attained by those only, who are well versed in the higher branches of the mathematical and mechanical science, and that they alone can appreciate the extreme beauty of the results, and of the means by which these results are obtained. It is nevertheless true, that a sufficient skill in analysis to follow the general outline,—to see the mutual dependence of the different parts of the system, and to comprehend by what means some of the most extraordinary conclusions have been arrived at,—is within the reach of many who shrink from the task, appalled by difficulties, which, perhaps, are not more formidable than those incident to the study of the elements of every branch of knowledge. There is a wide distinction between the degree of mathematical acquirement necessary for making discoveries, and that which is requisite for understanding what others have done.

All the knowledge we possess of external objects is founded upon experience, which furnishes facts; and the comparison of these facts establishes relations, from which induction, that is to say, the belief that like causes will produce like effects, leads to general laws. Thus, experience teaches that bodies fall at the surface of the earth with an accelerated velocity, and with a force proportional to their masses. By comparison, Newton proved that the force which occasions the fall of bodies at the earth's surface, is identical with that which retains the moon in her orbit; and induction led him to conclude, that as the moon is kept in her orbit by the attraction of the earth, so the planets might be retained in their orbits by the attraction of the sun. By such steps he was led to the discovery of one of those powers, with which the Creator has ordained, that matter should reciprocally act upon matter.

Physical astronomy is the science which compares and identifies the laws of motion observed on earth, with the motions that take place in the heavens; and which traces, by an uninterrupted chain of deduction from the great principle that governs the universe, the revolutions and rotations of the planets, and the oscillations of the fluids at their surfaces; and which estimates the changes the system has hitherto undergone, or may hereafter experience,—changes which require millions of years for their accomplishment.

The accumulated efforts of astronomers, from the earliest dawn of civilisation, have been necessary to establish the mechanical theory of astronomy. The courses of the planets have been observed for ages, with a degree of perseverance that is astonishing, if we consider the imperfection and even the want of instruments. The real motions of the earth have been separated from the apparent motions of the planets; the laws of the planetary revolutions have been discovered; and the discovery of these laws has led to the knowledge of the gravitation of matter. On the other hand, descending from the principle of gravitation, every motion in the solar system has been so completely explained, that the laws of any astronomical phenomena that may hereafter occur, are already determined.

Section I

It has been proved by Newton, that a particle of matter, placed without the surface of a hollow sphere, is attracted by it in the same manner as if the mass of the hollow sphere, or the whole matter it contains, were collected into one dense particle in its centre. The same is therefore true of a solid sphere, which may be supposed to consist, of an infinite number of concentric hollow spheres. This, however, is not the case with a spheroid; but the celestial bodies are so nearly spherical, and at such remote distances from one another, that they attract and are attracted as if each were condensed into a single particle situate in its centre of gravity,—a circumstance which greatly facilitates the investigation of their motions.

Newton has shown that the force which retains the moon in her orbit, is the same with that, which causes heavy substances to fall at the surface of the earth. If the earth were a sphere, and at rest, a body would be equally attracted, that is, it would have the same weight at every point of its surface, because the surface of a sphere is every where equally distant from its centre. But as our planet is flattened at the poles, and bulges at the equator, the weight of the same body gradually decreases from the poles, where it is greatest, to the equator, where it is least. There is, however, a certain latitude where the attraction of the earth on bodies at its surface, is the same as if it were a sphere; and experience shows that bodies there fall through 16.0697 feet in a second. The mean distance of the moon from earth is about sixty times the radius of the earth. When the number of 16.0697 is diminished in the ratio of 1 to 3600, which is the square of the moon's distance from the earth's centre, estimated in terrestrial radii, it is found to be exactly the space the moon would fall through, in the first second of her descent to earth, were she not prevented by the centrifugal force arising from the velocity with which she moves in her orbit. The moon is thus retained in her orbit by a force having the same origin, and regulated by the same law, with that which causes a stone to fall at the earth's surface. The earth may therefore be regarded as the centre of a force which extends to the moon; and, as experience shows that the action and re-action of matter are equal and contrary, the moon must attract the earth with an equal and contrary force.

Newton also ascertained that a body projected in space, will move in a conic section, if attracted by a force proceeding from a fixed point, with an intensity inversely as the square of the distance; but that any deviation from that law will cause it to move in a curve of a different nature. Kepler found, by direct observation, that the planets describe ellipses, or oval paths, round the sun. Later observations show that comets also move in conic sections. It consequently follows, that the sun attracts all the planets and comets inversely as the square of their distances from his centre; the sun, therefore, is the centre of a force extending indefinitely in space, and including all the bodies of the system in its action.

Kepler also deduced from observation, that the squares of the periodic times of the planets, or the times of their revolutions round the sun, are proportional to the cubes of their mean distances from his centre. Hence the intensity of gravitation of all the bodies towards the sun is the same at equal distances. Consequently, gravitation is proportional to the masses; for, if the planets and comets were at equal distances from the sun, and left to the effects of gravity, they would arrive at his surface at the same time. The satellites also gravitate to their primaries according to the same law that their primaries do to the sun. Thus, by the law of action and re-action, each body is itself the centre of an attractive force extending indefinitely in space, causing all the mutual disturbances which render the celestial motions so complicated and their investigation so difficult.

The gravitation of matter directed to a centre, and attracting directly as the mass, and inversely as the square of the distance, does not belong to it when considered in mass only; particle acts on particle according to the same law when at sensible distances from each other. If the sun acted on the centre of the earth, without attracting each of its particles, the tides would be very much greater than they now are, and would also, in other respects, be very different. The gravitation of the earth to the sun results from the gravitation of all its particles, which, in their turn, attract the sun in the ratio of their respective masses. There is a reciprocal action, likewise, between the earth and every particle at its surface. Were this not the case, and were any portion of the earth, however small, to attract another portion, and not be itself attracted, the centre of gravity of the earth would be moved in space by this action, which is impossible.

The forms of the planets result from the reciprocal attraction of their component particles. A detached fluid mass, if at rest, would assume the form of a sphere, from the reciprocal attraction of its particles. But if the mass revolve about an axis, it becomes flattened at the poles, and bulges at the equator, in consequence of the centrifugal force arising from the velocity of rotation,—for the centrifugal force diminishes the gravity of the particles at the equator, and equilibrium can only exist where these two forcers are balanced by an increase of gravity. Therefore, as the attractive force is the same on all particles at equal distances from the centre of the sphere, the equatorial particles would recede from the centre, till their increase in number balance the centrifugal force by their attraction. Consequently, the sphere would become an oblate, or flattened spheroid; and a fluid partially or entirely covering a solid, as the ocean and atmosphere cover the earth, must assume that form in order to remain in equilibrio. The surface of the sea is therefore spheroidal, and the surface of the earth only deviates from that figure where it rises above or sinks below the level of the sea. But the deviation is so small that it is unimportant when compared with the magnitude of the earth; for the mighty chain of the Andes, and the yet more lofty Himalaya, bear about the same proportion to the earth that a grain of sand does to a globe three feet in diameter. Such is the form of the earth and planets. The compression or flattening at their poles is, however, so small, that even Jupiter, whose rotation is the most rapid, and therefore the most elliptical of the planets, may, from his great distance be regarded as spherical. Although the planets attract each other as if they were spheres, on account of their distances, yet the satellites are near enough to be sensibly affected in their motions by the forms of their primaries. The moon, for example, is so near the earth, that the reciprocal attraction between each of her particles, and each of the particles in the prominent mass at the terrestrial equator, occasions considerable disturbances in the motions of both bodies; for the action of the moon on the matter at the earth's equator, produces a nutation in the axis of rotation, and the re-action of that matter on the moon, is the cause of a corresponding nutation in the lunar orbit.

399

If a sphere at rest in space, receive an impulse passing through its centre of gravity, all its parts will move with an equal velocity in a straight line; but if the impulse does not pass through the centre of gravity, its particles, having unequal velocities, will have a rotary or revolving motion, at the same time that it is translated in space. These motions are independent of one another; so that a contrary impulse, passing through its centre of gravity, will impede its progress, without interfering with its rotation. As the sun rotates about an axis, it seems probable, if an impulse in a contrary direction has not been given to his centre of gravity, that he moves in space, accompanied by all those bodies which compose the solar system,—a circumstance which would in no way interfere with their relative motions; for, in consequence of the principle, that force is proportional to velocity, the reciprocal attractions of a system remain the same, whether its centre of gravity be at rest or moving uniformly in space. It is computed that, had the earth received its motion from a single impulse, that impulse must have passed through a point about twenty-five miles from its centre.

Since the motions of rotation and translation of the planets are independent of each other, though probably communicated by the same impulse, they form separate subjects of investigation.

Section XXXVII
The known quantity of matter bears a very small proportion to the immensity of space. Large as the bodies are, the distances which separate them are immeasurably greater; but as design is manifest in every part of creation, it is probable, that if the

various systems in the universe had been nearer to one another, their mutual disturbances would have been inconsistent with the harmony and stability of the whole. It
is clear that space is not pervaded by atmospheric air, since its resistance would, long
ere this, have destroyed the velocity of the planets; neither can we affirm it to be a
void, since it seems to be replete with ether, and traversed in all directions by light,
heat, gravitation, and possibly by influences whereof we can form no idea.

Whatever the laws may be that obtain in the more distant regions of creation,
we are assured that one alone regulates the motions, not only of our own system,
but also the binary systems of the fixed stars; and as general laws form the ultimate object of philosophical research, we cannot conclude these remarks without
considering the nature of gravitation—that extraordinary power, whose effects
we have been endeavouring to trace through some of their mazes. It was at one
time imagined that the acceleration in the moon's mean motion was occasioned
by the successive transmission of the gravitating force. It has been proved, that
in order to produce this effect, its velocity must be about fifty millions of times
greater than that of light, which flies at the rate of 200,000 miles in a second. Its
action, even at the distance of the sun, may therefore be regarded as instanta-
neous; yet so remote are the nearest of the fixed stars, that it may be doubted
whether the sun has any sensible influence on them.

The curves in which the celestial bodies move by the force of gravitation are
only lines of the second order. The attraction of spheroids, according to any other
law of force than that of gravitation, would be much more complicated; and as
it is easy to prove that matter might have been moved according to an infinite
variety of laws, it may be concluded that gravitation must have been selected by
Divine Wisdom out of an infinity of others, as being the most simple, and that
which gives the greatest stability to the celestial motions.

It is a singular result of the simplicity of the laws of nature, which admit only
of the observation and comparison of ratios, that the gravitation and theory of the
motions of the celestial bodies are independent of their absolute magnitudes and
distances. Consequently, if all the bodies of the solar system their mutual distances,
and their velocities, were to diminish proportionally, they would describe curves
in all respects similar to those in which they now move; and the system might be
successively reduced to the smallest sensible dimensions, and still exhibit the same
appearances. We learn by experience that a very different law of attraction prevails when the particles of matter are placed within inappreciable distances from
each other, as in chemical and capillary attraction and the attraction of cohesion.
Whether it be a modification of gravity, or that some new and unknown power
comes into action, does not appear. But as a change in the law of the force takes
place at one end of the scale, it is possible that gravitation may not remain the same
throughout every part of space. Perhaps the day may come, when even gravitation, no longer regarded as an ultimate principle, may be resolved into a yet more
general cause, embracing every law that regulates the material world.

The action of the gravitating force is not impeded by the intervention even of
the densest substances. If the attraction of the sun for the centre of the earth, and

of the hemisphere diametrically opposite to him, were diminished by difficulty in penetrating the interposed matter, the tides would be more obviously affected. Its attraction is the same also, whatever the substances of the celestial bodies may be; for if the action of the sun upon the earth differed by a millionth part from his action upon the moon, the difference would occasion a periodical variation in the moon's parallax, whose maximum would be the 1/15 of a second and also a variation in her longitude amounting to several seconds; a supposition proved to be impossible by the agreement of theory with observation. Thus all matter is pervious to gravitation, and is equally attracted by it.

As far as human knowledge extends, the intensity of gravitation has never varied within the limits of the solar system; nor does even analogy lead us to expect that it should: on the contrary, there is every reason to be assured that the great laws of the universe are immutable, like their Author. Not only the sun and planets, but the minutest particles, in all the varieties of their attractions and repulsions,—nay, even the imponderable matter of the electric, galvanic, or magnetic fluid,—are all obedient to permanent laws, though we may not be able in every case to resolve the phenomena into general principles. Nor can we suppose the structure of the globe alone to be exempt from the universal fiat, though ages may pass before the changes it has undergone, or that are now in progress, can be referred to existing causes with the same certainty with which the motions of the planets, and all their periodic and secular variations, are referable to the law of gravitation. The traces of extreme antiquity perpetually occurring to the geologist, give that information as to the origin of things, in vain looked for in other parts of the universe. They date the beginning of time with regard to our system; since there is ground to believe that the formation of the earth was contemporaneous with that of the rest of the planets; but they show that creation is the work of Him with whom "a thousand years are as one day, and one day as a thousand years."

401

In the work now brought to a conclusion, it has been necessary to select from the whole circle of the sciences a few of the most obvious of those proximate links which connect them together, and to pass over innumerable cases both of evident and occult alliance. Any one branch traced through its ramifications would have alone occupied a volume; it is hoped, nevertheless, that the view here given will suffice to show the extent, to which a consideration of the reciprocal influence of even a few of these subjects may ultimately lead. It thus appears that the theory of dynamics, founded upon terrestrial phenomena, is indispensable for acquiring a knowledge of the revolutions of the celestial bodies and their reciprocal influences. The motions of the satellites are affected by the forms of their primaries, and the figures of the planets themselves depend upon their rotations. The symmetry of their internal structure proves the stability of these rotary motions, and the immutability of the length of the day, which furnishes an invariable standard of time; and the actual size of the terrestrial spheroid affords the means of ascertaining the dimensions of the solar system, and provides an invariable foundation for a system of weights and measures. The mutual attraction of the celestial bodies disturbs the fluids at their surfaces, whence the theory of the tides and the oscillations of the atmosphere. The density and elasticity of the air, varying with every alternation of temperature, lead to the consideration of barometrical changes, the measurement of heights, and capillary attraction; and the doctrine of sound, including the theory of music, is to be referred to the small undulations of the aërial medium. A knowledge of the action of matter upon light is requisite for tracing the curved path of its rays through the atmosphere, by which the true places of distant objects are determined, whether in the heavens or on the earth. By this we learn the nature and properties of the sunbeam, the mode of its propagation through the etherial fluid, or in the interior of material bodies, and the origin of colour. By the eclipses of Jupiter's satellites, the velocity of light is ascertained, and that velocity, in the aberration of the fixed stars, furnishes the only direct proof of the real motion of the earth. The effects of the invisible rays of light are immediately connected with chemical action; and heat, forming a part of the solar ray, so essential to animated and inanimated existence, whether considered as invisible light or as a distinct quality, is too important an agent in the economy of creation, not to hold a principal place in the connection of physical sciences. Whence follows its distribution in the interior, and over the surface of the globe, its power on the geological convulsions of our planet, its influence on the atmosphere and on climate, and its effects on vegetable and animal life, evinced in the localities of organised beings on the earth, in the waters, and in the air. The connection of heat with electrical phenomena, and the electricity of the atmosphere, together with all its energetic effects, its identity with magnetism and the phenomena of terrestrial polarity, can only be understood from the theories of these invisible agents, and are, probably, principal causes of chemical affinities. Innumerable instances might be given in illustration of the immediate connection of the physical sciences, most of which are united still more closely by the common bond of analysis, which is daily extending its empire, and will ultimately embrace almost every subject in nature in its formulae.

These formulae, emblematic of Omniscience, condense into a few symbols the immutable laws of the universe. This mighty instrument of human power, itself originates in the primitive constitution of the human mind, and rests upon a few fundamental axioms which have eternally existed in Him who implanted them in the breast of man when he created him after His own image.

ENDNOTES

1   Kathryn A. Neeley, Mary Somerville: *Science, Illumination, and the Female Mind* (Cambridge: Cambridge University Press, 2001), 53.

2   Martha Somerville, *Personal Recollections from Early Life to Old Age of Mary Somerville, with Selections from her Correspondence* (London: John Murray, 1873).

3   Martha Somerville, *Personal Recollections*, 53.

4   Martha Somerville, *Personal Recollections*, 344.

5   Martha Somerville, *Personal Recollections*, 345.

402

Bibliography

PRIMARY SOURCES

Aikin, Lucy. *Memoirs of the Court of Elizabeth*. London: Alex Murray and Son, 1869.

Ballard, George. *Memoirs of Several Ladies of Great Britain Who have been celebrated for their writings or skill in the learned languages, arts and sciences*. London: W. Jackson, 1752.

Barbauld, Anna Lætitia. *An Address to the Opposers of the Repeal of the Corporation and Test Acts*. London: J. Johnson, 1790.

Barbauld, Anna Lætitia, ed. *The British Novelists*. London: J. Johnson, 1820.

Barbauld, Anna Lætitia. *Civic Sermons to the People*. Number 1, London: J. Johnson, 1792.

Barbauld, Anna Lætitia. *Lessons for Children from Two to Three Years Old*. London: J. Johnson, 1787.

Barbauld, Anna Lætitia. *Lessons for Children of Three Years Old*. London: J. Johnson, 1788.

Barbauld, Anna Lætitia. *Lessons for Children from Three to Four Years Old*. London: J. Johnson, 1788.

Barbauld, Anna Lætitia. *Remarks on Mr Gilbert Wakefield's Enquiry into the Expediency and Propriety of Public or Social Worship*. London: J. Johnson, 1792.

Benger, Elizabeth. *Memoirs of the Late Mrs. Elizabeth Hamilton with a Selection from Her Correspondence, and Other Unpublished Writings*. London: Longman, Hurst, Rees, Orme, and Brown, 1818.

The British Lady's Magazine [London] 1 (1815).

Byron, Ada. "Notes on Menabrea's *Memoir on Babbage's Calculating Engines*." In *Scientific Memoirs*, by Richard Taylor. Vol. 3. London: 1843.

Carter, Elizabeth. *All the Works of Epictetus which are now extant*. London: S. Richardson, 1758.

Carter, Elizabeth. *A Series of Letters between Mrs. Elizabeth Carter and Miss Catherine Talbot, from the year 1741 to 1770 to which are added Letters from Mrs. Elizabeth Carter to Mrs. Vesey, between the years 1763 and 1787*. London: F.C. and J. Rivington, 1809.

Chapone, Hester. *Letters on the Improvement of the Mind, Addressed to a Young Lady*. Dublin: J. Exshaw, 1773.

Chapone, Hester Mulso. "A Matrimonial Creed; addressed by Miss Mulso to Mr. Richardson in consequence of his questioning her strictly on what she believed to be the duties of the married state." In *The Works of Mrs. Chapone*, vol. 2. Boston: W. Wells and T.N Wait and Co., 1809.

Cockburn, Catharine. *The Works of Mrs Catharine Cockburn, Theological, Moral, Dramatic, and Poetical, with an account of the Life of the Author by Thomas Birch, M.A., F.R.S.* London: J. and P. Knapton, 1751.

Cowden Clarke, Charles, and Mary Cowden Clarke. *Recollections of Writers.* Fontwell, Sussex: Centaur Press, 1969.

Cowden Clarke, Mary. *The Complete Concordance to Shakespeare: being a verbal index to all passages in the dramatic works of the poet.* London: C. Knight & Co., 1845.

Cowden Clarke, Mary. *The Complete Concordance to Shakespeare.* London: Bickers & Son, 1881.

Duncombe, John. *The Feminiad, A Poem.* London: M. Cooper, 1754.

Edgeworth, Maria. *Letters for Literary Ladies.* London: J. Johnson, 1795.

Elstob, Elizabeth. *Some Testimonies of Learned Men in Favour of the Intended Edition of the Saxon Homilies Concerning the Learning of the Author of those Homilies and the Advantages to be hoped from an Edition of them.* London, 1713.

Elstob, Elizabeth. *The Rudiments of grammar for the English-Saxon Tongue, First given in English with an Apology for the study of Northern Antiquities.* London: W. Bowyer, 1715.

Hamilton, Elizabeth. *Memoirs of Modern Philosophers.* Edited by Claire Grogan. Peterborough, ON: Broadview Press, 2000. First published 1800.

Hamilton, Elizabeth. *Translations of the Letters of a Hindoo Rajah.* Edited by Pamela Perkins and Shannon Russell. Peterborough, ON: Broadview Press, 1999. First published 1796.

Hamilton, Elizabeth. *Letters on the Elementary Principles of Education.* 2nd ed. Vol. 1. Bath: R. Crutwell, 1801.

Hays, Mary. "Art. XL. Translations of the Letters of a Hindoo Rajah; written previous to, and during the Period of his Residence in England." *Analytical Review,* October 1796, 429.

Hays, Mary. *Letters and Essays, Moral, and Miscellaneous.* London: T. Knott, 1793.

Jameson, Anna. "St. Mary Magdalene." In *Sacred and Legendary Art.* London, 1848.

Jebb, John. "Report of the Sub-Committee of Westminster." 27 May 1780. Reprinted in *The English Radical Tradition, 1763–1914,* edited by S. Maccoby, 35–36. New York: New York University Press, 1957.

Macaulay, Catharine. *The History of England from the Accession of James 1 to that of the Brunswick Line.* 8 vols. London: J. Nourse, R. and J. Dodsley, and W. Johnston, 1763–1783.

Macaulay Graham, Catharine. *Letters on Education with Observations on Religious and Metaphysical Subjects.* London: C. Dilly, 1790.

Macaulay Graham, Catharine. *Observations on the Reflections of the Right Hon. Edmund Burke on the Revolution in France, In a Letter to the Right Hon. The Earl of Stanhope.* London: C. Dilly, 1790.

Marcet, Jane. *Conversations on Chemistry.* London: Longman, 1806.

Martineau, Harriet. *Biographical Sketches, 1852–1875.* London: Macmillan & Co., 1877.

Martineau, Harriet. *Illustrations of Political Economy.* London: Charles Fox, 1832.

Martineau, Harriet. *The Positive Philosophy of Auguste Comte, Freely translated and Condensed*. London: Trübner and Co., 1875.

Montagu, Elizabeth. *Essay on the Writings and Genius of Shakespear, compared with the Greek and French Dramatic Poets: With Some Remarks Upon the Misrepresentations of Mons. de Voltaire*. London: J. Dodsley, Mess. Baker and Leigh, J. Walter, T. Cadell, and J. Wilkie, 1769.

Piozzi, Hester Lynch. *British Synonymy; or, An attempt at Regulating the Choice of Words in Familiar Conversation*. 2 vols. London: G.G. and J. Robinson, 1794.

Priestley, Joseph. *The History and Present State of Electricity*. London: J. Dodsley, J. Johnson and B. Davenport, 1767.

Shelley, Mary. "Life of William Godwin." In *Mary Shelley's Literary Lives and Other Writings*, vol. 4, ed. Pamela Clemit, xiii–xxviii. London: Pickering & Chatto, 2002.

Shelley, Mary. *Lives of the Most Eminent Literary and Scientific Men of France*. Philadephia: Lea & Blanchard, 1840.

Somerville, Martha. *Personal Recollections from early life to old age of Mary Somerville, with selections from her correspondence*. London: John Murray, 1873.

Somerville, Mary. *Physical Geography*. London: J. Murray, 1858.

Somerville, Mary. *On the Connexions of the Physical Sciences*. London: J. Murray, 1834.

Somerville Mary. *Mechanism of the Heavens*. London: J. Murray, 1831.

Strickland, Elizabeth. *Lives of the Queens of England, From the Norman Conquest*. London: George Bell, 1877.

Swift, Jonathan. *A Proposal for Correcting, Improving and Ascertaining the English Tongue in a Letter to the Most Honourable Robert, Earl of Oxford and Mortimer, Lord High Treasurer of Great Britain*. London: Benjamin Tooke, 1712.

Trotter, Catharine. *A Vindication of an Essay Concerning Human Understanding Written by Mr. Locke*, (1702). In *The works of Mrs. Catharine Cockburn, theological, moral, dramatic, and poetical. Several of them now first printed*, ed. Thomas Birch. London: J. and P. Knapton, 1751.

Vives, Juan Luis. *The Instruction of a Christen Woman*. 1524. Transcribed and edited by Virginia Walcott Beauchamp, Elizabeth H. Hageman, Margaret Mikesell, Sheila Ffolliott, Betty S. Travitsky, et al. Urbana: University of Illinois Press, 2002.

Wakefield, Priscilla. *An Introduction to Botany: in a series of familiar letters*. London: E. Newberry, 1796.

Wakefield, Priscilla. *Mental Improvement*. Edited by Ann B. Shteir. East Lansing, MI: Colleagues Press, 1995. First published 1794.

Wakefield, Priscilla. *Reflections on the present condition of the female sex: with suggestions for its improvement*. London: J. Johnson, 1798.

Wordsworth, William. *"The Prelude": a Parallel Text*. Edited by J.C. Maxwell. Harmondsworth: Penguin, 1971. First published in 1805.

SECONDARY SOURCES

Akkerman, Tjitske, and Siep Stuurman, eds. *Perspectives on Feminist Political Thought in European History from the Middle Ages to the Present.* London and New York: Routledge, 1998.

Altick, Richard D. *The Cowden Clarkes.* Oxford: Oxford University Press, 1948.

Ashdown, Margaret. "Elizabeth Elstob, The Learned Saxonist." *Modern Language Review* 20 (1925): 125–45.

Babbage, Charles. *Charles Babbage and His Calculating Engines, 1791–1871.* Edited by Philip Morrison and Emily Morrison. New York: Dover, 1961.

Barker, Hannah, and Elaine Chalus. *Gender in Eighteenth-Century England: Roles, Representations, and Responsibilities.* London: Longman, 1997.

Barker, Hannah, and Elaine Chalus. *Women's History: Britain, 1700–1850, An Introduction.* London and New York: Routledge, 2005.

Baron, Dennis. *Grammar and Gender.* New Haven: Yale University Press, 1986.

Baum, Joan. *The Calculating Passion of Ada Byron.* Hamden: Connecticut, 1986.

Beauvoir, Simone de. *The Second Sex.* Translated by H.M. Parshley. Harmondsworth: Penguin Books, 1983.

Bellamy, Joan, Anne Laurence, and Gill Perry, eds. *Women, Scholarship and Criticism: Gender and Knowledge c. 1790–1900.* Manchester: Manchester University Press, 2000.

Benjamin, Marina. *A Question of Identity: Women, Science, and Literature.* New Brunswick: Rutgers University Press, 1993.

Berglund, Lisa. "'Familiar talk': Hester Lynch Piozzi and Female Synonymy." Paper presented at the Dictionary Society of North America, XV Biennial Meeting, Boston, MA, June 8–11, 2005.

Bewell, Alan. "Jacobin Plants, Botany as Social Theory in the 1790s." *The Wordsworth Circle* 20 (1989): 132–39.

Bloomfield, P. *Edward Gibbon Wakefield, Builder of the British Commonwealth.* London: Longman, 1961.

Bolton, Martha Brandt. "Some Aspects of the Philosophical Work of Catharine Trotter." In *Hypatia's Daughters, Fifteen Hundred Years of Women Philosophers,* edited by Linda Lopez McAllister, 139–64. Bloomington: Indiana University Press, 1996.

Booth, Alison. *How to Make It as a Woman: Collective Biographical History from Victoria to the Present.* Chicago: University of Chicago Press, 2004.

Bowden, B.V. *Faster than Thought: A Symposium on Digital Computing Machines.* New York: Pitman, 1953.

Burnet, George L. "'That Cursed Barbauld Crew,' or Charles Lamb and Children's Literature." *The Charles Lamb Bulletin* 25 (1979): 1–18.

Burstein, Miriam Elizabeth. "From Good Looks to Good Thoughts: Popular Women's History and the Invention of Modernity, ca. 1830–1870." *Modern Philology* 97, no. 1 (August 1999): 46–75.

Burton, Sarah. *A Double Life: A Biography of Charles and Mary Lamb.* London: Viking, 2003.

Butler, Marilyn. "Culture's Medium: The Role of the Review." In *The Cambridge Companion to British Romanticism*, edited by Stuart Curran, 120–47. Cambridge: Cambridge University Press, 1993.

Butler, Marilyn. *Maria Edgeworth: A Literary Biography*. Oxford: Clarendon Press, 1972.

Butler, Marilyn, and Janet Todd, eds. *The Works of Mary Wollstonecraft*. Vol. 7. New York: New York University Press, 1989.

Chernock, Arianne. "Extending the 'Right of Election': Men's Arguments for Women's Political Representation in Late-Eighteenth-Century Britain." Paper presented at the 8th Gender and Enlightenment Colloquium, entitled "Gender and Enlightened Utopias," Centre for Eighteenth Century Studies, University of York, York, UK, June 7, 2003, York University.

Child, Elizabeth. "Elizabeth Montagu, Bluestocking Businesswoman." In *Reconsidering the Bluestockings*, edited by Nicole Pohl and Betty A. Schellenberg, 153–73. Special issue, *Huntington Library Quarterly* 65, no 1–2 (2002).

Clark, Anna. *The Struggle for the Breeches: Gender and the Making of the British Working Class*. London: Rivers Oram Press, 1995.

Clarke, Norma. *Ambitious Heights: Writing, Friendship, Love—the Jewsbury Sisters, Felicia Hemans and Jane Carlyle*. London: Routledge, 1990.

Clarke, Norma. *Dr. Johnson's Women*. London: Habledon and London, 2000.

Clarke, Norma. *The Rise and Fall of the Woman of Letters*. London: Pimlico, 2004.

Clery, E.J. "Bluestocking 'Feminism' and the Fame Game." *British Journal for Eighteenth-Century Studies* 28, no. 2 (Autumn 2005): 277–78.

Clery, E.J. *The Feminization Debate in Eighteenth-Century England: Literature, Commerce and Luxury*. Basingstoke: Palgrave, 2004.

Clifford, James L. *Hester Lynch Piozzi (Mrs. Thrale)*. 2nd ed. Oxford: The Clarendon Press, 1952.

Cooter, Roger. *The Cultural Meaning of Popular Science: Phrenology and the Organization of Consent in Nineteenth-Century Britain*. Cambridge: Cambridge University Press, 1984.

Christie, John, and Sally Shuttleworth. *Science and Literature, 1700–1900*. Manchester and New York: Manchester University Press, 1989.

Crook, Keith. *A Preface to Swift*. London: Longman, 1998.

Crook, Nora. General editor's introduction to *Mary Shelley's Literary Lives and Other Writings, by Mary Shelley*. London: Pickering & Chatto, 2002.

David, Deirdre. *Intellectual Women and Victorian Patriarchy: Harriet Martineau, Elizabeth Barrett Browning, George Eliot*. London: Macmillan, 1987.

Davies, Kate. *Catharine Macaulay and Mercy Otis Warren: The Revolutionary Atlantic and the Politics of Gender*. Oxford: Oxford University Press, 2005.

Delorme, Mary. "Facts not Opinions, Agnes Strickland." *History Today* 38 (1988): 45–50.

Demers, Patricia. *The World of Hannah More*. Lexington: The University Press of Kentucky, 1996.

407

Devoney, Looser. *British Women Writers and the Writing of History*. Baltimore and London: John Hopkins University Press, 2000.

Eger, Elizabeth. Editor's introduction to *Elizabeth Montagu*. Vol. 1 of *Bluestocking Feminism: Writings of the Bluestocking Circle 1738–1790*, edited by Gary Kelly. London: Pickering & Chatto, 1999.

Ehrenpreis, Irvin. *Swift, The Man, His Works, and The Age*. London: Methuen, 1967.

Elwin, Malcolm. *Lord Byron's Family: Annabella, Ada, and Augusta, 1816–1824*. London: John Murray, 1975.

Fara, Patricia. *Pandora's Breeches: Women, Science, and Power in the Enlightenment*. London: Pimlico, 2004.

Ford, Charles Howard. *Hannah More: A Critical Biography*. New York: Peter Lang, 1996.

Franklin, Caroline. *The Works of Anna Lætitia Barbauld with a Memoir by Lucy Aikin, 1825*. London: Routledge, 1996.

Gleadle, Kathryn. *The Early Feminists: Radical Unitarians and the Emergence of the Women's Rights Movement, 1831–1851*. New York: St. Martin's Press, 1995.

Gleadle, Kathryn. *Radical Writing on Women, 1800–1850*. Basingstoke: Palgrave Macmillan, 2002.

George, Sam. "Linnaeus in Letters and the Cultivation of the Female Mind: 'Botany in an English Dress.'" *British Journal for Eighteenth-Century Studies* 28, no. 1 (2005): 1–18.

Gretsch, Mechthild. "Elizabeth Elstob: A Scholar's Fight for Anglo-Saxon Studies." *Anglia: Zeitschrift für Englische Philologie* 117 (1999): 163–200.

Guest, Harriet. *Small Change: Women, Learning, Patriotism, 1750–1810*. Chicago: University of Chicago Press, 2000.

Gunther-Canada, Wendy. *Rebel Writer: Mary Wollstonecraft and Enlightenment Politics*. Dekalb: Northern Illinois University Press, 2001.

Habermas, Jürgen. *The Structural Transformation of the Public Sphere*. 1962. Translated by T. Burger. Cambridge, MA: MIT Press, 1989.

Hare, Augusta. *The Life and Letters of Maria Edgeworth*. 2 vols. Boston and New York: Houghton Mifflin and Co., 1995

Hawley, Judith. *Elizabeth Carter*. Vol. 2 of *Bluestocking Feminism: Writings of the Bluestocking Circle, 1738–1785*. Edited by Garry Kelly. Oxford: Clarendon Press, 1993.

Hawley, Judith, ed. *Literature and Science, 1660–1834*. 8 vols. London: Pickering and Chatto, 2003-04.

Haight, Gordon S. *George Eliot: A Biography*. Oxford: Clarendon Press, 1968.

Harrison, Brian, and H.G.C. Matthew, eds. *Oxford Dictionary of National Biography: From the Earliest Times to the Year 2000*. Oxford: Oxford University Press, 2004.

Hill, Bridget. "Priscilla Wakefield as Writer of Children's Educational Books." *Women's Writing* 4 (1997): 3–15.

Hill, Bridget. *The Republican Virago: The Life and Times of Catharine Macaulay, Historian*. Oxford: Clarendon Press, 1992.

Hill, Bridget. *Women Alone, Spinsters in England, 1660–1850*. New Haven and London: Yale University Press, 2001.

408

Hoecker-Drysdale, Susan. *Harriet Martineau, First Woman Sociologist.* Oxford: Berg, 1992.

Hoeckley, Cheri L. Larsen. Introduction to *Shakespeare's Heroines, or Characteristics of Women, Moral, Poetical, and Historical,* by Anna Murphy Jameson, 9–37. Peterborough, ON: Broadview Press, 2005.

Huskey, Velma R., and Harry D. Huskey. "Lady Lovelace and Charles Babbage." *Annals of the History of Computing* 2, no. 4 (1980): 299–327.

Johnson, Claudia. *Equivocal Beings: Politics, Gender, and Sentimentality in the 1790s.* Chicago and London: University of Chicago Press, 1995.

Johnston, Judith. *Anna Jameson: Victorian, Feminist, Woman of Letters.* Aldershot: Scholar Press, 1997.

Jones, Vivien. "The Death of Mary Wollstonecraft." *British Journal for Eighteenth-Century Studies* 20, no.2 (Autumn 1997): 187–205.

Jordanova, Ludmilla. *Nature Displayed: Gender, Science, and Medicine, 1760–1820.* London and New York: Longman, 1999.

Kelley, Anne. *Catharine Trotter: An Early Modern Writer in the Vanguard of Feminism.* Aldershot and Burlington: Ashgate, 2002.

Kelly, Gary. *Bluestocking Feminism: Writings of the Bluestocking Circle, 1738–1785.* London: Pickering and Chatto, 1999.

Kelly, Gary. "Sarah Scott, Bluestocking Feminism, and *Millenium Hall.*" In *Millenium Hall,* by Sarah Scott. Peterborough, ON: Broadview Press, 1995.

Kelly, Gary. *Women, Writing, and Revolution, 1790–1827.* Oxford: Clarendon Press, 1993.

Kennedy, Michael L. *The Jacobin Clubs in the French Revolution, 1793–1795.* Oxford: Berghan Books, 2000.

Knight, Frida. *University Rebel: The Life of William Frend, 1751–1841.* London: Victor Golancz, 1970.

Knott, Sarah, and Barbara Taylor. *Women, Gender, and Enlightenment.* Basingstoke: Palgrave Macmillan, 2005.

Kontler, László. "Beauty or Beast, or Monstrous Regiments? Robertson and Burke on Women and the Public Scene." *Modern Intellectual History* 1, no. 3 (2004): 305–30.

Le Breton, Anna Letitia. *Memoir of Mrs. Barbauld including Letters and Notices of her Family and Friends.* London: George Bell and Sons, 1874.

Le Breton, Philip Hemery. *Memoirs, Miscellanies and Letters of the late Lucy Aikin.* London: Longman, Green, Longman, Roberts and Green, 1864.

Lewis, Jan Ellen. "The Feminist Imagination." *Modern Intellectual History* 1, no. 3 (2004): 411–25.

Lewis, Judith S. "Princess of Parallelograms and Her Daughter: Math and Gender in the Nineteenth-Century English Aristocracy." *Women's Studies International Forum* 18, no. 4 (1995): 387–94.

Looser, Devoney. *British Women Writers and the Writing of History, 1670–1820.* Baltimore and London: Johns Hopkins University Press, 2000.

Mazzotti, Massimo, "Newton for Ladies: Gentility, Gender and Radical Culture." *British Journal of the History of Science* 37, no. 2 (June 2004): 119–46.

McCarthy, William. *Hester Thrale Piozzi: Portrait of a Literary Woman.* Chapel Hill: University of North Carolina Press, 1985.

McCarthy, William, and Elizabeth Kraft. "From the British Novelists." In *Anna Letitia Barbauld: Selected Poetry and Prose,* by Anna Letitia Barbauld, 375–76. Peterborough, ON: Broadview Press, 2002.

McLachlan, Herbert. *English Education under the Test Acts.* Manchester: Manchester University Press, 1931.

McNeil, Maureen. *Under the Banner of Science: Erasmus Darwin and his Age.* Manchester: Manchester University Press, 1987.

Miller, Florence Fenwick. *Harriet Martineau.* Port Washington, NY: Kennikat Press, 1972.

Mitchell, Rosemary. "A Stitch in Time?: Women, Needlework, and the Making of History in Victorian Britain." *Journal of Victorian Culture* 1, no. 2 (1996): 185–202.

Mitford, John. *A Description of the Crimes and Horrors in the Interior of Warburton's Private Mad-House at Hoxton ... called Whitmore House.* London: Benbow, 1822.

Moore, Doris Langley. *Ada, Countess of Lovelace.* London: John Murray, 1997.

Morrison, Philip, and Emily Morrison. *Charles Babbage and His Calculating Engine.* New York: Dover Publications, 1961.

Meyers, Mitzi. "Mary Wollstonecraft's Literary Reviews." In *The Cambridge Companion to Mary Wollstonecraft,* edited by Claudia Johnson, 82–98. Cambridge: Cambridge University Press, 2002.

Myers, Sylvia Harcstark. *The Bluestocking Circle: Women, Friendship, and the Life of the Mind in Eighteenth-Century England.* Oxford: Clarendon Press, 1990.

Neeley, Kathryn A. *Mary Somerville: Science, Illumination, and the Female Mind.* Cambridge: Cambridge University Press, 2001.

Nevill, John Cranstoun. *Harriet Martineau.* London: Frederick Muller, 1943.

Newlyn, Lucy. *Reading, Writing and Romanticism, The Anxiety of Reception.* Oxford: Oxford University Press, 2000.

Nichols, John. *Illustrations of the Literary History of the Eighteenth Century.* London: John Nichols and Son, 1822.

Nichols, John. *Literary Anecdotes of the Eighteenth Century.* London: H.G. Bohn, 1842.

Nokes, David. *Jonathan Swift: A Hypocrite Reversed, a Critical Biography.* Oxford: Oxford University Press, 1985.

O'Day, Rosemary. *Education and Society, 1500–1800.* New York: Longman, 1982.

Offen, Karen. *European Feminisms, 1700–1950: A Political History.* Stanford: Stanford University Press, 2000.

Ó Gallchoir, Clíona. "Gender, Nation and Revolution: Maria Edgeworth and Stéphanie-Félicité de Genlis." In *Women, Writing, and the Public Sphere, 1700–1830,* edited by Elizabeth Eger, Charlotte Grant, Clíona Ó Gallchoir, and Penny Warburton, 200–16. Cambridge: Cambridge University Press, 2001.

Parker, Rozsika. *The Subversive Stitch: Embroidery and the Making of the Feminine.* London: Women's Press, 1984.

Patterson, Elizabeth Chambers. *Mary Somerville and the Cultivation of Science, 1815–1840.* The Hague: Nijoff, 1983.

Peake, Catharine. Introduction to *Elizabeth Elstob, An Apology for the Study of Northern Antiquities*. 1715. Reprint, Los Angeles: The Augustan Reprint Society, 1956.

Pennington, Montagu. *Memoirs of the Life of Mrs. Elizabeth Carter with a New Edition of her Poems and Miscellaneous Essays in Prose*. London: F.C. and J. Rivington, 1807.

Perry, Ruth. *The Celebrated Mary Astell*. Chicago and London: University of Chicago Press, 1986.

Pope-Hennessy, Una. *Agnes Strickland*. London: Chatto and Windus, 1940.

Polkinghorn, Bette, and Dorothy Lampen Thomson. *Adam Smith's Daughters: Eight Prominent Women Economists from the Eighteenth Century to the Present*. Cheltenham: Edward Elgar, 1998.

Polkinghorn, Bette. *Jane Marcet: An Uncommon Woman*. Aldermaston: Forestwood Publications, 1993.

Porter, Roy. *Enlightenment: Britain and the Creation of the Modern World*. London: Penguin Books, 2000.

Porter, Roy. *Mind-Forg'd Manacles: A History of Madness in England from the Restoration to the Regency*. London: Athlone Press, 1987.

Reeves, Marjorie. *Pursuing the Muses: Female Education and Nonconformist Culture, 1700–1900*. London: Leicester University Press, 1997.

Rendall, Jane. "Writing History for British Women: Elizabeth Hamilton and *The Memoirs of Agrippina*." In *Wollstonecraft's Daughter: Womanhood in England and France, 1780–1920*, edited by Clarissa Campbell Orr, 79–93. Manchester: Manchester University Press, 1996.

Review of *Personal Recollections of Mrs. Somerville*, by Mary Somerville. *Quarterly Review* 271 (1874): 71-102.

Reynolds, Myra. *The Learned Lady in England, 1650–1760*. Boston: Houghton Mifflin, 1964.

Richardson, M.A. "William and Elizabeth Elstob." In *Reprints of Rare Tracts & Imprints of Antient Manuscripts, &c: Chiefly Illustrative of the History of the Northern Counties*. Vol. 1. Newcastle: M.A. Richardson, 1847.

Ribeiro, Alvero, and James G. Basker. *Tradition in Transition: Women Writers, Marginal Texts and the Eighteenth-Century Canon*. Oxford: Clarendon Press, 1996.

Rogers, Katherine M. "The Contribution of Mary Hays." *Prose Studies* 10 (1987): 131–42.

Rossington, Michael. "Sacred Monuments: Mary Shelley's *Lives of William Godwin and Mary Wollstonecraft*." In *Chamber Music: The Life-Writing of William Godwin, Mary Wollstonecraft, Mary Hays, and Mary Shelley*, edited by Gina Luria Walker. Romantic Circles Features & Events. College Park, MD: University of Maryland, April 2002. http://www.rc.umd.edu/features/features/chambermusic (accessed July 5, 2007).

Rothman, Patricia. *Women in the History of Mathematics: From Antiquity to the Nineteenth Century*. London: University College London, 1996.

Schnorrenberg, Barbara B. "An Opportunity Missed: Catharine Macaulay on the Revolution of 1688." *Studies in Eighteenth-Century Culture* 20 (1990): 231–40.

411

Secord, James E. General introduction to *Mary Somerville, Scientific Papers and Reviews*. In *The Collected Works of Mary Somerville*, Vol. 1. Bristol: Thoemmes Continuum, 2004: xv–xxl.

Seymour, Miranda. *Mary Shelley*. London: John Murray, 2000.

Shteir, Ann B. *Cultivating Women, Cultivating Science: Flora's Daughters and Botany in England, 1760–1860*. Baltimore: Johns Hopkins University Press, 1996.

Smith, Hilda L. *Women Writers and the Early Modern British Political Tradition*. Cambridge: Cambridge University Press, 1998.

Smith, J.W. Ashley. *The Birth of Modern Education: The Contribution of the Dissenting Academies, 1660–1800*. London: Independent Press Ltd., 1954.

Spongberg, Mary. *Writing Women's History since the Renaissance*. Houndmills: Palgrave Macmillan, 2002.

Stein, Dorothy. *Ada: A Life and a Legacy*. Cambridge, Massachusetts and London: MIT Press, 1985.

Stott, Anne. *Hannah More: The First Victorian*. Oxford: Oxford University Press, 2003.

Taylor, Barbara. *Mary Wollstonecraft and the Feminist Imagination*. Cambridge: Cambridge University Press, 2003.

Thompson, Ann, and Sasha Roberts, eds., *Women Reading Shakespeare, 1660–1900: An Anthology of Criticism*. Manchester: Manchester University Press, 1997.

Thorpe, Thomas E. *Essays in Historical Chemistry*. 1894. Reprint, Freeport, NY: Books for Libraries Press, 1972.

Todd, Janet. *Mary Wollstonecraft, a Revolutionary Life*. London: Weidenfeld and Nicholson, 2000.

Toole, Betty Alexandra. *Ada, the Enchantress of Numbers*. Mill Valley, CA: Strawberry Press, 1992.

Uglow, Jenny. *The Lunar Men: The Friends Who Made the Future, 1730–1810*. London: Faber and Faber, 2002.

Uglow, Jenny. "But What About the Women? The Lunar Society's Attitude to Women and Science, and to the Education of Girls." In *The Genius of Erasmus Darwin*, edited by C.U.M. Smith and Robert Arnott, 163–78. Aldershott: Ashgate, 2005.

Vargo, Lisa. Introduction to *Lodore*, by Mary Shelley. Peterborough, ON: Broadview Press, 1997.

Waithe, Mary Ellen. "Catharine Trotter Cockburn." In *Modern Women Philosophers, 1600–1900*. Vol. 3 of *A History of Women Philosophers*. London: Kluwer Academic Publishers, 1991.

Waters, Mary. *British Women Writers and the Profession of Literary Criticism, 1789–1832*. Houndmills: Palgrave Macmillan, 2004.

Watts, Ruth. *Gender, Power, and the Unitarians in England, 1760–1860*. London: Longman, 1998.

Webb, R.K. *Harriet Martineau, a Radical Victorian*. London: Heinemann, 1960.

White, Daniel E. "'With Mrs Barbauld it is different': Dissenting Heritage and the Devotional Taste." In *Women, Gender, and Enlightenment*, edited by Sarah Knott and Barbara Taylor, 474–92. Houndmills: Palgrave Macmillan, 2005.

Whitehead, Barbara. *Women's Education in Early Modern Europe, A History, 1500–1800.* New York and London: Garland, 1999.

Withey, Lynne. "Catharine Macaulay and the Uses of History." *Journal of British Studies* 16 (1976): 59–83.

Woolley, Benjamin. *The Bride of Science: Romance, Reason and Byron's Daughter.* Basingstoke: Macmillan, 1999.

Wordsworth, Jonathan. Introduction to *On Burke's Reflections on the French Revolution, 1790*, by Catharine Macaulay. Poole, Washington, DC: Woodstock Books, 1997.

Zinsser, Judith P., *Men, Women and the Birthing of Modern Science.* DeKalb, IL: Northern Illinois University Press, 2005.

Index

415